High Performance Sailing

High Performance Sailing

Frank Bethwaite

International Marine
Camden, Maine

Published by International Marine®,
a division of The McGraw-Hill Companies.
First published in Great Britain in 1993 by Waterline Books,
an imprint of Airlife Publishing Ltd.

10 9 8 7 6 5 4 3 2

ISBN 0-07-005799-0

Questions regarding the content of this book should be addressed to:
International Marine
P.O. Box 220
Camden, ME 04843

Questions regarding the ordering of this book should be addressed to:
The McGraw-Hill Companies
Customer Service Department
P.O. Box 547
Blacklick, OH 43004
Retail customers: 1-800-822-8158
Bookstores: 1-800-722-4726

Printed in Great Britain.

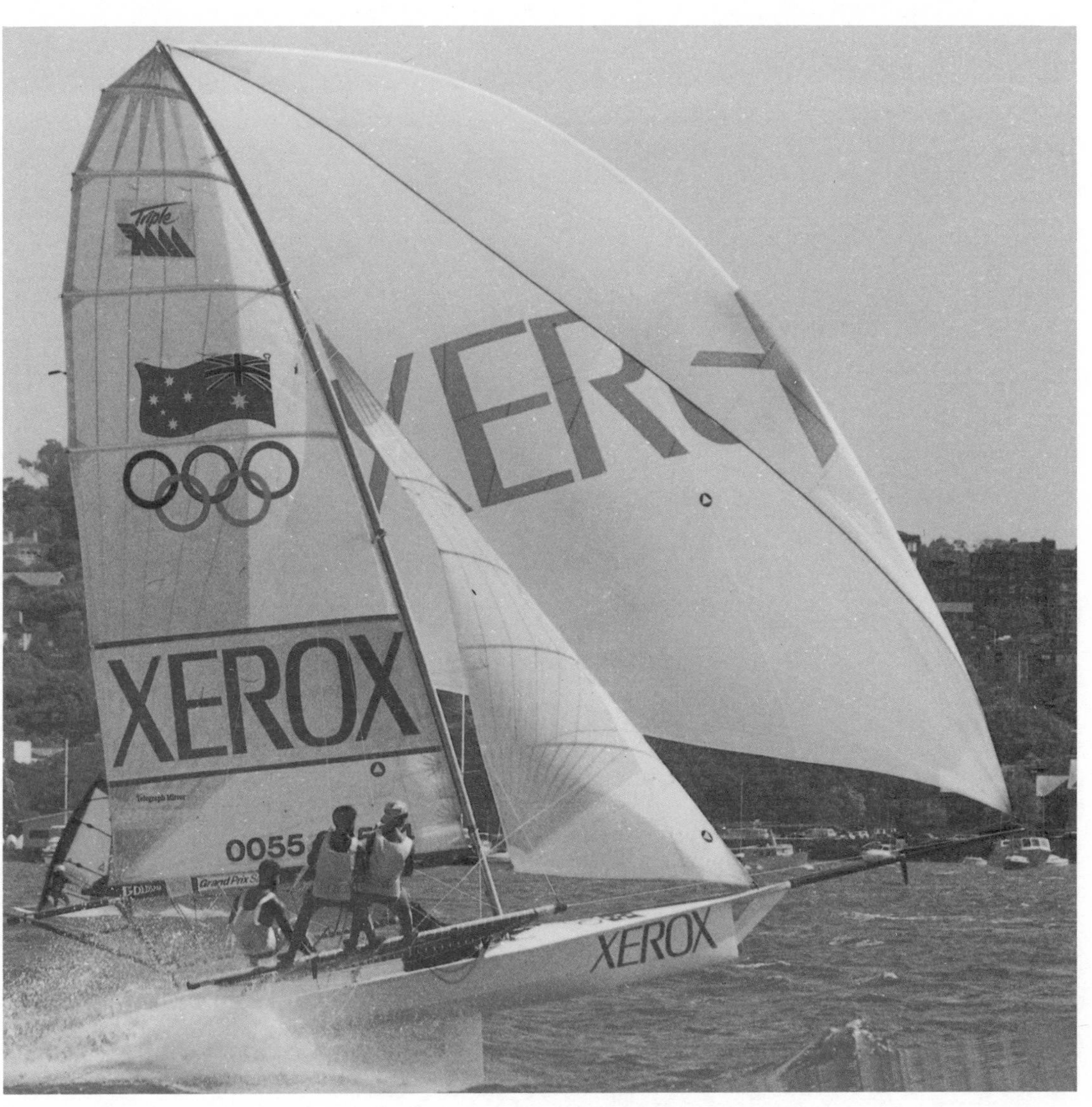
Triple
XEROX
0055
XEROX

Introduction

Some people like to sail.
Some people like to sail fast.
Some people like to get the windshifts right as well.
This book is written for those who like to sail fast and well.

This is a book about sailing faster. It is also a book for beginners, because so much of its content is new. In any new environment there are few experts.

During the past two decades there has been a revolution in the way some Australian skiff-class designers and sailors have thought about, designed, built , and sailed their boats. These classes are free from all restrictions and so create an environment in which new materials and technology can be tried, developed and optimised. The combined effect of these changes has been to achieve a spectacular increase in performance. This book is about the new ideas which have lead to these greater speeds and the faster sailing techniques which have been developed to achieve them.

In suitable conditions some high performance boats can now sail around a course at an average speed faster than the wind. The new ideas and handling techniques which have developed around these boats are proving faster when applied to conventional boats also. This 'spin-off' can help everybody sail faster.

The history of sailing is a story of two periods. There was a long period of thousands of years when nobody sailed for fun and throughout which the core ideas about sailing changed very little. This has been followed by a short period of about three hundred years, when increasing numbers of people have sailed for fun. During this time, a number of very important changes have taken place, of which the most recent is probably the most important of all. As yet, it is little understood.

Sailing began many thousands of years ago, when some innovative primitive held up a skin to 'catch the wind' and found that he could in this way escape the labour of paddling whenever 'the wind was fair'. When the wind was not 'fair' he accepted that he still had to paddle. So this sort of 'sailing' was simply a part of paddling and was thought of as hard work. Fun it was not.

As the centuries rolled by, sail-powered ships were developed for fishing, for trade, and for military might. The skin held up to catch the wind was replaced by woven sails, which on the bigger craft were always rigged on yards. These ships proved reasonably efficient for downwind and crosswind sailing but their performance when it was necessary to sail against the wind was dreadfully slow. For this reason, ideas about sailing throughout thousands of years did not change much. The belief was that all sailboats were necessarily heavy and slow. At their best, when sailing crosswind or downwind they could achieve a speed of one quarter to one half the wind's speed. When sailing to windward, the best that could be expected was about one tenth of this, so sailing to windward remained something to be avoided by all means possible.

Occasionally there were exceptions. Wherever the waterways were narrow and shipmasters had no option but to sail against the wind for much of the time, smaller boats of different kinds evolved. The beautifully shaped Arab dhows, with their lateen rigs, originated in the Red Sea area. In the narrow Bristol Channel in English waters, which is regularly swept by westerly gales from the Atlantic, a breed of fore and aft rigged cutters evolved. Both these boats possessed legendary seaworthiness, a reputation due primarily to their very good windward-sailing ability.
Another of these exceptions came from the East Indies. In 1661, John Evelyn recorded, 'I sailed this morning on the Thames with His Majesty (Charles II) in one of his yachts . . . vessels not

known among us until the East India Company presented that curious piece to the King, being very excellent sailing vessels . . .'

The sport of 'Yachting' had been born. This was the beginning of sailing for fun.

During the subsequent three hundred years of pleasure sailing, our expectations of performance have changed profoundly.

We start with the 'very excellent sailing vessels' of Charles II's era which could sail upwind and down on the Thames. Within a few decades, the fashion had changed. Yachts became modelled after ships of the Navy, to the point where they often carried a full complement of cannon and they took their pleasure in manoeuvring in squadrons. They had unthinkingly surrendered their previously good windward-sailing performance and manoeuvrability, and had reverted to all the limitations of the bigger vessels of the workaday world.

By the early 1800s the cannon had gone and yet windward-going ability had not been restored in English fleets. Across the Atlantic they had different ideas. The story of the schooner *America*'s windward-going speed advantage is well known and the race success of the American design was well deserved.

During the next century the periodic *America's* Cup challenges focused attention on 'total performance' on both sides of the Atlantic. Good windward-going ability was restored and detail improvements were developed although no fundamental changes occurred in the traditional ideas. Since 1661 these had crystalised into something like:

Racing yachts are always heavy.The fastest yachts can expect to sail upwind, crosswind and downwind at a maximum of either about one third to one half of the wind's speed; or at the speed of a wave of their own length, whichever is the slower.
Good big yachts will always sail faster than good little yachts, because of the wave length/hull speed nexus.

This then was the situation in 1925. Since then five revolutionary changes have occurred which have led to the modern high performance sailboat.

A Common Language
In 1925, Manfred Curry published his *Aerodynamics of Sails*. Curry had realised that sailboats follow aerodynamic law, and wrote a book about it.

The fundamental change here was that the technique of sailing ceased to be a mysterious art which could be understood only by the few who had been initiated. Curry explained a logical technology which could be read about in a book and therefore understood by everybody. It could be discussed with others in a common language.

Planing
The planing dinghy was developed in about 1935, primarily by Uffa Fox. More importantly, he described what he was achieving in many articles in the yachting media and also in several excellent books.

Prior to the planing dinghy, no sailboat had ever been able to sail for prolonged periods at a speed faster than the speed of a wave of its own length. The development of planing enabled a dinghy, for the first time in history, to sail steadily at much faster speeds. In terms of core ideas, the maximum speed achievable was no longer limited by the speed of a wave of the boat's own length, so the average speed to be expected around a course in suitable conditions was increased significantly.

At this stage, planing was achievable only when broad reaching or sailing downwind. Also, the maximum speed expected was still no more than about half the wind's speed. Even so, this change was to split sailing forever.

Prior to the planing sailboat, it had remained true that a good big boat would always beat a good little boat. The social consequence of this had been to reinforce the social order which existed ashore: he who could afford the biggest castle and longest boat would automatically win the races. Yachting had therefore tended to be an elitist sport.

The planing sailboat reversed all that. From 1935 onwards, those who have sailed fastest have been those who have been fittest, who have been the most skilful handlers of planing dinghies or catamarans or sailboards, and who have owned the lightest, most technically advanced, and always relatively small sailboats. The elitist barons were not amused. They expelled Uffa Fox from the Royal Yacht Squadron at Cowes. But Royalty often shows extraordinary common sense: the Prince of Wales quietly asked Uffa Fox to teach him to sail, and took him back inside.

Windward Planing

In about 1960, the windward-planing dinghy was developed. The combination of the recently-developed trapeze with a low, compact rig and a relatively light, easy-planing hull achieved the critical sail-carrying power to total-weight ratio needed to achieve windward planing. The Flying Dutchman, designed by Essen, was the first well-known boat which could routinely plane to windward in skilful hands.

The core change here was that the 'speed of a wave of its own length' limit to the maximum speed achievable no longer applied on any point of sailing. With the development of windward planing, boats were now free to sail at much higher planing speeds on all points of sailing, and the maximum average speed which could be expected in suitable conditions was further increased.

Tacking Downwind

As dinghies became progressively lighter, planed more easily and carried increasingly bigger sails, the point was reached in about 1958 when it became faster, in some conditions, to sail to the downwind mark by broad reaching back and forth instead of running directly downwind along the shortest distance. The first known case of tacking downwind when racing occurred in an Eighteen Footer world championships in Auckland, New Zealand. The boat which reached the windward mark first turned and sailed directly for the downwind mark. They observed the second boat to head off on a fast broad reach and assumed that it had retired and was returning ashore. But the broad reaching boat picked its layline perfectly, gybed and broad reached back to the leeward mark which it reached well ahead of the earlier leader. It had been planing freely all the time, while the earlier leader had for the most part been trapped in the 'forced' mode. The downwind tacker won both that race and the series.

The important change here was the realisation that in some conditions a boat can reach a downwind mark more quickly by tacking downwind and sailing a longer distance but at a substantially higher speed, than by running 'square' down the shortest distance but at a slower speed.

As a race tactic this was a major advance. As a technique for speed however, it turned out to be potentially much more important. Any boat which runs 'square' must necessarily sail downwind at some speed less than the wind's speed whereas any boat which tacks downwind has no theoretical limit to its speed. Ice yachts, for example, can tack downwind at average speeds many times the wind speed. So this development not only removed the last absolute restriction to a sailboat's speed, it unlocked a whole Pandora's box for future development.

The three performance changes noted above – the introduction first of planing downwind, and then of planing to windward, and then of tacking downwind – had between them removed all the old restrictions on the maximum speed which could be expected from a sailboat. The actual speed increases which had been achieved were substantial in percentage terms. Twenty years earlier, the highest average speed that either a fast dinghy or a small yacht could have achieved in a 'round-the-buoys' race, in the most favourable conditions, would have been about half the wind speed. By the early 1970s, the yacht was going no faster, but advanced dinghies such as the Flying Dutchman and catamarans such as the Tornado, had increased their speed nearly 50% to a maximum of about 70% of the wind's speed. But two thirds of the speed of a 10 knot wind is still less than 7 knots and 7 knots is not fast! Ice yachts can easily achieve 70 knots. Why were sail boats still so slow?

Total respect for performance

The fifth change has been an unprecedented research and development thrust that has substantially increased the speed of the recreational sailboat 'around the buoys'. It started less than twenty years ago and is still continuing. For a number of reasons, this activity has occurred primarily in Australia and principally in Sydney. It has been rooted in practicality. It has been directed not to straight line *dash* speeds with special boats which sail on one point of sailing only and only on flat water, but to the much more difficult business of winning races around closed courses in whatever the wind and the seastate may be. It has been a blend of many factors. Together they have increased the average speed which can be expected around a closed course, in suitable conditions, from about two thirds of the wind speed to something faster than the wind's speed – a near doubling of the speed in a mere twenty years.

Why this should have occurred in Australia is easy to see. In most countries, no unrestricted high performance classes exist. In any restricted environment, new technologies or new materials must necessarily be adapted within the existing order. In such applications, they can make, at best, only a small difference. Winged keels and Kevlar, when applied to 12 Metres, enabled them to sail perhaps one or two percent faster. Even to use fibreglass for a hull nearly caused an international incident. To use carbon fibre and achieve the same strength and stiffness at a fraction of the weight was deemed unthinkable. Such is the restrictive power of the established mindset.

The present Australian 12,14,16 and 18 foot skiffs are the descendants of the skiffs which used to service the old square riggers in the port of Sydney. Starting more than one hundred and sixty years ago – the first recorded regatta was in 1827 – these workboats raced for fun and wager under rules which were simple and appropriate, Namely:

The hulls shall be no more than 18 feet(or whatever)long.
The race starts at two o'clock.
The first yacht to cross the finish line shall be the winner.

As the decade and the century passed, the skiffs, now sponsored by great business houses, crowded on more and more sail. They had the good sense to retain their simple,'no restrictions, no excuses, no handicaps' rules. With rare brief exceptions in times of unusual stress, this freedom from restriction and open-ness to new ideas has been constant. It is the simplicity of these rules which has been the critical difference.

They have created an environment in which designers have been encouraged to create completely new designs of sailboats. Their designs make the best logical use of new technologies and materials as and when these become available. These new designs are then developed, refined and improved, with no restrictions at all except for a total respect for performance. It is this environment that has enabled them to blend all useful potentials into stunning craft which can now sail around a course at speeds the like of which the world has never seen.

Some who helped

Northbridge Sailing Club is one of those rare places where if you dream 'What if ..' over a cup of coffee, you will quickly be surrounded by a group as eager to find out as you are – and they will stay with you. We had to try three times to get the photographs of Fig 3. The technical results were identical every time, but the first try used pale blue spinnaker cloth which did not contrast well against the sky, the second try with white ribbons against the dark of the tree-covered hillsides ran into perspective problems, and it was the third try with black ribbons against a light sky which gave us the pictures you see. Over the years it has been this unfailing support and assistance by my club friends which made all of the club-based experiments possible.

I thank them for more than just their physical support. So often when you conduct a well designed experiment the immediate results may not be the most important lesson, and it takes a particular way of thinking to uncover that more important fact. Two examples:

The wind tunnel experiments showed that a number of mast shapes would eliminate separation bubbles, and that in the tunnel they were all about equally good. But on the water their performances were not the same. The most important lesson was that separation bubbles could indeed be eliminated but that in the real wind mast shapes which are critical will fail, and only the most tolerant mast shapes can do it successfully.

We learned an enormous amount from the flat-water tow tests. These were conducted principally over about a year, and accumulating fleet experience supported the test results. On the one day we continued our towing in waves, we saw no reason to doubt the results from the eighty-odd test passes completed that day. But in the down-wave tows at about wave speed the 'best' fleet-racing boats scored very badly and this coloured our design thinking for some years. It was only later that the penny dropped with some lateral thinker and he pointed out that the lowest-drag boats had slid most quickly down the wave faces and so had spent more of their time being hauled up the backs of the next waves and because of this the lowest-drag boats had scored the highest average drags in tow-tests conducted in that particular way.

I have quoted our experiments with confidence because not only have they been so thoroughly substantiated by subsequent fleet racing experience, but also because they have been so well thought through in the ways noted above.

As this book has developed a number of critics, referees and editors have shaped it. Adrian Morgan of Stanford Maritime was confident that there was a need for a good high-performance reference book. Rod Carr, the RYA Olympic Coach encouraged me to include a spectrum of classes. The Octopus literary board encouraged the inclusion of the whole of the 'Wind' and Water' sections so that it should become a 'Where to Sail' book as well as a 'How to Sail' book. Alan Payne's interest and confirmation that the principles outlined in Part Three are as relevant to heavy yachts as they are to sailboards and skiffs has extended the perceived scope of the work. Don McKenzie is an old NSC friend who is a life member of the New South Wales Yachting Association and for many years has been chairman of their training committee structure. His steady support of the book as a project, and his careful criticism of my accumulating text has helped me keep it accurate and balanced. Peter Coles, who edited for Tony Marchaj many years ago, has done it all before and has been unfailingly helpful in sometimes difficult circumstances.

I may have spent much of my life as a scientist, but I am a very practical person and I have tried to make this a practical book. In sailboat racing there is nothing quite so practical as winning, and so I have quoted contributions from champions from a wide spectrum of classes as examples of the ways in which the principles outlined can be used when racing in those conditions. In most cases the contributors are named. Where they are not named they are members of my family.

Mark helped with all the experiments. He designed 'Medium Dribbly', the break-through NS14 hull. He was Australian Olympic Yachting representative in the Flying Dutchman class at the Munich Games in 1972, – and again the Olympic Flying Dutchman class representative at the Montreal Games in 1976. He won the J24 class world championships in 1981. He won the Soling class world championships in 1981.

Nicola assisted with many of the later experiments. She won the Cherub class world championships in Adelaide in 1976. (She had been runner-up in Torquay in 1974). She was Australian Olympic Yachting representative in the 470 (Womens') class at the Seoul Games in 1988, where she scored a heat win and two seconds.In addition to her handling notes, she contributed much to the race preparation sections.

Julian assisted with many of the later experiments. He invented the asymmetric spinnaker. He designed the B14 class and the B18 Eighteen footer class. He won the Eighteen footer class world championships in 1991 and again in 1992 in one of his B18's. He sailed forward with Nicola to win the world championships in Cherubs in 1976. He sailed forward with Rob Brown to win the Eighteen footer world championships in 1986. Julian and I still conduct experiments whenever we have the time.

Units, bows and noses

The world cannot agree on a uniform system of units. My professional background is aviation, associated with science and meteorology. The ICAO units used internationally by the aviation industry were:-

Distance: Nautical miles, tenths and feet
Speed: Knots (nautical miles per hour)
Weight: Pounds

These are the units I have used except where metric appeared more appropriate.

Naval architects tend to draw bows to the right.
Aeronautical engineers tend to draw noses to the left.

Contents

Part One

Wind

Chapter One
The Racing Helmsman's Wind **1**
1.1 Where to sail? 1
1.2 Kiel 2
1.3 Marstrand 2
1.4 Keppel bay 3
1.5 Lake Garda 3
1.6 Rio de Janeiro 4
1.7 The different possibilities 4

Chapter Two
The Gradient Wind **5**
2.1 The wind's driving force 5
2.2 Circulation 6
2.3 Ups and downs 8
2.4 Fires in the sky 8

Chapter Three
The Two Surface Winds **10**
3.1 The two surface winds 10
3.2 Light airs 10
3.3 Breezes 10
3.4 Wind recording instruments 15
3.5 Factors which shape the wind 15

Chapter Four
Light Airs **20**
4.1 Steady light air 20
4.2 Thermal excitation 20
4.3 Thermal excitation over water 21
4.4 Thermal excitation over dry land 21
4.5 Isolated thermal 22
4.6 Isolated thermals over large areas 23
4.7 The cellular mechanism 23
4.8 Unsteady air – the cellular pattern 24
4.9 Roll mechanism 25
4.10 Pulsing air – the transverse roll 25
4.11 Oscillating air- the longitudinal roll 25
4.12 Ribboning air – the boosted longitudinal roll 26
4.13 Shore effects 26

4.14	Pattern size	26
4.15	Practicalities	26
4.16	What to look for	27
4.17	Sydney Harbour – Australian Intervarsity championships	29
4.18	Tallinn – Baltic pre-olympic regatta 1978	30

Chapter Five
The Breeze over a Cool Surface **32**

5.1	The onset of turbulence	32
5.2	The change of wind force on sails	32
5.3	The shape of the breeze	33
5.4	The gust mechanism	36
5.5	The fan	39
5.6	The effect of depth of the boundary layer	40

Chapter Six
Friction and the Wind-Wave Patterns **41**

6.1	Order – but where from?	41
6.2	Waves in the air – the friction mechanism	43
6.3	Oscillating surface waves	44
6.4	Regular or random	46
6.5	Transverse and other rolls	48

Chapter Seven
Heat and Thermal Patterns **52**

7.1	Surface heat in calm conditions	52
7.2	Surface heat in light airs	52
7.3	Surface heat in a breeze	52
7.4	Gusts plus surface heat	52
7.5	Wind-waves plus surface heat	53
7.6	Big wind-waves plus heat – the harmonic patterns	53
7.7	Small wind-waves – plus surface heat	57
7.8	The convergent/divergent pattern	59
7.9	The channelling winds	61
7.10	The two cell sizes	62
7.11	'Look for the speckled area'	62
7.12	The wandering breeze	62
7.13	Chilled air	63

Chapter Eight
Winds near Clouds **64**
8.1 The significant clouds 64
8.2 Frontal clouds 64
8.3 Roll clouds 65
8.4 Cumulus clouds – non raining 66
8.5 Raining clouds 69

Chapter Nine
Winds near Shores **73**
9.1 Starting points 73
9.2 The sea breeze mechanism 73
9.3 The quadrant effect 75
9.4 Refinements 78
9.5 The funnelling winds 82
9.6 Shoreline factors 83
9.7 The chilled wind situation 88
9.8 The land breezes 89

Chapter 10
Wind Appraisal and the *Stability Index* **92**
10.1 The parts of the puzzle 92
10.2 The kind of wind 93
10.3 The probable pattern 96
10.4 The stability index 99

Chapter 11
Race Preparation **102**
11.1 Principles and priorities 102
11.2 Preparation – overview 104
11.3 The water's waves and currents 105
11.4 Pre-regatta preparation 105
11.5 Pre-race preparation 107
11.6 Pre-start preparation 108
11.7 The winds 108
11.8 Pre-regatta preparation 108
11.9 Pre-race preparation 110
11.10 Pre-start preparation 113
11.11 In unsteady winds 113
11.12 In the steadier winds 114
11.13 In the quicker oscillations 115
11.14 In deep boundary layers 117

Chapter 12
Sailing the Wind Patterns **119**
12.1 The four groups 119
12.2 Sailing the unsteady winds 119
12.3 Sailing the wind-waves 122
12.4 Sailing through fronts 137
12.5 Sailing the cloud winds 137
12.6 The effects on wind of 'open' barriers 143

Part Two
Water

Chapter Thirteen
Waves **147**
13.1 The four wave systems 147
13.2 Wave motion 148
13.3 Regular waves 149
13.4 Chaotic waves 150
13.5 Swell 151
13.6 Standing waves 152

Chapter Fourteen
Depth and the Warm Surface Layer **154**
14.1 Depth 154
14.2 The warm surface layer 154

Chapter Fifteen
Currents and Tidal Stream **158**
15.1 Drive force 158
15.2 Friction effects and the velocity gradient 158
15.3 Flows through channels 158
15.4 Momentum effects 158
15.5 Flow over bars 159
15.6 Curves and eddies 160
15.7 Wind shear effects 160
15.8 Current and wave size 160

Preface to Part Three. 162

Part Three

The Boat

Introduction 163

Chapter Sixteen

The Quest for Speed **164**

16.1 Forces on a sailboat when sailing to windward 164
16.2 To sail faster 166
16.3 Changes of wind speed 167
16.4 The two wind speed ranges 169
16.5 Change of size 171
16.6 The emergence of ratios and weight 172
16.7 Historical performance limitations 171
16.8 Moving the crew to windward 174
16.9 The reduction of weight 174
16.10 The Eighteens and the third step 175
16.11 The dominance of ratios 178
16.12 The development of ratios 180
16.13 Downwind faster 180
16.14 Some unexpected observations 182
16.15 The dynamics of catamarans and sailboards 183
16.16 The application of ratios and the future 184
16.17 Different paths – same destination 184

Chapter Seventeen

Sails **188**

17.1 The starting point 188
17.2 Wings 188
17.3 The boundary layer 191
17.4 Sails behind masts 191
17.5 The separation bubble 194
17.6 Sails without masts 196
17.7 Super-critical and sub-critical flow 197
17.8 Dreams and realities 199
17.9 Modern rig development 204
17.10 Wingmasts – early development 207
17.11 The modern wingmast 209

Contents

Chapter Eighteen
Rigs **220**
18.1 The four rig groups 220
18.2 Group one – gaff rigs 220
18.3 Group two – early Bermudan rigs 221
18.4 Group three – the experimental years 222
18.5 Objects and dynamics 223
18.6 Modern rigs 227

Chapter Nineteen
Foils **232**
19.1 The foils – the centreboard, keel and rudder 232
19.2 Laminar flow sections 232
19.3 Surface texture 232
19.4 Modern foil development 234
19.5 Control at higher speeds 237
19.6 The drag of surface-piercing foils in wake 241
19.7 Centreboard area, point of sailing, wind speed and experience 243
19.8 Cambered centreboards 245
19.9 The rudder blade 245
19.10 Summary 246

Chapter Twenty
Hulls **247**
20.1 Experimental background 247
The motion of a dinghy hull
20.2 Summary 262
20.3 Skin friction 262
20.4 Form drag 263
20.5 Induced drag and leeway 264
20.6 Rudder deflection drag 264
Wave making drag
20.7 The three modes 265
20.8 Displacement sailing 266
20.9 The forced mode 267
20.10 Breakout and planing 268
20.11 The fourth mode 270
Drag in waves
20.12 Drag in regular waves – upwind and downwind 271
20.13 Drag in regular waves – crosswind 274
20.14 Drag in chaotic waves 274
20.15 Drag in swell 275
20.16 Concepts of mode sailing 275

Part Four
Handling

Chapter Twenty One
Scope **277**
21.1 Relevant conditions 277
21.2 High performance and other sailboats 277
21.3 Physical principles and administrative restrictions 277

Chapter Twenty Two
Handling to Windward **279**
22.1 Conventional and high performance handling 279
22.2 Sailing for speed, comfort and survival 280
22.3 The three handling regimes 281
22.4 In light airs 281
22.5 In moderate breezes – the vital changes 287
22.6 Sail trim techniques 288
22.7 Effects of fluctuations and gusts on technique 290
22.8 Handling in moderate breezes 290
22.9 In stronger breezes – the new factors 295
22.10 The trims for most power and least drag 296
22.11 Sail trim in 12 – 16 knots 297
22.12 Sail trim in 17 – 25 knots 298
22.13 Handling in stronger breezes 298
22.14 In rough air 302
22.15 Survival 304
22.16 To windward in waves 305
22.17 The effects of waves on performance 306
22.18 In waves and light airs 306
22.19 In waves and breeze – sail trim in 6 to 14 knots 309
22.20 In waves and breeze – sail trim in 15 to 25 knots 310
22.21 Handling in regular waves 311
22.22 Handling in chaotic waves 315
22.23 Handling in swell 316
22.24 Handling in waves and rough air 318

Chapter Twenty Three
Kinetics **320**
23.1 Introduction 320
23.2 Negative kinetics – the part power pause 320
23.3 Positive kinetics 322
23.4 Impulse 322
23.5 Energy recovery 323
23.6 Overtrimming (pumping) 325
23.7 Combined impulse and pumping 326

23.8 Surging 328
23.9 Other possible techniques 329
23.10 Summary 331

Chapter Twenty Four
Sailing Crosswind **333**
24.1 Crosswind sailing 333
24.2 Reaching dynamics 334
24.3 The design wind zones 336
24.4 The balance position 340
24.5 Steering for balance 341
24.6 Control at high speeds 344
24.7 In light air and flat water 346
24.8 In light air and waves 348
24.9 In moderate breeze and flat water 349
24.10 In moderate air and waves 351
24.11 Sailtrim crosswind in stronger breezes 352
24.12 Arc 1 – flat water and windward planing 353
24.13 Arc 1 – rough water 354
24.14 Arc 2 355
24.15 Arc 3 – zone A and flat water 355
24.16 Arc 3 – zone A and rough water 356
24.17 Arc 3 – zone B 357
24.18 Introduction to arc 3 – zone C 358
24.19 Arc 3 – zone C in steady wind and flat water 358
24.20 Arc 3 – zone C in gusts and channelling 358
24.21 Arc 3 – zone C in waves 359

Chapter Twenty Five
Sailing Downwind **362**
25.1 Sailing downwind – the principles and the performance factors 362
25.2 The fleeting dynamics of wind and wave 363
25.3 Rig characteristics and the properties of the delta planform 364
25.4 Hull characteristics 368
25.5 Handling in light airs and flat water 369
25.6 Two mode sailing 375
25.7 Handling in light air and waves 377
25.8 Downwind in breeze 379
25.9 Handling in blocking waves 380
25.10 Handling in surfing waves 382
25.11 Handling in mixed waves 384
25.12 Handling in chaotic waves 385
25.13 Handling in swell 386
25.14 Sailing the shifts 386
25.15 Handling in gusts 388
25.16 Practical handling downwind 392
Postscript 404
Index 409

Where so much of it started - Northbridge Sailing Club

Part One

Wind

Chapter One
The Racing Helmsman's Winds

1.1 Where to sail?

'The boats ahead were duelling up the rhumb line. We sailed to the right for the expected veer, found it, tacked and crossed them'.

'The wind was channelling gently, but the leading boat hadn't noticed. Downwind we found three separate channels one after the other, and passed him'.

Crews who know what to look for can often anticipate the next change and use it for great race advantage. They also have more fun.

The surface wind in which we sail is part of the lowest level of the atmosphere, called the atmospheric boundary layer. Within the air in this layer wave-like motions occur which are driven by both the present weather situation and also the temperature difference between the air and the underlying water and any nearby land. At the surface the wind blows only horizontally, but vertical flows in the motions above skew the surface wind from side to side and so cause oscillations which we can recognise as patterns. Three typical situations show something of the way this works.

Sea and lake breezes, funnelling winds and the up-valley 'ora' winds of mountain lakes occur in daytime when the weather-situation wind is light, there are few clouds to block the sunlight and the land surface becomes warm. These winds are part of shallow boundary layers usually only 200 to 300m thick. The analogy of water flowing along a shallow channel is apt, in that any waves will necessarily be small and will repeat quickly. Such winds are the steadiest and most predictable of all, in that their patterns show quick regular oscillations (two to four minutes each way) which can be anticipated with confidence. There are no substantial gusts and there are no longer-term features. These are the patterns which are typical of all boundary layers which are thin.

Away from shores at all times, or along shores when the land stays at about the same temperature as the water, as on cloudy days or nights, the weather system wind is the norm. The boundary layer is then 1,000 to 2,000m thick, and big wavelike motions can develop within these deep layers. On most days any lower clouds will have ragged peaky tops and on such days the motions in the air within these deep layers are like those in deep waters in which big waves and smaller waves are all jumbled together. Because some waves are big they take a long time to pass, so the principal features of these patterns repeat slowly. The typical weather system (gradient) wind has a pattern of stronger winds alternating slowly but not regularly with lighter winds, major shifts every 30 minutes or so but not regular, and strong gusts. In these conditions little prediction is possible.

Fortunately, there is an important exception. The Highs on a weather map are regions of subsiding air, and when a High is dominant this sinking squashes the boundary layer below to the point where the cloud-tops flatten, the motions within the boundary layer become orderly, and pilots then see the upper surface of the boundary layer as a wave system as regular as any waves on the sea (Fig. 6.8, p47). In these conditions the oscillations in the surface wind become as regular and predictable as the oscillations in a sea breeze. But because the waves in the thicker boundary layer are so much bigger, they take longer to pass and the oscillations they cause repeat much more slowly – 10 to 30 minutes each way is typical.

The skill of deciding, 'where to sail', is one half of yacht racing. Since so many helmsmen can do it consistently and well, it is demonstrably a skill, which can be acquired. The following examples show the ways champion crews analyse and use widely different conditions.

1.2 Kiel

At the Munich Olympics, in 1972, at which the sailing was from Kiel, the system used by the Australian team was that the team meteorologist (the author), moved onto the course area early each morning, and measured wind speed and direction every three minutes from 0730 until the finish. The morning plot was copied and passed to the individual crews on their way to the start areas pre-race. The early wind tended to be cool and the speed varied little. As each day progressed and warmed, the wind developed pronounced gusts and lulls, and its oscillations in direction became slower. Fig 1.1 is the plot of the wind on the day of the sixth heat. Its characteristics are typical of the winds during the later days of that regatta.

The Australian Dragon class yacht, crewed by John Cuneo, Tom Anderson and John Shaw elected to race by concentrating primarily on exploiting the changes in wind direction. They followed their compass and sailed the advantaged tacks. They ignored any differences in wind speed which they observed from time to time. They often separated widely from the rest of the fleet. They won most of their heats. They won them by wide margins. They won that regatta and a gold medal.

On the nearby FD, Star and Tempest course, with identical winds, the Australian FD crew applied exactly the same technique as the Dragon crew, and did *not* win. From their recent very successful international regatta placings they knew that they were sailing one of the fastest FD's in the world at that time. But what won for the slower and 'hull speed limited' Dragon did *not* win for the higher-performance FD. The faster boat reached the lay-lines too soon for the technique to work properly, and in any case it had already dropped behind those of its competitors who had observed areas of stronger wind and had systematically steered towards and into them, and had then sailed faster within them.

On the same course, the Australian Star Class yacht, crewed by David Forbes and John Anderson, elected to sail much more tactical races, in which they sailed the advantaged tacks only when this was consistent with not sailing into lighter air and not sailing away from their principal opponents.They finished consistently well, won some of their heats, and won that regatta and a gold medal.

No other example could so perfectly emphasise the importance of 'where to sail'. At the time of Kiel we did not fully understand the theory. For truly brilliant crews such as the two gold medal winners this does not matter – crews of that quality have the knack of being able to select and apply what works best for them and their boats, and never mind the theory. Years later, some earnest plodder will finally work out and explain what was happening in that situation, and why it can be that in the same wind and sea-state conditions different types of boat need different techniques and tactics to win.

1.3 Marstrand

At the 1974 world 505 championships held at Marstrand, Sweden, I measured the wind during two of the race days from halfway up the hillside on the south-western end of the island. From this height I could see the streaks on the water which are formed by the wind – the 'wind lanes' – all the way from the nearby shore for several miles upwind. On one day the wind, initially, was from the WSW, and was warm and moist. Thin stratus cloud minimised the diurnal heating. This was a classic 'warm air over cold water' situation in which warmer air was chilled by the water surface, and oscillated regularly. At about 1430 a change passed over, after which the air was colder and the wind stronger, and the oscillations occurred about six times more slowly. Fig 1.2 gives the wind speed and direction on this day.

The marking of the water surface caused by the wind was very even.There was no trace of 'channelling' – the tendency of the wind to blow in alternating stronger and lighter channels which are aligned with the wind direction. In the earlier lighter wind, the wind lanes snaked upwind in the form of horizontal waves, which flowed steadily towards me at about one quarter of the wind speed. I had previously watched the progress of similar waves both in Sydney, and also on the Ijsselmeer at Medemblik. The gap in the record of Fig 1.2 was due to a rain shower, during which I could not see very far. This was a day on which the wind's unsteadiness (apart from the isolated rain shower) was overwhelmingly a slow rhythmic oscillation of direction. Change of speed was minimal. In these conditions the fastest racing technique is always to sail the advantaged tacks and gybes, and this is true for all sailboats. The crews in the fleet below me tacked almost in unison as each new shift flowed over them. The winners were the ones who combined good boatspeed with playing this game most accurately.

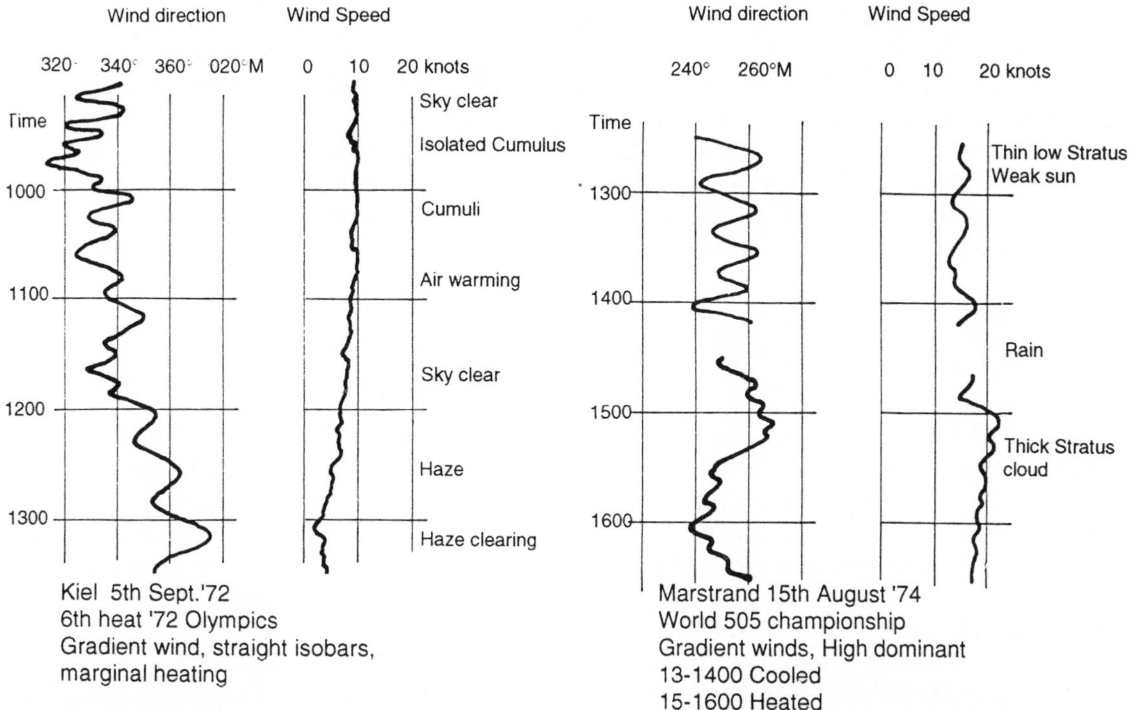

Fig 1.1 Kiel wind trace

Fig 1.2 Marstrand wind trace

1.4 Keppel bay

The 1988 Tasar world championships were planned to enjoy the warm sheltered waters inside the Great Barrier Reef and the warm south-east trade winds which prevail in these tropical latitudes at this time of year. This was dream stuff, and sailors world-wide responded enthusiastically.In the week before the regatta, one hundred odd crews enjoyed the warm-up races. The dreams began to come true. The climate was fine and mild, the warm winds steady and the shifts predictable, the fastest crews contested the lead, and confidence abounded.

An anticyclone moved through the Great Australian Bight. It slowed near Tasmania, grew to a huge size, stopped for awhile, and pulsed a great surge of cold polar air northwards over eastern Australia for two thousand miles toward the equator. For two days at Keppel Bay the wind blew with gale force, then it eased, but the High scarcely moved and the cold southerly air just kept flowing north more and more slowly. The change in temperature at Keppel Bay wasn't much – but it was enough to make the air a degree or two cooler than the warmer water inside the reef.

In chapter 7, the various patterns which result when air is heated from below are described. In this case, the heating was sufficient, for several days, to make the apparently steady trade wind 'boil' gently in a cellular pattern. From any high vantage point, the surface could be seen to be patchy in the pattern of a net, with the wind speed a little lighter in the holes, and a little stronger where the strings would be. The spacing of the holes was about 750 to 1,000m apart. From a helmsman's eye-level, even the nearest speed variation was scarcely visible to those who looked, and totally unnoticed by those who assumed that trade winds were steady, and didn't look.

Not surprisingly, only a handful of the 115 starters handled these most difficult conditions well. This regatta was won by those crews who knew when *not* to use the compass, who sensed patterned wind speed change across the course, and who were most successful in sailing to and staying within the bands of slightly stronger air.

1.5 Lake Garda

In the months prior to the Seoul Olympics, some of the crews from both Europe and Australia elected to train on Lake Garda, because it was one place where they were assured of consistently strong winds such as they anticipated at Pusan.

They came to know it quite well. For planing boats, which go faster to windward in stronger winds, the environmental factors reduced to, '. . . even there, everybody headed for the side of the lake, which was a sheer mountain wall, because the wind there was five knots stronger. This far outweighed the ten degree shifts in the middle of the lake.'

Note however, that for the crews of the hull-speed-limited keelboats (Stars), it didn't. Their fastest VMG was achieved by making full use of the windshifts in the lighter winds, so long as the speeds of these winds were *design wind speed* and upwards. Those who chose the side of the lake could sail no faster in the stronger winds, and were convincingly beaten by those who sailed just as fast in the lighter winds, *and* were able to take full advantage of the windshifts in the middle.

So in this situation, the question of 'the fastest way', depended entirely on the characteristics of the boat you happened to be sailing.

1.6 Rio de Janeiro

At the world Laser championships at Capo Frio, near Rio de Janeiro, in the late 1970's, one of the competitors was Tim Alexander, an Australian and a keen student of wind patterns. Tim lives in Sydney, which lies on the east coast of Australia. He later used two arresting phrases in describing the regatta. 'It was good to be sailing on the eastern side of a great southern hemisphere continent, with all the circulations going the right way'. And again, – 'The clouds were solid, low and isolated. They blew in from out to sea. When you looked upwind it was like watching a giant TV screen in the sky. You could usually see exactly what was going to happen minutes before it arrived'.

At the start of one race, Tim was squeezed out backwards and found himself last and with no wind, while the other one hundred and three starters moved away. Tim's response was to look at the sky upwind.He saw three clouds approaching.The first two were at a distance and spacing where it was worth a try to exploit the shifts around both. The third was too far away to be certain, but looked difficult.

As he regained air and movement, Tim concentrated absolutely on sailing to avoid the calm area just downwind of the first cloud, and to position himself so that he could tack and sail alongside and under its upwind shoulder. He accepted bad air and he took sterns to do it. He began to pass those who were caught in the calm. He exploited perfectly the arc of stronger inflowing air under the side and upwind shoulder of that first cloud. He judged his break-off so that he could sail to and repeat the technique with the second cloud. When he left the influence of the second cloud he was respectably placed in the fleet, and somewhat to the left of the rhumb line. The third cloud, now slightly further to the left, was going to be of no help, because he would have had to sail beyond the port lay line to use it.

Sometimes you can be lucky.

At exactly the right time, the third cloud began to rain! Non-raining clouds draw the surface wind inward, but raining clouds blow it outward. As the shower fell, the gust front poured outwards from its base. For Tim it arrived as a sustained, strong, backed gust. On port tack toward the left of the course he found himself lifted until he was able to point, for a while, almost directly at the windward mark. He rounded fourth.

Quite a recovery from 104th, during a first windward leg. Cloud winds can be useful.

1.7 The different possibilities

The Kiel , Marstrand and Keppel Bay examples all describe situations in which a wind pattern – a different pattern in each case – is uniform over a wide area.

The Lake Garda example is a situation in which a wind pattern is constant with respect to a shoreline – in this case, a mountainside.

The Rio de Janeiro example emphasises the different wind patterns which exist adjacent to both non-raining low-based clouds, and all raining clouds.These patterns move with the clouds.

In each of these five examples, boat speed alone could not win. Boat speed plus knowledge of tide and current could do a little better, but still would have had no hope of winning.It was not until good boat speed was combined with gifted use of the detail of the wind's flow, plus respect for the current, that superior performance over the race course became possible.

This 'other half' of sailing is challenging, fascinating, – and enormously rewarding.

Chapter Two
The Gradient Wind

2.1 The wind's driving force

The wind is driven by thermal energy. The sun heats the equator more than the poles. How this temperature difference leads to the world's complex wind flows is most easily understood if we build up the complete picture, in imagination, one step at a time.

As a starting point, imagine the world with its atmosphere, but without the sun, without clouds and without the earth's daily rotation. On such a planet, the atmosphere would be everywhere quiescent.

Let us, in imagination, now add the sun. The atmosphere is almost transparent to solar radiation, so the sunshine does not heat the atmosphere directly. It is the earth's surface which is heated. Because sunshine falls most directly on the equator, and not at all on the poles, the earth's surface temperatures become progressively hotter from polar to equatorial regions. Air in contact with the surface is heated by conduction, expands, becomes less dense and so rises from the surface. This rising is important because it permits the heated air to be replaced by cooler air which in turn is heated.

However, it is the expansion which turns out to be even more important, because due to expansion, the sequentially heated equatorial atmosphere becomes greater in total depth than the colder polar atmosphere. In practice these depths are about 18 kilometres at the equator and 9 kilometres at the poles. This means that the upper levels of the equatorial troposphere – the denser part of the atmosphere below the stratosphere – are at a greater height above the earth's surface than the upper levels of the polar troposphere. This difference in height causes the air at the upper levels of the troposphere to flow 'downhill' from its 18 kilometre height over the equator to its 9 kilometre height over the poles. Fig. 2.1 shows the factors at work.

This upper-level 'downhill' counterflow is critically important, because it creates the pressure differences which drive the circulation. As the upper level air flows away from the equator, the surface pressure is correspondingly reduced. As it heaps up over the polar regions, the surface pressure is increased. The denser surface air responds to this pressure difference by flowing at low levels from the higher pressure polar regions toward the lower pressure equatorial regions. As it approaches the hotter regions it is warmed, expands, and rises. At upper levels it flows downhill, back to the poles, where it subsides and is driven again by the pressure difference towards the equator.

The surface flow of this heat-driven cycle is what sailors call, 'wind'.

The above discussion has assumed a simplified model in order to concentrate on the basic point. Readers who would like more detail are referred to the standard texts on meteorology, which describe the further factors which cause the flow between poles and equator to become broken into identifiable segments.

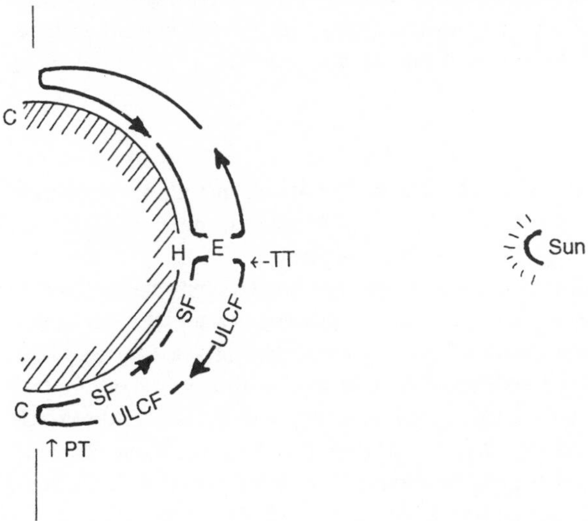

C=Cold polar surface
SF=Surface flow - wind
H=Heated tropical surface
E=Heated, expanded rising air
TT=Tropical Tropopause - 18Km high
ULCF=Upper level counterflow
PT=Polar Tropopause - 9Km high
Chilled air subsides over polar regions

Fig 2.1 The wind's thermal drive

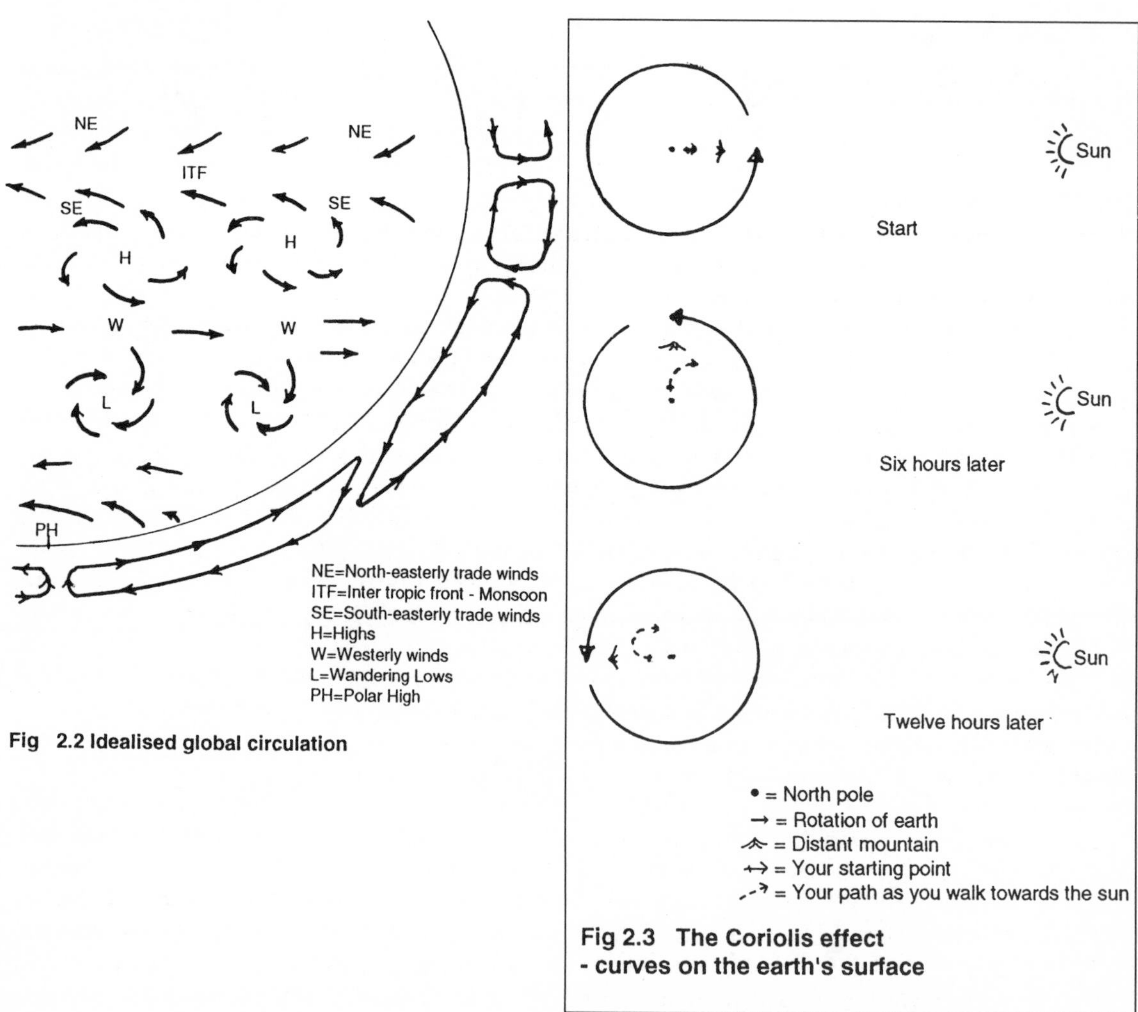

Fig 2.2 Idealised global circulation

Fig 2.3 The Coriolis effect - curves on the earth's surface

These cause vertical interchange in both the wandering depressions of the temperate latitudes and the great sub-tropical anticyclones, and also the easterly and westerly flows associated with these systems. Fig. 2.2 shows the sort of pattern which is most common over the great oceans of the southern hemisphere. The northern hemisphere is much less stable as it tends to be dominated more by the summer heat and winter cold extremes of the vast North American and Eurasian land masses. The basic point is that all of these systems are driven by heat, and the fundamental circulation at the surface tends to be from the poles towards the equator.

2.2 Circulation

Things in motion, such as wind, tend to continue in straight lines. The key to understanding the next bit is to realise that these straight lines are straight lines in space. The real world rotates. When we consider 'straight lines in space' over the surface of a rotating world, strange things happen.

Imagine that you are near one of the poles and that the sun, which we can regard as reasonably fixed in space, is low on the horizon. You decide to walk a 'straight line in space' by walking towards the sun. If you walk for a day, always towards the sun, you will have achieved your 'straight line in space' object. But because the earth will have turned beneath you as you walked, your footsteps will have traced a curve through about 360 degrees with reference to 'North' on the earth, and this curve will be deflected towards the right, i.e. it will be clockwise in the northern hemisphere, and towards the left and so be anti-clockwise in the southern. This principle will remain true at every other place on the earth's surface except at the latitude directly under the sun. Fig. 2.3 shows how your walk would appear to an observer above the North Pole.

So it is with the wind.

If you now imagine that a cubic kilometre of air surrounds you when you start to walk directly away from the North Pole, and that this wind is just starting its pressure-driven journey towards the equator, and that it happens to be moving at about your own speed, then you are thinking of a mass of about 1.2 million tonnes of air which is moving south at about 3 knots. It is being driven towards the south by the higher pressure over the North Pole. At the time you start, both you and the air happen to be moving south with respect to the earth, and towards the sun with respect to space.

Six hours later, as you walk, you will still be walking towards the sun. The air around you, responding with its own momentum to the 'straight line in space' principle, will also be still moving towards the sun. But beneath both you and the air, the earth will have rotated 90 degrees, and with respect to the earth, both you and the air will have curved to the right and be now moving west, not south. This is no problem for you, but it is for the air, because the higher pressure is still over the earth's North Pole, and this pressure is now accelerating the air to the south with respect to the earth, and no longer towards the sun, which will now be in the west. Strange things are happening.

Over the next hour, there is a parting of the ways. As you continue to walk towards the sun, your direction with respect to the earth will continue to curve to the right, from the west towards the north. But the air with all its mass and momentum (and your cubic kilometre is only one of tens of millions) cannot flow northward against the pressure which started its movement towards the south. Once the air has turned 90 degrees with respect to the earth, that is its limit. Any further turning will see the air trying to flow against the pressure gradient. So in practice the air will be continuously accelerated towards the south, the earth will turn beneath it, and the southward acceleration and velocity of six hours ago will become a westward velocity with respect to the earth six hours later. As the earth turns, the direction of the pressure difference remains constant with respect to the earth and so turns with it. This turning pressure difference continually both accelerates and turns the air.

The end result as far as the outflowing polar air is concerned, is that it ceases to flow toward the equator and is instead turned to the right and circles the pole in a clockwise direction in a system which we call 'the North Polar High'. In practice the circle 'leaks' a little, because surface friction slows the lowest-level air, and this slowed air is blown somewhat outwards for the same reason that air at rest is initially blown directly away from high pressure. So the air in fact flows in a near-circular spiral which delays but does not quite stop the flow of the air from an area of higher pressure towards lower pressure.

Air flowing outwards from the South Polar High is similarly turned, but to the left instead of the right, and so circulates in an anti-clockwise direction.

Wherever an area forms in which the air, for any reason, is at some higher pressure than the surrounding air, the same sequence will occur. The initial flow will be directly outward, away from the area of higher pressure. But as soon as the air starts moving and develops momentum, the turning pressure gradient will start to accelerate it in a progressively different direction and a near-circular flow, clockwise in the northern hemisphere and anti-clockwise in the southern, will establish around any area of higher pressure.

Conversely, wherever the air is heated and rises and so generates an area in which the pressure is slightly lower than elsewhere, the surrounding air will initially begin to flow directly inwards towards the lowest pressure. In the northern hemisphere the inflowing air will curve to the right due to the Coriolis effect (see below), exactly as does the outflowing polar air and will begin to swirl round the area of lower pressure in an anti-clockwise direction in a near-circular pattern which we recognise as a 'Low' on the weather map. This whole mechanism can be seen in microscale whenever you pull the plug from a flat-bottomed basin full of water. In ideal conditions the centrifugal force of the swirl can almost hold back the flow but there will always be some inward leakage of the slowed water at the bottom which will escape down the drain. In the atmosphere it escapes upward. In the southern hemisphere the circulation will be clockwise around a Low.

To summarise: the rotation of the earth causes the air, which initially starts to flow directly away from areas of higher pressure and directly towards areas of lower pressure, to turn almost 90 degrees and thereafter to flow in a near-circular spiral. Its direction of flow at any point will be approximately at right angles to the pressure gradient. This principle is called 'The Coriolis Acceleration', and the wind 'The Gradient Wind'. All that this means is that when you walk a straight line in space, your footsteps, or the shadow of a bullet, or the shadow of everything else that goes straight in space, will all trace curves on the surface of the rotating earth.

2.3 Ups and downs

Note particularly some simple but vital facts:

You can imagine the Highs on a weather map as the crests and the Lows as the troughs of a very slow-moving wave system. Under the crests the surface pressure is higher because the air is deeper or denser or both, and vice versa under the troughs. The surface air begins as always to flow from higher to lower pressure but the system is so big and moves so slowly that Coriolis changes the outflows and inflows into the near-circular spirals we are familiar with as Highs and Lows.

The near-circular outflowing spiral caused by Coriolis around a High merely delays and does not prevent, the outflow of air. The place of the air which escapes is taken by air from above which subsides toward the surface as it spirals. All high pressure areas are therefore areas of subsidence, of descending air, similar in principle to the polar Highs.

Conversely, the inflowing air which spirals around and into a Low pressure area, escapes upwards. All low pressure areas are therefore areas of convergence, of rising air, similar in principle to the rising air of the inter-tropic front.

2.4 Fires in the sky

So far we have built up, in imagination, a world with an atmosphere and a sun and have seen what happens to the atmosphere when the earth starts to spin.

Let us now add water. Water exists in nature in three forms: ice, water and water vapour.

If you are surrounded by ice and want water, you have to add heat to a chunk of ice to melt it. If you want to turn the water into steam, you must add more heat to bring the ice-cold water to the boil, and then even more heat to evaporate the boiling water into water vapour. The large amount of heat which is needed to turn ice into water and then water into water vapour, is called *latent heat*.

Latent heat also works the other way. Whenever water vapour turns into water, or water into ice, latent heat is released. If you put your finger near steam which is escaping from a boiling kettle, you will quickly realise how fierce this heating is.

You can now visualise the way in which every Cumulus cloud which you see in the sky acts as a vast furnace. The cloud is a mass of droplets of liquid water. At its base, as the water vapour in the air condenses into water droplets, it liberates exactly the same latent heat as burned your finger. (It happens at a much lower temperature but the amount of latent heat liberated per gram of water is exactly the same.) So the temperature within the cloud becomes warmer than that of the surrounding air. The warmed air rises. This sucks more air into its base. At the top, where the rising cloud meets dry clean air, the droplets evaporate, and the latent heat is re-absorbed. Fig. 2.4(a) shows the key facts. Heated from the bottom, chilled at the top, with a rising core several degrees warmer than the surrounding air and surrounded by a 'doughnut' of subsiding air which then turns inwards and flows towards the base – that is the dynamic picture of a Cumulus cloud. We will look at its effect on the racing helmsman's winds a few pages further on. (The sequence: 'subsiding air around a Cumulus cloud, and a strongly rising core within it', is every aircraft pilot's routine experience.)

When the cloud starts to rain, the part of the water which falls as rain is lost from the cloud and does not evaporate within the cloud system. So the dynamic picture of a raining cloud is much more energetic. Fig. 2.4(b) gives the key facts. It is heated from the bottom and only partially chilled at the top and so it has a heat surplus and grows bigger and lives longer.

If the cloud becomes really big, as in a thunderstorm, the dynamic picture changes violently. The upper levels start to glaciate – to turn into the characteristic giant feathery ice-crystal thunderheads. As the water droplets turn into ice they reverse the process. They liberate another burst of latent heat instead of absorbing it

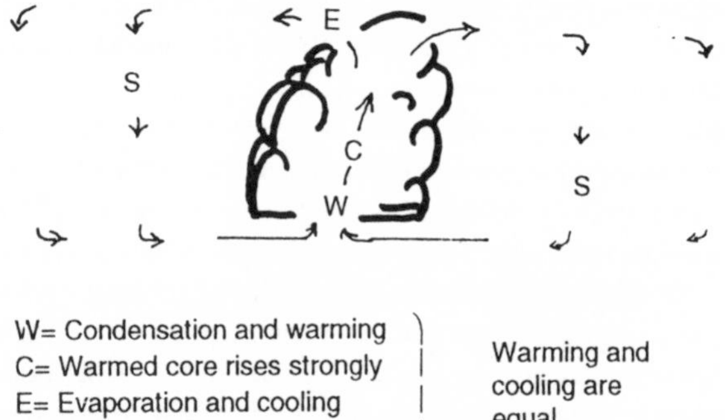

Fig 2.4(a) Heat dynamics of non-raining clouds

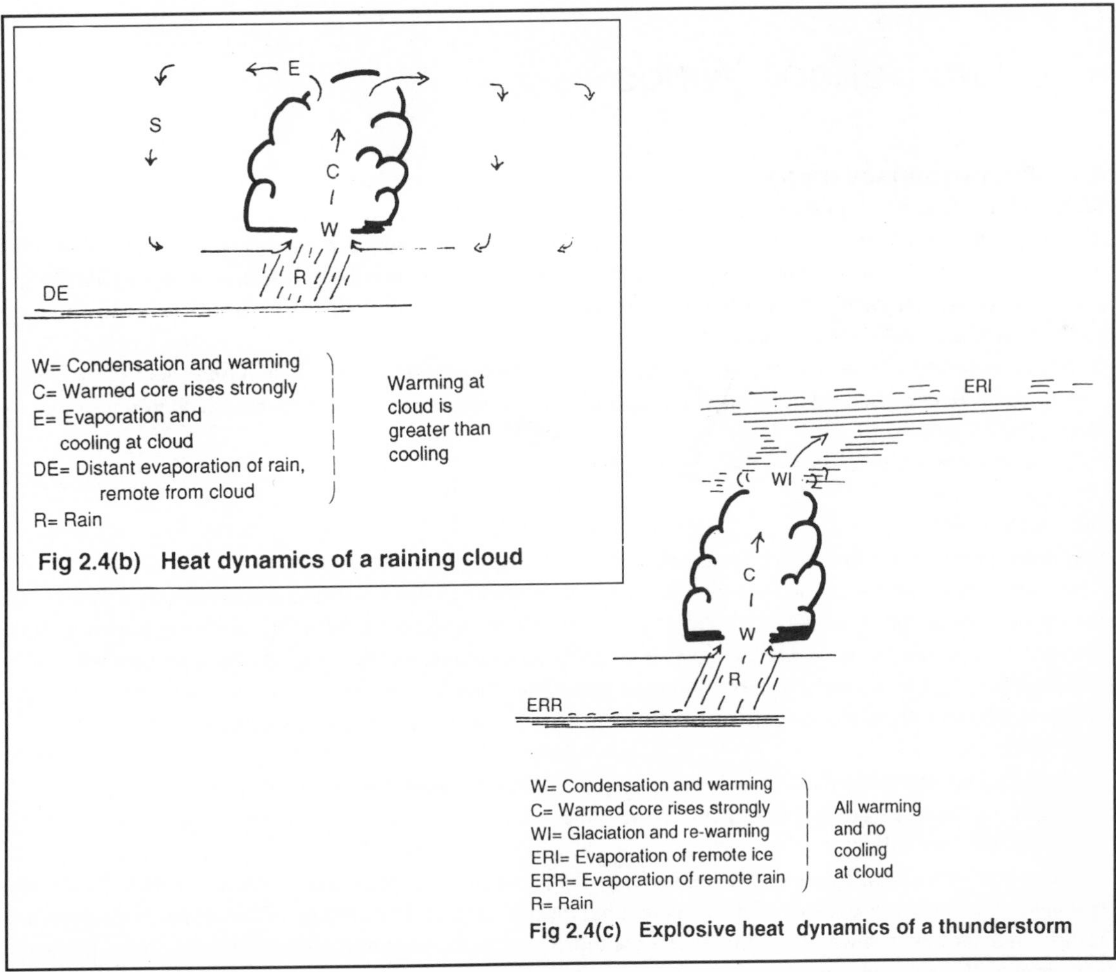

Fig 2.4(b) Heat dynamics of a raining cloud

Fig 2.4(c) Explosive heat dynamics of a thunderstorm

as they did when they evaporated. The ice-crystal top flows far downwind. It is usually hundreds of miles away and hours later that the ice sublimes into water vapour and re-absorbs its latent heat. So the dynamic picture of a raining thundercloud becomes: heated at the bottom, re-heated near the top and scarcely chilled at all. No wonder thunderstorms 'explode'. Fig. 2.4(c) summarises these dynamics.

I have described the Cumulus cloud situation because individual clouds are everyday things that we can relate to and sometimes we can watch their mechanisms working and understand what is going on. But on the global scale, the effects of water vapour and latent heat are breathtaking.

Look at a globe and you will see that most of the earth's equatorial regions are ocean. So the bulk of the sun's vast radiation energy falls on water and is totally absorbed in evaporating sea-water into water vapour. This means that a very large part of the total solar energy received by the earth is converted into latent heat. The low-level winds around the great sub-tropical high pressure areas – the relatively cloudless areas which, over land, are responsible for the earth's desert areas – carry this water vapour partly towards the equator and partly toward the poles. Near the equator the converging streams combine to form what land-dwellers call the monsoon, mariners used to call the doldrums and aviators call the inter-tropic front. The poleward flows meet and react with the outflowing cold polar air to form the wandering depressions (Lows) of the temperate regions. Both areas are the cloudy areas of the world. Within their clouds, latent heat which has been accumulated over millions of square kilometres and long periods of time is released within relatively small areas and short periods of time. This is the primary energy source which drives these systems. It greatly increases the local temperature and pressure differences, and the wind speeds and the unpredictability of these systems.

Latent heat, with its fierce heating of the clouds, is the great concentrator of thermal energy into small areas, and the de-stabiliser of steady-state systems.

Chapter Three
The Two Surface Winds

3.1 The two surface winds

So far, I have described how and why the winds blow. Sailors use only the ten, or at most thirty metres of the wind at the very bottom of an atmosphere which is many thousands of metres deep.

The behaviour of this surface wind is unique. It adopts one or the other of two forms. It curves, pulses and oscillates with a patterned beauty found at no other level.

The two forms are *'light airs'* and *'breeze'*.

The basic **light air** patterns are *'steady, unsteady, pulsing, oscillating'* and *'ribboning'*.

The basic **breeze** patterns are *'steady, wandering, pulsing, convergent/divergent, channelling', and 'harsh'*.

These patterns are discussed in the chapters ahead.

3.2 Light airs

Light airs are those winds which have the properties of a laminar boundary layer.

To understand the nature of light air, the analogy of water flowing down a stream is useful. Where the flow speed is slow, the surface is glassy and smooth. Water-logged leaves in the stream are carried along smoothly. In particular, leaves at the bottom scarcely move, leaves close to the bottom move very slowly, those a little further from the bottom move a little faster and so on. Further, all these leaves maintain a constant distance from the bottom as they move along. This is laminar flow.In the air, the situation is exactly the same.

Light airs are those winds with an average speed of about 5 knots or less.Their primary characteristic is that the flow speed is feeble near the surface and increases steadily with increasing height up to about 10m in 5 knots but less in lighter airs.

This is shown in Fig. 3.1(a). The ribbons are all of the same length and width, made of the same spinnaker cloth and are at 1 metre intervals to a height of 6 metres. The change of wind speed with height is clearly indicated by the way the ribbons stream more horizontally with increasing heights. Note the glassy appearance of the water surface.

In Fig. 3.1(a) the boat is stationary, so the ribbons are responding to the True Wind.

In Figs 3.1 (b) and (c) the boat is moving at about 2 knots across a 4 knot wind in a direction as if broad reaching, so in these pictures the ribbons are responding to the Apparent Wind. Fig 3.1(b) is a view from behind and Fig 3.1(c) is a view looking vertically up the ribbon halyard. The ribbons show that in light air there is an extraordinary change in the direction of the Apparent Wind with height, particularly when sailing crosswind. Nearer the surface where the True Wind is feeble, the Apparent Wind blows more from ahead. At height, where the True Wind is stronger, the Apparent Wind blows more from the beam. Therefore when sailing any high performance boat in light airs, sail twist is essential in order to optimise the sail's trim at each height to this 'twisted' Apparent Wind. Also, most of the sail's drive will be developed by the top 25% of the rig because that is where the stronger wind blows – so when sailing in light air the handling and trim of the upper sails becomes all-important.

Fig. 3.1(d) shows the extreme case in which the boat is moving at about 2 knots directly downwind, in a wind of about 4 knots at the masthead. The boat is overtaking the slower True Wind near the surface, so at low levels the Apparent Wind blows from ahead and the ribbons stream aft. At height, the stronger True Wind blows faster than the boat, so the Apparent Wind there blows from astern and the ribbons stream forward. This is why spinnakers, even masthead spinnakers, can be such an embarrassment when sailing fast boats downwind in light airs.

In this series of photographs, I have highlighted in white the dark background adjacent to the lower ribbons in order to improve the contrast and their visibility.

3.3 Breezes

Breezes are those winds which have the properties of a turbulent boundary layer.

If, back at our stream, we follow it to a stretch where the channel narrows and the flow speed increases, we will notice that at a particular point the surface becomes rippled with turbulence.This new turbulence does not grow gradually. It occurs suddenly. The flow has only two states – laminar or turbulent. There is no such flow-state as half-turbulent.

In turbulent flow, water-logged leaves are swept haphazardly towards and away from the bottom. Those which are swept towards the bottom arrive there with good speed and scrub the bottom before they are slowed by friction – except that usually, they are soon swept upwards again. We thus see that apart from being faster, this turbulent stream is different from the earlier laminar stream in three ways:

1 The motion is everywhere unsteady.

2 Flow speed near the bottom is almost as fast as higher up.

3 'Bursts' of fast water periodically scrub the bottom itself.

This situation is repeated exactly in the atmosphere. Breezes are winds with average speeds of about 6 knots or more. Their primary characteristic is that the change of speed with height is confined almost entirely to the one to two metres closest to the surface. Fig. 3.2(a) repeats the situation of Fig. 3.1(a). Wind speed at 2 metres is about 8 knots. It is clear from the angles of the ribbons that there is not much difference in wind speed between about 2 metres and 7 metres. All aviation experience suggests that if the wind near the surface is about 10 knots, it will be about 15 knots at 300 metres and nearer 20 knots at 1,000 metres. Over the height of any rig this sort of change of speed with height will be negligible.

Since the wind speed at all heights above about 1 metre is almost the same, the direction of the Apparent Wind will also be about the same. Figs 3.2(b) and (c) repeat Figs 3.1(b) and (c), except that the wind speed is about 8 knots and the boat speed is about 4 knots. The ribbons indicate that in a breeze, the direction of the Apparent Wind does not change significantly with height. This is totally different from the light air situation.

Comparison of Figs 3.1 and 3.2 make it clear that light air is not just a breeze which is blowing more slowly. It is an altogether different kind of wind, and the handling techniques which are fastest in light airs are therefore quite different from those which are fastest in breezes. In breezes the wind speed at all heights above 1 metre is about the same, every part of every sail is equally important and the sails should be trimmed accordingly. A square metre at the bottom of the mainsail will drive the boat just as hard as a square metre at the top. The direction of the Apparent Wind at the masthead will now be the same as at the boom. Twist (other than that needed to accommodate the deflected flow from the lower part of a fractional jib) should be minimised or eliminated.

Light air - as in Fig 3.1(a)

The boat is moving downwind at 2 knots.

Apparent Wind at masthead blows from astern.
Apparent Wind near the surface blows from ahead!

Fig 3.1(d)
Ribbon behaviour downwind in light air

Fig 3.1 Ribbon behaviour in light air

Light air
- about 4 knots at masthead
- boat stationary.

Upper ribbons stream more horizontally. Progressively greater droop of lower ribbons shows how wind speed becomes progressively less at lower levels.

Fig 3.1(a)

Light air
(as 3.1(a) above)
but moving at 2 knots in a broad reaching direction.
Ribbons viewed from astern.

Upper ribbons stream in Apparent Wind from abeam.
Lower ribbons stream in Apparent wind more from ahead.

Fig 3.1(b)

Exactly as 3.1(b) above, but ribbons viewed looking vertically upwards from the cockpit floor.
Bow is towards bottom of page, stern to top.

Fig 3.1(c)

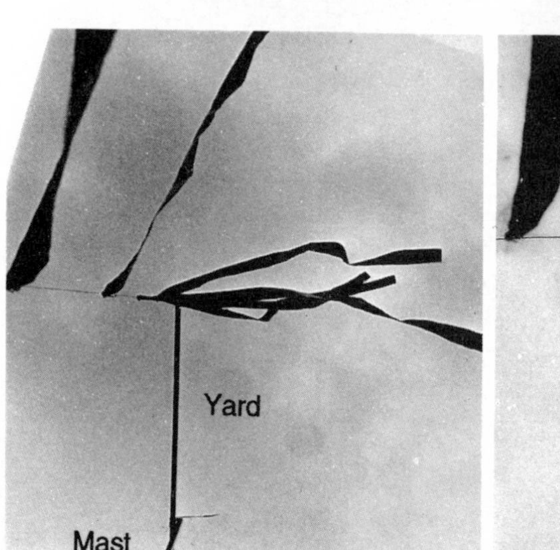

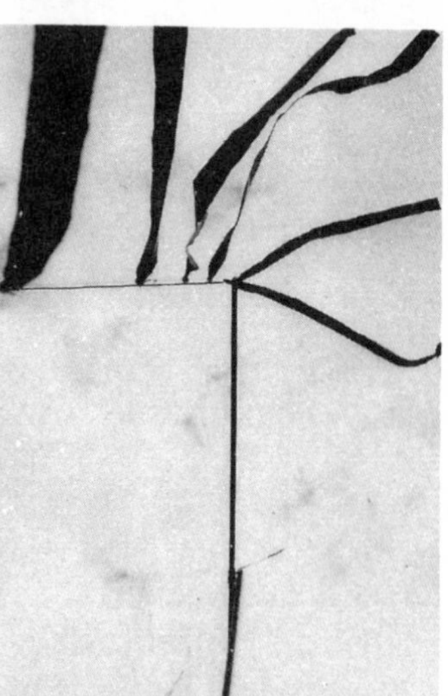

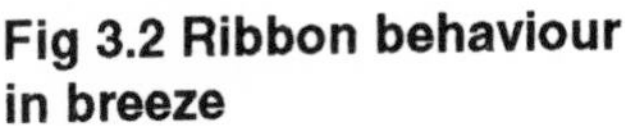

Fig 3.2 Ribbon behaviour in breeze

Breeze - about 8 knots at 2m - boat stationary.

Only lowest ribbon droops. All other ribbons stream at about the same angle. This indicates no increase of wind strength with height above about 1m.

Fig 3.2(a)

Breeze - as 3.2(a) above but boat moving at 4 knots in broad reaching direction.

Ribbons viewed from astern. Little difference in ribbon angle with height. Indicates little difference of windspeed with height.

Fig 3.2(b)

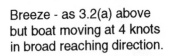

Exactly as 3.2(b) above, but ribbons viewed looking vertically upwards from the cockpit floor. Bow is towards bottom of page, stern the top.

Fig 3.2(c)

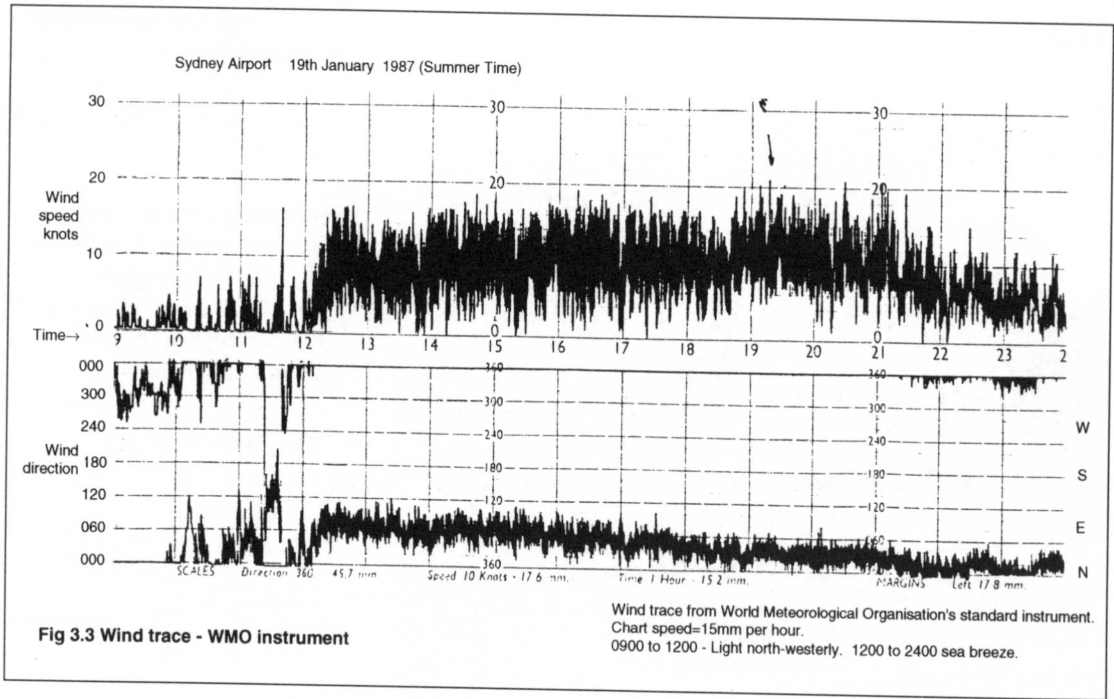

Fig 3.3 Wind trace - WMO instrument

Wind trace from World Meteorological Organisation's standard instrument. Chart speed=15mm per hour.
0900 to 1200 - Light north-westerly. 1200 to 2400 sea breeze.

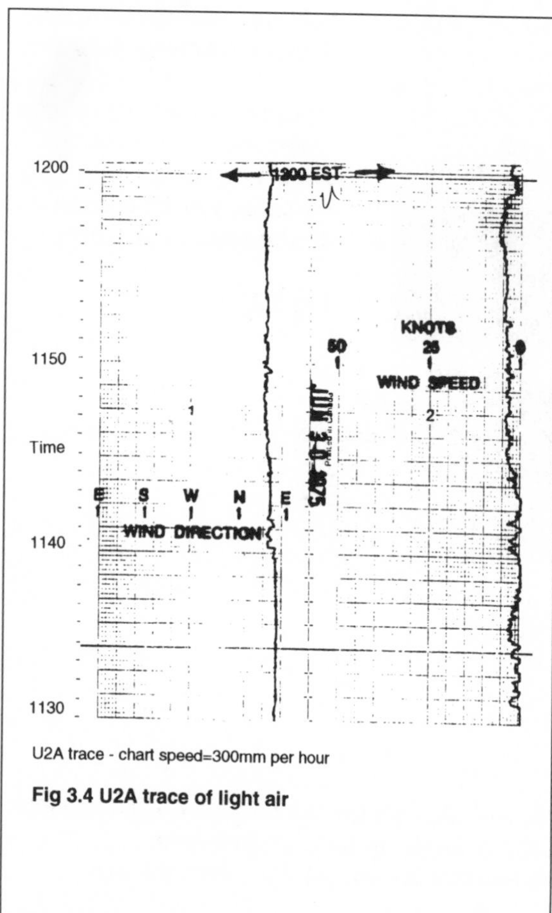

U2A trace - chart speed=300mm per hour

Fig 3.4 U2A trace of light air

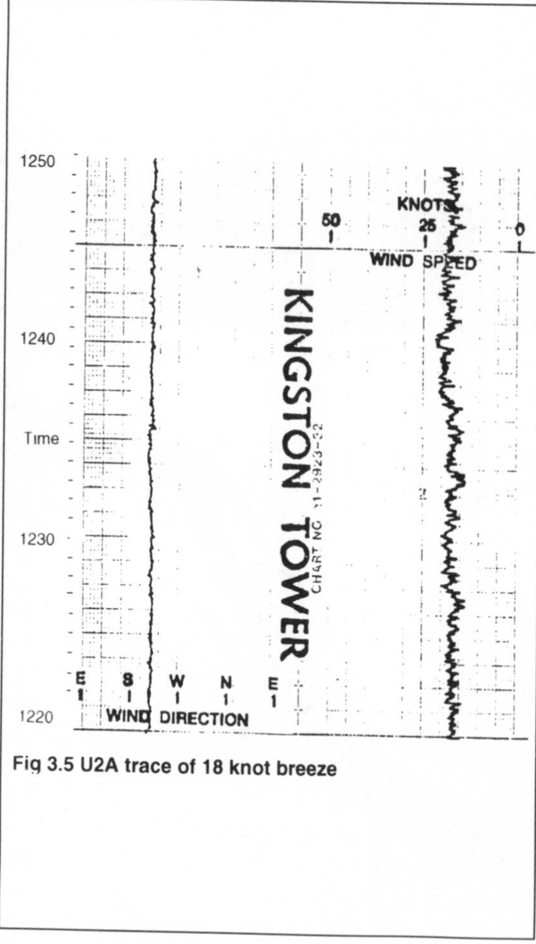

Fig 3.5 U2A trace of 18 knot breeze

3.4 Wind recording instruments

We cannot see the wind at all, nor can we feel it very accurately. In order to sense its flow, we customarily use indirect observations such as the movements of clouds, the behaviour of foliage or flags, and particularly the marks which the wind makes on the surface of the water. These are useful, but they vanish. In order to study the wind's structure and detail, we need records which do not vanish.

Fig 3.3 shows the wind trace of a day at Sydney Airport as drawn by the World Meteorological Organisation's standard instrument, the Dine's Anemograph. The broad information from this trace is superb; from 0900 to 1200 a light north-westerly veered to the north-east, then the sea breeze set in and blew steadily until dusk and faded until midnight, veering toward the north with Coriolis as the hours passed. In this instrument, the paper moves under the pens at about 15mm each hour. This speed is convenient in that each day's trace is only about 400mm long, and so is compact enough to file. But the slow chart speed so crowds the trace that it is not possible to analyse the fine detail of any individual gust or lull.

During the summer which preceded the 1976 Olympics in Montreal, with the sailing at Kingston, Ontario, the Canadian Department of the Environment installed an instrumented floating tower called the Kingston Tower, positioned eight miles offshore and in the sailing waters. Wind speed and direction were continuously recorded from 0900 until 1500 by an instrument (the U2A) which was modified to run its chart at about 300 mm per hour or 20 times faster than the W.M.O. instrument. Other measurements, including air temperature and water temperature, were also continuously recorded. As a result, we now have access to two hundred and forty hours of these superb 'open scale' wind records, eight miles removed from any land effect. Figs 3.4 and 3.5 are typical traces from this instrument.

The opening of the scale achieved by this faster chart speed enables us to look at the individual gusts, lulls, fluctuations, backs and veers of every wind. As a result we can now, for the first time, see clearly that there are a number of different wind patterns and we can also measure and describe the characteristic way in which each one blows. My thanks go to the Canadian Department of the Environment for making the Kingston Tower U2A records available to me, and for the co-operation of their officers both during those Olympics (I was then meteorological coach for the Australian Olympic Yachting Team) and for their subsequent permission to use excerpts from these traces in this book.

Traces drawn manually can be invaluable. For many years I have made a practice, whenever opportunity offered, of measuring and recording the wind speed and direction every two minutes or so for substantial periods, and then noted the associated meteorological factors. This accumulating data base now covers many different sailing locations world-wide, and has been decisive in developing an understanding of pattern. Figs 1.1 and 1.2 are typical of these traces.

3.5 Factors which shape the wind

3.5.1 Viscosity

Viscosity is the resistance of a liquid or gas to deformation. Air, like thick oil, possesses substantial viscosity. If you lay a tracer plume of cigarette smoke in a calm room and sweep your hand across it, the resultant swirls spin vigorously at first, but are soon slowed and brought to rest by viscosity.

The viscosity of air changes with temperature. Normal experience is with liquids. All readers will be familiar with the way thick oils and greases become 'thinner' when they are heated. Gases behave the other way. As a gas is heated, its molecules move faster and the increased inter-molecular 'turbulence' increases their linkage with each other; so viscosity increases with temperature. Air is a mixture of gases, and so obeys the gas law. As between two areas of air which are at slightly different temperatures, it is the cooler area which will be 'thinner'. It is this fact which is responsible for the formation of the descending 'curtains' of air which are such an important feature of the cell and roll patterns which are discussed in the chapters ahead.

3.5.2 Surface friction

Surface friction is caused by the combination of viscosity, with the fact that the fluid molecules which touch any surface always stick to it (i.e. they do not slide over it) for as long as they remain in contact. For this reason, there is never any surface 'slip' and the speed of the flow of the fluid at the surface is the speed of the surface itself. So surface friction is the force with which viscosity tries to drag the surface along with the fluid and vice versa. In the case of the wind, it is the force with which viscosity, acting from the stationary surface, tries to slow down and hold back the lower wind. Where the surface is physically rough, as in forested or built-up areas, friction due to obstruction is added to friction due to viscosity.

3.5.3 The boundary layer

The boundary layer is the layer of fluid between the surface and the distance from the surface at which full flow speed is reached.

In the case of an object of limited length, such as a hull or a sail or a centreboard, the boundary layer is very thin where first the fluid meets the hull or sail, and becomes progressively thicker as it approaches the stern of the boat or the leech of the sail. In this latter case, a typical thickness would be 25 to 50mm and thicker in light air.

In the case of a surface of unlimited length, such as the wind blowing over the earth's surface, the boundary layer thickens until some natural force opposes its thickening further. In this case, typical thickness can range from 10 to 3,000 metres.

Flow within the boundary layer may be either laminar or turbulent.

3.5.4 Laminar flow

Laminar flow is the flow pattern which results when fluid flows past a surface at less than some critical speed. The absence of slip means that the flow speed at the surface is that of the surface itself. Viscosity causes the flow speed to increase slowly with increasing distance from the surface, until at some distance full stream speed is reached. The essential point about laminar flow is that the flow speeds are so low (or other factors are at work) that the 'calming' influence of viscosity remains sufficient to prevent any turbulence, or to suppress it if it starts. As a result, the flow remains smooth and is organised as layer over layer of fluid molecules, each layer parallel with the surface, and with each more distant layer moving at progressively greater speed. There is absolutely no organised interchange of molecules between layers. The primary characteristic of laminar flow is this absence of movement of fluid particles towards and away from the surface.

The best example I have observed of this type of flow in nature occurred over low-lying flat terrain just south of the southern shore of the Gulf of Finland. En route from Tallinn to St. Petersburg, from dawn and for two hours thereafter during which we travelled about one hundred kilometres east, we passed within a short distance of many isolated communities each of which was dominated by a tall stack from which smoke flowed continuously. Every plume, without exception, flowed northwards straight and pencil-thin with sharp edges, and also remained at exactly its original height. Fig. 3.6 is from a sketch made at the time. There could be no better example of laminar flow, nor better proof that this flow was indeed laminar. This is classic 'steady light air'.

3.5.5 Swirl (Vortex)

The building block of turbulence is the vortex or swirl. Any mass of fluid which starts spinning will develop a life and coherence of its own. If you stir your coffee the upper ends of the spinning swirls will mark the surface for a long time. They slow gradually under the influence of viscosity until they are finally brought to rest. A more revealing insight can be gained if a tracer such as a few grains of ground pepper are stirred into a bowl of water. Each swirl can then be seen in three dimensions and its way of life followed as it writhes and intertwines, becomes larger and slower or smaller and faster, but never loses its individual identity until, after a surprisingly long time, its spinning is slowed by viscosity to less than some critical speed, and it suddenly ceases to be recognisable.

From the helmsman's point of view, the important fact about every swirl is that within it is a coherent core within which air spins progressively faster at increasing distance from the centre (it must, otherwise the swirl would disintegrate under centrifugal force). This coherent core is surrounded by a much larger cylinder of air which rotates progressively more slowly. Fig. 3.7 shows the way the speed changes. If we imagine a wind which is a mass of interwoven swirls, it will be clear that every time a swirl passes over a yacht, it will cause the speed to change twice, and each time the change will be sudden. This is the basic reason for the harsh 'spikiness' which characterises the traces of all winds except light airs and for the abrupt onslaught and decay of gusts and fluctuations. As an example, let us imagine the swirl of Fig. 3.7 to have a vertical axis, to be embedded in a 10 knot breeze, to have a core diameter of about 60 metres with a speed at its edge of about 1.5 knots, and that the breeze carries it over a yacht in the sense A-B-C. The helmsman will then experience a wind speed of 10 knots at A, a sudden increase to 11.5 knots at B which will sustain for six or seven seconds until it suddenly reduces to 10 knots again at C.

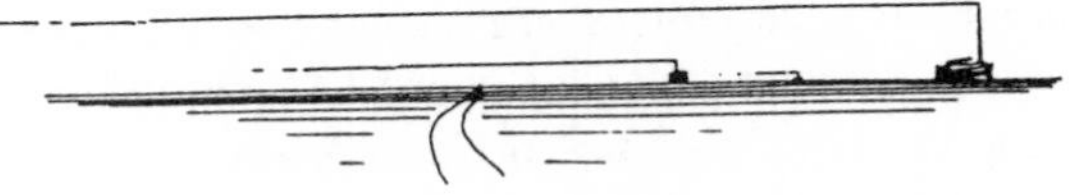

View looking east near Narva, Estonia. Wind south, 1 to 2 knots. Plumes remain pencil-thin for distances more than 5 miles.

Fig 3.6 Smoke plumes in laminar boundary layer

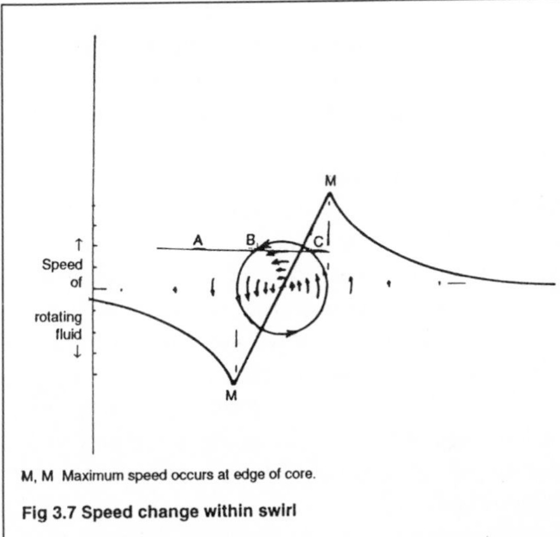

M, M Maximum speed occurs at edge of core.

Fig 3.7 Speed change within swirl

3.5.6 Turbulent flow

Turbulent flow is the flow pattern which results when fluid flows past a surface at any speed greater than the critical speed at and below which viscosity can suppress turbulence. The shearing force within the boundary layer caused by the surface film being held stationary, while adjacent fluid sweeps past, causes a rolling action. An analogy of the motion – which should not be pushed too far – is to lay a number of round pencils together on a table-top and roll them along under your hand. As soon as the energy of this rolling motion becomes greater – due to increasing flow speed – than viscosity can suppress, laminar flow collapses and turbulent flow establishes abruptly.

It takes the form of an interlocked mass of swirls. Given the continuous formation of swirls, not only at the surface but throughout the boundary layer, and the fact that two adjacent swirls which spin in the same direction will combine into one bigger swirl - then accidents of opportunity to grow will result in a mass of swirls of differing sizes. Smaller swirls rotate around larger ones, counter-swirls form between the bigger ones and skewing (by retarding one end and not the other) will cause mis-alignment. The end result is that some swirls will be skewed until their axes are vertical and others will be turned so that they lie more along the wind direction than across it. This results in particles within a turbulent boundary layer oscillating not only towards and away from the surface, and upwind and downwind, but moving crosswind as well when the turbulence is intense. This is the motion of a fully turbulent boundary layer.

It is distinguished from laminar flow principally by the fact that particles within a turbulent boundary layer will move freely towards and away from the surface. In practice this means that swirls which are formed near the outer edge of the boundary layer, and therefore possess almost the full stream speed of the fluid flow, will periodically sweep through the boundary layer until they impinge on and 'scrub' the surface. Under these higher-speed parcels of fluid (air in the case of the wind over the sails, water in the case of hulls and centreboards and rudders) the shearing action of surface friction is intense, and as a result the drag of 'skin friction' associated with turbulent flow is many times greater than that associated with laminar flow.

The thickness of a turbulent boundary layer caused by wind alone (i.e. without added heat) is about 500 metres in a 6 knot breeze, 1,000 metres in a 10 knot wind and 2,000 metres in a 20 knot wind. If the surface is heated, the boundary layer becomes thicker.

The rate at which flow speed increases with increasing distance from the surface, in conditions of turbulent flow, is shown in Fig. 3.8.An excellent example of this type of flow, occurring naturally, can be seen whenever a bush fire occurs on a windy day. Fig. 3.9 shows the smoke plume downwind from a grass fire near Goulburn, New South Wales on a hot summer's day when the wind was a 30 knot north-westerly. It was observed looking southwest, i.e. in a crosswind direction, and Fig. 3.9 was sketched from a distance of about 40 kilometres. The points of particular interest are:

1 Whereas in calm or light air conditions, the heat of the fire which caused the smoke will lift it fifty or a hundred metres at the most (e.g. the height of the smoke-stacks only in Fig. 3.6), the energy of turbulent

mixing lifts and diffuses the smoke through the entire 3,000 metres (or more) depth of the boundary layer when turbulence is present.

2 The slope of the upwind edge of the plume (A-B) is about 25-30 degrees to the horizontal. This indicates that the up and down velocities of turbulent mixing approach half the wind speed.

3 The slope of the upwind edge of the plume (A-B) is straight. This indicates that the turbulence throughout the boundary layer is uniformly intense. (This is consistent with aircraft operating experience.)

4 The vertical limit of the plume height (the level B-C) indicates the thickness of the boundary layer on this day (about 3,500 to 4,000 metres).

5 The upper surface of the boundary layer (B-C) indicated wave motion (C-C). This was so interesting that I stopped and observed these waves for about half an hour. The wave crests were about 10 kilometres apart, and moved in a downwind direction at about 10-15 knots. I have routinely observed these waves from aircraft.

When you climb or descend through any inversion you enjoy, briefly, a near-horizontal view which reveals waves in the cloud arrangement or the lenses of dust. I had never previously observed them from the ground, nor been able to estimate their speed.

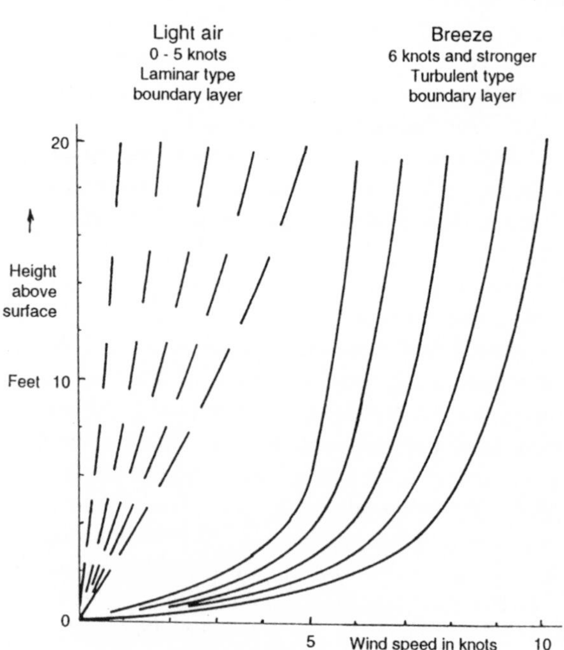

Note: Both surface temperature and surface roughness can alter the 5 to 6 knot critical speed, but only by a little.

Breezes maintain speed at low level - light airs do not.

Fig 3.8 Change of wind speed with height

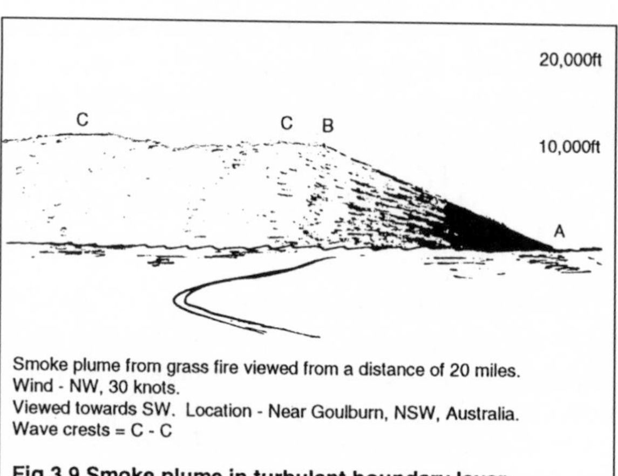

Smoke plume from grass fire viewed from a distance of 20 miles.
Wind - NW, 30 knots.
Viewed towards SW. Location - Near Goulburn, NSW, Australia.
Wave crests = C - C

Fig 3.9 Smoke plume in turbulent boundary layer

3.5.7 Velocity gradient

The rate at which the flow speed increases with increasing distance from the surface is called the velocity gradient. Note the essential difference between the velocity gradients of laminar and turbulent flows (Fig. 3.8). In turbulent flow, high flow speeds exist near the surface. In laminar flow, they do not.

3.5.8 Expansion and cooling

Due to conservation of energy, air will warm when it is compressed and cool when it expands. The pressure of the atmosphere decreases with increasing height above the surface.

Because of the 'towards-and-away-from-the-surface' movement characteristic of all turbulent boundary layers, a parcel of air near the surface at one moment may well be distant shortly thereafter.

In the lower levels of the atmosphere, say up to 3,000 metres, the rate at which air will warm or cool adiabatically when it is lifted or forced downwards will be about 1 deg.C per 100 metres. (3 deg.C per 300 metres or 1,000 feet.)

3.5.9 Atmospheric temperature

When the temperature of the atmosphere is measured at different heights, it is normally found to decrease with height at an average rate of about 2 deg.C per 300 metres (up to, say, 3,000m).

3.5.10 Buoyancy, negative buoyancy (sinking) and equilibrium

Since air which is forced upwards cools adiabatically at a faster rate – 3 deg. C per 300m – than the usual rate of decrease of temperature with height of 2 deg.C per 300m, it becomes progressively colder and therefore denser than the adjacent air at its new level. It therefore assumes negative buoyancy – the tendency to sink – and in the absence of other factors will soon sink back to its original level. This means that the atmosphere normally possesses positive equilibrium – a tendency to resist change. This equilibrium is why air flows around and not over, hills. The extreme example of this is the way the west wind diverts for many thousands of kilometres to flow around, and not over, the Rockies and the Andes. This fact governs the climates of North and South America.

Similarly, it governs the thickness of the earth's turbulent boundary layer. Air which is forced upwards mechanically by turbulence becomes colder and denser. It is therefore harder to 'hold up' the higher it is forced up. For this reason the thickness of the boundary layer caused by every wind of six knots or more is that thickness at which the mechanical upward 'shove' by turbulence is exactly balanced by the negative buoyancy (the downward force) of the cooler and heavier air which has been lifted. This is why (in cool conditions) lighter breezes have thinner boundary layers and only stronger winds with more turbulent energy and upward 'shove' can create thicker boundary layers.

HSP MkII Occasional glimpses of performance, but uncontrollable

Chapter Four
Light Airs

4.1 Steady light air

Fig. 4.1 shows the speed and direction traces of a 5 knot wind on a day when the water surface was cooler than the air.

This is the only wind in which a helmsman can look away for a few seconds and be reasonably certain when he looks back that the wind will not have changed. If the wind were always stable like this it would be so easy to sail well.

This wind can only exist in light air which is warmer than, or at the same temperature as the water surface or any nearby upwind land surface. It is seldom encountered during lake, harbour or river sailing on a warm day.

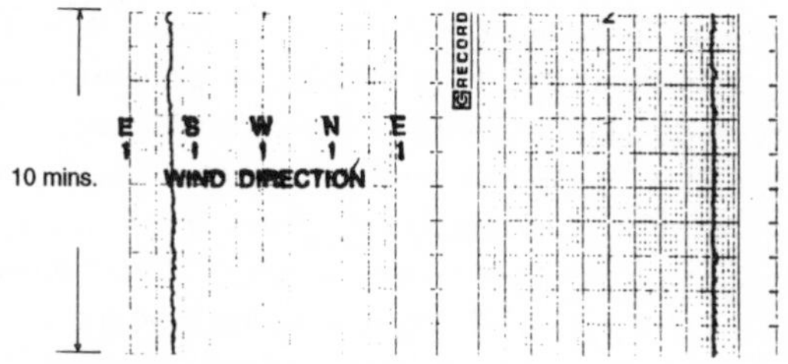

4.2 Thermal excitation

When air is heated from below, it begins to 'boil'.

In light air, this 'boiling' action will adopt one of three patterns:

1 **Isolated thermal**, which occurs when the heating is gentle.

2 **Cellular pattern**, which forms when heating is moderate.

3 **Roll pattern**, which develops when heating is intense.

The air can be heated by either the land or the water surface.

Figs 4.10(a) also (b) show how an isolated thermal would appear in calm air if we could see the air and observe its flow. The conceptual model of it is a wide, shallow doughnut – a three dimensional flow in which heated air rises in a concentrated central core and diverges outwards in all directions, usually at some relatively low level such as 50 to 100 metres. The outflowing upper air then subsides gently over a very wide surrounding area. At the surface, an inflow feeds the core for as long as it rises, which is often intermittently. Within this circulation the highest flow speeds occur at the surface where the inflow converges towards the core, just before it rises.

The circulation of the isolated thermal can form, exist within and be carried along by the slow flow of light air. Fig. 4.10(c) shows the surface wind pattern which results when an isolated thermal inflow pattern of 3 knots maximum is combined with a light air of 2 knots.

Because dry-land surface warms and cools so quickly and water does not, the effects of heating by land and by water are different.

Wind speed and direction both steady

Fig 4.1 'Steady' light air

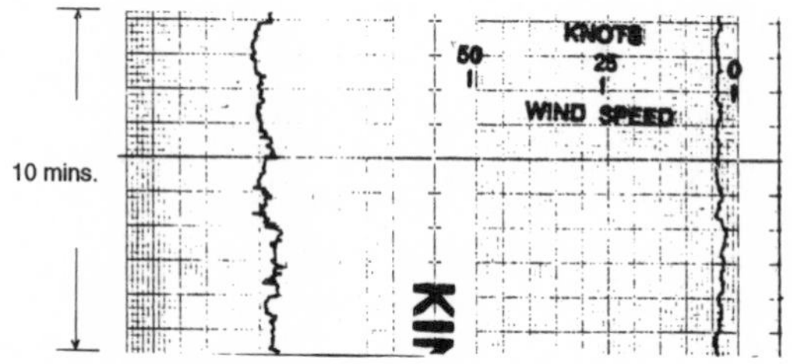

Wind speed and direction both unsteady

Fig 4.2 'Unsteady' light air

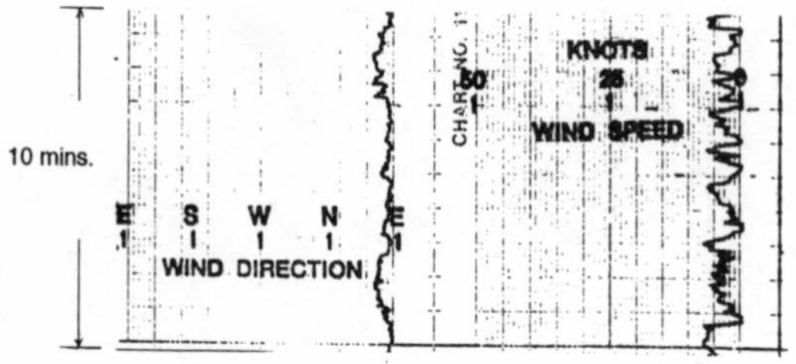

Speed very unsteady: direction less steady

Fig 4.3 'Pulsing' light air

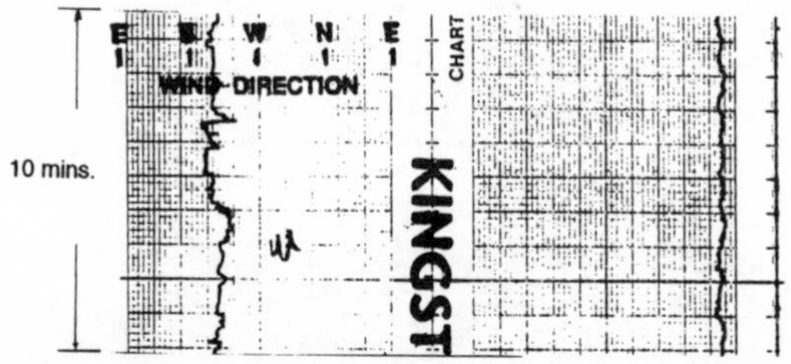

Direction very unsteady: speed less unsteady

Fig 4.4 'Oscillating' light air

4.3 Thermal excitation over water

The temperature of the water surface changes very slowly. Every day, the sun's energy heats, typically, the top 2 to 3 metres of water by something less than one tenth of one degree. This heat is lost by radiation at night. As a result, the water surface temperatures of the earth's oceans and great lakes are among its more stable features. Air is much more mobile and can sweep as wind from either the tropics or the poles into temperate latitudes within a matter of days, and still be recognisable as 'warm tropical' or 'cold polar' air. As it blows over the relatively unchanging water surface it will be heated or cooled as the case may be and this heating or cooling will be continuous throughout twenty-four hours of the day. Generally, the temperature difference between air and water will not exceed one or two degrees.

Note an apparent contradiction. A wind which 'feels cold' is traditionally expected to be steady. But when it blows over the local water, the chances are that it will be colder than the water surface and will thus be warmed by that water and so will 'boil' and become, in fact, one of the unsteadiest of all winds. Similarly, if the wind 'feels warm', this will excite memories of warm, fitful, puff-and-lull dry-land airs. But over water it will almost certainly be warmer than the local water surface, and so will be chilled and become serenely steady. Temperature differences of as little as 1 deg.C can make all the difference. This is far too small to estimate and hope to be correct. A thermometer is essential for certainty.

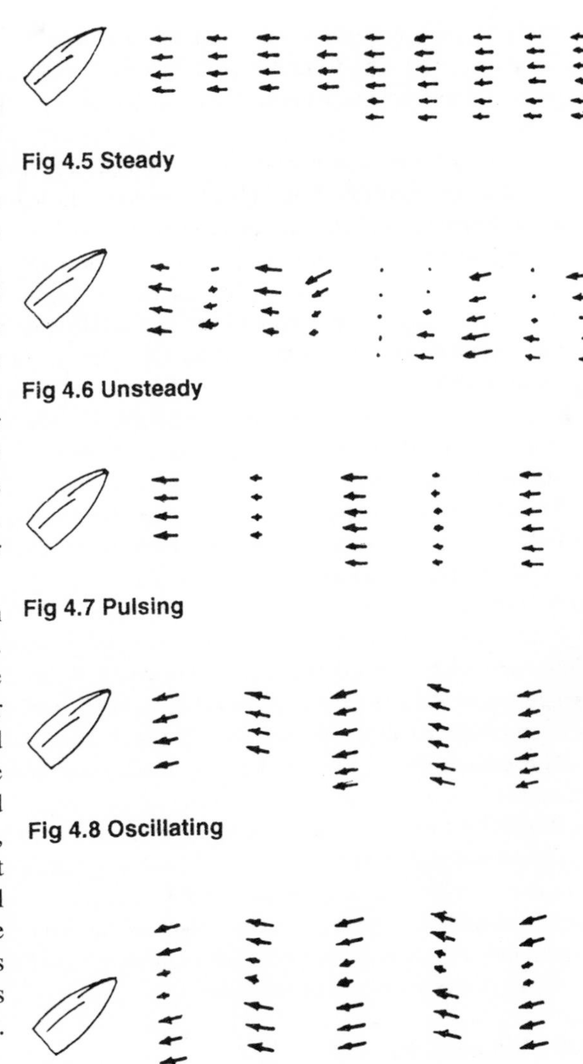

Fig 4.5 Steady

Fig 4.6 Unsteady

Fig 4.7 Pulsing

Fig 4.8 Oscillating

Fig 4.9 Ribboning

Arrow lengths indicate wind speed ← = 5 knots
Arrow directions suggests wind direction • = calm
Spacing of changes is typically 100 - 200 metres

Figs 4.5 to 4.9
Helmsman's visualisation of approaching air

4.4 Thermal excitation over dry land

The temperature of a land surface which is heated by the sun can change rapidly and substantially. Because only the top 5mm or so are affected, the land surface temperature-rise between pre-dawn chill and mid-afternoon maximum can exceed 50 deg.C. In this sort of situation there is never any doubt. The air – any air – will be heated strongly by such a hot surface but only for a few hours each afternoon. As a consequence, the heat patterns which result are usually in a state of growth or decay. There is very little of the 'steady state' situation which characterises cold air over warmer water. This fact is so important that it is worthwhile looking at an extreme naturally-occurring pattern which repeats each day, to get some idea of the sort of progressions and rates of change which are typical in different situations.

Near Lake Argyle, Kimberley Region, North West Australia.

As one part of a scientific study of how early monsoon clouds form, what sorts of clouds they are, and how long they last, it was my responsibility to observe from an aircraft this process near Lake Argyle for two periods each of about fourteen days. I chose an altitude of about 7,000 metres from which to make daily observations. The following progression was typical.

In the mornings the skies were cloudless and wind was fitful but calm on average.

At about 1300, tiny Cumulus clouds began to appear at an altitude of 1,000m to 1,500m in a widely separated and random pattern. They looked exactly like the 'fair weather Cumulus' so common over tropical oceans.

The first change was gentle. After about thirty minutes, randomness slowly gave way to a precise hexagonal arrangement. Some clouds moved a little and some new clouds formed. The pattern became exact and more compact, with the interval at 6 to 10km. Cloud top height increased to about 3,000m, with bases still at 1,000m. At the surface, dust plumes were raised by intermittent gusts which occurred in the areas directly below the bases of the clouds.

The next change, about an hour later was subtle and occupied 30 to 60 minutes. Some clouds evaporated, some appeared and some were reinforced. Almost imperceptibly, the hexagonal pattern vanished. In its place appeared parallel rows of clouds. The rows were spaced about 15 to 25km apart with the clouds along each row spaced closely. We could see 200km in every direction in an atmosphere which was crystal clear. The lines of the rows could not have been straighter if they had been drawn with a ruler. The cloud depth continued to increase. The bases were still at 1,000m and the tops now 5,000m.

Then followed a change which was not subtle. During the next 30 minutes every second row faltered, the clouds became wispy and then they evaporated. Simultaneously, in the intervening rows the clouds 'exploded'. They became huge and merged with each other in the direction along the rows. They grew high, with great glaciated tops which soared to 15,000 or 18,000m and entered the stratosphere. The play of lightning became continuous. Torrential rain poured from their bases. Fierce gusts of wind spread outwards from each shaft of rain. This pattern remained stable until 1-2 hours after sunset, after which all clouds progressively decayed and evaporated as the land surface cooled, and the other energy source – the latent heat of available water vapour – was exhausted. By 2200 the stars shone brilliantly from a cloudless sky.

Throughout their lives, the lines of the thunderheads did not waver. Their's was the ultimate 'roll' pattern.

While this example is extreme, it demonstrates perfectly the four key factors of 'progression', 'timing', 'dimension', and 'exclusiveness' which are present whenever air is heated. The sequence is always constant – first 'isolated thermal', then 'cell', then 'roll'. The pace is always deliberate. The relative dimensions of cell and subsequent roll are of the same order but with the roll spacing a little larger. Most importantly, the three-dimensional cell circulation and the two-dimensional roll circulation cannot co-exist. The presence of one excludes the other.

4.5 Isolated thermal

When the water surface is only slightly warmer than the air, isolated thermals can form in calm or near-calm conditions. At some point the film of warmer air at the surface becomes a little thicker than elsewhere. Once this occurs, it will thicken further until it achieves sufficient buoyancy to break free and rise. The analogy of drops forming and falling from the condensation film on a bathroom ceiling is appropriate.

This process can be watched over a land surface such as a level grassy airfield. Hotter air shimmers. If you lower your line of sight to a few inches above the ground, you can see the concentrated and widely separated shimmering areas hundreds of yards away, watch while one approaches and intensifies, then watch it vanish and a few seconds later feel the inflowing zephyr. This is an old technique in model aeroplane contests.

As the warm air rises it expands. Adiabatic cooling occurs. Because of this cooling, at some point in its rising the column's temperature will fall until it is exactly the same as the air already at that level. Once this height and temperature are reached, buoyancy is at an end. If the core rises a little further – say by momentum – its progressive cooling makes it cooler, and therefore denser than the adjacent air. In this situation the upwelling air diverges and escapes by flowing outwards and slightly downwards until it stabilises at its new equilibrium height. Meantime, the place of the inflowing surface air which feeds the base of the thermal core is taken by a gentle subsidence of the whole mass of air which surrounds the rising core. This organisation – a core which rises strongly, a surrounding large-area region which subsides gently, with outflow at the top and inflow at the bottom – is characteristic of all isolated thermals.

It is the inflow at the bottom which interests the sailor, because this becomes part of the wind he sails in.

Fig. 4.10(b) shows how this flow would look if it were possible to 'see' the air. Note that the inflow at the surface becomes progressively stronger the closer it is to the base of the rising core. In the extreme heating of the Kimberley example, this inflow was often reasonably continuous and strong enough to raise dust. In more gentle environments, thermals tend to be intermittent and are seldom more than a few hundred metres high.

To the sailor, isolated thermals appear as occasional, irregular, discontinuous puffs of slightly stronger air, say 3 to 4 knots, against a calm or light air background of typically 1 to 2 knots. They may blow from any direction and the direction of their surface wind will change as you sail past them or they blow past you.

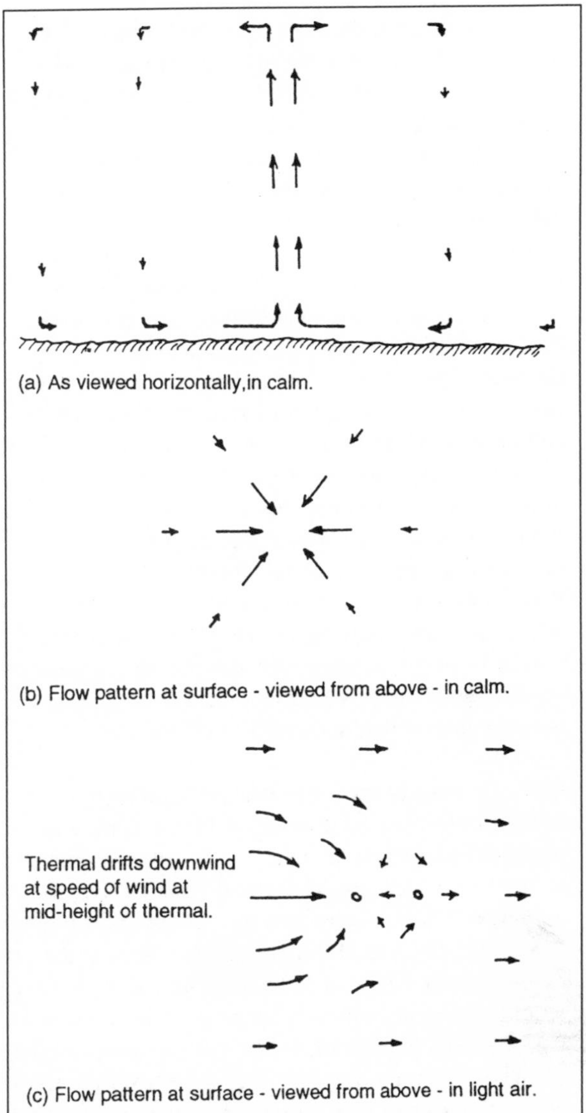

(a) As viewed horizontally,in calm.

(b) Flow pattern at surface - viewed from above - in calm.

Thermal drifts downwind at speed of wind at mid-height of thermal.

(c) Flow pattern at surface - viewed from above - in light air.

Fig 4.10 Surface flow pattern near isolated thermal

4.6 Isolated thermals over large areas

When air is warmed evenly by an extensive warmer surface – such as a large lake – the warmed air cannot and does not rise uniformly. Initially, some small area, over which the film of warming air becomes slightly thicker or hotter or both, begins to move upward. As it rises, the surface inflow common to all thermal excitation commences. Over the circular area affected by the inflow, subsidence must occur and this subsidence prevents any new core from starting within that area. As a result the next adjacent core in any direction must be at least some minimum distance away and this 'separateness' is the principal characteristic of the pattern which forms.

4.7 The cellular mechanism

Both experience and observation suggest that the Kimberley progression is the norm. Initially, the arrangement is one of widely spaced isolated thermals. If there is further heating they will concentrate into an arrangement which is haphazard and random. Up to this point, subsidence occurs over a very wide area and the strongest surface flows will be the inflows close to each core. This pattern is stable and it will continue for as long as the heating remains mild.

If the heating intensifies more cells will form to the point where the sky becomes crowded. Crowding forces the cells to adopt the most efficient packing arrangement, which is the hexagonal pattern. This follows exactly the behaviour of fluid in a shallow dish if it is heated evenly from below. Initially the cells are spaced randomly but quite quickly they adjust themselves to hexagonal spacing.

Fig. 4.11(a) shows how this hexagonal pattern would appear from above if it were possible to 'see' the air. Fig.4.11(b) shows the way the circulation would appear, viewed horizontally, if the pattern were to be cut along the A-A line. Fig. 4.11(c) shows the pattern of the flows at the water surface, as viewed looking downwards.

The development of the close-packed pattern has introduced a fundamental change to the nature of the surface flows. When the cores were widely spaced, the fastest surface flows were close to the base of each core. But not any more. The crowding of the cells has limited the area through which the air can subside. This has provided the opportunity for the cooler subsiding air to make use of its lesser viscosity.

In any mechanism with limited space, the motions will start and the highest velocities will occur in those areas where the gas has least viscosity. As was explained in Section 3.5.1, cooler air is 'thinner' than hotter air, so in the close-packed cellular (and also the roll) patterns it is the cooler descending air which will now move fastest.

The consequence of this is that the rising cores become diffuse and the flows beneath them become gentle. The descending air becomes concentrated, moves fastest, and takes the form of relatively thin 'curtains' of falling air. Along the lines where these meet the surface, the flows split and blow horizontally outwards in both directions away from the bases of the curtains. These have now become the strongest surface flows.

For the helmsman, these lines of diverging air are of the greatest practical importance because they explain why boats only one or two lengths apart can sometimes be in completely different winds. They also explain why these 'gusts' behave so differently from the gusts of a breeze – these become gusts which don't move towards you.

Flow pattern at upper surface of cell.

Section through A - A.

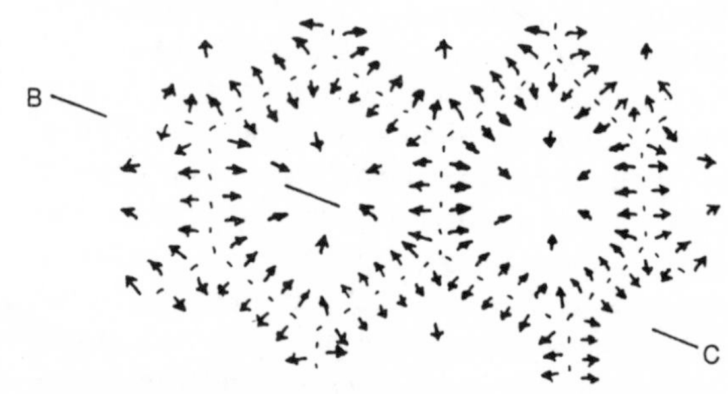

Flow pattern at water surface.

Fig 4.11 Hexagonal cell pattern and mechanism

4.8 Unsteady air – the cellular pattern

A thermal pattern such as Fig. 4.11 can form and continue indefinitely in calm air. It can also exist in light-air winds provided the thermal 'drive' is sufficient. If we imagine that the pattern shown in Fig. 4.11 exists and drifts in light air, in the direction B-C, then a helmsman initially at C would experience all the changing inflows along the line C-B, in addition to the light-air wind, as the pattern drifted over him. At this point it is useful to glance at Figs 4.1 and 4.2: Fig. 4.1 shows the trace of light air without any thermal excitation;Fig. 4.2 shows the trace of light air plus either a random or hexagonal pattern such as Fig. 4.11.

It is this which causes the great unsteadiness in both the speed and the direction of the wind. Fig. 4.2 is typical in that the 'feature size' – and to the extent that there is a sort of repetition in a basically random pattern – is of the order of 100m. This is unsteady air. Fig. 4.6 shows how it would appear to a helmsman if he could 'see' the air ahead.

The task of any helmsman who finds himself sailing in unsteady air is completely different from his task in steady air. In steady air, the racing helmsman's priorities are to accelerate his boat and then to optimise the camber, sheeting angles and twists of his sails for maximum VMG upwind and downwind and maximum boat speed crosswind.

In unsteady air, he will first need to make the choice whether he will sail along the curtains for maximum wind speed and boat speed, or toward the mark for minimum distance at some lesser speed. Either way, there can be no steady-state sailing because the wind will constantly change in both speed and direction as he passes through the diverging winds below the curtains and the intervening lighter-air cell centres. He will be repeatedly faced with the need to regain speed after some near-calm lull. In these constantly changing wind speeds there will be no single 'best' sail trim. The unpredictable changes of wind direction will tax his judgement of when to tack or gybe to the utmost. A further factor is that the ruffles on the water surface which indicate areas of faster-moving air will themselves move slowly in the direction of the pattern. They will not move in the direction nor at the speed of the puffs themselves. To make use of them he will usually have to sail to them.

4.9 Roll mechanism

In the Kimberley example, as the surface heating intensified, so the increasing thermal energy was absorbed by an increasing number of thermal cores. From isolated thermals to random cells to close-packed cells – the number of cores increased. But once the hexagonal pattern was established, the number of cells in a spatial array could be increased no more. There was no further room. For a while the cells became deeper. But the clouds were not yet raining and merely becoming deeper did not provide sufficient additional escape for the increasing amount of heat, both radiant and latent, being released.

In this situation, a different pattern was needed – some arrangement, without the cell pattern's limit to number, which could accept more cores.

The two-dimensional roll pattern is the answer. In it, the air rises along, and subsides between, parallel lines of cores. In this arrangement there is ample room for as many new cores as are needed. They can form in line with and between existing cores, and this way they simply boost the circulation instead of opposing it.

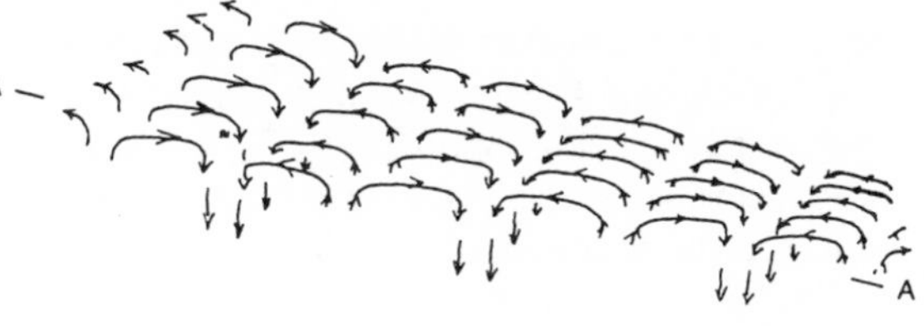

Flow pattern at upper surface of roll.

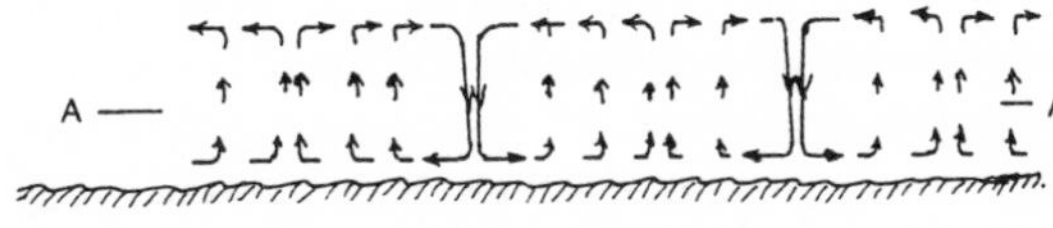

Section through A - A.

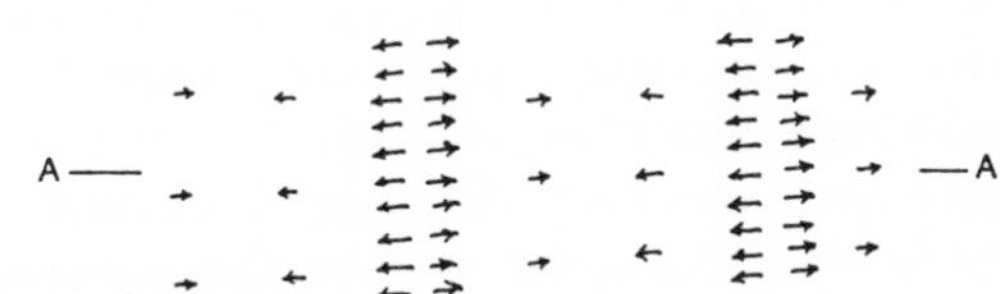

Flow pattern at water surface

Fig 4.12 Roll pattern and mechanism

This is exactly what happens in light air. It is at about one thousandth of the size and one millionth of the energy of the Kimberley turmoil but the principle is identical. As soon as the heating intensifies to the point where the cell pattern can no longer absorb the energy, the cell pattern vanishes and a roll pattern is established.

Fig. 4.12 shows what the essential mechanism of the roll circulation would look like if it were possible to 'see' the air. Exactly as with the cell circulation, it is the less viscous curtains of descending air which flow fastest and which split at the surface in lines each marked by two outflowing 'gusts'. The rising cores are diffuse and the surface flow speeds under them are minimal.

From the helmsman's point of view, the roll pattern will adopt one of three forms:

1 **Transverse**, which gives pulsing air.

2 **Longitudinal**, which gives oscillating air.

3 **Boosted**, which gives ribboning air.

A typical spacing between rolls in light air would be about 150 metres.

4.10 Pulsing air – the transverse roll

In light air, the alignment of the rolls is across – transverse to – the wind direction, the outflowing gusts under each curtain will add to the speed of the surface wind when they blow in the same direction, and reduce its speed when they blow the other way. The result is the pulsing pattern.

The trace of Fig. 4.3 is typical. A 3.5 knot surface wind is influenced by a transverse roll circulation in which the components alternate between plus and minus 3.5 knots. As a result the speed trace shows that 7 knot winds and calms alternate every 90 seconds on average. The direction, while not as steady as the direction in Fig. 4.1, is nevertheless relatively steady in relation to the extreme unsteadiness of the speed trace. This wind is 'pulsing'. Fig. 4.7 shows how this pattern would appear to a helmsman if he could 'see' the air.

4.11 Oscillating air- the longitudinal roll

Fig. 4.4 shows the oscillating pattern. While the speed trace remains relatively steady, the direction trace is wildly unsteady, with swings of up to 50 degrees. This is the sort of pattern which results when rolls caused by thermal excitation are aligned in a direction along, rather than across, the wind direction. Any helmsman sailing in this relatively steady-speed but rapidly oscillating to-and-fro (in direction) wind would describe it as 'quickly oscillating'. Fig. 4.8 shows how a helmsman would visualise this pattern if he could 'see' the air ahead.

4.12 Ribboning air – the boosted longitudinal roll

Another common light-air pattern is ribboning. The water surface is marked by long, often sinuous, upwind-downwind 'ribbons' of stronger air, usually about 50 to 100m wide, with intervening ribbons of lighter air and glassy water. This surface pattern is the result of a vigorous longitudinal roll circulation in which the depth of the rolls is sufficient to take the air to a height where the wind speed is significantly greater than that at the surface. The air at height is accelerated by viscosity, then descends rapidly in the curtains, and splits at the surface while it is still moving with some of this speed. Surface friction soon slows it to a drift, so everywhere except close to the curtains becomes glassy.

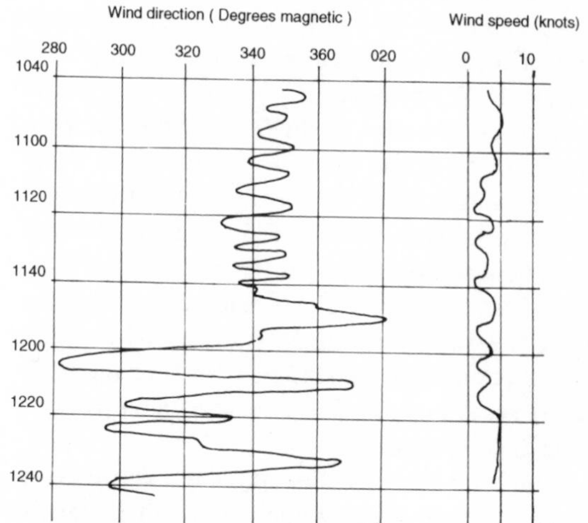

Lake Yarrawonga, Australia. 9th Sept 1976. Sky cloudless.
As the land surface around a small inland lake heats strongly, roll size increases abruptly at 1140 and oscillations become bigger and slower.

Fig 4.13 Change of pattern with great increase of heat

This pattern – in common with isolated thermals – does not show up clearly on the trace of a single anemograph. It is sketched conceptually in Fig. 4.9.

4.13 Shore effects

Figs 4.1, 4.2, 4.3 and 4.4 were measured 14 km offshore in Lake Ontario, Canada. The three thermal excitation patterns are therefore due solely to the relatively small differences between the temperature of the northerly 'polar' air and the surface temperature of Lake Ontario.

Fig. 4.13 was measured on the shore of Lake Yarrawonga, between NSW and Victoria. It shows a typical progression as the temperature of a dry-land surface immediately upwind becomes heated on a summer's day. As the temperature difference increased, the degree of unsteadiness became much greater. Yet as the form changes, and becomes more extreme as the day warms, it still takes a recognisable pattern which repeats and can be anticipated.

4.14 Pattern size

So long as the wind speed remains 'light air' the feature size remains compact. Even the wild direction swings of the Lake Yarrawonga example are only about 150-200 metres apart in an upwind-downwind direction. Light air pattern dimensions can be anticipated with reasonable confidence.

4.15 Practicalities

Light airs blow in at least five ways. What then, should we look for and expect as we sail? And how should we use what we see?

Just by looking at their traces, and by looking at the marks they make on the surface of the water, it is obvious that the unsteady, pulsing, oscillating and ribboning patterns are fundamentally different from the steady pattern. They are more complex and challenging. The consequences of this complexity on the way we should handle our boats and rigs are profound. To suggest a simple automobile analogy:

Racing in a steady pattern is like racing on a cleared freeway.

Racing in a pulsing pattern is like racing down a stretch of road with traffic lights every hundred metres which usually, but not always, turn red when you least want them to.

Racing in an oscillating pattern is like racing on a winding country road in thick fog – you have no idea where a curve may be until you are in it.

Racing in unsteady conditions is like combining the curves, the fog, and the traffic lights – it takes a particularly skilled and cool 'mindset' to excel in this exercise in probabilities and sail handling.

Racing in ribboning conditions is easier. The fog has cleared. Downwind is easy. But the fastest way upwind and crosswind through the lighter ribbons will call for a special blend of observation and anticipation.

'Steady air' has laminar flow characteristics and can be expected when the water or upwind land surface is cooler than the air, and the wind speed is less than 6 knots.

The unsteady, pulsing, oscillating and ribboning patterns can be expected when the surface temperature is warmer than the air, and the windspeed is less than 6 knots.

4.16 What to look for

(a) Progressions

It is always easier to find something if you know what you are looking for, so it helps if you know which pattern is most probable in the existing conditions. The following pointers, based on observation and experience, may be helpful:

When the upwind surface is solely water, the existing pattern is likely to continue.

When the upwind surface is dry land, and it is heating, the most likely progression is:

Steady – Unsteady – Pulsing – Oscillating – Ribboning

As the upwind surface heats, the patterns will progress. But they will progress no further than is justified by the upwind surface temperature.

(b) Appearances

Steady air

Steady air can be expected when there is no heating. This may be because the upwind surface is solely water which does not heat, or because the upwind land surface remains cool because of low sun, heavy overcast or drizzle, or the heating becomes less as the sun declines towards sunset, or when a previously warm upwind land surface cools due to intermittent heavy cloud shadow.

It is indicated by a uniformity in the ruffling of the water surface upwind, and a characteristic 'almost but not quite steady' feel in the wind force on the sails and the motion of the boat.

Unsteady air

Unsteady air can be expected when the upwind heating is gentle. It is recognised by alternating ruffled and glassy patches on the water's surface, arranged (so far as can be seen) in a random or checkerboard pattern, by differences in the intensity and shading of the ruffling and by the obvious facts that the boat is sometimes in moving air and sometimes not and that the wind's direction, as indicated by a sensitive wind-indicator, is unsteady in the extreme. For light air sailing, the wind indicator should be at the masthead. An indicator at any lower position, such as threads on the shrouds, is not of much use because the wind at lower level is so much slower.

The intensity of ruffling of the water surface indicates the local wind speed (unless there are oil slicks). Differences in shading and the way the light reflects will often give a clue about differences in direction. Above all, the fact that you are within a thermal pattern is revealed by the fact that 'the gusts don't come towards you'.

This is so important that it is worth describing in detail. In the next section, we will see that in almost all winds of six knots or more, the vigorous mixing is so overwhelming that the whole mass of air has no option but to move downwind as a well blended body. In this situation the future movement of every gust can be anticipated with reasonable certainty – it will move in a downwind direction at about wind speed. But in any situation in which the air moves in the vertical loops of a thermal pattern, those points on the surface where the local windspeed is greater than elsewhere will not move in the direction of that wind. In the simple case of an overall calm, within which is a stationary thermal cellular pattern, every 'gust' will also remain stationary. In this situation, you may be in near-calm. A four or five knot gust, a few yards away, may be blowing directly towards you. But whether that gust will move towards you, remain stationary, or move away from you, will depend entirely on the movement of the pattern which controls the circulation, and will have nothing to do with the direction of that or any other gust.

The shift from steady to unsteady usually occurs quite quickly. Typically two or three minutes are all that are needed for a helmsman to recognise, with confidence, that a new pattern is now operating.

In the case of intermittent heating of the land – due to irregular cloud shadows – the wind over the water just downwind of the intermittently heated land will itself alternate between steady and unsteady.

The unsteady pattern which forms over an upwind heated land surface will certainly influence the wind just offshore, but the distance downwind over water over which the wind will remain unsteady is very limited. Quite quickly the added heat and vertical momentum will be lost, and the pattern will attenuate to steady. If the heating becomes sufficient to drive the motion over the land to pulsing or oscillating, then the attenuation over the water will progress 'backwards' from pulsing through unsteady to steady with increasing distance downwind. The dimensions are frequently such that a fleet which races on waters one or two kilometres offshore in offshore light air may often find itself sailing in steady air at the leeward mark (furthest offshore, furthest downwind). It will progress through unsteady air as the shore is approached, and may enter strongly pulsing air near the windward mark close to the heated shoreline.

From a sufficiently high viewpoint – the ideal is a tower building at the water's edge – it is possible to see all this. Even faint rufflings, and the differences between rufflings, can be discerned from height at distances of several kilometres. It is easy to pick the parallel puffs and lulls of the pulsing or ribboning pattern.

It is frequently possible to recognise the ordered cellular shape of unsteady air, and to watch the whole pattern as it drifts slowly in the general direction of the surface wind.

The view from the helmsman's eye-level is radically different.

While it is still possible to see, faintly, the differences in ruffling at distances of half a mile or more (in flat water), the extreme foreshortening due to the low eye-level means that it is almost never possible to recognise either the pattern, or your position in it. You can 'read' the water surface with certainty only over the fifty metres or so immediately around you, and this, frustratingly, is seldom enough, in a subtly shifting pattern, to develop a logical game plan and position yourself with confidence on the basis of what you can see. However, if this situation is handled on the basis of observation plus probabilities, the resulting race performance can far outstrip that of any helmsman whose attitude is, 'it's the same for everybody', and makes no further effort. Some examples of this approach are given later.

Pulsing air

The pulsing pattern is easy to recognise. The water surface upwind adopts a 'banded' appearance with cross-wind lines of ruffled water alternating between glassy or lightly marked areas. For practical purposes, these are also 'gusts which don't move towards you'. In fact, because they move with the pattern, they generally do move toward you, but much more slowly than would normally be expected. There is a saving grace in this, because it makes one decision easier. When you are reaching in pulsing air, and you enter a calm patch, it will almost always pay to turn upwind and in this way reach the next patch of approaching air sooner. A turn downwind toward a patch of wind just to leeward so often sees it drift slowly away out of reach. And even if you catch it, you still have to traverse the calm band later.

Because the windier areas can be seen, it is possible to tackle the pulsing pattern by eye. The ruffling is wider, and the intervening calm is narrower, at some points than others. The helmsman who selects the more widely ruffled areas, and sails into and through them to pick his way among the adjacent narrower calmer areas, will sail much faster toward the next mark than crews who stay on one tack or gybe, or sail the rhumb line crosswind. In these conditions the most direct course can never be the fastest if it leads you into a calm which others sail around. Light air sailing calls for judgment as well as skill.

The pulsing pattern is less common than the others and tends not to last long.

Oscillating air

The oscillating pattern is common. The appearance of the ruffled water surface is more like that of steady air than the patchiness of unsteady or the banding of pulsing, but there is always a lack of evenness to it, although there may be none or few glassy areas. The oscillating pattern is recognised primarily by the fact that the wind speed is relatively steady (as compared with unsteady or pulsing air), and that it so obviously oscillates in direction. Oscillating patterns, like unsteady patterns, can last indefinitly. There are three ways of handling it. Two are simple and slower. One is fascinating and fast. It all depends upon what you sail.

If you sail a light roundish boat with a tallish rig which roll-tacks well, the fastest way upwind is to tack every time the wind direction changes through its mean direction, so that you never sail any disadvantaged tack. Because light roundish boats can generally be roll-tacked without loss of VMG, you lose nothing by tacking, so there is no reason not to tack.

If you sail any boat which takes a long time to tack, such as a yacht or catamaran, the losses from frequent tacking are so great as to be intolerable. As a result, the fastest technique is to 'snake' in following the changes in wind direction. In this way it is possible to maintain speed. Tacking is limited to either the minimum number possible – typical in catamaran racing – or to responding only to the major shifts which disadvantage you. In this situation it is faster to accept minor headers than the loss of VMG in tacking. The trick is to anticipate which will be the 'minor' headers.

But if you sail a boat with big sails and small wetted area, which is both fast in light air and also tacks well, then the situation will be one in which you must lose more than the roll-tacking Laser, but much less than the 12 Metre which needs about 45 seconds to re-acquire full speed. This is a situation which calls for much more skilful judgment. While you lose little from the tack itself, there is substantial loss (as compared with a competitor who does not tack) during the acceleration and winding up process which must follow each tack before full speed and pointing ability are restored. There is no bar to tacking, but the re-acquisition of speed takes on a new importance.

Another factor which is common to all boats with good light-air performance becomes particularly important in all light air which is unsteady for any reason. This is the fact that when any boat with speed sails into an area of lighter wind, the Apparent Wind – the wind across the deck – must necessarily blow from a direction more ahead. In the extreme case, if a boat which is moving at any speed at all sails into a calm patch, the Apparent Wind will blow from straight ahead for as long as the boat keeps moving. This will remain true regardless of the direction in which the boat may be turned in the meantime.

The practical point is that helmsmen of faster light-air boats will necessarily sense any change of wind speed as also a change of wind direction.

In oscillating light air, in which there is already high reward for judging correctly which are the major shifts of direction (so that the minor ones can be ignored), this extra factor raises the stakes and makes the situation much more interesting.

Ribboning air

Handling ribboning air calls for a mixture of the other techniques. Downwind is easiest – you sail to and stay in the nearest strongest ribbon. (Very high performance downwind tackers are different.) The fastest way crosswind is to sail more downwind in the puffs and more upwind – for best possible speed through the water – through the lulls. Also bias your path to cross the lulls where they are narrowest. This will decrease the time spent in the lulls. The end result is that you will spend a much greater proportion of your time in stronger air and this usually outweighs the extra distance sailed. Upwind will have some of the options of oscillating air but without the uncertainty. If your boat roll-tacks well you should tack to stay in the wind. If it does not, you will need your finest judgement to decide when the loss of speed from a tack will be greater than the loss of speed from accepting the lighter air ahead. There is no easy way.

What skilled crews do

In light airs, that helmsman will win who sails in a stronger wind for more of the time than his competitors. The whole point of discussing the 'patterns' is to enable a helmsman to recognise which one of the five possible patterns he is sailing in and so expand the meagre visual data into a coherent mental picture of the wind ahead. Around this he can structure a game plan which will exploit advantages which he believes will appear – although he cannot yet see them.

The two following examples indicate the way skilled helmsmen blend observation, a sense of pattern and the consequent probabilities into their racing technique.

4.17 Sydney Harbour – Australian Intervarsity Championships

In Australia the college boat is the Lightweight Sharpie, a long narrow sailboat of very light weight with big sails and a heavy crew (three). This puts it exactly into that class which tacks easily but takes substantial time to accelerate.

On the day in question the start was delayed due to calm until a light westerly appeared. Immediately following the start the wind began to back towards the south-west and became progressively lighter. The natural position of each boat made it impossible to tack onto port until the boat next to the right had tacked – for this reason, the boat which had started at the southern extremity of the line (at the pin end) was the last to be able to tack. The helmsman of this boat observed three factors:

1) The boats which had already tacked had been unable to accelerate well in the dying air and the harbour slop, and had not made much progress since tacking.

2) His own speed was still a useful 1 to 1.5 knots, although not in the preferred direction.

3) Fifty metres ahead, to the south, a line of air blowing some three to four knots had appeared. This was not moving towards him.

He used such movement as he could maintain to sail towards the puff, tacked in it and used that line of air to accelerate toward the west. So far, so good.

What happened next was that the puff (from the south-west) began to die and veer towards the west and north-west. This was so similar to the 'die-and-back' which had occurred after the start that he sensed pattern. So he did not tack onto starboard as the dying wind veered. Instead, he maintained his movement in the dying air, turning to starboard with it as it veered until he was heading almost north and was rewarded by another line of air ahead to the north-west which he sailed into, tacked, and accelerated in toward the west. Four times this oscillating pattern repeated before the westerly breeze filled in. By this time he was hundreds of metres ahead of the rest of the fleet, all of whom had tacked solely on wind direction. He held his lead to the finish and won. The others had not sufficiently considered either maintaining their own speed in light air or how best to handle 'gusts which don't move towards you'.

The key to winning in this situation was to mentally work out the total area pattern, and then to sail so as to maintain movement and manoeuvrability. To anticipate and plan to exploit puffs before they could be seen. To sail towards and into puffs that were virtually stationary on the water, and to handle the wind over the racing area in a far more imaginative manner than just sailing the most direct course to the next mark. The keys to that early break were observation, a sense of pattern and a game-plan to exploit winds which were anticipated before they could be seen.

4.18 Tallinn – Baltic pre-olympic regatta 1978

It has been my privilege to meet and work with many of the world's top-level Olympic crews. At this regatta the USA, UK and New Zealand teams offered to join with the Australian team (which I was then coaching) in our weather briefings and de-briefings, so as to build up and share as much Tallinn Bay weather information from as many observers and over as wide an area as was possible. In this situation, the contribution and light-air skills of three of the USA college-trained ex-Laser and Finn helms, John Bertrand, Stuart Neff, and Gus Walker, were outstanding – as was their sailing performance. They absolutely dominated the Finn fleet. Differences in awareness and approach between the different teams were revealing.

On one day, one Australian Finn helm reported that the 'wind seemed to blow in channels. Should I have sailed to the right or to the left in those conditions?'

On the same day, Gus Walker's report was as follows:

'Of the 470s which started ahead of us, those which sailed to the right were lifted and those which sailed left were headed as the wind backed. But those which had sailed left were much further away, so were evidently enjoying more air. I elected to follow them and sailed left. I was progressively headed. Occasionally, if the wind headed abnormally, I took a short hitch to the right on port tack, but tacked back to the left as soon as possible because the further left I sailed, the stronger the air became. Near the layline one 'channel' of wind became evident. It could not be seen because of oil slicks on the water, but could be felt. I tacked as necessary to remain in this line of stronger air – it was essential to sail to where this wind was because whenever I sailed out of it there was almost nothing anywhere else. This wind did not move across the water. I sailed well past the layline in following it but rounded the windward mark well ahead of the next Finn.'

Gus won comfortably that day. He, Bertrand or Neff won all the Finn races.

Note the several different factors that went into this approach:

1. The acute observation of boats which had started earlier.

2. The realisation that change of wind direction with time and change of wind speed with area were both present.

3. The election to go for the stronger-wind side of the course because a boat with stronger air will always sail faster, regardless of the wind direction, than a boat in a near calm.

4. The ability to overcome the handicap of being unable to 'read' the water surface (because of the oil slicks) by relying on 'feel' instead.

5. The ability to 'feel' the wind channel which could not be seen.

6. The sense of pattern which gave the confidence to tack to look for wind and find it and home in on it again whenever it was lost.

7. The willingness to sail beyond the layline when it was felt that the wind pattern (ie. the probable but not yet visible wind ahead) justified this.

At that time none of us had progressed to understanding the five light-air patterns. In view of what we now know, I feel that Gus accurately observed, used and reported a situation in which a pulsing pattern had established over the warmed land. It had extended offshore for about a kilometre, then attenuated over the colder water through unsteady air to steady air. The start was in steady air and those Finns which sailed to the right (ie. away from the upwind shore), remained in steady air, the surface speed of which was reduced by the extreme cold of the water surface temperature. Those boats which sailed left – towards the shore – enjoyed increasing wind and stronger winds in the puffs of unsteady air. Those who sailed far enough picked up the most offshore lines of a pulsing pattern. Gus was the helmsman who most quickly analysed the situation. He won the race. In my opinion he did more than just win. He did not just sail his Finn, he used his boat as an instrument to express his understanding of the subtle nature of the wind and the water. He deserved to win.

HSP MkIV Very fast in gusts, but not much else

Chapter Five
The Breeze over a Cool Surface

5.1 The onset of turbulence

At a wind speed of about 6 knots – 7 miles per hour – 3 metres per second, the turbulence caused by the shearing action of the moving wind over the stationary surface becomes greater than can be suppressed by viscosity. At this point the boundary layer abruptly becomes turbulent. The change is sudden and complete. There is no such flow-state as half-turbulent. It has to be either laminar or turbulent. Laminar-type surface flow is light air. Turbulent flow is *breeze*.

The different way in which the wind speed changes with height is shown in Figs 3.1, 3.2, and 3.8.

The energy of the turbulent mixing is sufficiently intense to obliterate immediately all the small three-dimensional cells or two-dimensional rolls which caused every preceding *unsteady, pulsing, oscillating*, or *ribboning* pattern. In its place appears the evenness of thorough mixing. As a result the surface 'patchiness' typical of light air ruffling, vanishes.

The greater wind speed which now periodically scrubs the surface raises a larger ripple which has a steeper face and so reflects less light. This darker ripple spreads evenly across the entire water surface. The establishment of this darker rippled surface signals the onset of the breeze.

The breeze's turbulence changes the nature of both the wind's direction and the wind's speed.

The wind direction traces drawn by the light airs of Figs 3.3 and 4.2, 4.3 and 4.4 are uncertain and wandering. The direction trace of the breeze in Fig 3.3 and in 3.5 is steady and ordered. Three separate reasons all contribute to this new orderliness. The first is the increased speed: this of itself increases momentum. The second is the increased depth through which turbulence initially establishes. This is a minimum of about 500 metres at 6 knots, in place of the 20 to 30 metres at 5 knots. This great increase in boundary layer depth, together with the increase in flow speed, increases the mass and the overall momentum of the boundary layer air which passes over any point by a factor of about fifty between the laminar-type 5 knot flow and the turbulent-type 6 knot flow. It is primarily this increased momentum which so steadies the direction of the turbulent breeze. The third reason is the turbulent mixing itself: this ensures that every particle is continuously influenced by the momentum of a whole mass of continuously changing adjacent particles, and this mixing makes it impossible for any particle or parcel of air to do other than 'stay in line'. The end result is that the direction of a breeze over a cool surface is about fifty times more predictable than that of light air. Nothing could be more different than the direction traces of the forenoon light air and the afternoon breeze of Fig. 3.3.

If we look at the speed traces of Figs 3.4 and 3.5, that of Fig. 3.5 is visibly more ordered than that of Fig. 3.4. This is only half the truth. The astonishing fact is that the turbulence of every normal breeze always contains within itself, like a heartbeat, a clear, recognisable and predictable pattern of gusts, lulls and fluctuations. Further, the average frequency at which both the gusts and the fluctuations repeat remains almost the same regardless of whether the breeze is only 6 to 7 knots or is strong.

5.2 The change of wind force on sails

Fig. 5.1 shows how the flow differences which occur between 5 knots and 6 knots affect the wind force on the sails of a dinghy. The 1 knot wind speed difference plus the fact that its full force is now felt over the entire sail plan instead of just the top, leads to a sudden three-to-one jump in the drive force. Fig. 5.2 shows how this wind force changes from calm to stronger breezes. When you know what to expect, you can feel it cut in at about six knots as if it had been switched on. Nothing can underline more clearly that the wind takes one or the other of two forms, and how different these are, than the discontinuity between 5 and 6 knots in Fig. 5.2.

The wind speed at which the boundary layer suddenly becomes turbulent is usually about 6 knots. When the surface is much colder than the air, it might be 7 knots. When the surface is either hotter, or physically rough (i.e. just downwind of reeds etc) or both, it might be 5 or 4½ knots. Further, turbulence takes a little time to establish or decay, so a 3-4 knot lull for a few moments in a 6-10 knot breeze will probably still feel like a breeze rather than light air. None of these qualifications matter much. The vital fact is that there are

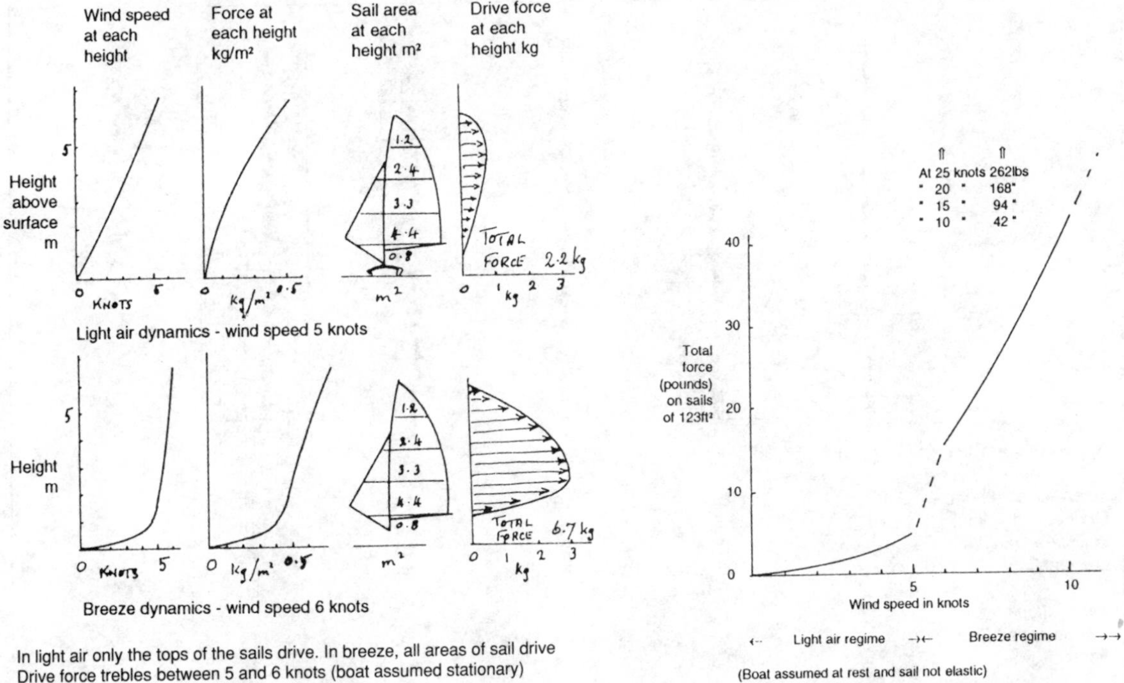

In light air only the tops of the sails drive. In breeze, all areas of sail drive
Drive force trebles between 5 and 6 knots (boat assumed stationary)

Fig 5.1 Change of dynamics between 5 and 6 knots

Fig 5.2 Change of sail force with wind speed

two sorts of wind, the change from one to the other is abrupt, it is easy to sense and feel, and the boat needs to be handled quite differently in light air compared with a breeze.

5.3 The shape of the breeze

Fig. 5.3 shows the speed traces of six lake breezes of speeds 6, 8, 10, 12.5, 15 and 20 knots. Note that each is characterised by gusts and lulls (marked 'G' and 'L'). If you look at them, foreshortened, by tilting the page away from you and looking at them upwards from the bottom of the page, you can see how each trace seems to be half gust, half lull, and very little in between.

Note particularly that, in addition to the obvious gusts and lulls, all the traces show, continuously, a second and much faster frequency. This is the fluctuation frequency. The notes below the traces of Fig. 5.3 tabulate the vital data about gusts and fluctuations at the six wind speeds.

The gust-lull sequence of these breezes normally sweeps a range of about 35-40% of the average windspeed. This is the difference between the average speed of the gust and the average speed of the lull. The periodic extremes are much greater. In Fig. 3.3 it is obvious that the extreme gusts are three to four times as strong as the extreme lulls. The average life of each gust is about 30 seconds, and the average life of each lull is similarly about 30 seconds. But, as a glance at Fig. 5.3 will make clear, gusts and lulls do not repeat regularly at any of the wind speeds.

Each trace of Fig. 5.3 shows, in addition to the more 'massive' gusts and lulls, a second, continuous, smaller, faster and more regular frequency. These typically sweep a speed range about one third of that of the gust-lull range, and they repeat about five times faster. These are the fluctuations. The combination of gusts and fluctuations together constitute the 'pattern' of every turbulent breeze. They fit together in a special way.

Diagrams which help in visualising this pattern are given in Figs 5.4 to 5.9.

Fig. 5.4 shows, first, how the average gust-lull pattern changes as the seconds tick away. Fig. 5.5 shows how the fluctuation pattern changes. Fig. 5.6, which is a combination of Figs 5.4 and 5.5, shows the average, continuous and everpresent wind speed pattern of every turbulent breeze. Note particularly that this very normal wind is in reality two separate winds, one a little stronger, and one a little lighter, which alternate continuously. It almost never blows at its mean speed at all. Further, the change from any speed to any other speed always occurs abruptly. This is why wind speed traces always look 'spiky'.

Figs 5.4, 5.5 and 5.6 show only the speed of the wind. Figs 5.7 and 5.8 show the direction as well.

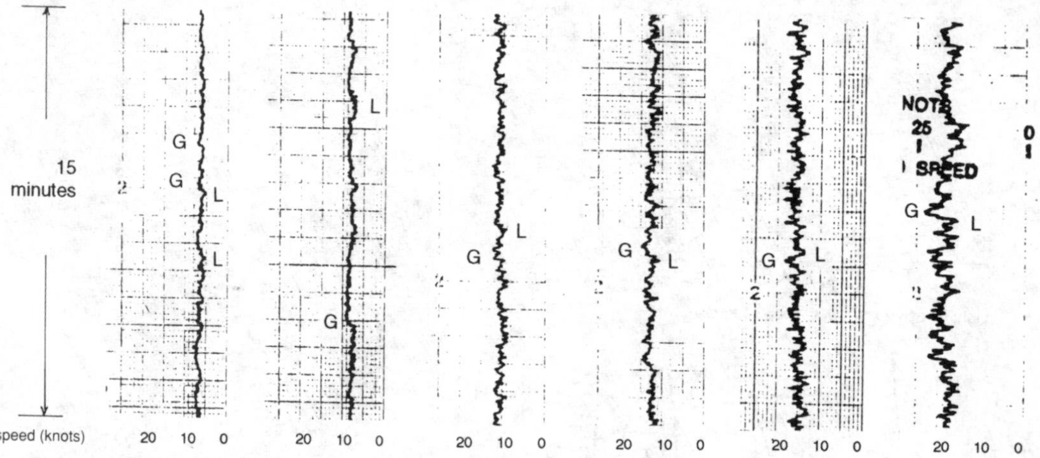

15 minutes

Wind speed (knots)	20 10 0	20 10 0	20 10 0	20 10 0	20 10 0	20 10 0
Mean speed (knots)	6	8	10	12.5	15	20
Gust speed (knots)	7	9.5	13	14	18	23
Lull speed (knots)	5	7	9	10	12.5	15
Gust factor%	33	33	30	35	37	40
Fluctuations:-						
Sweep speed (knots)		1	1.5	2	2.5	3
Factor%		12.5	15	15	16	15
Mean interval between gusts (seconds)	60	69	53	60	53	60
Mean interval between fluctuations (seconds)	-12	12	12	12	12	12

Fig 5.3 Speed traces of six cooled breezes

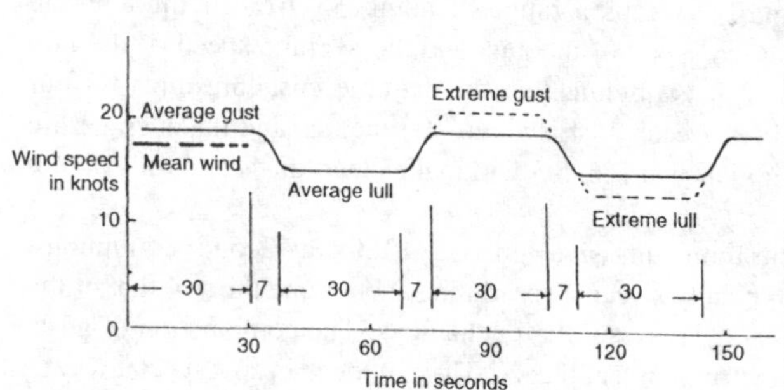

Fig 5.4 Gust/lull structure of real wind

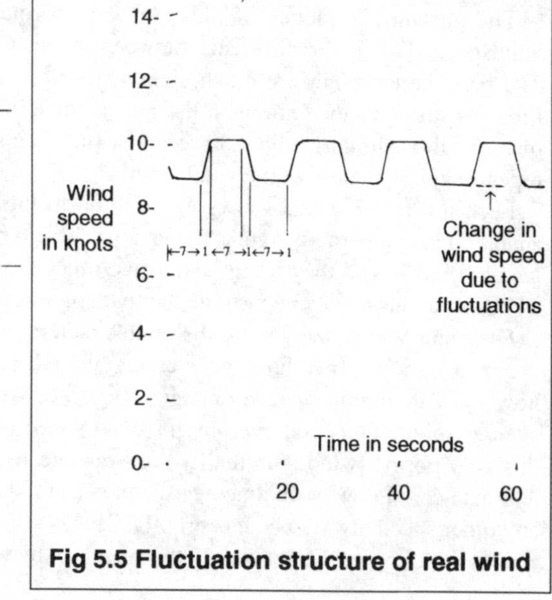

Fig 5.5 Fluctuation structure of real wind

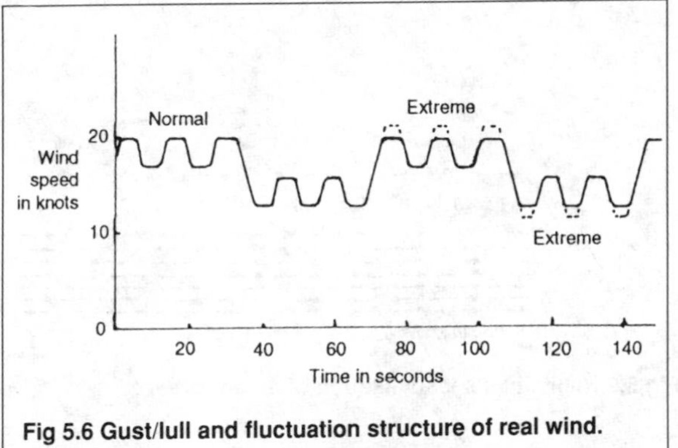

Fig 5.6 Gust/lull and fluctuation structure of real wind.

In Fig. 5.7 the average speed and the average direction of each gust and each lull over a half hour period of a cooled breeze have been measured and plotted to scale. It is as if you were in a hovering helicopter, looking vertically downwards, and somebody at 0 had a supply of magic thistle-down which would drift on the wind for, say, ten seconds

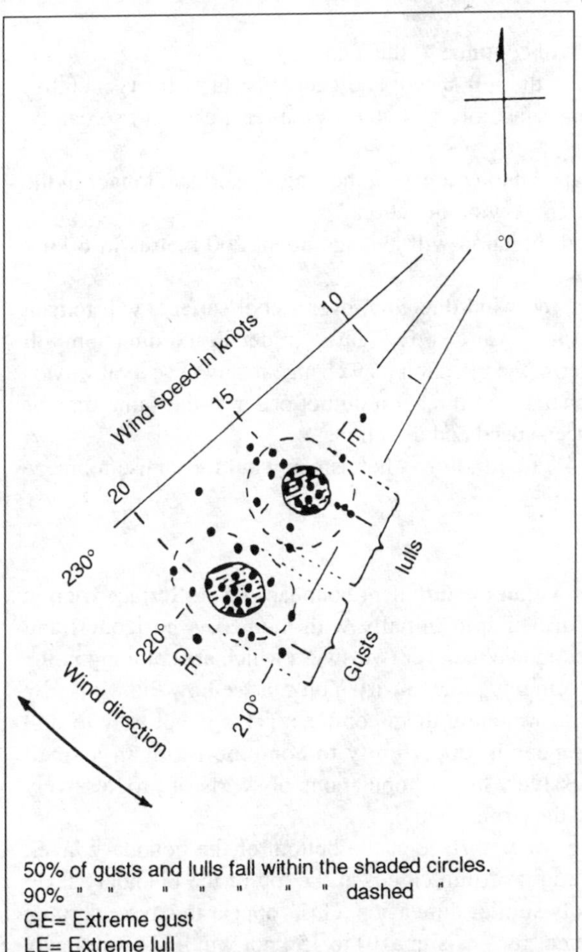

Fig 5.7 Plots of gusts and lulls

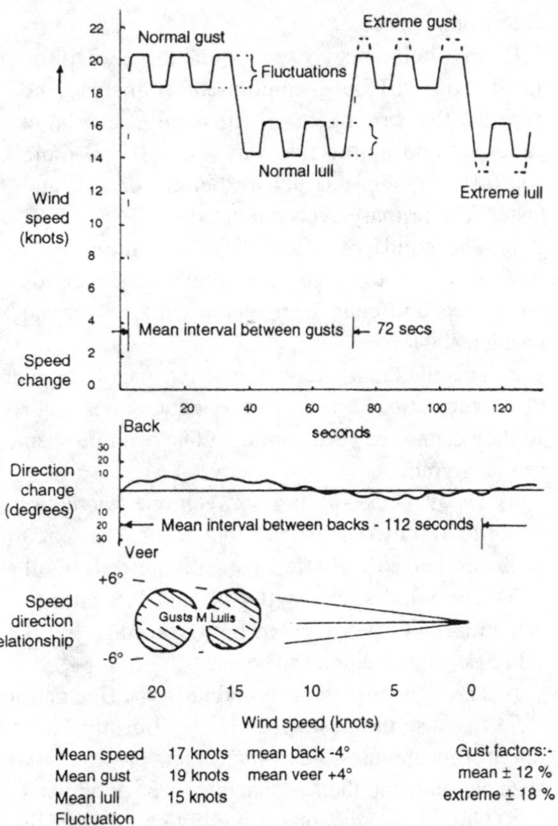

Fig 5.8 Signature of breeze without heat

and then stop. Each point marks the position at which the thistle-down released during that gust or lull would stop.

What Fig. 5.7. tells us is, that no matter how long the wind blows, almost all of the thistle-downs released in lulls will stop somewhere in the circle marked, 'lulls', and similarly that those released during gusts will come to rest within the circle marked, 'gusts'. Almost none will fall outside these two circles. Yet in this breeze these two circles do not even overlap.

No other diagram indicates so clearly that the cool breeze is usually not one wind at all, but two, and these alternate one after the other continuously. Note particularly that there is no systematic change of direction between the gusts and the lulls – in fact, the wind does not usually change its direction even at the same time as it changes its speed. There is no tendency for gusts to favour one tack or the other (except in some very special circumstances).

Fig. 5.8 sums up the information in Figs 5.3 to 5.7. It happens to display the behaviour of a wind which blows at an average speed of 17 knots, but Fig. 5.3 suggests that we will get the same sort of result from turbulent breezes, which are not heated, of any other speed.

If any helmsman expects the breeze to be steady, he will be disappointed. If instead, he expects the breeze to be unsteady, but in a patterned and predictable way, he will sail more comfortably, more safely, in better control, and faster. The primary expectations are:

1) The wind speed will fluctuate about 10 – 15% every ten to 15 seconds, typically 6 seconds puff, 1 second change, 6 seconds lull, 1 second change, and so on.

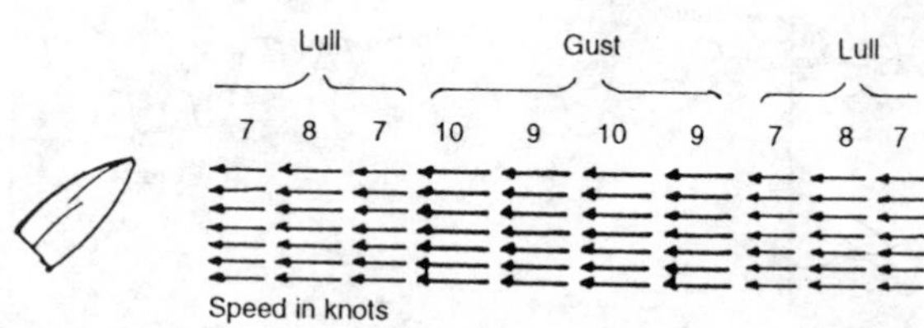

Fig 5.9 Helmsman's visualisation of a cool breeze

2) This fluctuation repetition is reasonably regular.

3) Fluctuations are not intense enough nor do they last long enough to mark the surface of the water, and so they cannot be seen coming. (They can be seen clearly on a visually sensitive surface, such as a field of growing grain).

4) The distance spacing between one fluctuation puff and the next is about 40 metres in a 6 knot wind, rising to 100 metres in a 20 knot wind. They are therefore much bigger than even the biggest recreational sailboats, and so will affect recreational craft of all sizes equally.

5) The wind speed will gust and lull alternately across a range of about 40% of the wind speed. Repetition will be irregular, but on average will be about 30 seconds gust, 5 seconds change, 30 seconds lull, 5 seconds change and so on.

6) Throughout both gusts and lulls, the fluctuations will continue to fluctuate.

7) Because the gust speed is significantly faster than the lull speed, and each gust lasts for (generally) one to four minutes, gusts mark their presence on the surface of the water, as darker areas, and so can be seen coming, and their onslaught can be anticipated.

8) Gusts typically appear as elliptical or lozenge-shaped darker areas on the water's surface, longer in the upwind-downwind direction and slightly shorter in the cross-wind direction.

9) Distance between gusts in the upwind-downwind direction will average about 200 metres in 6 knot breezes, rising to about 700 – 1000 metres in 20 knot winds.

10) Throughout this gust-lull and fluctuation pattern, the wind direction, over a cool surface, will remain surprisingly steady as between gusts and lulls over a time span of a few gusts. In detail, the direction will oscillate slightly as indicated in Fig 5.8. Over a longer term, the direction may change in any of several ways.

11) Except in special and rare circumstances, the changes in direction do not occur at the same time as the changes in speed, nor is there any correlation between speed and direction.

Fig. 5.9 displays with the same symbolism as Figs 4.5 to 4.9, how a helmsman would visualise a breeze which is not heated.

5.4 The gust mechanism

Gusts are individual swirls of air which form at height within the turbulent boundary layer. Surface friction ensures that the vast majority of swirls which are formed spin initially with their axes horizontal and crosswind and their tops moving in the downwind direction. Whenever two swirls which are spinning in the same direction approach each other, they combine to form one bigger swirl. You can see how this works by making two simultaneous swirls in a cup of coffee, and watching them combine. (This is not easy to do.) This process operates continuously. Random differences in opportunity to combine result in a small population of swirls which grow very big, and progressively larger populations of swirls of progressively smaller size. Some of the big ones become the gusts of the surface wind.

Observation of the marks made by the gusts on the water surface at the bottom of the boundary layer, and of the dimensions of the intermittent curls at the edges of thin clouds at the top of the boundary layer (we call these 'curlies') indicates that both are of broadly similar dimension. Gusts appear to have a definite cross-wind dimension – 200-300 metres would be typical for gusts in a 10 to 15 knot wind. (Theoretically vortices can have no free ends, so it is probable that some doughnut shape (toroidal) recirculation is present.) Such a rotating swirl of air would have a mass of between 10,000 and 30,000 tonnes and the coherence common to all swirls. Once started, this sort of mass takes a lot of stopping.

If we imagine that such a swirl should form about halfway between the surface and the upper limit of the boundary layer, then its speed would be intermediate between the surface wind and that at the top of the boundary layer. For a 10 knot surface wind, a typical wind speed at 1,000 metres would be 18 to 20 knots, so a swirl at mid-height could have a speed of about 14 to 15 knots. Once such a swirl forms, one of three outcomes will follow. Fig. 5.10 shows these diagrammatically.

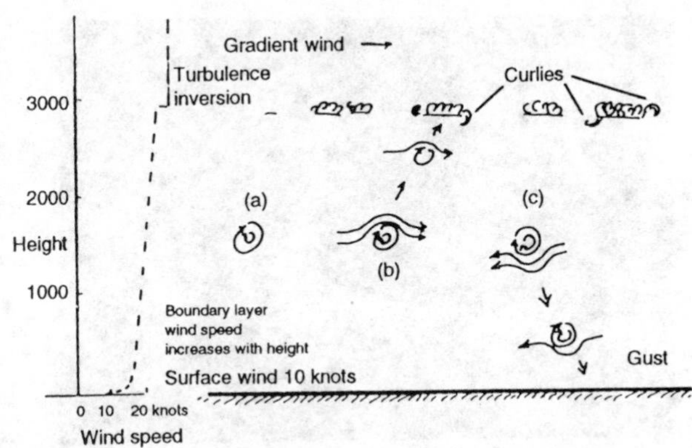

(a) Large swirl forms at mid-height.
(b) Swirl overtaken by faster air (large gust), circulation around swirl drives it upwards. If it encounters cloud it will form curlies.
(c) Swirl moves into slower air (large lull), circulation around swirl drives it downwards. It retains most of its original mid-height speed when it reaches surface, its greater speed appears as gust.

Fig 5.10 Gust mechanism

The first possibility is that no force will appear which will cause it to change its height. In this case the swirl will simply decay with time due to viscosity.

The second possibility is that the spinning swirl will, as a result of the general turbulent unsteadiness, encounter surrounding air which is moving a little faster than it is. When this occurs, the swirl will drive itself upwards with great aerodynamic force in the manner of an undercut tennis ball. Its own momentum will cause it to continue at about its original speed. Because of the velocity gradient, the higher it climbs, the faster will be the overtaking wind, and the faster it will climb, until it reaches the top of the boundary layer. On those occasions when small thin clouds mark the top of the boundary layer, the edges of these clouds will from time to time be twisted by these big swirls into the typical 'curled' shapes of Figs 5.10 and 5.11. These always form with their axes crosswind and their direction of spin such that their tops move downwind faster than their bottoms.

The third possibility is that the swirl will encounter air which is moving a little more slowly than it is. Within this slower air, the spinning swirl will behave like a tennis ball which is top-spun. It will propel itself downwards, and do so progressively faster as it meets progressively slowed air. At some point it must reach the surface.

At this point it will still be moving with the direction, and much of the speed, of the upper-level air within which it was formed and from which it has just arrived. Once it reaches the surface, its faster speed will cause it to adhere to the surface more strongly than the slower-moving air ahead of it. The result is that the whole rotating mass will undercut the slower air ahead. It will smear itself over the surface and move downwind with its greater speed, and this is what we recognise as a gust. Typically it will adopt an elliptical or lozenge shape, about 100 to 200 metres wide in the cross-wind sense (10 knot breeze) and longer in the upwind-downwind sense. These gusts have individual lives of from one to four minutes – they are bigger and last longer in the stronger winds. Once their momentum is dissipated (mainly by surface friction) they become the lighter wind of the lull and await their turn to be undercut and forced upward by the next energetic gust.

A particular point of interest is that neither Fig. 5.3 nor any other traces show any tendency of the gusts' extra speed to decay by systematic 'fading'. The higher speed of the gust usually appears to vanish as abruptly as it arrives. This again suggests some form of doughnut circulation, – or a horseshoe with its ends at the surface, – whose effect is to cause gusts to decay by becoming smaller rather than slower.

The sudden increase in the speed of the wind at the water surface makes the waves bigger. The initial increase is in the wave height and so the advancing faces of the waves becomes steeper. Because these steeper faces reflect less of the sky's light, the water surface under gusts appears as characteristic darker patches. Fig. 5.12(b) shows a typical Sydney harbour southerly gust pattern, as viewed from a height of about 100 metres. Sometimes it is possible to observe the gust pattern and the cloud 'curlies' at the same time. Always, if the gusts are big, so are the 'curlies', and vice versa.

When any turbulent wind, and particularly the stronger wind of a gust, 'scrubs' the water surface, it is in the nature of turbulence that some parts of the air in contact with the surface will be moving faster than others. The visual consequence of this is that the surface under the relatively slower-speed areas will remain 'shiny' while the surface under faster air will be darkened. The 'scrubbing' action of the air

Near Albury inland NSW.
Wind west 15 knots. View looking north.
Swirl diameters 200 to 400m.

Sydney
Wind south 20 knots. View looking west.

Fig 5.11 'Curlies'

Cloud wisps reveal swirls within the boundary layer. Wind west. 20 -25 knots at height, less at lower levels, blows left to right along valley. Mountains in the background are about 3,000 feet high. Boundary layer thickness about 6,000 feet, ill defined. Marlborough Sounds region, New Zealand.
(End of long fiord out of picture to right.)

Fig 5.12(a) Giant swirls within the boundary layer

elongates this darkening in a downwind direction. As a result, shiny streaks or 'wind lanes' appear between the darker areas. These indicate the direction of the approaching wind with absolute accuracy. Fig. 5.13 shows the appearance of an approaching gust as seen from a helmsman's eye level of about four feet. The wind lanes can be seen clearly. They show that the wind direction in the approaching gust will veer slightly with respect to the direction in the existing lull.

Some years ago the author discussed this gust mechanism with a dinghy helmsman friend and pilot who flies sophisticated STOL (short take-off and landing) aircraft out of Darwin, Northern Territory. Some weeks later he called back to report that he had tested the swirl mechanism in an unusual manner. Some of the strips he often served on a daily 'milk-run' were at the water's edge. When there was a breeze, and he observed a gust imprint on the surface just downwind of the strip he was approaching, he engaged auto pilot for the final stage of descent just prior to landing; i.e. as the aircraft passed through the airspace which he expected to be occupied by either a single swirl or a doughnut-type circulation immediately above the surface darkening adjacent to the strip. With the aircraft's speed steady and its attitude fixed by gyroscopes, he was able to sense short-period horizontal movements of the air by the change in indicated airspeed and the vertical movements by the lifting or sinking of the aircraft. He advised that, once he knew what to expect, the changes were easy to observe. He found the single and relatively big movements typical of a large single vortex, i.e. the aircraft sank sharply and airspeed increased (but not due to the sinking) as he entered the downwind upper edge of the swirl (flying in an upwind direction), and it lifted and the airspeed returned to its original value a few seconds later as he emerged from it. He had not, to that time, found any smaller double movements which would suggest a doughnut-type circulation.

View of part of Sydney Harbour from vantage point about 250ft above water. Wind South, 15 to 20 knots.
The 'footprint' mark of each substantial gust persists for 3 to 4 minutes and moves downwind 1 to 1.5 miles in that time. Points of interest are:-
1) The lozenge shape of each gust.
2) That about 50% of the surface area is occupied by gusts.
3) The wind lanes visible within the gusts.

Fig 5.12(b) The appearance of gusts from height

(a) Approaching gust, edge 200 feet distant.

(b) Ten seconds later, edge now 30 feet distant.

Approaching gust in 10 knot wind, viewed from a height of 4 feet. The foreshortening due to low eye-level, accentuates any curve in the 'wind lanes' - the shiny streaks on the water. In this case the wind lanes curve away to the right, so the wind within this gust will be slightly veered.

Fig 5.13 Approaching gust from helmsman's eye-level

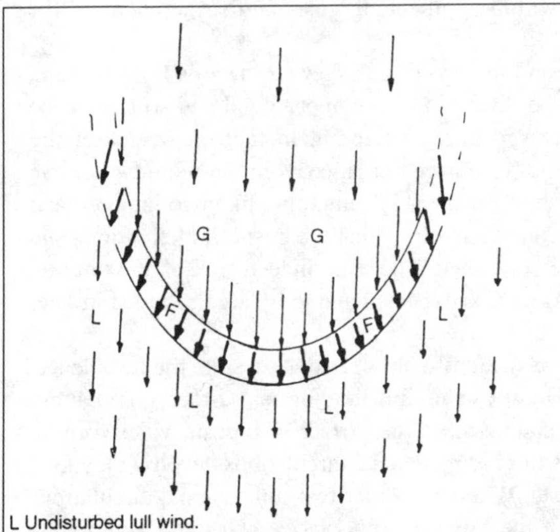

L Undisturbed lull wind.

G Gust wind which undercuts the lull wind.

F The 'fan', a fringe of air 25 to 50 feet wide which is displaced outwards by the advancing gust, in a direction away from the gust edge.

The fan passes over the water too quickly to form wind lanes.

Fig 5.14 The fan

5.5 The fan

As the mass of each gust advances, it undercuts and pushes aside the slower air ahead of it. The air just ahead of each advancing shoulder of the gust is moved forcefully, at almost the speed of the gust, in a direction angled outwards from the gust's direction. This is the 'Fan'. Fig. 5.14 shows its shape. Because it passes over each part of the water's surface so quickly, it makes no visible wind lanes. A helmsman ahead of an approaching gust will be able to see the wind lanes around him in the lull and also the wind lanes within the gust. Between the two there will be the fan. This will appear to the helmsman as a wind of a different direction which has a dimension of two or three lengths of a small boat.

If a close-hauled boat is heading into a gust from either side, the fan will appear as an abrupt brief header, (f – f, Fig. 5.14). If a close-hauled boat skims the shoulder of a gust, the fan can appear as a forceful and sustained lift. Alert crews who are aware of the fan can use this to free sheets, flick their boat onto a plane, and steer along the fan at greatly increased VMG.

But it is downwind that 'riding the fan' really comes into its own. Crews of high-performance, planing, downwind tacking dinghies, or fast catamarans, can steer to intercept the fan, and then bear away to accelerate in it and steer to stay in it. In this way they can ride it, broad reaching fast in the fan's skewed direction on the gust's shoulder – either shoulder – and with this technique they are able to steer sometimes almost directly downwind. In this way they can enjoy broad-reaching speeds in a directly downwind direction for as long as the gust and a usable fan lasts. You have to be alert, practised, and absolutely accurate, but it's devastatingly fast and tremendous fun.

5.6 The effect of depth of the boundary layer

Chapter 5 has introduced the breeze over a cool surface and its gusts. The six broadly similar lake breeze traces of Fig. 5.3 were chosen as typical examples. For simplicity, only these examples have been used in the discussion of mechanism.

Before we leave this introduction, let us establish some perspective. While the gusts of Fig. 5.3 are typical, they are only one part of a spectrum. The basic concept is the gust mechanism. For this to work, the boundary layer needs depth.

In the chapters ahead, we will see how much the depth of the boundary layer can vary. It can be very shallow, as in sea breezes or even shallower as in the anabatic and katabatic land breezes, or over abnormally cold water. Clearly, if the boundary layer is not deep, it cannot develop any relatively big swirls and so we will find that the shallower the boundary layer the smaller will be the gusts to the point where really shallow winds have no gusts.

Conversely, when conditions are such that the boundary layer is very deep, as is normal in gradient winds over sun-heated land, or over water just downwind of sun-heated land, the gust factor can be very large. In stronger winds the gusts themselves can be fierce. But the most important change for the helmsman is not the added speed and harshness of the gusts. The critical fact is that in strongly heated, strong-wind, deep-boundary-layer conditions, the directions of individual gusts can often be substantially backed or veered by significant angles from the wind's mean direction. These changes will almost always be random and so can never be predicted. But they can be anticipated visually. In these conditions, those crews who become skilled at observing the wind lanes within approaching gusts and so anticipating the wind direction within them can gain great race advantage.

Because the surface wind is slowed by surface friction and its direction is skewed towards low pressure, it would be natural to expect that the gusts would carry the direction of the upper wind and so tend to be systematically backed in the southern hemisphere or veered in the northern. In fact the scales of the mechanisms are such that no such general tendency occurs. No correlation appears in the records, nor can even the most analytical crews find any such pattern to use in practice. In something like two hundred and forty hours of (U2A) Kingston Tower traces, no single record occurs in which the gust/lull alternations and the back/veer alternations are even synchronised, let alone correlated. There are indeed special and unusual situations in which systematic direction changes either way can be expected and these are described in later chapters. But they are rare.

Finally, we will come across situations in which the air is heated so strongly that, despite the turbulence, it can rise and fall in circulations which are coherent. These can inhibit the normal surface gust pattern almost completely, because gusts which form in rising air cannot reach the surface, and gusts which form in falling air have no time to grow. When in these conditions three-dimensional circulations develop they give surface patterns of strange wandering breezes without gusts. When particular two-dimensional circulations develop they can give us gusts which blow continually in the same relative places, and these give us the channelling winds.

This is not the place to discuss these further patterns. But for perspective, let us remember that while gusts are the natural creatures of the breeze, and are almost universal, they come in different guises and they are not uniform.

Chapter Six
Friction and the Wind-Wave Patterns

6.1 Order – but where from?

One of the advantages of spending half a lifetime flying over the world's oceans was that I was one of a handful of people who knew that wherever you looked in the atmosphere, it possessed order. The far southern hemisphere is mostly ocean. There were few inhabited islands or ships to report weather. In the decades before weather satellites beamed their pictures of clouds and other data down to earth, weather office forecasters – in New Zealand in particular – were critically dependent upon the 'weather cross-section diagrams' routinely drawn by pilots. Pilots saw order. Pilots drew order. The weather bureau forecasters smiled. They knew that there could be no order.

Then came the initial photographs of whole weather systems from the early space vehicles. Revelation! Order! Unquestionably! It was our turn to smile. We had been twenty years ahead of them and had been using our understanding, sometimes routinely, and sometimes in unusual ways. As an example:

In the late 1940s a New Zealand airline ran a tenuous service across the southern Pacific. We used flying boats. Things were pretty primitive. Flights were long. There were no lights for night landings at the outlying islands, so you had to leave early and not loiter about decision-making if you were to arrive at your destination before dark. Facilities were minimal. Tahiti, for example, is a 3,000 metre mountain with a 1,000 metre-high island close offshore, both of which were often shrouded in cloud. There was then one generator which could run either the voice radio or the homing beacon, but not both together. There was no spare as a back-up. The locals regarded this as adequate. We, not surprisingly, did not, and treated Tahiti with great reserve. But back to *order*.

One morning at Papeete, Tahiti, I awakened before dawn for flight preparation. The weather had turned foul overnight. It was monsoonal with a strong westerly wind (directly onshore) and heavy continuous rain of the intensity one finds only in the tropics. Visibility was reduced in the rain to about 200 metres. As I dressed, the rain eased briefly. I slipped outside and noticed in the half-light that while there were still heavy clouds to the north, the wind had eased and veered to the north-west. Two minutes later the rain was thundering down again and the wind was strong and back in the west. I noted the time from habit.

At breakfast, the same sequence repeated. The heavy rain and the strong westerly eased but only for one or two minutes. The interval had been forty-three minutes. I spoke with my first officer and my flight engineer.

At the met. briefing at the weather office, the three of us and the forecaster awaited the next clearance. It came, right on the forty three minute interval. The forecaster regarded the idea of rhythm as ridiculous. I left him to his belief.

At Customs, all the civil authorities assumed that I would cancel in the appalling weather. I spoke with my purser, timed our run backwards (the passengers had to be ferried out to the flying boat via several trips on a launch) and ordered loading to proceed. The French (and some of the passengers) were incredulous. Another of the tiny clearances occurred, and on time. Nobody else seemed to notice it.

We started engines, slipped moorings, and taxied south, down the narrow marked channel inside the reef with its twenty seven degree 'S' bend. This channel had been blasted clear of coral heads to accommodate our two metre draught. It was hard to see the channel markers in the driving rain. The west wind was way above the cross-wind limit for take-off. I wondered if I hadn't pushed my luck too far. But our sums were right, and as we reached the southern end of the cleared channel – in fact, just as I was turning round – the rain cleared briefly, and the wind eased and veered momentarily north-west. I pushed the throttles open, coaxed the heavily laden ship onto the step, accelerated through the 'S' bends, lifted clear of the water, and airborne and away, drove straight into the wall of returning rain right over the township. What else is experience and observation for?

We knew about pattern. We used pattern. But at that stage of my life I was too involved with other things to ask myself, 'Why should there be pattern?' As far as sailboat racing was concerned, I unthinkingly accepted the then conventional wisdom, that any unsteadiness of the wind was usually due to the proximity of land and coastal hills, and that the further out to sea a course could be laid, the steadier the wind would be.

Ten years later, that wisdom was shattered forever.

One afternoon, in about 1960, my wife and I raced to windward south along the Sound of Middle Harbour (an arm of Sydney Harbour). Fig. 6.1(a) shows the topography. If there is any place in the world where the wind should be expected to curve smoothly around each of the 100 metre high, steep, alternating headlands, this is it. We started well, sailed fast, steered the perfect course to take advantage of the expected wind curve around each headland – and were soundly beaten by a slower boat which did *not* sail the 'perfect' course. Something unexpected was happening.

Fortunately, on that day the weather was cool and cloudy, and the post frontal southerly wind had not changed significantly during nor immediately after the race. We were so interested in what might have happened that we drove to a high downwind vantage point from which we could see the wind lanes upwind along the whole windward leg. The flow of the 10 to 12 knot southerly was initially as sketched in Fig. 6.1(a) – exactly as expected. But, as we watched, the pattern moved!. After seven or eight minutes, the curves had moved to blow as in Fig. 6.1(b). After fifteen minutes it blew as in Fig. 6.1(c). This was heresy! The primary curves of the wind opposed the lie of the headlands! The pattern continued to flow steadily north, and after thirty minutes blew again as in Fig. 6.1(a). We were so fascinated that we waited a further thirty minutes and watched while the whole pattern continued to flow downwind towards us and repeated another full cycle.

What we saw that evening dispelled forever my belief that unsteadiness in wind direction could be caused primarily by nearby hills or headlands. Whatever mechanism it was that made the surface wind on that day blow in horizontal waves which themselves moved downwind at about one quarter of the wind's speed – the force of that mechanism was so great that even the effect of a series of 100 metre high steep-sided headlands was as nothing compared with its power.

My approach to yacht racing took on a new dimension. I wanted to understand this mechanism so that we could anticipate and perhaps predict these waves. The previous chapters, and those which follow, flow from work which started following that afternoon.

The logical places to start were the weather offices. Unfortunately, most anemographs are sited in areas which are now so built up (and this includes the sites of airport instruments) that much of what the instruments measure are the turbulent wakes of upwind buildings. These wakes obliterate small oscillations. Some instruments, fortunately, are still sited in areas clean enough to show these oscillations when they occur. If they had at that time been noticed, they had not been studied. Weather bureaux libraries possessed nothing relevant. The basic reason is that weather offices tend to address the needs of metropolitan, rural, aviation, marine and recreational audiences, plus some special industrial applications such as forecasting the winds and waves around ocean oil rigs. None of these audiences is in the least interested in small oscillating shifts in the wind direction.

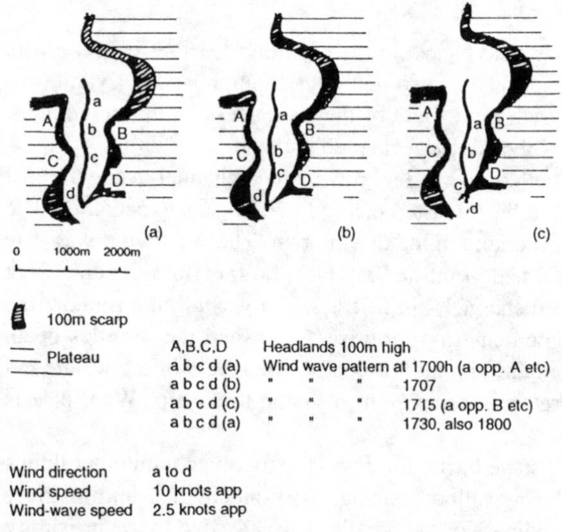

Fig 6.1 Movement of wind-waves past headlands

The scientific libraries were even more unhelpful. Oceanographic and other workers who necessarily dealt with the wind, all tended to develop elegant equations which would suppress the wind's unsteadiness and so enable them to use a single figure to represent the real wind's true complexity. This was exactly the approach I did not want. I was referred to one group who were endeavouring to work out whether an accidentally released radiation cloud would flow down one or the other of two adjacent valleys, so that they would know which one to evacuate. We did not seem to have much in common. (Years later, in the days following Chernobyl I remembered them and wished them luck.)

It seemed as if sailors were on their own. There seemed to be only one logical place to start – right at the beginning! It seemed to me to be essential to accumulate a series of records, in known conditions, of the actual behaviour of wind speed and direction over the waters on which we sail. I realised that it would take a long time but my hope was that an accumulating data-bank would ultimately contain sufficient information to analyse. From that time onwards, whenever I have been able to see wind over water, I have plotted its patterns and noted the associated conditions. My files are now several inches thick. It is primarily from this personal data-base, plus everything else that I have been able to lay my hands on, that a coherent logic of pattern and mechanism has finally emerged.

From time to time I have met other sailors who were interested. I would like to thank David Houghton of the British Weather Office in particular for his company during the workups to the Montreal (Kingston) and the Moscow (Tallinn) Olympics, for his introduction to the British Weather Office library and for his willingness to share ideas. The *Quadrant Effect*, mentioned later, is David's concept. I have developed this first as a tool for anticipating boundary layer thickness and then further to the *Stability Index* – a classic example of the benefit of sharing ideas.

In general, the bulk of a task is done when yesterday's complex mystery has become today's self-evident logic. So it is with wind patterns. It is now clear that there are four primary forces which drive the short-term changes of the surface wind: surface friction, inter-layer friction, surface heat and latent heat. We can now see how these four interact with a beautiful and self-evident simplicity. Depending upon which and how many of these four are present, the wind will adopt repetitive motions which are recognisable. These motions may never repeat exactly but they always repeat within sensed limits. They are stable in the sense that if they are disturbed temporarily by some greater force, they will restore themselves. Students of the science of chaos will feel very much at home with the concept.

I call these motions, 'patterns'. With a little logic and some supporting observation, a helmsman can now anticipate the way the wind will blow, and can then focus on the best way to exploit the expected shifts and changes for race advantage.

6.2 Waves in the air – the friction mechanism

In the absence of heating, the thickness of a turbulent boundary layer is proportional to the wind speed. It is about 500 metres in 6 knots, 1,000 metres in 10 knots, 2,000 metres in 20 knots etc. Throughout this thickness, particles of air are sometimes lifted and sometimes forced down by mechanical turbulence. They cool, adiabatically, as they are lifted. The result is that the air at the top of the boundary layer is cooler – sometimes several degrees cooler – than the air immediately above it. Fig. 6.2 shows the logic. This 'turbulence inversion' can separate the boundary layer air absolutely from the air above. At the bottom, friction with the land or water surface slows not only the surface wind but the whole boundary layer. At the boundary layer's upper surface a situation then develops where the warmer, lighter, faster air of the gradient wind blows over the cooler, heavier, slower air of the boundary layer wind. This is very similar to the situation of wind blowing over water, in that a lighter fluid is moving over a heavier one – the speed difference causes friction between the two – and this friction causes gravity waves to form on the boundary layer's upper surface exactly as the friction of wind over water causes waves to form on the water's upper surface. These waves in the boundary layer are called 'rolls'

At the time I made the sketch of Fig. 3.9, I looked to see if I could see these waves, because I have so often observed them when flying. A particularly good example of the force and scope of a turbulent boundary layer, and of the power of an inversion to keep two air masses separate, occurs when there are bushfires in eastern Australia. In High-dominant conditions, aircraft

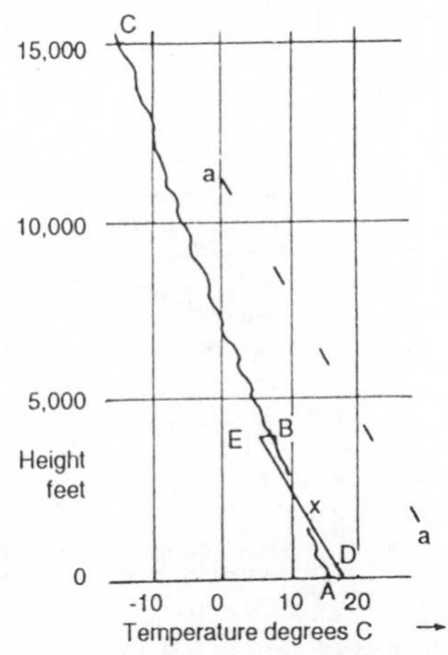

ABC = Initial temperatures at each height (lapse rate) - app 2° C per 1000 ft.
DE = Turbulent boundary layer. Forms in breeze.
a - a = Dry adiabat, 3° C per 1000 ft. Air forced down or up by turbulence warms and cools at this rate. In this way E becomes cooler than B.
BE = Turbulence inversion

Fig 6.2 Turbulence inversion

on the New Zealand – Fiji run, 1,500 nautical miles to the East, can find themselves flying over a lower atmosphere full of shimmering ash. In the old non-pressurised days we often flew close above it. Ash in the air below the inversion soiled the aircraft. Above it, the air was crystal clear. And when we flew just above the inversion, we could see the waves, like swell on the sea.

The effect of waves which form at the top of the boundary layer on the airflows which we sail in at the water surface is shown in Fig. 6.3.

The whole mechanism can be observed and understood at a smaller scale if you stand on a jetty over three or four feet of clear water, and watch how the waves move the seaweed at the bottom. In the chapter on 'waves' (See Part Two), the orbital motions of gravity waves in the water are described. Where the water is not shallow, the motion becomes progressively weaker until, at some depth, it vanishes. But where the depth is shallow when compared with the height of the wave, the presence of the bottom forces the water there to oscillate to and fro as a link between the adjacent up and down orbital movements. It is these to and fro horizontal movements at the bottom which wash the seaweed to and fro as the surface waves roll by. In the atmosphere, the boundary layer is usually shallow when compared with the height of the waves which form upon it, and the same mechanism as you can see working in shallow water also causes the air at the surface to move to and fro as the waves roll by overhead.

6.3 Oscillating surface waves

To complete our dynamic model of the atmosphere we now need a current to represent the wind – so let us come back to our jetty when the tide is flowing. If we watch the weed when there is current, but no waves, the weed will stream with the current and indicate steady flow. But if a boat passes by and makes waves with their crests aligned with the direction of the current and which therefore roll in a cross-current direction, the to and fro motions at the bottom induced by the waves will also act in a cross-current direction, and so will combine with and deflect the current first one way and then the other, and the flow will become sinuous instead of straight. The seaweed will indicate the resultant oscillations in direction.

This mechanism represents exactly the usual action of waves in the boundary layer. Fig. 6.4 shows the usual orientations of the wind flows at increasing heights, from the surface up through the boundary layer and into the gradient wind. It may come as a surprise that the direction of the relative wind 'BG' between the boundary layer wind 'OB' and the gradient wind 'OG' is approximately at right angles to the surface wind 'OS', but the logic says, 'yes'. The boundary layer wind 'OB' is slowed by surface friction, and so is skewed towards low pressure. At the upper surface of the boundary layer, the relative wind 'BG' is the vector difference between the skewed boundary layer wind and the relatively unskewed gradient wind. It is this relative wind which causes the friction which makes the waves, and the wave crests, 'cc – cc', will be approximately at right angles to this relative wind. At the surface, the surface wind 'OS' is slowed further by friction and skewed further by the pressure difference between the distant High and Low pressure centres. The end result is that the alignment of the wave crests will be approximately parallel with the direction of the surface wind, and the to and fro motions at the surface move across the surface wind. These are the motions which turn a steady wind into an oscillating wind.

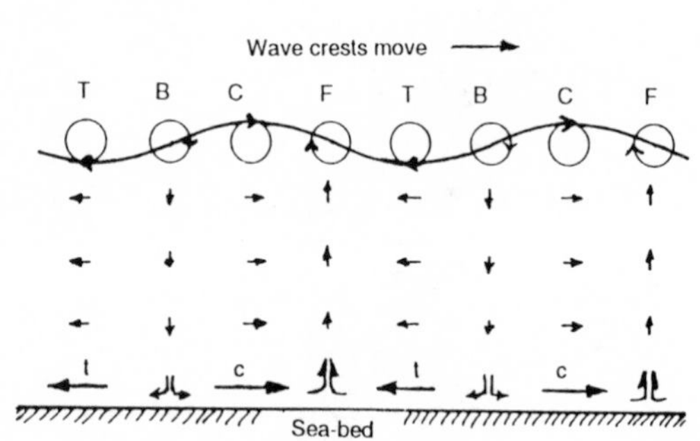

C Crest - water particles move to right
B Back - " " " downwards
T Trough - " " " to left
F Face - " " " upwards

At the sea-bed, the downflows under B & B split into horizontal flows c & t, which feed upflows f & f. As the wave moves c & t move to remain under C & T.

Fig 6.3 The flows on the sea-bed caused by waves

Figs 6.5, 6.6, and 6.7 are examples of the surface patterns caused by these wave motions.

All show oscillating winds, but all are different. Fig. 6.5 settles to regular oscillations with a repetition interval of about 30 minutes, but remains vague as to direction. Fig. 6.6 never settles: oscillations of up to 40 degrees repeat at intervals which vary from 20 to 50 minutes. Fig. 6.7 is even more irregular: the bigger oscillations

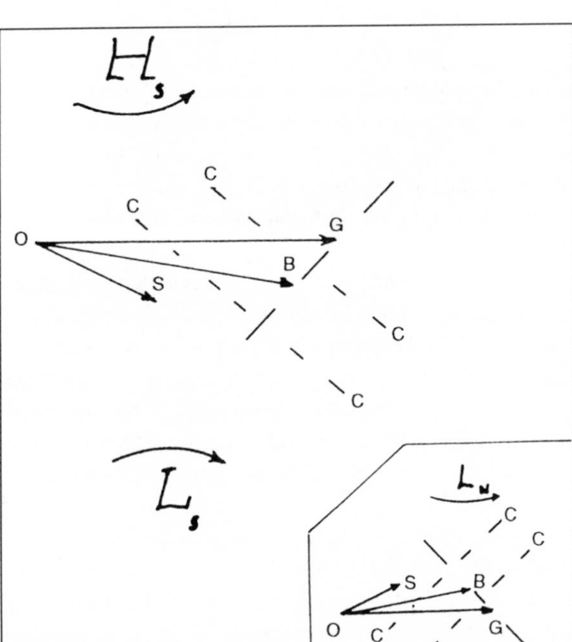

Hs Distant High - southern hemisphere
Ls " Low " "

HN Distant High - northern hemisphere
LN " Low " "

OG = Gradient wind above inversion
OB = Boundary layer wind below inversion
BG = Relative wind at inversion
c....c = Alignment of wave crests (perpendicular to BG)
OS = Surface wind

Alignment of wave crests is approximately parallel with surface wind.

Fig 6.4 Wind directions at different heights

repeat at between 40 and 80 minute intervals, but there is often a shorter, faster pattern within the big waves. The major backs and veers are huge. Any helmsman who could get these right would beat those who did not by very large margins. Fortunately, as we shall see later, it is generally possible to predict which patterns will be regular and which not.

At this point we must make a proviso. The roll orientation described is in fact the, 'longitudinal' roll. In it the wave crests are approximately parallel with the surface wind (hence 'longitudinal') and the to and fro oscillations move across the surface wind. This is the one which occurs most frequently, almost but not quite to the exclusion of all others. We will look at those others later.

In chapter 7 we will see that one of the heat mechanisms is so similar to the *friction roll* mechanism that it naturally combines with it and

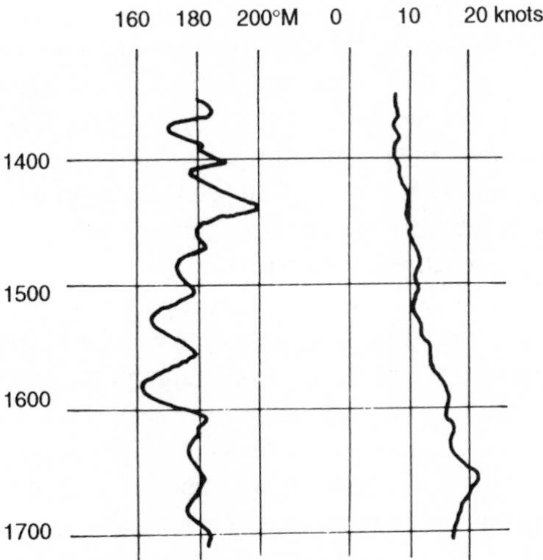

Port Phillip (Melbourne) 27th Feb 1976
Olympic selection trials

Fig 6.5 Gradient wind *straight isobars - cooled*

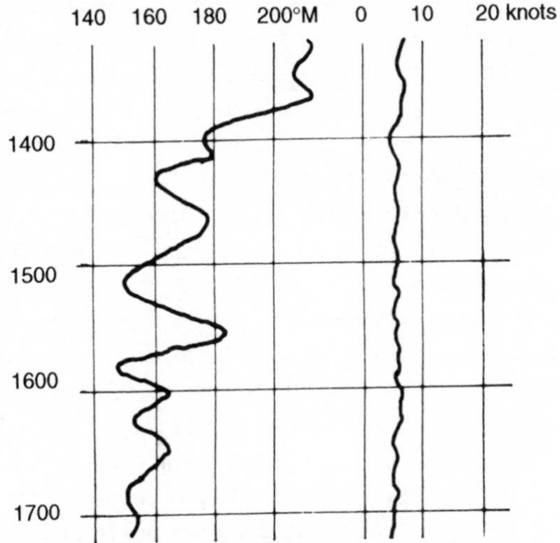

Adelaide, Sth Australia. 19th Jan 1988

Fig 6.6 Gradient wind *low dominant - cooled*

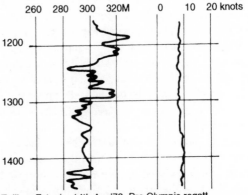

260 280 300 320M 0 10 20 knots
1200
1300
1400

Tallinn, Estonia. 14th Aug'78. Pre Olympic regatt.

Fig 6.7 Gradient wind *low dominant - heated*

boosts its effect.

The end result is that either the *longitudinal friction roll* mechanism alone, or this mechanism boosted by heat, is the one which occurs most frequently world wide. Wherever the wind direction oscillates, it is usually this mechanism which is at work. When the action is vigorous and the atmospheric humidity is high, thin clouds can form along the wave crests. Photographs from space vehicles, such as Fig. 6.8, frequently show areas of thousands of square miles uniformly covered with parallel lines of these 'roll' clouds, typically spaced about 2 miles apart.

It is sometimes possible to see these wave motions directly. Readers may have noticed that it is often possible to see the engine exhaust plumes from an aircraft if it happens to be flying almost directly towards or away from you. In conditions when the boundary layer is shallow, such as a sea breeze, it is sometimes similarly possible to see, from an aircraft, the smoke plumes from a power station if you line yourself up with them, at the right height, and look upwind along them from several miles downwind. When observed like this, they are seen to be not straight at all (except in steady light air). In roll situations they take the form of a helix, with the axis parallel with the mean wind direction. Wavelength usually appears to be about one to two miles per complete cycle.

An unusual sequence is worth describing. About fifty miles south of Sydney, near the city of Wollongong, are a power station, an airfield, and Lake Illawarra, a 10 by 20 mile lagoon separated from the sea only by a low and narrow strip of land. One Saturday many years ago when an interclub dinghy race was programmed on the lake. I happened to be scheduled to coach some airline cadets in flying techniques that morning. At about noon, well after the summer sea breeze had set in, I checked the plumes from the power station and noted that the helix was regular and particularly tight. The cadets dropped me at the local airfield. Two hours later I was enjoying some spirited dinghy racing. It was probably an unfair advantage, but I knew with absolute conviction that on that day it would pay to use the compass to the exclusion of almost all else because the oscillations would probably be regular – and they were.

6.4 Regular or random

If you watch waves roll onto an open ocean beach, their principle characteristic is their regularity. But if you move to some point where there is a submerged bar or rock ledge a little offshore, the big waves will break to seaward of it, and what will come in over the shallow bar and through the deeper channel between the bar and the shore will be nothing like the big waves offshore. Over the shallower bar, there will be only small waves, for the very good reason that you cannot have big waves in shallow water. Across the deeper channel between the bar and the shore, the waves tend to combine and become a little bigger. Three principles stand out, which we can accept intuitively because they are so obvious.

1. Big waves can exist in deep water.
2. Big waves cannot exist in shallow water.
3. Waves get smaller in shallower water, and vice versa.

Exactly the same principles apply with respect to the rolls in the atmosphere, but we need some imagination to appreciate the next step. In the ocean example above, the depth of the water was fixed by its density. At one tonne per cubic metre water is nearly one thousand times heavier than the air above it, and there is every good reason for assuming that the upper surface of the water will remain reasonably level, and so the depth of water will not change much from one minute to the next.

But in the atmosphere, if the temperature inversion due to turbulence is about three degrees Celsius (and it would seldom be more than this), this will mean that the air just below the inversion will be about one percent denser than the air just above, and not one thousand times denser. So it is only a relatively trivial force which controls the height of the upper surface and so the thickness of the boundary layer. This is why it is so sensitive to wind speed – the layer becomes deeper as the wind speed becomes stronger and the turbulence more energetic.

But the horizontal motions of the air due to the orbital motions of the waves will themselves alter the wind speed, to the point of nearly doubling it at one place and nearly zeroing it at another! So the practical result is that, as soon as waves (rolls) form in the boundary layer, they will themselves cause major and unpredictable changes to the height of its upper surface and so its depth – unless this is further controlled by some greater force. These depth changes will then make it impossible for the waves to be regular, exactly as did the change of depth of water over the bar. So the logic is that the 'natural' behaviour of the

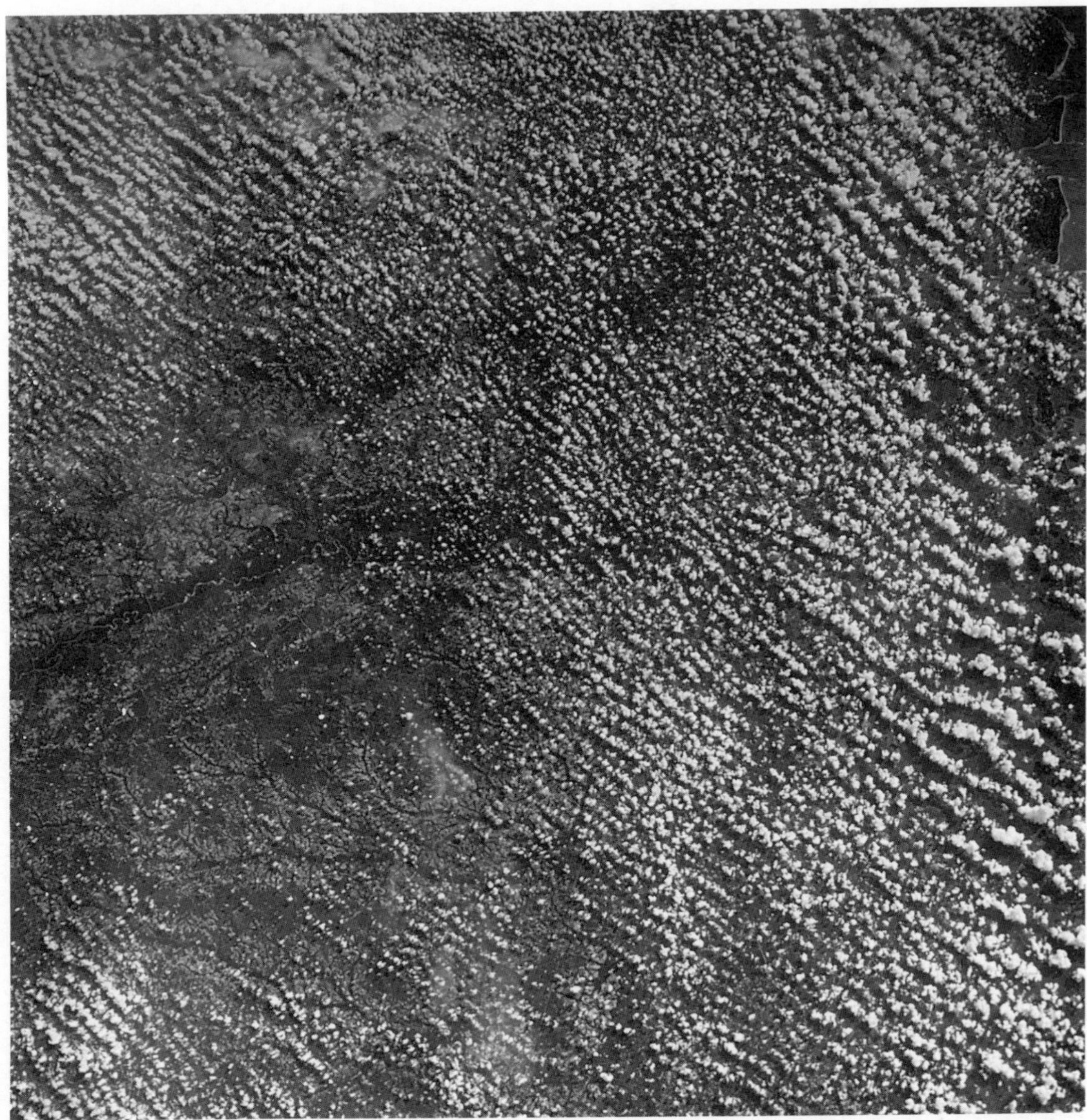

The Atlantic coastline southwest of Charleston, South Carolina, is visible in the upper right corner. Developing Cumulus cloud lines are oriented southeast-northwest over eastern Georgia and southern South Carolina. They are about 1 and a half miles apart near the centre of the picture.

Fig. 6.8 Roll clouds from space.
Photograph by courtesy of NASA.

resultant speed and direction changes of the surface wind will be an unpredictable jumble of bigger and slower and smaller and quicker oscillations. They repeat within recognisable bounds in that none will be longer than some period, and none shorter than some much shorter period, and their backs and veers will not exceed some amplitude, but their irregularity will be such that the only prediction possible is the irregularity itself. Fig. 6.6 is such a pattern.

This is the logic. But what about those beautifully regular waves which I had been admiring for decades from the flight deck?

In the years prior to the Montreal Olympics, I spent a lot of time studying the wind records in the area of Kingston, Ontario, where the sailing was to be conducted. The factors which control the climate there result in very frequent summer south-westerlies. I reached back into the July and August breeze records of the adjacent airport for year after year. (A little research had established that for winds stronger than 6 knots, the winds at the airport were the same as the winds at the recently installed Kingston Meteorological Tower offshore. Light airs were different.) Many of the records showed the expected random changes of speed and direction. But a surprising proportion showed a wind which, once it set in, was steady in speed, and showed smaller, ordered, rhythmic oscillations. There seemed to be two completely different sorts of south-westerly wind.

I checked to see if these 'steady' days were associated with recent fronts, approaching fronts, unusual temperatures, etc. Finally, the penny dropped. It was the isobar curvature over Kingston on the day concerned which separated the two groups perfectly. Figs 6.9(a) and (b), in which, for clarity, I have plotted only every tenth day's record, are from my notes at the time. On days when low pressure areas were nearby, the wind speed and direction wavered almost at random. But when high pressure was dominant, the wind speed, its direction and the rhythm of its oscillations all became regular and reasonably predictable. A little more dreaming, and the reasons became clear.

In regions of low pressure, the air spirals inwards, (the axis of the spiral is vertical), it converges and rises. When there is breeze, a turbulence inversion will form, on which waves will develop, and the resultant wind patterns will be unsteady for the reasons described above and shown in Figs 6.9(b), 6.6 and 6.7. A second reason for the unsteadiness is that the air in the Low will already be rising and cooling somewhat due to the convergence of the Low itself. In this situation air forced upwards by turbulence will not become much colder than the already cooled adjacent rising air, and so the temperature difference will be very small, and depth control minimal.

In regions of high pressure the air subsides. As it subsides, it warms by compression, exactly as air which is lifted by turbulence is cooled by expansion. So the subsiding air gets warmer. But the layer of air nearest the ground can't subside because the ground is there, and so it isn't compressed and doesn't get warmer – instead, it just spirals slowly outwards. Above it, the air which has subsided and warmed spirals outwards too. The result is two masses of air – an enormous mass of subsiding warmer air over a shallower layer of colder air, which are separated by what is called a 'subsidence inversion'. Fig. 6.10 gives the logic. This inversion is intensely stable, because it is continually reinforced by the steady subsidence of the thousands of millions of tonnes of air above it. Its height is typically one to one and a half thousand metres. It will always form, regardless of whether a turbulent breeze happens to be blowing or not.

When the breeze does blow, a turbulence inversion will form as it always does when the wind speed exceeds six knots. But when it forms under a High, the turbulence inversion will simply become absorbed by and blended with and will further intensify the much more intense subsidence inversion. This blended inversion will thereafter be controlled absolutely by the dominant subsidence component.

In the paragraph above we saw that waves would themselves vary the depth of a turbulence inversion, unless it was controlled by some greater force. The intense subsidence inversion which forms under every High is that greater force. This is the reason for the profound difference between the unpredictable traces of Fig. 6.9(b) and the predictable traces of Fig. 6.9(a).

'High dominant', or *'Low dominant'*. This is the first factor in the *Stability Index*.

6.5 Transverse and other rolls

The great areas of roll clouds which are so commonplace in temperate and sub-tropical latitudes are almost always aligned approximately with the surface wind. Over the oceans or the cool featureless areas of the

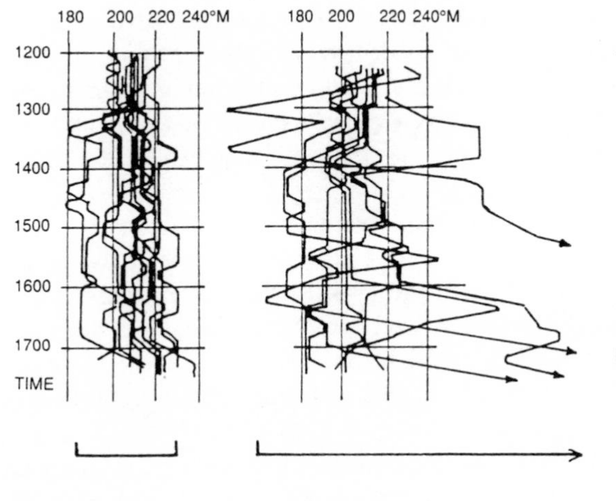

(a)
High dominant
Subsidence inversion

Wind directions predictable.
Changes of direction are small.
All directions lie within a narrow range.

(b)
Low dominant
No subsidence inversion

Wind directions not predictable.
Oscillations not predictable.
Wind directions back and veer irregularly.
Backs and veers sweep wide ranges.

Plots of directions of winds between south and west at Kingston airport, High dominant and Low dominant situations.

Fig 6.9 Effect of subsidence inversion

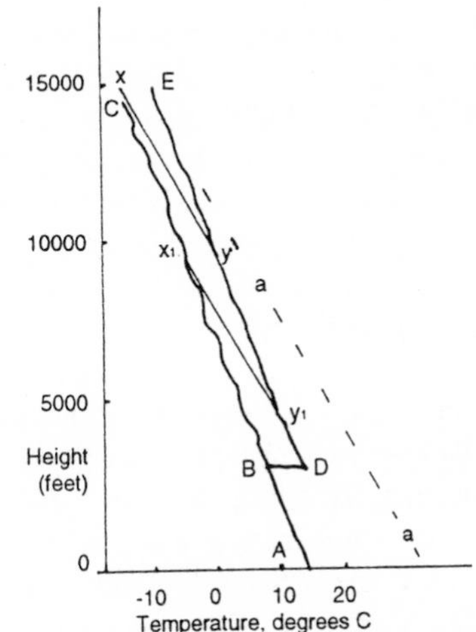

A - B - C = Initial temperatures of atmosphere at each height.
a---a = Dry adiabat - descending air heats at this rate - 3°C per 1000 ft.
x - y
x_1 - y_1 = Temperature change of air as it subsides 5000 feet.
Air at and above BD escapes by spiralling outwards.
Air below BD cannot subside due to the land or water surface below, so does not heat.
A - B - D - E = New temperatures of atmosphere after subsidence.
B - D = Subsidence inversion.

Fig 6.10 Subsidence inversion mechanism

continents, roll clouds almost never appear in any other way. But along discontinuities, such as coastlines, when the land is warmer than the water, or ranges of hills, two or three parallel lines of similar clouds will customarily form, and these lines will be parallel with the warm coastline etc, and not with the direction of the surface wind. Often these clouds lines will interrupt a wider pattern of roll clouds. In percentage terms the occurrence of these transversely aligned clouds is so trivial as to be statistically insignificant. But for the racing helmsman, the statistically insignificant 'transverse roll' turns out to be surprisingly important. The reason for this is that most of us sail close to coasts or lake shores or other discontinuities, and usually when they are warmest. We happen to spend most of our sailing time in exactly the places where these rare non-aligned clouds usually form and exist.

Fig. 6.11 shows how the to and fro motions of a transverse roll combine with the surface wind. The result is a pattern of alternately stronger and lighter winds, without systematic change of direction. Not infrequently, the 'stronger and lighter wind' pattern takes the form of alternating wind and calm.

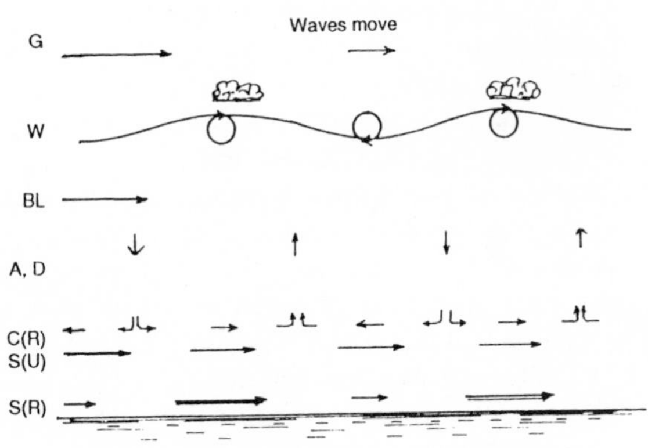

G = Gradient wind.
W = Transverse waves on upper surface of BL.
(Lines of clouds may mark crests.)
BL = Boundary layer wind.
A,D = Ascending and descending air under faces and backs of waves at W.
C(R) = Horizontal components of wind at surface due to waves (rolls) at W.
(Refer to Fig 6.3)
S(U) = Undisturbed surface wind.
S(R) = Resultant surface wind - |S(U) plus or minus C(R)|.

Wind speed increases under each crest, decreases under each trough.
Note that cloud lines, if present, mark crests.

Fig 6.11 Transverse roll mechanism

In the years 1949 to 1954 I developed the technique of soaring radio-controlled model gliders in the updraughts caused when onshore winds blew onto the coastal cliffs just north of Auckland, New Zealand. From the outset the object was to win the world endurance record for model aircraft with a flight of ten to twelve hours, so it was essential to be able to forecast the following day's wind with reasonable certainty. (We succeeded after five year's development in gaining the open world record with one flight of about eight hours, followed by a later flight of ten hours.) I chose the particular weather situation in which a large high pressure area centred to the south-east swept a north-easterly wind onto the north-west/south-east aligned cliffs near my home. These winds blew steadily for several days at a time, and so the following day's winds were easy to forecast with confidence.

The early models flew about as well as the seagulls. Later machines were much more efficient and flew very much higher. Throughout hundreds of hours of flying spread over five years, we were at first surprised by, but soon came to regard as normal, a 'stronger-wind – lighter-wind' cycle of about 60 minutes. Often, lines of thin clouds formed and blew overhead. During the stronger-wind part of the cycle, the model, and the seagulls, would fly hundreds of metres above the cliffs. During the feeble-wind part of the cycle, there was sometimes insufficient lift to support either the model or the seagulls in soaring flight. Fig. 6.12 was first published in a model aeroplane magazine in 1957.

The message is clear. If transverse roll clouds are visible, expect the wind speed to alternate in step with the movement of the cloud lines overhead as indicated in Fig. 6.11 If clouds are not visible, but the behaviour of the local seagulls suggests the same pattern, it is probably safe to assume a transverse roll and that this pattern will continue.

A most interesting observation is that this stronger-wind, lighter-wind pattern did *not* appear on the traces of either of two Weather Bureau wind recording instruments sited within thirty kilometres of the cliffs where we flew our models. One was at the weather office at the flying boat base about twenty kilometres to the south, at the entrance to Auckland harbour. This harbour develops strong funnelling winds. Another was at a joint military/civil airfield twenty five kilometres inland to the West. Often, after model flights of up to six hours, in which the cycling of the wind speed had been, sometimes, the major factor, I examined the two anemograph traces. Never was I able to detect, on either trace, any indication at all of the cycling which had been so prominent over the coastal cliffs a few kilometres away.

During this period I often took my models to Sydney, and joined Sydney modellers on their coastal cliffs. For whatever reason, the transverse roll cycle which is so prominent near Auckland is, in a similar weather situation, completely absent near Sydney. So don't rely on it anywhere, but don't be surprised if it appears.

In the same way that transverse rolls appear with unusual frequency at odd places, they similarly appear with unusual frequency at odd times. Very often, when the wind changes from something – say from a calm or from a wind from a different direction – into something else, the first few waves will be transverse, and the pattern will be: stronger, lighter, stronger, lighter, and then suddenly it will flick into a steady-strength breeze. For as long as the breeze accelerates in strength, it will remain almost steady in direction. Only when it steadies in speed will it begin to oscillate. Conversely, when it dies in strength, the oscillations will increase in amplitude. We call this increasing amplitude in a dying wind, 'the concertina effect'. Fig. 6.13 shows the concepts.

To summarise: Transverse rolls can exist at all times near physical or temperature discontinuities such as coasts, and as transient features as a part of any wind change. They are important for racing helmsmen. The stronger-wind lighter-wind cycle which they cause is easy to predict when roll clouds mark the wave crests, but difficult otherwise. They are intensely local. At a distance of a few miles offshore, or a few miles inland, they vanish. Near the entrance to any narrow waterway where funnelling winds blow, the stronger funnelling wind mechanism will usually obliterate any transverse roll mechanism.

Pattern in which wind speed increased and decreased as cloud lines approached and passed overhead.
Wind direction did not change.
Repetition interval was about 60 minutes
(in the 8 to 15 knot winds in which I flew my gliders).
Auckland, New Zealand, 1949-1954.

Fig 6.12 Observations of transverse roll winds
Diagrams originally published *M.A.N* March 1957

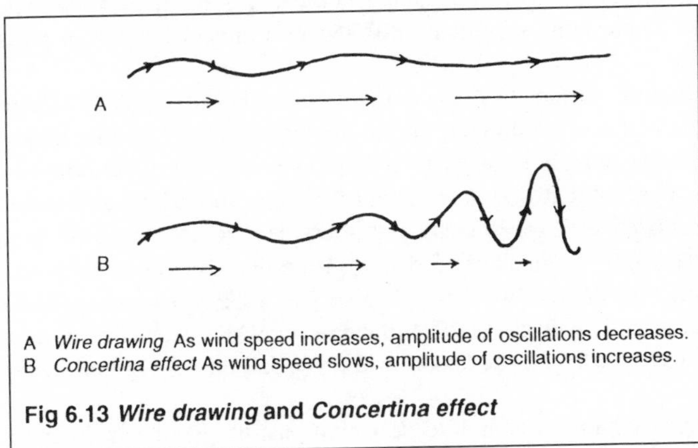

A *Wire drawing* As wind speed increases, amplitude of oscillations decreases.
B *Concertina effect* As wind speed slows, amplitude of oscillations increases.

Fig 6.13 *Wire drawing* and *Concertina effect*

Chapter Seven
Heat and Thermal Patterns

7.1 Surface heat in calm conditions

When the wind is calm and the water surface is warmer than the air, or the land becomes warmer than the air, the air will respond as in the Kimberley example, (Section 4.4). Gentle heating will cause isolated thermals and nothing more. More heating will cause random cells. Further heating will cause hexagonal cells. In calm conditions nothing less than fierce prolonged tropical dry-land heating will cause rolls.

7.2 Surface heat in light airs

The effect of a light wind is to accelerate the rate at which the motions pass through the progression: isolated thermals, then random cells, then hexagonal cells, then rolls, etc. In a calm-air situation, rolls do not appear until the heating is fierce. In light airs, even the gentle shear of the laminar-type boundary layer is sufficient to distort and weaken the cross-wind elements of cell patterns. This encourages roll patterns to form at a much earlier stage. The practical result is that the isolated thermal and the cell patterns are common to both calms and light airs. The 'roll-generated' pulsing, oscillating and ribboning patterns are never the creatures of calms. They can live only in light airs.

7.3 Surface heat in a breeze

At this point the picture changes fundamentally. Breezes, by definition, are those winds strong enough to have turbulent, energetic boundary layers 500 metres deep at the minimum, and usually several times this depth. Such boundary layers, as we have seen, will certainly contain gusts and lulls, and may also contain wave motions. So the logical approach cannot be 'surface heat plus breeze' because the cooled breeze already contains gusts and probably waves. The only logical approach is to look at 'gusts plus surface heat', then at, 'waves plus surface heat', and then at whatever may be left – which turns out to be the most surprising of all.

7.4 Gusts plus surface heat

Fig 7.1(a) shows 15 minutes of a Kingston Tower trace of a 'cooled' breeze, from a day when the air temperature was 24 deg. C and the water temperature was 23 deg. C. Fig. 7.1(b) shows 15 minutes of a 'heated' breeze, from a day when the air was at 19 deg. C and the water still at its customary 23 deg. C.
The obvious difference is that the speed trace of the heated breeze is much rougher. The gusts are harsher. This is not unexpected, but of itself it can win no races.
The less obvious difference is much more important from the racing helmsman's point of view. The direction trace of the cooled wind is steady. There is no significant difference in direction between gusts and lulls, nor between successive gusts.
The direction trace of the heated wind is different. Surface heat has not only made the speed traces harsher and the rates of change of speed more abrupt. It has so churned up the already turbulent air that major, irregular backs and veers appear. These are better thought of as gusts in their own right, but direction gusts, and not speed gusts. Practical observation suggests that they have about the same sort of dimensions as speed gusts. Sometimes they are in fact associated with speed gusts, but often they are not. Some of these gusts in Fig. 7.1(b) are backed, and some veered, by as much as 15 degrees from the direction of the mean wind. If you enter a gust and sail upwind in a 15 degree lift, this will give you a 22% increase in VMG compared with rivals who do not enter that gust. It will give a 75% increase in VMG over any adjacent crew who enter the gust but get it wrong and sail the 15 degree header while you sail the 15 degree lift. Fig 7.2 gives the vectors.

Surface heat has introduced potentially race-winning lifts and headers on a gust-by-gust basis. Because each direction gust is a coherent mass of air, the wind direction within each gust is usually reasonably steady. The direction differences, gust by gust, are random, so their directions can never be predicted. But you can 'read' the wind lanes within the approaching wind at a sufficient distance to enable you to determine which will be the advantaged tack or gybe, where will be the most advantageous path, and so be

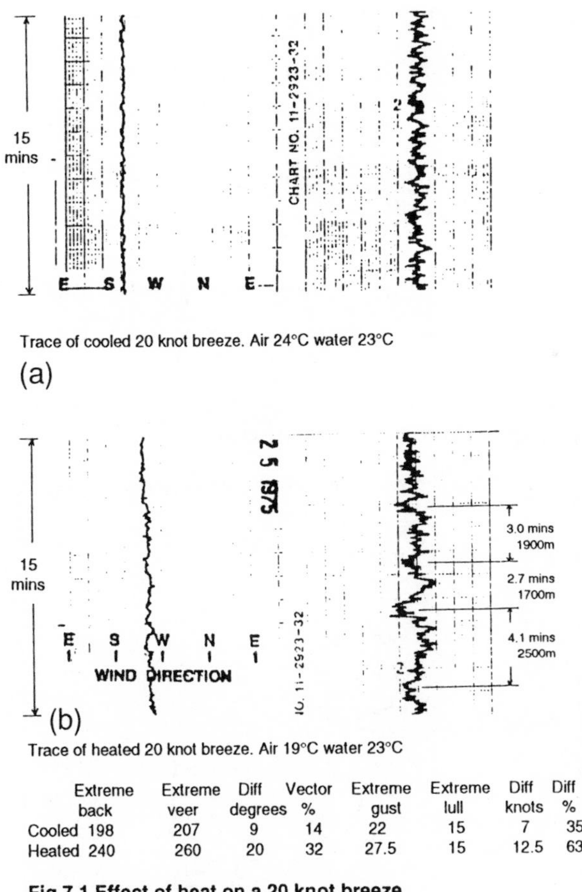

Trace of cooled 20 knot breeze. Air 24°C water 23°C

(a)

(b)

Trace of heated 20 knot breeze. Air 19°C water 23°C

	Extreme back	Extreme veer	Diff degrees	Vector %	Extreme gust	Extreme lull	Diff knots	Diff %
Cooled	198	207	9	14	22	15	7	35
Heated	240	260	20	32	27.5	15	12.5	63

Fig 7.1 Effect of heat on a 20 knot breeze

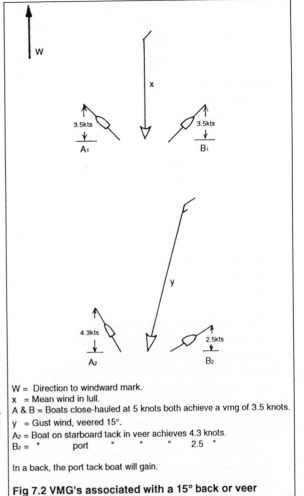

W
x
3.5kts
A_1
3.5kts
B_1
y
4.3kts
A_2
2.5kts
B_2

W = Direction to windward mark.
x = Mean wind in lull.
A & B = Boats close-hauled at 5 knots both achieve a vmg of 3.5 knots.
y = Gust wind, veered 15°.
A_2 = Boat on starboard tack in veer achieves 4.3 knots.
B_2 = " port " " " 2.5 "

In a back, the port tack boat will gain.

Fig 7.2 VMG's associated with a 15° back or veer

able to position yourself to take the greatest advantage of the approaching gust.

Another variation on this theme is that the two sides of a course can offer different types of wind. In Sect 10.4 an example is quoted in which there is land just upwind of one side of a regatta course (at 'x' in Fig 9.8) but not the other. When in a cold SSW'ly the clouds cleared and the land heated, the gusts on the western side of the course just downwind of the heated land became skewed either way as in Fig. 7.1(b), and offered massive 'lift' opportunities which were absent from the other side of the course.

This sort of race advantage is worth anticipating, practising, exploiting – and enjoying.

7.5 Wind-waves plus surface heat

The critical fact here is that although the driving forces are different, the circulating flows of the friction-driven rolls of Fig. 6.3, and those of the thermally driven rolls of Fig. 4.12 are identical. So in the case of rolls – waves in the air – it matters not whether they are driven by friction or by heat or by both. Each driving force simply blends with and boosts the other, and makes the total circulation more energetic. The forms which these more energetic waves take depends upon whether the waves are the big waves characteristic of a deep boundary layer, or the small waves characteristic of a much shallower one.

7.6 Big wind-waves plus heat – the harmonic patterns

For the sake of simplicity let us look at the simplest, most predictable case – a gradient wind underneath a High. As noted in Sect. 6.4, the boundary layer thickness in this situation will remain deep but be stabilised by the subsidence inversion. The surface oscillations of wind direction will be regular, and will be slow, as is always the case with the big waves which form in deep boundary layers.

Figs 7.3, 7.4, and 7.5 show typical traces, from various parts of the world, of gradient winds which blow under areas of high pressure and which are not heated. Fig. 7.3 is a winter ocean onshore wind measured just offshore from Sydney Heads. Fig. 7.4 is a summer ocean onshore wind measured just east of Auckland, NZ. Fig. 7.5 is a summer inland wind measured on the shore of Lac St Louis, Montreal. This lake, a widening of the St Lawrence River, is too small to generate any substantial lake breeze. All three are gradient winds, with no or insignificant surface heating, and stabilised by the subsidence inversion under a High. All show the simple slow rhythmic oscillating patterns which are caused by regular waves in a deep boundary layer, and are therefore expected in 'High dominant, not heated' situations. Fig. 6.5 is another of these patterns, but marginal. Its wanderings in direction would be disappointing to a crew, but the knowledge that its rhythm remains regular means that the 'part wave' final approaches to the windward mark can still be planned with greater confidence.

Figs 7.6, 7.7, 7.8 and 7.9 show typical traces, again from different locations, of gradient winds which blow under areas of high pressure and which are heated by warm surfaces. Fig. 7.6 was measured in Pittwater, a north-south harbour, north of Sydney which is separated from the sea by a north-south ridge of hills. The western slopes of these hills become very hot in the summer afternoon sun. Fig. 7.7 was measured at Medemblik, a Dutch sailing centre on the western shore of the Ijsselmeer, and about 20 miles inland from the sea-wall which separates the Ijsselmere from the North Sea. On this day a cold summer northerly blew inland over the warmer water of the lake. Fig. 7.8 was measured on a summer evening on the shores of Lake Eucumbene, a 20 mile long man-made lake 1,000 metres up in the middle of Australia's Snowy Mountains. The extreme case of Fig. 7.9 was measured 5 or 6 miles offshore on Lake Ontario when a cold polar summer northerly swept over the much warmer surface of the lake, and is confirmed point by point by the record from the adjacent Kingston Tower.

All four traces show quick harmonic oscillations superimposed on slow regular oscillations. This pattern is to be expected whenever 'High dominant' gradient winds are heated. The mechanism is analogous to that of smaller wind-generated waves co-existing with a swell Figs 7.6, 7.7, 7.8, 7.9 and 7.10.

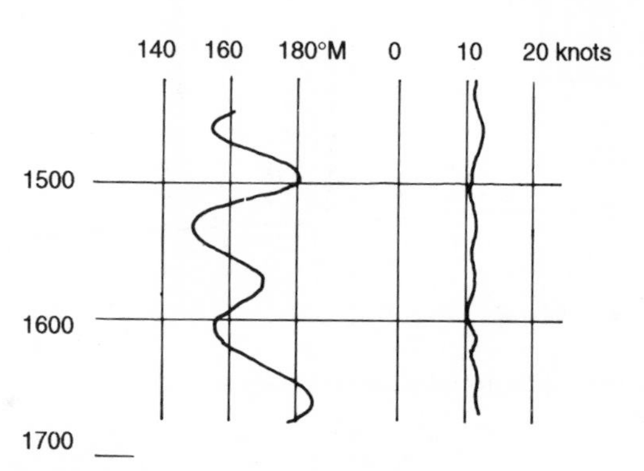

Sydney Heads. 10th June 1974 (winter)

Fig 7.3 Gradient wind *High dominant - cooled*

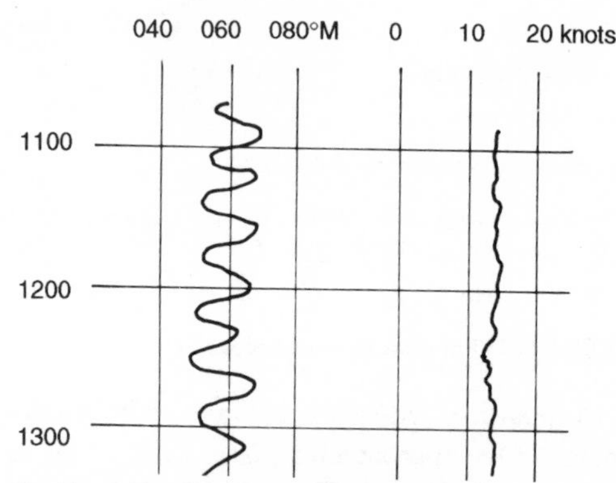

Auckland, New Zealand, 18th Jan 1974
Eighteen footer world championships

Fig 7.4 Gradient wind *High dominant - cooled*

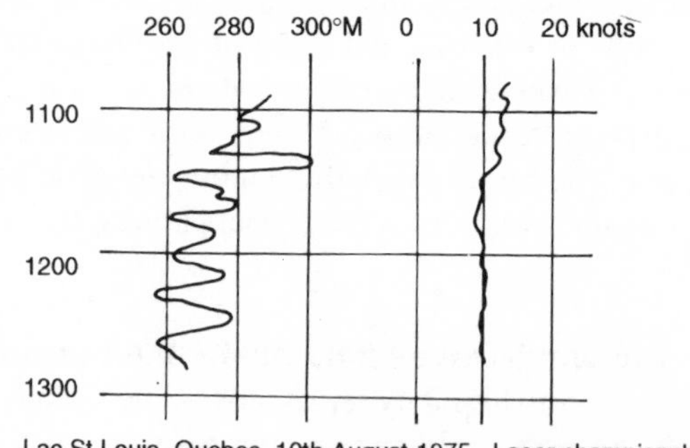

Lac St Louis, Quebec. 10th August 1975. Laser championships

Fig 7.5 Gradient wind *High dominant - cooled*

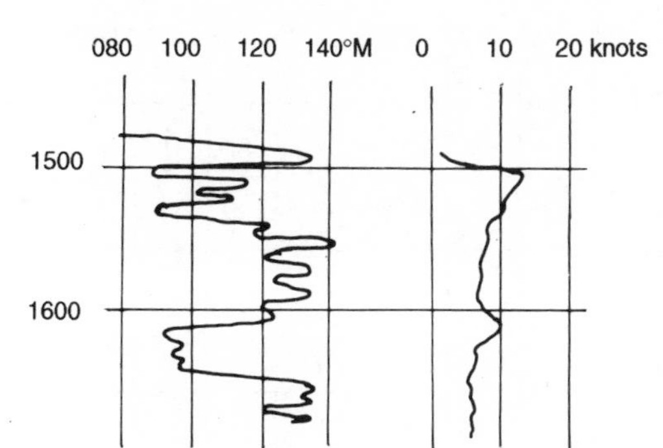

Pittwater, NSW. 1st Nov '75. Cherub championships

Fig 7.6 Gradient wind *High dominant - heated*

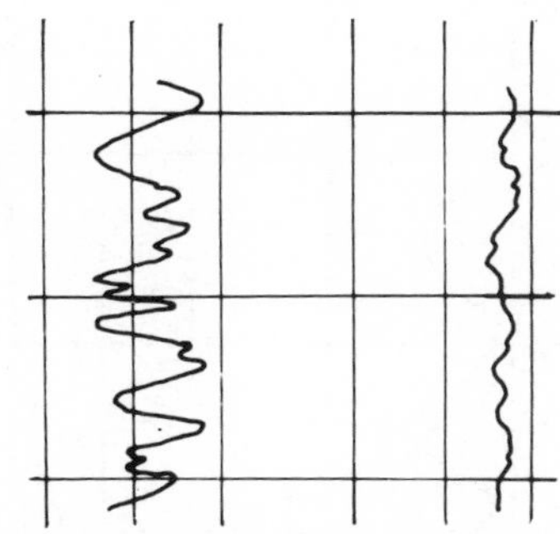

Medemblik, Holland. 10th Sept 1972

Fig 7.7 Gradient wind *High dominant - heated*

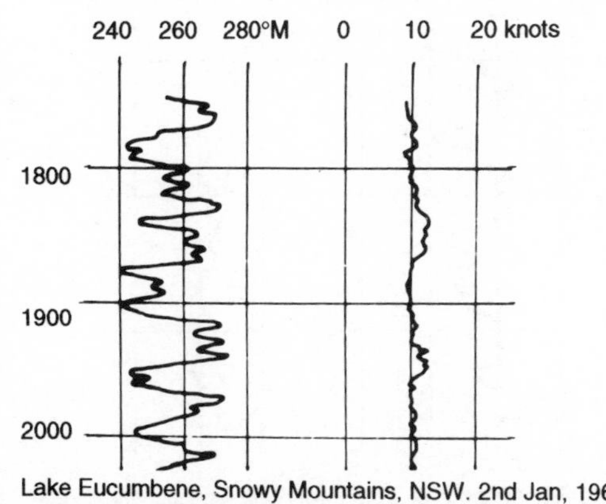

Lake Eucumbene, Snowy Mountains, NSW. 2nd Jan, 1966

Fig 7.8 Gradient wind *High dominant - heated*

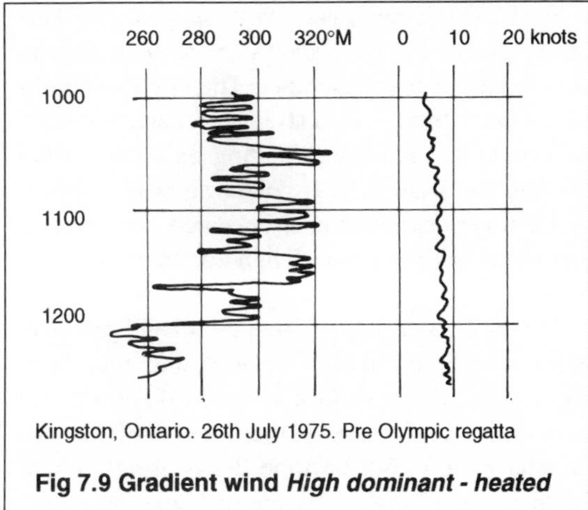

Kingston, Ontario. 26th July 1975. Pre Olympic regatta

Fig 7.9 Gradient wind *High dominant - heated*

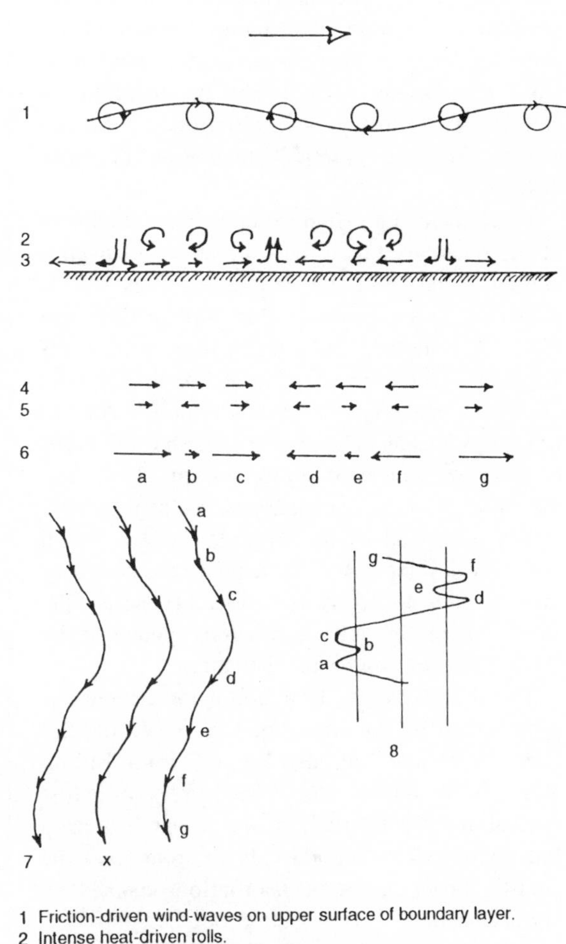

1 Friction-driven wind-waves on upper surface of boundary layer.
2 Intense heat-driven rolls.
3 (also 6) Final cross-wind component due to 1 and 2.
4 component due to 1
5 component due to 2
7 View from above of flow pattern of surface wind: the pattern itself flows slowly downwind.
8 Plot of pattern 7 as it flows over observer at x.

Fig 7.10 The harmonic mechanism

Fig 1.2 (Marstrand) is of particular interest. The earlier part of the trace shows the smooth pattern of warm air over cooler water. The rain must have been a weak front, with a stronger wind and colder air behind it. I remember putting on a coat, after the rain had passed. This colder air was warmed by the water, and harmonics appeared. The second part of the trace is a pure 'High dominant, heated' pattern.

The oscillations of the 'High dominant' gradient wind are almost always regular and therefore predictable. If the surface is warm there will be harmonics, and these sometimes confuse the broader picture, but become devastatingly clear when the wind makes its major backs or veers. Yachts which are ocean racing will enjoy the slow oscillations, with or without the harmonics. 'Round the buoys', racers will find the intellectual problem a little more challenging, because of the short leg-lengths. There is no reason why these slow oscillations should not be handled as confidently as the quick oscillations of the sea breeze, but the practical technique is quite different.

When there is no High to stabilise the thickness of the boundary layer, the oscillations of even a cooled wind will be irregular. Figs. 7.11, measured in Melbourne's Port Phillip Bay, and Fig. 7.12, another from the sailing waters off Kingston, Ont., and also Fig. 1.1 from the Kiel Olympics, and Fig. 6.6 from Olympic selection trials at Adelaide, all show the smooth oscillations of direction typical of cooled breezes. However, they also show the complete absence of regularity which is typical of the irregular waves which normally develop unless the depth of the boundary layer is very positively controlled. These are the slow, smooth, irregular oscillations typical of the 'Low dominant, not heated' situation.

The fourth group, 'Low dominant, heated', is represented by the traces of Fig. 7.13, another from Melbourne, and also Fig. 6.7 from Tallinn Bay. Both traces show the irregular slow oscillations characteristic of the waves in a deep but uncontrolled boundary layer, plus also the smaller faster harmonic oscillations caused by surface heating.

All of the, 'Low dominant' patterns are essentially random. None can be predicted. They should therefore be sailed opportunistically if ocean racing, or defensively if racing around the buoys.

If you think of roll circulations three

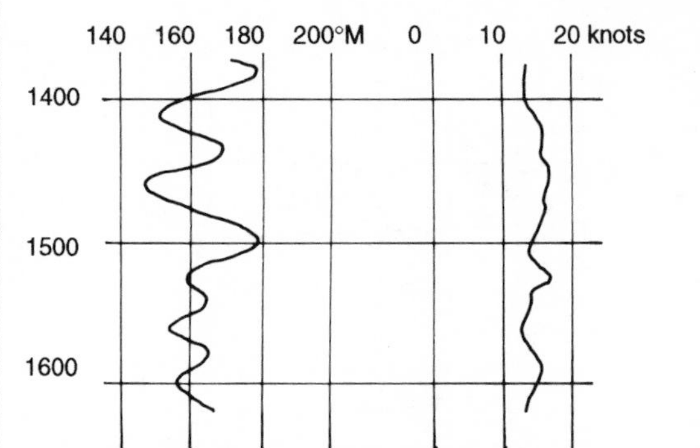

Fig 7.11 Gradient wind *Low dominant - cooled*

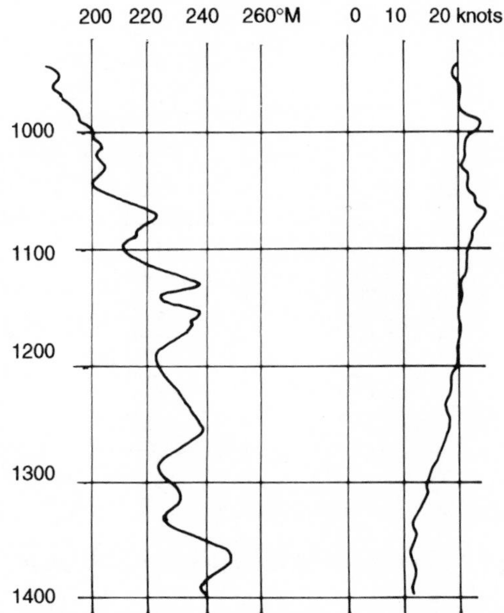

Fig 7.12 Gradient wind *Low dominant - cooled*

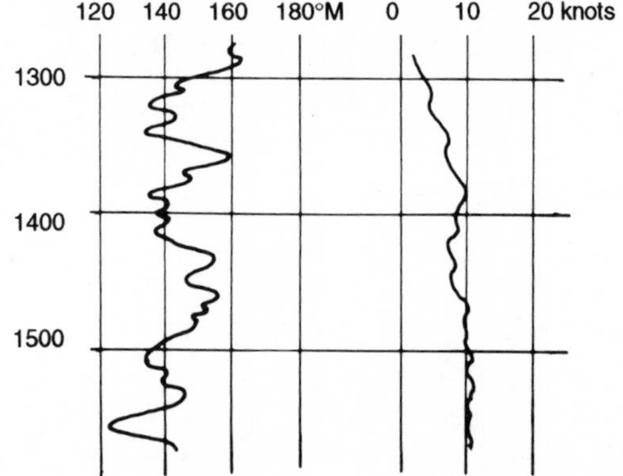

Fig 7.13 Gradient wind *Low dominant - heated*

dimensionally, it is obvious that the same motions as offer advantaged and disadvantaged tacks and gybes to the helmsman will offer updraughts and downdraughts to the glider pilot. I enjoy flying high performance sailplanes and have used this flying to explore more of the detail of these three dimensional flows. A common sequence is worth reporting, because it makes so many of the surface patterns so much more understandable:-

The town and gliding centre of Narromine, NSW., is far inland, with no hills, no water, and usually no clouds. Let us look at a typical day. The forecast is for a 10 knot SW gradient wind, with little subsidence (i.e. on the SE edge of a huge High). The cold calm spring morning warms. Mid-morning, birds begin to soar in the first thermals, and the day's flying starts. In these conditions, which are common, it is possible to soar to the top of the boundary layer, say to 1,500 metres by noon and 2,000 metres by mid-afternoon. You know when you are there because the roll updraughts concentrate dust into thin darker 'lenses' which you can see 'edge on' when you reach their level. These indicate, better than anything else, the alignment of the rolls. Typically the spacing between rolls is about 6 to 8 kilometres.

The vital observation is that in these conditions isolated thermals occur only in the updraught sides of the rolls. No thermals occur in the subsiding sides. In sailing parlance, a 'channel pattern' operates. The practical effect is that the classic soaring analogy – that your search for thermals is like that of a blindfolded man searching for trees in a forest – no longer applies in these roll conditions. Those who rely on it are soon back on the ground. But those who adjust their mental picture to that of a blindfolded man who searches for trees in a forest which has been cleared in alternate strips, and who therefore searches for trees only where the forest remains and who crosses the cleared strips quickly, can soar indefinitely. The practical situation, in a glider with a minimum sinking speed of 0.5 metres per second, is that you can fly in the updraught sides of the rolls with an average sinking speed of about 0.2 to 0.3 metres per second, and periodically encounter thermals which, when you centre in them, typically offer lift at between 3 and 5 metres per second to regain your height. But the rolls, which are simply waves, keep moving, and you must periodically move 'upwave' to stay near the gliding centre. When you enter the downdraught side of the roll, your sink is uniform at about 1.3 metres per second (the cooler descending air moves faster). This is continuous and with never a thermal. So you cross these areas of sink quickly and at right angles. The key lies in knowing the pattern and the orientation, so that you can adopt 'right angles' with confidence, and know that you will be through the sinking air within two or three minutes.

A crew who were to sail under this pattern would experience about 20 to 30 minute alternations of relatively steady air, under the downdraughts, followed by about the same period of unsteady and sometimes stronger air under the rising sides of the rolls.

7.7 Small wind-waves – plus surface heat

At this stage, we will foreshadow the 'winds near shores' chapter to the extent of stating that the depth of a sea breeze is often less than 300 metres, and that of a funnelling wind even shallower. The fundamental axiom, that 'big waves cannot exist in shallow water', applies. In these shallow boundary layers we find only small waves with quick repetition intervals. Figs 7.14, 7.15, 7.16 and 7.17 are typical sea breeze, lake breeze, or funnelling wind patterns. When these are not heated, their direction traces customarily take the form of a sine wave.

Fig. 7.14 is a sea breeze measured about three miles offshore from Adelaide, in St Vincents Gulf, South Australia. It was well established when I began to take readings, and there is nothing unexpected in this trace. It backs very slowly but continuously due to Coriolis. It oscillates for the first two hours at about a twelve minute cycle, as

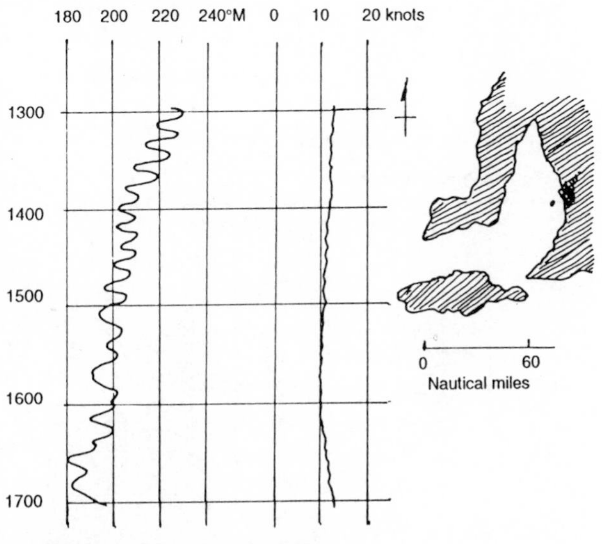

Fig 7.14 Sea breeze

regularly as any wind is ever going to oscillate. At 1500 hours Summer Time (1600 hours Sun Time) the waves begin to become larger and slower as the intense heating begins to diminish and the flow begins to become deeper. This is about as typical as any sea breeze can be.

Fig. 7.15 is measured offshore from Melbourne, Victoria, in the northern end of Port Phillip. The fact that its direction does not back with Coriolis indicates that it is a funnelling wind, which blows between two heated shores – these guide its direction between them as if on rails. Until about 1400 hours the direction trace is a little unsteady, probably due to the heated land 20 miles upwind. As the sea breeze mechanism intensifies, this unsteadiness becomes smoothed.

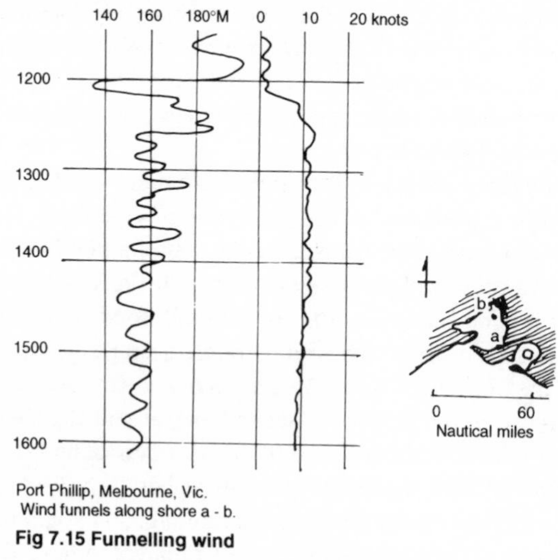

Port Phillip, Melbourne, Vic.
Wind funnels along shore a - b.

Fig 7.15 Funnelling wind

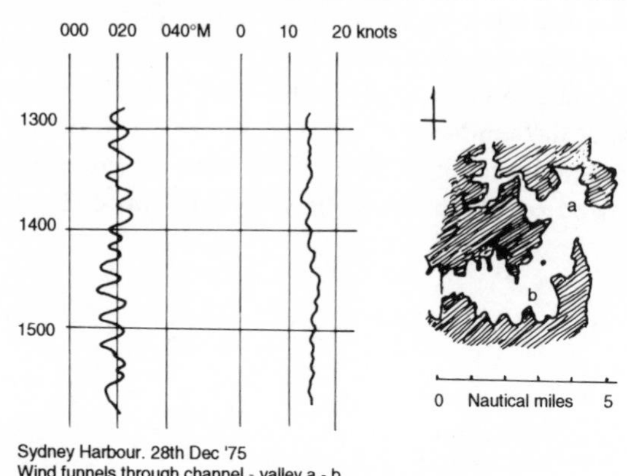

Sydney Harbour. 28th Dec '75
Wind funnels through channel - valley a - b.

Fig 7.16 Funnelling wind

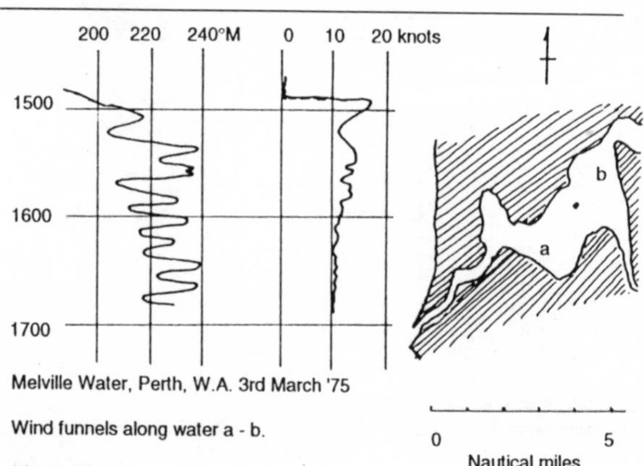

Melville Water, Perth, W.A. 3rd March '75

Wind funnels along water a - b.

Fig 7.17 Funnelling wind

Fig. 7.16 shows the prevailing Sydney Harbour north-easter. It funnels through the channel valley a – b and does not change its direction. Its strength is typically 12 to 15 knots and steady, with quick rhythmic oscillations. To keep you on your toes, the oscillations are occasionally punctuated by an off-beat one, caused by the heated peninsular upwind. By way of contrast, Fig 3.3 is of a typical Sydney sea breeze over the airport, 5nm south of the harbour. Nothing near the airport causes funnelling, so the wind direction there backs with Coriolis as it oscillates. It is only through the harbour valley a – b that the sea breeze funnels.

When these short waves are heated, the extra energy can alter the pattern in any one of a number of ways.

The most common effect is that the direction swings become wider and the repetition frequency becomes faster. Figs 7.17, 7.18 and 7.19 are typical. The mechanism is simply one of smaller orbits which rotate faster.

Fig. 7.17 is from Melville Water, a widening of the Swan River, in Western Australia. The city of Perth surrounds this estuary. This trace shows the first 90 minutes of what matures into a funnelling wind. The shallow water of the estuary is warmer than the cold ocean to the West, and the heated upwind land is close. The amplitude of the swings is wider than is usual (except for establishment periods such as in Fig. 7.15).

Fig. 7.18 is another funnelling wind measured in the outer sailing waters off Kingston, Ontario. Heating has increased the backs and veers until they sweep 30 degrees or more. Near-harmonics appear on most waves, and harmonics on a few.

Fig. 7.19 is from the island of Bahrain. On the west side of the island rhythmic backs and veers occur which are the biggest and fastest I have either observed, or experienced when sailing.

All observation so far suggests that the hotter the locality, the faster the oscillations, and the more intense the heating, the wider the swings. Sometimes, however, heated patterns take a different form.

7.8 The convergent/divergent pattern

When heating becomes more intense, the rolls become tighter and the pattern can progress to the point where convergent/divergent zones appear in an otherwise apparently steady wind.

The mechanism is that the circulation of the rolls is boosted by heat until it begins to concentrate the upward and downward movements of the air along the rolls. This leads to very narrow upwind/downwind lines of diverging air under the downflows and converging air under the upflows. The vertical flows suppress the gust mechanism, so the wind marks on the surface begin to look beautifully even. But the reality is that the wind is anything but even – instead, the wind directions can be very different close on either side of the lines where the vertical flows split at the surface.

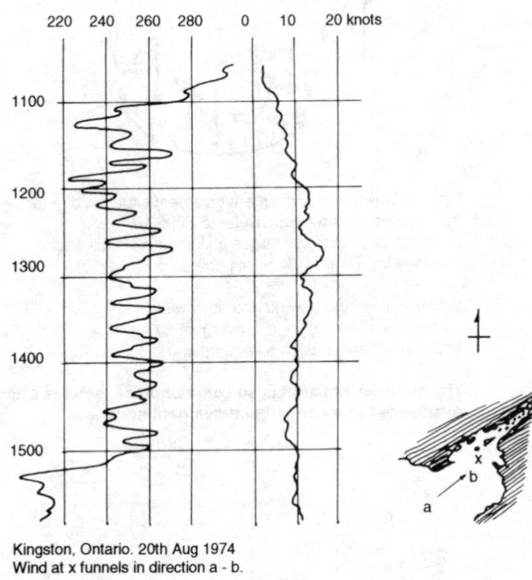

Kingston, Ontario. 20th Aug 1974
Wind at x funnels in direction a - b.

Fig 7.18 Funnelling wind - heated

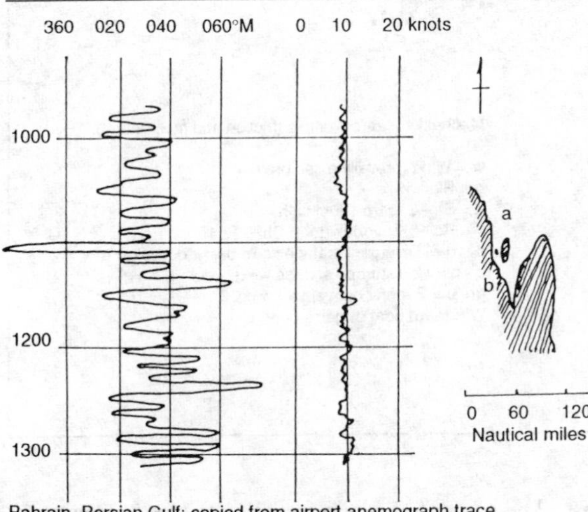

Bahrain, Persian Gulf: copied from airport anemograph trace.
Wind funnels through channel a to b.

Fig 7.19 Funnelling wind - intense heating

The mechanism and surface pattern are sketched in Figs 7.20(a) and (b). Racing helmsmen will recognise this immediately as the situation in which two adjacent boats of approximately equal performance suddenly cease to perform equally. One or the other has entered a wind of a different direction. The change was not anticipated because there were either no visual clues at all or they were too slight to be observed.

Normally, the second boat also enters the new wind within a few seconds. When this occurs the disadvantage is unfortunate but limited. But if the rolls happen to be much skewed from the upwind/downwind direction, the behaviour of two boats relative to each other, on one tack, can be very different for a long time. The worst case will be one in which one boat can just sail parallel and to windward of the convergent zone. This situation will cause the two boats to remain in their different winds – to the great disadvantage of the leeward boat – for as long as the helmsman of the leeward boat is prepared to put up with it.

I was first alerted to the existence of convergence and divergence in an unusual but most practical manner. During the years of development of hulls, rigs and foils described in Part Three, we routinely tested our ideas by conducting boat-against-boat tests. In these, two crews of equal ability sailed close to each other in near-identical boats. One boat changed nothing. The other alternated the new device or setting or whatever with a 'standard' configuration. Both boats towed fishing lines four lengths long with wooden clothes-pegs tied at two lengths and four lengths behind their sterns. The technique for each test run was for the crew of the leeward boat to wait, sailing slowly, until the other crew was sailing in a position directly crosswind of the leeward boat and abeam the 'two length' peg towed by it. Both crews then waited until the wind marks on the water for some hundreds of metres ahead looked as uniform as they were going to look on that day. When agreed, both boats accelerated smoothly. The windward boat, when up to full speed and in exact position,

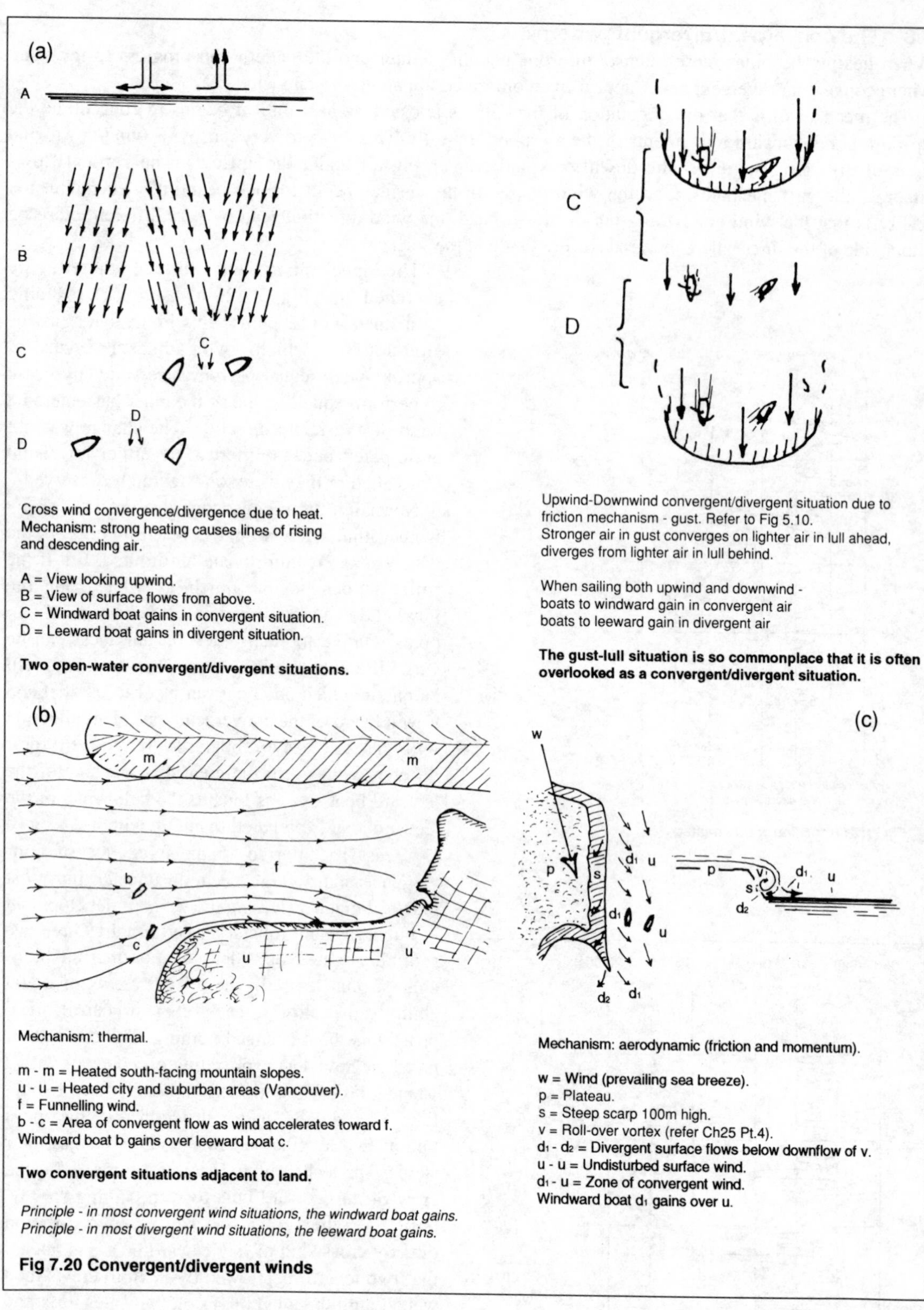

Cross wind convergence/divergence due to heat.
Mechanism: strong heating causes lines of rising and descending air.

A = View looking upwind.
B = View of surface flows from above.
C = Windward boat gains in convergent situation.
D = Leeward boat gains in divergent situation.

Two open-water convergent/divergent situations.

Upwind-Downwind convergent/divergent situation due to friction mechanism - gust. Refer to Fig 5.10.
Stronger air in gust converges on lighter air in lull ahead, diverges from lighter air in lull behind.

When sailing both upwind and downwind -
boats to windward gain in convergent air
boats to leeward gain in divergent air

The gust-lull situation is so commonplace that it is often overlooked as a convergent/divergent situation.

Mechanism: thermal.

m - m = Heated south-facing mountain slopes.
u - u = Heated city and suburban areas (Vancouver).
f = Funnelling wind.
b - c = Area of convergent flow as wind accelerates toward f.
Windward boat b gains over leeward boat c.

Two convergent situations adjacent to land.

Mechanism: aerodynamic (friction and momentum).

w = Wind (prevailing sea breeze).
p = Plateau.
s = Steep scarp 100m high.
v = Roll-over vortex (refer Ch25 Pt.4).
d_1 - d_2 = Divergent surface flows below downflow of v.
u - u = Undisturbed surface wind.
d_1 - u = Zone of convergent wind.
Windward boat d_1 gains over u.

Principle - in most convergent wind situations, the windward boat gains.
Principle - in most divergent wind situations, the leeward boat gains.

Fig 7.20 Convergent/divergent winds

called 'Start' and stopwatches were punched.

The task of the leeward boat was to sail her best. The task of the windward boat was to maintain position directly crosswind of the leeward boat and note any gain or loss of position by reference to the peg directly to leeward. Each test was terminated when the boats ran out of water, or one gained or lost one length (rare), or either crew suspected that the wind was not the same for both boats. At the end of each run the crews agreed their estimates of the wind speed and the result, this was noted, and another run commenced. At its best, this method will detect and repeat performance differences of about one metre in runs of two or three hundred metres, and we employed it frequently (and still do).

We were accustomed to sailing accurately in very close company. What we were not prepared for was to see, occasionally, the leeward boat suddenly drop to leeward one or more lengths when, from the wind marks on the water, it was passing through an area of apparently steady wind. But it happened. Not often, but without question. At that time we accepted it, abandoned that test run, and tried again. But the question remained. I have since understood that there can be both convergent and divergent flows. Convergent flows will separate boats which are sailing upwind, and concentrate boats which are sailing downwind. Divergent flows will do the reverse. The note above, and the tactical notes later, flow from that unanswered earlier question.

Convergent flows on a larger scale can develop by other mechanisms. Two examples:–

1. Near the entrance to any waterway which develops a funnelling wind, the surface flow will be convergent in that area in which the wind speed increases.

Fig 7.20(b) sketches the shape of English Bay, Vancouver, which is such a waterway, and indicates the area where the surface flow accelerates and converges. If two boats b and c start 'level' and sail toward a windward mark, b the windward boat, will draw ahead. C loses position because of the more adverse wind direction. B points higher because of the convergence of the flow.

2. A steady convergent flow will develop near any steep shoreline when the wind blows mainly along it but slightly offshore. Fig 7.20(c) shows the mechanism. A spiral 'roll over' vortex (refer to Section 25.2) will form close downwind of the crest and will remain fixed in that position. The down-flowing air of the spiral will split where it reaches the surface. The offshore half of this flow converges with the undisturbed wind further offshore. As in 7.20(b), boat d_1, to windward in this convergent flow will reach W sooner than U which started to leeward of d_1.

7.9 The channelling winds

This pattern can form when the heating becomes more intense. It is similar to ribboning light air, but occurs in stronger breezes and at about ten times the scale. In appearance, the wind blows in upwind/downwind channels, which can last almost indefinitely. Between them are intervening channels of much lighter wind. The whole pattern usually moves crosswind slowly. The speed difference is so great as to be visually obvious. Typical dimensions would be that the stronger-wind channels would be 200 to 300m across, while the intervening lighter-air channels would be perhaps twice that width. In common with ribboning light air, it is not possible to indicate the dynamics of a channelling pattern on a single trace. They are best conveyed by a diagram such as Fig 7.21.

The mechanism is an intensification of that of the convergent/divergent circulation shown in Fig 7.20. A longitudinal roll circulation is boosted by heat into a tight, energetic pattern which is relatively stable in position. The difference between Figs 7.20 and 7.21 is that in 7.21 the situation is such that air at height has assumed much of the speed of the upper wind. The downflowing circulations of the rolls bring this faster air to the surface, exactly like gusts, except that in the channelling mechanism the tightly organised circulation of the boosted rolls has fixed the areas of downflowing faster air and upwelling slower air relative to each other, in place of the randomness of the gusts of the cooled breeze.

Note particularly that the stronger-wind channels are also zones of diverging air. Because of this, it is normal to find, when tacking upwind along a stronger-wind channel, that, 'The boat won't point when approaching the core, but will point beautifully when through it'.

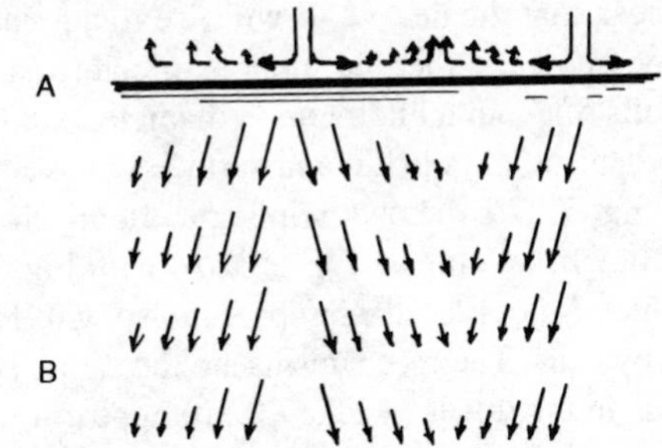

A *Mechanism*
Downflowing air is concentrated.
Upflowing air is diffuse.
Downflowing air brings speed of faster wind aloft to surface.

B *Surface pattern of channelling wind*

Fig 7.21 Channelling winds

7.10 The two cell sizes

When we introduced the breeze with its turbulent boundary layer, one of the points made was that the fragile light-air rolls and cells of about 100 metre typical size were obliterated by the onset of turbulence. Except for two special conditions, this statement will remain true. The key to both the dominance of the turbulence, and the two exceptions, is given by the relative depth of the boundary layer of each motion. The light-air cells or rolls we were discussing had a vertical extent of perhaps 50 metres. The initial depth of the turbulent boundary layer of a 6 knot breeze is ten times that depth. At that level of dimension and energy, there is no contest.

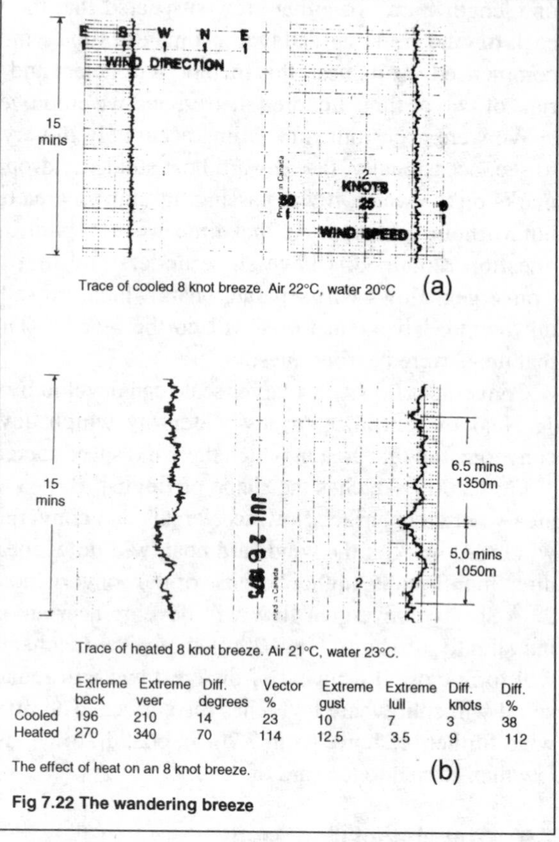

	Extreme back	Extreme veer	Diff. degrees	Vector %	Extreme gust	Extreme lull	Diff. knots	Diff. %
Cooled	196	210	14	23	10	7	3	38
Heated	270	340	70	114	12.5	3.5	9	112

The effect of heat on an 8 knot breeze. (b)

Fig 7.22 The wandering breeze

7.11 'Look for the speckled area'

You can see the largest of these cells on your TV screen every time a forecaster draws attention to the speckled appearance of approaching air which is going to be particularly cold. The surface temperature of polar snow and ice can be minus 20 to minus 40 deg.C, depending on position and season. Air in contact with this surface is cooled to about this temperature. Periodically, great surges of polar air burst out of the polar highs and sweep toward the temperate latitudes. When air at minus 20 deg.C meets water warmer than 0 deg.C, the boiling can be so vigorous its thickness can exceed the depth of the turbulent boundary layer. When this occurs huge cells form, typically 50 to 100km across. A giant cloud usually forms in the centre of each cell. These clouds are the specks of the speckled area.

7.12 The wandering breeze

Cells of about one hundredth of this size will form, and for exactly the same reason, on days when the air is heated strongly, the wind speed is between 6 and 9 knots, and a Low is dominant. The low wind speed means that the boundary layer will be relatively shallow. The Low dominant situation means that there is no subsidence inversion, and, more importantly, that the temperature of the (already converging and rising) atmosphere at increasing heights will be little different from that of the rising heated air as it cools. This in turn will mean that the heated air will rise to a greater height than is usual. This particular combination can make the depth of the thermal motions greater than the depth of the turbulent boundary layer, and in this situation cells of about a kilometre in diameter can form.

The mechanism, circulation and surface winds which result are identical in principle to that of 'unsteady light air'. Fig. 7.22(b) shows wind speed and direction traces typical of this pattern, which I call, 'the wandering breeze'. Compare Fig. 7.22(b) with Fig. 7.22(a) which shows the structure of a breeze of similar strength which is not heated. Compare it also with Fig. 4.2, unsteady light air, and note the similarities. Both are caused by cells. The mechanisms are the same. But the scale is very different. The cells which caused the unsteadiness in the traces of Fig. 7.22(b) appear to have been about 1,100 and 600 metres across. The cells themselves would have been embedded in, and drifted downwind with, a wind of about 7 knots. Diverging outflows of about 4 knots from the bases of the descending curtains would have combined with the 7 knot mean wind, to give gusts of about 11 knots when they flowed in the same direction, and lulls of about 3 knots when they flowed the other way, and also caused the 30 to 40 degree backs and veers when they blew in a cross-wind direction. This pattern when viewed from the air looks like a net, with darker lines of stronger air where the strings would be, and glassier areas of lighter wind in the 'holes' of the net.

The intensity of the unsteadiness can vary from the subtlest of differences, recognisable only to crews experienced in these particular conditions, to the sort of three to one speed differences and sixty degree wind shifts traced in Fig. 7.22(b), in which the bands of wind will be clear for all to see. These will, of course, be 'gusts which don't come towards you'. In fact they do, but much more slowly than one would expect. Normal technique is to sail to them, and then to sail to remain in them. When there is a choice when you are sailing crosswind, sail to the upwind gust, otherwise your advantage will probably be short-lived because the calm in the middle of the cell is likely to catch you later.

On the assumption that you will experience two changes of wind speed, and two changes of wind direction as you sail through each cell, when you sail upwind you can expect that there will be a significant change of something about every 200 metres or 2 minutes on average. It is as well to keep this in mind. All experienced crews see the gusts coming and flatten their sails for the stronger moments. But winning crews are more subtle and also see the lulls coming, and they are the first to make their sails fuller to 'power up' again as they approach each lighter patch.

I have dealt fairly thoroughly with the wandering breeze, because it is one of the commonest winds in which we race. It is also one of the most challenging to handle intelligently.

7.13 Chilled air

So far we have been looking at situations in which the temperature differences between the air and the water are small. This is the norm world-wide. One particular abnormal situation occurs in which the temperature difference is so large that the wind becomes different. This happens when an offshore wind blows over very cold water. There are two sources of very cold water. One is the polar seas. The other is ice.

On the global scale, air is progressively warmed by the earth's land and water surfaces as it makes its tortuous way towards the equator. The usual situation is that the warming air will be slightly cooler on average than the surface over which it flows, and that day by day it is likely to be only a little warmer or cooler than the local surface.

Again on the global scale, the primary ocean currents are the westward going equatorial drifts which split and become the Gulf Stream and the Brazil Current in the Atlantic basin, and the Japan Current and the Eastern Australian Current in the Pacific. The eastern seaboards of the world's great continents are all washed by warm currents. The shape of the north Atlantic basin is unusual in that it causes the warm Gulf Stream to wash the Atlantic coasts of France and the British Isles as well as the eastern American seaboard. Near all these coasts the temperature differences between the land and the warm water are usually small.

The eastern end of the Pacific is different. The cold Humboldt and Alaska Currents sweep from the polar seas and wash the west coasts of North and South America. Their surface temperatures are up to 10 deg.C colder than those of the warmer equatorial currents. By way of example, air and water temperatures both at about 23 deg.C would be typical for Sydney in the summer. But in Vancouver, a summer offshore wind temperature of 25 deg.C and a water surface temperature of 16 deg.C in the Georgian Channel and English Bay would be typical. San Francisco, offshore, is similar.

The other source of cold water is found in all the ice-prone lakes and inland seas such as the Great Lakes and the Baltic, where the water budget means that the water will be trapped within the system for years or decades. In these waters the surface temperature will warm and cool with the season. The example of Kingston, where the ice thaws in spring, but a warm surface layer has warmed to temperature equilibrium with the air at about 23 deg.C by mid-summer, is typical. Around these waters the land surface heats quickly during the spring months while the water heats much more slowly through a much greater depth (typically two to three metres). Throughout the spring and early summer an offshore wind can easily be five or ten degrees warmer than the surface of the water.

When offshore winds blow from a relatively warm land-mass over either the very cold ocean currents or the ice-cooled inland waters, the intense cooling of the lower air can so affect the turbulent mixing process and the boundary layer thickness as to alter your expectations about the wind.

I call this intense cooling 'chilling'.

Chilling is a shoreline phenomenon which occurs only when an offshore wind blows over very cold water. Its properties are discussed in chapter 9.

Chapter Eight
Winds near Clouds

8.1 The significant clouds

There are four sorts of clouds which can indicate to a helmsman the way in which the wind is likely to change in the minutes ahead. These are:

1 Frontal clouds – A single line of Cumulus (Cu)
2 Roll clouds – Parallel lines of Strato Cumulus clouds (SCu)
3 Non-raining, low-based Cumulus clouds
4 Raining clouds – The rain shower is the vital element

8.2 Frontal clouds

One single line of Cumulus, aligned more or less cross-wind, usually marks a cold front. Two rules are very useful because they are true for almost all of the time:

1. The wind will change direction under or close to the cloud line.
2. The wind will back in the southern hemisphere, and veer in the northern hemisphere.

It will be assumed that readers will be familiar with the way in which Highs, Lows and fronts move, from their regular display in the newspapers and on the TV channels.

The typical cold front situation is shown in Fig. 8.1. Cold air advances in the direction C – C. Warm air retreats in the direction W – W. The front itself advances in the direction x – y.

If the speeds and directions of the two winds, and the speed of movement of the edge of the cold air at the surface, are such that the advancing wedge of the cold air overtakes the warm air and forces it upwards, Cumulus clouds will be formed in the lifted warmer air above the advancing frontal edge, and the wind change will occur under or close to those clouds. This is the normal situation and is shown in Fig 8.1. This sort of front is called an 'Ana-front'.

Significant fronts are seldom missed from weather maps or forecasts. When the relative humidity of the air is either high or normal, clouds will form along the front. Many races have been won by alert crews who have observed the cloud line and recognised it as the expected front, and sailed to exploit the expected back or veer.

There are however two exceptions.

The dry front.

Sometimes, the air is so dry that no clouds form. The flows and the wind change are identical, but there is no cloud line to act as a clue to the wind change. This is a dry front. The defence against the dry front is to look at the forecast. If the relative humidity is low, there may be no clouds. If a front is forecast, a frontal passage with its back or veer is likely to occur, but its arrival can never be forecast with precision. In this situation, nobody can have any early-warning from the sky. The most advantageous technique, in percentage terms, is to sail defensively but slightly on that side of the leg which will be favoured by the expected change. Do not commit to any other strategy until the approach of the front is established by observation of whatever surface clues can be seen (smoke, upwind boats, etc).

The Kata front

On occasions the dynamics change. When the warm air retreats faster and the cold air, together with the advancing frontal edge moving more slowly, the warm air ceases to be lifted. Instead, it overtakes the cold air and flows 'downhill', sliding along the tapered slope of the cold air, in a similar fashion to cold air flowing down the side of a valley. Fig. 8.2 shows the relative movements. This sort of front is called a 'Kata-front'. In this situation no clouds form in the down-flowing air. Instead, they form in one or more lines ahead of the front, exactly as wave clouds form in the lee of a mountain range. Here, the significant change is not under the cloud lines. These cloud-lines can precede the surface front and wind change by an hour or more. In most areas Kata-fronts are rare. But in particular areas, e.g. in some parts of the Baltic in some seasons, they can be common.

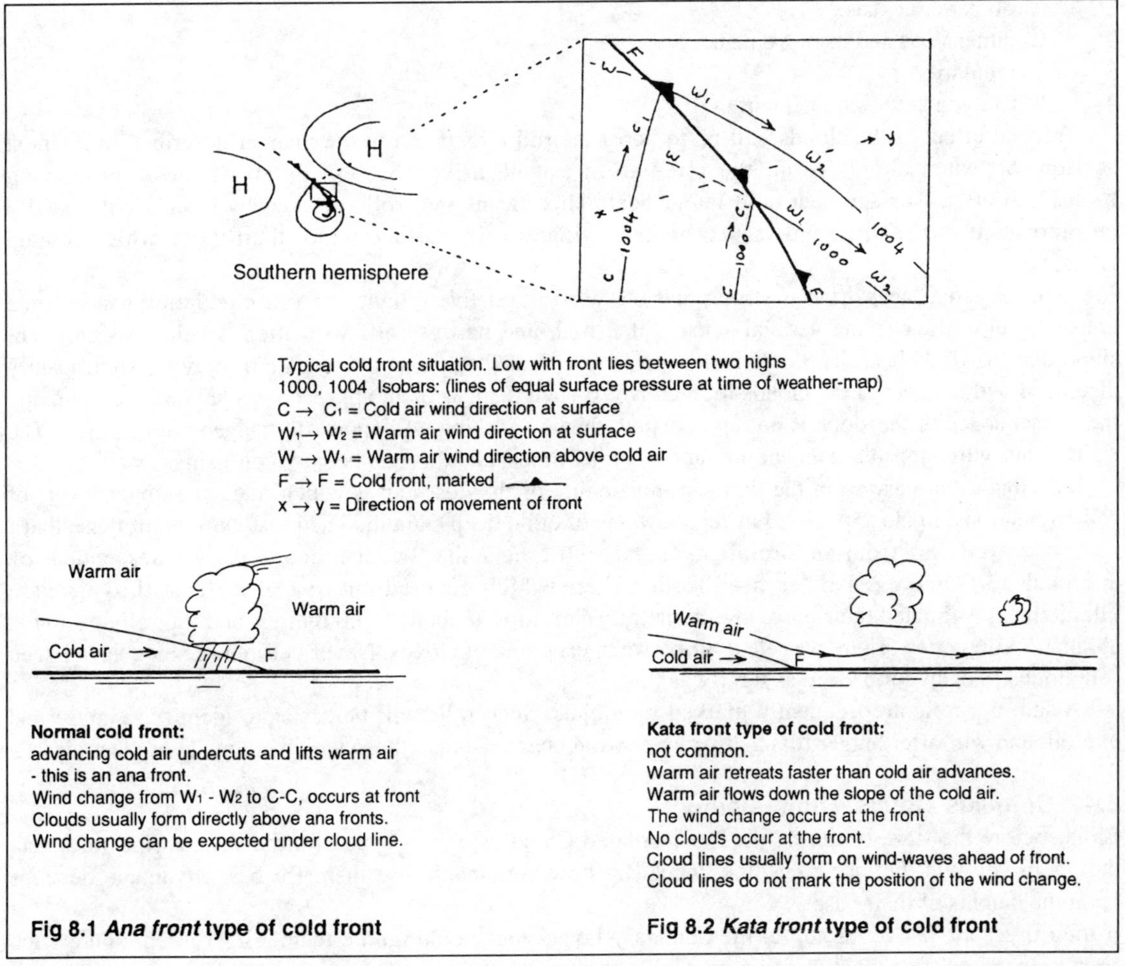

H
H
Southern hemisphere
Typical cold front situation. Low with front lies between two highs
1000, 1004 Isobars: (lines of equal surface pressure at time of weather-map)
C → C1 = Cold air wind direction at surface
W1→ W2 = Warm air wind direction at surface
W → W1 = Warm air wind direction above cold air
F → F = Cold front, marked
x → y = Direction of movement of front
Warm air
Warm air
Cold air
F
Normal cold front:
advancing cold air undercuts and lifts warm air
- this is an ana front.
Wind change from W1 - W2 to C-C, occurs at front
Clouds usually form directly above ana fronts.
Wind change can be expected under cloud line.
Warm air
Cold air
F
Kata front type of cold front:
not common.
Warm air retreats faster than cold air advances.
Warm air flows down the slope of the cold air.
The wind change occurs at the front
No clouds occur at the front.
Cloud lines usually form on wind-waves ahead of front.
Cloud lines do not mark the position of the wind change.

Fig 8.1 ***Ana front*** **type of cold front**

Fig 8.2 ***Kata front*** **type of cold front**

There is no defence against the Kata-front other than local knowledge. Fortunately, in most areas they are almost unknown.

Not all clouds which look like fronts are such. Rain clouds can be so big, that in the limited visibility of rain or drizzle, they fill the whole upwind field of view and may look exactly like an approaching front. Many crews have sailed to the right for the expected veer (northern hemisphere) and been sorely disappointed when it didn't arrive. The defence against the big cloud is in the forecast and the thermometer. Note particularly the forecast temperatures of the air ahead of and behind the front. Forecasts may be inexact in their timing, but they are usually correct as to sequence and factual details like air mass temperatures.

If the air temperature is still warm, the front has not yet passed. On the other hand, if the front has passed and the air temperature is cold – i.e. it is already at that temperature forecast for the air after the front has passed – then it is most unlikely that there will be another front, no matter what an approaching cloud looks like.

The deception of the big cloud is not unusual. It is just the most common trap.

8.3 Roll clouds

An essential part of the roll circulation is that in some places air rises and cools, and in others it subsides and warms. Wherever air rises, condensation will occur and a cloud will form if the air is sufficiently moist. It is therefore possible for all roll circulations to develop clouds and inevitable that a large proportion of them will do so. It is just a question of how moist the air happens to be.

'Streets' of roll clouds always mark the rising air, and the rising air only. All such clouds will therefore be of pure benefit to the sailor, because they make it visually obvious that:

1 A roll pattern exists.
2 Its dimensions and its movement.
3 Its regularity.
4 Where you are positioned within it.

A second effect of the clouds will be to boost the roll circulation in the manner described in the next section. So when clouds form, the circulation can be driven by any or all of the three driving forces – friction, surface heat, and latent heat. This means that rolls marked by clouds will usually be more vigorous, and so will cause bigger swings to the surface wind, than those which remain cloudless.

When the latent heat drive is strong and the wind is relatively light, the roll circulation can become unusually elongated in the vertical sense. Such high and narrow rolls will often develop a significant slope due to wind shear. The practical point here is that the surface wind pattern may be significantly displaced with respect to the clouds high above. If such displacement approaches a half wavelength, and the consequence of the slope is not appreciated, then everything will appear to happen out of phase. The right things will happen but apparently at the wrong times, and this can be very confusing.

Roll clouds can vary from the thinnest moistening of the dust lenses which mark the upper levels of roll circulations, to close-packed but regular lines of quite deep Cumuli. The most extreme of these that I have observed was from an aircraft over the Baltic near the Swedish coast. As we descended, on approach to Göteborg, I noted a uniform pattern which covered an area of at least thirty square kilometres. I estimated their bases at 300 metres, their tops at about 1,500 metres, and the roll spacing at about 1.5 kilometres. There was clear air between each line of clouds. Never before nor since have I seen roll clouds as deep nor packed as tightly as this.

To sum up, rolls are frequently marked by clouds. Such rolls will be easier to identify, analyse and exploit, and will offer bigger lifts and stronger wind channels, than those which are made of clear air.

8.4 Cumulus clouds – non raining

Either before the start, or during the race, isolated Cumulus clouds appear in the sky to windward. Can they help you win the race? Yes, they can! But how you should use them for best advantage depends upon the heights of their bases.

If their bases are above the top of the boundary layer, you should ignore them. High-based clouds such as these cannot affect what is going on within the boundary layer. There may well be a rhythmic wave pattern established within the boundary layer. Isolated Cumulus clouds at some higher level cannot disturb it. Concentrate on what is happening within the boundary layer, because only this can affect the surface wind in which you sail. Let other crews confuse themselves with faulty logic about distant clouds.

If their bases are within the boundary layer, but still relatively high – say higher than half the depth of the cloud – you can then be certain that there can be no rhythmic wave patterns. Cumulus clouds say, 'cell', in the clearest way possible, and cells and rolls cannot co-exist. They even show you where the centre of each cell is: at the position of the cloud itself. But at this height, the circulation around any cloud cannot and does not reach nor influence the surface, so your advantage lies in knowing that you are sailing through an unpredictable pattern of large cells. You should sail to play the percentages accordingly, and ignore the clouds.

When their bases are at a height of half the cloud depth or lower, the real fun begins. At this height the circulation around each cloud will reach and imprint into the surface wind in the most predictable manner. These local winds are some of the most advantageous and exciting you can enjoy, but your game plan has to be exactly right. Glance again at Section 1.6.

Clouds need understanding rather than rules of thumb. Let us look at some of their facts of life.

Fig. 8.3 develops the information introduced in Fig. 6.2. If dry air is lifted or forced down, it will cool by expansion or warm by compression parallel to the curves D..D (D = Dry air). If saturated air – such as the mist in a cloud – is lifted, it will cool by expansion along D..D, but simultaneously be warmed by the release of latent heat as more and more of the water vapour dissolved within it condenses out as the temperature falls. The end result will be that it will cool, but at the much slower rate W..W (W = Wet air).

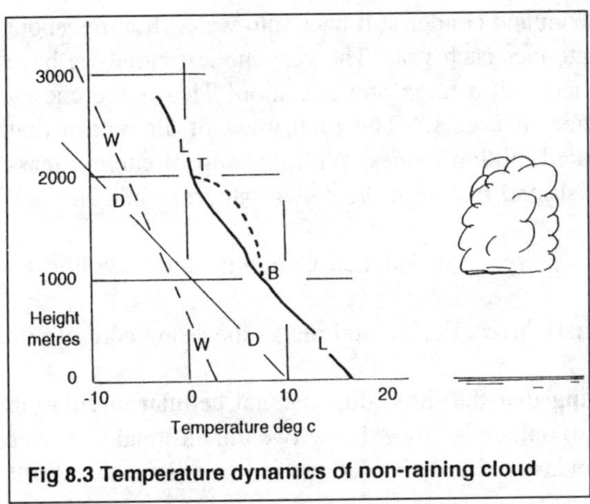

Fig 8.3 Temperature dynamics of non-raining cloud

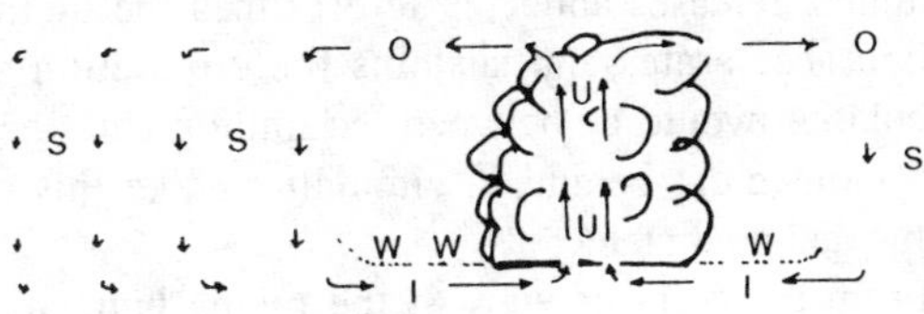

U = Updraught as warmed air rises
O = Outflow at cloud top level
S = Gentle subsidence over wide area
I = Inflow at and below cloud base level
W= Wisps of cloud sometimes form when inflow is strong enough to create turbulence.

Fig 8.4 Circulation around and below non-raining cloud

The actual temperature of the atmosphere at each height will change from day to day. When the whole atmosphere is converging and rising as it does when a Low is dominant, it is likely to be closer to the D..D curve – a trace such as L..L would be typical. (L = Low dominant).

If condensation begins to occur at, say, 1,000 metres, Point B Fig. 8.3 (B = cloud Base) on a day with an atmospheric temperature trace like L..L, the air will be warmed by the release of latent heat and will warm along a trace which is initially parallel with W..W. However, as soon as the air in the cloud becomes one or two degrees warmer than the surrounding clear air, the colder clear air at the top of the cloud will begin to sink into it, and so dilute the process. (A rain-making scientist friend of mine once quipped, 'What we need is an un-umbrella to keep the dry out.') This dilution will bias the trace away from W..W towards D..D. At some height this dilution, plus the heat loss of extreme evaporation into some layer of drier air at greater height, will cool the air at the cloud top to the temperature of L..L at that height. When this occurs its buoyancy will vanish. This will mark the end of its upward surge. A trace such as B..T (T = cloud Top) would be typical.

The natural stability of the atmosphere will prevent the air from rising further, instead it will diverge outwards. Similarly, the inflowing air which replaces that which rises through the cloud, will be drawn from a level not much below the cloud base. Fig. 8.4 indicates the circulation. I have occasionally observed the thin wisps of cloud which sometimes form in the turbulent boundary layer which develops between the accelerating inflow and the gently subsiding air above it when the inflow exceeds 6 knots. The line traced by these wisps is initially level. At a distance from the cloud approaching one cloud diameter, it begins to rise a little before it disappears.

In view of the gentle nature of the language used in the preceding paragraphs – 'mist', 'one or two degrees warmer', 'inflow and outflow' – it may come as a surprise that the thermal energy released by a modest Cumulus cloud can be enormous. A few figures give the scale. Let us assume that the cloud sketched in Fig. 8.4 is a little more than one kilometre in diameter, and about 1,000 metres high. At the latitude of Sydney in summer this cloud would have a temperature of about 20 deg.C at its base and about 14 deg.C at its top. At 20 deg.C air will hold about 20 grams of water vapour per cubic metre when saturated, and about 12g/m. at 14 deg.C. Let us assume that (because of the dilution by drier air), only half of this, say 4g/cu m. condenses out. Any pilot who flies through such a cloud would expect a sustained updraught of 150 to 300 metres per minute. Let us assume 200 metres per min. Since the cloud is 1,000m high, this means that the air within it changes completely every five minutes.

The area of the cloud base is about 1,000,000 square metres. It is 1,000 metres high, so its volume is 1,000,000,000 cubic metres. Each cubic metre carries 4 grams of liquid water, so the total mass of liquid water in the cloud is 4,000,000,000 grams or 4,000 tonnes. Because the air, rising at 200mpm changes itself every 5 mins, this means that 800 tonnes of water vapour is condensing into water and liberating its latent heat at the cloud base every minute, and the same amount is evaporating into and chilling the drier air near the cloud top.

To put this into perspective, a really big power station – say 2,500 mega-watt or 3,500,000 hp, will in the same minute evaporate about 30 tonnes of water into steam and condense it back into water. It burns about 15 tonnes of coal each minute to do it – 4 to 5 million tonnes each year. The very modest cloud we have assumed, releases about 25 to 30 times the thermal energy of a huge power station! This is the energy which accelerates and sustains the circulation sketched in Fig. 8.4 The total mass of air within that circulation would be between ten million and one hundred million tonnes. With that sort of energy, mass and momentum behind it, circulations like this establish and maintain their own patterns, and they are stable and predictable.

From the point of view of the racing helmsman, the presence of isolated Cumulus clouds within the boundary layer sends four messages about the wind:

1. Cellular circulation is established within the boundary layer. Each cloud marks the rising core of one cell.

2. There cannot be any wave patterns. The first thing that the three dimensional cellular circulation which forms around isolated Cumulus clouds will do is to obliterate any existing two dimensional waves or rolls with their sometimes regular oscillations. Three dimensional cell circulations and two dimensional roll circulations cannot exist together.

3. When the height of their bases is greater than about half their depth, the circulation around each cloud is not likely to reach the surface and will not influence the surface wind in any predictable way.

4. When the height of the cloud's base is about half the cloud's depth or lower, the inflow at the bottom of the circulation of each cell will reach and imprint on the surface and will bias the surface wind to the point of dominating it.

The fact that the circulation around a cloud which is above some critical height does not affect the surface wind was discovered by atmospheric scientists in the early 1960's. Many studies were conducted, world-wide, each of which contributed to the final picture. In one such study, two Australian scientists equipped an aircraft with sensitive recording thermometers on its nose and each wing tip, together with accelerometers, etc, and flew repeated passes at progressively increasing heights from twenty five to 1,500 metres during the hours when solar heating was increasing. The area was a section of the tropical coast of Queensland. They chose a flight path at right angles to the shoreline which would take them over three different surfaces. As they approached the coast they flew over a sea surface which was on some days warmer than the air. From the coast for several kilometres inland they flew over flat grassland. Further inland they flew over level forest. The programme was repeated for several days. The records from all days and over all surfaces revealed that there were three and sometimes four dynamically separate layers:-

1. In the lower layer, 200 to 300 metres deep, areas of rising air in simple thermal or the more complex cell form occurred which were about one degree warmer than the mean. (It is interesting to note that over the water the spacing found between these updraughts was typically 500 to 1,000 metres, and that this agrees exactly with the spacing implied by the Kingston Tower records on days when there was a wandering breeze.)

2. In the second layer, upward and downward motions of air still persisted at much reduced intensity, but the temperature had almost 'evened out'.

3. Above this was a layer in which the temperature was almost uniform and almost on the point of instability, and from which identifiable up or down air movements, which were bigger than normal turbulent motions, had disappeared completely.

4. On some days fair weather Cumuli formed, and a fourth layer developed at the height of their bases. In this layer the updraughts and subsidence associated with these clouds generated its own 'cloud-related' pattern. This pattern did not grow downwards.

At no stage was there any link or correlation between the surface patterns and the positions of these (not low) clouds.

The conditions in which these measurements were carried out ranged from calm to brisk breeze, and were altogether typical of the conditions in which sailors race and isolated Cumuli form. They make clear why the surface wind is not affected in any regular or predictable manner by the circulations around Cumulus clouds other than those with low bases.

As soon as Cumulus clouds develop with bases at a height lower than about half the cloud depth, the whole picture changes completely. When the bases are at about this height or lower, the circulation around the cloud reaches and imprints onto the surface.

Clouds come in an infinite range of sizes, from gentle wisp to mighty thunderstorm to compact tornado. To the extent that any cloud can be typical, let us continue with a cloud of the dimensions of Fig. 8.4. This happens to be about the size of the clouds which occurred and which were used in the Rio example.

We will call the undisturbed surface wind (away from the cloud) the 'remote' wind, and the surface wind influenced by the inflow, the 'cloud' wind.

When the remote wind is calm, the cloud winds look like Fig. 8.5.

Again, a few figures are revealing. The updraught through such a cloud would be about 200 metres per min over an area of 1,000,000sq m., so the volume of the inflow is about 200,000,000 cubic metres per minute. The area of the 'gap' between the outer edge of the cloud base and the surface is about 330 metres high, times 3,000 metres in circumference, i.e. about 1,000,000 square metres. 200,000,000 cubic metres of air per minute will flow through a gap of 1,000,000 square metres if the flow speed is 200 metres per min, or 3.3 metres per second, or about 6 knots. The wisps in Fig 8.4 were level, so the gap through which the inflow must pass will be twice as big twice as far from the cloud centre, and the flow speed half as fast. In Fig. 8.5 and subsequent similar figures the surface wind direction is indicated by the direction of the arrows and the flow speed by the length of the arrows. The typical speed in knots is written alongside representative arrows.

When the remote wind is 10 knots, the inflow combines with the remote wind component to develop the cloud winds shown in Fig. 8.6. There is an area of stronger wind upwind. There are pronounced inflows under both sides of the cloud. There is always a light air area and sometimes a calm patch downwind. All three factors – the stronger winds, the inflow, and the calmer patch – are of great tactical importance.

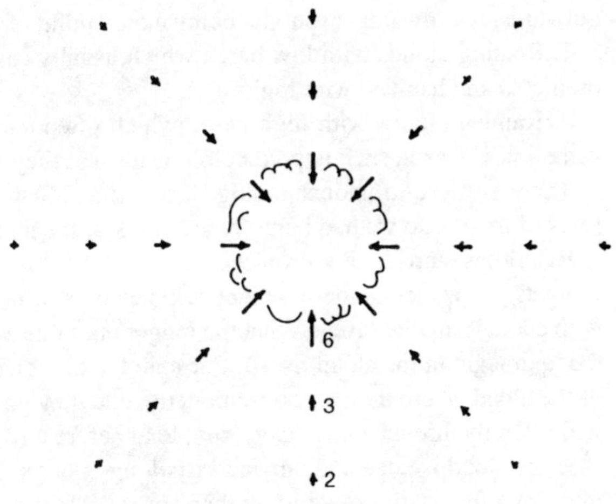

1 knot

Speeds suggested are typical, and indicate change of speed with increasing distance from cloud edge.

Fig 8.5 View from above of surface wind pattern under low-based, non-raining cumulus cloud.

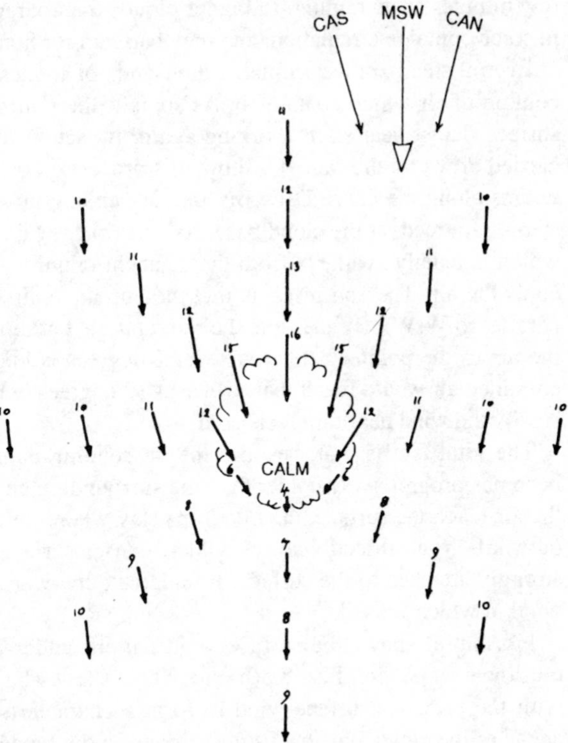

Surface wind pattern in 10 knot breeze near and under low-based, non-raining Cumulus cloud.

Note:
You sail in the surface wind -
but the cloud is steered by the gradient wind aloft - so
MSW = Mean direction of surface wind
CAS = Cloud approach, southern hemisphere
CAN = " " northern "

Fig 8.6 Surface wind pattern near non-raining cloud

8.5 Raining clouds

When rain falls, the pattern reverses. Non-raining clouds draw air inwards towards their bases and upwards through themselves. When their bases are low enough, the inflow imprints on the surface. Below raining clouds, the rain chills the air as it falls, and at the surface this cold air blows outwards away from the rain. The end result is that the surface wind near raining clouds flows outwards, not inwards. From the helmsman's point of view, there are two sorts of raining clouds:

1. Raining clouds with low bases which usually cause modest changes to the surface wind which can be predicted and handled with logic.

2. Raining clouds with high bases which often cause strong gusts followed by flat calms. These calms sometimes clear in such unpredictable ways that they can devastate an otherwise logical race plan.

There is more to understanding these effects than just big and small clouds, higher or lower bases, or rules of thumb, so we had better have a look at the mechanisms.

Raindrops start as tiny droplets, but these need to be big enough to fall fast enough to collide with the droplets below them, otherwise they will never grow into raindrops big enough to fall as rain. It is by colliding with enough smaller droplets that the bigger ones ultimately grow big enough to fall as a rain shower. Initially, the updraught in the cloud rises faster than the tiny droplets fall, and so they are all swept up towards the top of the cloud where they are concentrated while they grow. If you fly through the top of a Cumulus cloud, you will often fly through quite heavy rain, long before any visible rain appears below its base.

If the cloud is deep enough and lasts long enough, both the droplets and the total volume of liquid water in droplet form will grow bigger than some critical mass. At some time and some position within the cloud top, the increasing mass and increasing falling speed of all the growing raindrops is sufficient to cause that area of rain, and the air entrained within it, to start downwards through the cloud. This is the beginning of what becomes a downdraught which soon draws in and concentrates within itself virtually all the rain from the cloud top into one compact column. The process is almost complete by the time visible rain falls from the cloud base. The downdraught opposes the updraught through the cloud which is a fundamental part of its circulation – so the dynamics of the downdraught will usually destroy a small cloud which rains within a few minutes of its raining. In bigger clouds the updraught and the downdraught seem to manage to coexist in some complex circulation, and they can rain for hours.

Even a small shower contains thousands of tonnes of water. As it falls it entrains and drags down the column of air which contains it. As soon as the rain falls into the clear air between the cloud base and the surface, latent heat starts working again. Its action in this situation is to refrigerate the air entrained and carried down by the rain. To show this process, Fig. 8.7 extends Fig. 8.3. When dry air is forced down, it warms along the curve D-D. But the descending air entrained in the shower below the cloud isn't dry. It starts, saturated, at the cloud base. As it is dragged down it warms and becomes a little drier. Water vapour which is readily available from the adjacent raindrops immediately evaporates into it, and this evaporation cools the air. The end result is that the entrained air warms at the slower rate W-W. (In Fig. 8.7, B-12 is parallel to W-W). By the time the rain and the entrained air reach the surface, this refrigeration has cooled the air to the point where it is several degrees colder than the adjacent air. In the Fig. 8.7 situation the entrained air would reach the surface at 12 degrees, while the adjacent air would still be at 16 degrees. This is why the wind near rain feels cold.

The vital fact is that, because the descending column of air is continuously refrigerated as it falls, it becomes progressively colder than the surrounding air. It falls progressively faster. When the raindrops and the air reach the surface, the raindrops stay where they hit. But the plunging column of air splits and flows outwards in all directions as a colder, denser surface film. Because it is both heavy and fast, it remains strongly attached to the surface. It undercuts the warmer air in its path. It becomes for a while the surface wind in which we sail.

Fig. 8.8(a) shows the surface wind pattern under a relatively small raining cloud in a calm. There is outflow everywhere. Figs 8.8(b) and 8.8(c) show what happens when there is wind. The outflow combines with the previous surface wind to form a characteristic raining cloud wind pattern, with stronger winds ahead of the cloud, outflow from the sides, and a lighter air patch behind it.

When wind speeds are such that very little of the lighter-air area has winds of less than six knots, the raining-cloud wind pattern will be similar to that of the non-raining cloud, but reversed as in Fig. 8.8(b).

Raining clouds will almost always be deeper than adjacent non-raining clouds. If the difference in height is not great, the winds at mid-cloud height, which steer them, will be about the same, and so the same allowance should be made as for a non-raining cloud for the cloud's speed, and the skew of direction, as it approaches. A useful rule of thumb for the skew of such a cloud is to realise that the cloud moves sideways with respect to the wind direction at about half the boat speed, – to the right in the southern hemisphere, and to the left in the northern.

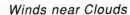

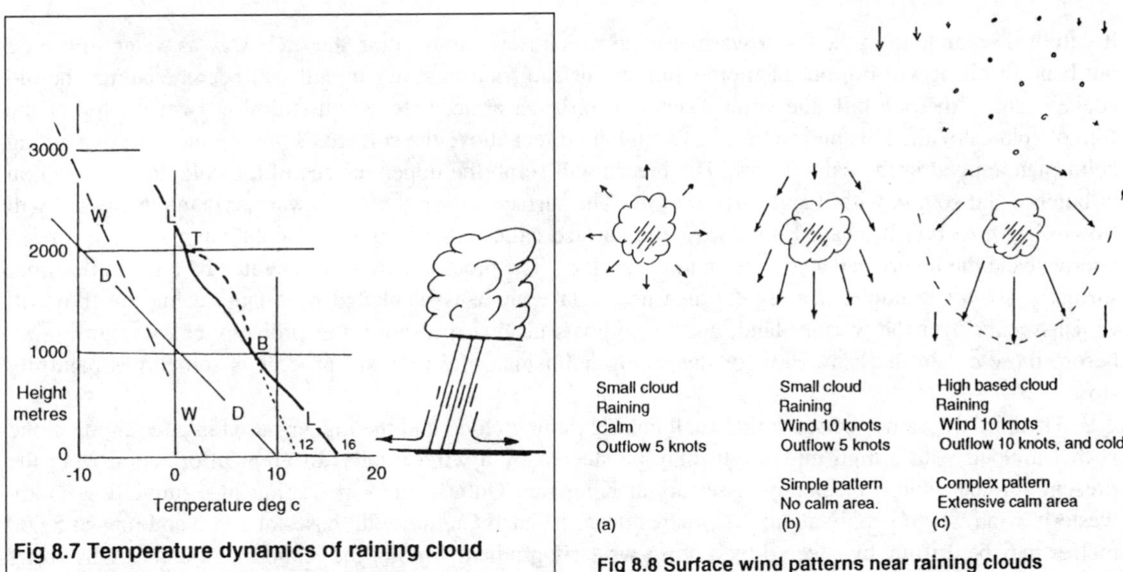

Fig 8.7 Temperature dynamics of raining cloud

Fig 8.8 Surface wind patterns near raining clouds

The height of the cloud base is of critical importance, but the sense is the reverse of the situation with non-raining clouds. The higher the cloud base, the more will the air entrained in the rain be cooled on its way to the surface, and the more of it there will be. Not only will the faster-falling air create stronger outflowing gusts. The greater volume from the higher column will make a deeper pool of colder air which will lie for longer on the surface after it loses its momentum.

Over and near salt water oceans, the lower atmosphere is both moist and also full of sea-salt particles which start as spray thrown up from the myriad bubbles which burst after each wave breaks. Some of the spray droplets evaporate before falling back into the water, and what is left is a salt crystal. These particles are carried aloft by turbulence, like the smoke particles of Fig. 3.9. These salt particles are both hygroscopic and also very much larger than any of the other particles which occur naturally in the atmosphere. When they are saturated within any cloud, the biggest of them are big enough to become the nuclei of droplets which are large enough to fall fast enough to collide with smaller droplets below, and so to start the rain process.

This rain process is very efficient. Because it requires an abundance of salt particles, it is confined to the oceans and the ocean shores, where the combination of ample moisture and abundant big salt particles means that clouds rain freely as soon as they attain modest depth. Once they rain, they decay and vanish, so individual clouds seldom become big. Consequently, the showers tend to be small, and the gusts they cause tend to be relatively modest and predictable. Raining clouds typically abound near coasts in temperate latitudes when the wind is onshore, and are frequently encountered by coastal sailors. The dynamics of Fig. 8.8(b) are typical of this most common situation.

Away from the oceans the salt particles soon fall out of the sky precisely because they are big. The other rain mechanisms are much less efficient than salt. So once the salt has gone, it is only much bigger and deeper clouds which can possibly rain. Further, away from the sea the air is usually drier, so these clouds tend to have much higher bases.

When a rain shower falls from a high-based cloud, it necessarily falls a long way through relatively dry air between cloud-base and ground. If you look again at Fig. 8.7 and imagine the ground to be further away from the cloud base you can see that rain below a high-based cloud must cool the entrained air more than will occur with a low-based cloud. Fig. 8.8(c) shows the surface pattern which is likely to occur below a high-based raining cloud when the surface wind is light or moderate. For the racing helmsman, there are three fundamental differences between Fig. 8.8(b) and Fig. 8.8(c).

1. The gust will be stronger, and will affect the local wind for longer, because the higher downdraught has more volume, falls faster, and has very much more momentum.

2. Particularly when the undisturbed wind is lighter, the 'raining cloud' wind pattern may include large areas with wind speeds of five knots or less in the area upwind of (i.e. behind) the cloud. In these slower-moving parts of the pattern the newly arrived cold air will simply lose its turbulence and becomes laminar.

It will then separate from the faster warmer wind which flows above it, in the same way as water will settle out beneath oil. It will run out of momentum as surface friction slows it, and will become calm. The old adage is apt – 'the rain kills the wind'. The undisturbed warmer breeze will still blow over the top of the film of cold calm air. This breeze, one or two hundred feet above the surface, is not of much use to a racing helmsman trapped in the calm below. The breeze will scrub the upper surface of the cold air with friction turbulence and so mix with it and carry it away. The surface will probably be warmer than the air, and will slowly begin to boil it away. Either way, the surface calm will last until the cold stagnant air has been removed and the breeze can again return to the surface. The process will be accelerated by a second warmer surface – so, for example, if a regatta area near a lake shore is blanketed by a large calm, the film will vanish sooner over the warmer land, and those boats nearest the shore will probably enjoy returning air before those out in the lake. But, for the racing helmsman, the removal process is sometimes painfully slow.

3. The third difference between the small coastal raining cloud and the higher-based inland raining cloud is that a cloud with a high mid-height may be steered by a wind totally different in direction from the present surface wind. For example, sailors at Kingston, Ontario, may be racing in a funnelling south-westerly wind which is only about 300 metres deep. Isolated Cumuli with bases at 2,000 and tops at 5,000 metres may be drifting by, steered by a north-westerly gradient wind at the 3,000 metre level. Alert crews will be conscious of these clouds, and aware of why their direction of drift is so different from the surface wind. They can ignore all non-raining clouds, because the wind they are racing in is a shallow surface wind beneath and separate from the gradient wind aloft. (refer next chapter). But if one of these big clouds rains, the rain and its plunging column of cold fast air will pierce straight through the funnelling wind, split at the surface, and sweep outwards in a gust which will be a major event in the afternoon's winds and racing.

The small salt-driven clouds can occur only over salt water, or near salt water in onshore winds. Over all other areas, only bigger, deeper clouds can rain. Even over the huge ocean-like areas of the Great Lakes, small clouds will not rain because the water there is fresh and there is no salt. Similarly, over ocean coasts but in prolonged offshore winds, there can be no salt particles, and so the expectations from small onshore-wind clouds which rain and the bigger higher-based offshore-wind clouds which rain are completely different.

Two-boat testing

Chapter Nine
Winds near Shores

9.1 Starting points

The lifetime experience of most sailors is so closely bound up with nearby shores that it is not easy to imagine sailing without one. The obvious characteristics of any shore are its height and its roughness. When we think further, there is also heat. What effect do each of these have on the winds we race in?

The height and roughness of the shore are easy to see. There has been a natural tendency to regard them as of principal importance in shaping the way the wind blows near shores. I was one of those who agreed with this approach – until that afternoon when we watched those horizontal wind waves serenely ignoring terrain which is both high and rough. (Fig. 6.1) In trying to learn 'why' I found myself concentrating more and more on the dynamics of the boundary layer, and the importance of heat in shaping those dynamics. Previous chapters have discussed some of the direct effects of heat on the different roll and cell patterns.

There is an even more important factor which governs the size and repetition frequency of wind patterns. It is the depth of the boundary layer. Exactly as big waves in the sea cannot survive over an offshore shoal, so big waves in the air cannot exist in a shallow boundary layer.

The mechanism which most frequently thins the boundary layer is the ultimate combination of heat and shore – the sea breeze. Within a few miles of shorelines the boundary layer of a sea or lake breeze or a funnelling wind can become very shallow indeed. So not only does the sea breeze change the wind direction. It also changes the nature of the patterns within the wind. The problem is that it is often not easy to recognise what is a sea breeze and what is a gradient wind – unless you know the mechanisms. So let us look at these mechanisms.

9.2 The sea breeze mechanism

The customary explanation of the sea breeze – 'that the air over the land is warmed and rises, so the cooler air from the sea flows in to fill the void' – is so simplistic as to be misleading. The truth is much more interesting.

The sea breeze in a calm.

Initially, let us assume that on a clear, sunny day, there is no gradient wind and that a little after dawn the surface of the land is at the same temperature as that of the sea. If, at this time, we measure the way the temperature and the pressure change with height at one point a little inland and another a little offshore, we would very likely find that both sets of measurements were similar in the way indicated in Fig. 9.1(a).

Let us assume strong sunshine during the next few hours. The sea surface warms by only a negligible amount through a depth of several metres. The top few millimetres of land surface warm strongly through many degrees. The land warms the air in contact with it by conduction, and that air expands and rises in shallow thermals (See Sect. 4.5 – Stability). These warm thermals mix with the surrounding air and in this way distribute the heat of the land's surface into the layers of air above them. For the sake of example, let us assume that the land warms the air 8 deg.C through its lowest 300 metres. This warmed air will expand about 10 metres, so all the air above 300 metres over the land will be lifted 10 metres. At the 300 metre level over the land there will now be an additional 10 metre mass of air above it, so the pressure at the 300 metre level over the land – but not over the sea – will rise by about 1 millibar. This is indicated in Fig. 9.1(b).

So far, not a molecule of air will have moved at the surface because no pressure difference has developed at the surface to move anything. But the expansion of the warmed low-level air has increased the pressure of the air over the land at all heights except the surface. No such pressure increase has occurred over the sea. This is the situation shown in Fig. 9.1(b).

What happens next is that the higher-level air over the land, driven by this pressure difference towards the sea, begins to flow offshore. This is exactly the same principle and the same mechanism as causes air which is higher over the heated equator to flow 'downhill' toward the poles (See fig. 2.1). And the result is exactly the same. The seaward drift of upper-level air reduces the total mass of air over the land and increases it over the sea. This in turn decreases the surface pressure over the land and increases it over the sea. This develops a low-level pressure difference towards the land, and this is the force which finally drives the air at the very lowest levels inland. This onshore flow is what we call the sea breeze. The important point is that the low-level onshore sea breeze can develop only after an initial upper-level offshore counterflow has first established itself.

Fig. 9.1(c) shows this pressure situation after the upper-level counterflow has commenced. The reduction of pressure difference in the offshore direction aloft has caused a pressure difference to develop in the onshore direction at and near the surface. Note that it develops first right at the surface, and that it is necessarily a very shallow mechanism. (The figures chosen for this example bring out nice simple numbers: 8 deg.C expands a 300 metre depth of air about 10 metres which happens to develop 1 millibar of hydrostatic pressure difference between the 300 metre level inland and the 300 metre level out to sea. In reality this sort of pressure gradient over four or five kilometres would cause a hurricane. The real life forces are only a fraction of these.)

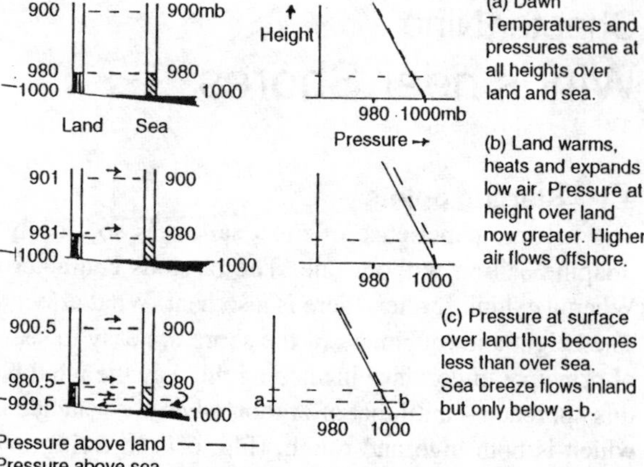
900
900mb
980
980
1000
1000
Land
Sea
Height
980
1000mb
Pressure
(a) Dawn Temperatures and pressures same at all heights over land and sea.
901
900
981
980
1000
1000
980
1000
(b) Land warms, heats and expands low air. Pressure at height over land now greater. Higher air flows offshore.
900.5
900
980.5
980
999.5
1000
a
b
980
1000
(c) Pressure at surface over land thus becomes less than over sea. Sea breeze flows inland but only below a-b.
Pressure above land
Pressure above sea
Fig 9.1 The sea breeze mechanism

Once the sea breeze starts to blow, air will continue to be warmed inland, will expand and rise, will mix with the air above and drift out to sea as a part of the deep counterflow aloft. To complete the loop, air must subside out to sea to replace the air which flows inland. These four factors – the warming of the land surface and the warming and expansion of the air over the land, the upper-level offshore counterflow, the subsidence out to sea, and the onshore flow of cool low-level air – must all be present before a sea breeze can develop.

The sea breeze when there is a gradient wind

When the calm is replaced by a gradient wind, very different things happen to the sea breeze according to the direction of the gradient wind. Let me describe what I saw as a pilot. In the late 1940's and early 50's I flew flying boats on the New Zealand – Australia and other routes. When we approached Sydney from the East on summer afternoons when there was a 10 to 20 knot south-easterly tailwind out to sea, we always seemed to land into a light 5 knot south-easterly in the harbour. But when we flew against a 20 to 30 knot westerly headwind over the ocean, we used to fly very low for the last 50 kilometres, because the surface westerly decreased to an uneasy calm about 30 kilometres offshore, and then progressively increased to about a 15 knot north-easterly sea breeze over Sydney. It blew at about 20 knots in the part of the harbour we landed on. (I now realise that this was a funnelling wind local to the main harbour only.)

Some years later, we flew landplanes into Sydney airport which is 10 kilometres south of the harbour and away from its funnelling wind. The Instrument Landing System glide slope beam which serves the north-east runway gave me another look at this strong summer sea breeze which developed when the gradient wind was in the West. For practise, one pilot would always make the approach 'blind' and fly down the 3 degree glideslope beam on instruments from about 1,000 metres altitude and 20 kilometres out. For the initial part of this approach, the aeroplane was usually in a strong westerly tailwind and needed to be throttled well back to descend fast enough to stay on the beam. At about 250 metres altitude it wriggled in brief turbulence and the indicated airspeed increased as it passed through the shear layer between the westerly gradient wind aloft and the north easterly sea breeze below and the temperature gauge dropped two or three degrees. From then on it needed much more power to hold the 3 degree glideslope to the threshold in the north-easterly headwind (the sea breeze) below the shear layer.

Why was the south-easterly wind so light in the harbour on hot sunny afternoons? Why did a westerly or north-westerly gradient wind cause so strong and shallow a north-easterly sea breeze?

Two more pointers. When I took my radio controlled gliders to Sydney and flew them over coastal cliffs with Sydney friends, in south-east winds we could soar them hundreds of metres above the coastal scarp. But in north-easters it was a fight to get them thirty metres higher than a 60 metre cliff. At first I wondered about technical causes. Then I looked at the seagulls. They were doing no better!

I sensed restriction above, remembered the shear layer on approach to the runway which was customarily present at a height of about 250 metres in these conditions – and became very interested in boundary layer thickness. Initially this was not an easy thing to measure, but fortunately changing life-style has since came to the rescue. The clouds of balloons which are now often released on festive occasions are superb indicators of any low-level wind change and the height at which it occurs. In recent years the privilege of observing numerous harbourside balloon releases has provided increasing insight into the typical boundary layer thicknesses over our sailing areas in different synoptic and quadrant situations.

In 1958 I moved to Australia to take up scientific flying (and to be able to see more of my family). The coasts of Australia – particularly its south and east coasts – are routinely washed by summer sea breezes of a regularity, strength and dimension rarely approached elsewhere in the world. I have been fortunate to be able to live, sail and coach within this sea breeze laboratory.

I would like to thank David Houghton for discussing with me his quadrant concept within the sea breeze (and lake breeze) mechanism. We meet from time to time and share ideas. David was as interested in my emerging pattern ideas at the Kingston Olympics as I was in his emerging quadrant ideas prior to the Tallinn Games. The following section combines David's quadrant ideas with my boundary layer thickness observations. It has developed into a useful tool for predicting wind pattern behaviour near shores.

9.3 The quadrant effect

This focuses on the effect of the direction of the gradient wind on the three factors which control the development of every sea breeze, namely – heating, the offshore counterflow, and subsidence. It is most easily understood if we look at it on a completely practical basis from the start.

The following method enables a helmsman to assess:-

1. When a sea breeze cannot develop.
2. The probability of a sea breeze in marginal conditions
3. When a sea breeze can and will develop.
4. What sort of wind patterns to expect in each case.

The method

Except when the gradient wind is so strong that there cannot be a sea breeze, the method has three steps:

1. Position the quadrants.
2. Determine the gradient wind direction.
3. Score the heat, subsidence, and counterflow factors, and total them.

Both the strength and the direction of the gradient wind are important, but in completely different ways.

Gradient wind strength

There is a gradient wind strength of about 20 to 25 knots in hot climates and somewhat less in cooler places, at and above which sea breezes simply cannot develop, regardless of all other circumstances. Conversely, there will be a wind strength – say 5 knots in a hot climate and less in cooler places – at and below which the wind direction will be irrelevant, and a sea breeze will develop when the heating is strong as if the gradient wind were calm. Between these two extremes, the strength of the gradient wind ceases to have any practical effect on the sea breeze mechanism.

Gradient wind direction

When the wind speed is less than the upper limit noted above, the direction of the gradient wind with respect to the coastline becomes all-important. This direction can be observed with certainty from the movement of low clouds, or be estimated closely from the direction of the isobars on the current weather map.

It is possible to position and number four quadrants, at any locality, in a simple manner which not only eliminates all compass directions, but also all the 'but in the other hemisphere . . .', confusion. All wind directions must necessarily fall within one of four quadrants.

To position and number the quadrants, imagine that you are standing on the shore and facing the land.

In the southern hemisphere call the quadrant to your left front 'one', to your right front 'two', and so on clockwise through 'three' and 'four'. In the northern hemisphere call the quadrant to your right front 'one', to your left front 'two', and so on anti-clockwise through 'three' and 'four'. Fig. 9.2 (a) and (b) are examples which give the quadrant positions for Sydney in the southern hemisphere, and for Kingston, Ontario in the northern.

The scoring system is to assign to each of the heat, counterflow and subsidence factors one point for maximum encouragement of a sea breeze, minus one point for minimum encouragement, and zero for intermediate.

Heat is essential. If there is no heat, there can be no sea breeze. Maximum heat will occur in summer, at and after noon, and when there are no or least clouds, which usually occur when the gradient wind is offshore, i.e. with a direction from quadrants one or two. In such conditions score one. If it is early or late in the season or the day and there is little heat in the sun, or if the offshore wind is full of broken clouds (as is typical in moist air and Low dominant conditions), score zero. For a moist onshore wind with continuous cloud cover which cuts off the sun's heating, as will often occur when the gradient wind is from quadrants three or four, score minus one. If the cloud cover is broken, score zero.

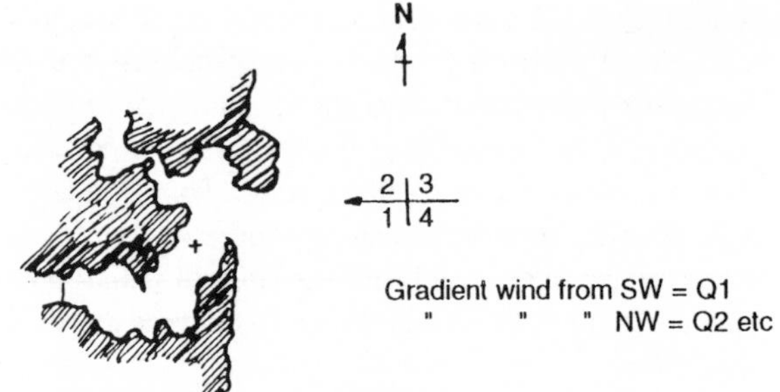

(a) Sydney, NSW (Southern hemisphere)

(b) Kingston, Ontario (Northern hemisphere)

Quadrant	1	2	3	4
Heat*	(0	1	0	-1)
Counterflow[a]	1	1	-1	-1
Subsidence[a]	-1	1	1	-1
Total	0	3	0	-3

* Heat scores are for example only. Adjust for cloud & season.
[a] Counterflow and subsidence scores are fixed by the quadrant.

(c) Sample score table.

Fig 9.2 Quadrant identification, and score table.

Counterflow is essential. Score one for gradient winds with directions in quadrants one or two because offshore winds encourage counterflow. Score minus one for onshore winds in quadrants three or four. As a refinement, score zero when the gradient wind blows almost along the coast – say within plus or minus twenty degrees of it.

Subsidence encourages counterflow and feeds the sea breeze. Convergence tends to block counterflow and so starves the sea breeze. What you are scoring here is the difference in direction between the surface wind over the rougher land and the smoother sea. When the gradient wind blows along the shore in the direction from quadrant one to quadrant two, there has to be an area of higher pressure inland and a low somewhere out to sea. The surface wind over the sea will be slowed a little and skewed perhaps 10 degrees. Over the rougher land it will be slowed more and skewed more – up to 30 or 40 degrees. This results in the two surface winds converging at the coastline. This convergence throws up a small pressure wave, often with clouds, which not only blocks subsidence, it positively discourages the offshore counterflow from starting in the first place, so convergence very strongly discourages any sea breeze.

Conversely, when the gradient wind blows along the coast the other way – from quadrant two to quadrant one – the low pressure must be inland. The surface winds then diverge at the coast, and the 'gap' thus formed between them both encourages the counterflow to start and also facilitates its subsidence to close the loop. The critically important point about this subsidence is that it is a very low-level phenomenon. By facilitating the counterflow at the lowest level, it is this factor, primarily, which makes sea breezes so shallow when the gradient wind is in quadrant two (and sometimes three). Score minus one for quadrants one and four. Score one for quadrants two and three. As a refinement, score zero when the gradient wind is within twenty degrees of directly onshore or offshore. Once you get the idea, an 8-column table is simpler because it enables you to put in those 'except' zeros without fiddling. It also reveals how fast the forces change when the gradient wind direction blows approximately along the coastline, i.e. between quadrants 2 and 3, and between quadrants 4 and 1.

Fig. 9.2 (c) shows the sort of table which would be drawn up by a crew prior to a major championship. Note that, once the quadrants are identified for a particular location, the scores on the counterflow line and the subsidence line do not change, because they are fixed by the orientation. The heat score is different. The 'heating' score should be determined by estimating what will be the heating in the hours prior to the race. To make these example tables complete, I have included (in brackets) heat scores which are typical.

The practical value of this table is that it enables a crew to anticipate with near-certainty when a sea breeze is impossible, when it is uncertain, and when it is likely. For example:-

(a) If the gradient wind is in quadrant 4, the score will be low because there will be convergence and the gradient wind opposes any counterflow. No amount of heat can cause a sea breeze to develop, no matter how much the onshore wind may feel like a sea breeze. A crew can be confident that the boundary layer will remain deep and the primary wind patterns will remain slow.

(b) When the gradient wind is in quadrant 2, only a little heat will be needed for a sea breeze to develop, and when it develops it will be stronger and shallower than when the gradient wind is in any other quadrant. A crew who understand this will elect, earlier than others, the side of the course likely to be favoured by its onset, and will expect quick oscillations.

(c) If the gradient wind direction is in either Q1 or Q4, whether or not a sea breeze can develop will be much less predictable because each quadrant will have one positive and one negative factor. This is where the eight-point table is so revealing. Whatever the conditions, the strength will not match that of a Q2 sea breeze.

(d) Remember always that deep boundary layers typical of gradient winds will have slow oscillations which may or may not be regular, while the shallow boundary layers of sea breezes will have fast regular oscillations. Whenever the wind changes from gradient wind to sea breeze, or vice versa, a crew should alter their windshift technique to suit.

Broad expectations

This system of quadrant positioning and scoring seems to be capable of explaining many important things about sea breezes. The broad expectations are as follows.

When the gradient wind is slightly offshore in quadrant one, the score will probably be 0 with good heating, or -1 with poor heating. The convergence will hold back the counterflow and inhibit subsidence. A sea breeze inland of the coast cannot develop unless the gradient wind is light and the heating intense. It is likely to be relatively deep and unsteady.

When the gradient wind is from inland in quadrant one, or from quadrant two, the score will probably be 2 or 3. A sea breeze will be most probable, and at its strongest. As the gradient wind direction moves from quadrant one through two, the divergence will increase and the sea breeze will become stronger and shallower, more free from gusts and more predictably uniform over an area.

When the gradient wind is almost along the coast in quadrant three, i.e. slightly onshore, the score will probably be 0, or -1 if heating is poor. The subsidence will be strong but the counterflow will be inhibited by the gradient wind. A sea breeze can form but only if heating is intense and the gradient wind light. Any sea breeze is likely to be very shallow, and will either be unsteady, or will form and vanish as the balance between heat and inhibited counterflow fluctuates. The direction of the gradient wind and the sea breeze will be approximately the same, but the boundary layer thickness will be very different, as will the windshift behaviour. This sector gives very unsteady winds.

When the gradient wind is more onshore in quadrant 3, the score will probably be -1, or 0 if heating is strong. The gradient wind opposes counterflow directly. There can be no sea breeze. On days with strong heating, the land's heat may accelerate the surface wind a little near the coast, and this boosted gradient wind may feel exactly like a sea breeze. However, it remains a gradient wind with a deep boundary layer, and will have all the big slow waves and potential unsteadiness (except in High dominant conditions), of all deep boundary layer winds.

When the gradient wind is from quadrant 4, the score is likely to be -2 or -3. There will be convergence near the coast which blocks subsidence in addition to its opposition to the counterflow. In this quadrant there cannot possibly be sea breezes, no matter how much they may look and feel like sea breezes. These winds remain pure gradient winds with normal boundary layer thicknesses of one to two thousand metres, and big, slow patterns.

Practical examples

The horizontal wind-waves which flowed up Middle Harbour (Fig. 6.1) were in a quadrant 4 situation. They were simply well developed, regular, roll oscillations of about the wavelength and frequency normal to a gradient wind with a 1,300 metre thick boundary layer stabilised by a subsidence inversion. Steep-sided 100 metre hills meant nothing to these 1,300 metre deep rolls.

The lighter south-easterly winds into which we landed when there were stronger south-easterly winds offshore were also in a quadrant 4 situation. These again were simply gradient winds. In the particular case of the Sydney environment, onshore south-easters are slowed partly by the friction of the city and partly by their being blocked by a mountain range 60 kilometres inland. As heating intensifies the mixing, the mass of blocked air becomes bigger and the onshore gradient wind has nowhere to go.

Success in Sydney Eighteen Footer racing has for decades been largely dependent upon the ability to choose the correct rig for the day. Alone of all the quadrants, tradition suggests (correctly) that a south-easter will become lighter – 'a sick sou'easter' – as the afternoon progresses.

The strong north-east sea breeze which is the local summer afternoon prevailing wind – the airport's main runway is aligned into it – is the purest quadrant 2 sea breeze. There could be no better examples than Figs 3.3 and 7.16.

The behaviour of my gliders in quadrant 4 winds was consistent with gradient winds with thick boundary layers. The lack of lift in the strong north-east sea breezes which developed in quadrant 2 (north-westerly) gradient winds was consistent with the sea breeze's very shallow flow, plus some subsidence. Further afield, the behaviour of the gliders in New Zealand in quadrant 4 winds was consistent with quadrant 4 expectation.

Further afield again, David Houghton, alone of the world's top sailing forecasters, was able to use this logic to predict 'no sea breeze' to his UK yachting team in Kingston, Ontario, on critical days of the Montreal Olympics. The quadrant effect goes far toward explaining the behaviour of the sea breeze, world-wide.

My own experience is that the quadrant effect is a very useful tool for gaining a feel quickly for any new location. It is broad-brush, don't expect miracles of accurate forecasting, but it does focus on the essentials and it needs only a little experience at any new location before it settles down and delivers very useful forecasts.

9.4 Refinements

Sea breezes, like other life forms, are born, they grow, they mature. Ultimately they die. They are all different. We sailed a UK championship at Falmouth. Only once during several days did a sea breeze appear during a race. It lived, clean and predictable, for a whole thirty minutes, then vanished. During the following calm, I was washed past the finishing line by the sluicing tide. This sort of ephemeral sea breeze is well covered by Alan Watts in his book, *'Wind and Sailing Boats'*.

They are not all like this.

Scale

Those who sail the east Australian coast anywhere between Brisbane, Sydney and Melbourne would expect, in summer heating, that a quadrant 2 sea breeze would be likely to set in between 9 and 10 am, and blow until dusk 11 hours later. The civil servants of Canberra, situated in the hills 150 kilometres to the West, often sail in the evenings – because the sea breeze which starts at 9 am in Jervis Bay keeps growing westward until it washes over Canberra in the later afternoon. Growth of this scale raises questions about both development, and also what happens when the shape of a coastline is complex.

Development

There are no surprises here. A sea breeze will grow no more than is justified by the heating. In the summer example above, the speed at the coast is usually 6 to 8 knots within minutes of onset, rises to a maximum of 12 to 18 knots between 2 and 4 pm, and is down to about 6 knots by 8 to 9 pm. It usually starts at right angles to the coast and backs with Coriolis throughout its life (Fig 3.3). As the sea breeze front moves inland, the direction of the wind immediately behind it starts at the original 'right angles to the coast' direction, despite the fact that the wind at the coast may by then have backed many degrees.

In the same situation but in winter's much lesser heat, sea breezes are rare, brief, and wash no more than 5 or 10 kilometres inland at most.

Widespread high clouds which cut off the heat slowly have an identical effect. When high clouds become denser or thinner, the strength of the sea breeze will develop or diminish slowly in response to the changed heating. But when the change in heating occurs quickly, an unstable pattern can develop. An example of this sometimes occurs when the surface air is moist and the heating intense. In this situation:

A quadrant 1 or 2 sea breeze develops strongly.

Dense Cumulus clouds develop inland. At some point they 'erupt' and their sheer density cuts off the heating almost completely.

The strength of the sea breeze surges briefly as the clouds erupt, then dies.

The clouds evaporate, because the feed of moist air has vanished.

Heating is restored.

The sea breeze develops again, and the cycle repeats.

Fig. 9.3 shows an example of this cycling. Typical cycle time, in Sydney, is in the 60 to 90 minute range.

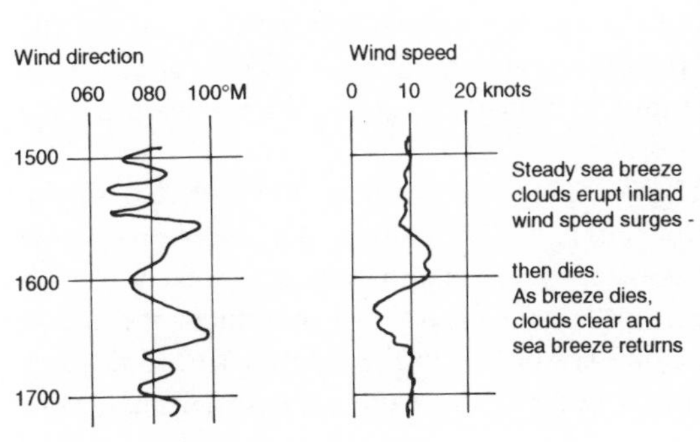

Fig 9.3 'Cycling' pattern - Sydney

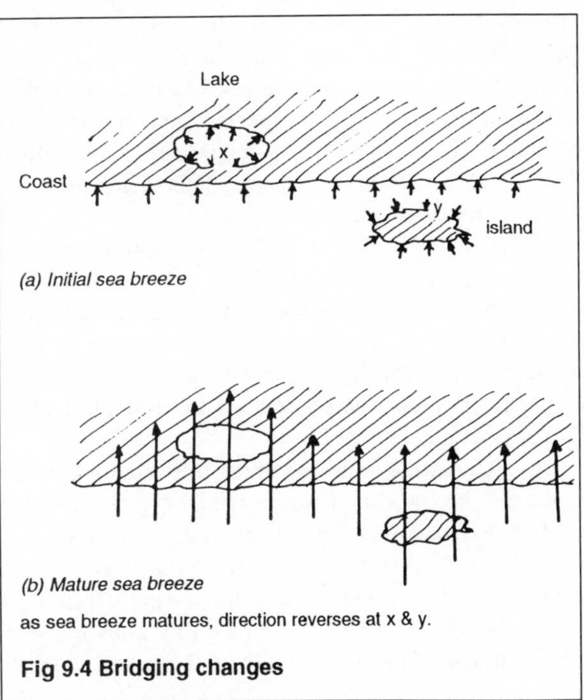

Fig 9.4 Bridging changes

Complex coastlines and 'bridging' changes

The first step in positioning the quadrants is to 'stand on the shore and face the land'. Where the coastline is simple, this presents no problem. But what happens when the coastline is convoluted?

The classic example is that of either an island or lake near the shore, as in Fig. 9.4. The initial sea breezes will blow directly onshore in every location, as in Fig. 9.4(a). If the heating remains feeble these directions will persist. But with increase of heating, they will blow as in Fig. 9.4(b). At 'x' and 'y' the direction has reversed as the sea breeze has developed more strongly.

These are 'bridging changes':

Usually, these changes of direction will occur suddenly. Their occurrence is reasonably predictable.

Their time of occurrence is not predictable.

In any such complex situation, the quadrants can be positioned correctly if you 'think like a sea breeze', and consider a series of elements of the coastline, each at a larger scale. In the example above of a shoreline with a lake or an island, the initial orientation will be 'to face the land' everywhere. The initial sea breeze at every point will be directly onshore, and if the heating is gentle this will be the breeze which will persist, and it will develop no further.

But if the day is such that you believe that heating will develop strongly, you should 'think big', ignore relatively small-scale details such as the lake or the island, and focus on the orientation of a stretch of coastline ten or twenty times as big. As the heat builds up, *that* will be the coastline to which the next stage of the sea breeze will relate. Sometimes this process can even continue to a third stage.

Two examples of this situation show how it works.

Fig. 9.5 is a map of the areas adjacent to Melbourne. Most of the Melbourne sailing clubs are based on the eastern and southern shores of Port Phillip Bay. Moorabbin airport, with its weather office, is 4 or 5 kilometres inland. Fig. 9.6 is a copy of the Moorabbin anemograph trace on a day which developed a strong, sustained sea breeze. This trace shows three separate sea breezes and the two intervening bridging changes. Initially, the direction at Moorabin and the nearby clubs was 240 degrees, i.e. almost directly onshore to the adjacent shoreline. It began to back with Coriolis to 220 degrees. At this early stage the sea breeze blew from the bay onto the shoreline A-B. If the heating had been feeble but sustained, the breeze would have stayed like this. In fact, the heating intensified, and at 1500 the direction changed suddenly to 190 degrees. (A practical point is that the brief reduction of wind speed prior to the change is one of the signals – another would have to be increasing heat – which would alert a Melbourne bay sailor that a bridging change may be imminent.) This was the first bridging change. The developing sea breeze now blew inland over the larger-scale shoreline C-D, and the whole of Port Phillip had become insignificant in the scale of this larger circulation. If the heating had remained at this moderate level, the breeze would have stayed like this.

Normally, it would be expected that the breeze would continue to back due to Coriolis. In this particular case this does not happen because the hills of the Mornington Peninsular act as a guide to the flow which resists such a change. This is an unusual but logical funnelling wind. So – for awhile – the direction remained steady.

The heating intensified further. At 1700 a second bridging change occurred, to 135 degrees. Again, the wind speed decreased briefly prior to the direction change. The mature sea breeze had now developed to such a scale that it swept inland across the whole of the predominantly east-west Victorian coastline E-F, and features such as either the Mornington hills or even the big shoreline indentation seaward of Port Phillip had become insignificant. This mature sea breeze backed slowly to 115 degrees as the earth turned, and continued to blow until after sunset at 2030 when the heating terminated for that day.

An even more extreme example of bridging changes occurs next door, 1,000 kilometres to the West in the St Vincent's and Spencer Gulfs. Fig. 9.7 shows the area near Adelaide, South Australia.

On a quadrant 1 or 2 day in summer – quadrant 2 to the whole SA coastline, that is – the sea breeze off Adelaide will set in gently from the West. As it develops, Coriolis backs it to the south-west, at which point it becomes a funnelling wind. (Refer next section.) Many Olympic trials, and one Laser world championship, have been won by knowing that the backing sea breeze will steady at about 215 degs and that a funnelling wind will thereafter oscillate closely around that direction.

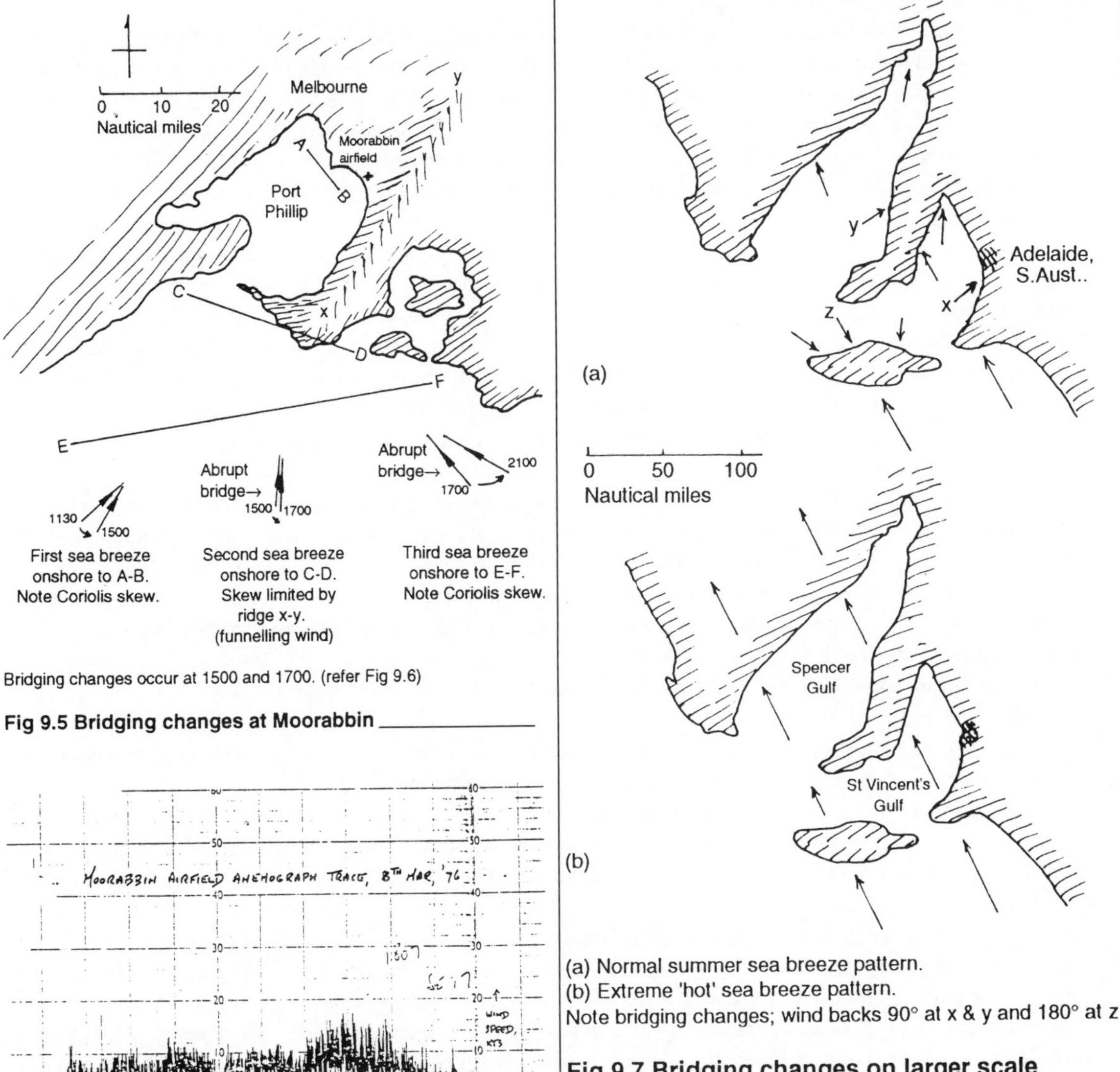

Bridging changes occur at 1500 and 1700. (refer Fig 9.6)

Fig 9.5 Bridging changes at Moorabbin

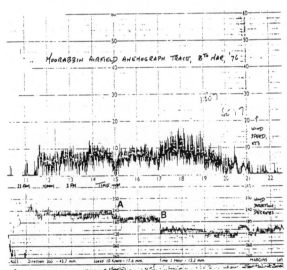

Anemograph (wind recording machine) trace; Moorabbin airfield.

Note abrupt changes of direction at A, 1500hrs; and B at 1700hrs.
These are bridging changes.
Note also the associated brief decrease in wind speed.
Refer to Fig 9.5 for topography.

Fig 9.6 Wind speed and direction trace of bridging changes

(a) Normal summer sea breeze pattern.
(b) Extreme 'hot' sea breeze pattern.
Note bridging changes; wind backs 90° at x & y and 180° at z

Fig 9.7 Bridging changes on larger scale

But – When the heating is at its maximum and the air is cold, the larger and more regularly-shaped Spencer Gulf, close by, develops a funnelling wind system of enormous scale and power. About early-afternoon, this can expand to include the St Vincent's Gulf flow. A bridging change occurs off Adelaide in which the wind changes from a strong funnelling SW into St Vincent's Gulf, and flicks instead into a SSE which is part of the larger Spencer Gulf system. This sweeps in from over the southern Mt Lofty ranges, and happens to be, near Adelaide, an offshore wind. It is unbelievable when first encountered, but becomes logical when you work it out. This is not itself a funnelling wind, because it backs a little thereafter with Coriolis.

The days on which it cannot occur, and the days on which it can and probably will occur, can be predicted by use of the quadrant effect. So there really isn't any need to be on the right hand side of the course, and out of all the fun, when it arrives.

9.5 The funnelling winds

When a waterway which is relatively long and narrow is aligned approximately with the direction which will be adopted by a quadrant 1 or 2 sea breeze onto the main coastline, and the shores of the waterway are each big enough to develop a sea breeze in their own right, a funnelling wind will develop along that waterway.

The funnelling wind is a special case of the sea breeze. It is driven by exactly the same mechanism and pressure differences which drive the sea breeze, except that in this case two shores, relatively close together, are both drawing low-level air from the same source. The inversion above the boundary layer prevents any infeed of air from above, so the total flow volume must enter through the mouth of the waterway. The result is that to meet this doubled demand the speed of the low-level airflow up the channel has to be much stronger than is the case with the normal two-dimensional sea breeze across a coast. Further, the increased demand keeps the flow very shallow indeed.

The funnelling wind is uniquely identified by the constancy of its direction. It will move towards and settle at its characteristic direction which thereafter remains fixed. It may oscillate, or adopt any of the patterns common within sea breezes, but these will all fluctuate around a direction which is as stable as the current of a river. In this it is completely different from the sea breeze which, after it initially settles, will back or veer steadily as it intensifies and matures.

Funnelling winds grow, become mature, and decay. In their early stages their dynamics are weak and they behave like sea breezes. When they decay, if the surface cools quickly, the tremendous momentum already built up has to go somewhere, and great folds in the airflow can then develop. In between, the mature funnelling wind has a number of properties which make it almost unique.

1. It is one of the most predictable of all winds, because it is driven by large and predictable forces which work over a relatively small area.

2. It is one of the shallowest of all surface flows, because two shores are both removing low-level air from below the inversion.

3. The depth of the flow is very even, because this boundary layer is controlled not only by subsidence above the inversion but also by accelerated removal of air from below.

4. It is the most uniform of all winds across an area. Because large pressure forces drive a thin ribbon of air fast, there is no opportunity for cells to form except at the downstream end of the flow. Any rolls which form can be only minuscule and absolutely regular because the boundary layer is so shallow and so uniform in its thickness.

5. Any oscillating pattern will repeat quickly, because only very small waves can form.

6. It is the steadiest of all breezes in the gust-lull sense. There is no substantial depth within which faster-moving gust swirls can form and descend. It therefore has the smallest gust factor of all breezes.

7. Near each shore, the flow will curve away from the primary, 'up the channel', direction and swing more onshore. This onshore curve is inherent in the mechanism, but it occurs in different ways in different places:

(a) This onshore curve will be more pronounced on the right-hand side of channels, looking towards the shore, in the northern hemisphere, and the left hand side in the southern hemisphere, due to Coriolis. (Moving particles tend to swing right in the northern hemisphere, and vice versa.) As an example on a very large scale, the funnelling wind which develops in the Gulf of Finland swings easily to the right into Tallinn Bay, but scarcely swings left into the Helsinki waterways at all. On a smaller scale, the funnelling wind which sometimes blows in English Bay, Vancouver, develops a pronounced swing to the right over Kitsilano, at the inner right hand end of the bay, but the swing to the left over Hollyburn, on the opposite left hand shore, is relatively small.

(b) The onshore swing will occur principally over the land and only to a negligible extent over the water surface at the coastal end of the waterway, but at increasing distance inland from the mouth of the bay will occur more and more over the water, particularly when the land is heated. In particular, if the waterway either terminates, or so contracts as to effectively terminate from the point of view of the funnelling wind mechanism, or if the onshore airflow is at all blocked, then the onshore swing may begin so far offshore that it occurs almost entirely over the water. The biggest swing will occur on the side encouraged by Coriolis.

8. The funnelling wind mechanism develops both convergent and divergent flows. Wherever a lighter sea breeze is drawn towards and accelerates into a waterway under an inversion, this flow must be convergent.

9. Of the two, the convergent flows can be very steady, and will persist for as long as the funnelling wind

blows. Divergent flows by their nature are much less stable, and will tend to break up into unsteady patterns which may mask the fundamental divergence. These geographically fixed convergent and divergent flows are of the greatest tactical importance.

10. The unusual steadiness referred to in 4, 5 and 6 above reaches its extreme in the areas where the flow converges and accelerates. If we imagine a spherical smoke puff to be released upwind of such an area, it will be compressed crosswind and elongated downwind as it washes downwind. Before long what started as a sphere of smoke will have become a long thin filament. The analogy of 'wire drawing' is apt. In such an environment embryonic cells or rolls are so quickly distorted towards filaments that they are unable to become established and grow. For this reason the flow in these areas may be completely free of even the slightest cell or wave pattern. The anabatic funnelling wind of Lake Garda is unusually steady for this reason.

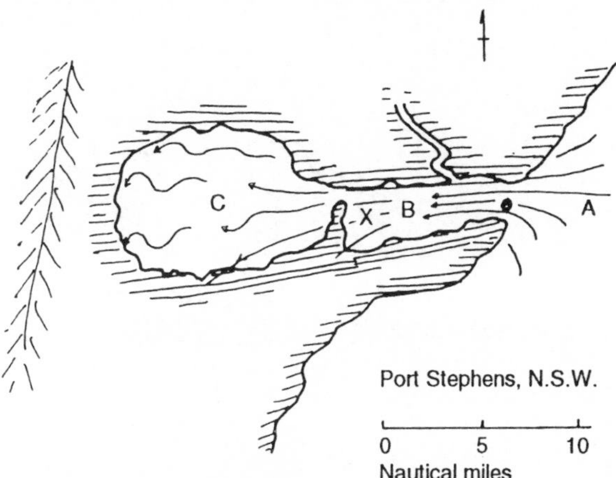

Fig 9.8 Convergence and divergence

11. In areas of divergent flow the reverse principle applies. Any small perturbation will be amplified in the crosswind sense, so the divergent areas are usually areas of extremes of unsteadiness.

9.6 Shoreline factors

Most of us sail near shores. Often we sail in bays or harbours which lie on the landward side of the coastline. Sometimes we sail out to sea. Sections 9.1 to 9.5 have introduced the larger-scale sea and lake breeze mechanisms which are the sailors' prevailing winds in many parts of the world when day-sailing in summer. The introduction to chapter six suggests that the influence of the height and friction factors – nearby hills or headlands, and the added surface friction of the roughness of cities or forests – which are so often quoted as of great local importance, often have an influence of only a few tens or hundreds of metres, and so may not be of widespread importance at all.

When we sail near coasts in cooler climates, or during seasons or in wind directions which develop no sea breezes, the special behaviour of the wind near shorelines will be governed by four factors.

1. The first is heat. As always, thermal excitation will cause profound and often surprising changes. When the surface temperature of the water is substantially different from that of the land surface, the effect of heat will be dominant.

(2, 3 and 4 are concerned with friction. When the temperatures of the land and the water surface are not much different, then friction factors will be dominant.)

2. The second is that the direction of the surface wind over the land will be different from the direction over the nearby sea because the greater surface friction over the rougher land skews the wind direction more.

3. The third is the orientation of the wind to the shoreline. This will largely govern where the change of direction will take place.

4. The fourth is convergence and divergence. This will largely govern the differences in wind speeds near the shore.

These friction factors combine to give five shoreline mechanisms and patterns. The simplest introduction is to sketch the basic expectations in each wind as they would be thought of by a crew about to sail a long windward leg on a cool day. In the case of offshore and onshore winds, I have assumed that the start is well out to sea, and the finish is inland, deep in a bay (and vice versa), so that the effects on both the seaward and the landward side of the coastline are shown. These five friction patterns are shown as Fig. 9.9 – Wind mainly offshore. Fig. 9.10 – Wind mainly along the shore, *Low* to seaward. Fig. 9.11 – Wind mainly onshore. Fig. 9.12 – Wind slightly onshore, *Low* inland . Fig. 9.13 – Wind slightly offshore, *Low* inland.

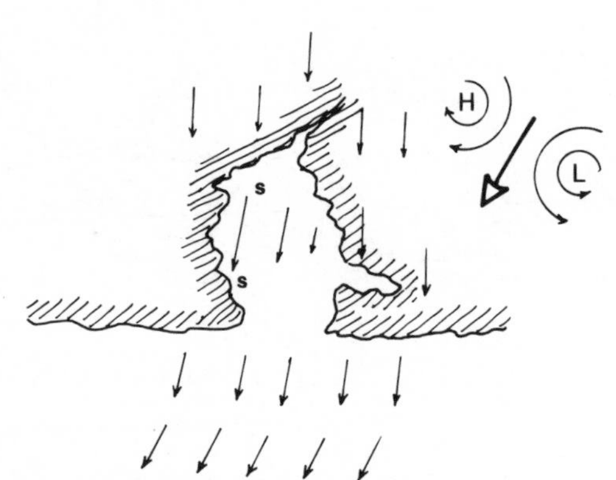

Features as Fig 9.91s except that:-
Wind veers and freshens offshore and in bay.
s - s Stronger wind in bay.

Fig 9.9n Wind offshore

Features as in Fig 9.11s, except that:-
wind backs over land, and becomes lighter.
s - s = Stronger wind in bay.

Fig 9.11n Wind onshore

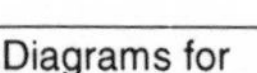

Diagrams for
Northern hemisphere

note that the principle remains true;-
Wind is stronger near shore - nearer High

L = Distant low
H = Distant high
→ = Gradient wind

Figs 9.9 to 9.13 (n) Shoreline effects - North

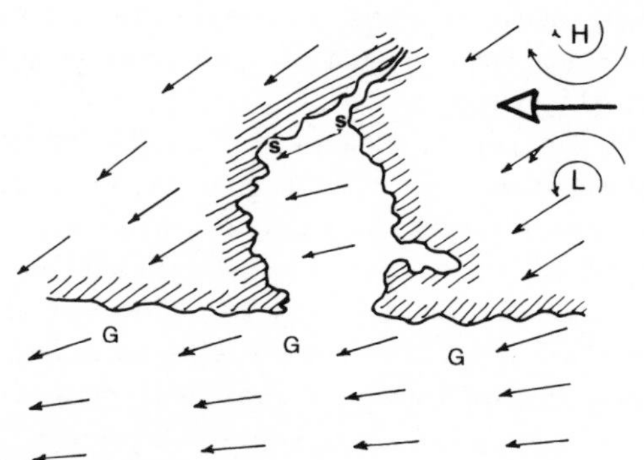

Features as in Fig 9.10s, except that
wind veers and freshens offshore and in bay.
G - G = Zone of convergence and stronger wind close offshore.
s - s = Stronger wind in bay.

Fig 9.10n Wind along coast,Low offshore

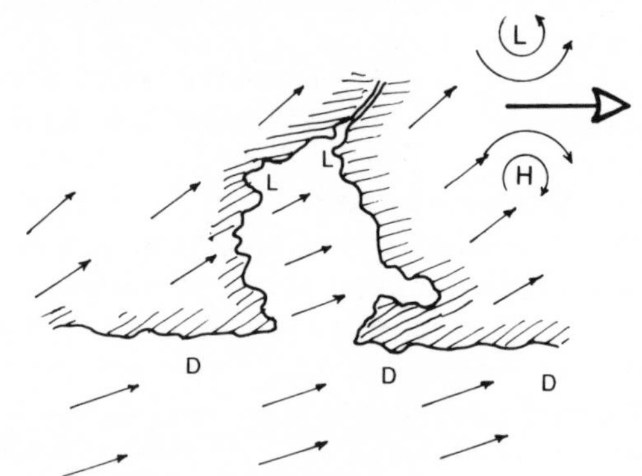

Features as Fig 9.12s, except that:-
wind backs over land and becomes lighter.
D - D = Zone of divergence and lighter wind near shore.
L - L = " " " " " " in bay.

Fig 9.12n Low inland, wind along coast

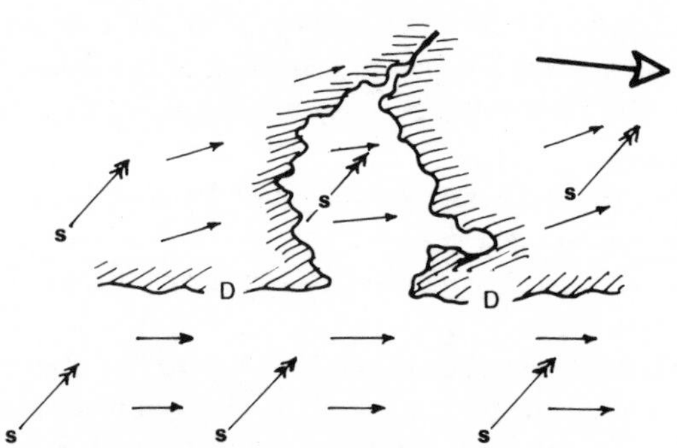

All as Fig 9.13s, except wind backs, not veers over land.
D - D = Zone of divergence and lighter winds - but,
s,s,s = if land heats even slightly, wind will back and freshen.

Fig 9.13n Low inland, gradient wind slightly offshore

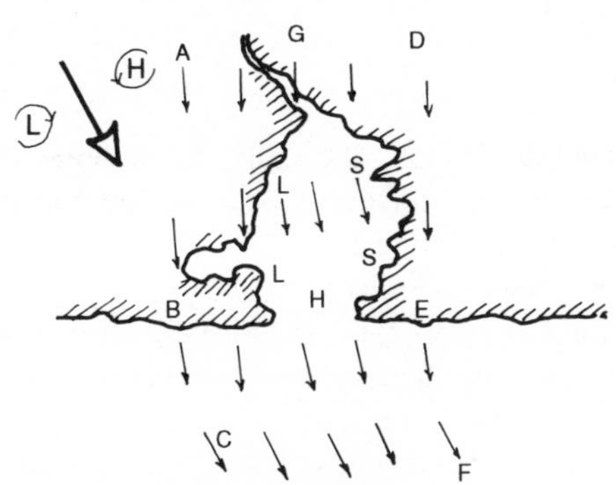

A - B, D - E = Over land, no change.
B - C, E - F = Over sea, backs and freshens.
G - H = Backs and freshens in bay.
S - S = Stronger in convergence between GH & DE.
L - L = Lighter in divergence between GH & AB

Fig 9.9s Wind offshore

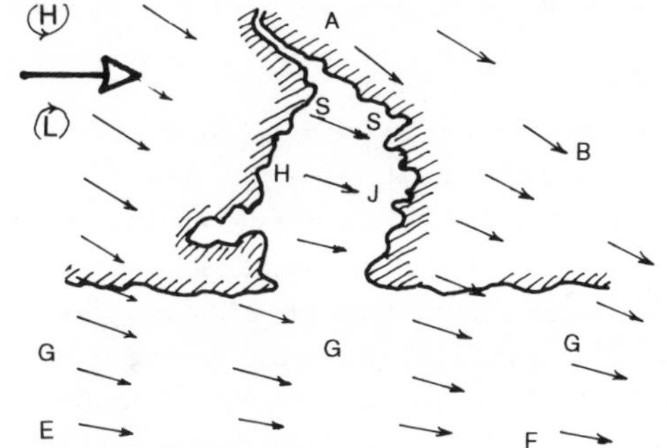

A - B = Over land, no change.
E - F = Over sea, backs and freshens.
G - G = Zone of convergence and stronger wind close to shore.
H - J = Backs over bay.
S - S = Stronger wind in convergence between H & A.

Fig 9.10s Wind along coast, Low offshore.

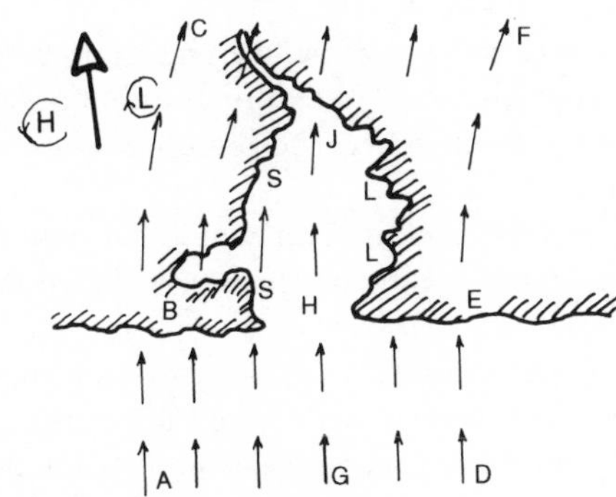

A - B, D - E = Over sea, no change.
G - H - J = In bay, no change.
B - C, E - F = Veers over land, becomes lighter.
S - S = Stronger in convergence between J & C.
L - L = Lighter in divergence between J & F.

Fig 9.11s Wind onshore

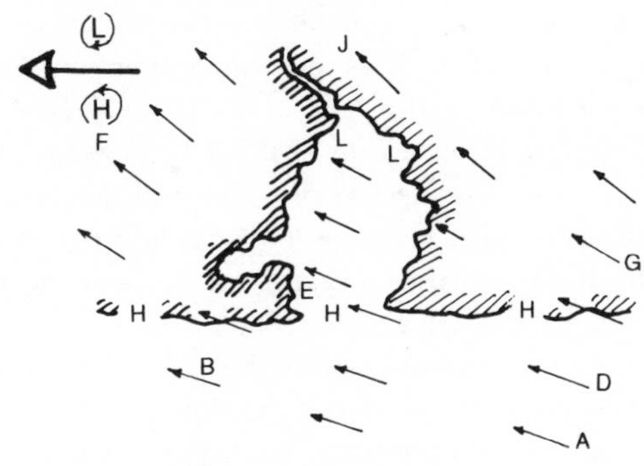

A - B, D - E = Over sea, no change.
E - F, G - J = Veers over land, becomes lighter.
H - H - H = Zone of lighter wind in divergence between BD & FJ.
L - L = Even lighter wind between E & J (divergence).

Fig 9.12s Wind along coast, Low inland

Diagrams for

Southern hemisphere

note that the principle remains true;-

Wind is stronger near shore - nearer High

L = Distant low
H = Distant high
→ = Gradient wind

These are the effects which commonly occur when there is negligible temperature difference between land and water. Disregard these principles if significant temperature difference exists or develops.

Figs 9.9 to 9.13 (s) Shoreline effects - South

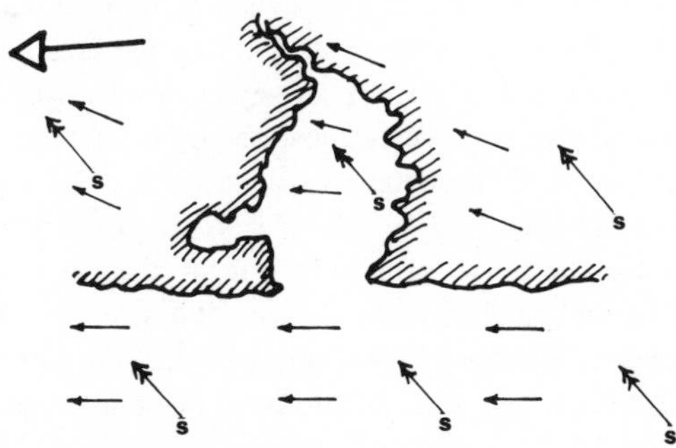

Broadly as Fig 9.12 above, but:-
if land heats even slightly, sea breeze effect will cause wind to swing onshore and freshen, as **s-s.**

Fig 9.13s Gradient wind slightly offshore, Low inland

In this area, there is no escaping the, 'but in the other hemisphere', proviso. For the convenience of readers everywhere, I have drawn reversed diagrams so that there is one for each hemisphere.

The mechanisms which are built into each of these diagrams are:

Friction

The effect of friction was touched on in describing the 'quadrant effect'. Basically, the unimpeded gradient wind blows almost along the isobars. Over the smoother sea, the surface wind is slowed a little, and is skewed about 10 degrees towards low pressure. Over the rougher land surface, the wind is slowed much more and is skewed towards low pressure much more – by about 35 degrees.

This is the fundamental effect of the shoreline, the wind direction over the sea will be different by about 25 degrees from its direction over the nearby land. In the northern hemisphere the wind will veer as it blows from land to sea. In the southern hemisphere it will back. (For quick recall, I use the acronyms VENOS=Veer North to Sea, and BASOS=Back South to Sea.) If you sail well inland or well out to sea, this is all that matters.

Closer to the coastline, either just to seaward, or just inland, as for example in harbour racing, the question of where and how this back or veer will occur becomes of the utmost tactical importance.

Winds which are mainly onshore and offshore will not be affected by a shoreline until they reach it.

An onshore wind (Fig. 9.11) will remain true in direction as it approaches any flat coastline. The back or veer will occur inland from the coast over a distance which in light airs will be short – say one kilometre – and in strong winds will extend further – up to perhaps ten kilometres.

If there are cliffs or hills more than about 200 metres high close to the shoreline, the oncoming wind will be slowed to windward of them, deflected along and around them if they are continuous, or funnelled through any gaps there may be between them, and the wind speed and direction close to windward of such hills will reflect these slowed and deflected flows.

An offshore wind (Fig. 9.9) will remain true over the land, and the back or veer will occur only to seaward of the coastline. Again, the stronger the wind, the longer will be the distance over which the curve will extend. Small bays, harbours or lakes of, for example, one to two kilometres size will be ignored by the stronger winds, but in light winds substantial curve can be expected between their windward and leeward shores. As noted below, any such curve will cause a wind speed difference to develop across the waterway. The wind speed will become stronger due to convergence on the side the wind blows towards, and lighter due to divergence on the side it blows away from.

Except when the wind blows directly onshore or offshore, it will be the other three factors which will most influence the position of the curve.

Orientation and convergence/divergence

When winds blow mainly parallel to the shoreline, the differences in direction due to friction cause convergence and divergence. The broad principles were introduced in Section 9.3. At this smaller scale and lower level, these motions become more obvious.

When the wind blows mainly along the coast and low pressure is to seaward, (Fig. 9.10), the slowed wind over the land will be skewed more towards the low pressure to seaward than the wind over the sea, and so the two wind directions, one over the land and the other over the nearby sea, will converge – they will blow somewhat towards each other. This 'Low Offshore – Convergence' (the acronym LOC is useful) situation will be true in both hemispheres. The congesting air will be forced both to accelerate and rise. There will usually be one or more bands of stronger wind, with the primary band over the sea close to and parallel with the coast. Other bands, parallel and diminishing in strength, may occur further out to sea. These may sometimes be capped with low clouds. Most of the change of wind direction will occur within the width of this band or bands. Because of the overall convergence, the weather will tend to be cloudy.

When the wind blows mainly along the coast but low pressure is inland (Figs 9.12 and 9.13), the slowed wind over the land will be deflected more towards low pressure and away from the wind over the sea. These two wind directions – the wind over the land and the wind over the nearby sea – will diverge, i.e. they will blow somewhat away from each other. Again, this, 'Low Inland – Divergence' (acronym LID) situation is true in both hemispheres. The upper air tends to subside into the area between them.

This causes a wide band of lighter winds which will extend further on the landward than the seaward side of the coastline. The change of wind direction will occur mainly within the width of this lighter-wind area. Generally, this zone will be marked by clearer skies or fewer clouds.

The reason for separating the 'Low Inland, Divergent' case into 'Slightly Onshore', Fig. 9.12, and 'Slightly Offshore', Fig. 9.13, will become clear as soon as we look at what happens when the land becomes warm.

The diagrams indicate the expectations which would be reasonable if friction, orientation, and convergence/divergence were the only factors to operate near a shore.

In the real world, all the other factors which effect the surface wind everywhere else – the change, wave, High or Low dominant, heat, and cloud factors – these will all continue to influence the surface wind in exactly the same way as is usual. They do not stop acting just because there happens to be a coastline nearby. All that the coastline does is introduce a few extra factors which make the local mix a little more interesting. Figs 9.9 to 9.13 seek only to draw attention to these extra factors.

For example, when the land surface becomes warmed by the sun, the customary isolated thermal, cell or roll patterns will form over the heated land. Wherever the wind blows offshore, – and whether the shore is the upwind edge of a small lake or a major coastline makes no difference – any boat which sails downwind and close to that shoreline will experience the full effect of these land-generated thermal patterns. This effect will attenuate with increasing distance downwind. This will also be the region within which the wind will back or veer. So the real-world situation is that the attenuating unsteadiness due to thermal excitation, and the back or veer in direction due to differences of skew, plus any crosswind increase or decrease in wind speed due to convergence or divergence, will all combine in the area immediately downwind of the shoreline.

This is the cauldron where most of us choose to sail! I am reminded of the ancient Chinese curse – 'May you live in interesting times'. Sailors could paraphrase this as, 'May you sail in interesting places'.

Gentle heat – a special case

This is what Fig. 9.13 is about. When the land becomes a little warmer than the sea, and there is divergence and there is an offshore component for counterflow, ('LID, Low Inland, Heated'), a micro-scale mechanism can develop which is similar to the beginnings of a sea breeze. It takes the form of a horizontal helix or spiral in the wind over the coast. The axis of the helix is horizontal and parallel with the coast. The helix skews the wind direction more inshore at the surface and offshore at height. It is flattened in the sense that it is always shallow but can be, in the extreme, several kilometres wide.

In this situation the wind near the coast can swing onshore through many degrees, and also freshen. The distance offshore at which this onshore swing begins can extend to several kilometres to seaward of the coastline, to the chagrin of race officers who may be trying to set courses far enough out to sea to avoid, 'land effects'. This heat-driven wind is common whenever these special conditions occur. It can co-exist with and within the flow of a mature sea breeze, wherever a few kilometres of the shoreline of a bay happen to be almost aligned with the local direction of the fully developed sea breeze.

From what has been written above, it will be obvious that this is one of those situations in which a small difference in the direction of the gradient wind and/or the heating can cause a big change in the strength and direction of the surface wind close to the shore. More importantly, this direction change will be the reverse of that which would otherwise be expected. As an example, let us assume a situation where low pressure inland causes a gradient wind which blows slightly onshore as in Fig. 9.12. In this situation there will be opposition to counterflow, so the, 'mini sea breeze', cannot develop.

Let us assume that the Low moves so that the wind direction changes to the point where it will blow slightly offshore, as in Fig. 9.13. In Fig. 9.12 the wind direction is slightly onshore and the wind speed is lighter at the shoreline (due to divergence), and is stronger both out to sea and also further inland. In Fig. 9.13 this situation remains, only the direction has changed. But if in the Fig. 9.13 case the land heats, the spiral can get going, and the wind near the coast will suddenly swing onshore again and simultaneously freshen to become strongest at the coastline.

So far, we have looked at shoreline effects which are bigger than, say, one kilometre. The mechanisms above are understandable and predictable on 'broad-brush' reasoning, and the evidence of their patterns appears on the traces of anemographs from appropriate sites.

When we focus on smaller detail, we find that, at a scale of say 100 to 500 metres there are sometimes small, exceptional flows which certainly exist and repeat predictably, but they are harder to understand. An example is that offshore winds will veer over the sea (in the northern hemisphere), in a curve some kilometres long. But on a smaller scale, David Houghton has observed that a cooled offshore wind will sometimes initially curve the other way, i.e. it will back for the first few hundred metres immediately offshore and only later commence its inevitable veer, as in Fig. 9.9n. David suggests that the surface wind responds immediately to the reduction of land-surface drag, and responds only later to Coriolis. Other, similar local flows exist. All that these small-scale, exceptional examples indicate is that the wind flows near shores possess great richness of variety.

9.7 The chilled wind situation

There are parts of the world where the water temperature can be many degrees colder than both the adjacent land surface and the air when the wind is offshore. Where and why these are likely to occur has been noted in Section 7.13 – *The chilled winds*. In these situations the wind will not be merely cooled. It will be chilled to the point where its density is increased so much that the dynamics are altered. The heavier air cannot be lifted so far by the turbulence, so the boundary layer becomes shallower, and more concentrated, and colder yet, and separated from the gradient wind above by a more intense inversion. Its depth remains greater than that of a sea breeze or funnelling wind, but is much less than is normal for a gradient wind.

These shallower, more stable flows behave differently.

The shallowness increases the wind-wave frequency.

The increased stability makes the changes in wind direction very smooth. There are none of the short term aberrations in wind direction which are a constant factor in all unchilled winds.

The increased stability also makes the wind speed very uniform across large areas.

The strangest effect is due to the abnormal influence of friction on the increasingly shallow and isolated layer. Normally, the smoother water surface results in the surface wind over the sea blowing faster than over the land, and this is what the differences of Figs 9.9 to 9.13 are all about. But if the chilling is intense enough the boundary layer can become sluggish to the point where it moves more slowly than the warm buoyant boundary layer over the nearby much warmer land.

When this occurs all the skew and convergence and divergence factors will reverse. This phenomenon can persist for a few hundred metres in a marginal case, and for fifty kilometres in a vigorous case. There is no way that a racing helmsman can be certain whether reversal is occurring or of the extent to which the reversal will apply.

The diagrams shown are offered as a useful guide as to the dynamic principles which apply when friction is dominant, i.e. when the air, land and water temperatures are not much different from each other. In places where the water is unusually cold and the offshore wind is chilled, temperature can dominate, to the point where the patterns can attenuate to zero and in the extreme case can reverse. In such situations all logic based on friction should be discarded.

There can be shades of this in places where both the land and the air become unusually hot in the afternoon. This can create a situation in offshore wind conditions in which water of normal temperature can appear abnormally cold to that particular heated air, and again a local shallow, slower boundary layer can develop and its skew can for a little way offshore be the reverse of that expected from friction factors alone.

I wish it were a simpler world, but it isn't. What comes out of this is that when you sail in places with 'normal' temperatures, the friction-based patterns and logic of Figs 9.9 to 9.13 can be helpful. But when you sail in places or at times when temperature differences become unusually large, then the temperature effects can and will override the friction effects to the point of eliminating them or reversing them.

The defence against being taken unawares by one of these exceptional patterns is to survey the whole racing area as completely as possible before any important race, and certainly prior to a major regatta. Successful crews usually launch early and sail at least the windward leg before the start. You should not only sail up the middle but also check the wind out to and along each layline as well. This may be more than one crew can reasonably accomplish, but there is no reason why two cannot do it.

In Section 4.19 I recounted an extraordinary example of wind analysis and tactics at a pre-Olympic regatta. The background to this had been given me by three brilliant Laser sailors some days earlier. Gus Walker, John Bertrand (the Californian) and Stuart Neff had elected to sail Finns for awhile and had come to Tallinn for the experience.

'Our Coach isn't here so we are on our own. We don't have much information about Tallinn Bay so we felt that the best thing we could do was to find out more about it. We think that the three of us are all sailing at about the same speed, so we have spent our days sailing in pairs. We start exactly together, sail on opposite tacks for two minutes, tack at two minutes exactly, sail for a further two minutes, and stop at four minutes exactly. We note and record the wind speed and direction, where we are in the bay, and whether the boat which sailed right or left finished ahead and by how much. We have repeated this to the point where we are now beginning to understand what is happening around the bay. We wonder if you can help us better understand why it is happening? May we join with your group and listen in on the briefings and contribute to the de-briefings so that we may all learn more about this bay?'

This is Laser type co-operation in action. Is it so surprising that these three newcomers to Finns, between them, were able to win all the Finn races, even though they were sailing against almost all of the helmsmen who had dominated that class for years?

9.8 The land breezes

There are two sorts of land breeze. The first is the 'downhill' Katabatic wind, or land breeze. The second is the 'uphill' Anabatic wind, which is not a common sailing wind.

'Downhill' – Katabatic winds

In previous chapters it has been pointed out that because only the top 6mm or so of dry land surface is heated by the sun each day, the rise in surface temperature of this small mass can be very large. Conversely, at night when there is no incoming solar radiation, the dry land surface will radiate the excess heat of this top 6mm towards the near-absolute-zero of space. Unless there are clouds or fog to act as a reflecting blanket, the surface can become very cold. The everyday experience of morning frost on the ground even though the air at face level remains warmer than 0 deg.C indicates how cold the surface can become due to radiation.

Exactly as air in contact with a warm surface is warmed by conduction, the air which lies over and in contact with a cold surface will be chilled. But the behaviour of the warmed and the cooled air is totally different. Air which has been warmed will rise as soon as it has been warmed a little, and so will make way for new air which in its turn will be warmed and rise. In this way the excess surface heat is transferred into a progressively thickening layer of air, all of which is only a little warmer than the air above. The presence of wind makes no difference to this process.

Chilled air is different. It tends to sink, because it is denser. Since air which is chilled by a cold surface is already on that surface, it will lie where it is if the surface is level and the windspeed is less than five knots. As the night progresses and the surface becomes colder, this denser heavier colder film of air simply becomes colder and thicker. The temperature difference which develops at the boundary between the chilled and the unchilled air can be much greater than anything we have so far considered. The cold air remains completely separate from the warmer air above, and can persist for several hours into a new day. It is everyday experience that when the arrival of a morning wind begins to move the air above – when, for instance, low clouds move across the sky, or the leaves of trees on rising land vibrate in an upper breeze, the calm cold film will persist for longest in the bottoms of the hollows or valleys – which is exactly where we find the water that we sail on.

In any wind of more than about six knots, turbulence will scrub the surface and mix the chilled air, as it is cooled, throughout the depth of the boundary layer. This will prevent initial separation of the cold air – there is never dew nor frost on the ground after windy nights. But if a lull of five knots or less admits laminar flow for a little while, the stagnant film will develop. Unless a stronger wind which returns thereafter is quite strong and persistent, it may simply blow across the top of the stagnant cold film because the cold film may grow faster than the wind aloft can scrub away its upper surface.

The marginal situation can be more than interesting. At the 1978 Balti Regatt, on one day the water temperature was about 6 deg.C and the air about 10 deg.C. The water chilled the lower air, and over about 98 percent of the surface of Tallinn Bay the surface was glassy for most of the day, and yachts moved at about half a knot or less. But here and there the breeze aloft ruptured the film, and patches of the water surface, 200 to 300 metres upwind/downwind and about 50 metres crosswind, shimmered in the sun with waves typical of a 6 knot breeze. The frustrating factor was that as each new patch appeared, the rupture immediately began to 'heal' from the downwind end, so the area of wind retreated 'upwind' much faster than any drifting sailboat could sail. Within a few minutes the chilled film had been restored and the surface was glassy again.

If the surface is not level, the situation changes. The chilled denser air will begin to flow down any slope. It thickens and flows faster as it sweeps up progressively more chilled air. New Zealand's Canterbury Plains slope uniformly from an elevation of about 400 metres near the mountains to sea level 80 kilometres to the East. Over this uniform slope the cold air flows evenly to the sea. Along several hundred miles of north-south coastline, this westerly wind blows every morning when the gradient wind is five knots or less and the night has been clear. There are occasional hills, and on these no frost forms above a height of about 150 metres, so these are essentially shallow flows. The northerly flow shown in Fig. 3.6 is similar.

Over the land, these Katabatic winds are the steadiest of all winds. Fig. 3.6 shows that light airs can be truly steady and without pattern. Katabatic breezes are so shallow that no mechanism other than turbulence can develop. In extreme cases the cold flow can be up to 15 deg.C colder than the air above. This can cause a density difference of about 5 per cent which in turn can suppress the depth of a turbulent boundary layer to perhaps one quarter of its customary value.

Where there are valleys to concentrate the flow, the cold air will behave more like a large river. In Sydney, the morning cold-air drainage out of the Cumberland Basin starts as an even drift generally toward the coast, but it progressively concentrates into and flows down the shallow winding river valleys. Ultimately it reaches the waterways, and flows out to sea as a series of sluggish cold jets between the various headlands. Higher up the hills the air is often calm. Where the country is steeper the winds can be stronger, such as the Katabatic wind which drains the mountain basin to the north of Riva and Torbole. This gives the famous strong and regular morning sailing winds between the mountain walls at the northern end of Lake Garda.

The land surface may cool at night, but the water doesn't. So as soon as a land breeze flows over water, it will immediately be heated, and heated very strongly. Within the shallow flow rolls will form where the temperature difference is greatest and the heating is strongest, i.e. closest to the shore. Downstream the patterns will normally sequence through waves and cells as the shallow airflow loses its drive force and loses speed as it warms. Before long it reaches the same temperature equilibrium with the water surface as the gradient wind of that area, and becomes a part of that wind. Normally this will be light air or nearly so, otherwise the land breeze could not have developed in the first place.

Crews who sail at night or early morning in lakes or near coasts will often enjoy land breezes. They will be strongest near the upwind shore. When they are small and weak they may be very shallow indeed – stories abound of brief periods when the upper and lower parts of a close-in ocean racer's rig were in different winds.

When you find yourself sailing in one of these winds, the key facts of the valley-floor wind will be:

1. It must necessarily be a very thin flow which has no option but to follow the curves of the valley floor, so its larger curves in direction will be as predictable as the flow of a river.

2. Because it is thin, it will have no gusts.

3. Because it is thin, any patterns within it will repeat quickly.

4. The air above this thin boundary layer must be hotter, so its depth will be limited by an inversion (similar the High dominant situation). Any patterns will therefore repeat regularly.

5. Its extent in distance and its life in time will both be short. As it flows offshore over warmer water the thin flow, strongly heated, will 'boil' and quickly break up. As the upwind land surface warms, the supply of cold air, and so the land breeze itself, will vanish.

6. Its behaviour will repeat, and can be anticipated but only by local knowledge. Because there will be large differences over short distances and times, the scale is too small for intuitive forecasting to expect to be accurate.

There are other sources of cold air. When cold post-frontal winds wash over the Swiss Alps, the upland valley basins can become full of very cold air. The weather system flows on. The cold air can remain trapped. For some days thereafter the pool of chilled air can escape through gaps in the basin walls, and flow down the river valleys, underneath the gradient wind of the moment, as relatively shallow cold winds so recognisable that they have been given local names. The *Mistral* is one example. In the case of these winds the land and the water surfaces over which they flow may well be at about the same temperature – as during any afternoon – in which case there will be no fierce heating over the water, and no sequence of patterns downwind from the windward shore.

'Uphill' – Anabatic wind

If a film of heated air develops in a hot pocket on the sloping side of some sun-heated valley, its buoyancy will cause it to rise. Over a hot surface which is level, it will separate from the surface and develop into an isolated thermal. But where the land surface slopes sufficiently, it will begin to flow up the slope. As soon as it begins to move it will tend to remain attached to the surface, As it flows upwards it will sweep up more and more heated air, and in this way a local wind mechanism develops in which a thin layer of heated air flows up the heated hillsides. Its place is taken by the cooler air from the valley floor, and this air in turn is replaced by air from further down the valley with exactly the same inversion mechanism as with funnelling winds. So the fully developed mechanism is one in which a valley-floor wind flows up the valley, and bleeds off up the heated hillsides. This is the Anabatic wind. These again are very shallow winds which cannot develop gusts. They are common in hot, dry, steep and hilly country. This is not where we usually find harbours and lakes and recreational sailboats. Lake Garda is an internationally famous exception.

HSP MkX This boat sails faster than the wind, both upwind and down, in some wind strengths

Chapter 10
Wind Appraisal and the *Stability Index*

10.1 The parts of the puzzle

The preceding chapters have tried to give some understanding of why the wind blows, why it gusts and lulls and backs and veers, how these alternations are driven and the particular pattern to be expected in each case, why these alternations are sometimes fast and sometimes slow and why they are sometimes predictable and sometimes random.

How can we use this understanding to help us finish at the front of the fleet or closer to it? Let us look at some real examples, to see what are the vital factors.

1. The Munich Olympics

You are on your way to winning the Dragon class' gold medal, but you don't know this yet. You are adjusting your sails better than others and so are the only competitor who can match the 'heavies' in the heavy conditions and the 'light air kings' in the light conditions, and everybody else in between. You have decided to sail a 'minimum-time' series, and have won the first two heats.

Your problem is that the previously compact oscillations have become slower and uncertain. Which way should you now steer as you approach each windward and leeward mark?

To win in these conditions, there is no question of covering any particular boat. Instead, in order to keep on sailing the minimum-time course and so keep on winning, you need to know all the skills of sailing the lifts for as long as there will probably be one or more full waves between you and the next mark; when and how to sail the headers in the part-wave situation which must always occur as soon as the distance between you and the windward mark becomes less than the full-wave distance; and when to acknowledge that you do not really know – and neither does anybody else – and how in these conditions to sail defensively for minimum loss whatever happens, and also for best position to exploit opportunity as soon as the picture becomes predictable. (John Cuneo kept his head, kept on doing exactly this, and won.)

2. The same Olympic regatta at Kiel, 1972

The last race of the Star class was sailed in a wandering breeze. As between Forbes and Pettersen, whoever finished ahead of the other would win the gold medal. Both boats started perfectly. Immediately after the start, Forbes used a momentary header to tack, cross, tack, and establish close-cover on Pettersen.

What did each boat most need to win?

In this situation it was pure match racing. Exploitation of windshifts for minimum time meant nothing. The only possibility for the boat behind to pass was to use one of the many random lighter-patch opportunities which could be expected, on probabilities, during the hours of the race. The method would be to encourage the leading, covering boat to sail into a lighter patch and break cover by staying in stronger wind and sailing around him. This calls for a perfect sense of the wind pattern of the wandering breeze.

The task of the boat ahead was harder. He had to sense the wind ahead so accurately that he could both avoid the lighter patches and also frustrate the efforts of the covered boat to sail him into them. (David Forbes did exactly this, stayed ahead of Pettersen and won the Star gold medal.)

3. World Laser championships, Rio de Janeiro (Section 1.6)

Immediately after one start, Tim Alexander found himself last in the big fleet. Some non-raining Cumulus clouds approached, one of which subsequently rained. He improved his position from 104th to 4th in the first windward leg. He was able to do this because he was the only helmsman in the race who knew exactly how to exploit both the inflows near non-raining clouds and the outflows near raining clouds, to maximum advantage.

4. World Tasar championships, Vancouver

In the final race, the finish line was just upwind of the convergent wind zone at the entrance to English Bay. A few hundred metres from the finish line the second and third boats converged with nothing between them. If one of them could finish second in that race, he would also finish second in the World Championship. What did he most need?

He needed to know the rather strange effect of a convergent wind on the positions of two boats in close company, so that when he tacked close to the other boat, he could do so on the side which would be advantaged in this converging-wind situation.

5. World Laser championships, Adelaide

You are on your way to winning the world Laser championships, but you don't know it yet. The race has started in a sea breeze. During the early beat, the wind backs steadily. What do you need to know to finish well?

You need to know about bridging changes and funnelling winds. Also the fact that the sea breeze, after this bridging change, will become a funnelling wind and what will be the direction of this particular funnelling wind. This means that you will know the direction at which this bridging change will stabilise and around which it will oscillate thereafter. So as soon as this 'progressive shift' reaches this direction you can switch from the fastest part-wave single-curve technique (of sailing the header first), to the fastest full-wave oscillating-wind technique of sailing the lifts.

Stuart Wallace had made it his business to become familiar with these waters (they were not his home waters) before the regatta. When this situation did occur during one race, his thorough preparation was sufficient to enable him to do the right thing with confidence and accuracy. He won the Laser world championship.

In each of the examples above, a different sense of priorities, a knowledge of a different wind pattern and a different sailing skill was needed to win. But a certain logic is common to them all. In each case the winning helmsman or crew

Recognised the kind of wind which was blowing and its probable pattern.

Decided whether the expected pattern was:

a) *Predictable and regular*

b) *Predictable but irregular (eg. clouds)*

c) *Unpredictable.*

Knew the minimum-time path upwind, crosswind and downwind through each pattern.

Knew the maximum-safety technique for close-covering and controlling an opponent upwind, crosswind and downwind through each pattern.

Adopted either the minimum-time or the maximum-safety technique which was correct in the tactical circumstances of the moment.

Let us look first at the way a skilled crew will forecast 'what pattern today?' and then at the tactics they will use to exploit each particular pattern.

10.2 The kind of wind

The best way to forecast 'today's pattern' is to approach the problem in two steps. First work out the kind of wind which will blow. Once you are confident of the wind type, it then becomes much easier to forecast the probable pattern.

In chapter 3 we saw that, everywhere, there can be either of two different kinds of wind, light airs or breezes. In Sections 9.2, 9.3 and 9.4 we saw that, near shores, there can be a third kind of wind, the sea breeze. In Section 9.7 we saw that in very special conditions there can be a fourth kind of wind, the land breeze. These four all behave differently because each wind is the surface flow of a different kind of boundary layer:

Light airs – have shallow, laminar-type boundary layers.

Breezes – have deep, turbulent boundary layers which may or may not be stabilised by an inversion at their upper surface.

Sea breezes and funnelling winds – have shallow turbulent boundary layers which are always stabilised by an inversion at their upper surfaces.

Land breezes – have abnormally shallow boundary layers which are always stabilised by an intense inversion. They may be either laminar or turbulent.

Before travelling

The best place to start is with the weather map and the forecast. Governments co-operate by adopting the methods and standards of an organisation called the World Meteorological Organisation. This has two primary functions. The first is to report and record, accurately and to a standard format, what the weather – rainfall, wind, temperature, etc. – actually was. The second is to try to forecast, for the benefit of the local population, what will be the weather tomorrow and further into the future. The service exists, no individual can hope to do better, so use it.

For a few days prior to, and during, any important regatta, cut the weather maps out of the newspaper and file them side by side in sequence. This will enable you to look at them and sense the flow, and particularly the rate of flow, of the Highs, the Lows, and the fronts. Note the air temperatures and the temperature range swept from warm pre-frontal to cold post-frontal winds. Find out the water temperature. Usually, newspapers give 'yesterday's' weather map and report, and 'today's' projected weather map and a forecast based on that projection. The better newspapers from other cities and continents are available world-wide, and this process can start some days before you travel. Television may be more vivid and up to date for the local viewer, but TV reports lack detail, and do not cover distant places.

If you compare each day's forecast with the following day's report, you will build up a very good mental picture of the reliability of the forecast. Forecasting is not easy, and it is not an exact science. A lifetime of long-range flying plus high-level sailing and coaching has left me with respect for forecasters in that they are usually reasonably accurate as to the sequence of what will happen, but much less accurate as to its time of occurrence.

From the point of view of both the pilot and the racing helmsman, the fact that the timing may often be wrong does not at all detract from the value of the information provided, so long as the sequence remains correct. You will help your own understanding of the weather at the regatta area by familiarising yourself with flow which is typical of that region, by establishing whether you can have reasonable faith in the sequence, and then mentally positioning yourself within the system flow so that your sense of sequence begins to align itself with reality. As you focus more closely on the weather, the wind type and the air and water temperatures at the venue, you will find yourself beginning to race in those waters, in imagination, long before you leave home.

A practical point: forecasters are human and have foibles. Beware the 'Sabbato Cataclysmic' – the apparently total break in the flow of the weather maps which sometimes occurs when forecasters change shifts, usually on a Sunday.

When you race in different places, your inbuilt sense of what is likely to happen may become disorientated in three primary respects:-

1. When you cross the equator and sail in the other hemisphere, only a major and continuous mental effort can align your thoughts with the reversed flows. It is like driving on the other side of the road – you can do it, but it takes constant conscious effort to override the habits of a lifetime, and this overt conscious effort so loads your mind at first that it tends to inhibit fluency and the ability to think ahead. I find two things helpful. If you sail with a partner who is committed and knowledgeable, and if you also deliberately allocate time for discussion before you launch for each race, you can then sail the forthcoming race, together, in imagination. This exercise enables you, together, to uncover in a relaxed atmosphere each of the factors which is likely to be important today, and to discuss and analyse in an unhurried way the effects of the reversed flows on each of these factors. The advantage of this process is that both of you will prime yourselves mentally, prior to the start, with the facts which are likely to be important during the race ahead. You can then discuss the unfolding patterns, fluently and with confidence, as you sail. You cannot hope to do better than this.

2. Weather systems pass by at different speeds at different latitudes. At 20 degrees south, over the tropical coasts of Queensland, weather systems tend to repeat at a frequency of about one every ten to fourteen days. Sydney, at 33 degrees south, is at about the latitude of the seven day repetition – in bad years we can have long sequences during which all the weekends are foul, and all the mid-weeks fine. Nearer 40 degrees south, over Melbourne, systems repeat at about a two to three day interval. At Marstrand and Tallinn, near 60 degrees north, it is normal for two entire systems to pass over in a single day. It is quite difficult to force the mind to override its inbuilt 'clock', and to think fluently in terms of a system flow which is faster than expected. The suggested exercise of cutting out the weather maps and considering the

flow, and the rate of flow, for some days prior to the regatta, is aimed at synchronising your mind with the local flow speed in a gradual and painless manner.

3. A third major disorientation can be the flow pattern at high latitudes. Most recreational sailing takes place in temperate latitudes. It is normal in Japan, North America, Europe, and Australia for the centres of Lows to pass between you and the poles. The effect of this is that most of us are accustomed to weather in which Lows between us and the poles move in a westerly direction, and the winds they drive are also predominantly westerly. Everything in this 'normal' situation flows from the west, and we become skilled in judging different rates of westerly flow. But when we travel to sail at higher latitudes, the Low centres will often lie between us and the equator. The Lows will still move from the west, but the winds between the Lows and the polar High will blow from the east. It is all perfectly logical, but it comes as a bit of a shock to the mind, particularly when the Lows pass by so fast!

Again, the exercise of filing the weather maps side by side and focussing on the system flow at the regatta venue for some time before travelling can establish some sort of familiarity before the event. Where the venue is in a different climatic regime and the regatta is important, this process of focussing on the regatta area weather, its wind types, air and water temperatures, and probable patterns, should start a long time before you begin to travel.

At the regatta

At the regatta, keep on filing and studying the weather map. Each morning, you should have a clear mental picture of:

The synoptic situation.
Whether the situation is High or Low dominant.
The gradient wind direction.
The boundary layer depth.
The expected air and water temperatures.
What changes are likely in the hours ahead.

Pre-race and while racing

Direct observation will establish whether you are sailing in light air or breeze.

Light air

1. Light air, particularly in marginal and changing conditions, is indicated visually by a glassiness of the water surface.

2. This glassiness of surface is just as apparent when there are waves as when the water is flat. Supporting sensory observations can be very useful when visual reference becomes unreliable as in rain, or when the water is fouled by oil. The following observations all indicate light air:

3. Feeble total force available from the sails.
4. Absence of periodic sudden increase or reduction of force with fluctuation and gust.
5. Absence of the feel of wind on the face.

Breeze

Breeze is indicated, in marginal conditions, by:

1. Pronounced surface ripple in place of glassiness.
2. The feel of wind on the face.
3. Substantial force from the sails.
4. Periodic and sudden increase and decrease in force with each fluctuation and gust.

Land breeze

A land breeze, of either light air or breeze strength, is indicated by five factors. If:

1. The night sky has been clear.
2. The hour is pre-dawn or early morning.
3. The locality is one at which land breezes are common.
4. The flow is several degrees colder than the expected daytime temperature.

5. The wind direction is that direction customary for the land breeze in that area.
That wind is a land breeze. This is the easiest of all winds to recognise.

The sea breeze
The sea breeze is established by elimination:
1. Winds which do not blow onshore cannot be sea breezes. ('Onshore' is used as in Section 9.4, i.e. consider bridging changes.)
2. Unless there is heating, there cannot be a sea breeze.
3. When there is heating, and the breeze is onshore, whether or not that breeze is a sea breeze or a gradient wind can be best established by use of the *quadrant effect*. Three further 'rules of thumb' can be useful when the situation is uncertain:
4. If there are clouds with bases lower than about 5,000ft, and their direction of movement is similar to the direction of the present surface wind, that wind cannot be a sea breeze.
5. If there are significant gusts and lulls, this indicates a deep boundary layer. This can be no sea breeze.
6. A funnelling wind can blow *only* from its typical direction. From any other direction it cannot be that funnelling wind. If it has significant gusts and lulls, it is no funnelling wind.

10.3 The probable pattern

Once the kind of wind has been worked out, it becomes easier to anticipate the probable pattern. Since all thermal patterns depend critically on the presence or absence of surface heating, it becomes essential to know the air and water temperatures accurately. Temperature differences as small as 1 deg.C can drive a vigorous thermal pattern which will be absent when the temperature difference is zero. Guessing the temperature is no longer good enough. A small thermometer has become a vital part of the racing crews' kit.

All water which is deep, or which flows as with the current of a river, or which is continually mixed by tidal surge, will remain constant in temperature for all practical purposes for the period of a regatta. Except in two particular situations, the water temperature need be measured only once:

1. Shallow water which does not flow, such as a shallow lake or a shallow bay in a lake, may warm detectably during several days of strong heating.
2. The upwelling situation. This can give a very big surface temperature change. It occurs when a warm surface layer is blown downwind by a strong and sustained offshore wind. In the Great Lakes of North America this is called 'upwelling'. A warm surface layer of water at 22 or 23 deg.C and perhaps 2 metres deep can be blown away from the shore and up to tens of kilometres downwind. Water as cold as 8 or 9 deg.C is then uncovered near the upwind shore for a few days. The effect on wind patterns of a surface temperature change of this magnitude is profound, because it will introduce chilling.

All of the many patterns described in the preceding chapters must develop within one of the four sorts of boundary layer. Summarised, these are:

1. The light air patterns.
The boundary layer of light air is laminar in nature, is shallow – 0 to 50 metres – in depth, has no finite upper surface, is feeble in energy, and is dominated by viscosity. It can accept no friction-driven energy from a wind above. It can develop no momentum-driven patterns within itself.

If the air is not heated from below, the flow will be steady. This situation is infrequent in temperate latitudes in daytime sailing.

When the air is heated, the motions and patterns will always be small – of the order of 100 metres repetition dimension – and will almost always be unpredictable except by direct observation of the lines of wind on the surface. The different forms which these heat-driven patterns can take have been described in earlier chapters. Summarised:

In light airs:

a) When the air is cooled the flow will be steady and without pattern.
b) When the air is warmed:

(i) In gentle heating the patterns will probably be unsteady (cellular); in moderate heating they will probably be pulsing; in stronger heating yet they will probably become oscillating or ribboning;

(ii) These patterns will be unpredictable other than by observation of their surface effects;

(iii) These patterns will all be small;

(iv) The distance from the mark at which 'part-wave' technique should be adopted will usually be about 50 to 75 metres.

2. The breeze patterns.

The boundary layer of the breeze is turbulent and deep – 500 metres minimum, usually 1,000 to 2,000 metres, and more when heated. It has a finite upper surface. It can accept friction energy at its upper surface, and can accept both friction and heat energy at its lower surface. It is dominated by momentum. It can develop momentum motions within itself (the gust mechanism). It can develop wave motions which are driven by friction from above or by heat from below or by both. The surface component of the orbital motions of these waves causes alternations in the direction or speed of the surface wind.

Because the boundary layer is so deep, the waves are large, and the interval between successive alternations in the surface pattern is long – typically 20 to 60 minutes when the observer is at rest.

In normal circumstances these wave motions themselves influence the local depth of the boundary layer in an unstable manner, to the point where the waves become irregular in size and spacing, and the consequent oscillations of direction and recurrent changes of speed of the surface wind pattern become irregular and unpredictable.

In the special yet frequent situation of a synoptic high pressure area, the subsidence inversion which is a part of every High will so stabilise the depth of the boundary layer that the waves will then roll regularly and the alternations of the surface pattern will become regular and predictable.

The boundary layer of the breeze can, in special circumstances, develop three-dimensional cellular motions which are driven by heat alone. Of these cellular motions only one, the wandering breeze, is of practical importance to the racing helmsman. Its typical dimension is of the order of 1,000 metres. Its pattern, like that of unsteady light air, is essentially unpredictable except that the lines of wind on the surface can be observed, and their movement can be better anticipated with a knowledge of the pattern mechanism.

When a three-dimensional wandering breeze situation exists, there can be no two-dimensional wave motions, and the gust mechanism will also be suppressed.

It is relevant here to point out the tactical implications of the wave and pattern sizes of the breeze. Wave frequencies of 20 to 60 minutes are reflected in surface pattern lengths of, typically, 2 to 5 kilometres in the static sense. When you are sailing to windward, the frequency at which you will meet the oncoming waves will be faster, and so the interval and the distance at which you will meet the alternations will typically become less, about 1 to 3 kilometres, and 10 to 30 minutes respectively.

For normal 'round-the-buoys' racing, world-wide, leg lengths of the order of one nautical mile (2 kilometres) are typical. It so happens that the typical wave-size within the boundary layer of the typical temperate-latitude gradient breeze causes the racing helmsman to experience oscillations in the direction of the surface wind at a dimension of about half to twice the length of the typical windward leg.

Nothing could possibly have been contrived which would lead to greater tactical uncertainty on every windward leg.

Summarised:

In Breezes:

a) Only in High dominant situations can wave patterns be regular.

b) In all other situations the motions within the boundary layer will probably be irregular and the patterns unpredictable.

c) In all situations the repetition frequency will be slow and the pattern-size will be large because the boundary layer is deep.

d) When the air is chilled by the water, the oscillations will be smooth and without short-term unsteadiness. (Figs 7.3, 7.4) In these conditions if you gamble and get it wrong, you will lose badly because there is no way to recover.

e) When the air is cooled, the oscillations will be slower, and some short-term aberrations are likely.

f) When the air is warmed by the water, the pattern will be characterised by continuous short-term unsteadiness superimposed on the longer-term oscillations, as in Figs 7.6 and 7.7. In these conditions, if you gamble and get it wrong, you can sometimes recover without disastrous loss by skilful use of the short shifts.

g) The distance from the windward mark at which part-wave or defensive sailing should be adopted will be, typically, 0.5 to 2 kilometres. Except when ocean racing, the leeward mark will sometimes already be within this distance of the windward mark.

3. The sea breeze and funnelling wind patterns

The sea breeze is an abnormally shallow boundary layer which is capped and stabilised by an inversion. Both shallowness and inversion are inherent in the surface sea breeze/upper-level counterflow mechanism. The friction of the sea breeze under the counterflow creates waves on its upper surface. The shallowness of the boundary layer keeps these waves small. The skewing of the direction of the surface breeze causes longitudinal waves and rhythmic oscillations in direction. The control by the inversion keeps them regular. Sea breezes which are developing or mature usually blow with a wave pattern of quick rhythmic oscillations which can be predicted with confidence.

These patterns tend to repeat faster in hotter climates or seasons. Repetition frequencies of 5 to 10 minutes, and upwind/downwind dimensions of 250 to 500 metres are typical in temperate latitudes.

The sea breeze is born each day. It generally establishes directly onshore, and then veers or backs with Coriolis.

In complex coastline situations, the sea breeze may change direction abruptly at some point or points in its development as it relates to progressively larger elements of the coastline. These abrupt changes are called 'bridging changes'.

As the sea breeze decays, the inversion will decay. The surface breeze may continue to blow for awhile due to momentum. In this situation it may thicken, and either slower and irregular or thermal patterns can then appear for awhile.

The funnelling wind is a special case of the sea breeze. It is stronger, its boundary layer is even shallower and it is more intensely stabilised. Its direction is constant – governed by the shorelines between which it blows. It is the most stable and predictable of all winds. Usually, there is negligible change of wind speed across the waterway apart from the fundamental 'stronger wind on the convergent side, and vice versa' factor (Figs 9.9 to 9.13). The wind-waves within it are small and repeat quickly. In the areas where it is accelerating, the oscillations of direction may be negligible (wire-drawing). Conversely, in the areas (if any) where it is slowing and diverging they will be exaggerated (the concertina effect) and large changes in speed will also develop. Summarised:

In sea breezes and funnelling winds:

a) Regular, quickly repeating oscillations of direction are normal.

b) The distance from the windward mark at which part-wave technique should be adopted will usually be about 200 to 400 metres.

c) Sea breezes will veer or back with Coriolis for several hours after onset.

d) Funnelling winds always blow from the same direction.

4. The landbreeze patterns.

The flow of a landbreeze will be steadiest and strongest at the point where the wind leaves the land. Over the water the initially cold air will be strongly and progressively heated, and will become progressively unsteadier and weaker with increasing distance offshore.

5. The cloud patterns.

The inflow pattern near a non-raining, low-based Cumulus cloud, or the outflow pattern near any rain-shower, will override all other patterns while the cloud or shower are nearby.

6. The shore patterns.

The proximity of a shoreline can cause the wind to back or veer, and to become stronger or weaker, as the shoreline is approached. Technically, these are geographic shifts rather than patterns which repeat within the flow. However, because they repeat as the boat moves toward and away from the shore as it sails around the buoys, the simplest mental approach for any crew is to factor them into their wind technique as they sail each leg.

10.4 The stability index

Two common threads run through the preceding sections. The first is that a few simple motions within the boundary layer each lead to recognisable patterns in the direction and the speed of the surface wind. The second is that while these motions are often unsteady and unpredictable, conditions sometimes occur in which they become regular and predictable. The racing helmsman who understands the pattern, and can therefore anticipate the wind's next change, has a great advantage over any rival who does not. If, in addition, he knows when the pattern is regular, and so can also correctly anticipate the time of arrival of that next change, his advantage becomes overwhelming.

Three factors govern the regularity of the motions within the boundary layer:

1. *The depth of the boundary layer*. Within deep layers, complex motions can occur. Within shallow layers, only simple motions are possible. The shallower the layer, the more predictable will be the motions within it.

2. *Whether or not the air is being heated from below*. When thermal energy is added to the boundary layer from a warmer surface, it will cause cell or wave motions which may be complex. When the air is cooled by the surface, these motions will be absent, and the resulting surface patterns will be simpler and more predictable.

3. *Whether or not the depth of the boundary layer is being controlled from above*. When friction energy forms waves on the boundary layer's upper surface, in convergent (Low dominant) or neutral (straight isobar) situations, these waves normally grow in an unstable manner. Some of them grow bigger for awhile at the expense of adjacent waves which become smaller, and nothing is then predictable except the disorder itself. This disorder is reflected in unsteady repetition intervals in the surface wind's oscillations. But when the height of the boundary layer's upper surface is itself controlled by a subsidence inversion, (High dominant, or sea breeze) the tendency of any wave to grow bigger and higher is firmly suppressed, and the wave trains become regular. In this situation the order and rhythm are reflected in regular repetition of the surface patterns.

The orderliness – the regularity – the confidence with which the character and time of arrival of the next change can be predicted is greatest when these three factors are all at their most stable extreme, and vice versa.

A second and vitally important factor is that the uniformity of the wind speed from time to time and from place to place across a regatta area will be steadiest when conditions are most stable, and most unsteady when conditions are most unstable.

The factors which control predictability can be combined into a simple '*stability index*'. It is constructed, scored and used as follows:

The stability index

Factor	**Least Stable**	**Neutral**	**Most Stable**
Convergence or subsidence	Low dominant	Straight isobars	High dominant
Boundary layer thickness	Gradient wind	Sea breeze	Funnelling wind
Surface heating	Air Colder than Surface	No difference	Air warmer than surface

Score each factor: 1 for least stable,
2 for neutral,
3 for most stable.
A fourth factor, '*change*', should be considered but not scored.

Consider approaching the race as follows:

Score 3 or 4 – Expect major and unpredictable changes in both wind speed and wind direction from time to time and from place to place. Assume that no prediction is possible. Sail opportunistically. Sail for wind speed, i.e. sail towards and to remain within the areas of strongest wind.

Score 5, 6 or 7 – When the air is colder than the surface, expect modest and unpredictable changes in both wind speed and wind direction. When the air is warmer than the surface, expect modest and unpredictable changes in the wind direction, with little change in wind speed. If a few regular backs and veers occur from time to time, expect such patterns to break into irregularity without warning. Sail defensively.

Score 8 or 9 – Expect wind speed to be uniform across the race area. Expect the present pattern (of wind direction oscillation) to continue predictably. Sail to plan, to exploit the predictable backs and veers.

As an example, the following is a description of how the *stability index* was used at one major championships. The location was Port Stephens, New South Wales, a harbour which is 25 kilometres long in the east-west direction, and 8 kilometres wide in the north-south direction, and which develops a funnelling wind from the east-north-east whenever the sea breeze blows from the east or north-east. The course area was about 6 kilometres inland from the coast, at a point where the funnelling wind was still accelerating, and so was usually free from the oscillations in direction which develop deeper into the harbour. (Fig 9.8)

Race 2. A weak cold front had recently passed over, so the synoptic situation was, 'Low dominant'. The wind was a moderate post-frontal south-south-westerly, so the wind was, a 'gradient wind'. The air, at 21 deg.C, was 1.5 degrees colder than the water which remained at 22.5 deg. throughout the regatta. The *stability index* was therefore 3, i.e. maximum instability. When sailing to windward, most boats sailed to the left of the rhumb line to take advantage of a stronger favourable ebb tide current through a deeper channel. Mid-race, the clouds cleared and we noticed that the gust marks on the water surface on the right hand side of the course, which was closer to the now strongly heating upwind dry-land surface of a low peninsular, indicated much greater instability. (Consider change). We broke right, hooked into a series of big, sharp edged gusts each of which lifted us about 20 to 25 degrees (some favoured port tack and some starboard), and gained ten places.

Race 3 (the following day). A High was now dominant. Skies were cloudless, heating was fierce, and an east-north-east funnelling wind of about 14 knots had developed by 1300. The air temp was 23 deg.C, water remained at 22.5 deg.C. The *stability index* was therefore 9, i.e. maximum stability. Start time was 1400, and negligible change in conditions was expected. We sailed the course pre-start, and observed that in the very steady funnelling wind, the oscillations were trivial or absent, but that a 7 degree geographic veer was present over the upwind half of the beat. We trusted the index, broke right after the start and shot the corner, and arrived at the windward mark with the leaders. (The author is well past the age at which he has any right to expect to be with the leaders in fresh breezes in this world-champion studded dinghy fleet. In lighter winds things are different.)

Race 4 (the following day). Conditions were identical with those of Race 3, except that this was a morning race with a start time of 1000, (0900 Sun Time). We launched at 0800 Sun Time, and sailed the course in a light but increasing funnelling wind. There were rhythmic oscillating shifts in this breeze, but we felt that this was another case where we should consider the 'change' factor. We reasoned that the cloudless day would continue to heat strongly for several hours, and that the funnelling wind would strengthen and mature. We reasoned that as the wind strengthened, the oscillating windshifts in the early lighter wind would vanish and the same geographic shift as we had observed the previous day would establish. So we decided, before the start, to follow the compass and sail windshifts for the first half of the race, and to shoot the corner in anticipation of a geographic shift during the second half. We followed the compass until the shifts vanished, and drew ahead of the people who shot the corner from the start because it had worked so well for them yesterday. We shot the corner later, and passed a few more crews who had abandoned the corner because it hadn't worked earlier in the race.

The regatta winner – a previous but not current world champion – used the *stability index* and broke back with a truly superb series performance. When those of us who had used this regatta as a test for the *stability index* compared notes, we concluded that its principal value had been that it had encouraged us to focus on the things that mattered. It had enabled us to plan our races with confidence and it had given clear meaning to any subsequent changes we had observed. The most telling statistic was that all of us had improved our position within the fleet.

The *stability index* is a powerful and effective tool on the water. It is also tremendous fun in the bar.

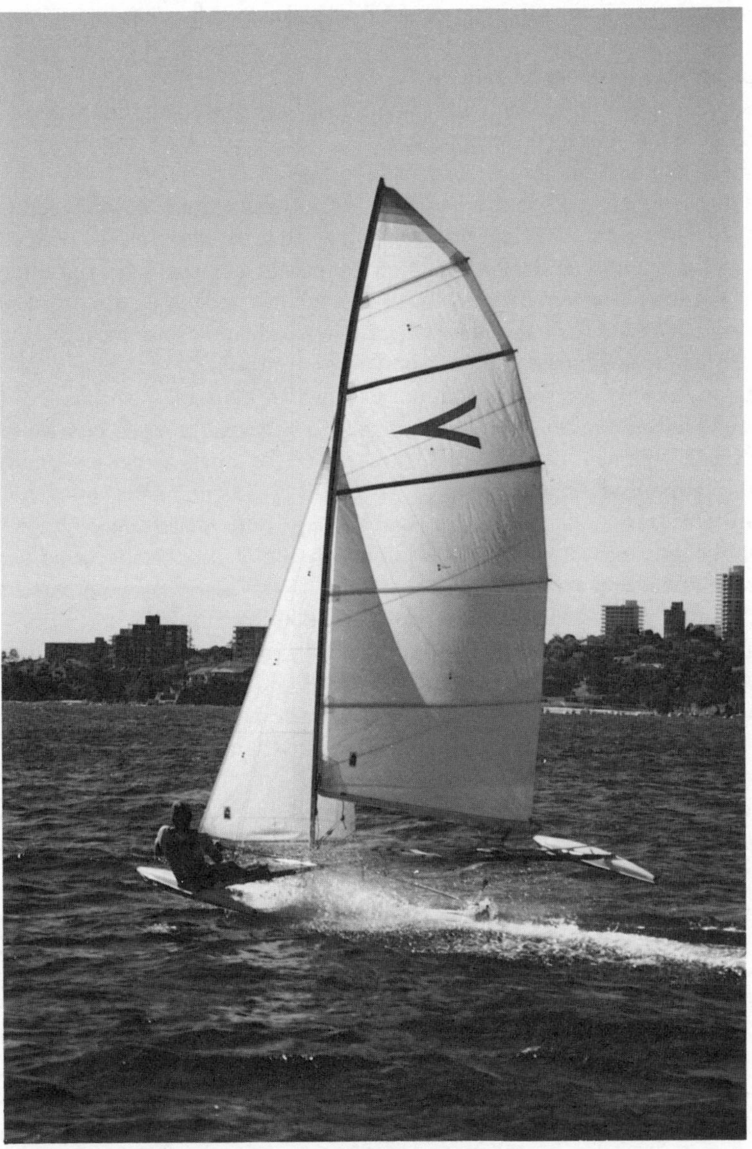

HSP MkXVII At last - simple, fast fun

Chapter 11
Race Preparation

11.1 Principles and priorities

This and the following chapter describe the different ways in which skilled crews prepare for their races and make use of their knowledge of wind patterns. In top level racing, this knowledge will be used in one of two ways. Depending upon the circumstances, crews will elect either to reach the next mark most quickly, or they will elect to reach the next mark ahead of a selected boat or group of boats.

The reasons behind these different approaches are best understood by considering the interaction of four factors:

1. The wind's predictable longer-term patterns.
2. The wind's unpredictable shorter-term gusts and fluctuations and lighter-air patches.
3. The environment of long distance 'ocean racing'.
4. The environment of 'round-the-buoys' type yacht racing.

Let us imagine that two pairs of boats, all of equal performance, race to windward in a wind which is steady except for regular wind-waves, and that one pair exploit the wind-waves perfectly while the other pair remain close to the rhumb line. In this situation the pair of boats which exploit the wind-waves will steadily draw ahead of the other pair. The two boats of each pair will enjoy almost identical wind, and so will remain close to each other. The exploiters will gain most when they are most distant in the cross-wind sense from the other pair, and will gain nothing when they are adjacent.

Let us now imagine exactly the same situation, except that the wind also has the random short-term gusts, fluctuations and lighter patches which are normal in any heated breeze. Over the long haul, the boats which exploit the predictable wind-waves will draw ahead of the others as before. But during the first few minutes, as the two pairs draw apart and begin to sail in different winds, the random effects of the unpredictable short-term gusts, lulls and lighter patches may briefly disadvantage either pair of boats to a greater extent than the growing but still small advantage due to the predictable wind-waves. What we see here is that when long-term probabilities and short-term random factors are both present, the probabilities will dominate in the long term, but the random factors may dominate initially.

In practical terms, if you predict the wind waves perfectly, and sail away from the fleet to exploit them, you will always win in the long term, but you have a very good chance of losing in the short term due to random factors which can never be predicted. This difference between the long-term and the short-term probabilities is at the core of the two different approaches adopted by successful helmsmen.

Yacht racing is structured, typically, in either of two ways.

If we think of an event such as an ocean race, it is always a single race which you either win or lose with no second chance. It is often a long race, sailed in an almost straight line through variable winds (Sydney to Hobart), or over a 'there and back' course around a single mark (Fastnet). There is little congestion or confrontation between boats between start and finish. This sort of race will be won by the crew which best combines boat speed with skill in exploiting the wind patterns and current patterns and so reaches the finishing line soonest. This is pure 'minimum time' sailing. When the first mark is 1,000 kilometres away, any brief initial disadvantage which may or may not occur due to unpredictable short-term differences in the winds as the boats begin to diverge can be properly ignored by any crew who set out to exploit the wind's predictable long-term patterns.

In this 'long-race' environment the most certain way to win will be to ignore the short-term random factors and exploit the longer-term predictable patterns. Over these longer time and distance spans, the random factors will tend to even out and affect all boats similarly.

When we think of any 'round-the-buoys' regatta, the environment is very different. It will usually be a series of six or seven shorter races. Each race is sailed over a course typically fifteen to twenty kilometres long which is structured as a number of laps each of which is composed of either two or three legs about 2 to 3 km long and with a rounding mark at each end. So each race is in reality a series of six to nine, short one-leg races. Competitors usually race in classes in which the individual boats are evenly matched.

A 'lowest total score wins' scoring system is used. This rewards consistency and penalises any bad placing harshly. This is an environment in which continuous congestion and confrontation are planned to occur at the start, at each rounding mark and at the finish. In this environment the priorities are completely different from those of the ocean race.

The new factors are:

1. Each race is made up of a number of legs – start to windward mark, windward mark to gybe mark, etc.
2. Every rounding mark makes a winner and a loser out of two boats which were previously side by side, because after turning they must necessarily leave each mark with one boat at least one length behind the other.
3. The effect of the 'Right of Way' rules gives great tactical advantage to the inside boat.
4. Every leg of every race therefore becomes a race in itself. The object during each of the nine leg-races is either to be ahead of the opponent at the next mark, or to be 'inside' him and overlapped in order to exploit the tactical advantage conferred on the inside boat by the rules.
5. The leg lengths are typically so short that the effects of the unpredictable short-term gusts, fluctuations and lighter patches remain significant throughout the leg.
6. In this more congested and confrontational environment, a small gain in either distance ahead (to break an overlap or to cross clear ahead of an opponent) or in tactical position (to gain the inside privileges at the next mark) will improve your race position by at least one place. But any loss, particularly if it is accompanied by loss of tactical advantage, is likely to lose several places. This is exactly the sort of lop-sided situation which already rewards conservatism and penalises inspiration, and it is further reinforced by the scoring system.

In this 'round-the-buoys' environment, the safest way to sail is to be tactically conservative. All practical experience, accumulated over decades, is that a wider hierarchy of skills is needed to win. These are crew work, boat speed, boat handling, tactics, understanding the water's currents and the wind's patterns (the course factors), fleet tactics, consistency – and race experience.

A world champion who had finished very well in a recent Olympics put it this way:

'Until your crew work is faultless you cannot hope to work up to consistent boat speed.'

'Until you are confident that your boat speed can match the speed of the best in your country, and match it in all wind and sea-state conditions and through all manoeuvres, you cannot be confident of consistency. Consistency is achieved by thinking conservatively, never gambling and never finishing badly. The top level crews are the ones who have developed the boat speed, the confidence and the maturity to think further ahead. They think in terms of winning this regatta, and the next one, and the next. They achieve this by thinking conservatively, sailing consistently faster than most people can hope to sail, and finishing well in this race, and the next one, and the next, and never finishing badly.'

'They never gamble. Any reasonably competent crew can win an occasional race if they are prepared to gamble. But while gamblers occasionally win races they more usually finish badly, so they seldom win regattas.'

'Until you are consistent, you cannot have the confidence necessary to protect your tactical rights, let alone improve your position by exploiting the tactical opportunities which occur from time to time due to random factors. You cannot even think of finishing well consistently until you can do this.'

'Until you are confident of your ability to at least maintain your tactical position, you cannot relax and sail to take full advantage of the wind patterns, current patterns and local biases and advantages which together make up the course factors.'

'Until you are confident of each of these four fundamentals – crew work, boat speed, tactics, and understanding of the course factors, you cannot be consistent enough to confront, match and beat the fleet – by which I mean the other three or four boats which might win. These by definition are the brightest and most experienced brains in the bunch, and they are sailing fast in the fastest boats. The rest of the starters don't matter.'

'The task of the crew who are going to win is to stay in touch with this fleet. If you don't sail away from them, they cannot sail away from you. Sail to beat the boat or boats that matter by a few lengths, and do this every race.'

'Beat them one by one by use of the wind patterns, but go only far enough to gain the tactical advantage you need to be ahead of or inside the selected boat or boats at the next mark.'

'Defend yourself from being disadvantaged by random effects by staying close to your competitors.'

'Never gamble to beat everybody by a leg. A win by a mile scores no more points than a win by a metre. If you separate widely from other boats, you can make big gains if you have anticipated well and nothing goes wrong. But you cannot avoid frequent big losses and consequent bad finishes due to the random factors. And if you have even one bad heat, you are unlikely to win the series.'

'It is only those crews who are not confident who gamble and shoot the corners. They sail away from the fleet because they are not confident of matching the boat handling and speed of the boats that matter.'

'At the Olympics we won one heat and came second in two, but we touched a mark another time and in re-rounding dropped from sixth to twentieth. In retrospect that probably cost us a medal. But when we analyse it, we have been sailing together for only eighteen months, and we are still improving. The few crews who beat us had all been sailing together for at least four years. We think our performance was reasonable.'

The principles which emerge are these:

1. In straight-line uncongested racing, skill in using wind patterns and current patterns will be all-important to success.
2. When wind patterns are used to the full, successful boats are likely to diverge widely from the rhumb line and from each other.
3. In congested and confrontational racing, many skills are needed. Fluency with wind patterns is only one of these.
4. When congestion is present, successful boats rarely diverge far from the rhumb line or from each other. Instead, they sail toward the side or area which they anticipate will be favoured by a wind shift or stronger wind only far enough to gain an advantage sufficient for tactical control. In this way they remain in close proximity with their selected rivals and thus defend themselves from the occasional advantages or disadvantages which occur at random from time to time between any two boats which are more widely spaced. Experience has demonstrated that this conservative policy results in higher average placings and higher series positions than any other.
5. When the winds are steadiest, the divergences between the top boats will be smallest. When the wind patterns are at their most unsteady extreme, even the most experienced and fastest crews may elect to diverge widely.

The sections which follow describe the techniques which best exploit wind patterns to reach the next mark in the minimum time. The extent to which you should modify them to achieve different tactical goals will depend entirely upon the importance of the fleet factors to you in the present race.

11.2 Preparation – overview

Preparation for a regatta, or for each race, falls naturally into three stages: pre-regatta, pre-race and pre-start.

This is a book about sailing. Nevertheless, in the interests of completeness, it is proper to point out that while skill in sailing can often win in club races, it is not, by itself, enough to go much further. If your goals are higher, nothing short of a determined campaign is likely to succeed. The previous quote, '*Those few who beat us had all been sailing together for at least four years*' makes the point. Sailing skill must necessarily be the basis of all regatta success, but by the end of any meaningful and successful campaign, you will have also developed the additional skills of Financial Controller, Business Manager, Marketing Manager, Senior Administration Officer, Psychologist, Nutritional Adviser, Master Boatbuilder, Sailmaker etc, – or you will already have failed to put yourself into any position from which you can hope to sail well. I will leave it to others to write about these executive, administrative and specialist functions.

Pre-regatta preparation.

The most efficient preparation takes the sequence noted earlier – until your crew work is flawless you cannot achieve consistent boat speed, until your boat speed is adequate you cannot stay with and race the fleet, until you can stay with the fleet you cannot relax and think 'outside the boat' to exploit the course factors, and until you can do all these things consistently and well you cannot confront and be confident of beating the boat or boats that matter.

It is up to you, your crew and your coach to sort out your crew work. The balance of this chapter will discuss the course factors – the water's waves and currents, and the next chapter how to make best use of the wind's patterns. Once you have mastered these three factors, you will be able to sail amongst the leaders. From that point on, the more effectively you work to maintain and improve these basic skills, and the more experienced you become, the more often you will win.

The course factors divide naturally into two parts – the water's waves and currents, and the wind's patterns. It does not much matter whether your object is to sail well in a regatta a few miles down the road next week, or to sail well in the next world championships for your class or the Olympic Games. The factors are the same. It is just a question of how seriously you address them.

11.3 The water's waves and currents

The principal fact about the water's waves and currents is that they are usually predictable. They can therefore be analysed as far in advance as you wish to do the work.

11.4 Pre-regatta preparation

As soon as you know the location, dates and starting times of the races, you can begin your preparations. A good starting point is to approach your local chandler and request the chart, pilotage notes, data on tidal currents, tidal predictions and the mean water temperature for the venue of the series. If you are close to their library, a search through the 'Pilotage Notes' of the last century is well worth while. The masters of sailing ships were wind-wise and weather-wise men, and their accumulated opinions about the winds in various places through the different seasons make interesting reading. The modern notes are directed primarily to the masters of powered vessels, and lack the wind detail which used to be such a feature of the reports of men who lived by the wind.

The waves you will race in will be governed by two principal factors, the water's depth, and the presence of any warm surface layer.

On the Manly circle, in the ocean off Sydney Heads, the bottom is 100 metres down on the continental shelf, and the great swells from distant storms and the smaller waves caused by the present wind can all roll and mix unimpeded. In a situation like this the water roughness is usually greater than one might expect.

The water in the hundred-odd kilometre wide channel between the Great Barrier Reef and the mainland in Queensland can become very rough, but in some places there is a coral shelf at a depth of between three and six metres for many kilometres offshore. The old adage holds, 'you cannot have big waves in shallow water'. So the surf which crashes ashore elsewhere is attenuated off places like Keppel Bay, and on courses laid over these shelves, yachts race in water no rougher than that of a large lake.

In spring when the ice has just melted, the waters of the Great Lakes off Toronto or Chicago are uniformly cold at all depths. When strong winds blow for a long time, these deep waters can spawn big waves. A few months later in the summer, the surface temperature will be about 23 deg.C, but the water two or three metres down will still be at about 6 deg.C. To the shallow warm surface layer, the denser cold water which lies below acts like a dynamically 'soft' shallow bottom, and prevents waves from becoming big. The Baltic is another sea which develops a warm surface layer during summer and autumn. In this and similar situations the density difference due to the warm surface layer is accentuated over wide areas by the inflow at lower level of a tongue of denser salt water from the ocean. Over this the less dense fresher water flows outwards as a surface film. The combined effect of these factors is such that hydrographic notes draw attention to the fact that a strong steady wind which will cause eleven metre waves in mid-Atlantic will cause only two to three metre waves in the Baltic.

There are some places where the waves will be long and big, and other places where they will be small. From a race preparation point of view, if your campaign is to race where there will be big waves, it will not be smart to do all your practising in water where there are only small waves, and vice versa.

Concerning current, there are two factors which are critically important.

The first is whether the speed of flow of the current will be relatively strong compared with the speed of the boat. If it is, then this will affect the way you will think about wind-waves. A strong adverse or favourable current can make a very large difference to the time you expect to take to reach a windward or leeward mark, particularly when the wind is lighter. This additional or lesser time will influence your judgment as to whether or not you think you will sail through 'at least one full wind-wave' before you reach the next mark.

The second factor will be the current gradient – whether the current speed is likely to be significantly different between any two places on the course.

If you sail in a tideless lake or lagoon, there will be no current and no current gradient.

When you sail near coasts, there will usually be flood and ebb tidal streams which repeat predictably. These will have been recorded in detail for the more important locations, and are published. Sometimes the flows are simple, such as the in and out flows in a featureless estuary. Sometimes they can become very complex indeed, such as the flood and ebb surges around both sides of the Isle of Wight, with its stronger flows mid-Solent and slacker water or reverse eddies along the shores. A deep channel can give a very different kind of gradient. In the upper reaches of Falmouth Harbour a narrow but 30 metre deep channel winds through mud flats which almost dry at low tide. The momentum of the mass of water in the channel maintains its flow direction for quite a long time after the tide has changed. This leads to a situation where, for a while, the shallow water over the flats can be beginning to flow inshore while the deep water in the channel may still be flowing outward, and vice versa. If there has been recent rain the river which feeds into the channel can flow strongly, in which case the narrow sinuous line of outward flow can persist for much of the flood with its inward flow over the shoals. In all these situations the currents repeat predictably. Often they are far too complex to be grasped quickly and intuitively while racing. In such cases careful pre-regatta study of the currents, plus a simple on-board aide-memoire, can be the basis of regatta success.

A simple and very practical aide-memoire is a length of adhesive tape which can be stuck to the deck. On this is written:

The predicted times and heights of high and low water for the regatta area for each race day and the preceding practise days,

Key sketches (often more than two) of the principal flood and ebb flow patterns in the race area.

The intervals after high and low water at which the critical flows establish.

This can be prepared months in advance, and it helps focus your mind on the race area and its current patterns. It is particularly valuable for confident re-planning on the water if the start of a race is much delayed by a series of general recalls, if a wind change occurs, or if a race to be resailed is signalled unexpectedly at short notice.

Note that throughout this pre-race preparation the current flows must necessarily be thought about and noted as currents in geographical positions (north of, south of, to seaward of etc). Not until the actual wind direction on the day enables you to estimate where the windward, wing and leeward marks will be placed does it become possible to think of the current flows in racing terms such as 'advantaged side, windward leg' etc.

There are some places where currents simply cannot be predicted. Fresh water and salt water do not readily mix. Wherever fresh water flows out to sea through a coastal opening which is large and deep, a tongue of denser salt water will penetrate far inland under the fresh water. Distant dynamics such as tide or swell near the coast can pulse this tongue. When this occurs, pulse-waves will flow along it at a speed which is very slow because of the small density difference. The overlying fresh water will flow away from the local present position of the submarine pulse crests and toward the troughs. Much the same thing happens whenever the relative masses of salt and fresh water change through natural causes, as for example where the tide normally causes salt water in a bay to surge back and forth regularly, but sometimes the bay is invaded by a massive fresh-water flow following heavy rain inland. The detail of flows such as these are beyond prediction.

To sum up:

The pre-regatta study of the wave and current environment can be completed by any prospective competitor anywhere in the world long before the regatta itself, provided that the data available from your local chandler or supplier is complete with respect to the area, and adequate in its description of the currents. In these cases, only last-minute checking for detail accuracy should be necessary at the regatta venue itself.

11.5 Pre-race preparation

If the data available has been complete and accurate, not much will remain to be done. But sometimes it isn't. The practical approach is to check. Four examples suggest useful techniques:

Keppel Bay and others. This is the apple technique. During pre-race sailing you throw an apple into the water alongside every spar beacon or moored or anchored vessel you see, and start your stop-watch. Sail back to pick it up one or two minutes later, and record the time interval, the distance drifted from the reference and the direction of drift. Keep going until you have recorded and analysed sufficient measurements to reveal the current speeds, and the intervals between times of high and low water and the onset and decay of the critical currents. Compare these currents with your predicted currents at those times. If the broad picture is confirmed – and usually it is – your confidence grows. Confident people tend to win.

If you sail on a lake which is a local widening of a river, such as Lac St Louis or Lac des Deux Montaignes on the St Lawrence and Ottawa rivers near Montreal, there will be a constant one-way current, which will be strongest in spring and slowest in autumn. The surface may look deceptively uniform but there can often be strong current gradients within this sort of flow. Because the current speed is relatively slow, flow remains laminar. This leads to sluggish flow where the water is shallow, and much faster flow through the deeper channels, some of which can be large. This sort of current detail is unlikely to be recorded or published, If you potter around pre-race in an outboard dinghy, you can anchor periodically and measure the currents, their differences and where the differences are greatest. A tide-stick is ideal. An apple is just as good. It is one thing to know that these current gradients exist. It is another to be able to use them, because it is sometimes not easy to know where these deeper channels are when you are racing – the water surface looks exactly the same everywhere. A major advantage of taking the time to go and measure the currents pre-race is that you will usually not only find areas of strong current but also work out ways of finding them again when you are racing later. This gives you a double advantage.

Kiel, 1972 Olympics. The Germans have a proverb: 'You can't call yourself a sailor until you can win at Kiel'. My task was to measure and analyse the wind patterns and the current patterns prior to and during the regatta. We were on the water in the regatta area from 07.30 each morning until practise or racing had finished for the day. We measured the current at about twelve different locations across the regatta area each morning, plus sample checks later. This data, analysed, satisfied us that there were no predictable patterns. This certainty, in turn, dispelled from the minds of the Australian crews the worry that local or European competitors might somehow have an understanding of Kiel's currents which would enable them to predict them and so have a race advantage. This gave the Australians confidence. Two Australian crews won gold. Even the certainty of chaos can be useful.

Brisbane River, 1975. In years past the Eighteen footers rotated their principal championships from Sydney to Brisbane to Auckland to Fiji. Sponsors prefer that the spectacular sailboats they sponsor should race where the public can see them. Sometimes this can lead to important races being sailed in unusual places, such as the big winding river which flows through Brisbane and its suburbs.

One skipper, David Porter, who was currently sailing superbly, had suffered a truly disastrous regatta in this river the last time around. He viewed the prospect of racing there again not with confidence but with dismay. The problem was that, despite very reasonable preparation, he had run aground so many times in places where the chart suggested that he should not have run aground.

The fix for this was twofold:

First, I checked the chart's fine print. It turned out that the detail of the dredged and marked shipping channel was accurate, but the detail of everything between the channel marks and the shorelines was indicative only.

Secondly, we armed ourselves with a three metre dowel plus the largest scale maps of the river we could find. We used maps with their detail of the land's features and structures, rather than charts, so that a helmsman who was racing could keep track of his position by reference to the conspicuous buildings and features on each shore. We set out in an outboard dinghy, always at low tide, to survey the bottom near the shorelines. The Eighteen with centreboard down needed 1.5 metres of water. We puttered along, probed the bottom with the dowel and established exactly where the two metre line lay. Whenever we found a bar or shoal, we nosed along it and across it and around it until it had no more secrets. We found shoals which were not on the original chart, and we found that some which were drawn on the chart had disappeared. We surveyed the whole ten kilometres of the course, both sides. David sat and watched all this as it was surveyed, and marked everything we discovered on that map on his knee. He pinned it to the wall of his room, and he lived and slept with that map and sailed with the memory of that map until the last race had finished. He never touched the bottom. He won.

11.6 Pre-start preparation

Pre-start observations can be vital in those unusual conditions when the currents cannot be predicted at all.

Kiel was such a place. The currents changed during the hours of a race. But if a crew observed the current pattern pre-start, and noted that the current at that time was more favourable on one side, it seemed sensible to sail more towards that side at least during the first beat.

Vancouver's English Bay is another. Normally the tide washes in and out, and this combined with a slow swirl in the bay gives an understandable and repeatable pattern to the currents. However, the estuary of the Fraser River is a few kilometres to the south, and the flow from this river remains attached to an unusually rounded intervening promontory. The fresh-water flow turns 180 degrees from west through north to east, and finishes by pouring directly into the southern side of English Bay. When the river is in flood, the sheer mass of this inflowing river water distorts the whole water budget of the bay and creates new patterns which cannot be predicted.

But they can be seen. The silt-laden river water is whiter in appearance, and does not quickly mix with the clearer salt water. The edge of the inflow can be observed directly. The crew's job pre-start is to observe which lot of water is going which way faster. Their job when racing is to sail into whichever water is moving more favourably. In this case it must all be done by eye.

11.7 The winds

The information available to you about future wind is of a different nature from that about current. The detail predictability of tidal streams is such that we can focus on a start at 1400 at a venue on the other side of the world on the second Tuesday of next September, and learn confidently that the northern side of the bay will at that time have a stronger westerly-going current than elsewhere. It is the nature of the wind also to repeat, but the wind's motions take the form of broader patterns and probabilities. If we accept this, and follow this track, it is surprising how much can be learned.

11.8 Pre-regatta preparation

Let us assume that your object is to sail well in a regatta to be held at a venue in a distant country some months hence. The information available would be, typically:

From the library of the Central Weather Office of your own country. General climatic information about the region which includes the regatta venue. Possible World Meteorological Service records of the daily flows of Highs and Lows over the part of the world which includes that region.

From the library of the Central Weather Office in the country in which the regatta will be held. A general description of the climate in the area of interest for each season. Such a description will normally include a detailed discussion of the prevailing winds. Mean wind speed and direction records from weather stations either near or representative of the regatta area. These may be means of all the winds observed, i.e. for the whole 24 hour period each day, or they may be the 0900 means, the 1500 means, etc. Mean air temperature records.

Wind roses are usually available from major weather offices such as airports. These reveal the direction and the frequency of occurrence of the most probable wind, and of the next most probable wind, etc. In addition, they reveal the proportion of time for each of the directions that the wind speed is light, moderate, or strong. They are normally available for specific hours.

There are sometimes research reports available in weather bureaux or university libraries about particular phenomena which can be useful to the racing helmsman, such as papers on aspects of the lake breezes or other winds of a particular coast.

From the library of the local harbour master (in addition to the charts, tidal streams, tidal prediction and 'Pilot' information). Information about the seasonal water temperatures. Possible access to old 'Pilots' or copies of those sections which describe the local winds. Possible research papers on aspects which include wind.

From the yachting media – descriptions of past regattas at the venue. While these are not usually mines of information about the nature of the winds, they do list who sailed fast, and correspondence with crews who have raced successfully in that locality can be most rewarding.

The interpretation of this data needs a little imagination, and sometimes a little detective work. Only once, to my knowledge, has a weather station been sited within the regatta area – that was the floating Bedford Tower installed by the Canadian Dept. of the Environment in the waters off Kingston, Ontario in the two years prior to the Montreal Olympics. In all normal situations the records from the nearest weather office are what is available. This will usually be a post office a few kilometres inland. It may be sheltered from the prevailing wind by a copse of tall trees, and so have profoundly different wind speeds from those at the coast. An airport at a greater distance may reflect an inland valley climate, and this can be even more misleading. Use whatever experience you have and whatever information you can glean to adjust the data you hold to what you think will be appropriate at the coast. Don't be frightened of being wrong. Most are. A classic case of mass misinterpretation was the initial assumption by the rest of the world, from the records of Pusan airport's inland winds, that the coastal winds off Pusan would also be light. They weren't.

From this information, you can work out:

1. The wind direction and speed which is most likely, and the direction and speed which is second most likely, etc. These will come from the prevailing wind data, and from the mean winds, and particularly from the wind roses.

In days gone by, this sort of data would have been regarded as complete information, and would have been all that a skilled crew would have expected to learn. According to these wind speed expectations, they would have endeavoured to practice in the predominantly light, moderate or strong winds expected at the regatta, and this would have been thought about as the best preparation possible.

The concept of wind patterns enables us to go much further, and predict whether the racing will be in regular patterns which call for planning skills, or unstable patterns which call for opportunistic skills, or one of the two principal intermediate situations. We can use the information above to estimate not only the wind speeds, but also;

2. Whether the air will be heated or not. If the mean air and water temperatures are about the same, it is reasonable to assume that the cooler polar winds will be heated, and the warmer tropical winds cooled. If the water is significantly colder than the air, as in ice-fed lakes in spring, or within the influence of the very cold ocean currents, the air will almost always be cooled and you will be in for an intellectual regatta.

3. Whether a High or a Low will usually be dominant. This information comes partly from the latitude. Over venues within the influence of the great sub-tropical anticyclones, such as Hawaii or the Bermudas, each High may last for a fortnight, and they experience Lows relatively rarely. Venues nearer the pole, such as Marstrand, Helsinki and Tallinn, are washed by Lows about once each day, and you have to be quick to recognise the brief intervening clearance as a High. In latitudes between, the description of the prevailing wind(s) may offer clues. At the simplest level, if the weather is cloudless, it is unlikely to be a Low. If they suggest rain or say nothing about the weather, it will probably be raining, and it cannot then be a High.

4. Whether or not sea breezes are common. This will come partly from the description of the winds, and partly from the quadrant. No offshore winds can be sea breezes. Because they usually start directly onshore, and then back or veer as they build, no quadrant four winds are likely to be sea breezes. Sea breezes cannot be light airs and except in rare circumstances they seldom exceed about 12 to 15 knots. If one of the common winds is a quadrant three wind of between 6 and 15 knots, and these are mentioned in the description of the climate, then those winds are probably sea breezes, and will have shallow boundary layers and will oscillate regularly and quickly.

The *stability index*. You can now estimate whether a High or a Low is likely to be dominant when the most likely wind blows and when the second most likely wind blows, the probable temperatures of the air and water, and whether any of the probable winds is likely to be a sea breeze. These probabilities, scored on the *stability index*, will reveal whether you are likely to sail in stable patterns in which planning will be everything, unsteady conditions which will reward opportunism, or something in between. This sort of information will be invaluable in enabling you to plan your practise, so that you will become accustomed to responding not only to the wind speeds and sea-state conditions but also to the patterns in which you expect to sail in the regatta.

Surprisingly, you can sometimes do better than go and practise at the venue itself. If you think about ice-fed waters such as the Baltic or the Great Lakes (e.g. the Kiel, Kingston and Tallinn Olympics), then in the spring when the water surface is still very cold the air will be chilled and the patterns will be at their most stable extreme. As the late spring and early summer weeks pass, the surface layer warms, and at some point it will reach the temperature at which it sometimes warms the air. Crews who may be practising in the area will experience a sudden change from always-regular to sometimes-unsteady patterns. This can be confusing if it occurs just prior to a major regatta.

Elsewhere in this work, I have quoted examples of sailors who have been years ahead of their time. Rodney Pattisson was one of these. He won a gold medal in a Flying Dutchman at Acapulco. In the months before the following Kiel (Munich) Olympics, he started practising, not in the still-cold waters of Kiel, but on the Spanish coast. As the sun moved north, so did Rodney – La Rochelle, Cherbourg, Medemblik, and finally Kiel. He had planned his practise so that in the months before the regatta he sailed continuously in the same sort of unsteady patterns as he expected to find, and found, at Kiel. He won. Pre-regatta planning can be helpful.

11.9 Pre-race preparation

From close quarters you can begin to be precise about the factors which were just educated guesses and probabilities from far away.

Before you launch or slip moorings prior to an important race, it is sensible to take a little time to review both the tactical situation and the day's probable wind patterns.

The tactical information will flow from the list of entrants and the score sheet.

1. Which are the boats in contention – 'the fleet'?
2. Where does each lie in the score ranking with respect to yourself?
3. What are your goals today?
4. What will be your race policy (confront, stay in touch, or sail minimum time) with respect to each boat in order to achieve these goals:
   a) At the start?
   b) When you meet during the race?

'4.' above calls for the most careful judgment. There has to be a single minimum-time path from start to finish. Selecting this path is strategy. What you do differently from this, because of the presence of another boat or boats is tactics. Remember that all tactics degrade strategy and slow the boat. If you must cover a boat, then engage in a tacking duel and cover. If you must luff, then luff. But accept the truth that while you do so every other boat will sail past both of you. Tactics are expensive, and should be used sparingly.

You will already have worked out the day's tides and currents. In your review of the day's probable wind patterns six basic factors should be observed and their inter-action evaluated:

1. Wind direction – orients the course and gives sense to current.
2. Wind speed – gives importance to current. Current dominates in light winds.
3. Thermal excitation – in heated air, look for stronger wind. In cooled air, look for shifts. In chilled air, look for reversed shoreline effects.
4. Boundary layer thickness – controls wavelength. and frequency
5. Subsidence or convergence – controls regularity.
6. Shoreline effects – chapter nine introduced the broader principles. The effect of the shore at each locality varies so greatly that only experience on those waters can enable you to make a balanced assessment. This is what the pre-regatta practise and warm-up races have been for.

Anticipation of the wind starts with the weather map. Each morning, get a newspaper which publishes the full weather map with its Highs, Lows and the isobars. Cut these out and file them in a notebook. (When I am coaching a group such as Olympic selection trials, I pin them, day after day, along a notice board.) As the days pass and the sequence grows longer, the nature of the systems and the ways that they flow in that area begin to emerge. Subconsciously you cannot do other than expect what you are accustomed to where you live – for example my experience of Sydney is of generally High dominant weather which repeats about once every seven days. Melbourne is a little further south but is washed by Bass Strait's weather, which has more Lows and repeats faster, so I tend to be surprised at how soon approaching weather arrives. This adjusting of your subconscious clock is important.

The direction of the isobars should give the direction of the gradient wind at the time for which the map was drawn, and the spacing of the isobars gives the expected gradient wind speed. If necessary, project the time to the present by altering your position on the map to arrive at the forecast gradient wind.

Observe the direction and the speed of the movement of any low clouds. If these are broadly consistent with the expectation from the isobars, accept this as a general confirmation of the accuracy of the map. If they conflict, reject the map or amend it. This may sound brutal, but clouds are real and now, they drift with the wind, and compared with their evidence, that of the forecast isobars is trivial. Sometimes, low clouds wash back and forth during periods of change. When you suspect that this may be occurring, observe their movement several times over an hour or two for certainty.

It will generally be found that while weather maps are not very accurate as to timing, they are reasonably accurate as to sequence. For example, if a front was forecast for today, it will probably arrive, but not necessarily at the expected time. So if the forecast for now was for north-westerly pre-frontal winds, but the clouds are now drifting from the south-west and the air is colder (southern hemisphere), all that has happened is that the front has arrived earlier than forecast. The weather map is still useful if you amend it by imagining that your position on it now is where the approaching south-westerlies are shown, and work from that point in your anticipation of what is likely to happen in the hours ahead.

From this point a procedure something like the following is useful:

1. The gradient wind direction will be given by the isobar direction, or by the observed direction of drift of low clouds. Once the broad wind direction is fixed, the course becomes oriented within the regatta area. The influence of both the stronger current streams, and of the shoreline factors as well, will then fall into focus and can be thought about in a way which is tactically useful, for example, 'left side favoured upwind until three o'clock, right side favoured after four.' etc.

2. The gradient wind speed is given by the spacing of the isobars, or by the observed speed of drift of low clouds. The regularity of the wind speed will be a mix of many factors. When the wind becomes light a strong adverse current stream can block all direct progress, and some longer circuitous route which avoids the adverse stream may be the only way to finish if the wind remains light, but will be a slower choice if the wind speed pulses. (This was sometimes the situation at the 1988 Pusan Olympics.)

3. For the thermal excitation factor, measure the temperature of the water in the course area once and carefully. Measure it again the next day to make sure. During the period of one regatta it will not change significantly except in very unusual circumstances. (An example would be a sustained strong offshore wind which blows a warm surface layer downwind and so exposes the cold water below.)

Measure the temperature of the air each day with the thermometer dry, in the wind and in the shade. If the wind is offshore, the air over the land may be heated, so measure the air temperature again in the course area after you launch.

When the air is warmed or heated, expect local changes in wind speed. Look for and use the stronger air.

When the air is cooled (air temperature up to say 3 degrees warmer than the water), expect little local change in the wind speed. Look for and use the favourable shifts.

When the air is chilled (air temperature say five degrees or more warmer than the water – this situation is common with offshore winds over ice-fed lakes in spring, or over the very cold ocean currents), expect little local change in wind speed, and the changes of direction to be very smooth.

4. In gradient winds the boundary layer will be deep, and the waves long and slow.

If there are clouds, and they are shallow with flattened tops cut off at a uniform height, these show the depth of the boundary layer clearly. If the clouds arrange themselves in bands or lines, the thicker bands indicate the wave crests. The backs and veers of the surface wind will be synchronised with the approach and passing overhead of each band. This situation is the easiest of all the slow patterns to read. (Watch out for harmonics within these slow oscillations if the air is warmed.)

In all gradient wind situations the surface wind direction will be skewed toward Low pressure from the gradient wind direction. Look also at the proximity and shape of the shoreline, and try to estimate the predominant shoreline effects.

If the gradient wind direction is from quadrant two or one consider the possibility of a sea breeze setting in. (It is less likely from quadrant one.) Sea breezes and funnelling winds are relatively easy to recognise. They blow onshore on sunny days when the gradient wind blows offshore. They have a characteristic cool steady feel about them. They have shallow boundary layers and so their directions oscillate quickly. Because an inversion is an integral part of their mechanism, these oscillations tend to be regular.

5. The curvature of the isobars will show whether a High is dominant, or whether they are straight or whether a Low controls. Clouds, if any, will be revealing. If they are the sort of shallow clouds mentioned in 4. above, these will confirm the subsidence inversion of a High and foreshadow regular wind-waves. But if the clouds are of uneven depth and have ragged tops with some higher than others, these are the signs of convergence, i.e. the straight isobar or Low dominant situation, and this foreshadows a day with irregular shifts.

Sometimes, big shallow Highs can be traps. What is drawn as a single large centre may in practice become two or more individual smaller centres. Between these the inversion may become weak or non-existent. Suspect this if areas of cloud (other than high cloud) appear without other explanation. (This pattern does not occur in deep, intense Highs.)

As soon as the wind direction, the wind speed, and the three *stability index* factors are evident, it is sensible to take a few quiet minutes to discuss their import and consider the day's likely winds and patterns. The essentials are:

1. *Wind direction* – this fixes the orientation of the course. This in turn admits both 'current' and 'shore effect' information into the race-plan, e.g. If you expect a stronger westerly-going current on the northern side of a west-facing bay, and today's wind will be easterly, then today the right side will be advantaged upwind, and the shoreline effects will be more pronounced towards the left.

2. *Wind speed* – this fixes the importance of the current in today's race. Current is never unimportant, but it becomes absolutely dominant in light winds.

3.a) *Warmed air* – this causes unsteadiness in wind speed. When the air is cooler than the water, it is reasonable to expect local wind-speed differences across the course, and little predictability in the wind's oscillations. On these days crews who look for and sail in the stronger-wind areas will win.

b) *Cooled air* – this causes steadiness in the wind speed. When the air is warmer than the water, differences of wind speed, if any, will tend to be associated with shoreline effects. There will be shifts of direction which will be patterned.

These patterns will be predictable, and may or may not be regular, i.e. on some occasions a crew will be able to predict with confidence that there will be no regularity, no predictable rhythm. In other conditions regular repetition can be anticipated with confidence. On cooled-air days it will be those crews who best handle these wind shifts who will win.

4.a) In *gradient winds* – the oscillations will be slow. The distance sailed in passing through one full wavelength may often be more than the length of a windward leg of a round-the-buoys race. In these conditions many windward legs will have single-curve or 'persistent shift' characteristics, while others will become more complex. The effect of adverse current, particularly in lighter winds, will often be to increase the sailing time on a windward leg to the point where it becomes an 'oscillating wind' rather than a 'single-curve' exercise despite the slowness of the shifts.

b) In *sea breezes or funnelling winds* – the oscillations will be quick and will tend to be regular.

5.a) In *High dominant* situations – the slow oscillations of the gradient wind and the quick oscillations of the sea breezes and funnelling winds will both be regular and can be anticipated.

b) In *Low dominant* or straight isobar situations – the slow oscillations of the gradient wind will be irregular and cannot be anticipated. The oscillations of the sea breeze and the funnelling wind will usually remain regular, but occasional aberrations may occur.

In practice, your assessment of the likely patterns will fall somewhere between the unstable extreme of unsteady wind speed and no order in wind direction, and the stable extreme of steady wind speed and smooth predictable oscillations. Between these there will be the two broad areas. The warmed winds will tend to have unpredictable lulls, and on these days a policy of sailing in the stronger wind areas will usually win. The cooled winds will have steadier wind speeds, and on these days sailing the advantaged tacks will usually win.

A final point. If there happens to be a convenient headland or tall building nearby, it is probably well worth climbing to look at the water surface from height. Watch it for long enough to sense the pattern flow. Nothing else is half so revealing.

With this information you can go onto the water and be confident that you will not waste your time.

11.10 Pre-start preparation

Your object before the start will be to acquire the information you will need during and after the start.

When wind speed changes are expected, the vital information will be pattern identification and familiarity.

When wind direction changes are expected, the vital information will be the frequency, amplitude, regularity and trend of the oscillations.

When both are present, the vital need will be understanding and experience. These situations are not easy to analyse on the water.

The *stability index* is a practical guide. A score of 3 or 4 suggests major changes in wind speed. A score of 5 or 6 which includes heating suggests intermediate conditions in which both the wind's speed and direction will be unsteady. A score of 6 or 7 which includes cooling suggests intermediate conditions with unsteady directions but steadier wind speeds. A score of 8 or 9 indicates steady wind speeds with regularly oscillating winds.

If the air is chilled the wind's speed is likely to be steady, regardless of other factors.

11.11 In unsteady winds

The fact that you may expect no predictable repetition does not in any way mean that the changes in wind speed and wind direction will be random. The speed will remain between minimum and maximum limits. The direction shifts will remain between limits. And the intervals between changes will similarly remain between limits. So each day's pattern will be a sequence of speed and direction changes which will never repeat exactly, and which will sometimes behave surprisingly, but which is recognisable because it will always remain within those limits.

When unsteady wind speeds are expected, your object during the race will be to spend more time in the stronger wind areas than your opponents. Wind direction will remain important, but less so than wind speed.

The time pre-start will be best spent in sailing through the puffs and lulls and backs and veers until their nature, appearance, spacing, life span, limits and movement become familiar and take the form of a pattern in your mind. Once the initial detail of the pattern becomes evident, wider detail can be added. Depending upon today's waves and today's light, it is often possible to recognise visually whether approaching puffs are backed or veered. The pattern repetition which is so obvious from height is harder to see from water level, but as you become familiar with the nearby surface indications, you can often see the most conspicuous features repeating in the distance, once you know what to look for.

The pattern repetition dimension of the wandering breeze is of the order of 1 kilometre. The lighter parts of a wandering breeze pattern are indistinguishable from light air and may develop transient pattern elements with the 100 metre repetition dimension characteristic of light air. Beware the trap of focussing so closely on the 100 metre elements that you miss the more important kilometre elements. Particularly in light airs, it helps to stand up occasionally. You can see further!

The life span of pattern features can vary enormously, usually in the sense that the lighter the wind, the longer they can last. A thermal pattern in a calm can last indefinitely. As light air and then breeze set in, cellular motions in particular become skewed and distorted and broken and they reform. The life span of the crosswind elements in particular tends to become relatively brief.

It will be the relative importance of each of these factors, together with the size and the tacking and gybing characteristics of your boat, which will determine the fastest way to sail in today's conditions. If, in a near-calm with long-life cells and curtains of air, you are sailing a boat like a Laser which roll-tacks and gybes fluently, your fastest way will be to approach and sail along the long-life lines of stronger air at the bases of the individual curtains, and this will be true both upwind and down. If in the same conditions you are sailing a boat which tacks slowly such as a Tornado, this technique will continue to work well for you downwind, but would be a disaster upwind. To increase the time you spend in the stronger areas of the wind when sailing upwind, you will have to work out some way other than tacking frequently. Which way will be best for you today? Your object, pre-start, is to answer this question, and get it right.

As the wind becomes stronger, your own mobility increases but the lives of the puffs will tend to decrease. If you have a manoeuvrable fast boat you can hunt the puffs successfully in the sense of reaching them while they still have some useful life remaining before they vanish.

Two special intermediate cases are worth describing.

One is the wandering breeze which is heated just enough to exist. It needs experience to recognise, and very sharp eyes and much more experience to identify the stronger wind areas as a pattern which can be exploited.

The other is the 'harmonics' situation such as in Figures 7.6 to 7.9 which can occur in 'High dominant, gradient wind, heated' situations. As presented in the figures they are obvious. On the water they are not at all obvious, and are difficult to identify particularly if the wind speed changes significantly which it often does. This is probably the only light air, unsteady wind speed situation in which it is fastest to sail the advantaged tacks systematically. You can do this only if you have identified the pattern.

11.12 In the steadier winds

In situations in which the air is not heated the wind becomes more stable. Two changes occur in the patterns:

1. Cooled breezes blow at steadier speeds. The conspicuous wind speed differences between one point and another which are such a feature of heated air vanish. Speed differences can still occur, but will be due to wider influences such as effects of shoreline factors.

2. The oscillations of direction which occur within this steadier flow are more deliberate and ordered than the finer-grain unsteadiness of heated air. These oscillations are relatively predictable. They may be quick or slow, regular or irregular

As the boundary layer approaches its stable extreme, the mechanism which develops will give both the steadiest wind speeds and the most regular oscillations.

In this new situation your object during any race ceases to be 'more time in stronger winds'. It becomes instead 'more time on advantaged tacks'. This leads to a completely different approach to pre-start preparation.

Preparation in the unsteady conditions of warmed air assumes continuous unpredictability of both wind speed and wind direction. This is a two-variable situation in which both speed and direction change continually, substantially and relatively quickly, and experience shows that those crews who concentrate on the wind speed factor are the crews who win. Preparation therefore concentrates on anticipation of, exposure to, and recognition of the nature and bounds of the day's pattern. A crew prepare themselves to respond with the best response possible to any of a number of cues to the next change in either speed or direction in a pattern which is essentially unpredictable. There is an overriding bias to go for the areas of greater speed rather than the areas of advantaged direction. This is pure opportunistic sailing.

Preparation in cooled, steadier conditions is essentially different, for three reasons.

1) The focus changes – it is the areas of advantaged direction which are now all-important.

2) The uncertainty changes – the shifts tend to repeat more slowly and in a more predictable manner.

3) The complexity changes – in place of two variables there has become only one, because wind speed, for practical purposes, can now be regarded as constant.

In this steadier, simpler environment successful crews concentrate on the detail of the backs and veers, their repetition interval, how many degrees they sweep, their trend, and their regularity.

To be confident of the repetition interval and the regularity of a pattern, one should trace that pattern through several full cycles. This is possible, pre-start, when the repetition interval is short, as in a shallow boundary layer. But when the frequency is slower, as in the deep boundary layers of gradient winds, several full cycles may occupy hours, and it is not practical to spend this sort of time on the water before every start. Further, while the response of an ocean racing yacht will be the same regardless of whether the shifts are fast or slow, the response of a 'round the buoys' yacht will be very different in the 'slow' shifts because the next mark will so often be less than one full wave-length ahead.

There are therefore two related reasons why the slow shifts need to be handled differently. Section 11.13 will consider the basics of the quicker oscillations, and Section 11.14 the slower shifts of gradient winds.

11.13 In the quicker oscillations

The wind oscillations will be quick – say 6 to 12 minutes full-wave – when the boundary layer is shallow, i.e. on those days when there is a sea breeze or a funnelling wind. The essential information pre-start will be the amplitude and frequency of the waves, the wind's mean direction, whether the mean direction is backing or veering with time, and the regularity of the pattern. In these conditions the following approach has been found useful.

Launch early so that you can sail the windward leg, and have time to spare. Measure the wind direction every minute if you can, and certainly not less frequently than every two minutes. There are five useful ways of measuring the wind direction:

1. Luff head to wind, read the compass.

2. Read the compass immediately prior to tacking. Tack. Read again as soon as you are stabilised on the new tack.

(a) The difference is your tacking angle.

(b) Half the difference is your pointing angle.

(c) The mean is the present wind direction.

(d) Any subsequent reading taken while sailing close-hauled in the same wind and sea-state conditions, plus or minus your pointing angle, will give the wind direction at that moment.

This procedure should be repeated several times to refine the accuracy. Note that most boats point higher in gusts than lulls. If this applies to your boat, and the day has significant gusts, either:-

(i) Tack and measure only in the lulls, – or (better)

(ii) Measure in both gusts and lulls, but indicate which are the gust readings, e.g. circle the gust points on the plot. This is more work, but gives more information.

3. After performing 2 above, sail close-hauled on either tack, read each minute, apply the pointing angle, plot.

4. Sail downwind of any flag on a stationary vessel. When directly downwind, read the wind direction across your compass. (Can also be used from upwind with big flags.)

5. Run directly downwind, carefully align your centreline with your wind indicator – both should point at the same point on the horizon. Read. Apply a correction of plus or minus 180 degrees.

Sail to windward on one tack from the start area for as long as it takes to pass through one or more complete wind-waves. Measure the wind direction as you sail. Start to draw a plot such as the inset in Fig. 12.2.

Tack and sail for long enough on the other tack to confirm the pattern through a second wave. Sail downwind back to the start area. Continue to plot the wind direction all the time. Expect your plot to show three completely different frequencies – a fast frequency as you sail to windward and meet the wind waves more quickly, a much slower frequency as you sail downwind and overtake the wind waves slowly, and an 'Observer Stationary' frequency during the time you spend near the start line. Fig 12.7 shows these three different frequencies.

In these short, quick, wind-wave conditions you can get additional and invaluable information if you can persuade another crew of about the same speed to co-operate. You should both:

(a) Start together from the start area,

(b) Sail to the windward mark, or the position where the windward mark will be, but with each boat sailing on an opposite side of the course. The leading boat should stop as the following boat approaches, and time the advantage.

(c) Compare opinions to confirm that the difference was not due to some abnormal factor.

(d) Start together and sail downwind, again each on an opposite side of the course.

(e) Stop, time the advantage, and again compare opinions near the position of the leeward mark.

If the same side of the course has proved faster both upwind and down at these different times, it is likely that there is either a geographic shift toward that side at the upwind end of the course, or that the wind is stronger on that side, or that the water is flatter, or some combination of all three.

If different sides proved faster, and there appeared to be no significant difference in the winds, suspect a current difference.

If these exercises have not revealed a wind-wave pattern with certainty, you do not have sufficient information to proceed as below. It may be faulty information gathering, or it may be that there are no wind-waves, or no regular wind-waves, today. In either case, amend your race plan and sail defensively.

If you have identified a quickly oscillating wind-wave pattern which is regular, you will now be able to read from your plot:

(a) The mean wind direction at present.

(b) Whether the mean direction has backed or veered since launch.

(c) Whether the mean direction changes toward the windward mark (Geographic Shift)

(d) The maximum back and veer expected.

(e) Your pointing angle, and the angle through which you will tack (double the pointing angle)

(f) Your compass readings on both tacks at the mean wind direction in the present wind and seastate conditions. These are the critical numbers to use when considering when to tack.

(g) Your compass readings on each tack at the times of maximum advantage. These are your adjusted layline directions in the present wind and sea-state conditions. Make a particular note of this factor. It is so common for 'tactics' diagrams to assume that the laylines are at plus and minus 45 degrees to the mean wind direction that we are in danger of accepting this as correct. It isn't. If the backs and veers are plus and minus 15 degrees, the laylines will become only 60 degrees apart, and any estimate of tacking position based on 90 degrees will result in consistent and massive overstanding and loss of position.

(h) The repetition interval upwind (and the longer intervals downwind). This factor is of vital importance in two respects:

(i) Failure of the direction pattern to repeat at the expected time is your earliest warning that the pattern may be failing to repeat regularly. (If you are well back in the fleet, the pointing angles of the boats ahead will indicate the wind's curves. But if you are near the lead, you will not have the privilege of this information, and must make use of other indicators.

(ii) In judging whether or not you expect to pass through one or more full waves before you reach the upwind mark, or whether you are within a half-wave length or less, a mental comparison between the time that you think it will take you to get there and the time that you expect the next wave or half-wave will often be a helpful back-up to your estimate of distance, particularly in lighter winds and tide.

Within the whole range of patterns, it is these predictable 'regular wind-direction oscillation' patterns which are associated with high values of the *stability index* which are the easiest to anticipate, to recognise, to measure and to exploit. They offer great race advantage because the VMG gain is so large. They are simple and relatively safe to use because the mechanism which gives these regular backs and veers tends usually to give the smallest changes of wind speed across the course.

Immediately pre-start. In the final minutes before the start:

(a) Decide, on the basis of the information you hold, whether you are certain that you will sail through one or more full wind-waves between the start and the windward mark.

If you are certain, use the full-wave technique suggested in the next chapter.

If you are not certain, sail defensively.

If you are certain you will pass through a half-wave or less between your present position and the windward mark, or if you become certain of this at some time after the start, use the part-wave technique.

(b) If you will sail through one or more full wind-waves:

(i) If your plot indicates that the mean wind direction has been veering progressively with time (normal sea breeze behaviour in the northern hemisphere, and vice versa in the southern), bias the mean wind direction and critical compass numbers about 5 degs further to allow for the expected change in wind direction due to Coriolis between the time of the last pre-start measurement, and the time you expect to approach the windward mark after the start.

(ii) In funnelling winds and also all gradient wind situations, make no such correction.

(c) Blend the 'tide' part of your race plan into your 'minimum time' plan. In practice this will mean deciding which areas you should avoid because the current there is less favourable or more adverse than elsewhere. The greater the remaining area you can use, the more freely you will be able to exploit the windshifts on both tacks.

(d) Also blend in the strategy to exploit any geographic shift you may have found. In practise this will mean sailing on the 'upwind' side of the rhumb line and planning to approach the upwind mark from the favoured side, e.g. closer to the starboard lay line if you expect the wind to veer at the windward mark, and vice versa.

(e) Continue to measure and plot the windshifts during the minutes immediately pre-start so that your plot remains up to date. By projecting the plot to and beyond the start time, you can see which will be the advantaged tack immediately after the start. If there are one or more general recalls, keep measuring and plotting the wind direction between the starts so that you can always project your plot to and beyond the next start. Each successive start will need to be planned anew.

(f) Your twin objects at the start should be first, to start well, and next, to adopt the preferred tack with minimum loss and delay. If starboard tack is favoured, this poses no problem. But half the time port tack will be favoured, and this will call for more thought.

11.14 In deep boundary layers

While sea breezes, lake breezes and funnelling winds are common in some places, in the global perspective they are rare. The more usual situation is the gradient wind with its deep boundary layer and slower and more complex and generally more unpredictable patterns. In the context of the *stability index*, no gradient wind can score higher than 7, which suggests that regularity and predictability are usually marginal. However, the particular case of 'High dominant, gradient wind, cooled' will often give slow oscillations with repetition intervals of between 20 and 60 minutes which are as regular as a sea breeze, provided that there are no upsetting factors such as steep or hot land upwind.

In these situations ocean racers will be relieved that they need tack only every 10 to 30 minutes. For all 'round-the-buoys' racers, the situation is different. This is the situation which is probably the hardest to sail accurately because a second uncertainty then becomes important: whether or not you will be likely to pass through one full wind-wave or something less, between the leeward and the windward marks. (The significance of this 'full-wave/half-wave' situation – often called oscillating winds and persistent shifts – is discussed in the next chapter.) A typical case would be a windward leg length of 2 to 3 kilometres, a tidal stream of plus or minus 2 kilometres per hour, a dinghy or catamaran with a VMG of 8 to 10 kilometres per hour, and a wind-wave repetition interval of, say 25 minutes. In currentless water the windward leg will be sailed in 15 minutes. If there is current and it is favourable, the time will become 12 minutes. If it is adverse, the time will become 20 minutes. The boat will be sailing upwind and meeting the wind-waves faster, so the effective repetition interval between wind-waves will be reduced to about 20 minutes. In this case a very modest 2 kph (1 knot) tidal current changes the expectation from 'one half of a wind-wave' to 'one full wind-wave', even when the wind-waves are predictable!

This sort of situation is never easy to get right. It will always be hard, from a distance, to estimate the 'full wave' situation. However, there is a saving grace. It becomes progressively easier to become confident of the 'half-wave' situation as you approach the windward mark. The more information you have, the sooner you will be able to shift from 'uncertain – sail defensively', to 'certain – sail to exploit'. The sooner you can exploit accurately, the greater the advantage you will gain from your more thorough preparation.

Because these wind-waves are so slow, an hour on the water before the start is unlikely to be long enough to enable you to recognise what may be a regular pattern. These are the days when it is essential to observe the back and veer extremes of the oscillations, and the changes in wind speed, if these are significant, for a longer time before the start. How you acquire the information does not matter. You can launch two hours before the start. You can let somebody else rig your boat and go on the water for the necessary time to make the measurements yourself. You can have somebody measure and plot the winds in the race area, and have them bring the information to you just before you launch, or you can pick it up from them when you get there. At a level which is more practical for an individual crew you can sometimes see from the shore the change of shadows on the hulls of boats moored offshore in relatively undisturbed wind as they swing back and forth in the shifts. When cloud streets mark the tops of the rolls, you can note the time of passing of each street.

While the wind direction may be so masked by nearby hills or buildings near the rigging area as to obliterate the detail of directional pattern, the wind speed is harder to suppress. Estimate the wind speed by periodically observing its effect on the most exposed trees, flags etc that you can see. Whatever you do and whatever you see, make a note of it and note the time. It is astonishing how a number of apparently unimportant details can reveal a pattern when they are assembled on a 'speed and direction against time' plot. The bottom line will be whether or not you have been able to acquire sufficient information, by any means, to be able to recognise any pattern before the start of the race.

Once you launch, start measuring and plotting exactly as suggested in the previous section, except that in these less stable conditions you should also plot your estimate of wind speed. Sail the windward leg, and plot as you sail. If you sense substantial difference in wind speed, take the time to assess whether there may be pattern to the differences. Is the stronger wind in channels? Does it build and fade in a general manner across the course. If so, is it general in area and regular? Consider the shoreline factor of convergence, and assess whether one side of the course may be generally stronger? As pointed out previously, the recognition of pattern in wind speed differences will almost always override the importance of wind direction differences.

If the speed is steady, note particularly how steadily the direction changes. The differences can be profound. In chilled gradient winds such as English Bay's easterlies in which the water may be 5 to 8 degrees colder than the air, the direction changes are so smooth that there is no opportunity at all to get back to the rhumb line without accepting the full loss of position if you have made the wrong decision about full-wave or half-wave. This becomes even more significant when the wind-waves are irregular. In gradient winds which are not chilled, such as Sydney's south- easters, in which the air may be at the same temperature as the water, there are small unsteadinesses to the direction which can be used to inch one's way back to the rhumb line with judicious short tacks, with substantially less loss. This sort of information is critical in situations when predictability is marginal, and the choice is between exploiting a probable pattern or continuing with defensive sailing. When the penalty for error is absolute, it pays to stay safer for longer.

As noted in the previous section, the 'harmonics' patterns are not easy to identify, but are immensely rewarding to exploit. If the air is even a little heated, take the time to check whether harmonics are present, and to try to understand their pattern.

If you have measured for long enough, and there is a pattern and you have identified it, you have the option of exploiting it. If you sail it correctly, you will gain much.

If you have not positively identified any pattern, you have no option but to sail defensively. If you sail carefully, you will hold your position with respect to others who sail carefully. You will lose to those who sail the pattern correctly and to a few of the gamblers. You will leave most of the gamblers behind.

If you gamble, you will probably lose badly.

Chapter 12
Sailing the Wind Patterns

12.1 The four groups

The tactics which best exploit the opportunities offered by differences in the wind speed and/or the wind direction from place to place fall naturally into four groups.

The first group relate to the 'stronger and lighter in speed' patterns and the 'back-and-veer in direction' patterns caused by cells and wind-waves which are everywhere to be found in open waters.

The second group relate to the winds near shores. These are locally slowed and skewed, more broadly convergent/divergent, have arrow-like funnelling wind and sometimes mighty sea breeze characteristics.

The third group relate to the patterns which exist only near isolated clouds or rain showers.

The fourth group is the effect of a moving open barrier – the fleet itself – on the wind. The effect of a compact fleet of boats on the nearby wind can be profound, and boats in the wrong position can be seriously disadvantaged.

12.2 Sailing the unsteady winds

Unsteady winds are those winds in which the wind speed varies significantly and unpredictably from place to place across the course. The cause of the unsteadiness is heating of the air by the water and/or the upwind land surface. In unsteady winds those crews will win who sail in the stronger wind areas for more of the time than their rivals.

The core technique in light and moderate unsteady winds is to visually identify the pattern and its stronger wind and lighter wind areas, anticipate its downwind drift, and steer to enter and remain within the stronger wind areas and to avoid the lighter wind areas to the greatest extent possible.

In stronger unsteady winds the same technique will apply when sailing downwind and crosswind. When sailing upwind, the wind's direction becomes more important.

The predictable fine-grain gusts and lulls normal in every turbulent breeze are not considered 'unsteady' in the sense above.

12.2.1 Unsteady light airs and similar patterns

In these conditions the future positions of areas of stronger wind cannot be predicted by calculation. But they can be anticipated to a useful extent by observing the present position of the lines of wind and the calmer areas between, assuming that the whole pattern will slowly drift downwind, and that it will probably persist for several minutes. The technique adopted should therefore be opportunistic. Sail toward and remain within the nearest line of wind. Anticipate the downwind drift of the whole pattern. Sail crosswind as necessary to reach and then remain within whatever upwind/downwind lines of wind may be available. The preferential seeking and sailing within the upwind/downwind lines of air has the advantage of avoiding to the greatest extent possible the large downwind-drifting calmer areas. This technique cannot work successfully all the time, because of the characteristically transient nature of light air thermal patterns. But to the extent that it is successful in increasing your time in the stronger winds, you will draw ahead of opponents who 'take what comes' and do not so skilfully chase the drifting lines of stronger air.

The mental approach to and the visual appearance of the most common light air patterns has been touched on in Section 4.16. The pre-race preparation for the actual conditions today, suggested in Section 11.10, is to work out from the known factors and from the *stability index* what the likely pattern will be, and to sail in this for an hour or so before the start so as to positively identify the pattern and get to know it. During this time the critical factors of this particular pattern can be observed, and the best technique to maintain movement by remaining within its stronger winds can be developed. Once its average repetition dimension plus some idea of the dimensions of the largest and the smallest cells are sensed, together with its speed of movement, the speed difference between the puffs and the lulls, and the life-span of the puffs, it will become easier to use your own mobility to sail into and then along the nearer puffs from time to time, and so to maintain good movement and the best possible VMG.

Three practical points are worth noting.

The first is that the wind will be just as unsteady along the starting line as it is everywhere else. Your object at the start is therefore to start where there is wind. The normally 'favoured' end of the line is useless if it is within a light patch, and there is wind at the other end. Reach back and forth a little upwind of the line, stay in the wind, maintain speed at all times, estimate where you think the best wind will be at the start, and dip below the line late and where there is wind and sail to stay in the wind. Everything else becomes less important.

The second is to resist the temptation of heading at all downwind to reach moving air. If on a reaching leg a line of wind appears just downwind – one which appears to be within reach – it is particularly tempting to steer downwind to enter it. All that usually happens is that it drifts downwind just a little faster than you can sail. The end result is that, having already 'lost' it, if you steer downwind you will usually increase the time you will spend in the calm, before you reach the next useful air. Patterns drift downwind. The next air will usually arrive from upwind. You will reach it soonest if you seek it upwind.

The third is that if in very light conditions a boat ahead is observed to enter a calm patch, it is more likely than not that there may be some moving air about half the pattern dimension away from it. A course which passes at about this distance (usually about 50 metres) from the becalmed boat will often succeed in maintaining air and movement.

12.2.2 In wandering breezes

The principles for sailing wandering breezes are broadly similar to those for handling unsteady light air, and for the same reason – no prediction is possible, so the response has to be visual and opportunistic. But unsteady light air and the wandering breeze are different animals, and so the detail has to be different. These differences are best appreciated by looking at each pattern from height.

Unsteady light air has a characteristic cell dimension of 100 metres. The cell centres are relatively calm. The lines of air between the cells are relatively narrow. The speed difference between the areas of more wind and less wind is sharply defined. Nobody can be in any doubt as to whether they are in the wind or not.

Wandering breezes have a characteristic cell dimension of about one kilometre. They have useful wind in the middles of the cells. They have more wind in the areas between the cells. The wind speed grades so smoothly between maximum and minimum that few sailors recognise that a pattern exists. Another smoothing factor is the absence of gusts – the three-dimensional cellular circulation which leads to the wandering breeze suppresses the gust mechanism.

In previous chapters I have likened the appearance of the wandering breeze pattern when viewed from the air to that of a net. Another impression. – Recently I addressed a group in Geelong, a city about thirty kilometres north of the Victorian coast of Australia and on Corio Bay at the western extremity of Port Phillip. A few days later came a call: 'The following day I climbed the cliff a few miles along the coast. There were all these funny oval shiny patches on the water. Can you run through that bit again . . .?' A cool moderating south-westerly had been blowing in cloudy weather over the thirty kilometres of land which separated Corio Bay from the cold Southern Ocean. Both the land and the water of the bay were slightly warmer than the air. These are exactly the conditions in which a wandering breeze develops. The shiny centres indicated wind speeds of 5 knots or less, and the stronger winds in the intervening areas were clearly turbulent – crews reported about 9 or 10 knots maximum. Pattern dimension was about one kilometre.

From what has been said, it will be clear that while the principles are the same as those for light air, the problem and the execution are different. There is wind enough to sail sensibly in the lighter areas. The bands of stronger wind are wider. So what is the problem?

There are three. The first is the foreshortening of vision which occurs when your eyes are at a low level. The pattern of 'funny oval shiny patches about a kilometre apart' which was so obvious from the cliff top is far from obvious from the low eye level of any small boat. But if you expect this pattern, and look for the cues, you can identify it and use it.

The second is that wandering breezes can be subtle. The wind speed difference between the calmer centres and the stronger bands can grade from the three to one of Fig. 7.22(b) or the probable two to one of David's 'funny oval patches' down to almost nothing, and the absence of gusts makes the appearance even smoother. There is a saving grace here. In the extremes the bands of stronger wind are easier to see but harder to reach quickly because of the relatively lighter wind in the middles of the cells. When the wind speed differences are smaller the stronger areas are harder to identify, but easier to reach because there is more wind.

The third is that it is the habit of most crews to concentrate too closely on their boats and not to look around enough. Beyond their boats, most do not look for even those things which are obvious, let alone the things which are subtle.

Enough of the difficulties. In wandering breeze situations those crews will win who most successfully sail around and so avoid the calmer patches. They expect, look for, find, and sail in the bands of stronger wind. The classic example must be Colin Beashel's advice to John Bertrand on the last downwind leg of the 1983 *America's* Cup races, advice which culminated in, 'stay where you are, John. There's more wind on this side, and here'. *Australia II* passed the defender which was in lighter air, and went on to win.

Note that this was in the ultimate match racing situation. We are not here considering boats which are far apart.

An understanding of the nature of the wandering breeze, and how to use it, can be useful.

12.2.3 In heated strong winds

When the wind is stronger than about 10 knots, thermal excitation ceases to express itself as the patterned kilometre-size cells of the wandering breeze, and instead takes the form of massive harsh gusts which are unpredictable and which often are also backed or veered in direction. Fig. 7.1(b) is typical of this pattern. Comparison of Figs 7.1(b) and 7.1(a) shows the degree to which the gusts of the heated wind are bigger and stronger and last for a longer time. It shows also the equally vigorous backs and veers caused by the heating. These shifts are absent from the trace of the cool wind.

The same basic principles apply in handling this form of unsteadiness as were needed in the lighter winds. The times and places of occurrence of the gusts are not predictable, so they cannot be planned for. But the gusts are big. They mark the water and so can be seen as they develop and approach. They last for two or three minutes. There is plenty of wind even in the lulls to enable a crew to position themselves to take the greatest advantage of each gust. So the basic technique remains the same – sail opportunistically, guided by visual cues plus a feel for the total pattern, with the object of increasing the proportion of time spent in the stronger-wind areas.

When sailing downwind, a crew should broad-reach towards and centre in the nearest gust, and steer to remain within its core. When that gust begins to decay the next gust should be selected and the process repeated. A practical point is that very great advantage can often be gained if the most suitable approaching gust within which to commence the downwind leg is selected during the last few seconds of approach to the windward mark. The rounding can then be executed with the object of centring the boat within that gust with the minimum delay.

When sailing crosswind, a technique of 'luff in the lulls, bear away in the gusts', will result in sailing both fastest and for the longest proportion of the time in the strongest winds.

When sailing upwind, a new factor is introduced by the relatively long-life backs and veers which appear in these heated winds. Analysis of the traces of which Fig. 7.1(b) is typical show:

1. The backs and veers are abrupt.
2. The backs and veers are not at all correlated with the gusts and lulls.
3. The backs and veers blow at directions between 10 and 20 degrees different from the mean wind.
4. The life of each back or veer is between 1.0 and 2.5 minutes.
5. There is no predictable rhythm to these shifts.

Further, we know that: -

a) The approach of each gust is visually obvious from the darkening of the water below it.

b) The direction of the approaching wind is visually obvious from the wind lanes on the water, and this is true in both gust and lull.

How to sail to make the best use of this more complex pattern will depend upon the characteristics of the boat you sail, plus a special skill.

1. Displacement boats cannot increase their windward speeds in gusts if the windspeed in the lulls is

already stronger than the design wind. Such boats should therefore continuously observe the direction, rather than the speed, of the approaching wind, and tack as and when necessary to sail the advantaged tacks. They should ignore the gusts except as in '3' below.

2. Windward-planing boats can increase their windward speed in gusts. Their fastest technique will therefore be to tack to sail the advantaged tacks as in 1 above, except that the position of each tack should be biased so that the boat will pass through the gusts to the maximum extent possible.

3. The 'fan' has been described in Section 5.5. The amount of air displaced by these massive gusts is substantial, and their fans are big enough to be features in their own right. They can therefore be aimed at with confidence and used for relatively long periods. While it is in the fan the boat enjoys not only the advantage of the lifted tack, but also the further advantage of the skew of the fan.

The technique to achieve this calls for aiming not just to meet the approaching gust, but a more precise aim to skim its 'outside' shoulder – (the right hand shoulder of a backed gust, and vice versa). As one gifted helmsman puts it, 'When you get it right, you don't go into the gust at all. You just sail around it and point impossibly high. But you have to be close!'

This calls for nice judgment.

It will be obvious that the fan can also be used by high performance downwind-tacking boats. One of the more inspiring sights in sailing is to watch good Sydney Eighteen footers pick up gusts at about mid-point and outrun the gust as they sail downwind along the fan until they reach the advancing edge of the gust.

12.3 Sailing the wind-waves

The steadier winds in which wind-waves develop are those in which the wind speed varies only a little from place to place across the course. The wind's direction backs and veers in a wave-like pattern which may be quick or slow, regular or irregular, but is usually predictable.

In steady-speed winds those crews will win who sail the backs and veers of these wind-waves to advantage for more of the time than their rivals.

Success in handling these wind-waves flows from understanding their nature, their probabilities, the way which is fastest through full-wave patterns, the different way which is fastest through part-wave patterns, sufficient modesty to acknowledge that mere man cannot always know everything, and patience enough to sail in a conservative way at such times until the probabilities become clearer. Let us look at the factors.

12.3.1 The nature of wind-waves

Winds which score 8 or 9 on the *stability index*, such as most sea breezes and funnelling winds, or the particular score 7 case of a gradient wind under a High and over a cooler surface, are the most predictable of all winds. They usually oscillate regularly. In these conditions, an observer who looks upwind from a high vantage point can often see a wave-like pattern traced by the wind lanes which extends indefinitely upwind and downwind. If he moves crosswind himself, as when flying crosswind in an aircraft, the pattern can be seen to extend indefinitely crosswind as well.

When the air is chilled the changes of direction are smooth and the pattern looks like Fig. 12.1(a).

As the air moves from chilled to cooled and towards warmed, the backs and veers may become sharper and the pattern begins to look more like Fig. 12.1(b).

When the air is strongly warmed, harmonics can develop and the primary pattern may become less regular, and look more like Fig. 12.1 (c).

We will call the loci along which the local wind direction is the same as the mean wind direction, i.e. 'n-n', 'p-p', 'r-r', the 'nodes'. The distance between any two nodes is a half wavelength. A full wavelength covers three nodes, e.g. 'n to r'.

The big waves of deep boundary layers have typical wavelengths (n-r, Fig. 12.1) of between 2 and 6 or more kilometres.

The smaller waves of sea breezes have typical wavelengths of 500 to 1.000 metres.

When the windspeed is moderate the change of direction between back and veer (the amplitude) is typically plus and minus about 10 degrees.

As the windspeed increases the amplitude becomes smaller, +/- 5 degrees is typical in 20 knots.

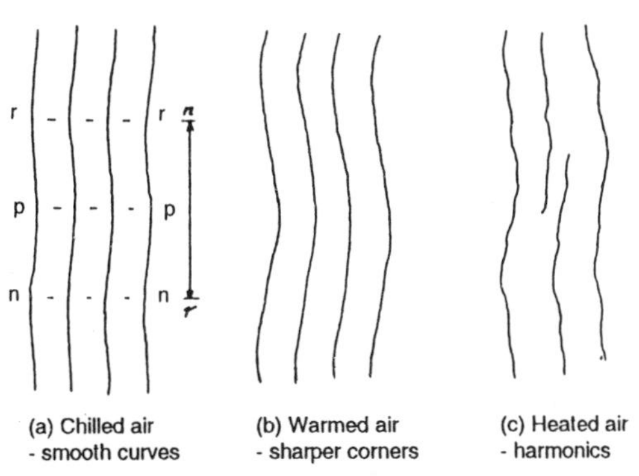

Fig 12.1 The appearance of wind-wave patterns from height

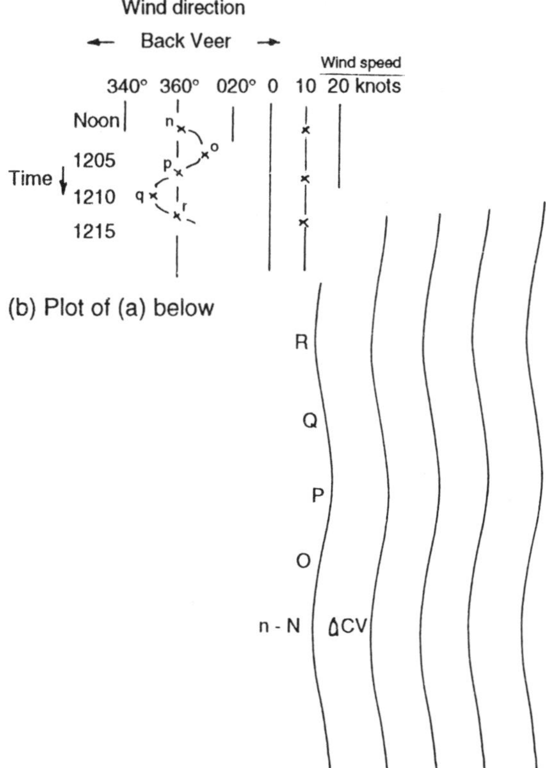

Fig 12.2 Method of plotting wind pattern

As the air becomes heated the amplitude becomes larger.

If the waves are watched for some time from a fixed position, the pattern will be seen to move bodily downwind, as in Fig. 6.1. The speed of movement downwind in that case was about one quarter of the wind's speed. This seems typical. Sometimes it appears to be less.

This downwind movement of the whole pattern means that it will wash over an observer at a fixed position, such as the starter on an anchored committee vessel ('CV'), at a particular speed. Let us imagine that an observer who looks upwind from height sees wind streaks on the water like 'N-O-P-Q-R' in Fig. 12.2. The wind blows in the direction from 'R' to 'N', and the whole pattern of curves moves downwind in the same direction but more slowly. A starter in a moored committee vessel CV measures the wind speed and direction at noon, notes that it is northerly at 10 knots, and plots point 'n' on his graph (Fig. 12.2 (b)). A few minutes later the pattern will have moved downwind and the veer at 'O' will be over the CV. The starter measures the 10 degree veer as 010 degrees, notes the time, and plots point 'o' on his graph at 1203. The pattern keeps moving and a few minutes later the node at 'P' has reached the CV. The starter measures 000 degrees, notes the time, and plots point 'p' on his graph at 6 minutes past noon. As further time passes the back at 'Q' and the node at 'R' each reach the moored CV, the starter keeps measuring and notes the time of each measurement and plots points 'q' and 'r' on his graph – and so on. The wind speed should be noted with each plot. Many of the wind traces which appear in this book have been plotted in exactly this way. I average the direction over 30 seconds, and measure every two minutes.

In the case of the small waves of a shallow sea breeze, the full-wave repetition interval from 'N' to 'R' (the frequency) is likely to be between 6 and 15 minutes. In the case of a gradient wind, it will probably be between 20 and 90 minutes.

If two motor-boats are anchored side by side and there are waves, both will pitch at the frequency of the waves. But if one begins to motor towards the oncoming waves and the other does not, the moving boat will meet each wave sooner, and will be forced to pitch at a faster frequency than the boat at rest. Technically, its movement toward the waves has increased its speed of closing with the wave train and reduced the period between each encounter.

In exactly the same way, a yacht which starts and races to windward will pass through the backs and veers of the wind-waves progressively sooner than they will reach the starter on the moored committee vessel. The faster the boat, the quicker the frequency will become. The effect of any windward-going tide will make the VMG faster yet – and an adverse tide in light winds can slow it surprisingly. The practical effect of sailing upwind is usually to make the windward-going frequency about half the frequency

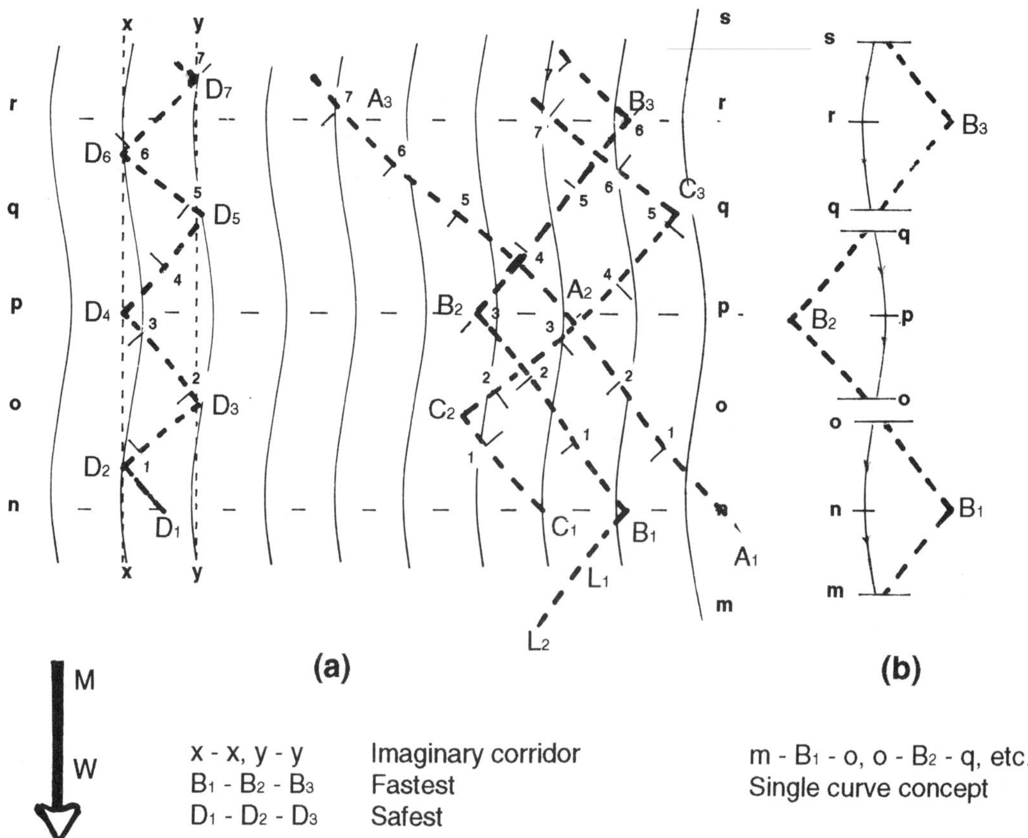

Fig 12.3 Full wave - minimum time and defensive techniques

measured by the starter or by a helmsman who manoeuvres near the start line. This faster frequency which results from the increased speed of closing with the wind-waves will not in any way alter the principles which follow.

There is no difference in principle between the way a crew will handle the shorter waves and rapid shifts of the shallow sea breezes and the longer waves and slower shifts of the deeper boundary layer gradient winds. But in practice the two winds call for an entirely different mental approach. In the shorter waves it is normal to pass through several complete waves between the leeward and the windward mark of any 'round the buoys' race. But in the longer waves of the deep boundary layer wind it is often uncertain whether or not you will pass through even one.

12.3.2 The probabilities of wind-waves.

Some wind-waves repeat more regularly than others

The sea and lake breeze traces shown in Figs 7.14 to 7.19 are typical of sea breezes and funnelling winds around the world. As a group, they are about as regular as wind-waves are likely to be, but none of the traces are free from occasional irregularities. The probabilities are such that a crew who plan on the expectation of regular repetition will usually be rewarded, but they must be constantly alert for irregularity and be able to detect it and accommodate to it without serious loss when it occurs.

The gradient wind traces shown in Figs 7.3 to 7.13 are a much more varied group. They all show the expected slower frequency. The 'High dominant, cooled' ones are as regular as any sea breeze. But when either or both of the stabilising controls (subsidence inversion or cooling) are removed, regularity becomes questionable and ultimately vanishes. However, in every case a semblance of pattern remains, in the sense that the amplitude remains between bounds and the interval between successive waves does not become less than something nor more than something. In this sense a crew can remain confident of a repetition pattern which, while not regular, will remain within those bounds.

12.3.3 The fastest way through full wind-waves

Fig. 12.3 and all similar subsequent diagrams are accurately drawn to scale on the assumptions that the boats sail to windward at steady speed and at 45 degrees to the True Wind. Also that the wind backs and veers plus and minus 10 degrees, that the windspeed is steady over the course area and that there is no current nor tidal stream. No dimension scale is implied because everything that follows will be as true when the waves are long as when they are short. 'M-W' is the mean wind direction. The curves 's-r-q-p-o-n-m' are the paths which would be traced by the shadows of thistle-down or smoke puffs released from 's'. Along the nodes 'r-r', 'p-p' and 'n-n' the local wind direction is the same as the mean wind direction. Along the line 'q-q' the local wind is backed 10 degrees, and it is veered 10 degrees along the line 'o-o'.

'A1-A2-A3' is the track of boat 'A' which starts on starboard tack from 'n-n' and does not tack. For the sake of the example which follows we will assume that the wind is a sea breeze which oscillates as in Fig. 12.2(b), that the wind-waves flow over a stationary observer at about one each 10 minutes and that a boat which sails to windward in the fastest way will sail from 'n' to 'r' in 6 minutes. '1', '2', '3', etc. mark the positions of each boat at 1, 2, 3, etc. minutes after starting from 'n-n'. 'A' takes 3 minutes to reach 'p-p' but 6.9 minutes to reach 'r-r' because it sails a 10 degree header – a disadvantaged tack with a lower VMG – all the way from 'A2' to 'A3'. A boat which sails on port tack continuously will take the same time to sail from 'n-n' to 'r-r'.

'B1-B2-B3' is the track of 'B' which starts from 'n-n' and tacks at each node, i.e. at 'p-p' and at 'r-r'. 'B' takes only 6 minutes to reach 'r-r', i.e. 54 seconds or 18% faster than 'A'. On each tack it is first progressively 'lifted' 10 degrees (from 'n' to 'o'and from 'p' to 'q'), and then headed 10 degrees from '0' to 'p' and from 'q' to 'r'. Note that this technique enables it to sail the advantaged tack at all times, and the disadvantaged tack not at all.

'C1-C2-C3' is the track of 'C' which tacks as soon as it is headed at 'o-o' and 'q-q'. The fact that this technique makes it appear to 'lift' all the time (eg. from 'o' to 'q' masks the fact that it sails the disadvantaged tack from 'o' to 'p' and from 'q' to 'r'). Because of this in smooth wind-waves such as Fig. 12.1(a) it takes 60 seconds or 17% longer than 'B' to reach 'r-r'.

When the curves are not smooth and the changes in direction are more abrupt, as in Fig. 12.1(b), the principle remains the same but it is necessary to tack more quickly.

When there are harmonics, as in Fig. 12.1(c), the boat will be alternately lifted and headed through many degrees every one or two minutes as it passes through the minor waves. In these conditions a crew should not tack until they are headed with respect to the mean wind. For example, if the mean wind is from 360 degrees (North) and the primary oscillations are plus and minus 10 degrees, i.e. from 010 and 350 degrees respectively, and the harmonics are +/- 8 degrees, then on starboard tack the wind direction will alternate between 018 and 002 degrees. It will be plain that the boat is lifted when it sails in the 018 degree wind. When it is headed by the 002 degree wind the fact that it has been headed 16 degrees will be obvious. What is not so obvious is that the 002 degree direction is still a 2 degree lift on starboard tack, so starboard is still the favoured tack despite the recent 16 degree header. In harmonic conditions a crew must not tack just because they appear to have been headed. They should tack only when the wind direction passes through the mean and the other tack becomes the favoured tack.

'D1-D2-D3-D4..' is the track of 'D' which sails within an imaginary corridor between 'D2-D4-D6' and 'D3-D5-D7'. Boat 'D' takes 6.6 minutes to reach 'r-r'. This is slower that the 6.0 minutes of 'B' but faster than all the others. Note particularly that 'D' does not spend half its time on each tack. The consequence of remaining within the imaginary corridor (which calls for nice judgement) is that the advantaged tacks become a little longer and the disadvantaged tacks become shorter, and so the time spent on each is biased in favour of the advantaged tacks. This is the 'defensive' technique.

When you sail to windward through one or more full waves, you should sail as 'B' when you have sufficient information and are confident of the wind ahead.

You should sail as 'D' at all other times.

All other options are slower.

12.3.4 The Basic Principle

There are two ways of thinking about the curves of Fig. 12.3.

The first is to regard the double-curve segment 'n-o-p' as a veer in which starboard tack will be advantaged, followed by a similar segment 'p-q-r' which is a back in which port tack will be advantaged, and so on. This mental picture is fine, but it is only a half truth which is not helpful except in full wave situations.

It is this concept which has lead to the artificial separation within yachting literature of the 'persistent shift' situations from the 'oscillating wind' situations. The reality is that they are simply different parts of the same continuum.

The more helpful mental picture is to regard all patterns as either one single curve or a series of separate single curves in the wind, such as 'm-n-o', 'o-p-q', 'q-r-s' in the inset Fig. 12.3 (b). In the case of full waves, the curves happen to be conveniently strung together.

Wherever there is a curve in the wind, the shortest-distance and therefore minimum-time path through it will be to sail always the shorter 'inside' path, i.e. 'm-B1-o', 'o-B2-q', 'q-B3-s' as in Fig. 12.3 (b). This focus on the single curves gives us a much better feel for the part-wave, single-curve elements which occur at the windward end of every leg, and which are such a feature of sailing in slow oscillations. When 'm-B1-o', 'o-B2-q', etc. are strung together, we get the optimum 'B1-B2-B3' path of 'B' in Fig. 12.3(a).

The principle of endeavouring to 'sail the inside of every curve' remains correct regardless of whether the curve is short or long, part-wave or full-wave. It is invaluable in enabling a crew to make sense of a confused situation and to reach a logical decision when the wave-lengths are intermediate and the probability of regularity is uncertain.

12.3.5 The start of the beat – one or more full waves expected

The start line or the leeward mark will usually lie somewhere between the nodes of the pattern. Regardless of the position of the leeward mark, ('L1', 'L2', etc. in Fig. 12.3 (a)) the fastest path will always be to adopt the 'lifted' tack immediately. This will necessarily be the 'inside' of the first curve.

If the wind direction is measured in the minute before rounding the leeward mark, this reveals which will be the advantaged tack and enables you to adopt it with minimum delay (when tactics admit).

In ideal conditions you should be sailing the headers downwind. When this is the situation, the advantaged tack upwind will be the opposite of the headed gybe downwind, i.e. if you approach the leeward mark headed on starboard gybe, port tack will be the initial advantaged tack upwind and vice versa.

When you approach the mark on a reaching leg, if the wind direction has changed to make the end of the leg tight, you should tack. If it is free and you need to luff occasionally for speed, do not tack.

If for tactical or other reasons you are not on the headed gybe, or are unsure, then the wind direction should be measured as noted for downwind in 'preparations', if it is possible to do this without significant loss.

12.3.6 The approach to the windward mark.

The windward mark or the finish line will also usually lie somewhere between the nodes of the pattern. In this part-wave situation, unlike the situation at the start of the beat, two other factors will influence how quickly you will reach it. The first is which tack you adopt. The second is where you start from.

1. Which Tack? Fig. 12.4 shows the principles from starting points on the node directly downwind of the mark.

Fig. 12.4(a) Mark one full wave upwind.

To sail the inside of every curve, adopt the advantaged tack first. Path ABC is shortest. All others are longer. Path ADC is 22% longer and slower.

Fig. 12.4(b) Mark ¾ wavelength upwind.

Again, adopt the advantaged tack first. Path ABC is shortest. All others are longer. Path ADC is 20% longer and slower.

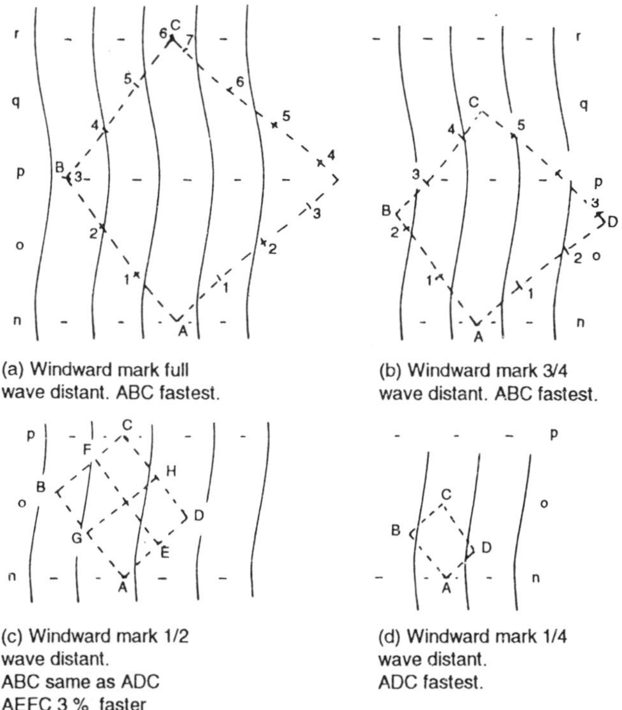

(a) Windward mark full wave distant. ABC fastest.

(b) Windward mark 3/4 wave distant. ABC fastest.

(c) Windward mark 1/2 wave distant.
ABC same as ADC
AEFC 3 % faster
AGHC 7 % slower.

(d) Windward mark 1/4 wave distant.
ADC fastest.

Fig 12.4 Part wave: minimum time paths from starting points on the node which are directly downwind of the windward mark

Fig. 12.4(c) Mark ½ wavelength upwind.

There are two curves, n-o and o-p which are equal and opposite. In this case paths ABC and ADC are of equal lengths. Path AEFC, which starts by sailing the headed tack first, is fractionally (3%) shorter than either ABC or ADC, because the gain through EF is greater than the losses through AE and FC. Path AGHC is a trap. It tries to be 'safe' by sailing a part of the lifted tack first and then sailing 'up the middle'. In fact it is 10% longer and slower than the ABC or ADC, and 13% longer than AEFC, because the loss through GH is greater than the gains through AG and HC. This is one of those cases where by trying to be careful and sailing 'safely, up the middle', you will be beaten by the boats on both sides of you.

For this reason, if when you reach the node you are uncertain but think that you are approaching the half-wave distance, it is safer to sail a little way into the headed tack before you go about.

12.4(d) Mark less than ½ wavelength upwind.

In this case the effective curve is n-o, and the inside of the curve lies to the right when a veer is expected. (When a back is expected the 'inside' will be to the left.) Path ADC, which sails the inside of the curve, is 11% shorter than ABC.

In 12.4(c) and (d) there is positive gain in 'sailing the disadvantaged tack first'. This is true if we define 'advantaged', etc. with respect to the mean wind. The reality is that the mean direction of the wind which remains to be sailed through when the mark is a half wave-length or less upwind of a node is not at all the same as the mean direction of the wind over a wide area. In this limited situation, the wide-area 'mean wind' has become irrelevant. The basic principle, 'sail the inside of the curve', remains true.

However, for practical purposes it is the wide-area mean wind which we tend to relate to throughout the race, and we think of tacks as 'advantaged' and 'disadvantaged' with respect to compass numbers based on this mean wind. So the practical advice is: 'When the mark is about a half wave-length or less to windward, sail the disadvantaged tack first.'

This advice is equally true regardless of whether the waves are long or short.

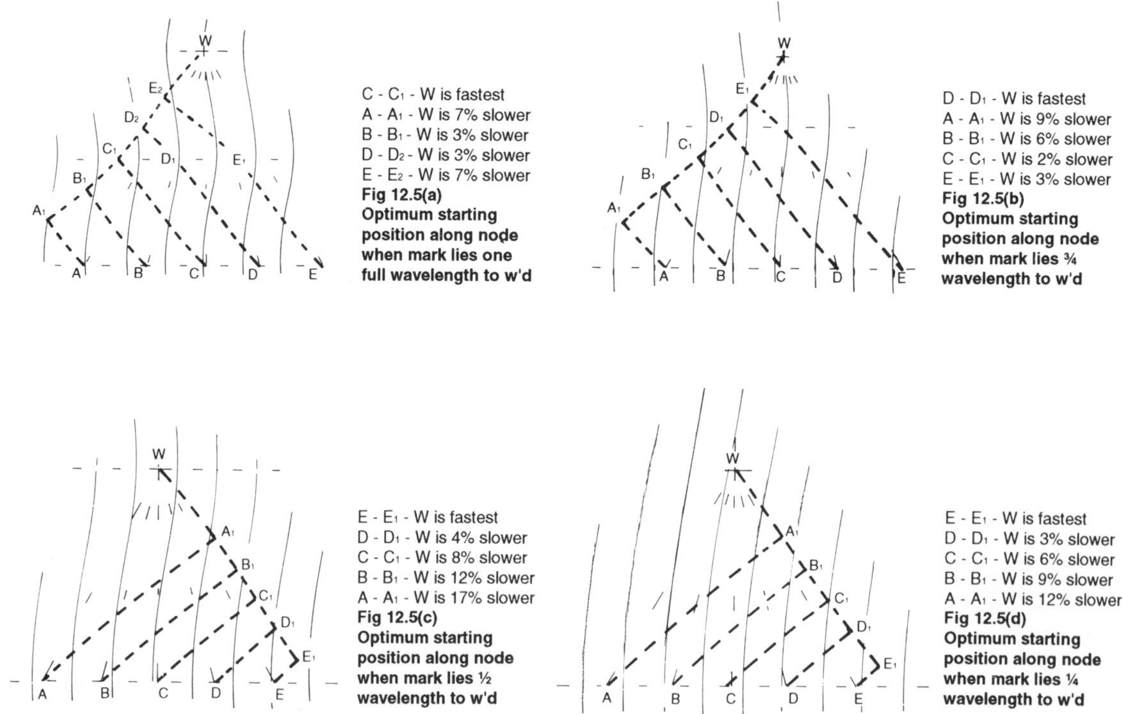

C - C1 - W is fastest
A - A1 - W is 7% slower
B - B1 - W is 3% slower
D - D2 - W is 3% slower
E - E2 - W is 7% slower
Fig 12.5(a)
Optimum starting position along node when mark lies one full wavelength to w'd
D - D1 - W is fastest
A - A1 - W is 9% slower
B - B1 - W is 6% slower
C - C1 - W is 2% slower
E - E1 - W is 3% slower
Fig 12.5(b)
Optimum starting position along node when mark lies ¾ wavelength to w'd
E - E1 - W is fastest
D - D1 - W is 4% slower
C - C1 - W is 8% slower
B - B1 - W is 12% slower
A - A1 - W is 17% slower
Fig 12.5(c)
Optimum starting position along node when mark lies ½ wavelength to w'd
E - E1 - W is fastest
D - D1 - W is 3% slower
C - C1 - W is 6% slower
B - B1 - W is 9% slower
A - A1 - W is 12% slower
Fig 12.5(d)
Optimum starting position along node when mark lies ¼ wavelength to w'd

Fig 12.5 Part wave: fastest starting positions from the nodes

2. Where you start from.

This section may prove surprising. The diagrams in most published tactical works reflect the widespread belief that boats which are equally far upwind in the crosswind sense – as for example a boat at the right hand 'corner' of the course, another at the left, and others on the line between them – should all reach the windward mark together. This is broadly true provided that there are still several wind-waves to be sailed through. It is when you approach the windward mark more closely or the wave is longer that the differences begin to emerge.

Fig. 12.5 shows the principles. For simplicity we will look at the fortunes of five boats which start from positions which are in line crosswind on the last node that they cross before they reach the mark. In each diagram boats A, B, C, D and E lie at angles of 30, 15, 0, -15 and -30 degrees from directly downwind of the mark. For realism, let us assume the smooth curves with +/- 10 degree veers and backs of Fig. 12.1(a), etc. and that a 14 foot boat which sails to windward at 5 knots will pass through one full wave every six minutes.

12.5(a) Mark one wave-length to windward, veer expected.

Path 'C-C1-W' sails the inside of every curve, and is fastest.

Path 'B' is headed between 'B1' to 'C1', and is 3% longer.

Path 'D' is headed between 'D1' to 'D2', and is 3% longer.

Path 'A' is headed between 'A1' to 'C1', and is 7% longer.

Path 'E' is headed between 'E1' to 'E2' and is 7% longer.

Boat 'C' arrives at the mark or finish first, from a starting position directly downwind of the mark, and after 360 seconds' sailing. Boats 'B' and 'D' arrive 11 seconds later, 6 boat-lengths behind. Boats 'A' and 'E' arrive 25 seconds later, 15 boat lengths behind.

12.5(b) Mark ¾ wave-length to windward, veer expected.

Path 'D-D1-W' sails the inside of every curve, and is fastest.

Boats 'C' and 'E' are headed from 'C1' to 'D1'and from'E1' to 'E2' respectively,and sail about 2% further.

Boats 'B' and 'A' are headed as they sail from 'B1' to 'D1' and from 'A1' to 'D1', and sail 6% and 9% further.

Boat 'D' arrives first, after 270 seconds, from a starting position 15 degrees to the right of directly downwind when a veer is expected.

Boats 'C' and 'E' arrive 5 seconds later, 3 lengths behind.

Boat 'B' arrives 16 seconds later, 10 lengths behind.

Boat 'A' arrives 27 seconds later, 16 lengths behind.

These differences begin to explain some of the 'how did he or she get there?' situations which occur so frequently near marks.

12.5(c) Mark ½ wave-length to windward, veer expected.

Path 'E-E1-W' sails the inside of every curve.

Boat 'E' arrives first, after 180 seconds, from a position 30 degrees right of directly downwind.

Boat 'D' arrives 5 seconds later, 3 lengths behind.

Boat 'C' arrives 13 seconds later, 8 lengths behind.

Boat 'B' arrives 21 seconds later, 13 lengths behind.

Boat 'A' arrives 27 seconds later, 16 lengths behind.

These substantial differences develop within the final half-wave distance of about 325 metres or 3 minutes from the mark, between boats which were equally close to the mark in the upwind/downwind direction.

The advice in 12.4 above that it is equally fast to adopt either tack when a half wave-length remains to be sailed remains true for all five boats. Which way you go will not help (other than tactically) if you have started from the wrong position.

12.5(d) Mark ¼ wave-length upwind, veer expected.

The position is broadly similar to 12.5(c).

Boat 'E' arrives first, after 90 seconds.

Boat 'D' arrives 2 seconds later, 1 length behind.

Boat 'C' arrives 5 seconds later, 3 lengths behind.

Boat 'B' arrives 9 seconds later, 6 lengths behind.

Boat 'A' arrives 13 seconds later, 8 lengths behind.

The diagrams of 12.5 and the tables above make it clear that when boats race within one wave-length of a windward mark or the finish:-

1. Boats which are equally close to the mark in the upwind-downwind sense cannot expect to finish together.
2. Whenever the distance still to be sailed is less than one full wave-length, the optimum starting position is not directly downwind of the mark.
3. Boats which start on the 'wrong' side suffer greater losses than the others' gains.
4. When the wind-waves are not predictable and regular, the safest starting position is directly downwind of the mark, but -
5. When the wind-waves are regular, very great advantage can be gained by biasing the path so as to arrive at the node near the optimum starting position for the back or veer expected and the distance still to be sailed. This calls for very deliberate estimation of the oscillation pattern for more than one wave-length ahead.

When the wind-waves are regular, calculation and estimation ('guesstimation) of the remaining distance, number of waves and optimum final starting position is properly based on anticipation of repetition.

When the waves are not regular, the fact that patterns repeat within bounds can be used. There has to be some shortest probable distance for a half-wave. Sail defensively close to the rhumb line until close to this distance, then:

1. If approaching a node, sail first for the optimum starting position on the node for a half-wave or less.
2. If within a back or veer, sail as suggested in 'Part-wave legs' that follows.

12.3.7 Part-wave legs (persistent shifts) – less than one full wave expected

When the waves are so long that the legs of the course are shorter than one wave-length, the whole leg will be sailed in a part-wave. This situation is sometimes referred to as a persistent shift, although as is clear from Figs 12.4 and 12.6 there is frequently more than one curve involved. Part-wave legs will necessarily start either on or near a node, or at or near the midpoint of a back or veer.

When the start line or the leeward mark is on or near a node, the possibilities are as shown in Fig. 12.4, and the whole leg should be sailed exactly as you would normally sail the approach to every windward mark. For practical purposes, you estimate that the mark:

1. Lies beyond a half-wave distance, as in 12.4(a) and (b). In this case sail the advantaged tack first (starboard if veer expected, and vice versa)

2. Lies at about a half-wave distance, as 12.4(c). In this case sail the disadvantaged tack first, and follow the path 'AEFC'. Quite apart from being he fastest path if your estimates are exactly right, this path keeps you reasonably close to the rhumb line, and so is a sensible choice in marginal situations.

3. Lies closer than a half-wave, as in 12.4(d). In this case sail the disadvantaged tack first. Tack before you reach the layline, partly because you expect to be 'lifted' strongly as you approach the mark, and partly to retain some tactical flexibility.

When the start line or leeward mark lies at or near the mid-point of a back or veer, the situation simplifies as in Fig. 12.6:

12.6(a) Full-wave.
Adopt advantaged tack. Sail 'a-b-c-d' as in 12.4(a).

12.6(b) ¾ wave.
Adopt advantaged tack. Sail beyond node at 'y-b', so as to spend greatest possible time 'b-c' in most advantaged 'lift'. Paths 'y-b' and 'c-d' are close to nodes and little headed. Path 'a-y-e-d' is longer and slower than 'a-b-c-d' because 'e-c' is headed more than 'y-b'.

12.6(c) ½ wave.
Adopt advantaged tack.

12.6(d) ¼ wave
Sail inside of curve 'a-b-c'. Nothing else makes sense.

Fig. 12.6 shows that the shortest path when starting between nodes and expecting less than one full wave is always to sail the advantaged tack first, and hold it either to the next node, as in (a), (b), and (c), or to the lay line, as in (d). It is only when starting at nodes and for wave-lengths about a half-wave or less that the technique of adopting the headed tack first should be used.

12.3.8 To windward when confident of the pattern

Immediately after the start:

(a) If starboard tack is favoured, never tack unless a short tack becomes essential to clear your wind, and you are lucky enough to have a gap in the fleet to windward to enable you to do this. Before you make any tack in a crowded fleet, be very certain that this will be more profitable than 'hanging in there', and waiting for the fleet to thin. If there is clear air close to leeward, a quick close-reach for one or two lengths to clear your wind to leeward of a boat or boats close ahead will probably lose you much less than two tacks, particularly if you sail a fast boat. When in doubt, do not tack.

(b) If port tack is favoured, and you have started well, do not tack and sacrifice good position if nobody else has tacked. The fact that, for awhile, everybody is sailing in the wrong direction – and this often happens – is overridden by the fact that you are well placed in the fleet. Dirty wind from the front line will soon thin the fleet behind, and enable you to adopt port tack a little later with little loss to any boat. But if you have started badly, tack immediately, take sterns, and go for clear air on the favoured tack. Nothing else makes sense.

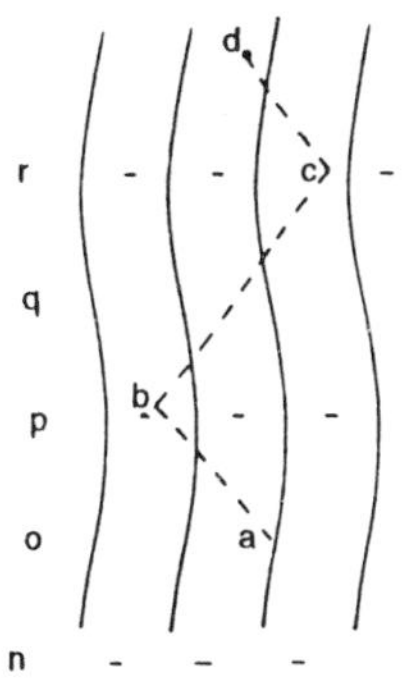

(a)
Mark lies one full wave to windward.
a - b - c - d fastest.
Adopt advantaged tack first.
Tack at nodes.

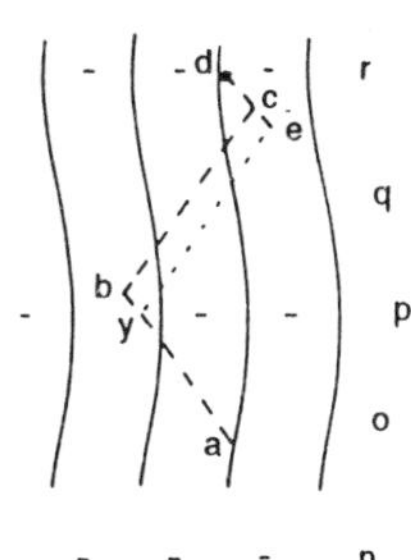

(b)
Mark 3/4 wave to windward.
a - b - c - d fastest.
Adopt advantaged tack first.
Tack beyond node.

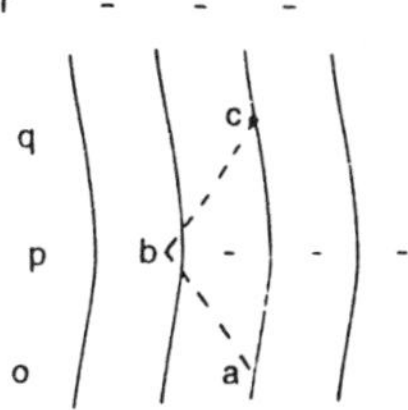

(c)
Mark lies 1/2 wave to windward.
Sail inside of expected curve.
Adopt advantaged tack first.
Tack before layline.

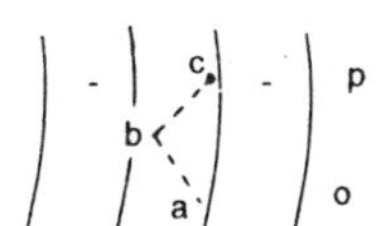

(d)
Mark 1/4 wave to windward.
Sail inside of expected curve.
Tack before layline.

Fig 12.6 Part wave: minimum time paths from start between nodes.

(c) Lock into the windshift pattern. The pre-start work you have done will enable you to do this at least as well as the few others who were prepared to do this work, and enable you to do it sooner and better and more accurately than everybody else. Do not be fazed if you find yourself among the leaders.

(d) Do not tack until you are certain that the wind has reached or passed its mean direction as it oscillates. There is no law that prevents the wind from wriggling. As it approaches its mean, there are often momentary swings past the mean. If you tack on one of these, and it was only a momentary swing, you will lose a little to those who waited and tacked accurately, ('B', Fig. 12.3). But the principle damage will be to your confidence, because suddenly things will start to go wrong in your mind. One crew member should follow and time the windshifts all the time, so that you know not only that the wind direction is approaching the mean but also that the time is approaching when you expect that it should. I am always fascinated by the grease-pencil graphs on the sides or the decks of top-level Solings and Etchells, and the squeaky-clean topsides and decks of the scrubbers. There is a lesson there about what is most important in the minds of those who win. Be sure that the wind is at its mean before you tack.

Fig. 12.3 shows your course through the pattern when you sail this way. If only it were this easy! In real life, you cannot see the wind. You must therefore sense its pattern, and also sense that the wind is 'lifted' or 'headed' by comparing your boat's present heading with what its heading would be at what you believe is the wind's mean direction.

This is the critical part. Your efforts to exploit the wind's curves will be effective only if the model of the wind which you hold in your mind truly reflects the wind's reality. All else must be futile. Your most important task, then, is to observe and visualise the wind's present pattern, and to accept, mentally, any changes which occur with minimum delay, so that your mental model is always accurate enough to be useful. If the pattern is clear in your mind, what to do about it, and doing it, are easy.

There are several useful ways of sensing the pattern, and exploiting the curves, when you sail upwind.

The simplest method (which is particularly effective in unsteady winds), is to sense the direction of the nearby wind by observing the headings of adjacent boats. This method is direct. The rule is, 'if a boat on the same tack, either ahead or behind, is pointing significantly higher than you are, or a boat on the other tack is pointing lower than expected, you must be in a header, so tack'. The great advantage of this method is that the present pattern in your area is continuously revealed, and as well, the direction of the mean wind is constantly revealed and corrected. Use this method, always, when you are in close company, and never forget to keep looking over your shoulder, at the boats behind, particularly when you are in the lead.

12.3.9 Fleet sailing.

The technique above, slightly extended, is what fleet sailing is all about. Whenever opportunity offers to cross a competitor, take it. As Hans Fogh puts it- 'When God gives you a break, put it in the bank'. Tack, cross ahead, tack again, and establish yourself in a position between the competitor (or the 'fleet') and the next mark.

When you are sailing in conditions in which there is no regular pattern this technique can be further extended to become 'percentage sailing'. If you are uncertain but think it equally likely that the wind may shift either way, position yourself so that about half the fleet are on either side of you. If you are uncertain but think it is more likely to back, sail so that about 40% are to your left and 60% to your right. This is the technique used most of the time by top-level sailors when conditions are unsteady.

If in these conditions you elect, instead, to 'minimum-time' sail, and let the backs and veers run their course and tack on the nodes, you may well sail a shorter path to the mark and finish further ahead. This is the technique of the ocean racer. But if you are sailing around the buoys and do not have the luxury of being able to wait forever for the next back or veer, and the wind direction does not behave as you expect, you may well finish further behind. You will also be subject to any differences in wind strength and other variables, and these may not be to your advantage. The difference between fleet sailing and minimum-time sailing is safety *now*. The fleet sailor, a few lengths in front, is safe from most of the uncertainties about wind direction and variables in wind speed, and that is what he wants.

There are prices to pay for this short-term safety. One is that you will not be as far ahead as you might have been and so your margins become less (all tactics degrade strategy and slow the boat). Another is that you cannot effectively block either a single competitor or a group of competitors when you are sailing downwind, and so 'safety' only works for some of the time. A third is that you cannot be in two places at once, so whenever the fleet splits, you are back to square one – you have to make the right 'minimum-time' decision, or you lose. There is no safety in staying in front of a boat which is going the wrong way.

A good example of this comes from the last Soling race of the Tallinn pre-Olympic regatta in 1979 – the race after the two-cloud example noted in Section 12.5.2. The four Solings which could win were indeed at the front of the fleet at the last leeward mark, in the order, let us say, of A, K, C and D. The wind-waves were irregular. 'A' fleet-sailed ahead of C and D who elected to sail defensively. 'K' sailed away on the other tack. 'A' elected to stay with C and D – when the fleet split he had no option but to choose to stay with one part of it or the other. As they approached the windward mark some minutes later, 'K' crossed in front of the other three, and won the race and the series. He had 'minimum-time' sailed a difficult part-wave leg well enough to beat the group who had sailed defensively. 'A' finished second in the race and in the series. Skill in percentage sailing the fleet is no defense against minimum-time sailing, split fleets, nor on downwind legs.

Percentage sailing will fail as soon as the wind shifts become regular. Wind-waves are usually only a few hundred metres long. If you imagine a fleet which is spread over a few hundred metres and within which every boat is exploiting the windshifts correctly, then half the boats will be on port tack and heading to the right, and half on starboard and heading left. In these conditions any boat which sails to keep half the fleet to port and half to starboard will necessarily sail in headers for half the time and so will be beaten by every other boat, and this will remain true regardless of that boat's position in the fleet. The safest technique, as soon as the *stability index* suggests regular windshifts, is 'don't sail headers' – even little ones. The percentage sailing which wins in unsteady winds should be discarded as soon as the shifts become regular, even if they are very small.

12.3.10 Defensive sailing.

When you are not confident of a regular pattern, sail defensively.

If you have started well, stay on starboard tack with the leaders, until the fleet has thinned, you can tack without loss of position, and you judge that you have sailed as far from the rhumb line as is prudent. Tack, cross the rhumb line, and again judge your distance from it the other side, and repeat. Consciously prolong slightly the tacks which more directly approach the windward mark, and shorten slightly the unfavourable ones, but never allow yourself to be tempted too far from the rhumb line. If there is no predictable pattern the wind may swing either way – and half the time it does!

Sailing for too long and too far from the rhumb line on a 'favoured' tack will leave you badly disadvantaged when the wind keeps swinging the same way. The object of defensive sailing is to defend against exactly this.

12.3.11 Windward-sailing techniques.

In the absence of nearby boats, a landmark ahead on each tack gives continuous and accurate indication of your heading, but it tells you nothing about the mean wind. This you must begin to sense in your mind. In the classic sea breeze situation, after you tack (at 'B1', Fig. 12.3), you can expect to watch your heading 'lift' about ten degrees during one to two minutes, 'B1' to locus 'o-o'. (A hand's width including thumb at arm's length is about 10 degrees.) Your heading will remain steady for awhile at 'o-o', and then 'head' for one minute or more, 'o-o' to 'B2'. At what you judge is the mid-point of the oscillation, you should tack, at 'B2' and expect to watch the process repeat on the other tack. There may be wriggles in the wind at any time, but so long as you have a secure sense of both the windshift pattern and also its rhythm, you can recognise these as momentary wobbles and ignore them.

If you lift more than expected, and particularly if the direction fails to return to what you expect to be the mean at the time that it should, accept this as a warning that the mean may have shifted, perhaps temporarily, perhaps permanently. In this situation it is usually safer to assume such a shift and tack. The principle reason why this is safer is that a return toward the rhumb line is the natural response whenever you adopt defensive sailing, and so this response has two chances out of three of being the correct response whenever there is any uncertainty. If you lift less than expected, assume that the wind has probably shifted a little the other way.

Reliance on landmarks ahead will obviously fail if there aren't any.

A more sophisticated method is to use diagonal marks on your deck or cockpit floor. Use tapes to trial the method and establish where the permanent marks ought to be so that you can see them and sight along them when you want to. Compare their alignment with a distant landmark which is upwind or downwind at the orientation of the mean wind. So long as the direction of the relevant diagonal compared with the distant mark (allowing for parallax) indicates that you are pointing higher than you would at the wind's mean direction, this indicates that you are 'lifted' on that tack, *provided*, that the direction of the mean wind has not changed.

This method is one of the easiest to grasp mentally. You can see the heading change while you sail. It will indicate exactly when to tack, and it is probably the most direct of all the methods in alerting you to a possible change in the direction of the mean wind. As in the paragraph above, if you sense non-standard shift of direction, assume that it is probably due to a change in the direction of the mean wind and tack back towards the rhumb line until certainty and confidence are restored. This method fails in haze or when there is no suitable distant object.

For serious racing only a compass will provide continuous heading information in haze or rain or in the absence of useful landmarks. It is therefore an essential piece of equipment, but it has two drawbacks.

The first is that it requires another and different mental skill to interpret a number read from a compass in a way which is meaningful in understanding what the wind is doing over an area. The critical point here is that just following compass numbers without relating them to the overall pattern can only work if the preliminary information gathering was completely accurate, *and* the pattern has not since changed even a little. If the pattern has changed a little, just following compass numbers is about as useful as the right street directory in the wrong city.

The compass' second drawback is that it is such a convenient thing to concentrate on when things go slightly wrong. When winning crews become uncertain, they concentrate on the environment outside the boat, and on the future. They adopt defensive sailing, look outside the boat, absorb all the area information visible, and keep on absorbing it and analysing it until the corrected pattern becomes clear in their minds. They then decide the compass numbers which will best help them exploit this new (i.e. corrected) pattern. Only then does the compass get looked at again.

In the same situation, lesser crews concentrate harder on the boat and the past. They focus on their compasses, read them twice as often, and mutter evil things about temporary shifts. It is all so much easier. The only problem is that they are now trying to exploit a pattern which no longer exists, and so they fall further behind. Do not expect from a compass anything more than a number against a lubber line which indicates your heading now. It is not a crystal ball. It is not responsible for the wind.

12.3.12 Realities.

The regular-wave situation described above is the ideal. It exists frequently, the technique is achievable, and it wins. But sometimes things go wrong, either because of a mistake, or the sheer pressure of traffic forces you toward one side of the course to avoid impossible air. The result in each case is that you find yourself too far to one side of the course for mental comfort. When this occurs:

(a) Mentally discard the single 'mean wind' division between port-tack favoured and starboard-tack favoured shifts. Instead, think of the shifts as in three parts: a port-favoured extreme, a starboard-favoured extreme, and a zone in the middle in which you can go either way without much loss.

(b) For 'percentage sailors' who sense that regular shifts are emerging but are not yet sufficiently confident of them to abandon percentage sailing, this technique is invaluable. Use the middle bits for percentage positioning. But sail the extremes as lifts.

(c) This middle zone can also be used to obtain any tactical position you want. You will lose a little, but much less than if you approach the windward mark from too close to either lay line and are forced to sail a header on the final approach to the mark. A far worse situation occurs when the wind shifts a little, and you sail for longer than you should on a tack which appears to remain 'lifted'. This will leave you still downwind of the mark after your competitors have rounded it. The moment you sense this happening, get back towards the rhumb line, and the sooner you do this the less you will lose. To delay action in this situation is the quickest way to the back of the fleet. The defense against this is to time the tacks. One crew member should always keep the time. If the expected time for one tack expires, but the wind direction has not begun to return to its original mean, this is the best and earliest warning you can get that its mean has probably shifted. To restore control: . . .

(i) Change your estimate of the mean direction. If you find yourself to starboard of the rhumb line, assume that the mean has shifted to port, i.e. anti-clockwise, and reduce the compass numbers by whatever seems reasonable and vice versa. (A correction of about half the total swing or a little more seems adequate on most occasions).

(ii) Tack without delay to regain the rhumb line, and sail close to it until you are confident of the new mean wind and where you are in the pattern.

As you approach the windward mark, start early to estimate how many more tacks you will need to reach it. As the number falls towards two, i.e. a little more than one full wave length, bias your position to the left or right of the rhumb line so as to start your final approach from as near the optimum position as possible, as in Fig. 12.5.

12.3.13 Sailing crosswind through wind-waves

As between sailing directly towards the mark, and sailing any other course, the crosswind legs offer least gain. The leading boat will normally sail straight lines in clear air, and will usually increase its lead by doing so. The steadier the wind speed, the truer this will be.

On crosswind legs in big fleets, relative success will usually depend much more upon minimising the disturbance or slowing of your wind by adjacent boats than upon any elegant plan to exploit the wind-waves. However, two particular situations frequently occur in which race advantage can be gained by exploiting the expected change of wind direction.

All planing boats with spinnakers will have one wind angle at which they reach fastest without spinnaker, and another wind angle at which they broad reach fastest with spinnaker. In the case of light, fast boats the speeds at intermediate wind angles are often so much slower that it is often faster to sail an offwind leg partly reaching at maximum speed and partly broad reaching at maximum speed rather than sailing directly for the mark at some lower speed. If you sail such a craft, and a back or veer is expected during a reaching leg, you can shorten your distance and time if you elect to 'two-sail' reach through the headed part of the wind-wave, and use spinnaker through the part where the wind is more free.

Another technique appropriate to such craft is to exploit the curves by, 'snaking'. It is sometimes possible to luff and bear away as appropriate through the backs and veers and in this way maintain consistently the wind angle needed for highest speed. Sail high of the mark when lifted but sail low, back to the rhumb line and below it, when this becomes possible through the headed curves. A boat sailed this way can sometimes sail at continuous high speed throughout the leg. A rival who sails directly for the mark will sail a slightly shorter distance, but will alternate between high speed and some slower speed as his wind angle changes.

12.3.14 Sailing downwind

In many classes of boat, the quickest way to the leeward mark is to head directly for it. For these boats the oscillations in wind direction will make only a trivial difference.

In most classes the fastest way will be either to luff a little for clearer air onto a short-pole spinnaker,or to tack downwind. Part Four includes the handling techniques but we are here concerned with how best to exploit the wind's oscillations of direction.

For boats which do not sail directly downwind, the downwind legs become the mirror images of sailing upwind, but with three major differences. These are:

1. When sailing downwind, the headers are the advantaged gybe. This is the reverse of sailing upwind.

2. If you keep the windshifts in your mind as you approach and round the windward mark, you can adopt the advantaged gybe without uncertainty. The rule is: If starboard tack is advantaged upwind, port gybe will be advantaged downwind and vice versa.

At the leeward mark, the reverse situation will apply – when the favoured approach is port gybe, adopt starboard tack without hesitation, and vice versa.

3. The wind-waves usually move downwind at about one quarter of the wind speed. Most sailboats sail upwind and downwind at somewhere between one third and two thirds of the wind's speed. Let us assume half the wind's speed for the sake of example. The consequences of these speeds are:

(a) When sailing downwind you will be sailing a little faster than the wind-waves, and overtaking them. So, if there are boats both ahead and astern, it will be the boats ahead, i.e. downwind of you, which will indicate to you the wind direction you will shortly be sailing in. Look behind, i.e. upwind, for the gusts and the channels, but look ahead, i.e. downwind, for the direction of the wind you are about to enter. (A proviso is necessary here. If you sail a high-performance boat which can move downwind faster than the wind, you look ahead for everything. There is no point in looking at and preparing for that gust close behind and upwind, because it falls further behind as you sail away from it. These boats give a new meaning to the term 'tactics'. Your object, as you sail downwind, is to hunt the headers from behind, so as to head more directly for the leeward mark, and to 'snake' to pick up the best sequence of available gusts, again from behind, as you do it. It's fun.)

(b) The frequency at which you will pass through each wave will be much slower than the windward-going frequency. A useful analogy here is to think of the waves on the water. If you board a moored motor boat when there are regular waves on the water, it will pitch at a certain frequency as each wave lifts the bow. If you motor upwind, the frequency at which you pass through the waves will increase. This is the situation of a sailboat sailing upwind into the wind-waves. If you turn around and motor downwind at exactly the speed of the waves, you will stay in a trough and pass none. If you motor a little faster, you will overtake the waves, but very slowly. This is exactly the situation of a sailboat sailing downwind through the wind-waves.

Fig. 12.7 is an unusual plot which shows this very well. The occasion was one of the periodic New South Wales 'State Squad' coaching clinics, in which top-level sailors are invited to attend sailing school for two days. One of the exercises is to set long upwind – downwind courses, start the group, slowest first (Lasers

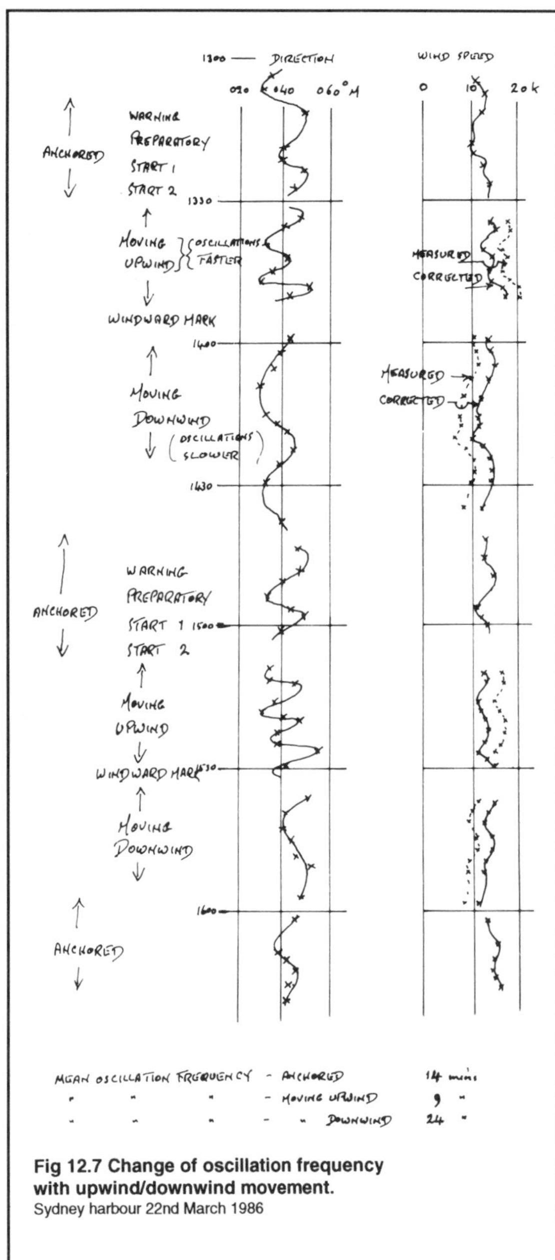

Fig 12.7 Change of oscillation frequency with upwind/downwind movement.
Sydney harbour 22nd March 1986

and Finns), so that they all arrive at the windward mark about together, and finish them at the leeward mark. On such occasions the sailing coaches follow the individual boats. I choose to motor directly upwind and downwind in line with the most downwind boats of the fleet. I measure the apparent wind as I go, and note the tactics of each boat with respect to the backs and veers. At the debriefing after the sailing session my wind plot is thrown, enlarged, onto a screen, and we can then discuss the wind tactics used by each crew with precision.

Fig. 12.7 shows two things very well:

The first is the three wind-wave frequencies. The differences between the frequency when moored, (we act as starter), and the faster frequency when moving upwind, and the slower frequency when moving downwind, are all clear to see.

The second is a point made when discussing wind pattern progressions. The swings become bigger and faster and more unsteady toward the upwind mark, because there was heated land a few hundred metres further to windward. The simple way to think of this is to realise that there would be vigorous thermal excitation over the land, and that this pattern attenuates with increasing distance downwind over the cooler water. From the point of view of the sailors, this exercise called for exploiting predictable swings at the downwind mark, but called for a shift through defensive to opportunistic sailing as the windward mark was approached. The wider swings near the windward mark also closed the laylines closer together, and so made the approach sector nearer to 60 degs rather than the 90 degs usually envisaged.

Sheethand calls approaching gusts.
Forward hand assesses when to tack.
Skipper checks opposition.

12.4 Sailing through fronts

As a cold front passes over, the wind will veer in the northern hemisphere, and back in the southern. The wind change is often abrupt, and is frequently marked by a gust front following a lighter period.

Fronts are tactical factors of everyday importance to ocean racers. Forecasters can usually predict the time of occurrence of a front within a few hours, and yachts which are sailing long legs can plan to exploit the back or veer accordingly. Most fronts are visible as they approach. Dry fronts and Kata-fronts are invisible and will be problems.

For round-the-buoys competitors, a front is usually more of a meteorological event than a tactical factor. However, if a front is known from the forecast to be imminent, it is reasonable to assume that its approach will be visually obvious for the final 30 minutes or so. Ignore it as a wind pattern factor until it is seen to be approaching. Only when it is identified and the leg or legs it will affect become known should all effort be directed to exploiting the approaching back or veer.

Warm fronts are, by their nature, diffuse. The clouds thicken. The rain becomes continuous and heavier. Over the next few hours the wind backs (southern hemisphere) or veers (northern) progressively. The clouds thin. The rain eases. The warm front has passed. For ocean racers, this amounts to a back or veer during a single leg. For round-the-buoys crews, it was simply the weather that race was sailed in – a slow, predictable, progressive back or veer.

12.5 Sailing the cloud winds

12.5.1 Sailing under roll clouds (Refer to Section 8.3.)

Roll clouds mark the crests of rolls. The backs and veers of the surface wind will be synchronised with the passing overhead of each cloud street. If the roll pattern happens to be sloped, the expected change at the surface may either precede or follow the passage of the cloud street overhead by up to about fifteen minutes.

For practical purposes, roll clouds are almost always associated with slow regular wind-waves. They confirm their presence, mark their dimension and frequency, and indicate to you where you are at any time within the pattern. They give you the confidence to plan and sail minimum-time techniques in slow oscillations.

12.5.2 Sailing near non-raining Cumulus clouds (refer Section 8.3).

From a tactical point of view, the inflows shown in Fig. 8.6 develop into a mental picture of the surface wind flow something like Fig. 12.8. The areas of greatest windshift advantage are under the crosswind and upwind edges of the cloud. There is sustained stronger wind in the area upwind of the cloud. The disadvantaged area is the light air and calm patch just downwind of the cloud. The optimum places to start from when sailing to windward are 'S(s), S(s)' in the southern hemisphere, and 'S(n), S(n)' in the northern. Substantial advantage can still be expected crosswind of the cloud and within about one diameter of it.

This would be easy to do if the cloud stayed still. It doesn't. You have to hunt it, and skilfully. There are two traps:

1. The cloud will not move at the speed of the surface wind remote from the cloud, but at the faster speed of the wind at about the cloud's mid-height, because this is the wind which drives it and steers it. A sensible rule of thumb is to assume a speed half as fast again as the remote wind.

2. The cloud will not move in the direction of the remote wind, but in the direction of the steering wind, which will usually be the gradient wind. The surface winds in which we sail are always skewed towards low pressure because they are slowed by friction. The end result is that a cloud will approach from about fifteen degrees to the left of the 'up the surface wind' direction in the southern hemisphere, and from about fifteen degrees to the right of it in the northern hemisphere.

The sailing technique for maximum race advantage is to aim for a point slightly outside either crosswind edge of the cloud and about half a cloud diameter downwind from it – positions 'S, S' in Fig. 12.8. Bias your position to the right in the southern hemisphere, and to the left in the northern, to allow for the skew in the cloud drift direction. The cloud will approach and pass surprisingly fast, so aim to get into position very early or it will have gone before you get there and the opportunity will have been lost. The worst mistake is to get yourself trapped in the patch of light air or calm downwind of the cloud while your opponents enjoy stronger air and lift under its shoulders.

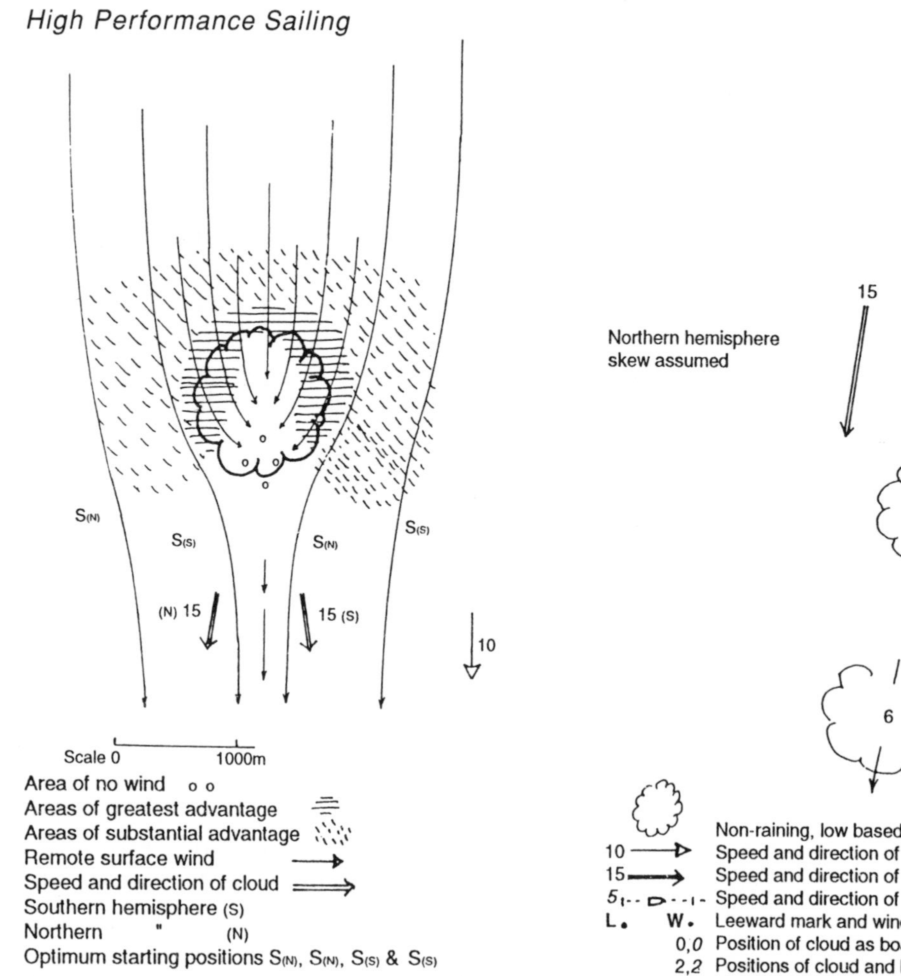

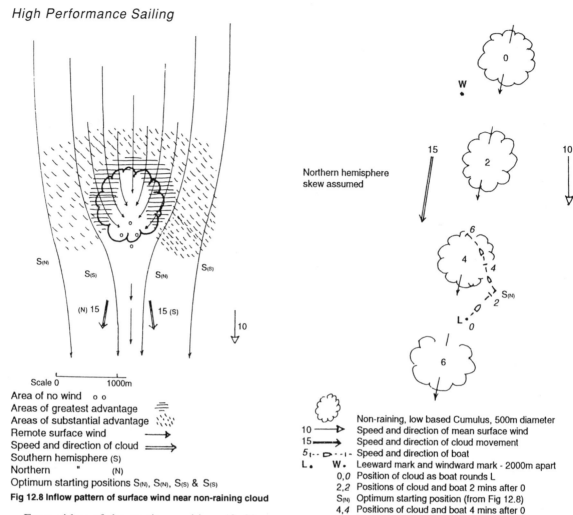

Fig 12.8 Inflow pattern of surface wind near non-raining cloud

Fig 12.9 Dynamic concept of cloud-hunt upwind
(Northern hemisphere)

From either of the starting positions 'S..S' you can expect to enjoy a massive sustained lift as the cloud sweeps by you. The very typical example shown would give a lift averaging thirty degrees for more than two minutes. This works out at more than one minute's clear gain on any boat which did not use the cloud wind in this way.

Fig. 12.9 is drawn to scale, and indicates how fast things happen when you are sailing upwind. The wind speed is assumed to be 10 knots, the cloud's speed 15 knots, the boat's VMG nearly 5 knots, and the speed of closing as between cloud and boat nearly 20 knots – so the cloud approaches and goes past very fast. The fact that the boat speed is relatively slow means that there is almost no margin for error, and the skew in the cloud drift makes things complicated if you forget to apply it from the beginning. However, every cloud you get right can put you about one minute ahead of those competitors who did not have the opportunity, or had it and didn't try, or tried but got it wrong. The dimensions chosen for this example are about the size of the clouds referred to in Section 1.6.

Fig. 12.10 (to the same scale and legends) indicates the optimum technique downwind. The speed of closing is halved, so there is more time. The principal benefit is the avoidance of the calm, and the enjoyment of the much stronger wind from a broad-reaching wind angle for two or three minutes. This could double the speed of a fast planing boat, and would have to be worth a good deal to a displacement-limited keelboat.

Two points:

1. The vital initial action is to sail crosswind, and fast, to avoid the approaching calm patch. Any boat which were to run direct from W towards L would be becalmed briefly and in lighter air for several minutes, and would lose at least one minute to a boat in undisturbed wind.

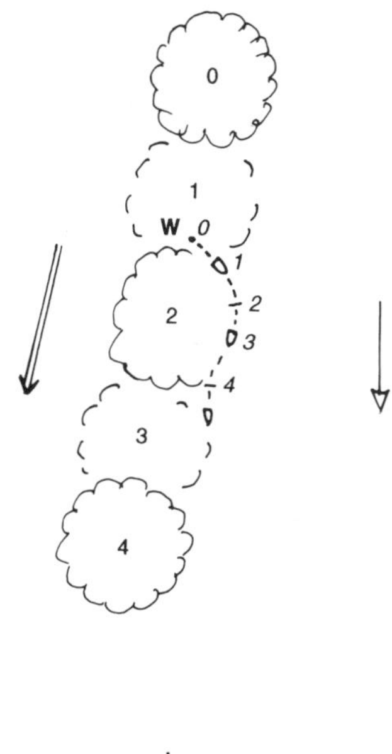

Scale and legend all as Fig 12.9
Northern hemisphere skew assumed.

Fig 12.10 Dynamic concept of cloud-hunt downwind

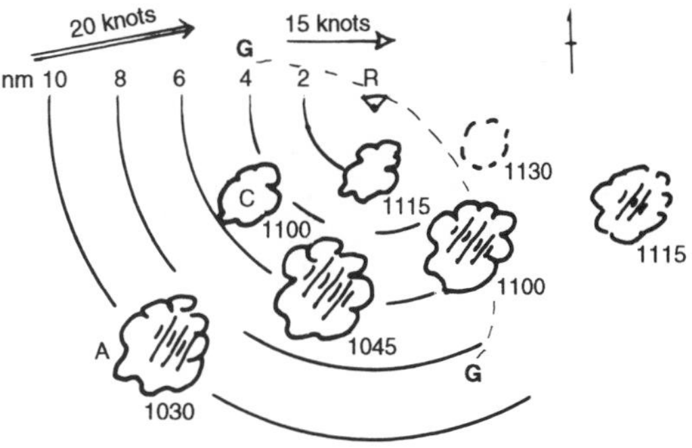

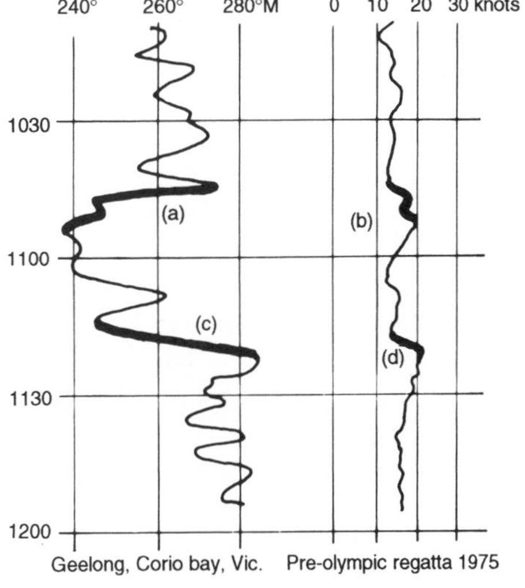

Geelong, Corio bay, Vic. Pre-olympic regatta 1975

R	Regatta area
A	Big raining cloud passes to south
G - G	Big raining cloud gust front at 1045
(a)	Gust front backs wind 30° and
(b)	Gust front increases wind speed 7 knots.
C	Large non-raining cloud passes close to south
(c)	Inflow veers wind direction 40° and
(d)	Inflow increases wind speed 6 knots

Fig 12.11 Effects on wind of passing clouds

2. If you sail a very high performance boat – one which can tack downwind at a speed substantially faster than the wind speed – you can aim for boat position '2' and then hold that position while you 'ride' that cloud broad-reaching downwind 'at cloud speed' for as long as the cloud lasts and goes your way. It's fun!

To give an idea of scale, Fig. 12.11 shows the substantial dynamics associated with a big non-raining cloud. The trace was drawn during one morning's racing at a pre-Olympic selection regatta at Geelong, Victoria. The surface wind was westerly at about 15 knots. At 1030 a huge isolated Cumulus appeared upwind, began to rain very heavily, and swept by about 5 kilometres to the south, still raining extremely heavily. Its outflow (refer next section) caused the back and gust which starts at 1046. Fifteen minutes later a big non-raining cloud swept by with its near edge about 1 km to the south. Its inflow caused the veer and gust which starts at 1115. Another example from the smaller end of the spectrum, in which a quick-thinking helmsman used two minuscule Cumulus clouds simultaneously, comes from Tallinn. At the 'Balti Regatt, 1989', the final on-site pre-Olympic practise regatta before the 1980 Olympics, the world's top crews competed. In the Soling class, five races had been completed. From the big fleet, the number of crews who could possibly win had narrowed to five. Let us call one of these 'A', and another 'U'.

Before the start of the sixth race, 'A' observed that there were isolated small low Cumulus clouds. As start-time approached, 'A' noticed that one cloud directly upwind, which had previously been rather long, had broken into two separate clouds which were still unusually close together.

Both 'A' and 'U' started well. About two minutes after the start, 'A', instead of crossing 'U', tacked and applied the closest and most aggressive cover. 'U' tacked to clear, but 'A' responded and continued to apply the tightest cover. Four times this happened, then 'U' tacked again, but 'A' did not.

What happened next was a masterpiece of planned tactics. 'U', relieved that this stupidity was over, sailed straight ahead – straight into the calm patch downwind of one cloud. 'A', on the other tack, was already close to Posn 'S', (Fig. 12.8) with respect to the other cloud, and from there enjoyed the stronger air and prolonged lift under the shoulder of the second cloud. 'U' never recovered and finished twenty ninth. 'A' rejoined the leaders, finished second and shared the points lead. The number of crews who could possibly win had been reduced to four.

Wind patterns near clouds can be useful.

12.5.3 Sailing near raining clouds. (Ref. Section 8.5).

Fig. 12.12(a) shows the wind pattern around a small raining cloud such as a coastal cloud in a breeze. The cold downdraught from the cloud is adding mass to the surface flow, hence the outward flow-lines and the stronger winds downwind of the cloud. The dynamics are assumed to be moderate and the wind upwind of the cloud keeps blowing in the same direction although at a reduced speed. These dimensions and factors would be about the same as the raining cloud referred to in Section 1.6 (Capo Frio).

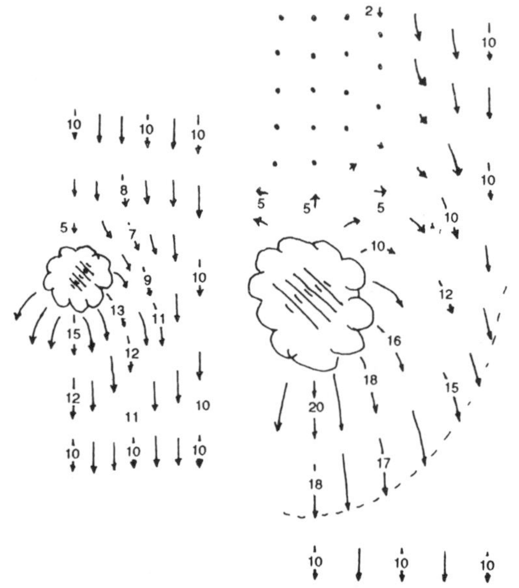

(a)
Surface wind pattern near small, low-base raining cloud.

(b)
Surface wind pattern near large, high-base raining cloud.
Note: Gust front ahead of cloud, also area of calm (cold stagnant air) behind cloud.

Fig 12.12 Wind patterns near raining clouds

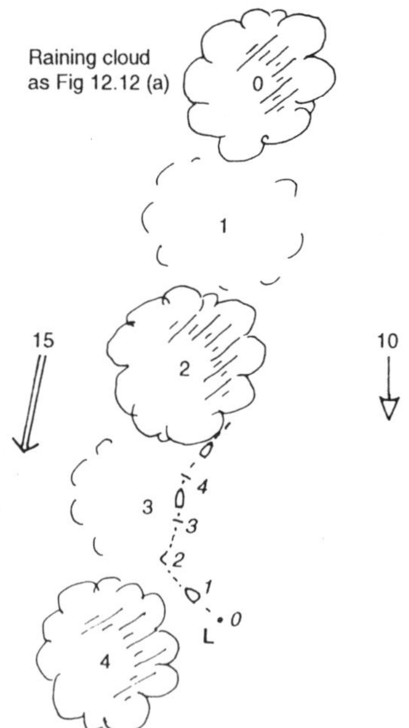

Scale and legend as Fig 12.9
Northern hemisphere skew assumed.

Fig 12.13 Dynamic concept of cloud-hunt (raining cloud) upwind.

Fig. 12.12(b) shows a typical pattern around a bigger, higher-based cloud. The stronger winds downwind, and the outflows, are the same but stronger. To windward of the cloud, the situation is very different. The outflow is so strong that it has reversed the wind direction immediately upwind of the cloud, and reduced the wind speed to something less than 5 knots over a wide area. This cold, slowed air soon becomes first laminar, then stagnant, and remains calm until it is removed by heat or turbulent scrubbing. A big raining cloud can be likened to a road-making machine which lays down a carpet of cold calm air behind it.

Raining cloud-hunt, upwind

Fig. 12.13 shows the dynamics of hunting small raining clouds, upwind. The scale and legend are the same as in Fig. 12.9. With a small cloud, you have one single object – to exploit the stronger winds and the skewed winds for optimum VMG. This is best achieved by starting from a position almost directly downwind of the cloud. Commence your tack away from the cloud's line of drift so that you pass under its advancing shoulder and crosswind edge. The tack should be started early rather than late, because in the skewed wind you will be 'lifted' so much that you may, for awhile, be pointing so high as to be sailing almost directly upwind. A useful rule of thumb is to start outwards about the time that the stronger wind first reaches you. As can be appreciated from Fig. 12.12, things happen fast, but at best you should expect about a 30 degree lift for about 2 minutes, which would put you about one minute further ahead than you would otherwise have expected to be. The outflow pattern downwind and crosswind of the cloud is wide enough for significant advantage still to be enjoyed within about one cloud diameter.

If the cloud is larger, and you sense calm behind it, your objects become twofold – exploit the stronger-wind back or veer, and avoid the calm. This suggests caution in going too close. There is little point in achieving another thirty seconds' VMG gain if you then spend 5 minutes in flat calm. Better make a wide tack away from the cloud's line of drift, and keep going. This is one of those times when it may pay to sail well past the layline. Wind will return soonest to the boats furthest upwind and furthest crosswind from the centreline of the cold-air carpet. The quickest way to a windward mark in the centre of the cold air may be to sail upwind alongside the cold air (but never entering it) until you are abeam the windward mark, so you can enjoy the shortest distance and reaching speed as the breeze returns. The basic point here is that the fastest way will often be a question of logic rather than technique.

A good example of this was a summer evening race which I watched at the Royal St. Lawrence Yacht Club in Montreal. The critical factors were a raining cloud, current, and the temperature difference between land and water. The sailing waters were Lac St Louis, a widening of the St Lawrence river.

The early evening land surface was still warm. The river flow was gentle. Shortly after the start of an upwind, up-current leg toward the WSW, a big high-based cloud which had drifted in from the NW rained a mile or two to the north. The light westerly breeze chilled and freshened and swung well toward the North as the outflowing air reached the river. Most of the fleet freed sheets and headed for the mark. One or two crews chose to sail closehauled to the northern shore. As the minutes passed, the chilled air slowed and stopped. The boats in mid-stream, although close to the mark, began to drift backwards in the current. Those close to the warm shore in near zero current drifted backwards less. The breeze returned over the warmer land before the calm cleared from the colder water. The boats near the shore picked up this breeze soonest, inched upwind and upcurrent as the breeze filled in, and were already around the mark by the time the returning breeze reached the fleet in mid-stream ten minutes later.

Crosswind

If you have the option, and the performance, arc downwind of any approaching cloud and cross its line of drift in the stronger winds. If this is not possible, arc well upwind of a small cloud to avoid the lighter wind areas close upwind of it.

If it is a large cloud which lays a carpet of calm air across your path, the further you go upwind the sooner you will have wind again. But be cautious about going too far. There is no law that requires a carpet of cold air to clear in a progressive and orderly manner.

Downwind

How you can best handle the cloud winds for race advantage downwind will depend on the performance of the boat you sail. For clarity, let us think of boats as either:

(a) Yachts and heavy dinghies which can sail downwind at about hull speed or half the wind speed, whichever is the lesser.

(b) Conventional 'fast' craft, such as 505's, FD's, Tornado's, etc., which can achieve about ¾ of the wind speed in some conditions.

(c) Lightweight high performance craft such as Eighteen footers, and the modern lightweight fourteens, etc., which can substantially exceed the wind speed in some conditions.

If you sail a hull-speed-limited displacement boat, then sail in the strongest winds directly downwind of the cloud until the cloud's edge is over you. At that point turn either way to escape crosswind and so avoid the lightest-air area directly upwind of the cloud. In this way you can increase your boat speed from 5 knots in a 10 knot wind to say 7.5 knots in a 15 knot wind for the two minutes during which you can expect to enjoy the stronger winds close downwind of the cloud while the cloud, which is drifting at 15 knots, overtakes you at 7.5 knots. Two minutes at 2.5 knots faster will give you a lead of about 100 to 150 metres over a boat which remained in 10 knot winds.

If you sail a conventional fast boat, tack downwind in the stronger winds ahead of the cloud. Manoeuvre as it slowly overtakes you so that you take up a position near one of its advancing shoulders where you can enjoy both the stronger wind and the outwards skew. If you get it right, the skew will enable you to broad-reach at maximum speed on a heading directly downwind. In the 12 knot winds under the shoulder of the cloud in the example, you can probably achieve about 10 knots. The cloud will overtake you at about 5 knots, so you will be able to enjoy about 3 minutes of this. Coupled with an initial (say) two minutes in the stronger winds, your total gain would be about 3 knots extra speed for 4 to 5 minutes, or 400 to 500 metres.

If you sail a high performance boat which can tack downwind faster than the wind, and you position yourself to stay in the skewed strong winds near the cloud's shoulder, you can sometimes exceed the cloud's speed of 15 knots. This will give you a margin of speed which will enable you to hold your position at the cloud's shoulder for as long as the cloud lasts and goes your way. The speed advantage over a similar boat in the undisturbed wind would be about 5 knots, or nearly 200 metres per minute. Five minutes of this and you will be half a leg in front.

These are the techniques and possibilities for a relatively modest raining cloud.

If the cloud is big and high-based, and you sense calm behind it, then use logic to escape the calm. A small temporary gain in the stronger winds, followed by minutes languishing in a calm, is no way to win a race.

Sometimes clouds are huge. The trace of the 30 degree backed gust from the raining cloud in Fig. 12.11 is not unusual. The race officers and I all anticipated the backed gust and expected it to arrive about when it did. Note that in this extreme case the back lasted for longer than it takes to sail one leg, but made no difference to the mean wind later in the race.

In the extreme, these 'thunderstorm fall-out gusts' from high-based thunderstorms can be destructive, so a safety and survival note is relevant. There are two points. The first is that the wind speed, for awhile, may be of such force that all thought of sailing a light unballasted boat is futile, and only survival measures can be relevant. The second is that these thunderstorm fall-out gusts don't last long, so even the most temporary measures can be effective. A third point – that they are intensely local – is not of much solace when you are in one.

A Sydney example which is unlikely to be forgotten occurred many years ago. A big high cloud drifted towards the coast from the west, and suddenly grew huge and became a violent thunderstorm. Its base would have been at about 3,000 metres and its top somewhere in the stratosphere at about 15,000 metres. The initial very heavy rain reached the ground about 2 kilometres to the north-west of where we were sailing. Houses were unroofed. We had no warning. The gust front was measured by several yachts at more than 70 knots, and lasted six to seven minutes. Our club fleet all stayed with their inverted boats until it moderated and nobody was hurt. The gust swept on over the northern harbourside suburbs and rattled progressively fewer windows. It never reached the southern shore of the harbour, about 7 kilometres from its original impact point. After the initial 6 minute gust it eased progressively, and became a flat calm 30 minutes later. The sea breeze returned about an hour after the gust onslaught.

History records two crews as less lucky. One hundred and seventy years ago, a similar big high-based cloud rained at 0200 over a squadron in the western end of Lake Ontario, north-west of Niagara. The schooners *Scourge and Hamilton* were both heeled in the initial gust until their masts were near horizontal, water entered their deck openings and they foundered with the loss of most hands. The story of their history, the storm, their loss and recent relocation contains a classic description of a 'thunderstorm fall-out event'.

At the other end of the scale is a practicality which I have seen responsible for the loss of several races. As a pilot, I am well aware of the initial periodic disorientation which affects all trainee pilots when they are first introduced to instrument flying. Their senses insist that the aeroplane is not level or is turning. The instruments indicate that it is straight and level. The mental conflict can be quite disturbing at first, and is common.

I was not prepared for its marine form. My first experience was 20 years ago during a race when a misty drizzle shower became fog. We were sailing to windward among the leaders in a 100 boat fleet. The rain had stuck all the tufts to the sails and at that time I sailed without an independent wind indicator, and with only a small compass placed where only my forward hand could read it. Wind was steady at about 4 or 5 knots. In the fog, despite about 30 years of flying and 40 years of sailing experience, my senses insisted that the dinghy was turning when the compass said it wasn't. I recognised the disorientation for what it was, and adopted 'instrument sailing' – steering exactly according to what my forward hand called from the compass, regardless of what I felt. When we emerged to windward of the shower we were hundreds of metres ahead. It was clear from discussion with the other competitors later that they too had all become disoriented. In the years since I have learned that this is commonplace with yacht helmsmen in fog or in rain, particularly at night in a confused seaway.

It seems still to be both unexpected and commonplace. While helms who sail in countries where fog is common must necessarily become familiar with this and accommodate to it, I have experienced or observed several occasions since that first experience in which boats which were well-placed before they entered drizzle emerged having lost position hopelessly. Clearly, not everybody knows about it, so it seems worth mentioning.

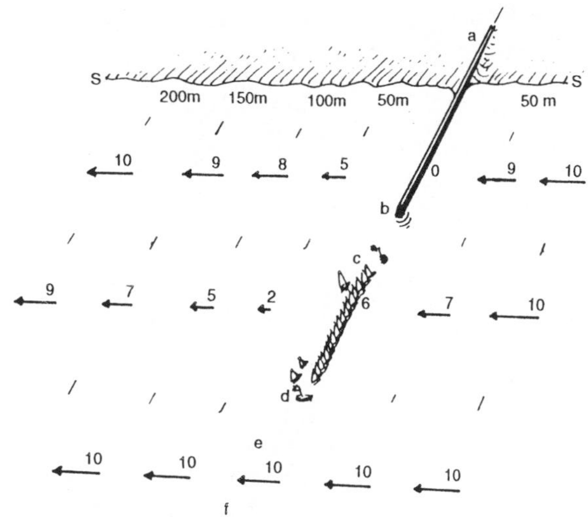

Sea wall and rigs both assumed to be 7m high

Fig 12.14 Wind speeds near solid and open barriers

12.6 The effects on wind of 'open' barriers

Three situations occur in every 'round-the-buoys' race in which the effect of the fleet itself on the wind over and near the fleet is so important that all but a few boats will be slowed. All three are special cases of the effect of a discontinuous barrier on the speed of the surface wind. This subject was first researched by agricultural science workers who looked at the properties of different types of hedgerow windbreaks. Alan Watts, in *'Wind and Sailing Boats'*, looks at the consequences of this work on individual sailboats which sail close downwind of trees and groups of buildings. My purpose here is to draw attention to the further effects of a fleet of sailboats on one another.

Measurements of the way the wind speed changes as it approaches, blows over or through, and streams away downwind from different types of windbreak or barrier show surprising differences between the effects of a dense barrier and the effects of a more 'open' barrier. Fig. 12.14 assumes that a 10 knot wind is blowing parallel to a shoreline 's – s', that a solid sea-wall 'a – b' which is 7 metres high extends offshore crosswind, and that 'c – d' is a big fleet of Lasers or Finns or any other class with rigs about 7 metres high which have just started. The area 'e – f' is open water. The figures give the wind speed at distances of 50m, 100m, etc. upwind and downwind of each obstruction, and the lengths of the wind arrows are to scale.

Over the open water the wind blows unimpeded at 10 knots.

As the wind approaches the solid sea-wall, it begins to be slowed about 50m upwind, slows to nothing at the wall, is up to half speed again 50m downwind and has regained its full speed within 200m of the solid barrier.

The wind's behaviour as it approaches and streams away from the close-spaced yachts is very different. Its speed slows progressively from about 50 metres to windward but not to zero because the barrier 'leaks'. The surprising differences occur downwind. The slowest average speed occurs not at the barrier itself but about 35 to 70 metres downwind, where the mean speed falls to the surprisingly low value of about 2 knots. Further downwind the speed increases again, but much more slowly than is the case behind the solid barrier. As a result, the wind speed downstream of the open barrier is both slowed more, and the slowing extends further downstream than is the case with the solid barrier.

In any yacht race, there are three occasions when yachts necessarily sail in close company in the crosswind sense – at the start, on the first reaching leg, and when approaching a leeward mark. Whenever even three or four boats sail sufficiently closely together, their grouped sails will act as an 'open barrier' which will reduce the windspeed for a much greater distance downwind and over a much wider area than the distance and area affected by any single boat, or by the three or four individual boats prior to their approaching each other sufficiently closely. This situation is a trap because it occurs relatively rarely, but is

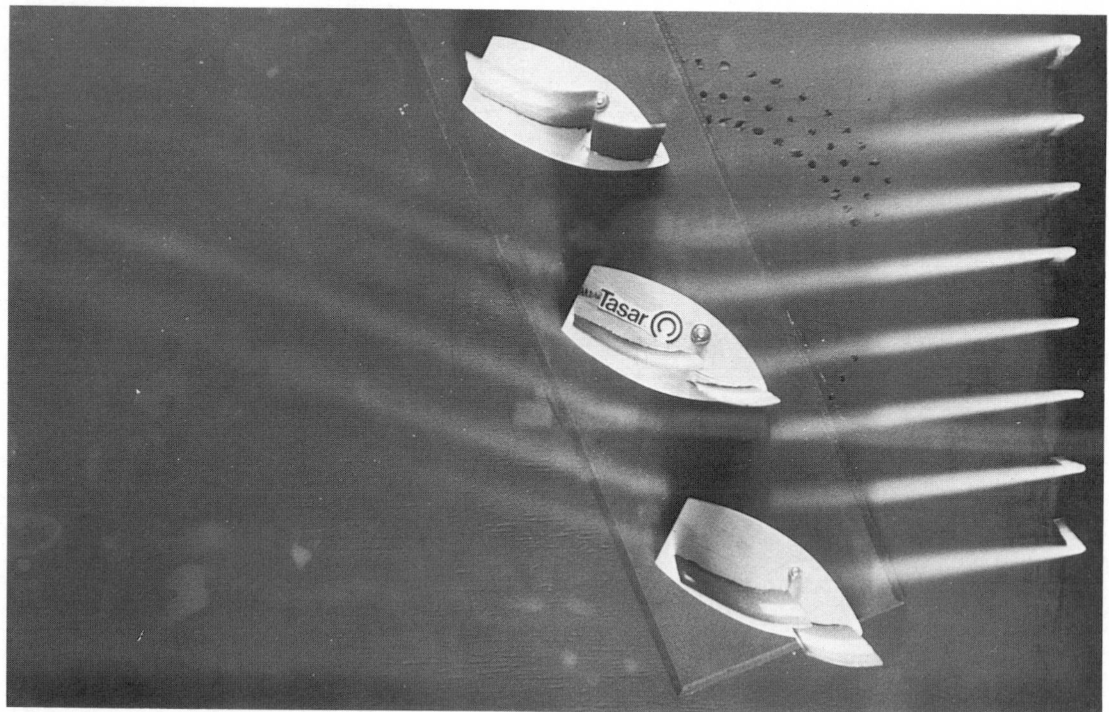

Models and sils in wind tunnel arranged to represent front row of boats at start. Smoke plumes at mid-height of sails show pattern of stream lines.

Fig 12.15 Stream lines around model sails

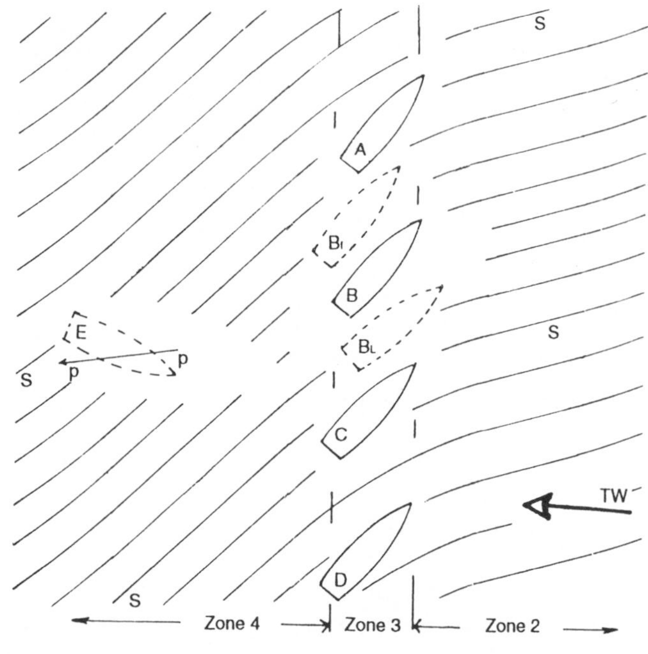

TW True Wind

S - S)
S - S) Stream lines of apparent wind related to A,B,C,D all on starboard tack

p - p Apparent wind related to port tack boat E

Fig 12.16 Wind pattern near front rank at start

so overwhelming in its effect when it does occur. All boats which lie within, or are caught within, the much larger area of reduced wind will sail more slowly. This situation will occur only when three conditions exist:

1. Large numbers of boats. This means, generally, a regatta rather than a club fleet. Most club fleets are not numerous enough to give densely clustered boats.

2. Relatively large numbers of crews fast enough to contest the lead aggressively. Again, this occurs, generally, only in major regattas. In most club fleets, even large ones, only a few boats are consistently fast. These few boats race each other. Generally, it is only at major regattas which attract the top crews from many clubs that the situation exists where relatively large numbers of contestants will both start well and will reach the first windward mark almost simultaneously.

3. The wind speed is in the moderate range. The viscous nature of light air's laminar flow blurs the concept of distinct zones more towards a horizontal lens of slowed air, slowest in the middle, which envelopes the whole fleet. And in winds stronger than the design wind sailboats are able to slow and bend the wind progressively less, so the relative disadvantage diminishes with increasing wind strength to the point where it vanishes in strong winds.

12.6.1 Barrier Effects at the Start

The first and obvious case is the start. This is a special case for two reasons.

The first special aspect of the start is that the barrier suddenly changes from negligible to substantial at about the time of the start. Prior to the start, the line of eased sails affects the wind relatively little. Just before the start all boats 'sheet on', and the barrier abruptly becomes much denser. At that instant the new barrier begins to slow the wind, but it has not yet slowed it. Not until about ten to fifteen seconds later will the wind speeds near the new barrier have been slowed to the values noted above.

The second special factor is that for tactical reasons the boats will almost all be on the same tack. They will therefore not only slow the wind but also deflect it.

Fig. 12.15 is a photograph of the way smoke plumes in a wind tunnel at half the height of the sails are deflected by the sails of a line of model boats arranged all on one tack as if starting. Fig. 12.16 is an analysis of Fig. 12.15 which represents the actual situation near the front line of boats a few seconds after any start.

Until the fleet sheets in, the effect on the wind of the streaming sails is negligible, and the wind speed and direction over every boat is little different from the windspeed away from the fleet. It is only when the fleet sheets in at the start that it suddenly becomes an 'open' barrier. The mass of air which will wash over the sails of a 100 boat fleet during the next fifteen seconds in a ten knot wind will be about 400 tons. The total sideways force of 100 boats on the wind will be about 100 pounds per boat or 5 tons total. The effect of this force after about fifteen seconds is shown visually in Fig. 12.15 and diagrammatically in Fig. 12.16. For practical purposes the fleet itself has within these few seconds divided the wind over and near it into five zones. (Zone One lies just to the right of Fig. 12.16, and Zone Five far to the left.)

Zone One is the relatively undisturbed wind two or three lengths ahead of the fleet.

Zone Two extends from the undisturbed wind to the front line of boats. In it the oncoming wind slows from ten to about six knots and veers about 5 to 7 degrees. The streamlines in Fig. 12.16 show the Apparent Wind as it relates to the front line of boats.

Zone Three is the front line of boats, and is only one boat length in extent. In this short distance the wind is backed about 25 degrees by the cascade of sails.

Zone Four extends downwind from the front line for about ten boat-lengths. In it the wind falls even lighter and slowly straightens to its original direction.

Zone Five extends from ten to about forty boat lengths downwind from the frontline. In Zone Five the wind speed very slowly regains its undisturbed value.

Some practical points emerge which may be helpful:

1. Set up your boat for optimum performance not in the speed of the undisturbed wind, but in the much lighter wind speed you will sail in immediately after the start. Good starting technique, plus superior performance during the time you must sail in these lighter winds, are the keys to emerging among the leaders one to two minutes later.

2. The massive 25 degree curve within the space of one boat length in Zone Three means that the way to break clear of the front line is to point, not to foot. Consider boat 'B' in Fig. 12.16. If it bears away at all for speed as 'B(f)', it will move forward, but at the expense of moving into a wind which is more headed and so it will fall behind boat 'A'. But if it points higher as 'B(h)' it will immediately enter a more favourable wind direction and so will be able both to consolidate its gain and then extend it.

3. The massive adverse header immediately behind the front line means that no boat can remain there on starboard tack. In practise this means that among any group of boats which sheet on at the start, those in the position of 'B(f)' or worse will 'hang in there' for the initial 5 to 10 seconds, but as the wind adopts the pattern of Fig. 12.15 they will thereafter quite quickly drop back through and to the downwind end of Zone Four. This causes a gap to open up immediately behind the front rank, and it begins to open about fifteen to twenty seconds after the fleet sheets on.

4. The development of this gap sometimes makes it possible for a boat in the position of 'B(f)' to tack and sail out of trouble along the gap. Boat 'E' is drawn at the angle it would adopt if it sailed close hauled in the deflected wind 'p – p'. It suffers reduced wind speed, but gains from the enormously advantaged direction of the deflected wind. In practise, if the circumstances of the moment make it possible to accomplish the critical part – a tack which manages to keep clear of starboard tackers – it can then free sheets and have performance to spare as it sails along the open gap skimming the sterns of the front rankers. This is possible if and only if it can sail close enough to the front rank. If it is more than about two lengths back the wind is dying and straightening too much for the ploy to work.

12.6.2 Barrier Effects on Reaching Legs

In major regattas, boats can bunch so closely as they leave the first windward mark, that they can form an open barrier. When this occurs, the wind in which they themselves sail and the wind nearby in which other boats will probably be sailing will be so reduced that it will dominate absolutely the performance and fortunes of all boats affected. More damaging from a tactical point of view is the situation in which boats, and particularly boats to windward, bunch unexpectedly for any reason. A common cause of this is the situation in which most boats of a fleet sail high on the first reaching leg, each keeping its wind clear from the shadow of the boat behind and to windward. This spacing is insufficiently dense for there to be a significant effect on the wind of boats to leeward, But when towards the end of the leg they turn a little more downwind, they become closer together in the crosswind sense (i.e. as viewed upwind/downwind), the critical density is reached at which their wind shadows interact, and the 'open barrier' wind pattern downwind of 'c – d' in Fig. 12.14 suddenly develops. When this occurs boats to leeward suddenly find themselves with only a fraction of the wind they expected.

12.6.3 Barrier Effects at the Leeward Mark.

In exactly the same way as the fleet diverges after the start, it must necessarily converge as it approaches any downwind mark. The example given above, which often occurs in big-fleet racing at the end of a reaching leg, must necessarily occur at the end of every running leg in which any large group of boats approaches the mark without much upwind-downwind separation. For boats to leeward, the escape is to anticipate the occurrence and the position of the area which will be affected, and move sideways sufficiently to retain faster speed in the undisturbed wind until they are in a position to make the shortest practical crossing of the lighter air area en route to the mark on a reaching point of sailing.

Should there be current in a direction against the wind, a situation can easily arise in which, due to this barrier effect, no boat within or near a group can make progress although isolated boats can retain adequate speed for manoeuvrability.

The practical differences between small-fleet and big-fleet racing are due at least as much to the barrier effects of the fleet itself on the nearby wind as to the tactical consequences of the presence of numerous competitors.

Part Two
Water

Chapter Thirteen
Waves

13.1 The four wave systems

Water provides the level, inviting, sparkling, mostly unobstructed surface on which we sail. From the point of view of the helmsman, this surface has four basic states.

It will have either:

1. No waves and no current.
2. Waves, but no current.
3. Current, but no waves.
4. Both waves and current.

Boat handling has to do only with waves. Current (and in this chapter, I also mean the word to include tidal streams) has to do with navigation and tactics. However, the shoals and channels which cause differences in current also cause differences in waves. From the practical point of view no commentary on waves can be complete without some discussion of the factors which change waves, such as current, depth and the warm surface layer.

Sailboats sail fastest in flat water (except when surfing is possible). The handling techniques and sail shapes which are fastest in flat water are not the fastest through waves. Different techniques and sail shapes must then be used for maximum speed.

When waves are present, they arrange themselves in any one of four different systems or some combination of these. Because there are four different wave types, so there are four different techniques to use when racing through them. The four sorts of waves, and the ways in which they are formed, are:

1. *Regular waves* are wave-trains caused by the local wind. These are the most common of all waves. They always move in the direction of the wind. They start small and slow, either at a windward shore or when the wind starts. They grow relatively quickly initially. After the first two hours they will have developed to a size at which they roll at a speed typically about two thirds of the wind speed. Thereafter they grow more slowly, and may reach a speed of about nine tenths of the wind speed after twelve to twenty four hours. The ultimate nature of these waves will depend largely on the depth to the bottom (Sect 14.1), and on the presence and depth of any warm surface layer (Sect 14.2).

2. *Chaotic waves* are usually caused by the wakes of moving boats. Neither their regularity nor direction are predictable. Often they are abnormally steep and short. Chaotic waves can also be caused by the reflection of regular waves by irregular cliffs and sea-walls.

3. *Swell.* Very big waves developed within energetic storms can travel long distances. As they flow outwards for distances of thousands of kilometres they attenuate in height but not in either wave-length nor speed. In this way they become the long, low, fast moving waves which we recognise as swell. Their direction and frequency are absolutely predictable. The direction of the local wind may be quite different from the direction of the swell, and any local wind will have not the slightest influence upon the swell unless that wind is strong and sustained.

4. *Standing waves* Current which flows over a shallow uneven bottom will develop standing waves. These will always lie at right angles to the direction of the current. At practical current speeds they are always small, but can be critical in light airs. A particular property of standing waves is that when regular waves and standing waves combine, the resultant system tends to have the size of the regular waves but the direction of the standing waves, i.e. the standing waves bias the direction of the much bigger regular waves to an unexpected degree.

13.2 Wave motion

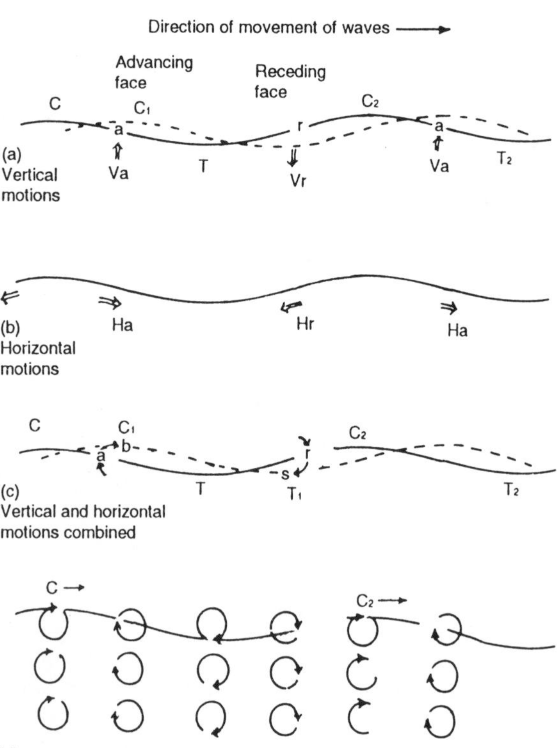

Fig 13.1. Elements of wave motion

All waves, however caused, have a common form and characteristics. The form is governed by the fact that gravity will cause any heaped-up fluid to flow 'downhill' towards the nearest lower surface. This means that wave motion must contain horizontal movement as well as vertical. Particles do not simply move up and down. They move sideways as well. The up and down and to and fro motions combine into the simplest possible motion – circular – and this becomes the basic motion of all gravity waves.

Fig. 13.1 shows instantaneous cross-sections through two waves of a wave-train, in which crests C and C2 and troughs T and T2 are sketched, 'frozen' in their movement from left to right.

If we consider the vertical movement of the water particles, it is clear that every particle such as 'a' which lies on or within the advancing face of the wave must rise as the surface level rises as the crest moves from 'C' to 'C1' in Fig. 13.1(a). Similarly every particle such as 'r' which lies on the receding face must fall as the surface level falls from 'C2' to 'T'. These vertical motions on and within the advancing and receding faces are shown by the arrows 'Va' and 'Vr'.

If we consider the horizontal movements of particles 'a' and 'r', they must all flow 'downhill' away from the heaped-up water, under the force of gravity. The directions of these horizontal movements are shown by arrows 'Ha' and 'Hr', Fig. 13.1(b), and will always be away from the crests regardless of the direction of movement of the crests.

When we combine the vertical and horizontal movements, Fig. 13.1(c) shows why the water within any wave system adopts its simple circular orbital motion. As particle 'a' rises due to 'Va', it is accelerated to the right by 'Ha' to reach 'b' by the time crest 'C' reaches 'Cl'. Similarly, particle 'r' not only falls due to 'Vr' – it is swept to the left by 'Hr' to reach 's' as trough 'T' reaches 'Tl'. Similar reasoning applies from 's' to 'a' and from 'b' to 'r'.

The complete picture of the motion of the particles both at and below the surface is shown in Fig. 13.1(d). The particles rotate in an orbit which has a diameter equal to the height of the wave from trough to crest. They make one rotation around this orbit for every wave which passes. The practical effect is that the water in and near the wave crests moves in the direction of the wave motion with a significant speed, while the water in and near the wave troughs moves in the reverse direction. It turns out that it is these changing horizontal speeds, at least as much as the vertical movements, which so affect the performance of any sailing boat. Note that the water below the surface moves in exactly the same manner. For this reason, the local speed through the water of a keel, centreboard or rudder is affected by waves just as much as the topsides of the hull. In water of relatively uniform temperature and great depth, the orbital diameter becomes progressively smaller at increasing depths. Submarine commanders advise me that a depth of about ten times the wave height is usually sufficient to escape all significant motion due to surface waves.

The waves described here are called, 'gravity waves'. One of the important characteristics of gravity waves is that a wave of the same length always travels at the same speed. Whether it is a relatively steep, young wave, or an old attenuated wave (like swell), makes no difference. The formula is Speed (knots) = $1.32 \times \sqrt{\text{length}}$ (Length is the wave-length expressed in feet). Fig. 13.2 shows how the wave speed increases with increasing wave-length. The hull speed of a boat is about the same as the speed of a wave of the same length. (Refer to chapter 18 – Hulls.Part Three.) Trivial speed differences will occur due to density differences caused by changes of temperature and salinity.

13.3 Regular waves

In light airs, i.e. in winds of 5 knots or less, the wind speed at the surface is near zero. The shear between this slowly moving air and the water surface is so weak that the surface remains shiny. Only a ruffling is caused by winds of 3 or 4 knots.

In winds of 6 knots or more, the greatly increased shear of the wind on the water surface due to the onset of turbulence in the boundary layer is sufficient to cause waves. At their smallest, in a 6 knot breeze, they form a regular ripple in which the waves are distinctively steeper and sharper crested than the smoother and more polished rufflings of light airs. Because the slopes are steeper they reflect less of the light from the sky, and so appear darker. It is these differences in shading which enable skilled sailors to 'read' the upwind water surface and so anticipate approaching gusts, etc. The ripple always moves in the direction of the wind. The stronger the wind, the longer the time for which it blows, and the longer the unobstructed distance from the windward shore (the 'fetch'), the bigger the waves will become unless the water happens to be very shallow, or there is a pronounced warm surface layer.

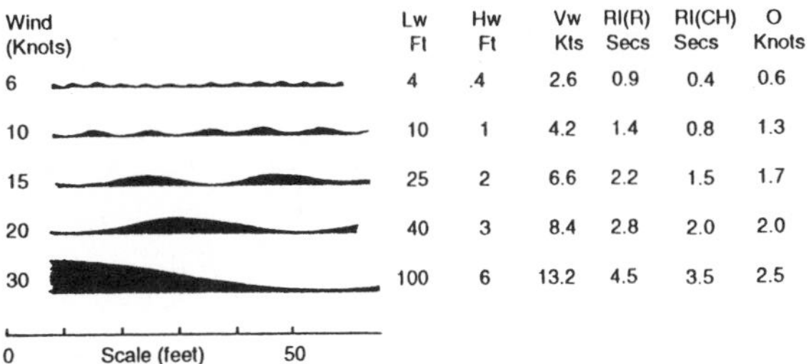

Wind (Knots)
Lw Ft
Hw Ft
Vw Kts
RI(R) Secs
RI(CH) Secs
O Knots
6 4 .4 2.6 0.9 0.4 0.6
10 10 1 4.2 1.4 0.8 1.3
15 25 2 6.6 2.2 1.5 1.7
20 40 3 8.4 2.8 2.0 2.0
30 100 6 13.2 4.5 3.5 2.5
0 Scale (feet) 50

W = Wind speed The waves suggested are typical, in open water, after 2 hours of the wind stated.
Lw = Wave length.
Hw = " height.
Vw = " speed.
RI(R) = Wave repetition interval, boat at rest.
RI(CH)= " " " boat close hauled at 5 knots.
O = Orbital speed.

Fig 13.2 Properties of regular waves

Oceanographers' observations of wave sizes in the open ocean show that if, for example, a breeze starts and blows steadily from one direction at about 10 knots for two hours over a stretch of water unobstructed for about ten kilometres or more, the wave height will grow from nothing at the windward shore to about 0.3 metres high, trough to crest, some kilometres downwind. If the wind speed is 15 knots, the wave height will become about 0.6 metres, and in 20 knots about 1 metre. If both time and the unobstructed distance are increased substantially, say to 10 hours and 50 kilometres, the waves will continue to grow but much more slowly, and may ultimately stabilise at about double these heights. Waves which are 'young', i.e. increasing in size with time and unobstructed distance, tend to have a height from trough to crest of about one tenth of the distance between their crests. Waves which are 'mature' i.e. stabilised and no longer increasing in size, tend to have a height about one twentieth of the distance between their crests. Because most small-boat sailing takes place in daylight hours when heating is occurring, and one of the consequences of heating is, generally, to make the boundary layer deeper and so the surface wind stronger as the day's heating progresses, it follows that most small-boat sailing takes place in areas where the waves are 'young'.

For a variety of reasons the waves which are formed within any area will not all be of exactly the same height – in practise wave-trains tend to take the form of a few well-formed sequential waves a little higher than average, followed by a series of smaller and less regular waves. However, the direction of movement of all the waves, the distances apart of their crests and their speed of movement will all tend to be about the same. It is this widespread regularity of the total pattern which is the primary characteristic of the regular waves which form in open water.

Fig. 13.2 shows, to scale, the wave lengths and heights, and tabulates the wave speeds, the repetition intervals past a fixed object, and the orbital speeds of young waves typical after two hours in winds of 6, 10, 15, 20 and 30 knots in open water which is deep and free from any 'warm surface layer' effect.

It also gives the shorter repetition interval appropriate for a boat which sails close-hauled at 5 knots towards the oncoming waves.

If the water is either shallow, or a pronounced warm surface layer exists, the nature of these waves will change.

The effects of shoal bottom are discussed in Section 14.1.

The more complex effects of a warm layer are discussed in Section 14.2.

Summarised, if the warm layer is deep, wave size will be relatively unaffected. If the layer is two to three metres deep, the waves will initially be unchanged, then will become higher and steeper than the waves in

Fig. 13.2, but finally will become limited in height and so smaller. If the layer is intense but very shallow, a second system of small steep irregular waves will form on and combine with the normal 'regular' waves.

13.4 Chaotic waves

The second way in which waves can be formed is mechanically, by boats. These waves come in sets – the wake of every moving boat must include a port-side bow and quarter-wave, a starboard-side bow and quarter wave, and a set of stern waves. Fig. 13.3 shows the pattern. The bow and the quarter wave systems roll sideways both ways away from the line of the boat's wake. Between these the stern waves follow the boat and move at exactly the speed of the boat. They will all be largest nearest the boat, and diminish progressively at greater distances. Each boat will create one set of these three wave systems, and once these have passed the water surface will revert to its previous state.

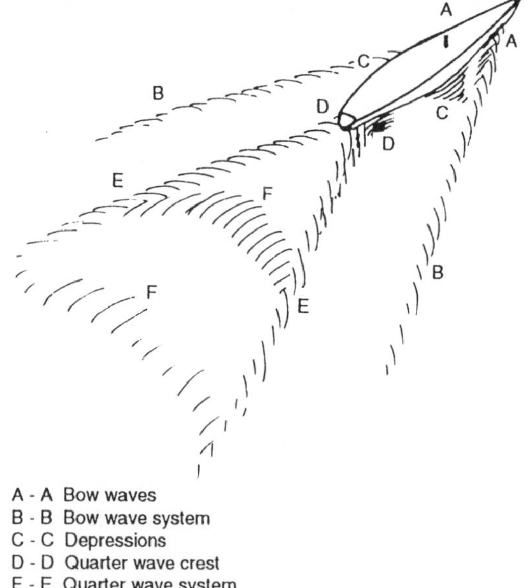

Fig 13.3 Wave systems generated by displacement hull

The size of these waves will depend upon the weight, length, and speed of the boat – in the simplest terms, these waves represent the energy wasted by the boat, so the more efficient the boat's use of its energy, the smaller the waves it will make. It is therefore not surprising that a rowing skiff will scarcely mark the surface of the water, and that a huge freighter or tanker will make surprisingly small and gentle waves. Both hulls are designed to be as efficient as possible. It is regrettable that this concern for efficiency is so seldom observed in the design of recreational motor boats, many of which merely waste fuel by raising unnecessarily big waves which are out of all proportion to the size and speed of the boat.

Combinations of two wave systems

When two regular wave systems intersect, there are three possible outcomes:

1. When they meet at some speed and angle which is neither parallel, nor equal and opposite to the first, an interference pattern will be created in which the continuous crests are transformed into lines of separate 'hills', and the continuous troughs become lines of separate 'holes'. Hills and holes all advance in some intermediate direction at a constant speed, and so in this case the future position of any hill or hole can be anticipated. The hills will be higher, and the holes deeper, than the crests and troughs of either of the contributing systems.

2. Sometimes the second wave system is equal in size and opposite in direction from the first. This situation routinely occurs whenever any vertical water barrier, such as a vertical cliff face, or a sea wall, reflects waves which approach it at right angles; or when two similar ferries on opposite routes pass and their respective bow and quarter waves meet. In this situation the result is a series of standing waves which do not move. Instead, the water pulses up and down, with crests twice as high, troughs twice as deep, and the intervening slopes up to four times as steep, as those of either contributing wave system. The effect of substantial standing waves on light air performance can be catastrophic.

3. Very often, the situation occurs in which a second wave system is generated which is almost identical and parallel with the first. If we imagine an existing wave system, and that another is generated within it which is fractionally faster than the first, then as each faster crest overtakes and matches a slower crest, the combined wave will double its height. A little later, the faster crest will overtake and match a slower trough, and this combination will yield almost flat water. All swimmers and surfers will recognise this as the normal surf system – a few big regular waves followed by a period of confused smaller waves, and then the big waves come again, and so on. This is simply the result of two nearly identical wave systems which move alternately into phase (big waves) and out of phase (small waves) with each other. It may well be that

the faster system is generated by the gust winds, and the slower by the lull winds of the normal breeze.

Combinations of three or more wave systems

When three or more wave systems intersect, the situation abruptly becomes one in which no anticipation at all is possible. Individual hills and holes appear, exist for a second or two, and vanish. If they move, each individual hill or hole may move in any direction. Their sizes are uneven. But characteristic of all chaotic systems is the increased height and depth of the hills and holes and the increased steepness of the interconnecting slopes. This increased roughness is an integral part of all interference systems.

This sort of seaway is characteristic of any busy harbour. When ferries, tugs and other work-boats move nearby with sufficient speed to cause big wakes, it is not surprising that the water becomes rough even when the wind is near-calm. When, in these conditions, the wind becomes strong enough to generate significant regular waves, a mixed situation results which is part predictable and part unpredictable, and which shifts subtly from almost regular in the remoter bays to almost chaotic near the busy traffic lanes. Since the fastest technique through regular waves is rhythmic, and the fastest technique through chaotic waves is opportunistic, these conditions are among the most difficult and challenging to race in.

It is often not appreciated that a large fleet of sailboats which race over the same course will of themselves generate sizeable chaotic waves. This occurs because the act of racing causes large numbers of adjacent boats to sail in the same directions and at almost the same speeds. Each moving vessel will create the three wave systems shown in Fig. 13.3. The wedge of the bow will heap water up on each side of the bow at 'A' and 'A'. These two crests roll away sideways as the bow-wave systems 'B' and 'B'. The water under the hull is forced by the hull's advancing bulk towards the only place it can go – to accelerate backwards into the advancing void under the stern. As it gains speed the pressure drops and the depressions 'C' and 'C' form on each side of the hull. As this aft-moving water meets the static water under the stern it creates a pressure surge which forces the water upwards into a crest at 'D'. This crest dissipates its energy partly by rolling away sideways in both directions as the quarter-wave systems 'E' and 'E', which closely follow but never overtake the bow-wave systems 'B' and 'B'. The crest also accelerates forward toward the retreating troughs at 'C' and 'C'. This forward acceleration at the surface reacts with the aft-directed impulse of the slowed water below the surface to start a circulation. In the same way as waves cause an orbital circulation, this circulation causes waves. This third system, the stern waves, form with their crests perpendicular to the boat's heading, they follow the boat at exactly the boat's speed, and they lie between and attenuate quickly as they become wider between the receding quarter waves.

Each of these three wave systems will combine with the almost identical system generated by each adjacent boat. The systems will combine in the algebraic sense, i.e. for half the time the effects will be additive, with waves nearly twice as high where the systems are exactly in phase, while for the other half the water will be flatter, and completely flat where the systems are exactly out of phase. When twenty or thirty similar wave systems combine in this way, some of the resulting sets of waves can become surprisingly big. All three systems from all the starboard tack boats will then interfere with those of all the port tack boats. Those of early boats which have rounded the wing mark will interfere with those of later boats approaching the mark. It is not surprising that in these conditions waters which were previously placid can become very disturbed indeed.

Two points follow from this. First, that big-fleet racing tends to be rough-water racing, and the further back you are in the fleet the rougher the water becomes and the more will your boat lose speed relative to the leaders. This is particularly true at the start of the race. Leaders enjoy not only clear air, but flatter, faster water. The second is that the combinations of stern-waves from the boats ahead can often combine into a set of waves which are big enough to surf, even when close-hauled. The technique is to position the boat between the advancing face and the crest of the wave. This gives the maximum additional thrust and enables the boat to maintain its speed while pointing higher. It should be held on the wave in that position by pointing as high as possible for as long as the wave remains a useful size.

13.5 Swell

When the world's great high-energy wind systems – tropical cyclones nearer the equator and deep depressions nearer the poles – either remain stationary for awhile, or move in such a way that their very strong winds blow in the same direction over a substantial area of ocean for twenty hours or more, the wind-driven waves which are formed will roll faster and grow larger and higher until their speeds approach those of the winds which drive them.

Typical wind speeds within these systems, and the wave speeds which they can generate in the circumstances noted above, and the wave lengths and associated repetition periods (the intervals between successive crests) are:

Wind speed (knots)	Wave speed (knots)	Initial wave height (Metres)	Wave length (Metres)	Repetition interval (Seconds)
35	30	8	160	10
50	40	12	300	13
70	50	16	450	17

The momentum possessed by systems of huge waves such as these is so great that they can roll (in the absence of strong opposing winds) for two thousand kilometres or more. As they age and fan outwards from their source their height becomes progressively smaller, but their speed and length change little. In this attenuated form they are generally known as 'swell'.

To the helmsman, swell waves have five characteristics which are unlike those of all other wave systems:

1. They are absolutely regular in their repetition.
2. They are absolutely predictable in their direction.
3. Whether or not there is a local wind, will affect the swell's properties not at all.
4. The long interval between successive crests means that a boat will spend considerable time on each slope. This factor has important consequences from a momentum point of view, and is responsible for the reversal of technique which applies as between regular waves and swell.
5. When the wind is light, the substantial orbital speed of the water may exceed the speed of the low-level wind – in which case the lower sails (but not the upper sails) may be blown 'aback' for half of each wave cycle.

The fourth and fifth properties noted above dictate why the techniques of racing in swell in light air and the lighter breezes have to be so different from either the regular-wave or the chaotic-wave techniques.

13.6 Standing waves

Whenever a current flows over an obstruction in shoal water or an abrupt change of depth, a wave will form (Fig. 13.4). The restricted area through which the current can flow forces an increase in the current speed. As the speed increases the pressure reduces, and the level of the surface drops. (The extra speed comes from this 'downhill' flow.) Where the flow leaves the obstruction the flow reverts to its earlier lower speed. The impact of the faster current against this slower water creates a local pressure which forces the surface water upwards again in the form of a wave crest. This wave will maintain its position adjacent to the obstruction, and so is called a 'standing wave'. If the bottom is relatively shallow for some distance, and sufficiently uneven to form, in effect, a closely spaced series of separate obstructions, the result will be to excite a series of standing waves which will tend to adjust themselves into a wave train in which all the waves near that shoal area will become regular in height and wavelength, and will have their crests at right angles to the current (Fig. 13.5).

In normal conditions these standing waves will be minuscule, but in strong river current and very light air they can sometimes interact with the speed of the boat and excite it to pitch bow up – bow down at its resonant frequency. If this oscillation is allowed to develop, it can slow a boat in light air to a surprising extent. (The fix is simple – forward hand and helmsman should move their weights very smoothly toward the bow and the stern respectively, so as to maintain the boat's trim, but by separating their weights they will slow the boat's natural frequency, like making a pendulum longer, or increasing the diameter of the balance wheel of a watch). In this way they can 'de-tune' their boat's natural frequency from the wave's exciting frequency, and resume smooth and fast sailing again.

The other important property of standing waves has already been mentioned – they frequently combine with and bias the direction of regular waves. This commonly occurs in tidal estuaries. The end situation is one in which a wind which may blow diagonally to the current will cause substantial regular waves, but the wave crests become aligned more across the current than across the wind. From a handling point of view

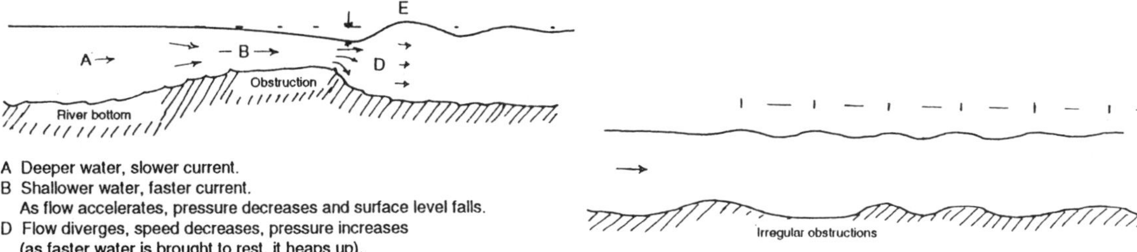

A Deeper water, slower current.
B Shallower water, faster current.
As flow accelerates, pressure decreases and surface level falls.
D Flow diverges, speed decreases, pressure increases
(as faster water is brought to rest, it heaps up).
E Standing wave crest.

Fig 13.4 Standing wave mechanism

Even if obstructions are irregular, wave train will be regular.

Fig 13.5 Wave-trains of standing waves

this creates an asymmetric situation both when tacking upwind and also when tacking downwind. In the windward-going situation one tack may be almost directly into the waves, while the other may be much more along the waves. The fastest sail trim and handling for the high-resistance into-wave situation is not at all the same as the optimum trim and handling for the much smoother cross-wave situation, so this will call for different handling on one tack compared with the other. Downwind, depending on the boat's characteristics, surfing will probably be possible on one gybe but not the other. But with fast boats which tack downwind faster than the waves, the waves will get in the way and slow the boat on one gybe, and not in the other, smoother-water, direction. These factors are discussed in Part Four.

B14 on Botany Bay

Chapter Fourteen
Depth and the Warm Surface Layer

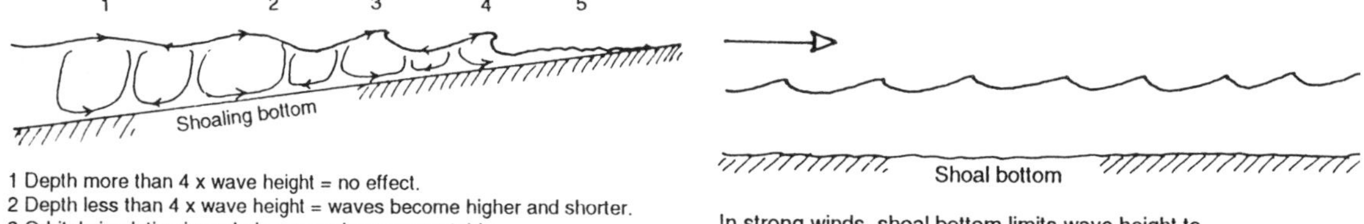

1 Depth more than 4 x wave height = no effect.
2 Depth less than 4 x wave height = waves become higher and shorter.
3 Orbital circulation impeded = waves become unstable
4 " " " = - and break.
5 Orbital momentum
dissipated in break turbulence = Wave height small.

Fig 14.1 Effect of shoaling bottom on approaching waves

In strong winds, shoal bottom limits wave height to about one quarter of the depth.
The stronger the wind, the shorter and steeper the waves become, and the more they break.

Fig 14.2 Shoal bottom limits wave height

14.1 Depth

In shoal water, waves become higher and shorter. The wave heights suggested in Fig. 13.2 assume that the water is deep, with no current and is of reasonably uniform temperature. They are the smallest waves which can be expected from those winds.

It is an everyday observation that where the depth becomes shallower, as on a shelving beach, waves will heap up and become higher before they break. Fig. 14.1 shows the mechanism. As the shoaling bottom restricts the orbital circulation at depth, the unspent momentum appears as an increase in wave height. As the wave slows there is some shortening of wave length.

If the bottom rises toward the surface, and then levels off at some constant but shoal depth, the waves will heap up at the upwind edge of the shoal. They may or may not break. Over any shoal bottom the waves will stabilise at some smaller size and steeper shape than the 'deep water' size and shape for the same wind. They will remain constant at this size for as long as the bottom remains at a constant depth. Regardless of the wind strength, the wave height cannot much exceed about one quarter of the depth. Fig. 14.2 indicates this situation.

If the bottom continues to shoal, the waves will continue to build. When the slope of the water surface approaches about 9 degrees – a slope of about one in seven – the heaped-up water becomes unstable and the wave-break process starts.

14.2 The warm surface layer

All water, like all land, is heated by the sun by day, and radiates its heat towards space by night. The sun's radiant energy penetrates the translucent water and heats the top two to three metres a little, a different process to that found on land where only the top few centimetres of its opaque surface are heated strongly. Because the absolute temperature increase in the water each day is very small, little of it is lost by re-radiation. The warmed water is less dense than colder water so it rises to the top like cream on milk. The end result of this process is that the surface layer of bodies of water becomes warmer than the deeps, and more so in tropical latitudes than nearer the poles.

It turns out that the depth of this warm surface layer is of importance to the racing helmsman. There appear to be at least three characteristic depths. Each of these is associated with different wave characteristics:

1. Layers fifty to one hundred metres deep are associated with simple waves of unlimited size.
2. Layers two to three metres deep are associated with simple waves of limited size.
3. Very thin layers about one metre deep are associated with complex patterns of two sizes of waves.

Deep layers

Those whose business it is to study the temperatures of the oceans at depth (– and for submarine warfare with sonar this is a very important study indeed –) advise me that in the windy areas of the open oceans, orbital motions of the big waves typical of these areas mix the warm water with the colder water below it to a depth of up to 100 metres. When the warm surface layer is thoroughly mixed into the colder water below for a depth as deep as this, the temperature difference between warm and cold water is small and the influence of the warm surface layer on wave size and characteristics is negligible.

Near shores, mechanical mixing will occur wherever current is forced through obstructions or past the promontories of a broken coastline. The floods and ebbs which constantly sluice past the British Channel Islands and into and out of the Solent, will mix the water there at least as thoroughly as the big waves of the open ocean. This mechanism mixes the water thoroughly, and because it repeats with every tide it mixes it continuously. It does the same in all harbours or bays with constricted and tortuous waterways. Two Australian examples are very different but typical:

Port Phillip Bay, on which the city of Melbourne is located, is a large relatively shallow body of water but with a very constricted entrance. The full water budget of every flood and ebb is forced through this narrow entrance and around several sharp corners nearby.

Sydney Harbour, in geological terms, is a complex of contorted steep-sided faults with jagged corners within a large sandstone and basalt formation. It would be hard to imagine any better shape for inducing turbulence and mixing, so while the tidal flows are relatively small in volume, the mixing mechanism is unusually efficient.

Wherever the warm surface layer is deep, the substantial waves developed by moderate and strong winds will not be limited in size, and will tend to be simple in form.

Characteristically, when sailing to windward, it will be easy to handle the boat with a wave-by-wave technique. Downwind, when you surf these simple waves, there will be nothing to stop you and a fast boat can surf a single wave for several hundred metres.

Layers two to three metres deep

Even in the open oceans, there will be little mixing in those areas where the prevailing winds are light and big waves are rare. In such areas the layer can become so thin and the temperature difference between itself and the colder water below can be so intense that the surface layer becomes quite mobile. Even relatively light winds can start it moving over the cold water below, and it blows downwind at a significant fraction of the wind speed. In these circumstances light-air windward performance is affected exactly as if the boat were beating into an adverse tide – the boat feels 'dead' and it won't point properly. This was often the situation at the Olympic sailing venue at Acapulco. The waters of the Mediterranean off Barcelona appear to be similar.

Shorelines will not affect a warm surface layer unless both strong current and obstruction are present. Where current is gentle and the coastline featureless, the warm surface layer will persist to the beach.

In enclosed waters – particularly those which start cold because they are ice-fed – a massive and intense warm surface layer 2 to 3 metres deep can develop in summer. When the layer develops in early summer, swimmers often sense the colder water with their feet. Later it is at a greater depth. Fig. 14.3 shows a temperature trace which is typical of the situation throughout the Great Lakes during August.

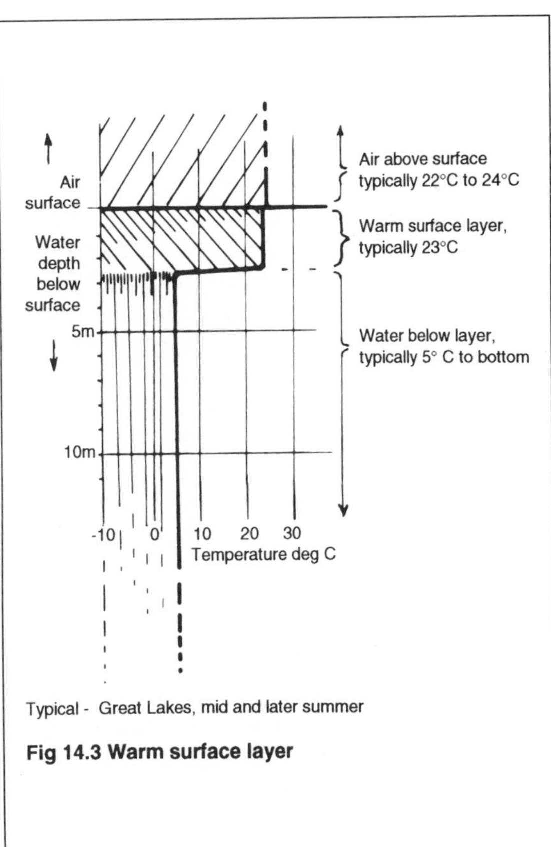

Fig 14.3 Warm surface layer

Warm surface layers such as this will affect the characteristics of waves in two ways. The most useful way to describe these effects is to compare the waves which form in these 2 to 3 metre layers with those which form in the deep layers in three different wind speed ranges:

a) In the wind speed range from calm to about 10 knots, there is no difference. The orbital motions of waves up to about the 0.3m height typical of 10 knot winds do not reach the denser cold water below, and so are not affected by it.

b) In the wind speed range from 10 to about 25 knots, the orbital motions of the progressively bigger waves will reach the denser cold water below. The effect will be that the denser water will interfere with the 'natural' orbital circulation in a manner broadly similar to the effect of a shallow bottom. This will cause the waves to become higher and steeper and more likely to break than the comparable deep water waves. My observations of the wave heights in two typical places – Sydney Harbour, which is well mixed, and Kingston Ontario in August when it has a well developed warm surface layer, suggest the following differences in wave height:

Wind speed (Knots)	Wave height(Metres)	
	Sydney	Kingston
10	0.3	0.3
15	0.6	1.0
20	1.0	1.8

These higher waves will normally be of simple form, and in these conditions normal wave-by-wave handling techniques will continue to be fastest. I recall one Canadian Starboat Olympic helm commenting, 'You have to go out there determined that you will not mishandle one single wave'. He was a Great Lakes sailor. Only those who have spent their lives in relatively regular waves could make a comment like that.

c) In winds stronger than 25 knots, i.e. in storm conditions, the effect of the warm surface layer on wave height reverses. The maximum height of the waves becomes limited and to a surprising extent. For example, sustained 40 knot winds can develop waves 10 to 12 metres high in the North Atlantic, but the same sustained winds will develop waves only 2 to 3 metres high in both the Great Lakes and the Baltic Sea in late summer. This is because the denser cold water below the warm surface layer continues to act rather like a shallow bottom, and big waves cannot develop in shallow water.

Thin layers

Intense layers which are thinner yet – say one metre – can occur in hot regions where layers are forming. Swimmers sense colder water from the hips down. These thin layers have insufficient mass to suppress the formation of wind-driven waves of normal size, i.e. the size to be expected having regard to the wind speed, how long the wind has been blowing, and the distance from any upwind shore (the fetch). Instead, these very thin warm surface layers make their presence felt by superimposing a system of small waves on the bigger waves. These small waves always become steep and irregular, and are typically up to a metre high. The total wave system ceases to be simple in form. In this system all the waves roll downwind in the same direction, so this is not a chaotic-wave system. Rather it is a complex system of bigger faster waves which roll downwind under small slower waves. Within this total system nothing is regular nor are the wave sizes uniform. A sea-state condition of this nature will need to be handled, both upwind and down, in a way which is different from either flat water or regular waves.

One example of this situation occurs off Adelaide, in the Gulf of St Vincent. The gulf is open to the Southern Ocean, which is very cold. Kangaroo Island lies across the entrance to the gulf and protects it from the ocean swell so there is no mixing from regular big waves. The openings between the ends of Kangaroo Island and the peninsulas which border the gulf are so wide that the floods and ebbs flow so gently that no mechanical mixing occurs. The summer climate is hot. The shores are shallow. Breezes are brisk. At a recent major regatta held in January, the warm layer was about one metre deep. In the prevailing 20 knot winds the bigger waves grew to about 1.5 metres, occasionally 2m, and superimposed on these bigger waves were smaller waves occasionally 1 metre high but usually less.

This mixture of smaller waves with bigger waves has far-reaching consequences on handling technique and sail trim. Without pre-empting the fuller discussion in Part Four, it will be helpful to touch on two situations here:

To windward

When sailing to windward in the simple waves typical of both the deep and the moderate depth warm surface layer, all sailboats except high-performance dinghies and catamarans will sail faster if they luff through the wave crests and bear away in the wave troughs, so as to minimise the time spent in the downwind orbital flow in the crests, and maximise the time spent in the windward-going orbital flow in the troughs. This can be accomplished efficiently with practise by adopting a wave-by-wave technique, and boats handled in this way will win. The fastest sail trim for this purpose will be fuller and more twisted than the fastest flat water setting – this is sometimes referred to as 'trimming for a wider groove'.

When sailing to windward in the complex waves of the thin layer, the potential speed advantage will continue to be dominated by the orbital flows of the big waves. But a new factor, wave impact drag, will be dominated by the more numerous irregular steep small waves. So to gain extra windward-going speed it will still be desirable to luff through the crests of the big waves. But as the small waves become steeper and more energetic in stronger winds, the impact drag suffered when bursting through them will destroy the momentum of light boats. When luffing up the face of an advancing wave, momentum is essential to carry the boat through and over the crest. If two steep small waves are encountered on the way up the face of a large wave, this may mean little to a heavy yacht which can never go fast in any winds, but can virtually stop a lighter boat, and the lighter (and faster) the boat, the worse it will be affected. In the extreme case the race to windward may be won by a crew who revert to a technique and sail settings little different from those used in flat water.

What comes out of all this is that the fastest technique to use to windward through waves is likely to depend partly on windspeed, and partly on the thickness of the warm surface layer and the consequent complexity of the wave pattern, and partly on the momentum of the boat you sail – and not at all on a simplistic – 'in waves luff through the crests and use fuller and twisted sails' approach.

Downwind

When sailing downwind in simple waves, practise and skill and forceful kinetics can accelerate a naturally fast boat from its normal 'half the wind speed' pace to the 'two thirds of the wind speed' velocity necessary to 'catch' a wave and initiate surfing. But once a boat is surfing, there will be nothing to inhibit the surf until the wave decays, so each surf can usually be prolonged.

When sailing downwind in the complex waves of the thin warm surface layer, the same practise and skill and forceful kinetics will be needed to catch any big wave to initiate surfing. But once the boat is surfing, there will then be the added problem that the smaller slower waves ahead will be blocking waves, and to maintain the surf on the face of the big faster wave it will be necessary to sail over or through these smaller slower waves. To negotiate the lowest points of the slower smaller waves ahead and sail through them whilst you surf the faster bigger wave calls for a more practised and elegant skill than that needed to surf any simple wave system.

Nobody who has sailed in these complex waves would ever say ' . .. determined not to mishandle a single wave'. In the thin-warm-surface-layer, complex-wave situation, such a statement makes no sense at all.

To sum up:

Where the warm surface layer is either absent as in polar seas or is deep, moderate and fresh winds will generate wind-driven waves which will be relatively simple in form, regular, and their height will depend on the wind strength.

Where the warm surface layer is both intense and two to three metres deep, waves in winds up to about 10 knots will be unchanged. Waves in winds from 10 to 25 knots will be higher and steeper. Waves in winds stronger than about 25 knots will be much lower than those in waters with deep warm surface layers. All these waves will be relatively simple in shape and regular.

Where the warm surface layer is intense but very thin, moderate and fresh winds will generate a complex wave system. Large fast waves will develop which will not be limited in height. Superimposed on these will be small steep irregular slower waves. The combined system will be complex and irregular, and will need handling and sail trim techniques different from either flat water or regular waves.

Chapter Fifteen
Currents and Tidal Stream

15.1 Drive force

Current is driven primarily by slope, and occasionally by wind. The important point about slope is that it drives all water equally. When the tide comes in, the rising sea level offshore drives all water inland with exactly the same force. It is this fact that enables us to predict the changes in current and tidal stream speed from place to place with reasonable certainty.

15.2 Friction effects and the velocity gradient

Fig. 3.8 is as true for water as it is for wind. Wherever there is flow there must be a boundary layer, and it must be either laminar or turbulent. The flow speeds associated with tides are relatively gentle and the boundary layers are normally laminar. In slow water, as in light air, surface friction slows the movement at the bottom to almost nothing. Above the bottom, given the uniform drive force, the flow speed will become faster with every additional metre of depth up to about four or five metres. The consequence of this is that the flow speed at the surface will be slowest where the water is shallowest, and fastest where it is deepest (Fig 15.1(a)).

15.3 Flows through channels

Where a wide estuary accommodates the flow of a substantial river system, the bottom of the waterway often takes the form of one or more deeper channels which are continuously scoured by the current. These are flanked by wide shoal silted areas. The channel(s) will be aligned in the direction of the current, and carry the flow of the river at low tide. In these areas the mechanism above slows the shallowest water. The deeper water in the channel(s) is less affected by surface friction and can flow faster. Fig. 15.1(b) shows the principles. The practical result is that there will be differences in current speed at the surface as between the deeper water and the shoals. These differences become tactically important when racing, particularly in light airs. The rule is:

In adverse current sail over the shoals and cross any channel quickly.

In favourable current sail the channel.

15.4 Momentum effects

The differences in flow speed between channels and shoals can lead to momentum effects at the change of tide. A common example would be a wide estuary which retains a single deep channel but is otherwise silted so completely that the mud may almost dry at the extreme lows of the tide cycle. Except at these extreme lows, there will be water enough for dinghies and small yachts to race at all tides across the whole estuary. If the channel is, for example, 30 metres deep and 200 metres wide (I am thinking of the estuary above Falmouth in England), there would be about (1,000 x 200 x 30), i.e. 6 million tonnes of water in each kilometre of several kilometres of channel, and

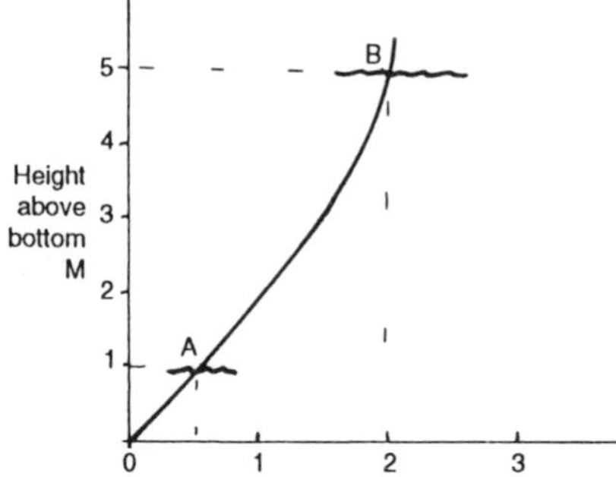

Typical flow speed of current above bottom (knots)

A Flow speed at surface of water 1M deep - 0.5 knots.
B Flow speed at surface of water 5M deep - 2 knots.

(a)

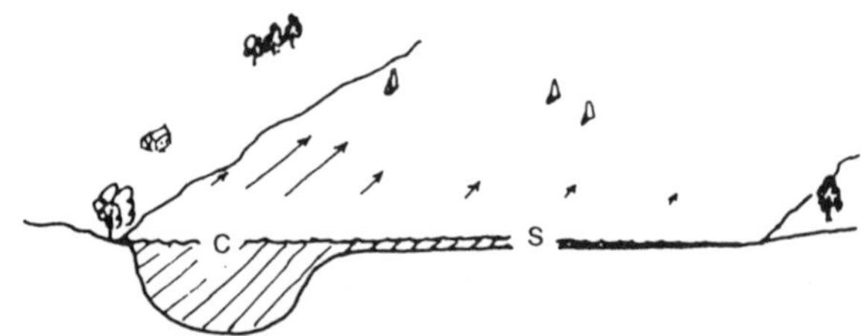

Cross section of estuary with channel and silt shoals.
C = Typical flow speed through channel - 2 knots.
S = Typical flow speed over shoals - 0.5 knots.

(b)

Fig 15.1 Effect of depth on surface speed of current

this enormous mass will ebb at two or three knots. At the change of tide, the almost motionless water over the shoals will respond immediately to the change in slope. The mass in the channel, due to its momentum, will take the form of a jet, separate from all the other water, and it will need time to slow, stop, and accelerate in the reverse direction. The time lag may approach one hour. During this time, the directions of flow and the speed differences between shoal water and the jet in the channel can take complex forms, particularly where the channel bends.

Where the steady outflowing current of a river and the oscillating currents of tidal flood and ebb combine, the ebb current will be stronger than, and flow for longer than, the flood. The acceleration effects will tend to favour the ebb at both changes of tide.

The practical outcome of all these effects will be pure local knowledge, and a beer with a knowledgeable local can be most rewarding.

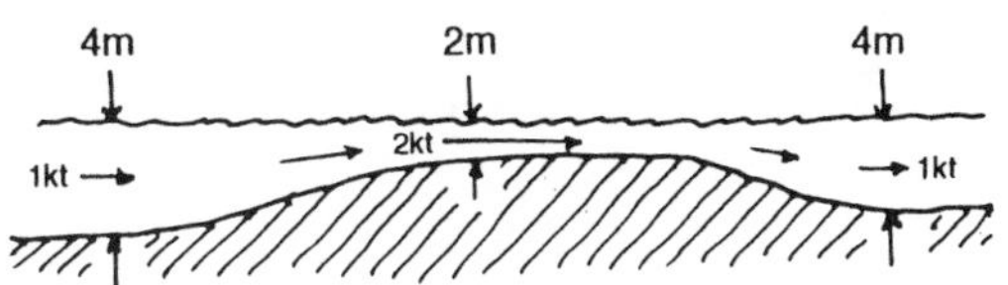

Where current speed is not sufficient to scour a channel, continuous bars can form.
Over a continuous bar, current must flow through a smaller total cross-section area, and so must flow faster.
'Faster current over shoal' is the reverse of the normal situation.

(a)

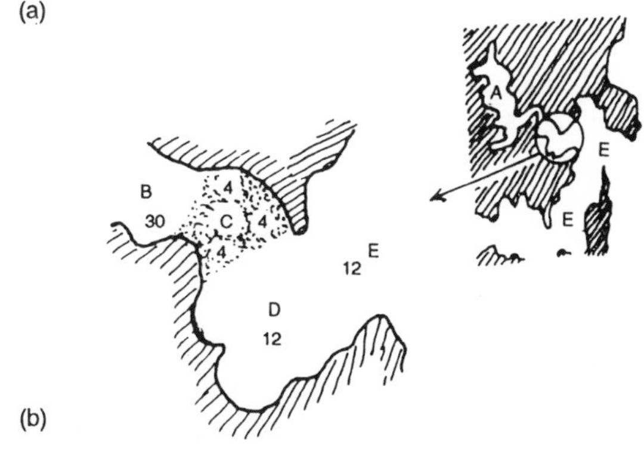

(b)

Tidal range typically 1.25M

(c)

A Upper middle harbour, 10 sq km water surface, no rivers.
BCD 'The sound'. Depth at B 30M; at C 4M; at D 12M.
E Main harbour and ocean.
F,H Areas of feeble current.
G Areas of faster current.
J Eddy.

Fig 15.2 Current flow over bar

15.5 Flow over bars

When a wide estuary or harbour does not accommodate any significant river flow, and the tidal ebb and flow is not sufficient to scour a channel, the shape of the bottom often takes an arrangement in which a deposit of sand or silt will form as a bar across the flow.

In bar situations, the current speeds between shoals and deeps reverses. The bar acts as a restriction, like a Venturi. In exactly the same way as the current in a stream must flow faster where the stream is narrower, so it must also flow faster where the depth is shallower, and the shallower the bar, the faster the current will be. Fig. 15.2(a) shows the principle, and 15.2(b) and (c) show a practical example – Sydney's Middle Harbour – and indicates the way the current speed changes with depth across this shoal. In this case an arm of the harbour with a surface area of about 10 square kilometres but without any significant river flow is connected with the main harbour and sea through 'The Sound' within which lies a sand bar. Fig. 15.2(b) shows the geography and depths. The tidal range varies from 0.9 to 1.6 metres, say 1.25m on average. The volume of water which moves across 'C' during each tide is therefore about (10 x 1,000 x 1,000 x 1.25) = 12,500,000 cubic metres. The flow is strongest at mid-tide, so the flow per hour then is about 4,000,000 cubic metres per hour. Shoal 'C' is about 400 metres wide and 4 metres deep, so has a cross-section area of about 1,600 square metres. A volume of 4,000,000 cubic metres per hour will pass through a cross section of 1,600 square metres if it moves at a speed of 2,500 m/hr (2.5 kph) or about 1.25 knots, which is exactly what we race in. The important point is that the tide through the deeps is a negligible quarter knot or less, while over the bar it flows much faster. Fig. 15.2(c) shows the flood-tide expectation.

Note the essential differences:

When channels are aligned with the current, the flow will be fastest where the water is deepest. But when bars without any channel lie across the current, the flow will be fastest where the water is shallowest.

15.6 Curves and eddies

Where a waterway is curved, centrifugal force will cause the current to flow most strongly on the outside of the curve, and most slowly on the inside. The stronger current will usually cut a deeper channel, and the faster flow through the deeper channel will accentuate the difference in speed of flow as between the inside and the outside of the curve.

If the curve is substantial, and the shoreline is smoothly curved, the flow will remain attached to the shoreline as described in Section 11.6. But if the shoreline is not smoothly curved, an eddy can form on the inside of the curve. Figure 15.3 shows the principle, and the eddy at 'J' in Fig. 15.2(c) shows a practical example.

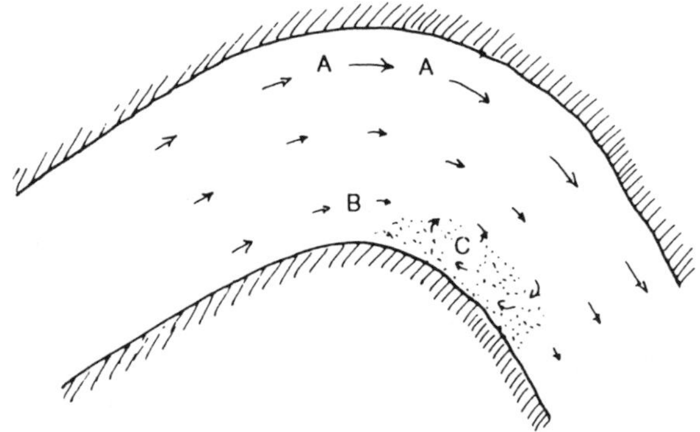

A = Stronger current on outside of curve scours channel.
B = Weaker current on inside of curve.
C = Shoal and/or eddy can form beyond curve.

Fig 15.3 Current flow around curve

The differences in current speed as between the inside and the outside of the curve, and particularly any reversed direction of flow within the eddy, will be tactically important. The flood-tide eddy shown in Fig. 15.2(c) can be critical when racing in the lighter morning winds before the sea breeze sets in.

15.7 Wind shear effects

When the wind is both abnormally strong and abnormally sustained, its friction on the water surface can drive water downwind to a significant extent. There will be two effects.

The first will be an abnormally high water level at a lee shore which is downwind of any long fetch, for as long as the wind keeps blowing. This fact, combined with possible extreme high tides, can cause catastrophic flooding. In the deeper water the larger waves caused by the strong wind can roll unbroken right to the flooded shoreline where they break with damaging force and add to the general misery. Times and places such as these are not where we race our boats for pleasure.

A second effect is that strong sustained winds can blow a warm surface layer downwind away from windward shorelines. This happens from time to time in places like the Great Lakes. For a few days afterwards the surface water will be abnormally cold. In this situation the notes in Chapter 9.7, 'Chilled wind effects', may be appropriate despite the late-summer season.

15.8 Current and wave size

When current flows against the wind, the waves become bigger, and vice versa. The primary reason is that, as far as the water is concerned, the current speed is added to the wave speed, and so the Apparent Wind becomes stronger and the waves become bigger. If the water is at all shoal, the usual increase in wave height due to shoal water simply adds to the increase due to the stronger Apparent Wind.

From the point of view of any crew, the increase in wave size is much greater than the perceived increase in wind speed, and the racing conditions become more difficult because of the difficulty of achieving and maintaining good speed through waves which are higher and steeper than those expected. The saving grace is that the current is necessarily favourable, and so the boat continues to point well even if the boat speed does not satisfy.

The converse situation – the smaller waves which occur when the current flows with the wind – may be merciful in themselves but the situation leads to even greater frustration, because while the boat can move through the smaller waves more easily, there will be less wind to drive it, the current will be adverse, and 'the boat won't point properly' because of the vector skews which accompany adverse current. These are discussed in Part Four.

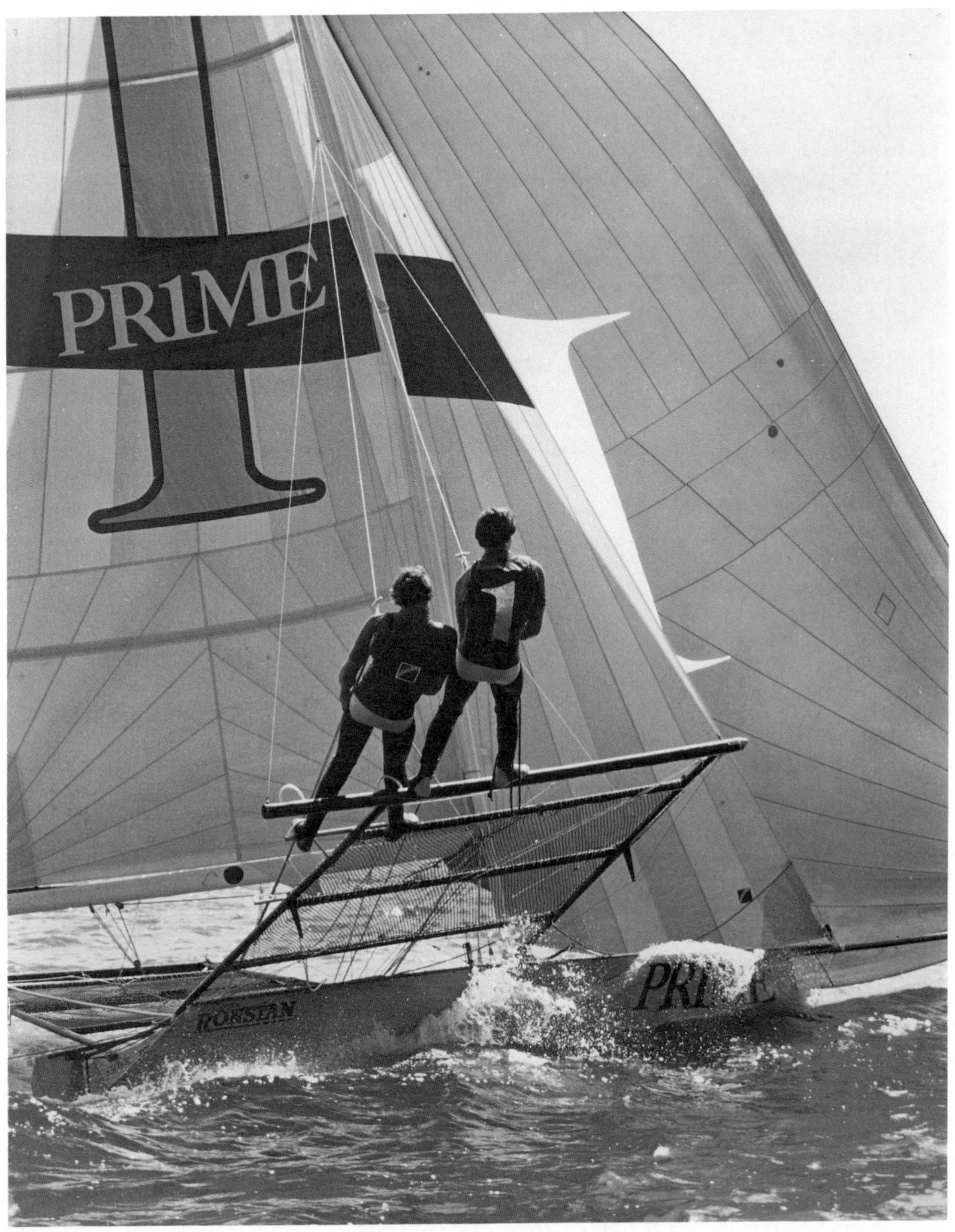

Prime MK III - Julian's third two hander, was a remarkable boat. Built from long-grain balsa and epoxy/glass/carbon, the hull with the fittings attached weighed 99 pounds, and the total sailing weight including crew was 550 pounds. Wing-span tip to tip was 26.5 feet, mast height 36 feet and sail area downwind with the big rig was 1400 square feet. Julian won one heat of the 84/85 Eighteen Footer Worlds.
Exactly as I had kept the underwater shape of the Dribbly IV when designing the Tasar, so Julian kept the underwater shape of *Prime Mark III* when designing the B18.

Preface to Part Three

Alan Payne is one of Australia's most respected yacht designers. Some highlights of a long life spent among fast yachts are that he designed *Gretel I* and *Gretel II*, the first two of the ultimately successful series of Australian *America*'s Cup challengers, and he has contributed to the final performance of many of those which followed. Few designers in the world can be in a position to know more than Alan about what makes a big yacht sail fast.

Readers will gather from the descriptions in the chapters ahead, of our many experiments and the results we have subsequently achieved, that I am confident of what I write concerning the smaller, lighter, faster boats with which I have spent most of my time.

Alan and I have known each other for years, but because we worked at different ends of the size range we met only rarely. When we did, we always seemed to agree on the basics of whatever new principles had recently emerged.

I was delighted when Alan expressed interest in my manuscript, and immediately invited him to read it and comment. Our subsequent discussions uncovered fascinating information about the subtle way priorities and dynamics change as boats grow bigger. All of Alan's 'big boat' information has been incorporated into the text.

Alan's contributions have added greatly to the range and the authority of the following chapters. I value his co-operation and thank him for it.

Frank Bethwaite

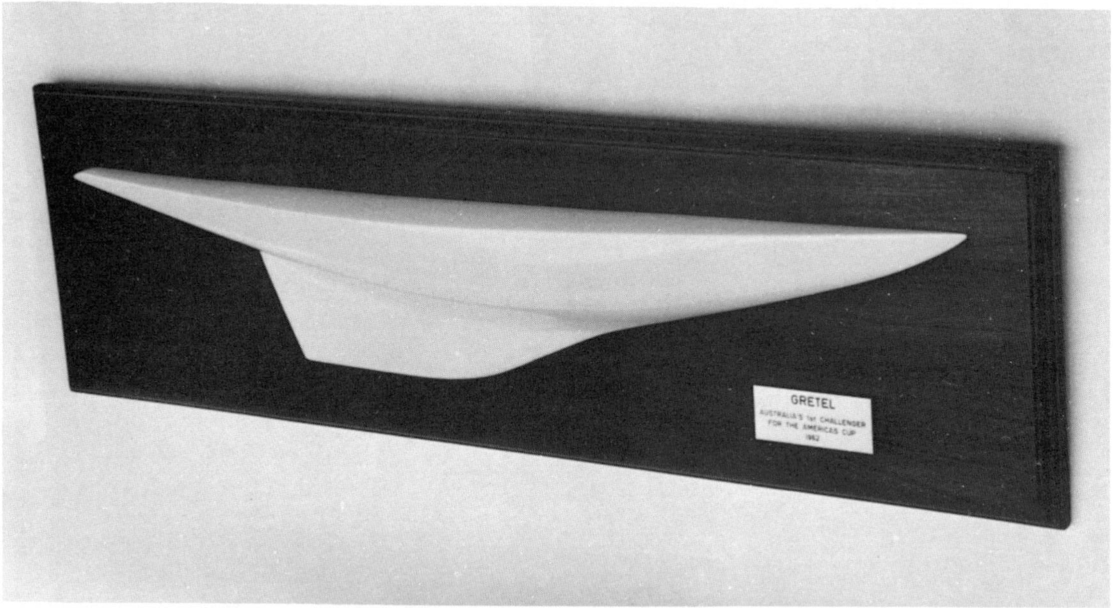

Half model of *Gretel I*

Part Three

The Boat

Introduction

I have contributed really very little to this book, but I am particularly pleased to have taken part. This is a book about making one's own discoveries – finding things out, and then making use of the findings. My own inclination has always been towards that, if I could manage to do it.

There are already a number of helpful books which make the connections between the classic theories of fluid flow, and the things that happen to us in our sailing boats. This is all very well, and Frank Bethwaite makes those same connections in this book, but with a different emphasis. The other books have often given me the impression that there is the chapter to explain this, and the chapter to explain that, and all the chapters put together add up to everything having been explained and accounted for. I don't suppose that the various authors would claim to have done that, but I think that is the impression that the reader gets. To me as a yacht designer, this is just a little annoying.

I find that there are still plenty of mysteries. No doubt the solutions to these mysteries are linked with the laws of fluid flow, but we haven't found all the links just yet.

Frank's book is based on combining theory with real-life experimentation. I have great enthusiasm for full-scale tests and trials with real boats. If somebody wants to tell me how they tried this and that, I am always interested to know what happened. I'm surprised that more yachtsmen aren't interested in comparative trials, or experimental measurements, in preparation for racing. We can all try things out, especially if we form a little group with two or three boats, and it can be as much fun as the racing itself.

Home-made trials can point us towards intriguing discoveries, which surely we would never have made simply by poring over our fluid-dynamics textbooks.

No doubt the new computational fluid dynamics will be as useful, eventually, as it has become to aircraft design. However, in respect of all the advances we have made in boat and sail design, I think that the amateurs and 'practical men' have at least as good a record, up to the present time, as the fluid dynamicists and the naval architects such as myself. Even with the computer added, I'm not sure that this situation will change.

So read Frank's book, and start a new sailing life, trying things out according to his advice.

Alan Payne

Skiff racing can be close

Chapter Sixteen
The Quest for Speed

16.1 Forces on a sailboat when sailing to windward

If a perfect rig is mounted on a perfect hull, but one without a centreboard or keel, and it is sailed upright, it will not to sail to windward. The 'wing in the air' (the rig) produces a force '0S' (Fig. 16.1), which is roughly at right angles to the sails.

The bottom of any planing hull is necessarily reasonably flat, and so is unable to produce much cross-boat force (unless it is heeled to put the chine deep in the water). As a result, in Fig. 16.1, 'upright, no keel nor centreboard', situation, the boat will accelerate in the direction 'OS' until the hull's drag increases to the point where it becomes equal and opposite to the sail force 'OS'. This situation, with the hull's centreline headed in the direction 'heading', but the boat tracking across the water in the very different direction 'OS', will neither win races, nor be much fun.

The best way to think about any sailing boat is to regard it as an assembly of three basic components:

1) A wing in the air (the sails and rig).
2) A wing in the water (the centreboard, or keel, plus the rudder).
3) A form of low-drag flotation (the hull).

The force provided by the hull is primarily upwards, to keep the boat and crew from sinking. In the case of the very fast sailboards, the hull at rest is not big enough to do even this – it has to be moving fast enough to develop dynamic lift before it can support its rider. The hulls of most modern sailboats, except multihulls, are reasonably flat, and for this reason they can be usefully thought of as if they were saucer-shaped, i.e. free to move equally easily in all directions.

The keel or centreboard is a 'wing' which 'flies' through the water. Like the rig, it produces a force roughly at right angles to its surface 'OC', Fig. 16.2(b).

When a sailboat sails to windward or on a close reach, the forces acting on it when viewed from ahead, i.e. those forces which act across the boat, take the arrangement shown in Fig. 16.2(a). Appreciation of these forces is helpful in understanding which boats can and which cannot sail fast. For Fig.16.2 we will use figures typical of the many popular classes of non-trapeze conventional dinghies about 14 to 15 feet long which are of approximately similar performance and are well understood, such as the GP14, Enterprise, Albacore, etc. These boats weigh about 350 pounds (300 for the hull and 50 for the rig and foils) and are designed to be crewed by two adults who will typically weigh about 310 pounds themselves and 330 pounds dressed for sailing and wet, so the total weight at which the boats are designed to sail is about 680 to 700 pounds. We will assume that the water is flat, that the True Wind is 12 knots, that the boat's heading when sailing to windward is 45 degrees from the direction of the True Wind, and that the boat speed through the water is 4.5 knots. The triangle of velocities in Fig. 16.2(c) shows that the Apparent Wind becomes 15.5 knots, and blows at 12 degrees from the direction of the True Wind, and at an angle 'across the deck' of 33 degrees from the bow. These speeds and angles are reasonable, in that they are suggested by theory and confirmed by observation and measurement.

The leeway angle is different. Other authors have reported that they have found it hard to measure. We took one of our own designs – the marque shown in Fig 20.12 – which is designed to sail to windward in the design wind, with its centreboard running at an angle of attack of 3 degrees (i.e. with a leeway angle of 3 degrees), and towed a thread with a small weight at its end. While two of us sailed the boat, a third read the angle of the thread across the aft deck from the bow of a following motor-boat. It never showed anything like 3 degrees. It did not read even half a degree on any of a number of runs. We tried the direct observation approach. An observer stood on one shore of a narrow bay without tide and the crew sailed from near the shore on a fixed heading, which was about close-hauled, directly toward a conspicuous object on the other shore. The observer moved if necessary, until he was sighting along the boat's centreline at the aiming point on the far shore, and watched to see how much the boat drifted to leeward of the line of sight. It didn't drift to leeward either.

In no way do I suggest that the centreboard does not meet the water at about the three degrees necessary for the force to be developed. All that we report is a measurement difficulty in that the measured leeway angle of this typical dinghy with a deep efficient centreboard (which is strong, stiff and firmly secure in its case), is much less than appears theoretically possible. Something is happening which we do not yet understand. Efficient keel yachts are also designed to have leeway angles of about 3 degrees. In their case this angle is confirmed by model tests, observation and full-scale measurement.

For the sake of simplicity I have drawn Fig 16.2 and subsequent diagrams, as if the leeway angle with respect to the centreline is zero – which is about what we measured.

Fig. 16.2(a) shows how the (low-speed) balance forces work when they are viewed from ahead. The crew, who would typically weigh about 310 pounds dry, will probably weigh about 330 pounds wet, and when 'hiking' as hard as they can, their weight 'W' will act about 4 feet to windward of the hull's buoyancy 'B'. This produces a righting moment of (4 x 330) or about 1320 pounds/foot. Because the hull is upright or very nearly so, it contributes nothing toward the righting moment. The sail's force 'S' acts about 10 feet above the centreboard's force 'C' and so a sail force of 132 pounds will produce a heeling moment equal and opposite to the crew's righting moment. (132 pounds of sail and of centreboard force x 10 feet separation equals 1320 pounds/foot heeling force. 330 pounds of crew weight and of buoyancy force x 4 feet separation equals 1320 pounds/foot righting force.)

Fig. 16.2(b) shows how the forces work when viewed from above. If the centreboard were infinitely efficient, the force it would develop would be at right angles to the water flow, in the direction 'OX'. Because this is a real world in which nothing is perfect, the centreboard suffers both slight hydrodynamic drag and also some tip loss, so the actual force 'OC' acts at an angle of about three degrees aft of 'OX'. To balance the sail force 'OS' of 132 pounds across the boat, the centreboard (when the boat is sailing to windward) must develop an almost equal force, which is represented by the vector arrow 'OC'. (For the sake of simplicity, throughout this and subsequent examples we will consider only the 'cross-boat' forces. This simplification will not affect the principles under discussion. In practice the sail and centreboard forces will be directed slightly forward and aft respectively, and so their total forces will need to be fractionally greater than the cross-boat forces quoted.)

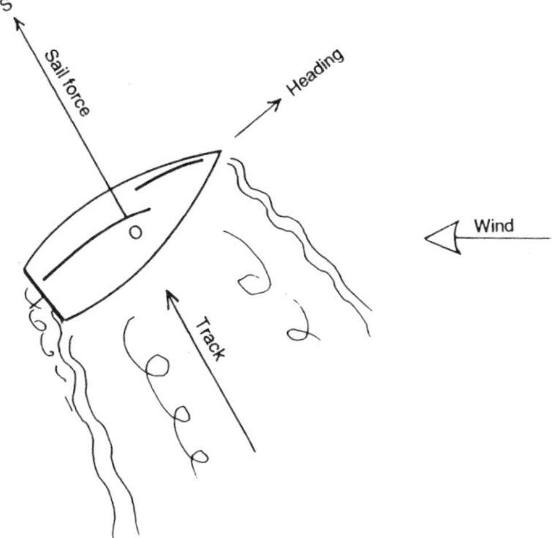

Fig 16.1 **Performance of flat-bottomed boat without centreboard**

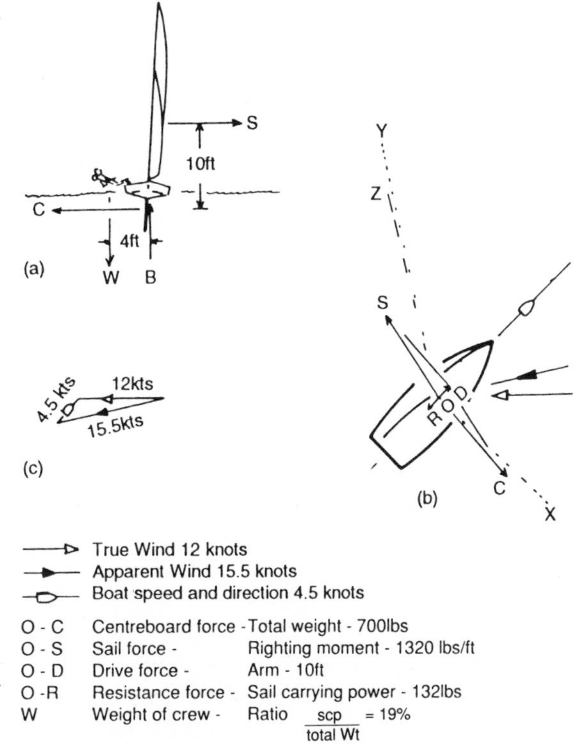

Fig 16.2 Principal forces when sailing to windward

If the rig were theoretically perfect, it would develop a force 'OY' at right angles to the Apparent Wind.

If it were as efficient as a glider's wing, the force would lie within one degree of 'OY' along 'OZ'.

Unfortunately this is a real world in which our rigs are anything but streamlined and in fact develop substantial drag. They are also squat and so suffer substantial tip loss. They are also relatively small and so we must work them at angles of about 20 to 25 degrees to the oncoming wind – instead of the glider wing's 1 degree. For all these reasons the line of force 'OS' lies quite a long way downwind of 'OY'.

If we complete the parallelogram of forces 'OSDC', the drive force 'OD' appears. The crew can control this drive force. If they point high, it will be small. If they bear away a little and ease sheets, 'OS' will swing forward and 'OD' will become larger.

The resistance of the hull plus the foils at 4.5 knots is about 25 pounds. This is represented by the vector arrow 'OR'. Provided that the crew maintain a drive force 'OD' which is equal and opposite to 'OR', the boat will keep sailing. In practise, competent crews will adjust the trim of their sails relative to the centreline, and adjust their boat's heading relative to the Apparent Wind, until 'OS' lies at the angle to 'OC' which will give them the drive force 'OD' which will give them the speed they want. This will be the drive force which is equal (and opposite) to the hull's resistance 'OR' at the desired speed. Successful crews then refine the trim of their sails to minimise drag so as to achieve this drive force at the highest possible pointing angle, and re-refine this trim every time even a small change in the wind or sea-state condition occurs, so the retrimming process is virtually continuous.

These three force vectors, 'OS' (sails), 'OR' (hull), and 'OC' (centreboard) absolutely dominate the art of sailing to windward. Everything that happens in the boat must affect one of these three arrows. If the sail is too flat it will lack 'power' and 'OS' will be shorter. If it is too full, power will be restored, but the sails' drag will rise because of the larger separation bubbles, and 'OS' will swing in a downwind direction, and so 'OD' will become shorter unless the boat is sailed further off-wind (pointed lower) to restore the angle between 'OS' and 'OC'. If the sail is allowed to twist too much, 'OS' will also swing downwind. If the centreboard or rudder are not maintained highly polished and free of blemish, or if they pick up weed, which is not noticed and cleared by the crew, 'OC' will swing aft and again the boat will have to be pointed low to restore performance. If the crew sit too far aft, or allow the hull to heel, 'OR' will become bigger, and again the boat will have to be pointed lower for sufficient angle between 'OS' and 'OC' to compensate.

It is interesting to look at the figures which have emerged. The total sailing weight is about 700 pounds. The sail force which the crew can hold up against the wind, in the cross-boat sense, is about 132 pounds, or 19% of the total weight. I call this the *'sail carrying power'* of the boat. The drive force needed to sail to windward at an efficient speed is about 25 pounds. Twenty five pounds is about 20% of the sail carrying power, and about 3.6% of the total weight. These figures of a sail carrying power of about 20% of the total weight, and a drive force requirement of between 3 and 4% of the total weight, are entirely typical of both these conventional dinghies and also of most 'performance' keelboats.

When sailing to windward, I find it useful to think of 'OS' and 'OR' as two rubber bands which are continually under the direct control of the crew. The crew's job is to trim the hull fore and aft, and hold it upright, so as to make the tension in 'OR' as small as possible, and to trim the sails so as to make the tension in 'OS' as large as possible consistent with its pointing as far forward as possible. Provided that the centreboard and rudder blade are maintained in flawless condition, 'OC' looks after itself – except for the small matter of weed, which can sometimes reduce performance subtly, and catastrophically.

6.2 To sail faster

If we want to sail faster, it is interesting to look at how the forces will change, and what effect these changes will have on our speed, if we sail in stronger winds, or make the sails bigger, or make the hulls bigger, or make the boats lighter, or move our weight out further, or when we move into sailboards or catamarans or trimarans.

Most works on design emphasise the importance of the speed / length ratio and of skin friction, almost to the exclusion of all else. This is very proper for heavy boats. However, heavy boats don't sail fast. Most ocean races are won at average speeds of about one third to one quarter of the average wind speed – which is usually about one half to two thirds of the hull speeds of the competing yachts. Many of the present ocean racing records were established many years ago, which suggests that boats with heavy keels are still sailing today at exactly the same speeds as they sailed yesterday – provided, of course, that they are still as well sailed and as well maintained.

The actual speeds, forces, and ratios of Fig. 16.2 represent about the best that can be achieved from any of a group of popular, well developed, well understood conventional monohull dinghies. For this reason Fig. 16.2 is a very good starting point from which to move, in imagination, as we try to understand the ways in which it might be possible to sail faster.

In the notes which follow, we will assume equal excellence of design in all cases.

Initially, we will consider only the, 'sailing to windward', situation which is described in Fig. 16.2. This is a sensible approach for three reasons. First, sailing to windward has always been the most decisive point of sailing from the point of view of race success. Secondly, looking at only this one point of sailing will help keep the story simple. But most importantly, when we come to look at the performance of truly high-performance craft – those which can routinely sail faster than the wind – we will find that because the Apparent Wind at these speeds must necessarily blow always from ahead, these boats must therefore sail with close-hauled or close-reaching sail trim at all times and on all points of sailing. So, in the end, we have no option but to discard the force diagrams with the Apparent Wind on the beam or aft, and it is only the close-hauled force diagram which remains relevant.

16.3 Change of wind speed

Let us look first at what happens as the wind speed changes.

In a calm, there can be no sail force, no drive force, and no movement beyond that achievable by kinetics.

As the wind speed increases from light air to the 12 knots assumed in Fig. 16.2, the sail force 'OS' will increase from nothing to 132 pounds. In light air the crew will balance their weight centrally. As the sail force increases, they will move their weight progressively outwards. As the drive force increases, the boat will sail progressively faster as the wind speed increases towards and reaches 12 knots. At this point the crew will be fully, 'hiked'.

Up to this point the boat's Velocity Made Good (VMG) to windward will increase approximately as the wind speed increases. (The VMG is most easily thought of as the speed at which the boat approaches the windward mark when the windward and leeward marks are truly up and down the True Wind. Technically the VMG is the component of the boat's speed measured in the direction of the True Wind which the boat is sailing in at the moment, and is the end result of the boat speed and pointing angle chosen by the crew.) This is shown by the curve '0-A' in Fig. 16.3. The sail force and drive force will increase approximately as Apparent Wind speed (squared). Hull resistance will increase approximately as boat speed (squared) – it will be greater in waves. So it will usually be true that in wind speeds of less than the design wind, the stronger the wind, the faster the boat will sail, and the faster will be its VMG.

What happens next is surprising. We will assume that the crew are and remain fully 'hiked'. As the wind speed continues to increase beyond 12 knots, if the crew do nothing the sail force must increase and the boat will begin to heel. This will increase hull drag ('OR' in Fig. 16.2) and the boat will sail more slowly. If they wish to keep the boat upright the crew must either point higher to 'feather' the boat, and again sail more slowly, or they must ease sheets to reduce the sail force in order to prevent the boat from heeling, or use some combination of the two. The heeling force of 1320 pounds/foot is the maximum that they can accept. So, although the wind speed may continue to increase, and much greater sail power will become potentially available, this potentially greater sail force cannot be used because the boat cannot be held upright, and so the drive force cannot increase further. (In the case of a yacht, it will heel beyond its optimum angle and sail more slowly because of its rapidly increasing hull resistance.) It is not possible, therefore, for the boat's speed nor its VMG to increase any further in the progressive manner in which it increased between calm and 12 knots.

The wind speed at which the crew have to start pointing higher or easing sheets is the point at which the progressive increase of boat speed with wind speed ceases. This wind speed is called the *'design wind'*. It is shown as 'A' in Fig. 16.3. In practical terms, in winds of up to the design wind, the crew will be 'looking for power'. In winds stronger than the design wind, the crew will need to shed power. *What happens next depends upon the type of rig.*

As the wind speed increases, two primary factors *will always* change, while a third *may* change. The first helps the boat go to windward faster. The second slows it. The third optimises the conditions of the moment.

1. The first factor is that when the boat speed remains constant and the True Wind speed increases, the direction of the Apparent Wind will shift progressively towards that of the True Wind. This will mean that a boat which sails at the same angle to the Apparent Wind will sail progressively closer to the True Wind, and so will increase the component of its speed in the 'up the True Wind' direction i.e. its VMG. will

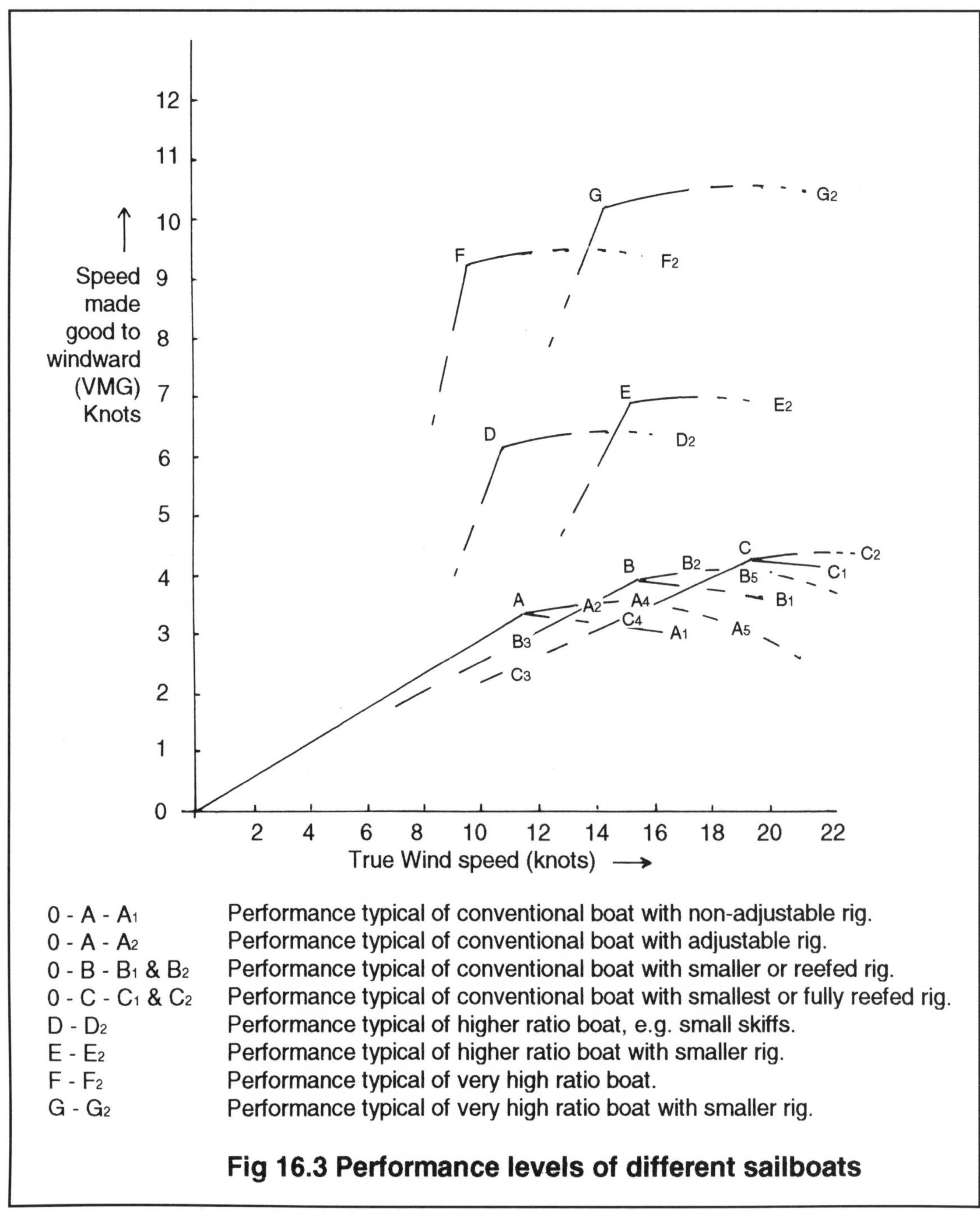

Fig 16.3 Performance levels of different sailboats

increase. In practical terms, in stronger winds and flat water the tacking angle will become smaller.

2. The second factor is that the aerodynamic drag of everything in the wind – the mast with all its shrouds and halyards, the sail, the hull, and the crew themselves, will increase as the square of the speed of the Apparent Wind.

These two factors are roughly equal and opposite, and so tend to mask each other in normal sailing wind speeds of say, up to 25 knots. It is self-evident that on those occasions when a sailboat, any sailboat, is caught out in winds of 40, 60, 80 knots or more that there will be some wind speed at and above which progress to windward becomes impossible. This simply acknowledges that at these unusually high wind speeds, the speed (squared) drag increase becomes the dominant factor.

3. The third factor is the shape of the sail(s). If the shape of the sails cannot be changed – as with the largest sail of a sailboard, or the rigid glider-wing sails of some large catamarans, the boat's windward-going speed will become slowly but progressively less. ('A-A1', Fig. 16.3)

If the shape of the sail can be adjusted, then by skilfully flattening the upper sails and allowing them to twist away slightly in the progressively stronger winds, it will be possible to reduce the sail's aerodynamic drag a little. More importantly, allowing the sail to twist a little will lower the height at which the sails' force acts. This, together with a slight raising of the centreboard, can reduce the distance (arm) between the raised centre of pressure of the centreboard and the lowered centre of pressure of the sails. The effect of these changes can give a small increase in the maximum sail force which can be accepted and also to the drive force which is developed. (If the arm were halved, the acceptable sail force would be doubled before the boat would heel.) In practise, the maximum improvement achievable before the rig becomes hopelessly inefficient appears to be an increase in drive force of about 10 to 15 per cent. This needs skill and good technique to achieve, but can be used to achieve either a better pointing angle or a little more speed up to some higher limiting wind speed, or some combination of both. This approach is indicated as 'A-A2' in Fig. 16.3.

If the design of the boat is suitable, this increase of sail force, combined with a lower pointing angle, can be used to initiate windward planing. The critical difference between displacement sailing and planing is the drive force needed, about 3.5% to 4% of the boat's total weight for displacement sailing at hull speed, but about 10%, or three times as much, for free planing.

While many dinghies can plane, only a few can point high enough while planing to achieve a VMG which is faster than displacement sailing more slowly but at a higher pointing angle. The Flying Dutchman and 505 are typical of design styles which can just plane to windward with success. This whole subject is looked at in detail in Part Four.

If all or part of the rig can be changed – as by reefing or changing headsails on a yacht, or changing the entire rig, as is the practise with sailboards and some Australian skiff classes – a faster speed can be achieved in stronger winds by shifting to progressively smaller rigs. This will be at the expense of slower speeds in lighter winds. The effect of changing to a smaller rig size and particularly to a lesser rig height in stronger winds is shown as 'O-B-B1' and 'O-C-C1', in Fig. 16.3. If these rigs are themselves adjustable, improved performance into yet stronger winds can be achieved, as in 'O-B-B2' and 'O-C-C2'.

The apparent contradiction – that higher speeds can be achieved with smaller rigs (provided that there is enough wind) – is due to the greater sail force achievable with the lower rigs. But note that a smaller rig will always give a slower performance than a larger rig in all wind speeds which are less than about the design wind for the larger rig. If one of three crews believes that the wind will average 12 knots and wear their biggest rig, and the second crew guess that it will average 16 knots and wear their No 2 rig, and the third estimate 20 knots and wear their No 3 rig, then in 12 knots their windward-going VMG's will be as 'A', 'B3' and 'C3', with 'A' fastest. In 16 knots their VMG's will be as 'B', 'A4' and 'C4', with B fastest. In 20 knots their speeds will be as 'C', 'B5' and 'A5', with the smallest rig the fastest and the biggest rig very much the slowest. The frequently expressed belief that the biggest sails are fastest could not be more wrong in strong winds. The ultimate example is the Skeeta ice yacht, a very clean but heavy (800 pounds) frame, 25 feet wide and 30 feet long, with a tiny 75 square foot sail to handle the 50 to 100 knot Apparent Winds encountered as they sail at up to six times the wind speed. Another example is the tiny sail area used in gale winds by the 'speed' sailboards which are currently the fastest sailboats to be timed across an official course.

What Fig. 16.3 shows most clearly is that, at their best, conventional yachts and dinghies can sail to windward in wind speeds of up to about 10 to 12 knots at speeds of about one third of the wind speed, and that in stronger winds their performance, as a fraction of the wind speed, becomes less. No matter how well they are handled, conventional craft are just not capable of boat speeds – when sailing to windward – which remotely approach the speed of the wind in any conditions.

16.4 The two wind speed ranges

A second fact revealed by Fig. 16.3 and the subsequent similar figures is that there are two entirely different windspeed ranges in the windward-going performance diagrams of almost all sailboats.

1. In the windspeed range between calm and the design wind, there is no doubt. All boats will sail faster

in stronger wind. This means that, in reality when the wind is never steady, it will always be faster in light and moderate winds to head towards and sail within the stronger wind areas. In this windspeed range, and regardless of all other performance differences, a boat in more wind will always sail faster, and in every direction, than a comparable boat in less wind.

To sum up:

IN LIGHT AND MODERATE WINDS, FOR ALL BOATS, IT WILL BE WIND SPEED WHICH WILL WIN.

2. But when the wind is stronger than the design wind, there will be three choices, according to the characteristics of the boat you choose to sail.

(a) The first group are the boats which never plane, and which can never much exceed hull speed in any conditions. This group will include all keel yachts except the lightest, and all the heaviest dinghies. These boats will by definition be 'up to speed' at the design wind when sailing to windward, and in winds of this strength will also be up to their hull speed on all other points of sailing. They therefore cannot sail significantly faster in any stronger wind on any point of sailing. In this situation there is no advantage to be gained by seeking any stronger-wind area.

Conversely, there is now every advantage to be gained from using the advantaged tacks and gybes which are offered by windshifts and in this way sailing shorter distances to reach the next mark. Race advantage will therefore lie in seeking and sailing in those areas in which the wind direction is more favourable, and this will be true both upwind and down.

To sum up:

IN STRONGER WINDS, FOR NON-PLANING BOATS, IT WILL BE WIND DIRECTION WHICH WILL WIN ON ALL POINTS OF SAILING.

(b) The second group will include all the boats which cannot plane to windward, but which can plane or go faster in stronger winds on other points of sailing. This group will include all conventional planing dinghies, and all catamarans, and some of the older style slender deep keelboats which sail like catamarans downwind and some of the lightest dinghy-shaped keelboats which can also exceed their hull speeds a little in very strong winds downwind.

When sailing to windward in winds stronger than the design wind this group will be in exactly the same position as group (a) above. They will be up to speed, will be able to sail no faster in any stronger wind, and so will reach the windward mark soonest by sailing the shortest distance through the water, i.e. by sailing the advantaged tacks.

But when sailing downwind, the stronger the wind the faster the planing boats will sail, and there is no limit to their increase in speed. The other boats in this group will be able to enjoy a smaller but still significant downwind speed advantage in the stronger wind areas.

To sum up:

FOR DOWNWIND PLANERS, IT WILL BE WIND DIRECTION WHICH WILL WIN UPWIND, AND IT WILL BE WIND SPEED WHICH WILL WIN DOWNWIND.

(c) The third group will include all the high-performance planing dinghies and sailboards which have sufficient power to plane to windward at increasing windward-going speeds in stronger winds. It is self-evident that these boats will also go faster downwind in stronger winds. In their case their speed continues to increase in stronger winds on all points of sailing, and this overrides the limit which other boats suffer when winds become stronger than the design wind. The end result is that whether the wind is lighter or stronger makes no difference to these boats – the stronger the wind, the faster they go, and this will remain true in all wind strengths and on all points of sailing. The classic example is the ice yacht.

To sum up:

FOR WINDWARD PLANERS, IT WILL BE WIND SPEED WHICH WILL WIN IN ALL WIND STRENGTHS AND ON ALL POINTS OF SAILING.

(A practical example of (b) and (c) in action is given in Section 1.5 (Lake Garda)).

16.5 Change of size

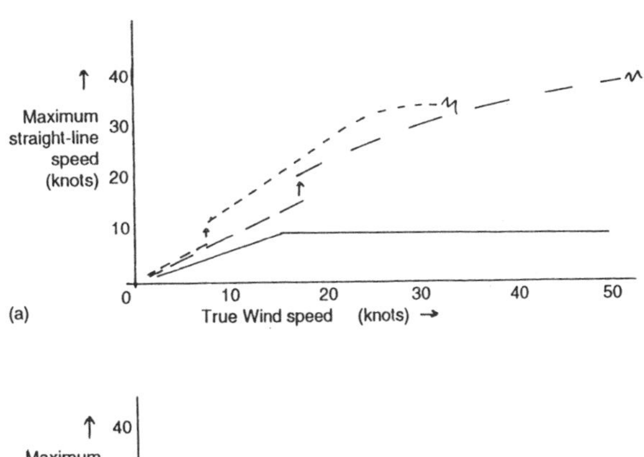

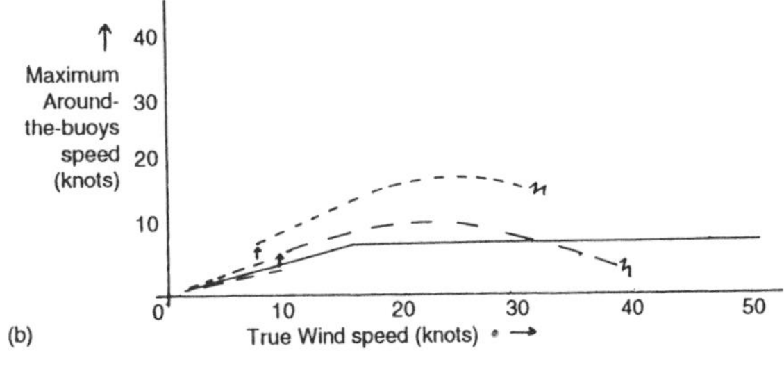

— — — Sail board - Displacement 50 pounds.
- - - - - - - Skiff - Displacement 500 pounds.
———— Maxi - Displacement 50,000 pounds.

Fig 16.4 Effect of change of size on speed.

As boats become bigger, five factors work to change the performance which can be expected. One, the speed-length ratio, increases the average speed to be expected from bigger boats in moderate winds. Two, three and four – the ability to plane, the ratio of sail area to wetted area, and the ratio of the sail-carrying-power to the total weight – all limit whatever extra speed can be expected in stronger winds. The fifth, the cube/square law, is always in the background. The way the first four factors work can be sensed if we look at the performance of a sailboard which weighs say 50 pounds, an eighteen foot skiff which weighs 500 pounds, and a maxi ocean racer which weighs say 50,000 pounds, and see what speed each of them can offer as the wind becomes progressively stronger. We will assume that the crews do everything that they can to optimise their performance. In the case of the maxi, they will change sails. In the case of the skiff, they will change rigs as well as sails. In the case of the sailboard, they will change their hulls as well as their rigs as well as their sails. Nothing is barred.

Fig 16.4(a) shows the maximum straight-line speeds that can be expected as the wind speed increases.

The maxi will increase its performance from nothing in a calm to about 10 knots in 15 knots of wind. Within this wind speed range it can sail at about 0.7 of the wind speed. In all stronger winds it can go no faster, and simply continues to sail at 10 knots.

In winds up to about twelve to fifteen knots sailboards with hulls big enough to rope-start can sail on a tight beam reach at about 0.8 of the wind speed. As soon as the wind becomes strong enough to enable much smaller sinker boards to water-start and sail, the lighter weights and much smaller wetted areas of these specialist boards enable their sailors to achieve speeds on a close beam reach of about 1.2 to 1.3 times the wind speed in winds up to about 20 knots, reducing to about 0.8 to 0.9 of the wind speed at 50 knots. The break in the sailboard plot in Fig 16.4(a) indicates this changeover from rope-start board to sinker board.

The sailboard is remarkable in that it remains controllable in very strong winds, and needs very little water to sail in. Sailboard enthusiasts have discovered a number of locations around the world where very strong converging funnelling winds blow with unusual steadiness over water which is absolutely flat. Sometimes this takes the form of a cross-wind water-filled trench which they have dug themselves. In these conditions they can achieve 80% or more of the wind speed, and 80% of a 50 to 60 knot wind is 40 to 48 knots, and this is the range within which the current world straight-line speed records lie.

In light airs the eighteen foot skiff sails a little faster than the maxi. As soon as the breeze sets in at 6 knots it begins to plane steadily on a broad reach at about 1.5 times the wind speed, until in winds of 20 to 30 knots and boat speeds of 30 to 35 knots the combination of increasing boat speed over increasingly rough water reaches the limit of control and it becomes necessary to slow down for survival.

Fig 16.4(b) shows the highest average speeds which can be expected in the much more practical 'round-the-buoys' situation, and particularly in the 0 to 25 knot wind speed range within which almost all recreational sailing takes place.

The maxi can expect to average about 80% of its straight-line speed, i.e. it can expect to average a little more than half the wind speed in winds up to about 15 knots. In stronger winds it will sail no faster so its average speed will fall as a proportion of the wind speed..These are in fact about the speeds at which big yachts complete ocean races.

Sailboards lack the sail area to sail downwind fast, and so they enjoy only modest round-the-buoys performance in light to moderate winds. In stronger winds the sailboard lacks the sail-carrying-power to sail fast upwind, and further the configuration of the speed boards is addressed to beam reaching only to the extent that performance to windward becomes marginal or absent.

The skiff, which tacks downwind as well as upwind, can average at its best about 1.1 times the wind speed around the buoys when the wind is steady and blows between 6 and about 20 knots. In stronger winds it continues to increase its average speed, but both the dynamic limit to close-hauled speed through the water of about 15 knots, and also the fact that the times needed to set and drop the spinnaker do not decrease both reduce the average speed/wind speed ratio.

Summed up, all three sizes have their strengths, but in each case at a price.

Sailboards are the smallest of boats. They are unusually controllable and can sail at about 80% of the wind's speed in very strong winds. In specially selected locations and 50 to 60 knot winds they can sail faster than any other sailboats. For several reasons their round-the-buoys speeds are unremarkable.

The skiffs are bigger boats – about ten times heavier – which have developed the sail-carrying-power, the ratios, the flexibility and the adjustability to achieve very high round-the-buoys speeds in a wide range of practical wind and sea-state conditions. Their average round-the-buoys speeds are far in advance of all other contemporary sailboats, and the factors responsible are the subjects of the following chapters. The fact that they also happen to be fast in a straight line is purely incidental. They lack the sailboards' strong-wind straight-line speeds, and they lack the maxi's sea-keeping ability.

The maxi is one thousand times heavier than the sailboard and one hundred times heavier than the skiff. It is supreme in passage racing in open water in conditions in which a crew need to live aboard. But to achieve this it has had to surrender all the factors which enable the skiff and the sailboard to achieve their extra speeds in sheltered waters.

The fifth factor, the cube/square law, works this way. A brick which is twice as big in all dimensions as another brick will weigh (2 x 2 x 2) = 8 times as much. But a sail which is twice as big as another sail has only (2 x 2) = four times the area. So if you make a sailboat – or an aeroplane – twice as big as another, it will logically finish up weighing eight times as much but with only four times the sail area or wing area, and so it will inevitably have a worse sail area to total weight ratio, and poorer expectation of performance. I know that boats – and aeroplanes – are hollow, and this makes a difference. Further, in the real world big boats and big aeroplanes are usually much more carefully designed and built than smaller ones, and this care in design and added expense in construction has enabled big boats and big aeroplanes to avoid the disadvantages of the cube/square law so far. But it is always there in the background. Just making something bigger can end up being very disappointing because it is likely to be too heavy and with inadequate power.

16.6 The emergence of ratios and weight

In the Fig. 16.2 situation, the total sail force which the crew can accept is about 132 pounds. This turns out to be about 20% of the boat's total sailing weight. This figure is typical for conventional dinghies. For keelboats it is much less. The reason for this is that in the case of dinghies and sailboards so much of their total sailing weight is people, and people can move their weight to balance the boat. The situation in the case of keelboats is that the ratio of crew weight to total weight becomes much smaller. For example, in the case of a 60,000 pound 12 Metre, the entire crew might weigh about 2,000 pounds, or only about 3% of the total weight. Given this relatively small sail-carrying-power in the 'across-the-boat' direction as a starting point, it is clear that at any reasonable pointing angle the 'forwardly-directed' drive force cannot possibly be more than about 3% to 4% of the total weight. So long as we are content to sail to windward in the displacement mode and at hull speed or less, this does not matter – a drive force of about 3% to 4% is all that is needed to achieve hull speed. For this reason the windward-going boat speeds of all well-designed boats tend to be surprisingly similar at about their hull speeds in moderate winds. The more efficient boats point higher and achieve higher VMG's.

It was noted above that the minimum drive force needed for efficient planing was about 10% of the total weight. To get a drive force of 10% at any reasonable pointing angle, we will need to increase the sail-carrying-power / total weight ratio to something much greater than 20%. To do this there are three approaches we can follow:

1. We can move the crew further to windward to increase the righting moment.
2. We can make the whole boat lighter.
3. We can combine both – move the crew to windward, and also make the boat lighter.

Traditionally, boats have been built heavily partly because they operate in a severe mechanical and chemical environment and so there has been everything to be gained by making them robust, strong and durable, and partly because it is less expensive to make things heavily than lightly – steam-rollers cost less per pound than aeroplanes. The resultant heavy weight seems not to have been considered important.

While practical sailors have traditionally adapted efficiently to the effects of changing wind speed and changing boat size, there seems, until very recently, to have been a series of mental blocks in the consideration of change of weight and change in sail carrying power. This is most clearly revealed by the history.

16.7 Historical performance limitations

Early planing motor-boats, like early aircraft, were characteristically underpowered. It quickly became evident that if they were too heavy, they simply did not plane. The development in the late 1930's of the first planing sailing dinghies focussed attention on the same problem. Only the lightest sailing dinghies which could be built by the best traditional boat-building methods then available could sometimes plane.

In the days before waterproof glues, all boats needed to be built with fastenings which passed right through the pieces to be joined and clamped them together from both sides, in the manner of a bolt and a nut. This is called 'through-fastening'. For light woodwork very thin copper nails were used together with a form of washer called a rove which had an undersize hole at its centre. The nail was driven through the pieces to be joined. The rove was driven down the exposed pointed end of the nail until it touched the wood, the excess of the nail was cut off except for a small 'stand-out', and this stand-out was then peened over to spread it and so clamp the rove permanently onto the nail. This operation required two people, one outside the boat and one inside, and both needed to know what they were doing.

Heavy planks need only a few sturdy fastenings. But the planks from which the International Fourteens were built were of soft light mahogany and only about 4 mm thick. They needed to be fastened every 50mm, otherwise the boats leaked. The ribs were only about 10mm wide and 4mm thick and were spaced about 100mm apart. This was what was involved in building a 'light' boat by traditional methods. Because of the immense amount of detailed handwork involved in hand-rivetting together the thin mahogany planks and the myriad matchstick-like ribs, these boats were very expensive.

In days when dinghy hulls which weighed thirty to forty pounds per foot of length were sold at 'one pound Sterling a foot', the International Fourteens which weighed twenty pounds per foot cost up to £300. No wonder there were so few and that they enjoyed such a reputation. And as well as their cost image, their lighter weight enabled them to plane. The necessarily heavier boats which could be built more quickly and for less cost with simpler heavier structures could never plane. For some reason, despite the brilliant example of Manfred Curry's adaptation of aeronautical aerodynamic technology in the 1920's, no effort was made in the decade of the 1930's, nor for many years thereafter to adapt aeronautical structural technology to sailboats. As a result, all boats except a privileged few remained relatively heavy. Planing downwind remained a rare and exotic experience, and sailboat average speeds changed little. Then came the 1939-45 war, and recreational sailing was forgotten for a decade.

When sailing revived in the 1950's, the scene was set for three far-reaching changes. One occurred quickly in the northern hemisphere. The second occurred more gradually in the southern. The third has followed inevitably.

The notes which follow endeavour to give an accurate, 'broad-brush', history of these developments. I am aware that some features of small and innovative classes pre-dated the developments described here, as in the case of the 10 Square-metre Canoes, the sliding plank of which did exactly the same job as the trapeze and pre-dated it by several decades. But even at their most numerous, there were only a handful of canoes, and they failed to influence current opinion. Trapezes, on the other hand, quickly 'caught on' in their thousands, and changed the whole perception of what a racing sailboat should be.

16.8 Moving the crew to windward

As part of a post-war revival exercise, the IYRU, in the early 1950's, set up the first of a series of competitions to encourage new designs. The outstanding boats to emerge from this first competition were the Flying Dutchman by van Essen, and the 505 prototype by Westell. What set these two boats apart from almost all previous craft was their use of a trapeze to move the forward hand's weight further to windward, and so increase their righting moments and sail-carrying-power / total-weight ratios. As a result, both boats were able, in fresher breezes, to windward plane. This was considered revolutionary. It captured the imaginations of the sailors of the era. It was a significant factor in the subsequent revival of popular sailing.

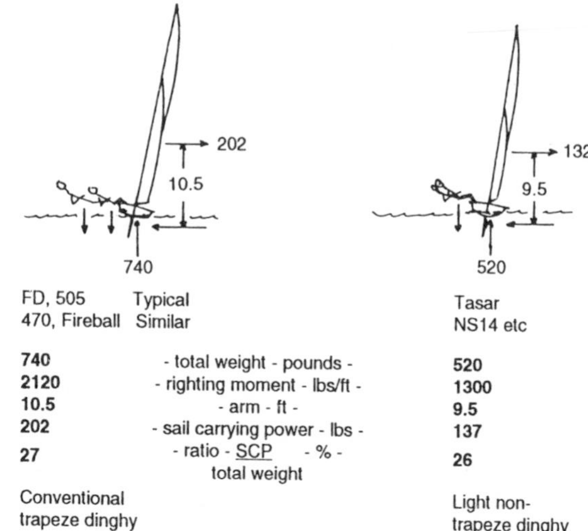

Fig 16.5 Dynamic forces on conventional trapeze dinghies and on lightweight non-trapeze dinghies

These boats could achieve the 10%, 'drive force / total weight' ratio necessary for efficient planing at a pointing angle sufficiently close to the wind for their planing VMG, in some wind and sea-state conditions, to be faster than their VMG in the displacement mode. Although the two boats are quite different as regards stability, their force diagrams are surprisingly similar, and are shown in Fig. 16.5. Note the difference between the sail-carrying-power ratio of the GP14, Enterprise, Albacore, etc. of 19%, (Fig. 16.2) and the 27% of both the FD and 505 in Fig. 16.5. The GP14, etc. cannot windward plane at a VMG faster than its displacement-sailing VMG regardless of the skill with which it is handled. The FD and the 505, when well handled, can just exceed their displacement-sailing VMG's when windward planing. This sail-carrying-power ratio of about 27% seems to be the threshold for practical windward planing.

Use of the trapeze spread rapidly throughout racing dinghy fleets world-wide. Performance levels increased a little. The sense of challenge, achievement and satisfaction, when sailing in this new manner, increased a lot. The first approach – moving the crew further to windward, had been introduced.

16.9 The reduction of weight

The pre-war insensitivity to structure weight was changed for ever by an unconscious choice made half a world away in the early 1950's.

At about that time 'plastics' became available, world-wide, to light industry and for amateur use. 'Plastics', came in a multitude of forms. Of these, two were of particular interest to the sailing fraternity. One was, 'Fibre Reinforced Plastic', FRP, or 'Fibreglass'. Its principle advantages are that it is relatively inexpensive and it can be easily moulded into complex shapes. The other was a range of truly waterproof adhesives – the ureas, resorcinals, epoxies, etc.

For whatever reasons, the northern and the southern hemispheres made different choices.

The northern hemisphere, for the most part, chose fibreglass. This had the advantage of enabling the best existing designs to be duplicated by moulding from a common mould. This simpler industrial process was relatively inexpensive and required little skill. The skin thickness which became industry standard resulted in dinghies which weighed about 20 pounds per foot. This happened to be exactly the same weight as the lightest, fastest, and most expensive of the hand-made pre-war dinghies – the International Fourteens. Everybody was happy. Duplicates of, 'millionaires', boats could now be bought for a reasonable price, and they performed as well as the expensive boats they copied and much better than the heavier 30 pounds per foot (or more) boats they replaced. On the basis of these relatively inexpensive 20 pounds per foot FRP dinghies, with their performance further boosted a little by the new trapeze, the dinghy boom of the late fifties and sixties was started. It was based primarily on the adoption of new materials and methods of construction which were less expensive. But there had been no reduction in weight to get below that of the best of the pre-war dinghies, no change in dynamics, and performance levels remained relatively unchanged from those of the best of the lighter pre-war timber boats.

Australians went instead for plywood and timber. Their plywood manufacturers were quick to adopt the new water-resistant adhesives, and offered an abundant range of aircraft-quality marine ply, in strengths and densities which ranged from the light spruce-like Klinkii to the toughiest, ash-like, Eucalypts. For decades, wooden aircraft such as the famous Mosquito had been built from glued plywood. These had proved strong and robust in service despite their light weight. (As a point of interest, they had been built with glues based on casein or similar. This was sufficiently waterproof for an aeroplane which was intermittently soaked with rain, but it was not good enough and ultimately softened when used in a boat which was continuously saturated.) By adapting to boat building both the lightweight construction technology which had been developed for wooden aircraft and also the new marine plywoods and waterproof glues, a new generation of dinghies was developed. These were relatively featherweight craft which weighed about 10 pounds per foot, but proved to be astonishingly robust. They were tough enough to be cartwheeled over rocks in squalls, or blow off roofracks at highway speeds – accidents which simply destroy any heavy through-fastened structure – but these new boats accepted this sort of punishment and suffered astonishingly little damage. These became the norm throughout Australia and New Zealand. They were hand-built and so cost more than fibreglass, but they were easy to build and the prices were reasonable. Often they were home-built.

We quickly learned that the traditional designs of the heavier-weight hulls were useless – they touched the water only in the middle. Research and development such as that described later in this book commenced. It has spanned 30 years and is continuing. It has changed the proportions and dynamics of unballasted sailboats into a completely new breed.

At exactly the right time – after Australian designers had already spent fifteen years optimising the dynamics of their designs to these lighter structure weights – the aerospace industry developed the foam sandwich technology for the lunar lander. One immediate spin-off for the marine industry was that craft of half the weight of conventional 'fibreglass' construction could now be duplicated from moulds by this new process at a reasonable cost. The early examples of this technology weighed about the same 10 pounds per foot as the lightest hand-built plywood boats. How strangely history repeats itself!

The performance increase achieved by this reduction of structure weight proved in fact to be almost exactly the same as that achieved from the use of the trapeze on conventional boats. The figures given in Fig. 16.5 show that the 'sail-carrying-power / total weight' ratio of the most highly developed of the Australian recreational, i.e. non-trapeze, non-spinnaker, dinghies – the Tasar (Fig 20.13) is a good example – it turns out to be identical with that of the FD and the 505. It is not surprising, then, to observe that on the water these lighter recreational non-trapeze and non-spinnaker boats sail around a course at about the same speed as the heavier conventional trapeze-and-spinnaker racing dinghies of about the same size, such as the Fireball and the 470. In performance terms, the average, 'round the buoys', speed of the best of these lightweight recreational boats has been raised from about one third of the wind speed to about one half of the wind speed.

The second approach, that of reducing the structure weight, had been accomplished.

What came next was a technological explosion.

16.10 The Eighteens and the third step

The third surge of development, that of combining both the moving of the crew to windward and the reduction of structure weight, soon followed. This was pure Sydney Skiff, and needs explaining.

Sydney is a metropolis based on a narrow deep-water harbour. It enjoys a warm climate and regular, fresh, summer-afternoon sea breezes. In the late 1700's and early 1800's the men who used skiffs to service and victual the square-rigged ships which served the Port of Sydney began to race their workboats for wager and pleasure on Sundays. The population, which lived by ships and understood sailing, began to watch and wager. The harboursides are steep, and there are many vantage points from which one can look down on the water and so follow and enjoy the tactics of individual boats within a fleet. Not surprisingly, skiff racing quickly became popular both as a participant and also as a spectator sport.

The bureaucrats of the time were, in some respects, surprisingly sensitive. This spontaneous emergence of interest in sailboat racing was officially encouraged by formal 'regattas'. The first 'Royal Naval Sailing Association's Regatta' took place on January 26th, 1827. This was the world's first scheduled sporting (as opposed to naval) regatta. It has been an annual fixture ever since, and is the world's longest running sporting sailing event. Inevitably, those early workboats carried their owners' names. As those early entrepreneurs prospered and founded great business houses, the practice of keeping one or more skiffs on the water has carried on, both for the love of the sport and for the continuing exposure of the enterprises' names. Not infrequently, the crack skippers of yesterday have become the chairmen of the boards today.

The sailors who crew the skiffs have never been professionals. Over the centuries they have contributed their time, skill, enthusiasm – everything but all the money. The sponsors have contributed, depending on the race record of the skipper, some or all of the cost of a craft which would normally be far beyond the reach of the usually young crews. The end result is that the top crews have been able to drive stunning craft with an athleticism and at speeds which properly excite admiration.

Sydney skiff sailors have always been a turbulent lot. They crowded on sail and still more sail. They have probably never agreed about anything other than survival. Lack of agreement when times were fair, lead naturally to the 'no restrictions' ethic. But a threat to survival was something else.

Two examples:

1. For some years following 1968 there was a difference of opinion between the relatively new RYA or IYRU-based organisations and the traditional skiff clubs. The IYRU-rule followers endeavoured to apply Rule 26 (no advertising, introduced in 1968) to all craft, and objected to the continuing display of the owners' logos on the skiffs' sails. This was unwise. It is interesting to look at dates:

Sydney's first skiff races	circa 1800 – 1820
Sydney's first 'official' regatta	26th January, 1827
Yacht Racing Association (UK)	Founded 1875
Int'l Yacht Racing Union (IYRU)	Founded 1908
IYRU Rule 26 (No Advertising)	Introduced 1968

From the Australian skiff point of view, Rule 26 came a little late – about one hundred and fifty years too late.

The attempt to enforce Rule 26 was resisted. Skiff sailors are men of strong resolve – they have to be to handle the sail they carry. They countered by continuing to sail the 'Board of Trade' rules they had always sailed, and they held their courses, often at high speeds. The crunch came in the law courts after the collisions. The RYA (or IYRU) rules apply only amongst boats which agree to set aside the internationally agreed 'Board of Trade' rules, and the skiffs had not so agreed. Life became legally impossible for the 'royals'. For a few years, sailing in Sydney became anything but dull. But quite soon a most sensible compromise was worked out. The skiff clubs joined with the 'royals' in an umbrella, self-policing, Australian Yachting Federation. The federation which normally follows IYRU rules formally agreed to accept the skiffs' historically based 'advertising' by permanently excepting skiffs from Rule 26, and damn what the rest of the world might say. The skiffs agreed to join with and support the objects of the federation and to race under the IYRU rules, except Rule 26. Harmony and uniformity of rules in sailing in and sharing the narrow waterway were restored. It is interesting to see how the IYRU and the IOC are now following this same path.

2. At the other extreme was an attempt by an international sports promotion company to gain commercial control of skiff racing. This was messy, brutal and hopelessly inefficient. Costs, prices and expectations spiralled upwards. At the end the promoters walked away with nothing, having contributed nothing but having inflicted massive damage by pricing the sport out of the reach of its traditional supporters. This left the skiff movement shattered and paralysed. After about a year during which the dust slowly settled, a top-level cabal of cool planners reasoned that the path to recovery lay in developing a top-line skiff which could be purchased and campaigned at a cost within the promotion budgets of local businesses. This was about one third of the inflated price of the recent skiffs, and the only way to achieve this sort of cost reduction without sacrificing technical quality was to agree, for awhile, to go 'One-design'. To get the project underway a design study was commissioned, and the advertisement which appears as Fig.16.6 was produced.

The key point about this $50,000 full-page advertisement was that it was donated by three Sydney business houses all of whom felt strongly that the skiffs should be supported in practical ways in times of stress! The merchant bank, which was sponsoring one of the new skiffs, paid half. The advertising agency prepared the advertisement for nothing. The newspaper accepted the half and donated the other half. The advertisement was successful in reviving faith in the survival of the Eighteens. Fig. 20.15 shows one of these boats – this one happens to be paid for by its owner (me) and so does not carry any sponsors name. A number of the new boats were sponsored by other business houses and formed the core of a renewed fleet. The Eighteens were back, visible, viable and healthy. That is the level of commitment of some of the great business houses of Sydney towards its skiffs when their survival is threatened. A truly delightful aspect of this exercise is that the 'budget' boat, once worked up, proved to be convincingly faster than all the previous designs at three times the cost.

Fig 16.6 $50,000 full page advertisement – *donated*!

I have mentioned these incidents in the skiffs' history because they make several points. The skiff group are a turbulent crowd. Their politics are fierce. But they are highly intelligent and very, very effective, as is indicated by the way they responded to both threats to survival recounted above. It is exactly this lateral-thinking approach that has enabled them to avoid all restrictions, to ignore all technical conventions and social mind-sets, and to focus on and adopt whatever it may be that they think may enable them to sail faster. And in sailing faster they have been brilliantly successful.

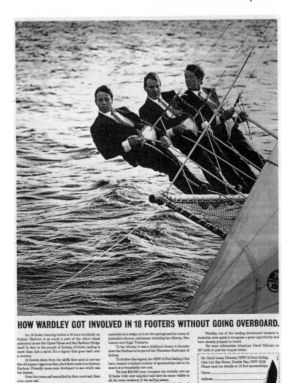

Sydney still loves them. There may be five hundred sailboats on the crowded main harbour on a Saturday or a Sunday afternoon. The Royal Sydney Yacht Squadron puts 45 to 50 Etchells 22's across the starting line in its club races. Twenty or thirty of all the boats may be Eighteen footers. You pick them instantly because they are the ones which are moving three times as fast as almost anything else on the harbour. From start to finish of their races the harbourside vantage points are crowded. When the skiff race finishes the vantage points empty. There may be four hundred and seventy other sailboats still racing, but it was the skiffs which the crowds came to watch.

This is the environment within which the recent dramatic performance advances have occurred.

One year, in their quest for speed, two crews built big buoyant boats with huge sails. Despite the skill of their crews, both boats performed far below expectation.

This prompted a lateral thinker to dream of a different approach – a more slender and altogether smaller boat, with smaller spars and sails which would take advantage of the cube-square law in reverse and finish at a much lighter overall structure weight. He reasoned that if he crewed such a boat with only three people, but all of them used trapezes (up to that time the skipper had always steered from the gunwale with his feet in the boat), this approach could achieve a significantly higher 'power-to-weight' ratio than had been possible up to that time. Thus was born the concept of the, 'three-hander'. Prior to this time, all Eighteen Foot Skiffs had sailed with crews of at least four. It required several years of continuous development to optimise the design, structure, rig technology and handling to the point where the performance of this new machine matched that of the highly developed four-handers. But the three-hander development didn't stop there. It continued, and the potential of the three-hander was so good that it soon outclassed all previous designs.

In the quest for speed, these three-handers are significant, because they were the boats which distinctively separated out from the traditional racing boats such as the FD's, 505's, Lightweight Sharpies, Tornados', etc. Photo 16.7 shows David Porter, the man who had the vision and perseverance to bring the three-handers on stream, sailing his first three-hander in 1970. Fig. 16.8 shows the force diagram of this boat. Note that by using all three approaches – use of the trapeze to move the weight of all crew members further to windward, use of light plywood to reduce the structure weight, and use of the cube/square law in reverse to create a still smaller and lighter boat – he achieved a Sail-carrying-power to total weight ratio of 30% with his 'big', rig, and about 35% and 40% with his No.s 2 and 3 rigs respectively. (These three rigs typically cover the wind-speed ranges of 0 to 15knots, 8 to 25knots, and 14 to 35knots respectively. The design assumptions are that with the big rig some of the time will be spent in light air and displacement sailing; with the No. 2 rig that the wind will average 10 to 15 knots and that the boat will be planing at all times; and that with the tiny No. 3 rig the wind will never be less than about 18 to 20knots.)

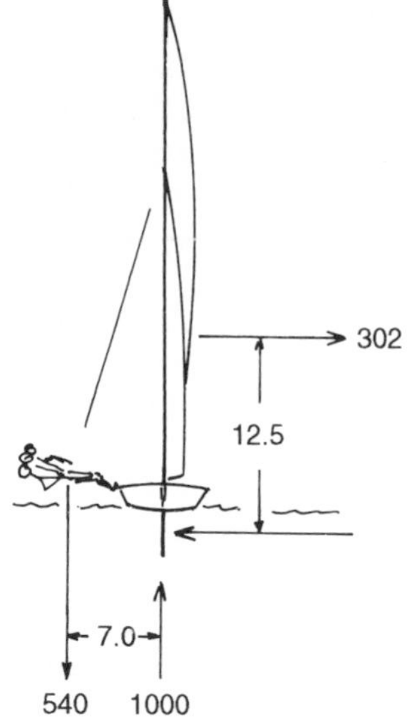

Weight of boat = 460 lbs
Weight of crew = 540 lbs
Weight of boat plus crew = 1000 lbs
Righting moment = 3780 lbs/ft
Arm = 12.5 ft
Sail carrying power = 302 lbs
ratio $\frac{\text{scp}}{\text{total wt}}$ = 30 %

Fig 16.8 Forces on 1970 Eighteen

In winds of about eight knots or more these boats planed cleanly on all points of sailing. Since the average Sydney summer afternoon sea breeze is about 11 to 12 knots this meant that these boats planed almost all of the time – far more so than any other boats in the world at that time. Because of this, their designers and crews were able to focus on the planing mode with a new intensity. The new performance levels are shown in Fig 16.3, D and E.

The third approach, that of both moving the crew to windward and also reducing the structure weight, had been started.

16.11 The dominance of ratios

Over the next few years we learned that the performance level of these high-performance boats was overwhelmingly governed by the three ratios:

1. Sail Area/Wetted Area – governs light air performance.
2. Sail Area/Total Weight – governs downwind breeze performance.
3. Sail Carrying Power/Total Weight – governs upwind breeze performance.

This does not mean that the effects of the displacement/length ratio and the speed/length ratio cease to operate. It is just that they cease to be of much importance. And again and for the same reasons as previously, for the fastest boats, only the 'upwind' ratio remains relevant, because they now sail with the Apparent Wind forward of the beam for almost all of the time.

In Fig 16.8 a crew of three, each averaging about 180 lbs dressed for sailing and wet, trapeze against the gunwale of a boat seven feet wide at the deck. The centre of buoyancy is displaced about 6 inches to leeward of the centreline. So the righting moment is (3 x 180) = 540 lbs x 7 ft = 3780 lbs/ft. The arm between the Centre of Effort of the centreboard and the CE of the sails is about 12.5 ft. for the big rig, and progressively less for the No.s 2 and 3 rigs, which also use shorter centreboards, respectively. This boat can therefore stand, 3780 divided by 12.5 or approx 300 lbs of crossboat sail force with the big rig, and more with the others. The total weight is about 540 lbs crew plus 460 lbs boat – about 1000 lbs with the big rig, and about 50lbs less with the smallest.

So the ratio 'sail carrying power / total weight' is 300/1000 or 30%, i.e. this boat can develop and use a sail force of nearly one third of its own weight when sailing to windward with its biggest rig, and progressively more when using the smaller rigs.

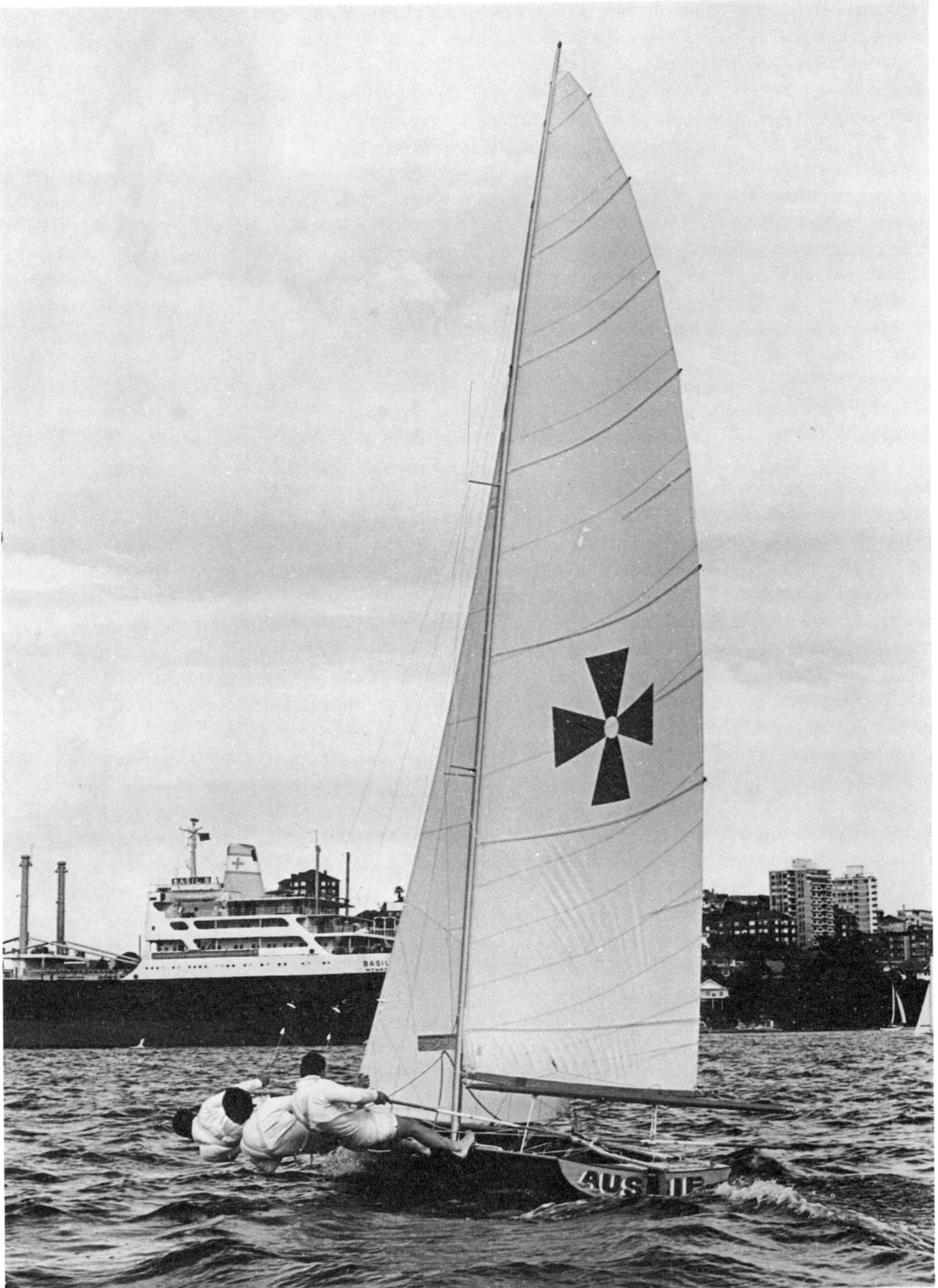

Fig 16.7 David Porter's *Aussie* c1970 – an early three-hander eighteen footer

It turns out that this figure of about 30% is critical for practical windward planing. From the hull drag graphs in chapter 20, it will be seen that a thrust of about 3.5 to 4% of the total weight is sufficient to drive a small-boat hull at its hull speed, but the much greater thrust of at least 10% of its total weight is needed to drive it through the forced mode and to the point where it is planing cleanly. To achieve a 10% drive force at any reasonable pointing angle needs a sail carrying power capability of at least 30%.

In the case of the FD, 505, 470, etc. – and the lightweight non-trapeze craft like the Tasar – their basic sail-carrying-power / total weight ratio is about 27%. None of these designs, with their sails sheeted firmly, and the upper sails driving well, can windward plane. But in stronger winds, if the sails are flattened to reduce drag and the sheets freed a little to spill air from the upper leeches, and the centreboard is lifted a little, the centre of effort of the sails becomes lower, and that of the centreboard becomes higher, and so the distance between the centres of effort of sails and centreboard is reduced. In this trim the sail-carrying-power/total weight ratio is increased to about 30% – and off they will go. Their pointing angle is somewhat lower than when displacement sailing because of the slacker sheet. It takes skill, but they can do it.

The three-hander Eighteens were different. With their built-in ratio of 30%, you couldn't stop them from planing, even with the big rig sheeted firmly! This is the importance of that 10% difference in ratios from 0.27 (27%) to 0.30 (30%).

And to think that it all started with that unconscious choice of plywood over FRP.

16.12 The development of ratios

The next stage saw the flowering of all the seeds which had been sown. As the full importance of both righting moment and total weight became appreciated, skiff crews who had until that time trapezed against the gunwales, found themselves moving out a little on frames, then further out onto stub wings, then far out on wings which spanned, ultimately, 28 feet. Hulls became progressively lighter as aerospace technology was adopted without compromise, and costs which are routine for the aircraft industry, but astronomical for recreational sailboats, were accepted. This lead to very strong and stiff hulls which approached 5 lbs per foot of length, and righting moments previously undreamed of.

Iain Murray was the designer, builder and helmsman who was principally associated with the main thrust of this development. For some years he dominated the class, and it was his influence which kept the machinery light, simple, practical and reliable as year by year the span of the wings increased. The increasing sail-carrying-power of the progressively wider wings threw increasing loads into the rigs.

Andrew Buckland, who sailed with Iain, was primarily responsible for developing the bigger, stronger, lighter, hydraulically adjustable rigs which absorbed the increased power with remarkable efficiency and reliability. He introduced hydraulic rig adjustment and achieved sufficient sail-shape adjustment to keep the rigs efficient through a wide range of Apparent Wind speeds. Fig. 20.16 shows the state achieved by the art at that stage.

The bottom line was that the, 'sail carrying power / total weight' ratio had been doubled to nearly 60% with these wide wings and big rigs, and more with the smaller rigs (Fig. 16.9). These boats, when sailing to windward, could develop and use a sail force of nearly two thirds of their total weight! This means that, even when sailing hard on the wind, they could call on up to double the drive force needed for planing. Because in the planing mode (and only in the planing mode) the drag of a well-designed hull increases directly as speed increases, this doubling of thrust results in a doubling of speed, and windward going speeds of 14-16 knots through waves became routine. This upwind performance level (as VMG), is shown as 'O-F-F_2' and 'O-G-G_2' in Fig. 16.3.

16.13 Downwind faster

By this time the boats were sailing upwind, and two-sail reaching crosswind, at speeds never before achieved by any sailboat. But downwind had become a problem. The boats had the power, and the crews had the skill, to carry almost any spinnaker. But the sheer size of a 1,200 square foot spinnaker, the practical difficulty of carrying all the associated loose gear – the spinnaker pole, halyard, sheets, braces, uphauls and downhauls – and the substantial minimum times needed to set, gybe and drop such a spinnaker and its pole when sailing around a closed course in a small boat at high speed had become a nightmare.

But under all this there was a more important theoretical problem. When carrying a spinnaker which was cut deep enough to be controllable, these powerful boats couldn't point high enough to go downwind fast.

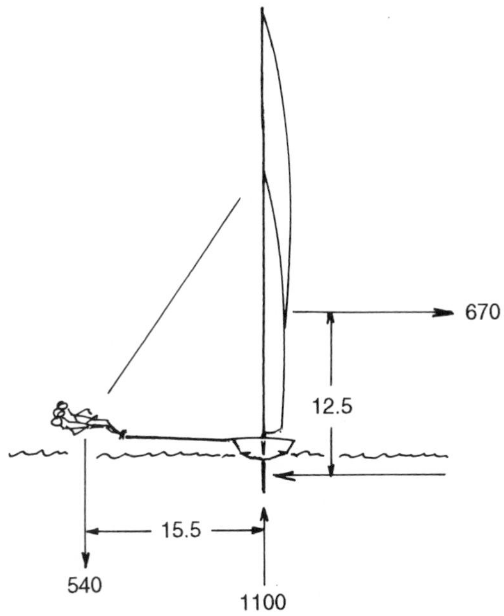

Weight of boat = 560 lbs
Weight of crew = 540 lbs
Weight of boat plus crew = 1100 lbs
Righting moment = 8370 lbs/ft
Arm = 12.5 ft
Sail carrying power = 670 lbs
ratio $\frac{\text{scp}}{\text{total wt}}$ = 61 %

Fig 16.9 Forces on 1988 Eighteen

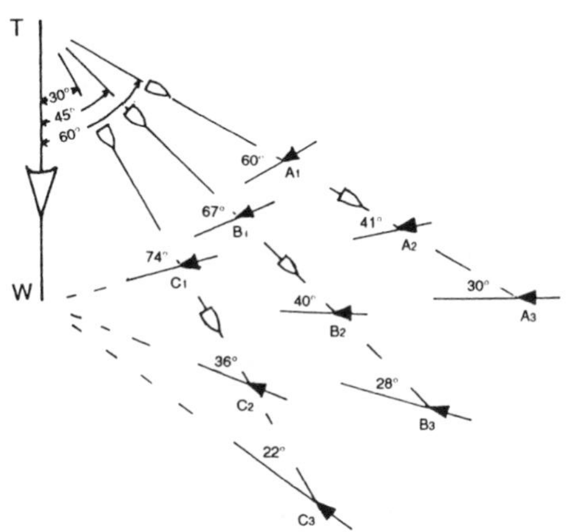

TW = True wind

In A_1 A_2 A_3 the boats heading is luffed 60° from directly downwind
In B_1 B_2 B_3 the boats heading is luffed 45° from directly downwind
In C_1 C_2 C_3 the boats heading is luffed 30° from directly downwind

In A_1 B_1 C_1 the boats speed = the wind speed
In A_2 B_2 C_2 the boats speed = 1.5 × wind speed
In A_3 B_3 C_3 the boats speed = twice wind speed

So angle TB_2W is the angle of Apparent Wind from the *bow* when tacking downwind at 1.5 wind speed and luffed 45°.

Fig 16.10 Apparent Wind angles when tacking downwind at high speeds

This problem is shown as a vector diagram in Fig. 16.10. 'TW' represents the True Wind of 10 knots. 'TA1', 'TB1', 'TC1' are the tracks of three boats which are tacking downwind at a boat speed equal to the wind speed (10 knots), and at angles to the downwind wind direction of 60, 45 and 30 degrees respectively. 'A1W', 'B1W', and 'C1W' represent the Apparent Wind speeds and directions. The angle of each of these Apparent Winds from the bow is 60, 67 and 74 degrees respectively. Not too many conventional spinnakers remain set when the Apparent Wind is within 60 degrees of the bow.

'TA2', 'TB2' and 'TC2' repeat 'TA1', etc. but in this case the boat is assumed to be sailing at a boat speed of fifteen knots, or one and one half times the wind speed. These speeds are routinely achieved and measured. Note that the angles from the bow of the apparent wind have become surprisingly similar at 41, 40 and 36 degrees respectively. Because the real wind is never steady, these angles will fluctuate and will sometimes be a few degrees less. What we see here is that unless a spinnaker can remain set and drawing efficiently when the apparent wind is about 35 degrees from the bow, no boat can sail downwind faster than one point five times the wind speed.

When you sail out of a gust and into a lull, you will be sailing at about twice the wind speed for a few seconds, and the situation will be as shown by 'TA3', 'TB3' and 'TC3', and the Apparent Wind angles will then become 30, 28 and 22 degrees respectively. To put these angles into perspective, Fig. 16.2 shows us that when a GP14, Enterprise, Albacore, etc. sails to windward hard on the wind, the angle of the Apparent Wind across the deck is 28 degrees. But this is less than the Apparent Wind angle – 'T-B3-W' – as applies to 'B3' in Fig 16.9!

Nothing can underscore the difference between modern high-performance faster-than-the-wind sailing and conventional sailing more than this comparison: that to make use of the new power and performance potentially available it is necessary to be efficient downwind with spinnaker up at the same Apparent Wind angle from the bow which is accepted as normal when sailing upwind in conventional boats. This also explains perfectly why I have discarded discussion of all force diagrams except the 'cross-boat, windward-going' diagram.

If you now imagine a boat with a spinnaker which begins to collapse at say 35 degrees, the nature of the problem becomes clear. Whenever either the boat accelerates freely, or the wind becomes momentarily lighter, it is necessary to luff and slow down to keep the spinnaker full, and the end result is that you either find yourself luffed so far that you are not going downwind efficiently, or you hold a reasonable course but at some speed slower than your potentially achievable speed, and all because you cannot point high enough with the spinnaker set to sail downwind fast. As the wings became wider and the boats sailed faster this problem emerged, and the faster they sailed the worse it became.

Julian Bethwaite is another of the class' lateral thinkers, and it was he who analysed this problem correctly and solved it. He invented the asymmetric spinnaker.

At one stroke he threw away all the loose equipment – pole, braces, uphauls etc. – and in so doing cleaned up the boat and made it lighter. He fitted a simple bowsprit, and co-operated with his sailmaker in developing a sail with a flat leech and a suitably shaped luff which would point as high into the Apparent Wind as was called for and yet be easy to control.

This sail has ushered in a revolution. It is so simple and practical. It simplified, lightened and tidied the boat. Because there is no 24 foot spinnaker pole to set, gybe and stow it has enormously reduced the times to set, gybe and drop the spinnaker from 30 to 40 seconds to 5 or 6, and this reduction of 'dead' time has greatly increased average speed. It is as simple to gybe as a jib. It can be cut to point as high as is necessary. It has removed all the pointing limitations of the old gybing-pole spinnakers. It has enabled modern high-performance sailboats to point as high into the Apparent Wind as they need, to achieve their full speed potential downwind.

Fig 20.18 shows an early asymmetric spinnaker on one of Julian's Eighteens. Fig 20.16 taken a few years later shows the sort of downwind performance these boats could by then achieve with their small rigs in a sustained 25 knot gust. This photograph was taken in heavy rain and from a long distance away. As a point of interest, the aft wing beam marks the stern of the boat. The boat is moving at about 35 knots. The rig is loaded to the point where it is deflecting visibly, but these remarkable machines have been developed to the point where they are able to accept this sort of punishment week after week, and can still be relied upon to finish, My guess is that it will take the C Class catamarans another fifteen to twenty five years to develop this sort of gut reliability – the ability to sail fast and finish in *all* reasonable wind and sea-state conditions.

16.14 Some unexpected observations

It is only to be expected that some of the lessons learned along this path have been unusual. Three examples:

Wing-span

It has been found that there is an optimum which depends primarily on wind roughness and partly on traffic. At an offshore, sea breeze location with little conflicting traffic, the boats achieved highest average speeds with wing-spans approaching 10 metres. But until recently, for most of the world's Eighteen Footers sailing occurs on Sydney Harbour. The afternoon sea breeze in the harbour is rougher than the morning breeze or the breeze offshore because of the thermal excitation it receives as it passes over the heated land near the coast. It was quickly found that as the wind became rougher, the optimum span became smaller. Conflicting traffic has the same effect. Because the Eighteens sail about three times as fast as most of the other boats on the harbour, and the harbour is crowded when they race, they tend to give way to all other sailboats simply by weaving around them. Dynamically, this is the same as roughness. Strangely, the optimum span is also different for different crew weights, in the sense that lighter crews in their smaller boats are more nimble and so can handle and go faster with slightly larger wings. The two-handers shown in Fig. 20.18 and page 161 proved fastest with 8m wings, while the three-handers sailed fastest with 7m wings.

Spinnaker shape

In Part Four, some of the particular advantages of a jib without overlap are discussed. The spinnakers used by the Eighteens are identical. Because the boats tack downwind at speeds much faster than the wind, the Apparent Wind on this point of sailing blows, typically, from about 45 degrees from the bow. This would be regarded as a close reach on most craft. So the asymmetric spinnakers are cut with long luffs, flat leeches, and, for greatest drive, no overlap. Area is of secondary importance.

Air roughness effects

This is a strange one. The boat which sails downwind at the speed of the wind will suffer most from wind unsteadiness! To get a feel for this, imagine that there is a wind blowing of 10 knots mean speed, with gusts to 12.5 knots and lulls at 7.5 knots. We will ignore the smaller faster fluctuations. If you stand on a motor boat which is at rest, this is the wind you will feel. Its gust factor will be 50%. (12.5 gust minus 7.5 lull = 5 knots. A 5 knot gust/lull range in a 10 knot wind gives a gust factor of 50%.)

If the boat now motors downwind at 5 knots, you will feel a wind of 5 knots average. The gusts will be 7.5 knots and the lulls 2.5 knots. The gust/lull range will still be 5 knots, but because the average speed of the apparent wind is now only 5 knots, the gust factor has increased to 100%. This is a typical situation with any boat which runs directly downwind. Obviously it accelerates in the gusts and loses speed in the lulls, but during the seconds before its speed has adjusted it suffers the full 100% gust factor.

If the boat now increases its speed to 10 knots, you will feel an average calm, but this average calm will be the average of intermittent puffs of up to 2.5 knots which will blow from all directions. The gust factor has become infinite! This is a situation in which it is not possible to think of 'sailing' in any normal manner. The practical solution is, of course, to tack downwind in wide broad-reaching gybes. The wider the angle the faster the boat will sail and the smaller the gust factor will become and the easier the boat will be to control and the easier it will be to keep it moving fast. So it turns out that in practice it is much more efficient to sail very fast in wide gybes rather than on headings closer to the rhumb line but which suffer gust factors so great as to periodically depower the boat.

An interesting point is that contemporary Eighteens now sail downwind substantially faster than the wind, and so they have passed through the worst of this particular hazard and are now beginning to sail in apparently steadier winds again. At present it is the crews of the faster lightweight Fourteens which are following the Eighteens' technology which are experiencing the surprises.

16.15 The dynamics of catamarans and sailboards

Catamarans

Catamarans march to a different drummer

Their advantages are that their slender hulls escape the forced mode drag rise (Chapter 20), and their sail carrying power / total weight ratios can be very high. Their disadvantages are that the total wetted area of their twin hulls is necessarily greater than that of an equally well designed monohull, their slender displacement hulls cannot plane, they are unable to heel in light airs and so cannot twist their sails into efficient light air shapes by gravity and they cannot be driven hard offwind otherwise their fine bows bury. The end result is that their light air performance is disappointing. Once turbulence sets in at about six knots and twist is no longer necessary for efficiency they come alive and take off as if somebody had thrown a switch. Their moderate air performance should be superior – if it isn't, there is something wrong with the design. In conditions where conventional boats get trapped in the forced mode, good catamarans just go faster. In strong winds the honeymoon is over. The fact that their displacement hulls do not plane means that their wetted area does not decrease and their drag rises inexorably. Their strong-wind upwind performance is therefore not as good as one would expect from their moderate-wind speeds, and their cross-wind and down-wind performance is limited by the fact that regardless of the wind strength, if you drive them too hard the lee bow will go under and you will abruptly stop sailing in the upright mode!

Catamarans are superb moderate-wind recreational machines. They are too slow in tacking to respond efficiently to windshifts or tactical situations, so they leave racing crews frustrated. In light airs and in strong winds their performance is not as good as modern monohulls.

Sailboards

By reducing the size of their craft to the absolute minimum, the sailboard sailors have exploited the cube-square law in reverse to their maximum advantage.

Sailboards have three principle advantages:

1. The relatively low cost of the machine has encouraged experimentation at full size. There has been no unnecessary delay in development because somebody played with models and believed that they were following a good idea only to find that they had made a mistake with the scale effect. Development has been rapid and effective, and the better sailboards have achieved greater performance increases within a decade than conventional keelboats have achieved in a century.

2. The direct manipulative control of the sail enables sailboarders to respond to the wind's unsteadiness much faster than is possible through any artificial system of ropes and pulleys. They can therefore sail under control and aggressively in winds in which conventional boats have no option but to adopt survival techniques.

3. The geometry which has been adopted by designers of efficient sailboards happens to give the machine a sail-carrying-power / total weight ratio of about 50%, but at the cost of a rig so squat that the tip losses are so great that they destroy upwind efficiency, plus the fact that the bulk and aerodynamic drag of the human frame are large in relation to the total machine, and this again reduces the potential of the upwind performance.

The end result is that sailboards have the potential to go very fast crosswind in very strong to gale force winds, and this they do superbly well. They go fastest on water which is completely flat, and when they find the right combination of a 50 to 60 knot wind, and a stretch of artificially flat water just downwind of a low wave-break which lies at the correct angle to the wind, they can break world records on those occasions when they judge the gust right. If the lull arrives before they have completed the 500 or 250 metre course, the minuscule hull tends to sink. It should be noted that they are not efficient enough yet to be able to sail faster than the wind. They simply sail under control in winds much stronger than other sailboats care to face.

Fig 20.17 shows a sailboard at its crosswind fastest. Because of the disproportionate tip loss from the low rig plus the drag of the rider their upwind performance is relatively poor, and their downwind performance is unremarkable because both their 'sail area / total weight', and their 'sail area / wetted area' ratios are relatively low. So despite their brilliant crosswind potential, the best 'upwind, downwind and around-the-buoys', speeds they can achieve in normal wind and sea-state conditions are unremarkable.

16.16 The application of ratios and the future

For some years the Eighteens were the only craft which could sail with the modern faster-than-the-wind performance level which they had developed and demonstrated to be achievable. This is no longer true.

A very practical and affordable light-hull-weight one-design 14 footer, the design of which has brilliantly adapted modern Eighteen Footer technology, is shown on pages 332 and 403. It has a 'sail carrying power / total weight' ratio of more than 40%, and higher yet when reefed. This is sufficiently above the 30% windward planing threshold for truly high performance. Its downwind performance is astonishing; its rig proportions and angles are all biased to enable it to by-pass the 'maximum unsteadiness' problem noted in Section 16.14. Helming from trapeze is a peculiarly Australian trait. It is practised by young sailors for fun and so has become as commonplace as the ability to ride a skateboard. However, it appears to be unusual elsewhere. Not everybody can or wants to helm from a trapeze. By the innovative use of wings instead of trapezes on this boat – 'regard the wings as a part of the deck' – its designer has managed to offer modern performance without the necessity to steer from a trapeze to all who want to sail fast.

16.17 Different paths – same destination

In 1969 Bernard Smith wrote a book titled, '*The 40 Knot Sailboat*', in which he suggested that if an efficient sail were to be angled partly upwards so that its force would both drive the hull and also partly support its weight, and the 'hull' were to take the form of three canted centreboards which were thickened enough to float and support the weight of the machine at rest, then a new form of sailing should be possible which promised very high speeds. He called his craft an 'Aero-hydrofoil' and reported limited success with models, and less success to date with man-carrying prototypes. I corresponded with him, and visited him.

He showed me movies of models moving at spectacular speeds across small ponds. I became enthusiastic. Over the next twenty years, apart from breaks such as the two years to develop the Tasar, another year to design and develop the Laser II, etc, I have built and sailed a total of nineteen man-carrying prototypes, and along the way have re-invented the wheel. I called this frolic my 'High Speed Project'.

Early trials with a slender hull and outrigger with canted foils, which we towed with a motor boat to get a feel for the dynamics of this sort of foil-borne platform, suggested first that the hulls had to be surprisingly strong to resist the twist. Mark I broke. A stronger Mk II taught us further that fences were needed on the foils to keep the water and the air separate and each going the right way. We were learning fast. However, when Mk II had been modified until everything behaved as it should, we were left with the conviction that it was fine at rest, and reasonably efficient at its design 'foiling' speed of about 25 knots, but in between its drag as it climbed out of the water was so great that only a huge sail could have been expected to provide sufficient drive force to accelerate it. The trouble with this approach is that, if ever you do get up to speed, a huge sail is exactly what you do not need in those stronger Apparent Winds. Bernard's tiny balsa models had been so light (the cube/square law in reverse) that he had not been faced with this problem. I therefore decided to use slender featherweight hulls instead. These could be lifted out of the water to reduce their drag just as easily as thick foils. This approach enabled me to get on with the main act – developing and learning how to handle the canted 'Captive Kite' rig which was to be the engine of any new creation.

Marks III to Mark IX were all anti-proas, slender main hulls with smaller outriggers to leeward. All were double-ended, so that they would sail both ways, and thus keep the outrigger (which carried the base of the canted mast) always to leeward. All showed promise at particular wind speeds and on particular points of sailing. As prototype followed prototype, they became more practical, in the sense that with Mk III, I spent 99% of my sailing time either upside down, or 'taken aback' with the wind on the wrong side of the sail, the boat going the wrong way and completely stable and unable to be controlled to make it go the right way, or other similar delights when things went wrong with the machinery aloft. With Mk IX, I could sail properly for perhaps 50% of the time, so there had been progress. But when I appraised the whole project – where we had come from during our years of effort and where we could reasonably expect to go with further development – I decided that there were practical disadvantages in the double-ended proa set-up which could never be overcome even with all my perseverance – and that these far outweighed all its possible advantages. I abandoned it.

Mk X was not a proa. It was a trimaran, with a slender main hull with a bow and a stern and a stern-hung rudder and a bottom flat enough to plane. It had tiny tip-floats in the manner of a flying boat which were for static stability only. As soon as any speed was attained the idea was to balance on the main hull with the floats clear of the water. This was much more successful. My 'sailing properly' time increased to about 90 to 99%, and we could routinely achieve speeds of about 25 knots through the gusts in strong winds. Mk XI had a redesigned bottom to plane a little sooner. In light airs the sail was so big and the wetted area so small that these boats were able to move well in the lightest zephyr and achieve at best about double the wind speed when sailing crosswind. This was technically exciting for us and impressive to the crews of becalmed yachts and catamarans through whose fleets these strange craft sailed as if by magic. We spent several pleasant years with Mk X and Mk XI and their various rigs. These boats had become fun to sail. However, by the time we had learned all we were going to learn from them, three further facts had become clear:

1. There is no such thing as a steady wind. One of the more valuable spin-offs from my initial search for a steady wind was that I began to look at the real wind's structure. This work to date has developed into Part 1 of this book, and nobody suggests that there is not a great deal more yet to be learned.

2. Any concept which is based on supporting some of the weight of a boat by the force from a canted sail can only work efficiently if the upward force is continuous. I developed my boats to the point where they could 'fly' beautifully through gusts which were from the right direction and at the right speed. But as soon as I sailed out of the gust and into the lull, the boat simply fell back into the water and nearly stopped, and I then had to wait for the next gust and re-accelerate all over again. I realised that Bernard Smith's models had similarly worked well but only in the gusts. We had never discussed the lulls. Ten years later, we see the 'sinker' sailboards experiencing exactly this same problem. They break world speed records in the gusts, and sink in the lulls. If they make their hulls big enough to float in the lulls

they lose their speed edge in the gusts.

Once one assumes that the wind can never be steady and that all sailboats must necessarily sail in a wind which continually sweeps a gust/lull range, it becomes clear that to have any chance of superior performance a boat has to be both fast enough to sail very fast in the lull and controllable enough not to stagger or be overpowered in the gust. A few dreamings and calculations then reverse the usual theoretical picture. It becomes far more efficient to support the weight of the boat on the denser water with either a planing bottom or possibly foils, than to hang it below a kite in an unsteady wind. This was the first lethal blow to the captive-kite rig.

3. A second was even more damning. I finally realised that any asymmetric (i.e. efficient only when it works one way) rig which has to be flipped from side to side has in fact all the drawbacks of a square-rigger, in that if you point too high the rig must be 'taken aback'. For slow ships which broad reached around the world this did not matter. But when you are looking for speed, the more successful you become at sailing faster the more will the Apparent Wind come from ahead, and never more so than when you sail with speed out of a gust and into a lull. So, for really fast boats, the captive-kite rig is doomed, because the faster you go the worse it becomes. It is also a brute to control. The 'captive-kite' rigged Little America's Cup challenger which broke up because it could not be controlled in a strong wind fared no better than I had fared with the same types of rig many years earlier.

We appraised progress a second time. I abandoned the captive-kite rig.

Mk XII was a slender planing trimaran with a bow, a stern-hung rudder, and tiny flying boat style tip floats for static stability only. It had a conventional symmetrical fore-and-aft rig. I had re-invented the wheel, but I was convinced. I had tried all the other hull platform and rig set-ups, had learned their strengths and their weaknesses, and had concluded from bitter experience that this relatively conventional trimaran set-up was superior in the practical world of real unsteady wind and often big waves to all of the others. It was practical, controllable and fast. At its heart Mk XII had a force set-up and critical ratios very similar to those of a typical Eighteen of its era. Its performance proved to be about the same also.

It was my good fortune to have reached this stage, and these conclusions, at about the time that my younger son Julian, who works with me and who has been in the thick of all the Eighteen's ferment of development, reached the almost identical stage and conclusion, and had to invent the asymmetric spinnaker so that he could move to the next performance level with his designs. Each of us had followed totally different paths for more than ten years – his through raw competitive development within a younger mans' 'no-restrictions' fleet and mine through a more theoretical meander – and yet we had arrived at the same technical destination at about the same time. We conclude from this that, together, we are unlikely to be very wrong in our approach to fast sailboats.

Fig. 16.11 shows a single-handed HSP quietly going about its business of cruising at a speed of about 1.5 x wind speed. Once you get the feel for the enormous changes in the Apparent Wind as it winds up, and adjust your thinking to maintaining that Apparent Wind through the changing True Wind, it matters little which way you point it. It just goes, and there are few more pleasant ways of passing an afternoon than to explore a new lake or harbour in this machine. Fig 20.19 and the photo on page 319 show HSP Duo Mk XVIII, a two-hander. This one is a little faster, a little more serious. When handled properly it can cruise downwind at very nearly double the wind speed.

These two are unlike any other boat to handle. I still enjoy my frolic. They are such tremendous fun to play with.

Speed with control in stronger winds. Balmoral, Middle Harbour.

Fig 16.11 HSP Mk XVII

Chapter Seventeen
Sails

17.1 The starting point

In a world in which aeroplanes are commonplace, the understanding of how aeroplane's wings work is also commonplace. Because sails look like wings, it used to be believed that sails and wings worked in the same way. *They don't.* Nevertheless, this was a not unreasonable belief, because there was so little evidence to the contrary. That this should be so was due to an unusual historical coincidence.

The wings which were used in the early, under-powered, slow-flying days of aviation were shaped exactly like modern headsails – thin and deeply curved. Their task, like the headsail, was to develop a large cross-wind force ('lift'), from a relatively slow airflow. Some very efficient wing sections were developed empirically, but at that time aviation was more of a hobby than a science, little research was undertaken, few records were kept and until recently almost none of these survived in the literature of the science.

As soon as more powerful engines were developed, aircraft became able to fly faster, to carry substantial loads, and to be generally useful for military purposes. The priorities changed. At the higher speeds now attainable, the over-riding consideration became to reduce drag. To this end, formal research was commissioned. The now-familiar low-drag streamline shape was developed, and this was adopted for wings as well as for many other applications. The world is obsessed with speed, and almost all of the subsequent research has concentrated on and reported the properties of bodies in ever faster airflows. Because formal scientific aeronautical literature started from about this time, almost the whole of the earlier low-speed experience was simply ignored as irrelevant.

It so happens that while wings of tear-drop shape are superbly efficient at higher airspeeds, their efficiency collapses at the low airspeeds typical of the pioneer aircraft and the still lower speeds at which sailboat sails work. This is the coincidence which has lead to the present confusion – that exactly this whole subject area of low speed flow, the whole of the area that behaves so differently, happens to be the subject area which is missing from the literature of aerodynamics.

For many decades, the science and understanding of low-speed airflows was much neglected. Tiny amateur groups, such as the more serious model aeroplane enthusiasts experimented and published accurate data, and were able to design superbly efficient low-speed wing sections for models. F.W Schmidt in Germany, and the Low Speed Aeronautical Research Association (LSARA) based at Cranfield in England, contributed outstanding work. Recent years have seen this whole situation improve. The advent of aircraft which can hover and fly at very low speeds has prompted industrial research. There is now much published low speed data. This shows that, at the wind speeds in which yachts sail, the detail flows are fundamentally different and that sails don't work like 'high-speed' aeroplane wings at all. The essential differences are discussed in this chapter.

The section on '*Wings*' summarises the high-speed situation.

The section on '*Sails behind masts*' introduces the basic concepts of low-speed airflow. Figs 17.1, 17.2, 17.3, and 17.4 and Figs 17.6, 17.7, 17.8 and 17.9 could not be more different.

The section on '*Sails without masts*' introduces the concept of 'knife-edge' leading edges, their strong points and their traps.

The final sections discuss the evolution and development of the modern wingmast and wingmast rig. They show how a little thought and perseverance have managed to achieve high speed efficiencies in low-speed environments.

17.2 Wings

Fig. 17.1 shows the smooth flow of wind around a slender section such as the wing-tip of a glider. Smoke plumes have been introduced into the flow so that we can see where the air goes – the 'stream' lines.

Figs 17.2, 17.3 and 17.4 show in diagram format, the airflows, pressures, and total forces around a typical light aeroplane wing section at about 200 miles per hour. Fig. 17.2(b) shows that the airflow is

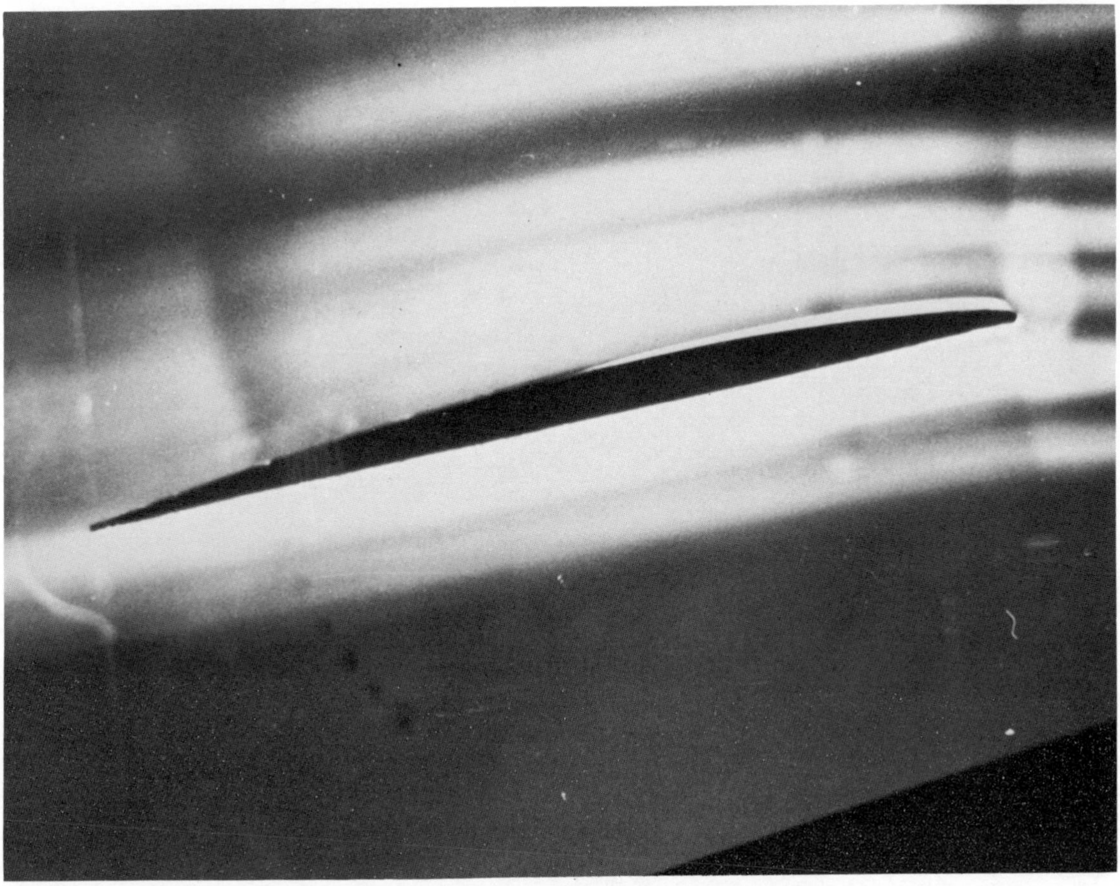

Fig 17.1 Smoke tracers show stream lines around wing

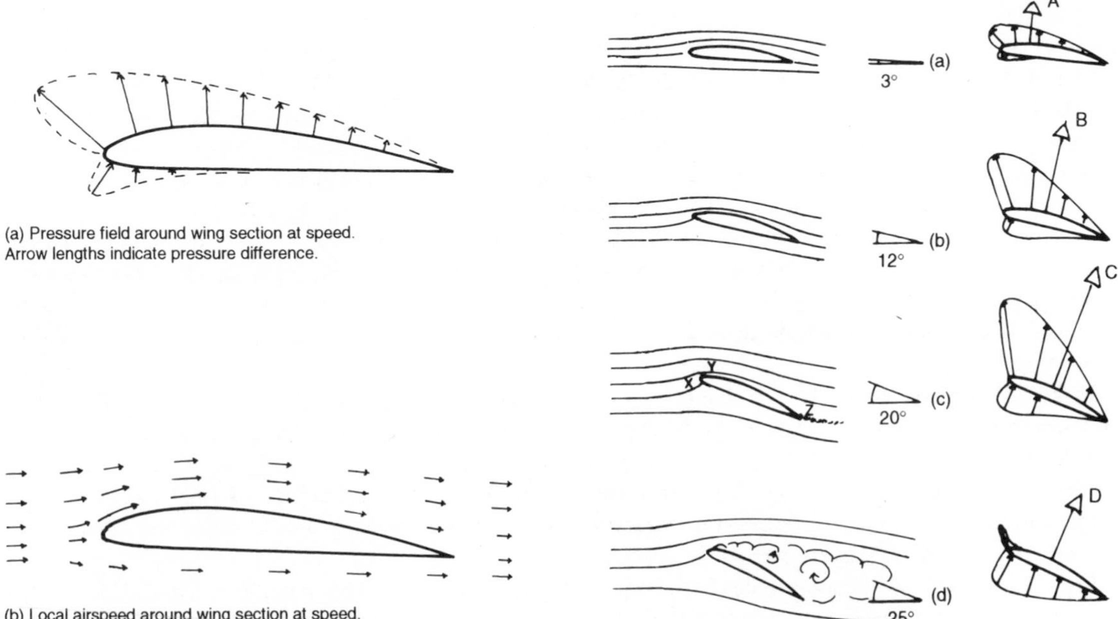

(a) Pressure field around wing section at speed.
Arrow lengths indicate pressure difference.

(b) Local airspeed around wing section at speed.
Arrow lengths indicate local speed and direction.

Fig 17.2 Airflow, airspeed and pressure distribution around wing section at speed

Fig 17.3 Change of airflow and pressure with change of wing angle to high speed flow

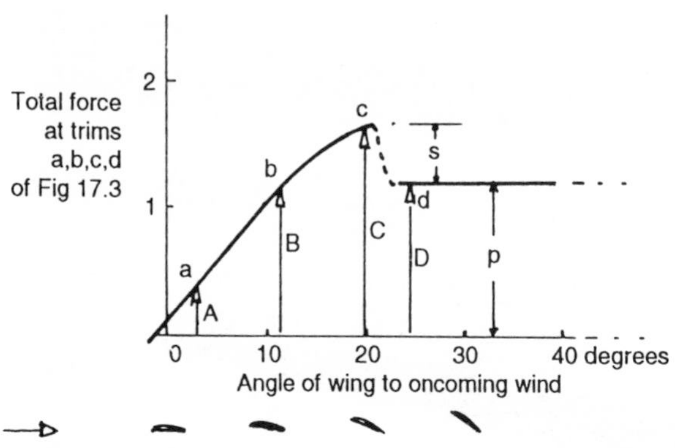

Fig 17.4 Change of total force with change of angle to wind - wing

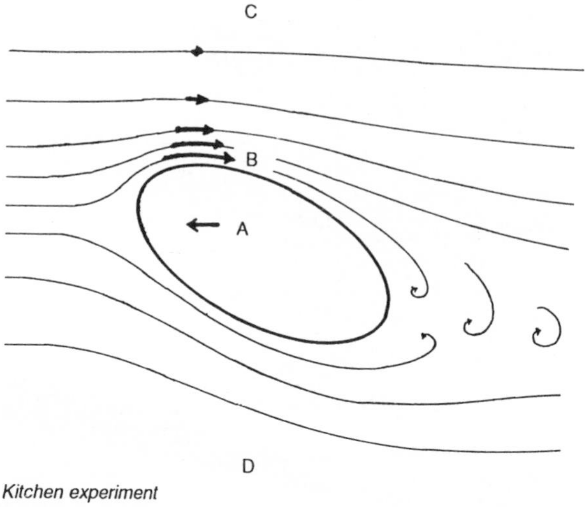

C
B
A
D

Kitchen experiment

As bottle A is moved to the left, particles at B accelerate strongly to the right and the surface level at B becomes lower.
(The faster the flow, the lower the pressure.)
Particles at C and D remain motionless.

Fig 17.5 Acceleration of fluid near moving foil

everywhere smooth (except within the turbulent boundary layer), and that the surface flow is everywhere in the downwind direction. The faster airflow which occurs over the forward upper surface shows in 17.2(b). Where the flow becomes faster, the pressure falls. To understand this, it is useful to think of the reverse situation – where an obstruction such as a spinnaker slows the wind, the pressure rises and this is what pushes the boat along. The converse is also true – where the flow speeds up, the pressure falls. You can see this in action in the kitchen experiment of Fig 17.5. This faster airflow where the flow diverges, and the forwardly directed suction associated with it which is shown in Fig 17.2(a), is the characteristic of all efficient wing sections.

The way in which the airflow accelerates over this area can be seen in a simple kitchen experiment. Fill a basin with water. For a tracer sprinkle the surface with particles which float – ground pepper is excellent. Find a bottle of elliptical shape, and move it, at an angle, sharper edge first, and half immersed, through the water as in Fig. 17.5. Note how, as the bottle is moved one way, the tracer particles nearest the bottle are accelerated in the other direction. (If you cannot find an elliptical bottle, your own hand is not a bad substitute.) This local acceleration is the key to efficient flight – and to efficient sailing.

Figs 17.3(a), (b) and (c) show that the airflow pattern, the pressure pattern, and the force pattern all change and increase in an uncomplicated manner as the angle of the wing to the airflow – *the angle of attack* – is increased. We will see later that this is due to the high initial speed of the air. Because it is moving so fast to begin with, it can stand considerable slowing before it is brought to rest, or reversed. Until it is brought to rest, no fundamental change will occur. Note, however, how critical is the situation in 17.3(c). At 'x', there is a substantial suction. At 'y', there is no suction. Air at 'y' tends to be driven by this pressure difference from 'y' towards 'x'. Only its initial high speed keeps it moving from 'x' towards 'y'. It slows as it flows against the adverse pressure. Already at 'z' it has become sluggish, and a 'wake' is thickening.

In Fig. 17.3(d) the inevitable has happened. The sluggish air at 'y' has been driven forward, by the pressure difference, toward x. This is 'adverse pressure gradient' separation – the classic aircraft 'stall', in which air sweeps forward suddenly from the trailing edge. As it moves forward, it splits the flow completely off the suction surface. The entire suction force is lost – suddenly. The total force abruptly reduces to the 'pressure only' force on the pressure surface, which remains almost unchanged thereafter, regardless of further increase of angle.

Fig. 17.4 shows how the total force changes as the angle is increased. The maximum force, at 'C', is the sum of both pressure 'p' and suction 's' forces. Once separation has occurred – the 'stall' – then, only the pressure force 'p' remains, and this is directed much further downwind. As a result, there is not only greatly reduced 'lift', but also substantially increased drag.

17.3 The boundary layer

Aircraft wings tend to be shaped the way they are because they are designed to work in airflows which are so fast that, while the flow near the surface may slow in places, it is never expected to stop.

At the much slower wind speeds at which we sail, the surface flow is often stopped or reversed. What happens to the sails' performance and efficiency in these conditions depends critically on the nature of the boundary layer, and whether this is energetic or feeble.

In Part 1, 'Wind', the ideas were introduced that, whatever the wind speed might be at height, the wind speed at the surface itself is always zero. There must therefore be a layer through which the wind speed changes from nothing at the surface to the full speed of the undisturbed wind, and this is called the boundary layer. The manner in which the wind speed increases with increasing distance from the surface will always take one of two forms: laminar or turbulent.

In the case of the wind, the earth's surface is effectively infinite in size, and so there is no point at which the process starts or stops. For this reason, the thickness of the atmosphere's boundary layer over wide areas is everywhere about the same. In light air (laminar type flow) its thickness is 100 metres at most, and often more like 10 metres. In turbulent breezes, it will be 500 metres at least, and up to 3,000 metres in strong winds. Over a wing, sail, or centreboard, a boundary layer will always exist and within it the flow will be either laminar or turbulent, exactly as it is over the land or water. But there are two new factors. One is the leading edge of the sail or centreboard. The other is the small and finite chord – the dimension in the downwind direction – between the leading edge and the trailing edge. These new factors introduce a tremendous change of scale.

Regardless of the speed of the wind, the flow will always be laminar and very thin at and just behind the leading edge of a sail. In strong winds, it quickly becomes turbulent. As the wind speed becomes progressively less, the extent of the sail downwind from the leading edge, which will be washed by laminar flow, becomes progressively greater until, in very light airs, the boundary layer may remain laminar right across the sail. The change of scale as between the earth's surface and the sail's surface is enormous. Instead of the earth's boundary layer thickness of hundreds or thousands of feet, the thickness of the boundary layer over the sail, in strong winds, increases from one tenth of an inch or less near the leading edge, to perhaps an inch at the leech. As the wind becomes lighter, the boundary layer becomes a little thicker.

17.4 Sails behind masts

Figs 17.6, 17.7, 17.8, and 17.9 show the totally different behaviour of the air flow around a typical small yacht or dinghy mast and mainsail in a 10-15 knot breeze. This is about one tenth of the speed of the flows of Figs 17.2, 3 and 4. In this case, because the air is moving so slowly to begin with, almost anything will stop it. On the pressure surface, this is not very important because it affects the local and total pressures only slightly. But over the suction surface, the difference is critical.

Fig. 17.7 shows that, instead of flowing everywhere smoothly, the flow divides into five zones. These are:

1. Attached flow zone (a-b)
2. Separation bubble zone (b-d)
3. Re-attachment zone (d)
4. Attached flow zone (d-f)
5. Leech separation zone (f-z).

The smoke plumes in Fig. 17.6 show how different is the flow from Fig. 17.1, and how distinct are the first three zones.

From the point at which the oncoming air meets the mast ('a', Fig. 17.7) to the point 'b' at which it separates, is the first zone. The surface flow accelerates as it flows around the mast, then slows, and then separates as air or water always separate when their speed over the surface falls to zero. The completeness and distinctness of the flow separation can be seen in Fig. 17.6.

The separation process can be observed and understood in another kitchen experiment. Again, fill a basin with water, and sprinkle the surface with a few grains of ground pepper or similar. Move a half immersed round object like a tumbler slowly across the surface. The first four or five diameters of movement will show, first, the abnormal 'starting flow' state, and then the progressive change to the 'steady flow' state

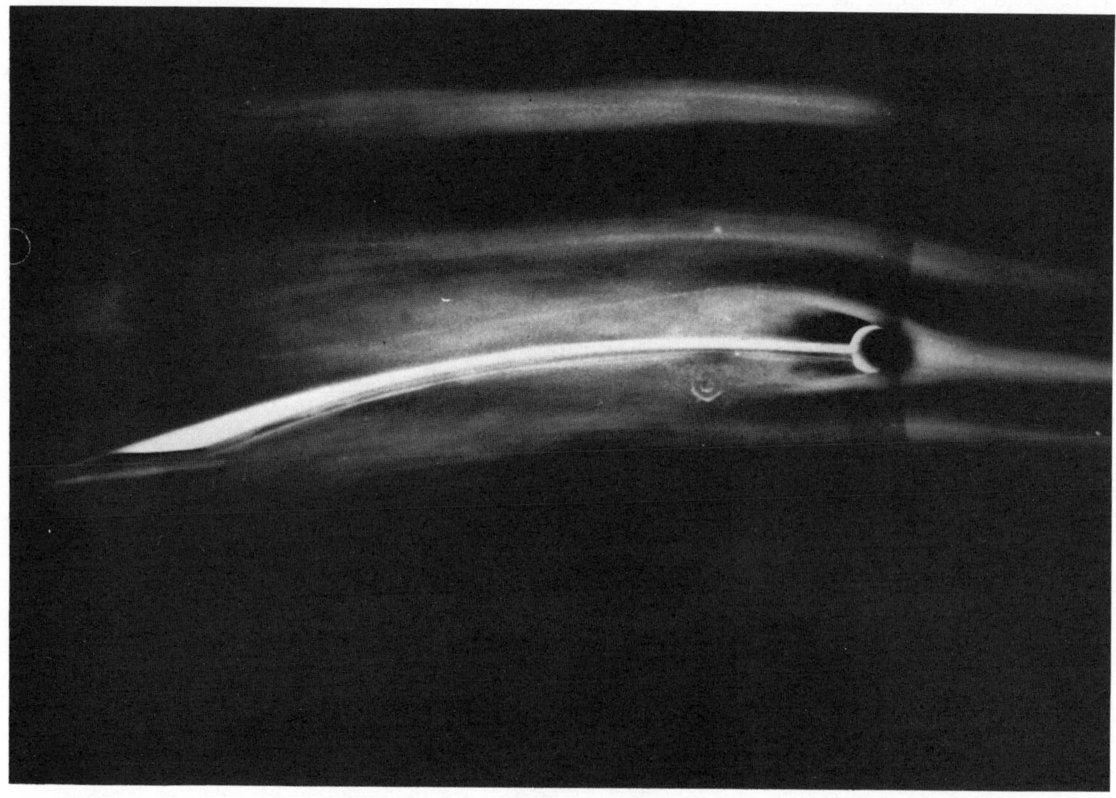

Fig 17.6 Smoke tracers show stream lines around sail behind mast.

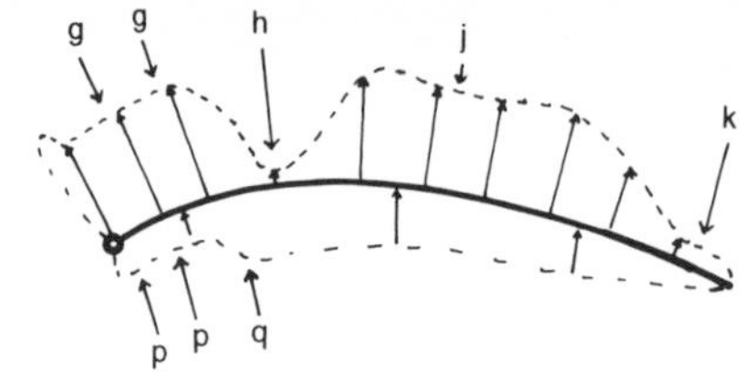

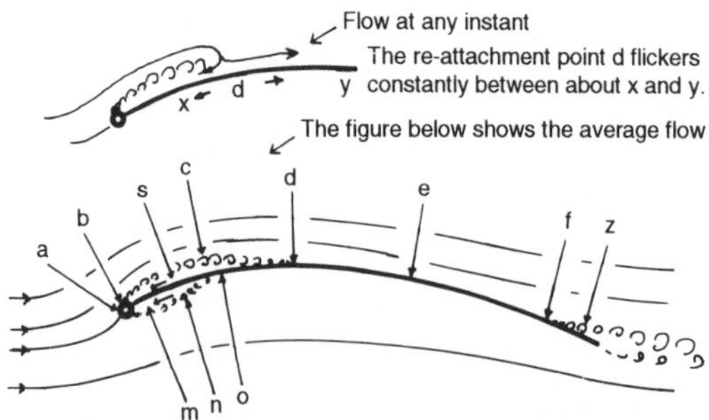

a Wind meets mast - stagnation point
b Flow separates from mast
c Free shear layer - over
s Separation bubble
d Flow re-attaches to sail (refer to inset)
e Zone of attached flow
f Flow separates from sail
z Free shear layer at leech
g Uniform reduced suction over s

h Greatly reduced suction near d
j Useful suction over e
k Zero suction over z

n Free shear layer
m Separation bubble
o Flow re-attaches to sail
p Uniform reduced pressure over m
q Pressure jump at 0

Fig 17.7 Typical flow pattern around sail behind conventional mast

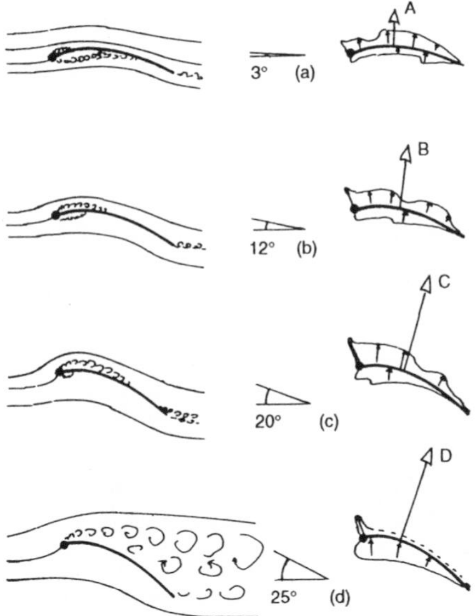

Fig 17.8 Change of airflow and pressure with change of trim angle of mast plus sail to wind (i.e. low speed flow)
Compare with Fig 17.3

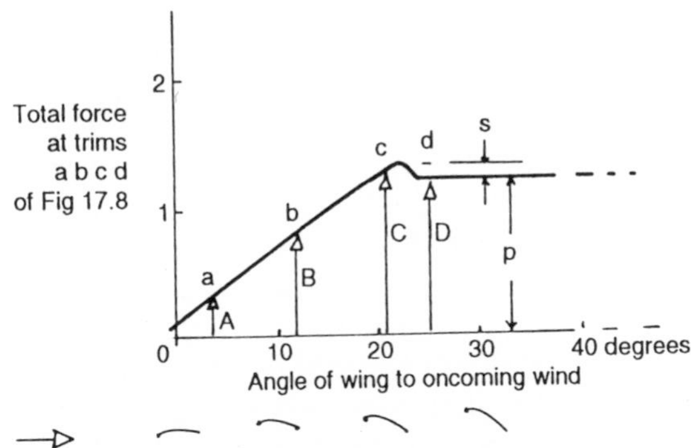

Fig 17.9 Change of total force with change of trim angle of mast plus sail to wind

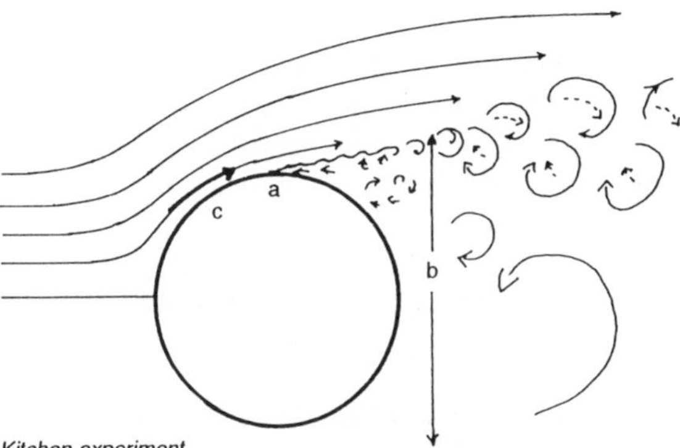

Kitchen experiment

c = Zone of highest speed and lowest pressure.
a = Point at which flow separates (except at high Reynolds numbers).
b = Turbulent wake.
Drag is usually proportional to wake thickness.

Fig 17.10 Flow around bluff object such as mast

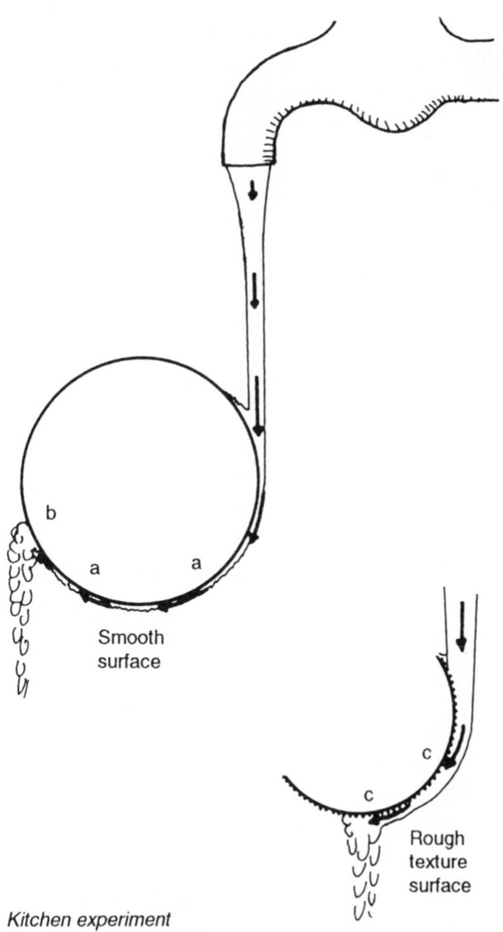

Kitchen experiment

a - a = While flow retains speed, it remains attached.
b = Where flow comes to rest, if falls off.

c - c = Speed within texture is zero, so flow falls off at lowest point regardless of speed beyond texture.

Fig 17.11 Flow around smooth and rough tumblers

with its characteristic and clearly visible flow separation.

Note particularly that the point at which the flow separates from the tumbler is where the surface flow speed becomes zero. Almost always this will prove to be true. The general flow pattern is sketched in Fig. 17.10.

Another particularly revealing demonstration of this, is to hold the tumbler horizontally under a smooth stream falling from a tap, as in Fig. 17.11. The water will curve around the bottom of the glass far beyond the horizontal and can remain attached for some distance up the other side so long as it has speed. At the point where it comes to rest, it will fall off.

If a rough-textured tumbler is tried, the behaviour will be completely different. The water will then always fall off at the bottom regardless of its initial speed. The rough surface will bring to rest not only the molecules which touch the surface but also the layer of water which lies within the texture of the roughness. This stagnant layer will then control the behaviour of all water 'outside' itself, regardless of how fast that water may be moving. This is why frost on an aeroplane's wing causes such severe loss of lift – the air near the surface is brought to rest by the roughness of the frost. Similarly, crumpled sails sail slowly.

17.5 The separation bubble

From the point, ('b', Fig. 17.7,) at which the flow separates from the mast, the flow then divides into two levels. The unslowed air continues downstream, but its inside limit is no longer the mast or sail, but a thick layer of stagnant air called a separation bubble. This can be seen clearly in Fig. 17.6, and is shown as 's' in Fig. 17.7. Between this stagnant air and the moving air lies a 'free shear layer'. This is extremely unstable, and breaks up quickly into a mass of swirls which rapidly grow larger, and 'reach outwards' into the free stream, and 'reach inwards' towards the sail's surface. This is indicated in Fig. 17.10, and can be seen in Fig. 17.6. Further, because all the initial swirls are caused by the friction between the moving air and the stagnant air in the bubble, the strongest swirls all spin in the same direction. Every swirl must be, to some extent, embedded in the circulation around an adjacent swirl – for this reason, all the swirls, once formed, will tend to rotate around each other. As each swirl of a pair moves inwards, it must become briefly embedded in the stagnant air of the bubble. The outer swirl of that pair will then tend to be swung around the embedded swirl, and so inwards towards the surface of the sail. This is indicated by the dotted arrows in Fig. 17.10. For this reason, the shear layer between the bubble and the moving air always curves inwards as it thickens and extends downstream, and so at some point will usually impinge on and re-attach itself to the surface of the sail.

This too can be seen in a similar kitchen experiment. As before, apply a tracer to a water surface, and then draw either a flat or a gently curved half-immersed server or spoon slowly across it. If the angle is too great, the separation will be complete. At a slightly smaller angle, the separation bubble, the free shear layer, the swirls and the subsequent re-attachment, and even the second separation zone near the trailing edge, will all be present and can all be seen as they develop.

The separation bubble ('s' Fig. 17.7), which lies between the point of separation, 'b', and the re-attachment zone, 'd', is the second of the five zones.

Its size will depend on three factors.

(1) The smaller the mast, (2) the smaller the trim angle of the sail to the wind, and (3) the fuller the sail, the smaller will be the length of the bubble on the suction surface. A bigger mast causes a bigger bubble. Increasing the angle of the sail to the wind causes the bubble to become longer. Flattening the sail also causes the bubble to become longer. All this can be seen clearly if two or three horizontal rows of tufts are taped to one side of a sail. Within the bubble the tufts will blow forward. By watching back-lighted tufts as the sail's fullness, twist and trim angle are changed, and at the same time feeling the boat's response, a crew can learn much about the nature of this flow, and the forces developed.

The re-attachment area 'd' Fig. 17.7 is the third zone. Because the free shear layer ('c' Fig. 17.7), is turbulent and unstable, re-attachment occurs over an area rather than at a point. This zone marks the boundary between the forward-flowing air within the separation bubble, 's', and the aft-flowing boundary layer, 'e', of the fourth zone. Because air in this re-attachment zone has great turbulence but no mean speed in any direction, tufts in this zone agitate rapidly but at random, with no indication of direction at all. Also, because the surface flow has little or no speed, the suction is much reduced. Because the actual point(s) of re-attachment oscillate rapidly and continuously across the re-attachment zone, the reduction of suction shows up as a deep dip, 'h', in the pressure diagram of Fig. 17.7, rather than a 'notch'. At any particular instant the flow would look like the inset in Fig 17.7.

This absence of suction is the key to the forward flowing tufts in zone 'c'. In the absence of the mast and separation bubble, the sail would expect to enjoy high speed flow and large suctions near the leading edge as in Fig. 17.2. But because the flow has separated and the bubble exists, the local airspeeds within the bubble are all low and so the suction is low. Further, the bubble forms a channel through which the higher-pressure air 'h' of the re-attachment zone can flow forward and continuously reduce the larger suctions which would otherwise exist further forward. The free shear layer acts rather like a leaky membrane which encloses the bubble, but through which air can pass to a limited extent.

The end result of this mechanism is that separation bubbles are in effect, 'internal leaks', which act to destroy the higher and desirable forward, lee-side suctions which would otherwise exist. The free movement of air inside the bubble causes the suction 'g' (Fig. 17.7) over the zone outside the bubble to be everywhere about the same. The low speed of the air keeps the suction relatively small. This is totally unlike the suction diagram in Fig. 17.2. The re-attachment zone 'd' shows up in Fig. 17.6 as that area where the smoke puffs are least blurred, because they move with least speed.

The zone with re-attached boundary layer 'e', between the re-attachment zone, 'd', and the second separation point, 'f', is the fourth zone. The re-attached turbulent flow accelerates and develops suction, 'j'. This zone corresponds to the entire luff-to-leech attached flow in Fig. 17.2. Note particularly the vital difference. In Fig. 17.2 the flow starts with full stream speed, and is further accelerated towards the very low pressure at 'L'. In Fig. 17.7 the flow speed starts from near-zero. Inevitably, the suction developed, the 'power' of the sail, will be substantially less. Further, because of the lack of the large forward-directed suctions near the leading edge due to the 'internal leak' of the bubble, the sail's total force, which is caused by the sum of all the pressure differences between the windward and leeward surfaces, will be generated on average nearer the leech, and so will be directed more across the boat than forwards.

In Figs 17.7 and 17.10 the boundary layer is laminar between the extreme leading edge and the point of separation, 'b'. The free shear layer becomes turbulent ('c', Fig. 17.7). The re-attached flow, already turbulent, remains turbulent (except in winds of say 2 knots or less). Once turbulent flow reattaches to a surface, the wind speed at the surface is restored very quickly.

A good example of this is to observe a visually sensitive surface such as a field of growing grain, which has a low hedge or wall as an upwind windbreak. In light airs, the restoration of surface flow speed downwind of the hedge is a long slow process. But in the turbulence of breezes, the point at which the flow re-attaches is clear to see, and from there downwind the turbulence scrubs the surface with almost equal vigour. So it is in zone 'e'.

The pressure difference between the suction, 'j', (Fig. 17.7), and the normal atmospheric pressure at the leech, 'k', tends to drive the stagnant air at the leech, 'z', forward. The wedge of stagnant air splits the flow away from the sail at 'f'. This is the second separation point (the first was at 'b'). The separated flow between 'f' and the leech is the fifth zone. Tufts within this zone will hang limp in light airs, or stream gently forwards, against the wind, in a breeze.

The actual position of 'f', will be determined by the balance between the flow speed at the surface, and the suction at 'j'. Given stronger winds, flatter sails, and small suction at 'j', the attached turbulent boundary layer in zone 'e', will sweep strongly across the sail all the way to the leech, and no separation will occur. This is the normal, 'going to windward in moderate or strong winds' condition. But in conditions in which a crew are 'looking for power' as in light air or when reaching, trailing edge (leech) separation will occur just before the sail trim reaches the angle at which total separation (as in Fig. 17.3(d) and 17.8(d)) occurs. Because it necessarily occurs a little before total separation, with its attendant loss of power, the ability to use a tuft near the leech to detect its onset becomes a vitally important sail trimming aid. This is the logic behind the 'leech ribbons just popping in and out' trim technique.

On the pressure surface, the flow pattern is broadly similar. There is the same separation from the mast, the free shear layer ('n', Fig. 17.7) which encloses a separation bubble, 'm'. The pressure, 'p-p', over the separation bubble, 'm', is constant, exactly as is the suction, 'g', over the bubble, 's'. Similarly, there is a pressure jump, 'q', which corresponds to the suction dip, 'h', over the re-attachment zone, 'o'. On the pressure surface there is nothing to cause surface flow to come to rest and so develop the suction-side trailing edge separation 'f-z', and 'k', and so the re-attached flow zone downstream of 'o' continues uninterrupted to the leech.

Figs 17.8(a), (b), (c), and (d) correspond with Figs 17.3(a), (b), (c), and (d). At a small angle the separation bubble on the pressure surface is large. It becomes progressively smaller as the sail's angle to the oncoming wind is increased. On the suction side, the reverse process takes place. At small angles the separation bubble is small and short. As the trim angle is increased, it grows progressively larger and longer. Note how the dip in the suction diagram moves progressively further aft as the angle is increased, and how the second separation point moves forward to meet it. When the dip – the re-attachment zone – meets the second separation point, total separation occurs (Fig. 17.8(d)). This is classic, low-speed, 'long separation bubble' separation, which starts from the leading edge and moves aft. It is totally different in nature from the high speed, aeronautical, 'adverse pressure gradient' separation, which pilot's call 'the stall', which flashes forward from the trailing edge.

In comparing Fig. 17.8 with Fig. 17.3, note particularly the absence at all angles of the large forwardly-directed suctions which so dominate Figs 17.3(a), (b), (c). The loss of these large suctions is due primarily to the re-distribution of pressure outside the separation bubble by the, 'internal leak', mechanism inside the bubble – and the separation bubble is caused by the obstruction to smooth flow by the mast itself.

The diagram which shows the change of total force, Fig. 17.9, shows a much smaller maximum force than Fig. 17.4. Both diagrams (Figs 17.9 and 17.4) show the same contribution to total force from the pressure surface – this is the residual pressure force which remains in both cases after separation has occurred. The reduced total force of Fig. 17.9 is due solely to the way the conventional mast causes a separation bubble, and this inhibits the development of substantial suction.

17.6 Sails without masts

If we take the mast away, and consider the performance of a sail set on a wire, such as a headsail, the situation becomes much better, but two further factors appear. These are:

1) knife-edge separation.

2) the effects of laminar flow.

Knife-edge separation is easy to see and to understand. If a knife-blade is held sharp-edge-upwards in the falling stream of water from a tap, Fig. 17.12, the slightest misalignment of the blade with the water (except when it falls very slowly) will result in separation from the 'suction' surface (Fig. 17.12 (a) and (b)). A gently curved spoon will show similar separation, but this time from the 'pressure' surface, at all angles less than that at which the spoon edge aligns with the oncoming flow (Fig. 17.12 (c) and (d)).

What we see from the sharp-edged knife and spoon, is that water can flow smoothly over each of them, but in each case at only one angle – the angle at which the sharp edge aligns exactly with the oncoming flow.

Sails behave similarly. In the case of the wind, the oncoming flow is deflected by the pressure and suction fields over the sail, but it remains true that only when the luff of the sail is exactly aligned with this deflected flow will the air flow smoothly over both sides of the sail.

Fig. 17.13 shows the practicalities for a very flat sail of 5% camber. At a trim angle of 5 degrees, a small separation bubble forms behind the leading edge on the pressure surface. At about 10 degrees, the flow over both surfaces is smooth.

The way the total force increases is shown in Fig. 17.13(e). At 5 degrees and 10 degrees, the force rises steadily.

At 15 degrees, the flow separates due to knife-edge separation, and a separation bubble forms on the suction surface. It increases in size rapidly as the trim angle is increased further. By 20 degrees (Fig 17.13(c)) it covers more than half of the suction surface. The 'internal leak' mechanism common to all separation bubbles destroys the peak suction which would otherwise occur, and the rate of increase of the total force is less than would be expected. This is shown in Fig. 17.13(e). In the absence of the internal leak, Force 'X' would be expected at a 20 degree trim angle. Instead, the sharp-edged sail can only produce Force 'Y'. This is why very flat sails are so slow in lighter winds.

At about 25 degrees, the flow separates completely, and the total force increases no further.

A particularly revealing way to understand the flow shown in Fig. 17.13(c) (20 degrees) is to listen to the surface flow with a stethoscope, while a probe (a fine hollow tube) is moved progressively from the leech to the luff on the suction side of a sail set up in a wind tunnel. At the leech, if the flow has separated as in Fig. 17.7 'f' and 'g', the stagnant air will be quiet. As the probe is moved forward to point 'f', a low roaring is heard. This is the characteristic noise of turbulent flow, and is heard in every aeroplane in flight, and in an automobile when travelling at speed on a freeway. As the probe is moved forward the loudness increases and the pitch rises as the turbulence becomes more intense. At the re-attachment point ('d', Fig. 17.7) the loudness becomes a maximum but the frequency becomes irregular. Further forward, within the separation

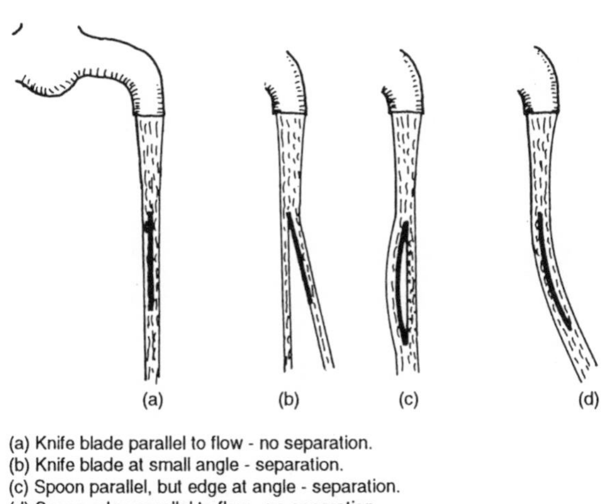

(a) Knife blade parallel to flow - no separation.
(b) Knife blade at small angle - separation.
(c) Spoon parallel, but edge at angle - separation.
(d) Spoon edge parallel to flow - no separation.

Fig 17.12 Knife edge separation

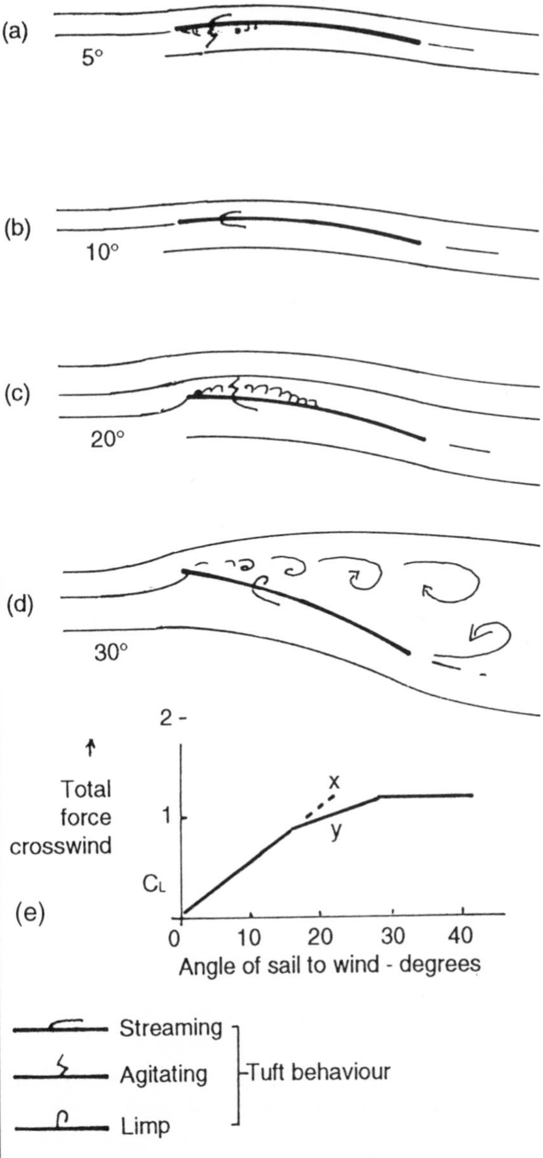

bubble, there is an uneasy quiet punctuated by an occasional 'crash' as a random vortex sweeps by. If the probe is lifted away from the surface, the coarse turbulence of the free shear layer is heard. Further out, there is only the quiet rushing noise of laminar flow passing the probe edge. Back on the surface, the uneasy quiet of the separation bubble maintains until, right at the leading edge, the probe meets the free shear layer as it separates. At this point the intense, fine grain turbulence is heard as a scream. Further forward again, only the rush of the smooth oncoming air can be heard.

Fig. 17.14 shows the flow patterns and forces for a full sail (15% camber). At all except very large trim angles an enormous separation bubble will form within the deep hollow of the windward surface. To bring all this air to rest produces substantial drag – downwind force – and this is why such full sails are so slow to windward.

At larger trim angles of between 25 degrees and 35 degrees (the exact angle will depend upon the shape of the leading edge), the flow becomes 'clean' across both surfaces. Both windward and leeward tufts stream smoothly, and at these trims full sails – such as spinnakers cut for broad reaching or tacking downwind, or wingmasted mainsails – can develop a total force much greater than that which can be developed by any combination of conventional mast and sail. Fig. 17.14(d) shows how the force changes with increasing trim angle. The maximum force, at point 'C', is the total of the pressure force, 'p', and the suction force 's' exactly as it was in Fig. 17.4. As the trim angle is increased further, knife-edge separation occurs from the leading edge on the suction side, the total force increases no more, and shortly thereafter the flow separates completely, suction force is lost, and the total force reduces abruptly to 'p'.

(a) 5°

(b) 10°

(c) 20°

(d) 30°

(e) Total force crosswind C_L — Angle of sail to wind - degrees

Streaming
Agitating
Limp
Tuft behaviour

Fig 17.13 Flow, force and tuft behaviour over a flat sail without a mast

17.7 Super-critical and sub-critical flow

At this point we must make a proviso. The high total force 'c' in Fig 17.14(d) is attainable only if the wind is strong enough for the boundary layer to be turbulent. In light winds, the effects of laminar flow begin to be important.

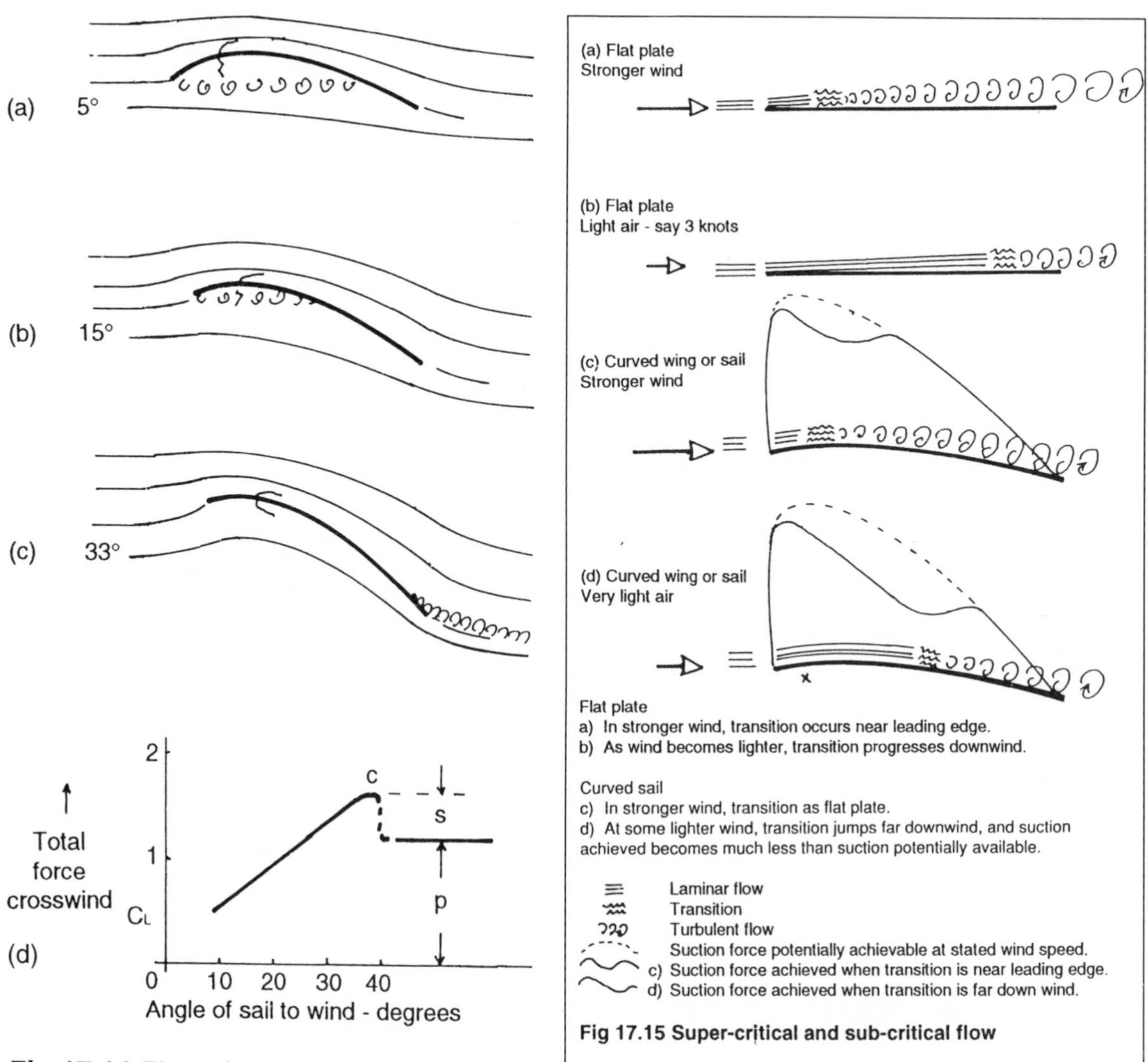
(a) 5°
(b) 15°
(c) 33°
Total force crosswind
C_L
(d)
c
s
p
2
1
0 10 20 30 40
Angle of sail to wind - degrees
(a) Flat plate
Stronger wind
(b) Flat plate
Light air - say 3 knots
(c) Curved wing or sail
Stronger wind
(d) Curved wing or sail
Very light air
Flat plate
a) In stronger wind, transition occurs near leading edge.
b) As wind becomes lighter, transition progresses downwind.
Curved sail
c) In stronger wind, transition as flat plate.
d) At some lighter wind, transition jumps far downwind, and suction achieved becomes much less than suction potentially available.
Laminar flow
Transition
Turbulent flow
Suction force potentially achievable at stated wind speed.
c) Suction force achieved when transition is near leading edge.
d) Suction force achieved when transition is far down wind.

Fig 17.14 Flow, force and tuft behaviour over a full sail without a mast

Fig 17.15 Super-critical and sub-critical flow

Figs 17.15(a) and (b) indicate this process as it applies to a flat surface. At and below some critical speed – in practice about one to two knots of Apparent Wind speed, depending on the size and roughness of the surface – viscosity can suppress the feeble turbulence and the flow can remain laminar for an indefinite distance. At windspeeds slightly greater, the flow will remain laminar for a long way before the increasing shear force triggers transition and turbulence. The stronger the wind, the greater the shear force becomes, and the shorter the length which will be swept by laminar flow before transition and turbulence occur.

In Fig. 17.15(c) and (d), the effect of laminar flow on the suction diagram of a curved sail is shown. The dashed line indicates how the suction would change at high speeds, such as the aircraft's 200 miles per hour.

The solid line of Fig. 17.15(c) shows the lesser suctions actually achieved by a perfectly trimmed real headsail in light wind. The reason for the dip in the suction diagram over the forward part of the sail is that the laminar flow beneath it acts rather similarly to a separation bubble. Because the flow speed near the surface is so feeble the adverse pressure gradient slows it almost to a stop. This slowing causes the boundary layer to thicken, and this thickening changes the effective shape of the sail, as experienced by the 'high speed' air outside the boundary layer, in a way which always reduces the total force which would otherwise be available. At some point, the surface flow is brought to rest. The zero-speed flow then separates, exactly as in Fig. 17.7, 17.10 and Fig. 17.11 at 'b', and a free shear layer forms. This is intensely

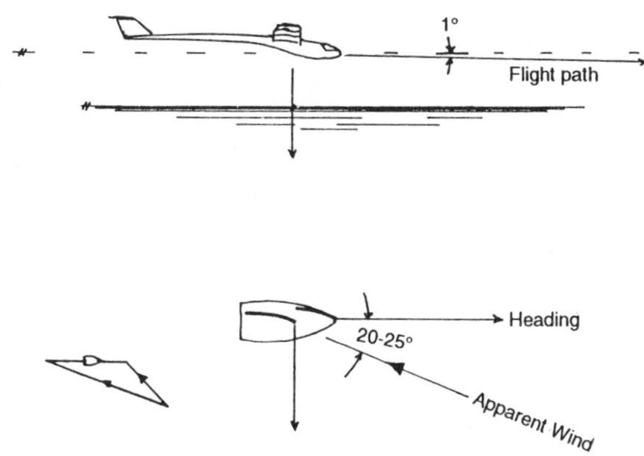

Gliders can fly within 1° of the horizontal.
Sailboats can sail within 20-25° of the Apparent Wind.

Glider wings at their best are about 20 times more efficient than sailboat rigs at their best. (Ice yachts are better.)

Fig 17.16 Wings and rigs at work

(a)
Aspect ratio
(Ratio of span to area)

The smaller the aspect ratio, the more the pressure leaks around the tip.
Glider - aspect ratio 30
Yacht - aspect ratio 6

(b)
Range of trim angle

The smaller the range needed, the more the section can be optimised.
Glider needs 1° to 2.5°
Yacht needs 0° to 90°

(c)
Twist

The effect of twist is to reduce still further the aspect ratio. In effect, the top of the rig is discarded, and the remaining lower rig suffers massive tip leakage.
Glider - twist 0°
Yacht - twist up to 20°

(d)
Airflow
(Refer Figs 17.1 and 17.6)

Glider - clean
Yacht - broken

Fig 17.17 Glider wing and yacht rig - the essential differences

unstable, and so becomes turbulent and, because it is so close to the surface, it immediately re-attaches. The turbulence spreads rapidly outwards through the boundary layer. This is transition. Its trigger is the short separation bubble.

What we see here is that short separation bubbles can be useful. They are one of the mechanisms whereby the boundary layer triggers into turbulence. As soon as turbulence establishes, particles moving at high speed sweep inwards and 'scrub' the surface. With this restoration of flow speed and energy at the surface, the air at the surface starts moving again against the adverse pressure gradient, and suction quickly re-establishes.

Fig. 17.15(d) shows that, in very light winds, laminar flow persists for a greater distance downwind from the leading edge before the boundary layer trips into the turbulent state, and the loss of suction is greater. Fundamentally, this is caused by the inability of laminar flow to maintain speed at the surface against an adverse pressure gradient when the wind speed is slower than that which is critical for that sail shape. In practice, while the change from the flat plate Fig. 17.15(a) situation to the (b) situation is progressive, the change from the cambered sail (c) situation to the (d) situation occurs with a jump.

Flow as in Fig. 17.15(c) is described as super-critical, and is 'powerful'. Flow as in Fig. 17.15(d) is sub-critical and can never be powerful. The fuller the sail, the higher the wind speed at which the flow loses power in this way. This is why in light airs a flatter sail, of say 8% camber, which operates super-critically and relatively powerfully, can be faster than a 12% camber sail which has dropped to sub-critical flow.

17.8 Dreams and realities

The difference in efficiency between a glider's wing and a conventional yacht's sail is enormous. The best gliders can glide about sixty feet forward for every foot that they sink. This is a gliding angle of 60:1, or about 1 degree. The sailing equivalent is sailing to windward. Most yachts tack through about 80 to 90 degrees, i.e. they can sail at about 40 degrees to the True Wind or about 25 to 30 degrees to the Apparent Wind. The glider manages 1 degree. This is a difference in efficiency, not of percentages, but of orders of magnitude! (Fig. 17.16.) The best model aeroplane wings, despite their much lower operating speeds, can achieve almost the same efficiency as glider wings.

If we compare the glider's wing and the yacht rig more closely, to try to understand why the yacht sail is so inefficient, four differences stand out. (Fig. 17.17.)

The first is that the glider's wing is long and slender, and the yacht sail by comparison, is short and squat. One of the facts of life of all aerofoils, whether they be wings, sails, centreboards, or keels, is that fluid from the pressure side will always 'leak', by skewing outwards and flowing around the tip towards the suction side. The effect of this leak is similar to the loss of effort experienced when climbing uphill in soft sand – some of the gain in height of each step is lost because the foothold itself yields downwards. Long-span wings like those of gliders experience minimal tip leakage, and can be compared with a firm foothold. Short-span wings, such as those found on *Concorde* or a space shuttle, experience very great leakage at low speed, as can be seen from the extreme angles they need to adopt when approaching to land. Shallow keels suffer similarly – this explains the substantial leeway suffered by yachts with stubby keels when sailing to windward. Stubby rigs – and also twisted rigs – have the same disadvantages as short-span wings at low speed. In lighter winds, because of the leakage of air and pressure around the low tip, it is often necessary to point 10 to 15 degrees lower than with a tall slender rig just to achieve the same working pressure difference. It is easy to see why gliders are designed with such long wings, and that these are one of the principle reasons for their efficiency.

The second difference is the angle to the wind at which the sail and the glider's wing work. The glider's wing, except in the moments of slowing flight before landing, always works within a narrow range of between about 1 degree and 2½ degrees. Another fact of life about wings is that they always achieve their best ratios of lift/drag – or pointing angle – at these very small angles. Yacht sails are profoundly different, because in practice they have to be able to work at trim angles which may be anywhere between 0 degrees and 90 degrees, depending on the wind strength and the point of sailing. Only between the angles of 0 degrees and 35 degrees (Point 'C' in Fig. 17.14) can the sail be thought of as behaving like a wing, but even then the difference between the glider's 2½ degrees and the sail's 35 degrees is clearly very great.

The third difference is twist. Look at any aeroplane or great sea-bird in flight. Their wings are beautifully designed, with either no twist at all, or very little, and every part of the wing meets the air at exactly the right angle. Now look at the yachts on the harbour or in any magazine. Twenty degrees of twist is not uncommon. Twist may be aesthetically pleasing, but it is aerodynamically catastrophic, because only some tiny part of so twisted a sail can be working at its best angle. Further, because the tops of twisted sails are virtually streaming downwind, and are not contributing their proper share of the total force, the effect of twist, technically, becomes similar to that of an untwisted sail lower in total height and of smaller area (the concept is shown in Fig 17.17 (c). The loss of effective area is bad enough, but it is the reduction in effective height which is most damaging, because this greatly increases the inefficiency and loss of pointing ability due to the leakage of air around the tip. Summed up, twist makes stubby rigs out of tall ones.

It is principally in steady-breeze and relatively-flat-water conditions that untwisted sails will prove faster. In light air twisted sails will always be faster. And when rougher water and/or unsteady breeze makes the airflow itself unsteady some deliberate twist will usually be faster. But in this latter case elasticity – which encourages the leeches to twist open temporarily at the moments of greatest force – will be faster yet. Elasticity is really momentary twist.

The fourth difference is the detail of the airflow over the two aerofoils. The glider's wing enjoys the clean flow of Fig. 17.1. The conventional yacht rig suffers the blemished flow of Fig. 17.6.

If we admire the efficiency of the glider's wing, are conscious of the inefficiency of the yacht's rig and the reasons for it, and consider what we can do to improve each of those four differences to make the yacht sail better, it becomes clear that while we can do little about aspect ratio and operating angle, we can do a great deal about twist and airflow. Let us look at each of these in turn:

Aspect ratio

The typical dinghy or yacht rig shown in Fig. 17.17(a) has an aspect ratio of 6·4:1. The glider has an aspect ratio of 30:1. To achieve, with the same sail area, an aspect ratio of 30:1 on the dinghy would require a mast 45 feet high with a sail three feet wide (Fig. 17.18(a)). Such a sail would be impossible to set without uncontrollable twist.

If we could, by some means, control the twist, then the weight of a 45 foot mast and sail would be impossible to handle even in a calm. And if we could find some magical infinitely strong and weightless material, so that we could make such a rig and handle it in a calm, as soon as the wind began to blow the boat would heel far over because the centre of pressure on so high a rig would act at more than twice its usual height above the deck.

So it turns out that even if we could, with great skill, sail with such a magical rig, the boat would sail only slowly because we could accept only half the force from the double-height rig. So the modest reduction in 'tip-leakage' loss (induced drag) gained from the very high rig turns out to be of no practical benefit at all to the performance of the yacht as a whole, because of the loss of more than 50% of the drive force. In practice, the fastest rig height turns out to be a mechanically reasonable compromise between the greater 'power' of a squat rig and the higher pointing ability of a taller rig.

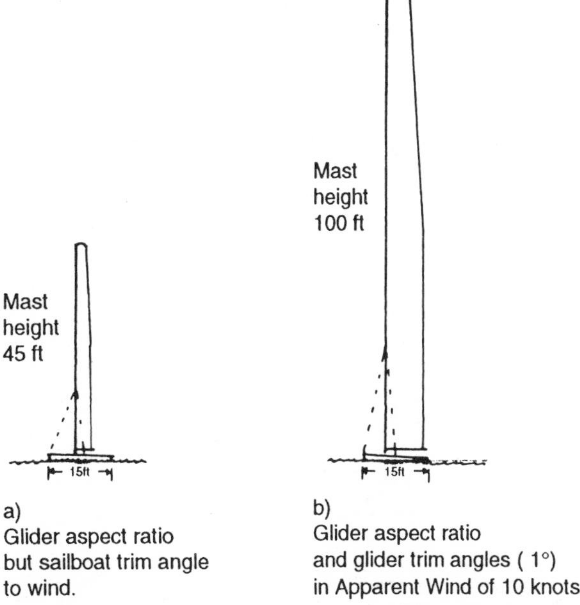

Fig 17.18 Rig sizes needed by 15 ft dinghy for glider equivalence

Range of trim angle

In the example just quoted, the sail area was assumed to be the same as the dinghy, and so the trim angles would have to be the same, i.e. seldom less than 10 degrees, and often 30 degrees to 40 degrees. To achieve the glider wing's 2.5 degree trim angle in 'normal' winds, it would be necessary to make the sail between 4 and 10 times bigger, i.e. (for aspect ratio 30:1) the mast would need to be between 90 and 140 feet tall, (Fig. 17.18(b)). If a 45 foot mast on a dinghy stretched the imagination, a 100 foot mast is in 'cloud cuckoo' land!

Twist

Here we come back to reality. The conventional yacht mainsail is a triangle of flexible fabric set between a mast and a boom, and controlled by a sheet attached to the boom. In a calm, the free edge of the fabric – the leech – lies straight, and the sail has no twist, as in Fig 17.19(a) (b) and (d). As soon as the wind blows, the leech is forced to leeward and all of this movement to leeward appears as twist in the set of the sail as in Fig 17.19(c) and (e). So whether twist is wanted or not there is no escaping it. The consequence of this is that much handling lore reduces to ways of optimising performance in the presence of twist which is not wanted but which cannot be avoided.

Two modern developments enable crews to control twist positively to the point of eliminating it.

The first is the fully-battened sail with a roach. The way this works is shown in Fig. 17.19(f) to (j). In light air, if the sheet is pulled tight, the threadline, 'T', between the head, 'H', and the clew, 'C', tries to become straight. The leech 'L' is then driven by the curve of the battens to windward of the plane defined by the mast and boom. This is called 'hooking' and is shown in Fig. 17.19 (g). When the wind blows, the threadline 'T' adopts the same sort of curve to leeward as is adopted by the leech of the conventional sail, but in the fully battened sail this threadline supports the battens near their centres and the aft ends of the curved battens can then lie near, or on the zero-twist plane as is shown in Fig 17.19(h) and (j). Such a rig requires careful development before it will achieve and repeat the proper changes of shape with zero or

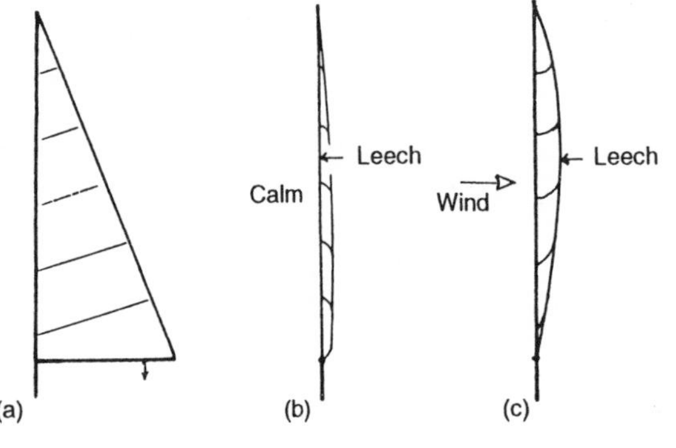

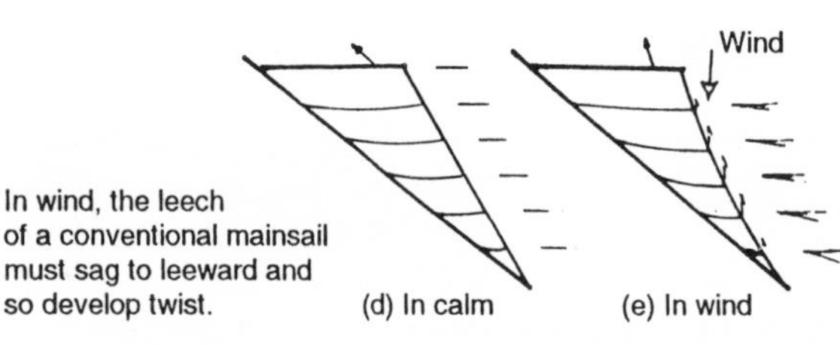

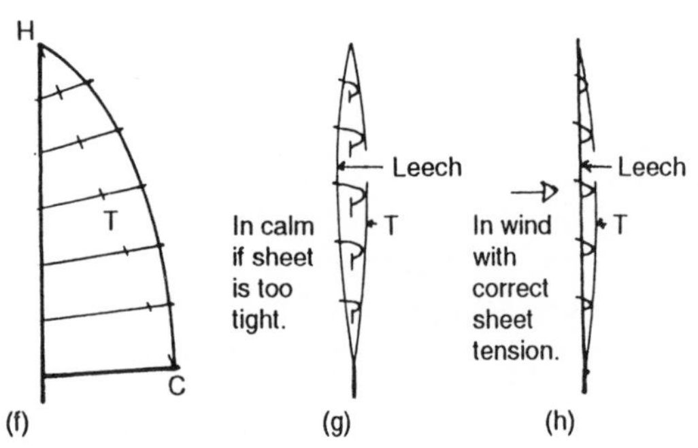

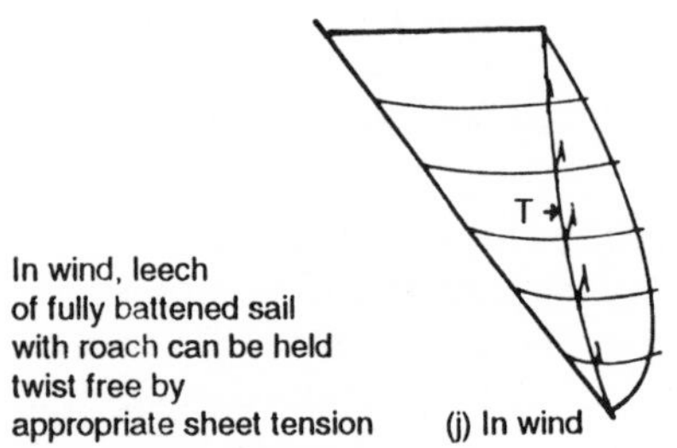

T
In wind, leech
of fully battened sail
with roach can be held
twist free by
appropriate sheet tension
(j) In wind

(a) and (f) = View from side
(b) (c) (g) and (h) = View from astern
(d) (e) and (j) = View from above

Fig 17.19 Control of twist

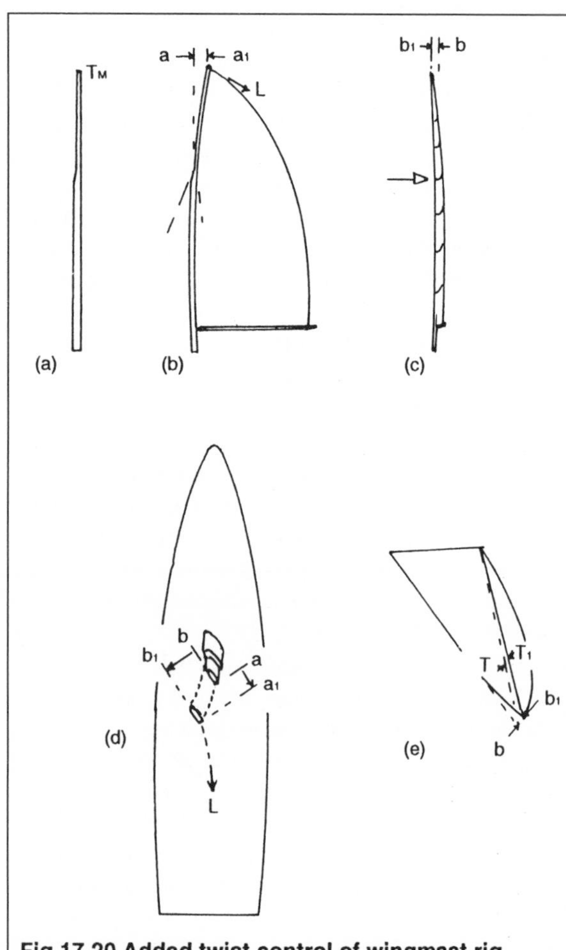

Fig 17.20 Added twist control of wingmast rig

small twist as the wind speed changes from light to strong. But once it is developed, it enables a helmsman to put his leech where he wants it . In stronger winds, he need only pull his sheet harder to keep the leech at or near zero twist, and the traveller then adjusts angle. Fully battened sails are faster than leech-batten sails primarily because they enable crews to control twist better. They can be very fast when intelligently handled. The key to handling them is the conscious adjustment of sheet tension to match changing wind strength. As the wind speed increases the sheet tension should be increased to maintain a zero or small and constant twist. Above all, when the wind speed reduces, the sheet tension *must* be eased, or the upper leech will 'hook', and the boat will slow.

The second development was a by-product of the over-rotating wingmast rig. In the course of development, we found that if the topmast were made relatively stiff 'fore and aft' (in the plane of the major axis) and relatively flexible sideways (in the plane of the minor axis) then a new property appeared which gave three very great advantages.

The property is that the rotated masthead ('TM', Fig. 17.20), when pulled aft by mainsheet tension, 'L' will bend both backwards (from 'a' to 'ai'. Fig 17.20(b) and (d)) and also sideways in the windward direction (from 'b' to 'bi' Fig. 17.20(c), (d), and (e)). The effect of this is to draw the threadline 'T' to windward of the plane of the mast and boom (from 'T' to 'Ti' Fig. 17.20(e)). This accentuates the control of twist described in Fig 17.19. In light air this can drive the mainsail upper leech far to windward – so light air sailing calls for careful control of twist with a very slack sheet.

The first advantage is that since twist can be controlled with a lesser sheet tension at any wind strength, the practical consequence is that the upper leech becomes more elastic and the boat sails faster. The second advantage is that to deflect the top of the mast and sail to windward like this is extremely efficient aerodynamically – sea-birds droop their wing tips for the same reason. The third advantage is that the windward-deflected topmast gives a very firm upper leech and relatively untwisted sail when reaching, and this results in much greater 'power' and higher crosswind speeds, particularly in strong winds. This principle has been used for years in the rigs of the fastest ice-yachts. Only in this way could they manage to set their sails almost twist-free in the very strong apparent winds and high aerodynamic side loads which their relatively tiny sails develop at high speeds. What our rigs did was to extend into the light air range the wind speeds in which we could enjoy this unusual efficiency

In retrospect, there was a period of many years during which we were consciously focussing on other elements of our rigs, while in fact our principle problem was that we had not yet understood the different nature of the two winds. In light airs twist is essential. In breeze it should be greatly reduced or eliminated. Until that fundamental dawned, we could not apply it because we had not thought of it, and so we continued to set our sails in unenlightened ways. In this situation, no amount of development of mechanical capability or control technique could give us superior performance over the full range of wind speed from drift to strong breeze. Only when we finally got twist right in our minds, could we blend control of twist with control of shape, in a manner in which both tended to change automatically and in the right sense, when the wind speed changed. We were then immediately rewarded with real improvements in speed and handling.

Airflow

Early efforts at improving rig efficiency in the C Class 'Little *America*'s Cup' catamarans took the form of glider-like rigs. It is fair here to acknowledge that recent work by Lindsay Cunningham and others has been successful to the point where they have now developed glider-like rigs which are superbly efficient within a narrow 'window' of True Wind speed. Between about 7 and 12 knots of True Wind they are superb, and are much more efficient than any other sailboat with the possible exception of the best of the ice yachts, and their potential for further development is outstanding. But these are still early days. In light airs the thick sections are not efficient, and in winds stronger than about 15 knots these machines are not yet strong enough nor controllable enough, so theirs is not yet a general solution to the problem of improved efficiency.

About 30 years ago two beliefs became widespread. One was that the flexible sailcloth, from which all conventional sails are made, was itself somehow responsible for the generally poor efficiency of sails as compared with aircraft wings. The other, conversely, was that only soft-fabric sails could retain performance, however poor, in light airs.

Two subsequent developments showed that both these beliefs were wrong. The first was the work of low-speed aerodynamic research groups who were interested in the performance of model aeroplane wings. They discovered the physical reasons behind the two-mode behaviour of glider-like solid wings at low speeds. In the simplest terms, the lower the operating speed, the thinner the wing needed to be, and the finer the leading edge radius (but never sharp). The area just behind the leading edge always needed very careful shaping. Given this information, model aeroplane designers were at last able to develop solid wings which are superbly efficient at low speeds. These findings, which revolutionized model aeroplane performance, were directly applicable to yacht sails. It was immediately clear that it was the final shape which was important, and whether the structure was made of aluminium, balsa, or stretched sailcloth made absolutely no difference.

The second development was a practical one. When the very heavy synthetic sail-cloths were first developed, the fastest ice-yacht classes exploited the strength and stability of these fabrics in fully battened sails set behind flexible wingmasts which could be turned until they aligned with the on-coming wind, and which then 'popped' – hooked the masthead to windward in the manner of Fig 17.20. At a stroke this gave the ability to control and eliminate twist. The best of these ice-yachts can now achieve speeds on clear ice of five to six times the wind speed. At these speeds, even when beam reaching, the Apparent Wind necessarily blows at an angle of 10 degrees or less from the boat's centreline – and less again when sailing to windward and downwind (Fig. 17.21). In this way these boats demonstrate that fabric sails can work efficiently at angles as small as 6 to 8 degrees. When this is compared with the 20 degrees or so optimum of normal yachts, it is clear that these fabric sailed, wing-masted, and relatively twist-free ice-yacht rigs are already about three times more efficient than the best conventional sailboat rigs.

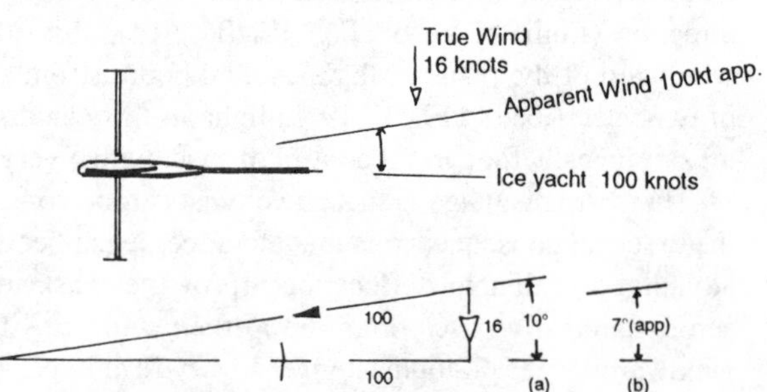

Skeeta ice yacht can sail at six times wind speed.
On beam reach, Apparent Wind blows from 10° from bow.
Close-hauled and downwind, wind blows from 7°(app) from bow.

Fig 17.21 Apparent Wind angles of ice yacht at speed

Three more pieces of information were needed before the efficient low-speed wingmast became possible.

One was the understanding of the long separation bubble, with its 'internal leak' penalty.

The second was the realization of the increasing extent to which sails are washed by laminar flow at low speeds, and the 'suction loss' penalties which attach to laminar flow at the larger trim angles, as shown in Fig. 17.15.

The third was the realization that a sub-critical, laminar flow boundary layer could be triggered into super-critical turbulence by a 'trip turbulator'. This is either a tiny obstruction, or a knife edge, so proportioned and placed that it initiates turbulence within the boundary layer without causing separation. (A number of passenger aircraft use trip turbulators. These are the rows of small projections which appear on the upper forward surfaces of the wings when the landing gear or flaps are lowered.) Because a turbulent boundary layer can keep flowing against an adverse pressure gradient about four or five times as great as will stop laminar flow, the benefit of a trip turbulator is that it makes it possible to enjoy much greater 'power' from sails in lighter winds. Fig. 17.15(d) shows how potential force is lost due to laminar flow in light airs. If a trip turbulator is placed at about 'x', (Fig. 17.15(d)) it will trigger the boundary layer into the turbulent mode much closer to the leading edge, and the flow will become similar to the flow in Fig. 17.15(c). The suction force will increase from the Fig. 17.15(d) sub-critical 'large loss' situation to the Fig. 17.15(c) super-critical 'small loss' situation, even in very light airs.

Note that trip turbulators are useful only in those cases where increases in suction forces are needed and are available by the tripping of laminar flow into turbulence, and a small increase in drag does not matter. There is a penalty, which is the extra drag caused by the trip itself. (There may be gains other than the increased lift, such as a thinner total wake, in which case the overall drag may become less – this whole subject area is complex.) In the case of sails in light airs the extra drag is a minuscule addition to the total 'hull plus foils plus rig' drag, and is a price well worth paying for the substantial extra 'lift' and drive force gained.

It is sometimes suggested that a rough surface will behave in the same way as a trip turbulator. This is not true. All that happens with a rough surface is that the flow close to the surface is everywhere brought to rest, and suction is then everywhere destroyed (Fig. 17.11(b) – rough tumbler). A trip turbulator is one single critically-shaped and positioned 'trip' on an otherwise smooth surface.

17.9 Modern rig development

In 1959, a small group of Sydney men and women decided to develop a dinghy class for their own enjoyment. We elected to base its rules very broadly on those of the respected International Fourteen, but we deliberately chose to discard the archaic 'mindset' approach to limitations which merely foster rule cheating, and to substitute instead the 'natural' limits of length, beam, minimum weight and actual sail area. We believed that this approach would encourage basic experiment and that the class would thus develop with least distraction into a boat which would offer 'most fun, and highest performance, within the strength of a man and a woman to handle in the water and out', which was our object. This decision was to have far-reaching consequences.

As we looked at the rigs and sails of the best of the existing classes, and considered the possibilities, three vital facts stood out:

(a)

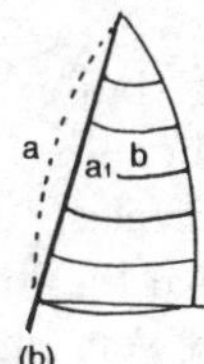

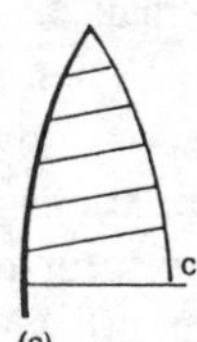

(a)
Sail flat on ground; note curve of luff. Mast naturally straight, but flexible.

(b)
Sail hoisted on mast. Cloth at *a* is moved to a_1. Sail becomes full at *b*.

(c)
Mast is bent mechanically until it matches luff curve. Upper sail becomes flat as in (a). Clew at *c* is pulled out to flatten lower sail.

Fig 17.22 Basic mechanism for controlling mainsail fullness

1. Very great advances in the design of high-lift devices for wings had transformed the aircraft industry in recent decades. Slats and flaps had been developed which could be extended when needed to form deeply curved wings with great lift capability at low speed for take-offs and approaches, and which could be tucked away to give thin blade-like wings of minimum drag for high-speed cruising flight.

2. The group included aerodynamicists, pilots, scientists and engineers who understood that if these aerodynamic advances could be adapted to sails and rigs, they would greatly increase sailboat performance.

3. Conventional sailboat design had, up to then, failed to respond in any way to these aerodynamic examples.

Those of us who were experimentally active within the group decided that our first goal would be to control the shape of our sails, so that, like birds and pilots, we could make our sails deeply curved and 'powerful' in the lighter winds and off-wind points of sailing, and flatter in the stronger winds. For years, helmsmen had changed from fuller to flatter sails on strong-wind days, but this was about as sensible as using, for the whole of any one day, only one gear of a motor car's five speed gear box. We wanted to change shape and power every time we changed our point of sailing or the wind changed strength.

Those were the earliest days of 'bendy' spars. We started by combining a flexible mast with powerful outhaul, downhaul, and vang controls, and then experimented with mast stiffness, sail cut and batten stiffness until we had developed a practical rig which could be set to any desired fullness from very full, with the mast nearly straight and the foot of the sail eased, to completely flat, with the mast bent to match the luff curve of the sail and the foot taut. (Fig. 17.22.)

Once we began to get the feel for this sort of thing, we learned that mast taper was all-important for sail shape, mast stiffness controlled the sail's 'power', and that rig springiness (which is quite different from mast stiffness) was important for sustained speed in rough-air conditions. All the time we measured, recorded and compared the mechanical properties, the absolute performance, and the race results. We quickly learned that the sloop rig was indeed faster than the cat (single-sail) rig, and began to focus on detail such as:

What was the fastest planform, i.e. How much of the allowable sail area should go into the jib?

How much should the jib leech overlap the mainsail luff?

How high up the mast should the forestay attach?

Within a few years we had optimised each factor. The class' newsletter regularly published both the static and the dynamic measurements of the winner of each major championship, and included not only the dimensional measurements of the boat, foils and rig, but also dynamic detail such as:

The wind and sea-state conditions in which the championship had been sailed.

The weight of the crew.

The static (unforced) shape of the mast-sail-batten combination, including the jib, i.e. the depth of camber near the foot, at mid-height, and near the head, and where the deepest point of the camber occurred.

The stiffness of the lower mast (butt to hounds) both fore and aft, and sideways.

The stiffness of the topmast, both fore and aft and sideways.

The rig controls, if these were innovative.

A narrative of how the boat had been handled and how the controls had been used to achieve the winning performance.

Very soon the class' builders were able to produce and duplicate mast-sail-batten combinations with stiffness and springiness figures accurately adjusted for differences in crew weight. Above all, these were rigs which enabled crews to adjust their sail shapes, easily and whilst sailing, across the whole range from very full to completely flat.

This sort of control had never previously been achieved. We had shifted responsibility for sail shape from the sailmaker to the crew. No longer was the question, 'Do you have a good heavy-weather (or whatever) sail?'. It was now, 'Do you know the fastest sail shape to set up for heavy weather?'.

In the early days, it soon became clear that crews who adjusted these rigs fluently began to sail several percent faster than those who did not . Our work was beginning to yield practical results. We were surprised, however, when we compared notes about our adjustments. The broad details were agreed, but it always seemed to be the finer detail, about which we were not yet agreed, which yielded so much of the extra speed. The more we learned, the more, it seemed, there was to learn. There was a further problem – the personal one. Different people meant slightly different things by the words 'full', 'medium', etc. We needed to develop a more precise language. But despite all this, we were sailing faster. We were having tremendous fun! It was an exciting period to enjoy sailing.

Upper tufts and leech ribbons stream
Middle tufts and leech ribbons agitate
Lower tufts and leech ribbons limp

indicate

Lower sail oversheeted
Too much twist

All tufts and leech ribbons stream
(except for those in separation bubble)

indicate

Sail trim near correct

Upper tufts and leech ribbons limp
Middle tufts and leech ribbons agitate
Lower tufts and leech ribbons stream

indicate

Upper sail oversheeted,
either
In light air - not enough twist
In breeze - upper leech 'hooked'

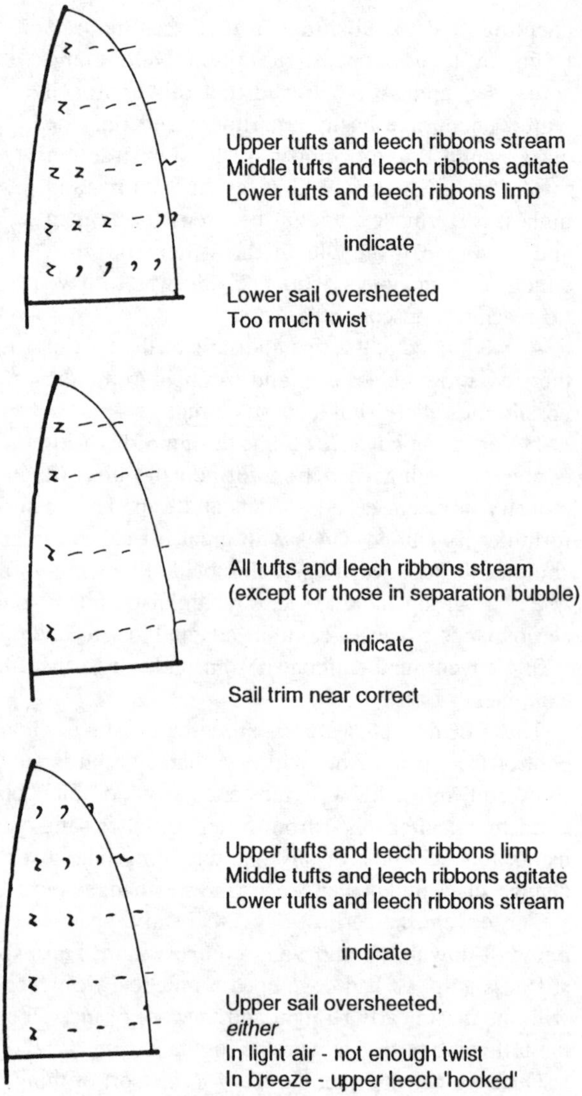

Fig 17.23 Flow patterns revealed by lee-side tufts

The next development came when an observant crew, Kevin and Angela O'Neill, noticed that a loose thread on their jib did not always stream as expected, and discussed it. This sounded strange and disturbing. Others of us fitted loose threads, and true enough, they behaved strangely. Thus were tufts (or tell-tales) born in Australia. I am advised that one of the International 14 group ('Shorty' Trimmingham?) was similarly fitting tufts to his sails in England at about the same time. We quickly learned that tufts on the jib were useful – they were beautifully accurate steering indicators.

However, we very soon realized that what the tufts were really doing was revealing the local state of the boundary layer. We fitted tufts to our mainsails, made the sails flatter and fuller, and the tufts responded with a precision which was beautiful. This lead us to the critical third step – to use the behaviour of the tufts to shape our sails, and thus to achieve, not a shape that we thought that we wanted, but the airflow pattern that we knew that we wanted. (Fig. 17.23.)

I always find it fascinating to re-read Dr Manfred Curry's book, '*The Aerodynamics of Sails*' published in 1925 more than 65 years ago, in which he described his 'experiments with down'. (We would have said 'tufts'.) Fig. 17.24 is from his book, and it shows the flow patterns he observed around sails which we would now consider a little too full, and also a little overtrimmed. When we covered the same ground 40 years later, we flattened our sails slightly and eased the trim a little, and the tufts on the suction side changed their behaviour to look like Fig. 17.25(b) – and our speed increased. Manfred Curry, for all his genius, could not alter his sails' shapes, and so could not take that simple further step.

To sum up how far we had progressed to that point:

We had learned how to adjust the shape of our sails.

We had learned how to use tufts(tell-tales).

We had learned that we could control the behaviour of the tufts (i.e. the boundary layer) by adjusting the shapes of the sails when the wind speed changed.

We had learned that those crews who adjusted their sail shapes, so that they sailed with the most powerful sails it was possible to set with the tufts still streaming smoothly, sailed faster than boats had previously sailed.

These were tremendous achievements, but we were far from finished.

We had also learned one more thing – that there was always a great area of turbulence behind the mast on both sides of the sail which we could never eliminate with any shape, try as we might. (We now know that these were the separation bubbles.) This demanded action. All our accumulating experience had lead us to believe that whenever we had revised our sail shapes to make our tufts stream smoothly by eliminating the turbulence which had previously made them agitate, we had sailed faster. If we could clean up these last stubborn areas of massive turbulence, we believed that we should be able to sail faster yet.

We decided that our next goal should be to smooth this flow. This lead us straight to wingmasts.

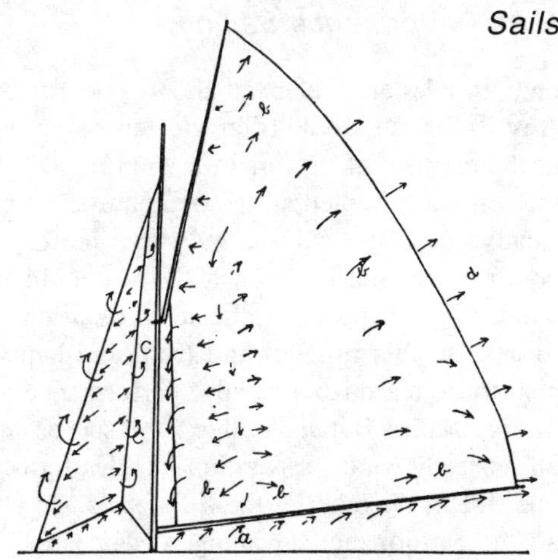

Lines of Flow on windward Side of Sail.

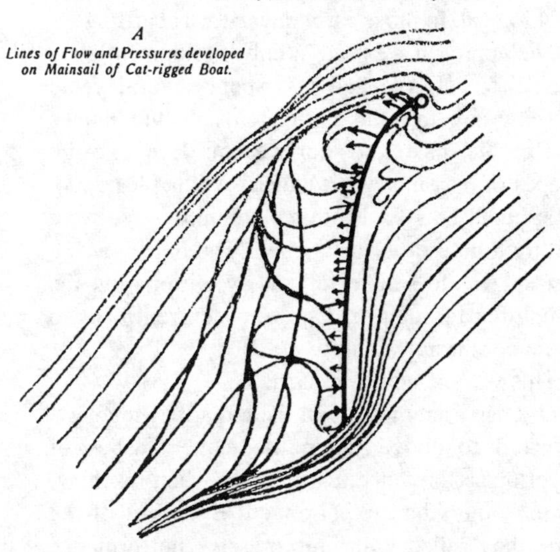

A
Lines of Flow and Pressures developed on Mainsail of Cat-rigged Boat.

Fig 17.24 Flow patterns observed by Manfred Curry in 1925

17.10 Wingmasts – early development

There was nothing new about wingmasts. However, there was everything new about the way we approached them. By 'wingmasts', we had in mind small masts so shaped and turned that they could reduce or eliminate the turbulence over the sail behind them. It was not our object to adapt glider wings.

Wingmasts, by their nature, had always tended to be small and thin across their minor axis, and long in the major axis, and so were, as a group, always very stiff in the plane of the sail. Because of this, these masts could not bend sufficiently for adjustment of sail fullness, and so the sail shape could not be much changed. As a result, the Fig. 17.13 (20 degrees), or 17.14 (15 degrees) situation, with a separation bubble on one side or the other, was the norm in practice. No matter how efficient the wingmast, the flow would be 'clean'

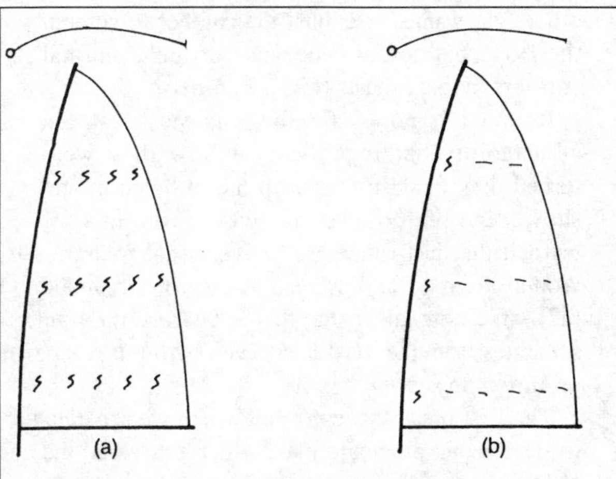

(a)
Lee side flow pattern reported as normal by Curry, (Fig 17.24).

(b)
By flattening the sail a little, and easing the sheet a little, and controlling the twist accurately, we achieved this flow pattern, and sailed faster (with round masts).

Fig 17.25 Early tuft control

Conventional round mast.
Diameter adjusted for correct flexibility, but aerodynamics are inefficient.
a_2 and a_3 are no better than a_1; because flow separates ahead of fairing.
(Refer Figs 17.6 and 17.10)

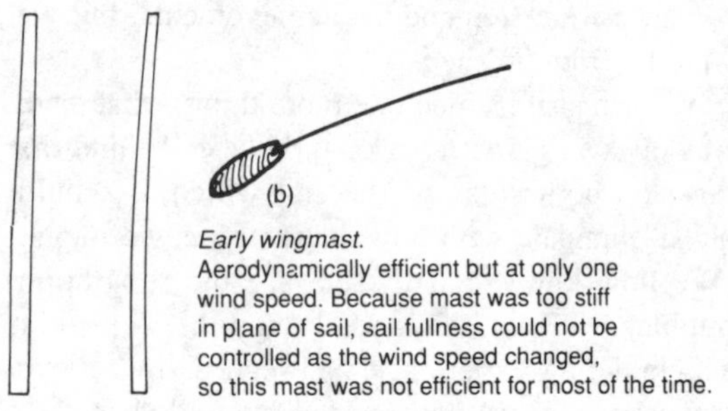

Early wingmast.
Aerodynamically efficient but at only one wind speed. Because mast was too stiff in plane of sail, sail fullness could not be controlled as the wind speed changed, so this mast was not efficient for most of the time.

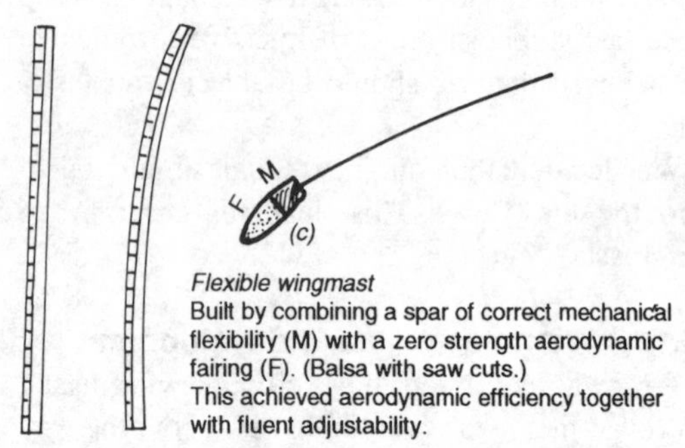

Flexible wingmast
Built by combining a spar of correct mechanical flexibility (M) with a zero strength aerodynamic fairing (F). (Balsa with saw cuts.)
This achieved aerodynamic efficiency together with fluent adjustability.

Fig 17.26 Development of flexible wingmast

on both sides of a fuller sail at only one trim angle. Any flatter sail would offer greater tolerance, but at the expense of power. In a wind tunnel, when the sail was trimmed at this optimum angle to the steady artificial wind, the measured performance could be revolutionary. On the water, in those winds which happened to be about the right speed to call for this fullness and trim, and happened also to be reasonably steady, performance could be spectacular. But at all other wind speeds, and in all unsteady winds, separation bubbles formed on one side or the other of the fuller sails and almost all the performance advantage disappeared. Now that we know about separation bubbles, it is all very logical. In those early days, it was baffling.

The approach we used in our development class was different. We had just spent several years learning how to build and match sails and battens to flexible masts, so that we could change the shapes of our sails as we sailed. We had learned a little about how to use this new ability. We were sailing a little faster as a result. The object, as we saw it, was to sail faster yet by eliminating the remaining turbulence. It never occurred to us to surrender the adjustability.

This was the new approach.

Our early attempts, with the too-stiff wingmasts referred to above, gave the same flashes of superior performance, particularly when reaching, which others had experienced. But most of the time they sailed with unimpressive performance and fluttering tufts on one side of the sail or the other. We wanted to adjust the camber to smooth the flow, but couldn't because of the abnormal stiffness of these masts (Fig. 17.26(b)).

Rounder, more flexible masts restored adjustability but regardless of how they were turned they failed to clean up the turbulence, and showed no performance increase. From this we learned that just rotating a conventional round mast – so that the leeward surface of the sail is wrapped around the mast and sweeps away from it smoothly and so 'looks' clean – is futile. (Fig. 17.26(a1) and (a2).) We now know that this is because the round mast presents too blunt a leading edge, and the flow separates from the mast itself even before it reaches the sail (in the manner of Fig. 17.10) so this approach promised no answer.

The first break-through came when we separated the mast's mechanical and aerodynamic properties. By using a round or square mast which possessed the correct flexibility but was the wrong shape, and adding light non-structural fairings to it to make it the right aerodynamic shape (Fig.17.26(c)), we were suddenly able to enjoy both the adjustability of the flexible mast and the efficiency of the wingmast. Those early rigs were too stiff, and the sails too full. Because they were so stiff, they were critical to handle, and brutes to keep adjusted to the wind's subtle changes. But those crews who persevered with them achieved unbeatable speed in almost all conditions.

A strange signal confirmed that these new rigs were indeed fundamentally different. Our fourteen foot boats had all been built with the centre case positioned so that the leading edge of the centreboard was vertical and about one foot or a little more behind the mast. As we became fluent with the new rigs the boats all developed lee helm. To correct this we cut a triangle off the aft top of the centreboard, so that we could angle the tip forward under the boat to restore balance. This forward movement of a foot or more of the centreboard tip was needed to balance the powerful new suction close behind the mast! We now know that with a good wingmast rig the leading edge of the centreboard needs to be within about two inches of the mast.

We were on our way.

The steps which followed were all pure development, mixed with a little invention, and spanned several years.

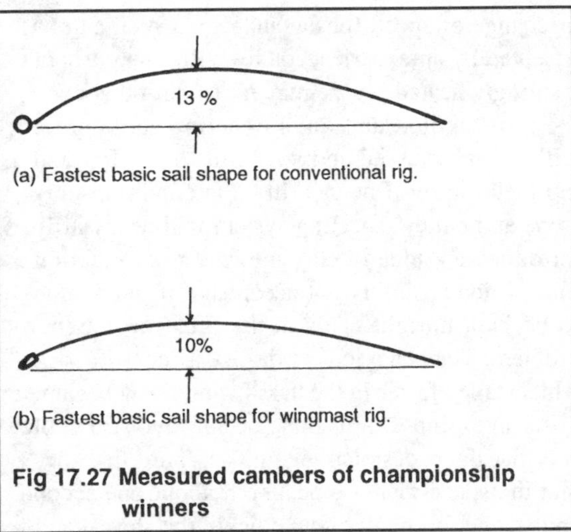
13 %
(a) Fastest basic sail shape for conventional rig.
10%
(b) Fastest basic sail shape for wingmast rig.

Fig 17.27 Measured cambers of championship winners

17.11 The modern wingmast

We had already established that the fastest light and medium air shape for a conventional sail is about 13% camber. We learned, little by little, that the fastest camber for a wingmast sail is about 10% (Fig. 17.27). Of this 10%, the rotated mast contributes about 2%, and so the sail itself need add only another 8%. Once we had developed a 'feel' for this optimum shape, we soon arrived at a mast-sail-batten combination which adopted this shape naturally when sailing, and was easy to adjust around it. No wonder those early rigs with their far-too-full sails had been such brutes to adjust!

From this base, we experimented. Stiffer masts with flatter-cut sails were not very adjustable, but could sail fast with a slack sheet and without becoming too full in light airs. They were also very fast in strong winds. But in the medium-wind range, and when sailing across the wind, they lacked power, and were slow.

Very flexible masts with much fuller sails gave rigs which were fluently adjustable in shape, but had to be sailed with almost constant sheet tension, regardless of wind strength, otherwise the sail would become much too flat or too full. As a result, they were slow in light airs because they were either too full (with sheet slack) or twisted the wrong way, (sheet tighter). In cool steady winds these rigs would have one particular wind speed at which their performance was superior. At all other wind speeds performance was well below optimum, except in two cases. These rigs were invariably fast when sailing across the wind. Also, whenever the wind became hot and rough and the gusts harsh, these were the rigs which were not only most pleasant to handle, but were often the fastest. In these conditions it seemed that their soft elasticity more than compensated for all their other shortcomings. This lesson was not lost, and lead later to the development of 'two-mode' mainsail control.

The next step was to combine the best features of both rigs. We combined sails of moderate fullness with masts of moderate stiffness, together with battens in the upper sail which were just stiff enough to flatten the naturally fuller sail to the flatter camber which operated super-critically and was fastest for light airs. The camber of the lower sail was controlled by the outhaul. These rigs proved to have all the desirable properties. In light airs the upper sail would automatically adopt the correct camber, and this was as true when sailing cross-wind and down-wind as when close-hauled. We call this arrangement an 'active batten' rig. In moderate winds, aerodynamic suction and pressure flexed the upper battens fuller for optimum 'power'. When the crew needed a flatter sail again in the stronger winds, either severe sheet and downhaul tension, or use of a powerful vang, or some combination of both would bend the mast and flatten the upper sail as desired. (Crews of yachts with fractional rigs were quick to adopt this technique – except that they use backstay tension instead of vang.) The lower sail's battens were softer, and its fullness was controlled directly by the outhaul. This arrangement, with an active batten upper mainsail, and a fully battened but 'passive' lower mainsail, we call a 'composite' rig.

As we gained experience, we became aware of the difference between 'gust factor' and 'gust onslaught'. A wandering breeze may have a three to one gust factor, but it all happens slowly, and poses no control problem. The gusts of a cool turbulent breeze increase their speed from lull to gust much faster, but at a rate of change of speed (onslaught rate) which can be accepted by an experienced crew. But the gusts of a strongly heated breeze may hit so hard that even the most skilled and quick-reacting sailboarder will be embarrassed and will shift to a softer and more elastic rig if he can. In these conditions any 'rope and pulley' sheeting system will necessarily introduce an added delay into the total reaction time which is simply not acceptable if the boat is to be kept upright. This is the 'gust onslaught' problem. The behaviour of those earlier 'soft' rigs which sailed faster in the harsh winds now became explainable.

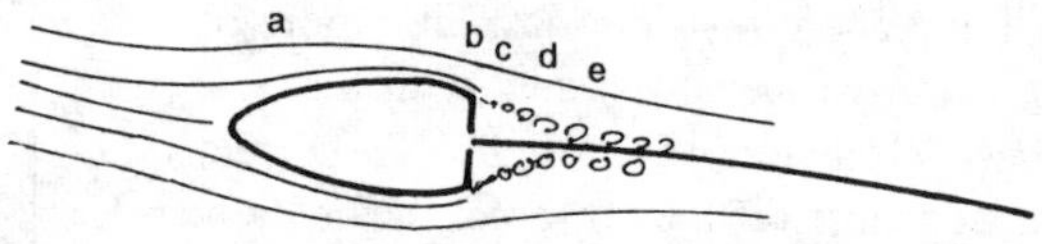

a Flow accelerates over shaped wingmast -
b is turned inwards -
c and is separated from the knife edge.
d The free shear layer becomes turbulent -
e and immediately re-attaches, turbulent, to the sail.

Fig 17.28 Mechanism of trip turbulator on modern wingmast

As an example let us imagine a heated strong breeze, with lulls of about 10 knots, gusts of say 25 knots, and that the occasional gust hits so hard that the 'rate of change of speed' – the 'gust onslaught' is such that the speed increase occurs in about one second. In these conditions a boat with a 'hard' rig will heel and stagger no matter how quickly the sheet-hand responds – and a reaction time of one third of a second is at the quick end of human capability. The time taken by the boom and its machinery to start to move outwards is added to the basic 0.3 second response time of the crew, and the practical situation is that the rig remains sheeted hard for the first half-second or so of the gust's peak speed, and the boat heels uncontrollably. But if an adjacent boat has a 'soft' rig which yields easily, the rig will yield a little and almost instantaneously. The practical effect of this is that the crew have about another half second within which to react before the boat begins to heel significantly, and this is long enough for a smart crew to free the sheet and so 'keep the boat on its feet' even through gust onslaughts like that. Another major advantage is that the yielded sail drives forward more, and so drives the boat faster.

Once we reached the understanding that 'hard' rigs were fastest in steady winds, but 'soft' rigs were fastest in the harsh gusty stuff, it was only a matter of time before somebody came up with another bright idea. One innovative designer had already developed a traveller control system in which the traveller track was curved upwards at the ends to compensate for the lengthening of the standing part of the mainsheet from floor block to boom block as the boom swung out. This gave a boom movement which remained horizontal when the sheet was cleated and the traveller was played. Because the boom could not lift at all, this arrangement gave the 'hard' rig which sailed fastest in the steadier airs. We soon found that if we reversed the technique and cleated the traveller well to windward and played the mainsheet the boom could then rise against a tensed vang, and the rig, handled that way, would be springy and 'soft' and sailed fastest in the harsh winds. Intermediate positions of the cleated traveller to give a more vertical mainsheet provided intermediate elasticity. We had added control of elasticity to our handling techniques.

As these primary factors came under control, and superior moderate and strong wind performance in all wind and sea-state conditions began to be achieved, a problem was recognised at the other end of the wind-speed range. The substantial fall-off in performance caused by sub-critical flow in light airs became evident and was recognised for what it was. A variety of trip turbulators were tried and found useful. The final solution was beautiful in its simplicity. By shaping the mast as in Fig. 17.28, and rotating it until it faces the Apparent Wind, the on-coming wind is split by a leading edge of the optimum radius to preserve low-speed efficiency without knife-edge separation. The flow is then accelerated as the section thickens (Kitchen Experiment 17.5). It is then gently turned inwards and abruptly separated from the knife edges while it is still moving fast. The free shear layers thus formed are unstable and become turbulent immediately. Almost immediately thereafter they meet the sail's surface and re-attach, fully turbulent. In this way we achieved the advantages of a 'trip' turbulator without any of the drag penalties of a normal 'trip'. Adoption of this knife-edge square-back mast section greatly increased the very light air 'power' of these wingmast rigs.

Rigs of this type soon became dominant. With experience, we optimised the mast stiffness, sail fullness, and batten stiffnesses which were fastest for each weight of crew – and suddenly found ourselves in possession of rigs which were completely adjustable mechanically, and reasonably efficient aerodynamically provided that they were adjusted correctly. Not only the increased efficiency, but also the need to adjust, was something new in sailing.

Prior to these rigs, crews necessarily had to 'make do' as best they could with relatively inefficient rigs with little adjustment capability. Because the rigs were inefficient, adjustment was relatively ineffective – no amount of fiddling can ever get rid of the separation bubbles behind a conventional mast. It was therefore widely believed that the ability to adjust was not important and not needed by top-level crews.

What we had done was to lift the efficiency of the rigs, but this was achievable if and only if the rigs were correctly adjusted. We had removed all limits to adjustment – we could now get whatever sail shape and elasticity we wanted – but we had introduced the new need to adjust, because the new rigs were no better than the old ones unless they were properly adjusted.

Without realising it, we had with this change lifted sailing to a new level. Handling these rigs in the myriad different wind and wave conditions has become the new challenge. As the years have passed and we have learned progressively more about the different patterns adopted by the wind and the waves, so we have increased our knowledge about which are the fastest sail shapes and elasticities and handling techniques to use through each. As we have learned more, so have we continued to share our knowledge, and to increase our fleet speeds relative to conventional 'benchmark' fleets. As we have learned, we have enjoyed our sailing more. Nobody suggests that there is not still more to be learned and enjoyed.

A look at the differences

Figs 17.29 to 17.33 show something of the forces and flow patterns around conventional rigs, and the different forces and flows achieved by the new rigs.

The pressure distribution diagrams of Figs 17.2 and 17.3 are from standard aerodynamic reference texts. Those of Figs 17.7, 17.8, and 17.15 are measurements from my own wind tunnels (there were three in all). Fig. 17.29 is from a report by Stuart Wilkinson of the Ship Science Dept. of Southampton University, and shows how the same diagrams appear when they are produced more elegantly by modern techniques.

In the top left hand figure of 17.29, the line 'A' to 'B' represents the mast and sail, with the mast at 'A' and the leech at 'B'. The suction diagram above 'AB' is the same as the suction diagram 'gghjk' in Fig. 17.7, but in Fig. 17.29 it relates to a 100 inch sail of 12.5% camber set behind a mast 1.03 inches in diameter and trimmed at 2.5 degrees in a 15 knot wind (or a 50 inch sail in a 30 knot wind, or a 200 inch sail in a 7.5 knot wind). The diagram above the line 'CD' shows the different suctions when the sail is trimmed at 10 degrees. The solid diagram between 'AB' and 'CD' shows how the suctions change as the trim changes from 2.5 degrees to 10 degrees. The top right hand diagram shows this same solid diagram when viewed from another angle – 'A1-B1' repeats 'AB', and 'C1-D1' repeats 'CD', etc.

The lower two diagrams are exactly the same in principle, but the mast diameter has in this case been increased from 1.03% to 18.2% of the chord.

I have labelled the zones and the features of the suction diagrams exactly as they are labelled in Fig. 17.7. A point of interest in the diagram between 'EF' and 'GH' is the way the reattachment zone 'd' and the second separation point 'f' drift together as the trim angle is increased, and how this diagram shows this feature more vividly than diagrams 'a', 'b' and 'c' in Fig 17.8.

Fig. 17.30 shows the balance, model holder, end plates and a sail with one of the 8 masts in position which we used for our '2' x 2'' project in 1969. We arranged the use of Sydney University's Department of Aeronautical Engineering's big wind tunnel, but ran it at so slow a speed that we had to make our own special balance to measure the small forces accurately.

The background to this was our search for some way to eliminate that stubborn turbulence which we had found behind the mast-sail junction with conventional masts. For about a year we had been systematically reducing this turbulence over a model sail by evolving progressively 'better' mast shapes and observing the results in a simple and practical way. We had made a model holder which would hold a model sail 2 feet square between end plates which kept the flow over it reasonably straight. We mounted this on an arm long enough to run it through 'clean' air, and set it at controlled angles out of the window of a car. We found a supermarket parking lot which was well lighted but deserted on weekend nights, and which happened to be bordered by weeping willows which revealed even the slightest movement of air. On nights when the air was still we made runs the length of the lot at 11.5 and 23 miles per hour – (10 and 20 knots respectively). A two foot sail at 20 knots develops the same flows and forces as a 4 foot sail at 10 knots, and this was the speed range which interested us. Fine thread tufts on both sides of the sail revealed the turbulence exactly. The tufts were staggered so that the shadows from the backlighted tufts were clear and unambiguous. It was

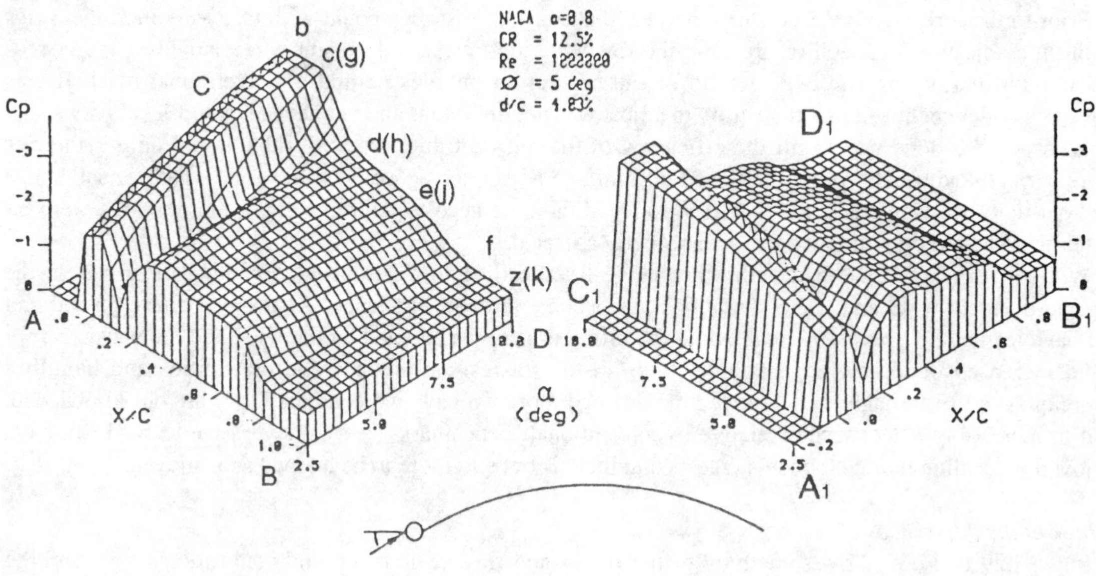

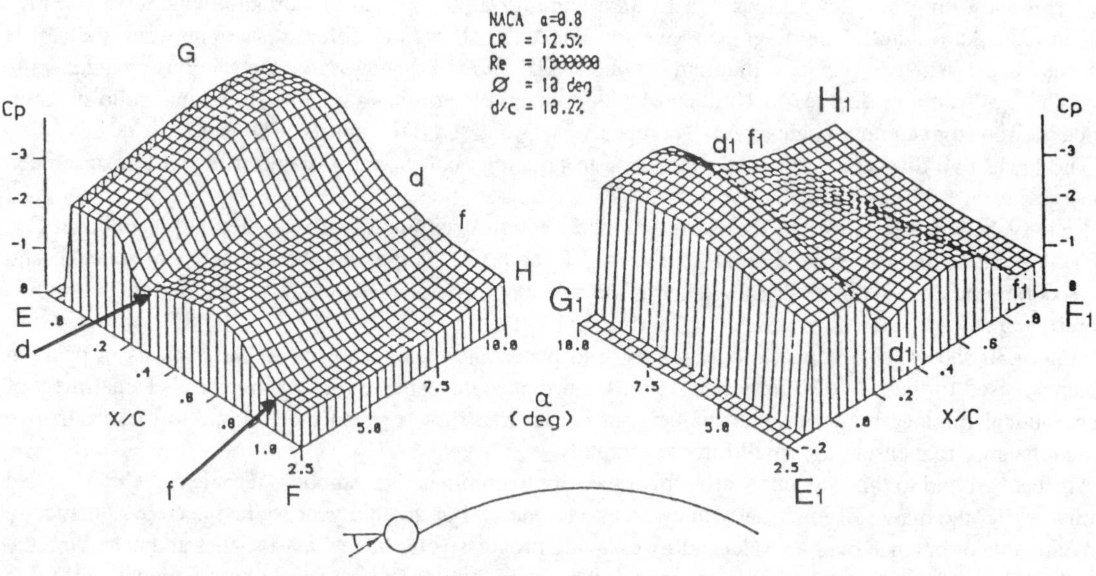

Fig 17.29 Diagram from *Investigations into 2D Mast/Sail Interaction* by Dr Stuart Wilkinson, Ship Science Dept., University of Southampton

Fig 17.30 Model and balance in wind tunnel

all very practical and after several months of work we had managed to eliminate the turbulence almost completely. We now wanted to measure the forces so that we could know what differences we had achieved and whether what we had done would enable us to sail faster. We could think of no simple and practical way in which we could extend the convenient 'car' technique to let us measure forces with sufficient accuracy to compare small differences. The tunnel was available. It was time to use it.

Dr Pat Smith, a scientist in our group, ran the tunnel. Colin Thorne and Charles Mansfield, both engineers, between them designed, built and calibrated the balance. Colin and Pat produced the report '*Wind Tunnel Tests on a 2' x 2' Rig*'. I had made all the models and the model holder. I modified the holder to fit onto the balance so that we could use the same models in the tunnel. It was pure amateur enthusiasm, professional science and tremendous fun. The wind speed chosen gave a Reynolds number of 300,000, which is about right for a four foot chord dinghy sail in 10 knots of breeze. (Wilkinson chose 1,000,000, which is more in the yacht range of an 8 foot sail in 15 knots.) To arrive at the lift and the drag forces, we measured the drag at each angle of the model holder and end plates without any mast and sail, and subtracted these drags from those measured with the masts and sail in place. Apart from this, the forces plotted are as measured. The left hand and bottom scales are in coefficient form – refer to the note 'Some useful figures' at the end of this chapter.

Fig. 17.31 shows the properties of a sail set behind a conventional round mast. The sail was 24 inches from luff to leech, cambered 1.6 inches (7%), and set behind a round mast one inch in diameter (4%). The dashed line 'C-D' shows how the crosswind force (lift) increases as the trim angle increases to a maximum of 1.23 (left hand scale) at 25 degrees (top scale). The drag force associated with each lift is shown by the solid curve A-B.

The inset diagram which shows the zones, demonstrates how the separation bubble (R) plus the reattachment zone (U) over the pressure surface, cover most of the sail at small trim angles, but become smaller and vanish at an angle of about 18 degrees.

On the suction surface the reverse happens. At small angles the separation bubble and reattachment zone are small but they grow quickly and progressively until by 25 degrees the whole of the suction side flow is disturbed.

As one lot of turbulence grows the other gets smaller, but there is no trim angle at which this rig is clear of turbulence. Between the mast and the leech this rig always stops or reverses a lot of air. This is exactly what a spinnaker does in order to drive a boat downwind. Downwind force is drag, and the drag of this entirely conventional rig is high simply because it slows, stops or reverses so much air at all trim angles.

Fig. 17.32 shows the very different flows and forces from the same sail at the same camber in the same breeze but set behind one of the experimental wingmasts. The lift force increases to a maximum of 1.46, nearly 20% more than the conventional rig. This gives faster sailing when maximum sail force is needed, as in patches of light air

The inset diagram which shows the zones is completely different from that of Fig 17.31

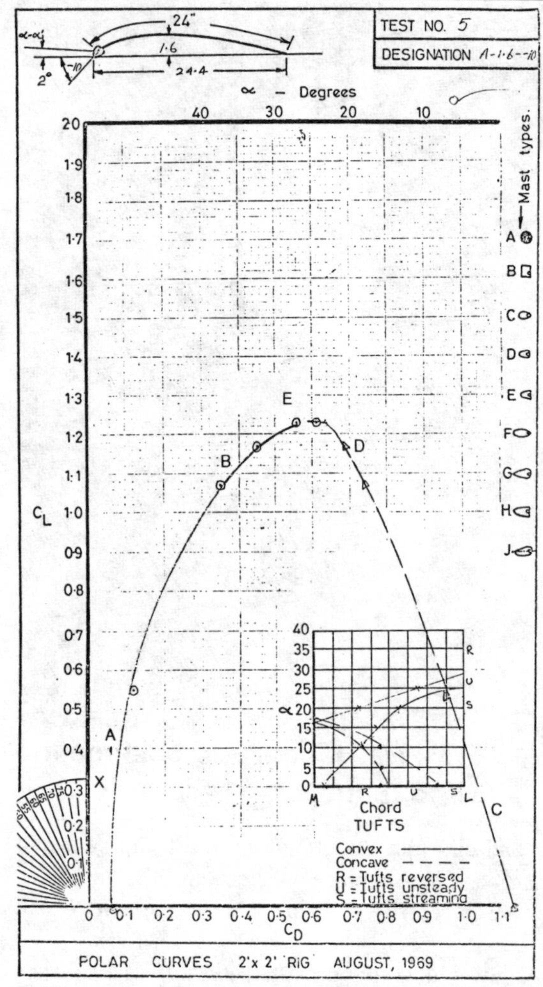

Fig 17.31 Round mast set at -10° to sail of 7% camber

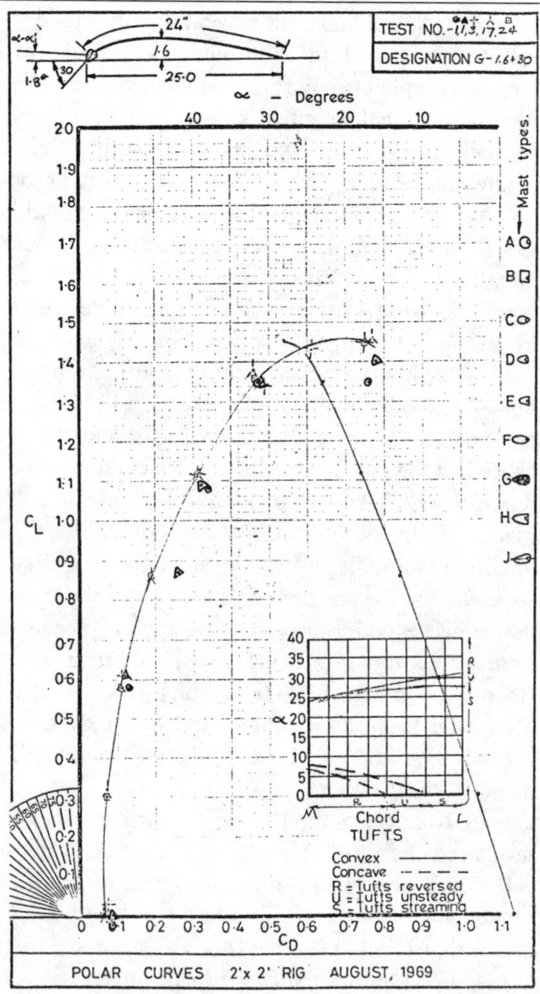

Fig 17.32 Mast type G set at 30° to sail of 7% camber

The designation gives the mast type (at the right of each page), its angle (diagram top left) and the sail camber. I have repeated this information in the title at the foot of the diagram.

In each diagram the solid curve A-B is the plot of the lift (crosswind force}, given on the left hand scale as CL (coefficient of lift), and the drag (downwind force) which is given on the bottom scale as CD (coefficient of drag)

The higher this curve, the greater is the crosswind force, and the faster the boat will sail on all points of sailing up to the design wind for that point of sailing.

The further to the left, the less is the drag, and the higher the boat will point in all winds when sailing close-hauled, and the faster it will sail in all Apparent Winds from forward of the beam.

The dashed curve C-D is the plot of the lift against the angle of attack (trim angle of the sail to the Apparent Wind) which is given in the top scale in degrees.

To keep the two curves A-B and C-D well separated, the drag scale at the bottom increases from left to right, while the angle of attack scale at the top increases from right to left.

Some useful notes about coefficients are given at the end of this chapter.

The inset diagrams show how the behaviour of the boundary layer changes as the angle of attack (left hand scale of inset) is increased from 0 degrees to 40 degrees. The edge of the inset marked 'M' represents the mast, and 'L' the leech. The solid lines show how the boundaries between the areas where the tufts stream (S), are unsteady (agitate) (U), or are reversed or limp (R) on the convex side of the sail change as the angle of attack is increased. The dashed lines give the same information for the concave (pressure) side of the sail.

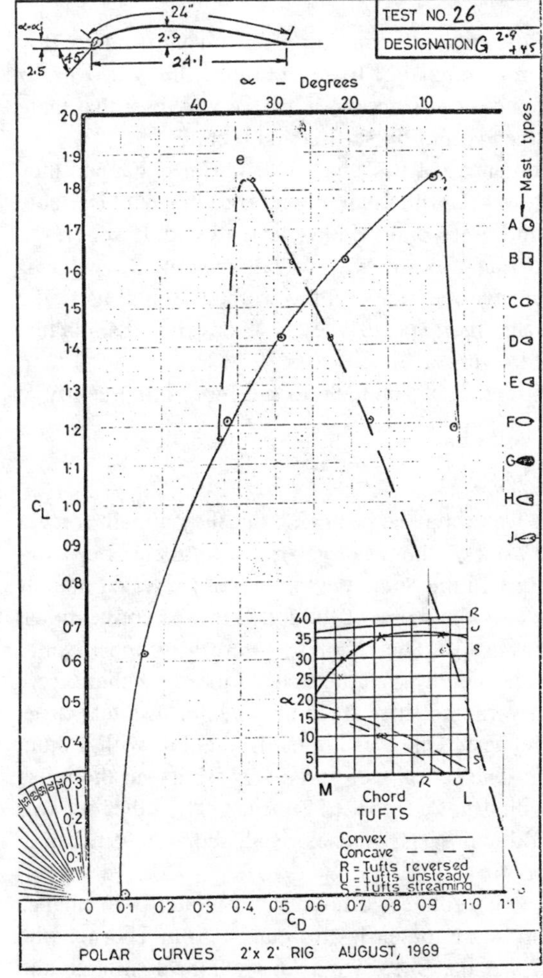

Fig 17.33 Mast type G set at 45° to sail of 12% camber

The 'R' areas show the sizes of the separation bubbles.

The 'U' areas show the extent of the re-attachment zones.

The 'S' areas show where the sails are working efficiently with attached flow.

The information in these insets greatly extends the scope of the information given in finer detail in Fig 17.29.

Between 7 and 25 degrees this rig runs turbulence-free. Because it stops little air, its drag is consistently less than the drags shown in Fig 17.31. At the trim angles typically used when sailing to windward in strong, medium and lighter breezes, the drag of the wingmast rig measures less than the drag of the conventional rig by 15%, 23% and 28% respectively. This advantage would be expected to appear as the ability to point higher at the same speed in light to moderate winds, or to windward plane higher and sooner in stronger winds, and this is exactly what we had found on the water.

It does not help very much to increase the camber of sails behind conventional masts, because the separation bubbles leak almost all the extra suction away.

The situation behind wingmasts is very different. Fig. 17.33 shows the forces developed by a sail cambered at 12% set behind a wingmast. At small trim angles the drag is very high because of all the air which is stopped or reversed in the huge separation bubble on the pressure side. Such sails are useless for sailing to windward. But as the large trim angles used for reaching are approached the flow cleans up on both sides of the sail, and the maximum crosswind force achievable is 1.84, or about 50% greater than that able to be developed by a sail behind a conventional mast. This is the secret of the fast reaching speeds of wingmast-equipped dinghies and catamarans. It is achievable if and only if the sail is both deeply cambered and correctly trimmed and set almost completely free from twist. Note that inaccuracy, such as slight overtrimming, will lose one third of the drive force.

Nobody suggests that we cannot do better. The leading-edge slatted and double-slotted flapped wings of many big aircraft can achieve lift coefficients approaching 3 on final approach, so we can sail faster yet if we are prepared to do the work.

These three diagrams between them summarise, with measured numbers, most of what we had observed, and most of the work that we had done, over the previous ten years. We had reduced the going-to-windward drag by 20%. We had increased the off-wind drive force by 50%. We had greatly increased the speed of our boats. We had not been wasting our time.

But the benefits are only for those who are prepared to adjust their sails to the right shape and the right twist and to trim them to the right angles as they sail. It will take a long time before this is properly appreciated, particularly by top-level sailors from conventional classes.

An example:

At the first Tasar world championships in 1981, two of the entrants were Terry Neilson and Andrew Roy who were shortly to become world Laser champion and runner-up. In my opinion the world Laser championship is the hardest championship of all to win, and those who win it are the very best that there are. So when Terry and Andrew entered, I assumed that they would finish first and second.

They didn't. In each race they started well, and moved ahead at first, but as conditions changed they faded. I was Race Director at that regatta, and was able to speak with them in a relaxed manner. To quote Terry – 'Sure, we can sail. But we have been practising in Lasers, and we have teamed with Laser crews, and because we change nothing in Lasers we thought that was the way to sail to win. But what is happening in these boats is that as soon as conditions change the men and the women around us fiddle with their rigs, and there is nothing we can then do to match their speed. They have developed skills that we do not have, and we had better learn them if we want to win'.

So there it is. With these new rigs the performance is there, but you have to sail more intelligently to get it. Be alert, be accurate, or be last.

This is the new challenge.

It is worth recording that the ways of the wind and the water may be beautiful, but they remain forever complex and they can still lay traps for the unwary. Our work on the water generally paralleled our work ashore as reported above. But two of us still fell into a trap. In the Sydney wind tunnel we tested models of eight mast shapes. One was square. This was undoubtedly the worst of the lot. One was conventional round. This was so bad we were committed to improving it. The other six were all experimental wingmast shapes, intended to be rotated to whatever angle should prove fastest. Of these six there were two each of three basic shapes. One shape was blunt forward and finer aft in the manner of a tear-drop. One was ovoid except that aft it was cut slightly 'squareback'. One was almost triangular, with a blunt point forward, and an exaggerated squareback shape aft. One set of each three was 'short' in the sense that the fore and aft dimension of the full scale mast would not exceed 2.75 inches. The other set was 'long' in the sense that the fore and aft dimension would approach 4 inches. Both sets would finish at about 1.75 inches wide.

When the results were all in, the ovoid 'short' mast, when rotated, offered wind tunnel performance figures about as good as any other. It was certainly going to be the easiest to make. Colin Thorne, who was the group's theoretician, immediately said, 'Let's make one'. I may be a lateral thinker and innovative, but I am a pragmatist, and had my doubts. But I felt obliged, so I said 'Let's make two', and did. One went onto Colin's boat and one onto mine. There followed months of frustration. Occasionally it flew. Usually it floundered. Colin persevered. I seethed. Finally, I broke and fitted a 'long squareback' which was the other mast to perform superbly in the tunnel. I couldn't hold the boat. At the next State championships, Julian and I won five firsts and a second from a hundred boat fleet. It wasn't all due to the mast but it sure helped.

We performed a post-mortem. The problem was another manifestation of being 'over-critical'. At its best, the suspect mast – the short ovoid – was good. But it needed only a little variation in the angle at which the wind arrived – a little gust or backwind – to separate the flow, and once separated it wouldn't easily re-attach. This had not been a problem in the smooth wind of the tunnel, but was obviously an important consideration in the unsteady winds of the real world. The long squareback was a dream. You couldn't shake it. No matter how it was upset, efficient flow immediately re-established. That was the difference.

Years later, demand outran our ability to hand-make wooden spars, and I needed to design a 'short' section for alloy extrusion. I re-ran the wind tunnel programme for many months to optimise the leading edge radius, the position of the maximum width, and the shape ahead of the knife edges, and my sole criterion was 'tolerance'. I tried the most tolerant section in timber. It worked. I paid much fine gold to have the three dies for the sleeving sections made, and tried the result. Despite being 'short' it works, and superbly. It ought to. We didn't arrive at that shape quickly, or without thought.

Fig. 17.34 looks at these different flows in another way. In this case an 8 inch balsa 'mainsail' and a 4 inch 'jib', both cambered at 10%, are mounted in one of my wind tunnels. They are set at an angle to the wind as if the boat were beam reaching. The airspeed is about 15 knots, and smoke plumes are being

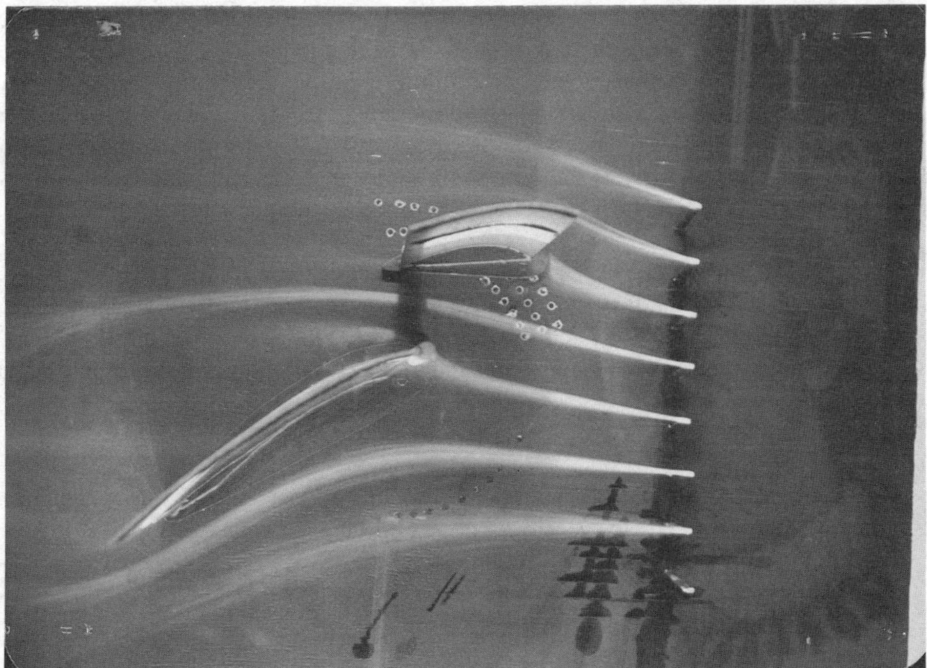

(a)

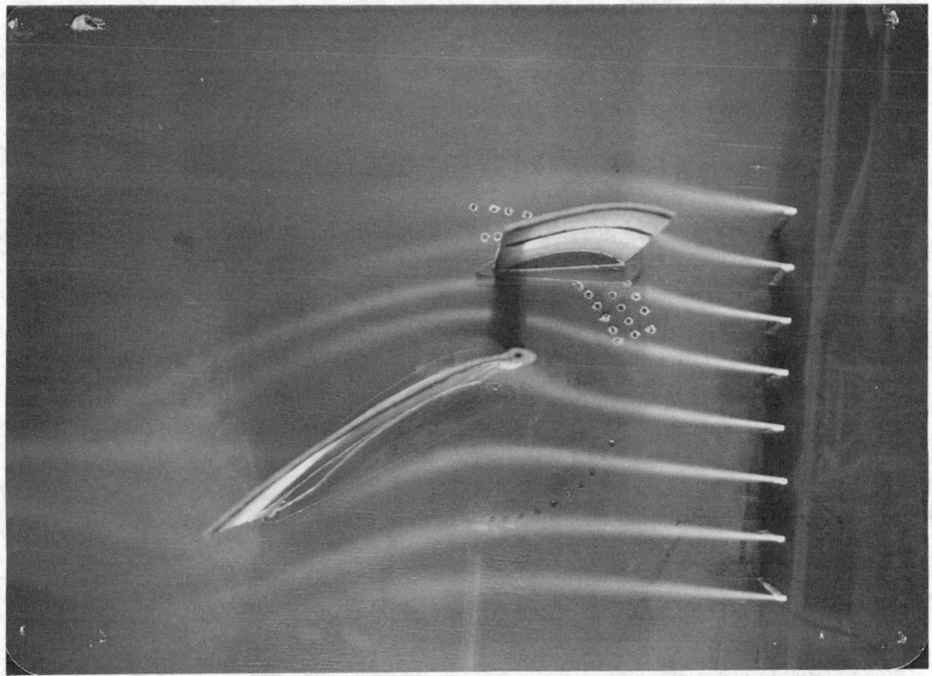

(b)

Settings and speeds are identical in both pictures, except:-
(a) Has round mast
(b) Has wing mast

In (a) Flow is separated from both jib and mainsail.
in (b) Flow remains attached to both jib and mainsail.

Fig 17.34 Model of jib and mainsail in wind tunnel

introduced into the flow so that we can see where the air goes. All settings are identical as between the two photographs, except that there is a round mast fitted in the top photograph, and one of the new short squareback wingmast sections in the lower. In the upper picture the flow has separated from the leeward side of the mainsail – it is streaming off to the left nearly horizontally. In the lower picture it is still attached, and the smoke plumes show the flow still following the leeward (suction) surface of the mainsail. What we see here is the new short shape at work, and also that the presence of a jib does nothing to correct the fundamental inefficiency of a conventional mast.

Coefficients and Reynolds numbers – some useful figures.

When we measured the forces on the model sail in the wind tunnel, we could have stated that 'At 10 degrees of trim, the crosswind force was 3.82 pounds'. This is nice and simple, but not very useful. You, the reader, might wonder what the force might have been yesterday, when that gust hit, and want to work it out.

Coefficients

By reducing the forces to coefficients, anybody can work out a force by using the formula:

Force = Coefficient x Area x Density x Speed x Speed. (The density of water is 1.0).

Force is in pounds.

Area is in square feet.

Speed is in feet per second.

Let us work out two examples.

1. A rudder blade has an area of 2 square feet, is moving at 10 knots through the water, and is angled at 5 degrees to the flow. What will be its drag?

From Fig. 19.1, the coefficient of drag of either section at 5 degrees is about 0.006.

One knot is about 1.69 feet per second.

Density of water is 1.0.

So:

Drag Force = (0.006 x 2 x 1 x 16.9 x 16.9) pounds = 3.42 pounds.

2. A dinghy with a sail area of 123 square feet and a wingmast rig is sailing to windward at 5 knots in a 12 knot True Wind, with its sails trimmed at 17.5 degrees to the Apparent Wind. What is the total crosswind force from its sails?

The density of air at sea level averages 0.0012. (This is roughly one thousandth that of water.)

The speed of the Apparent Wind will be 15.95 knots (= 26.95 ft per sec).

From Fig. 17.32 the coefficient of lift at 17.5 degs will be 1.1.

So:

Force = (1.1 x 123 x 0.0012 x 26.95 x 26.95) = 117.9 pounds

Those two examples should take most of the mystery out of coefficients.

Reynolds number

Technically, this represents the ratio of momentum compared with viscosity. Low numbers approach viscous flow.

For practical purposes, when you see a Reynolds number quoted, you can bring it down to a windspeed across your sails, or a water speed across your centreboard, by using the VL (Velocity times Length) number used for decades by model aeroplane designers:

VL 1.0 = RN 4,700 (in air at sea level) and = RN 61,000 (in water).

V = Velocity in feet per second.

L = Length – Chord – distance in the direction of flow – in feet.

The same two examples:

1. The rudder blade would have a chord of about 8 inches, or .67 feet.
   So:
   RN = 16.9 (ft per sec) x 0.67 (ft) x 61,000 = about 700,000.
2. The rig of 123 square feet is 20 feet high, so has an average chord of about 5 feet.
   So:
   RN = 26.95 x 5 x 4,700 = about 650,000.

And that should take the mystery out of Reynolds numbers.

The ability of tear-drop shape wing sections to generate high crossflow forces begins to collapse below Reynolds numbers of about 500,000. Provided that big crossflow forces are not needed, they are still superbly efficient as low-drag shapes, and are therefore used for centreboards and rudder blades.

Two of the Author's wind tunnels. Following the 'car' work and the Sydney University Tunnel measurements (Figs 17.30 - 34), three tunnels were built. The first was temporary and flimsy but demonstrated usefulness and provided a sound design base for the second, which was used for refining the 'long' wingmast shapes and also for learning more about jib - mainsail interaction with wingmast rigs. The third smaller tunnel followed some years later - it possessed a wider speed range and also a useful level-of-airflow-roughness range was used intitially to develop the tolerant 'short' wingmast shapes now used on the Tasar.

Chapter Eighteen
Rigs

18.1 The four rig groups

The natural life of a great class appears to be about thirty to forty years. Sometimes it is longer – for example, the Snipe and the Star classes both date from the 1930's. Any discussion of 'modern' rigs must therefore include at least the life-span of classes now sailing, i.e. the last 50 years.

During this period, rigs have changed profoundly. The changes have fallen into four easily recognisable groups.

The first group includes the gaff and gunter rigs which were almost universally used in the 1920's and early 30's. For example, both the Snipe and the Star started their lives with gunter rigs. Their one-piece-mast Bermudan rigs were in each case introduced as a mid-life rule change. Gaff rigs were surprisingly adjustable. But strangely, the literature of the period almost never discusses adjustment of sail shape – it was one of those things which seemed to be taken for granted.

The second group comprises the early Bermudan rigs which were adopted almost universally in the late 1930's to the 50's. These rigs were almost totally non-adjustable. The only way of setting up a sail of different shape was to buy a different sail. As a result, the fad of chasing sailmakers for multiple sails of slightly different shapes became common.

The third group includes all the early experiments with different ways to adjust the shapes of Bermudan mainsails while sailing, together with a growing knowledge of the importance of dynamic response.

The fourth group are the highly developed modern rigs. In different classes the mechanical arrangements and the adjustment techniques are often different, but outstanding rigs are all characterised by three properties, namely:

1. The rig tends to change the shape of the sails in the right manner as the wind speed increases or decreases slowly.

2. As the wind speed, sea-state condition and point of sailing change, the crew can adjust the rig, simply and easily, to the exact sail shape and elasticity that they need.

3. The rigs' short-term dynamic response to gusts, and particularly to the harsh onslaught of the gusts of rough winds, is either naturally 'fast' or can be adjusted to be fast.

Rigs which combine these three properties represent the current state of the art. They cannot yet begin to match the lift-to-drag efficiency of the best long, slender, flexible, glider wings, in which the dynamic response to gust is to yield but with a subtle momentary twist in the 'fast' sense. There is no reason why our rigs cannot be developed further and become much more efficient yet. Speeds approaching those of ice yachts should ultimately be achievable on the water.

But, as they stand, the best of the modern rigs are incomparably more efficient than anything the world has previously seen. The astonishing increase in both the fastest 'dash' speeds achieved by sailboards, and the near doubling of 'round the buoys' speed achievable by the fastest skiffs are the best indicators of just how significant have been the advances in rig efficiencies in recent decades.

18.2 Group one – gaff rigs

The essential point about a gaff rig was that the angle between the gaff and the mast could be adjusted. In practice, this gave exactly the same control of shape of the sail as a modern flexible mast. When the gaff was set nearer vertical, the leech of the sail was drawn forward toward the mast, and so the sail set fuller. As the head of the gaff was permitted to fall progressively away from the mast, the sail set progressively flatter. The limit was reached when a girt – a tension line in the fabric – developed between clew and throat. If the gaff were then eased even further, the sailcloth aft of and above the girt flapped loosely. This was a very convenient emergency way to 'depower' in an unexpected squall, but the abnormal stretching along the girt did the sail no good at all. (Fig. 18.1)

Modern synthetic sail cloths date from the 1960's. In the days of gaff rigs, sails were made from cotton or other natural fibres. These stretched with use. They stretched during any prolonged race in a brisk wind. As the hours passed slackness and wrinkles developed and it was customary to 'twitch up the halyards to take out the stretch'.

It is interesting to look at this practice from a modern standpoint. Because crews were committed to constantly adjusting their throat halyard, peak halyard and outhaul tensions to compensate for stretch and to keep the sail 'looking right', they in fact adjusted their sails fuller in lighter winds because this 'looked right' – and flatter as the breeze increased. Nothing appears in the literature about deliberate adjustment of shape. It is all about how to handle stretch. But gaff rigs were fluently adjustable and were in fact continually adjusted whilst sailing. People just didn't talk about it!

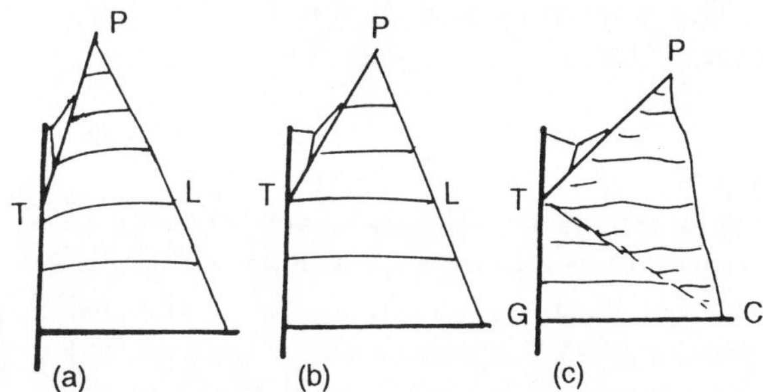

(a) Peak P drawn forward: sail becomes fuller T - L
(b) Peak dropped slightly: " " flatter T - L
(c) Peak dropped further : sail girts across T - C
" sets firmly TCG
" streams TCP

Fig 18.1 Basic adjustability of gaff rig

Gaff rigs possessed two other subtle but major advantages. The optimum shape for a wing or sail is elliptical. The tapered quadrilateral shape of a gaff rig approximates an ellipse more closely than does any triangle. For this reason good gaff rigs proved much more efficient to windward than might be expected. Their second advantage has to do with the fact that when the leading edge of a wing or sail is swept back far enough, the separation bubble begins to rotate, and it then forms a 'roll-over' vortex which scrubs the suction surface vigorously and delays separation until extreme angles are reached. The drag is horrendous, but the lift which can be achieved is spectacular. The best aeronautical example is the extreme attitude and relatively low speed at which delta-winged aircraft such as the Concorde approach and land. Dr Manfred Curry in his 1925 book, '*The Aerodynamics of Sails*' published the figure which is shown as the inset in Fig. 25.1, which displays very clearly the 'lobe' of greater force developed by a gaff sail on a crosswind point of sailing. On this angle to the wind, and particularly if the boat is heeled, the gaff appears to the Apparent Wind to be a heavily swept-back leading edge, and the consequent roll-over vortex delays separation and is responsible for the 'lobe' of increased drive force. The luffs of the rectangular sails of square-rigged ships were angled for the same reason and were outstandingly efficient when broad reaching.

I have drawn attention to this property because – sixty years later – it has re-appeared as one of the principle features of very fast sailboats. The near-horizontal upper luffs of the asymmetric spinnakers carried on the long bowsprits of the Australian 18 and 14 foot Skiff classes attack the wind at a similarly swept-back angle. The consequent roll over vortex maintains attached flow and increased drive force up to extreme angles. When tacking downwind in unsteady winds the angle of attack from moment to moment can change greatly. The roll-over vortex has the property of preventing separation during momentary very high trim angles. It is largely this 'tolerance' factor which maintains and stabilizes the drive force and enables the boat to maintain a relatively steady speed through the very unsteady Apparent Winds which are suffered by all high-performance boats downwind. (Refer Section 16.14) In this situation these lower aspect ratio, swept-back sails are more effective in delivering high performance than the more vertical-luffed spinnakers which are set on short spinnaker poles can ever be.

18.3 Group two – early Bermudan rigs

These were amongst the simplest of all rigs – and the least enjoyable. One mast, either naturally stiff, or stayed to be stiff. One boom, one mainsail, one mainsheet and one jib plus jib sheets. The crew's ability both to trim and adjust was limited to hauling in or easing the sheets. But it remained true that a fuller sail was faster in lighter breezes, and a flatter one on stronger days. The only way to change the shape was to hoist a different sail. So it became the norm to have a bag of sails with different fullnesses. In this situation, it was not the crew which sailed best who won. It was the crew which could afford the most sails, and was also the best at guessing what would be the predominant wind speed during the forthcoming race.

There was much frustration, particularly amongst those who had indeed purchased the correct sails, but who so frequently found themselves using the wrong ones because they could not foretell the wind well enough.

This was the motivation which started them experimenting.

18.4 Group three – the experimental years

These started the exciting years. Those who elected to experiment started with the example of the fluent adjustability of the sea-bird's wing, the memory of the controllability of the gaff and gunter rigs, and the more recent model of the aircraft pilot and his ability to alter his wings' camber and lift by extending slats and/or flaps. As a first goal they wanted machinery with which they too could alter their sails' camber whilst sailing.

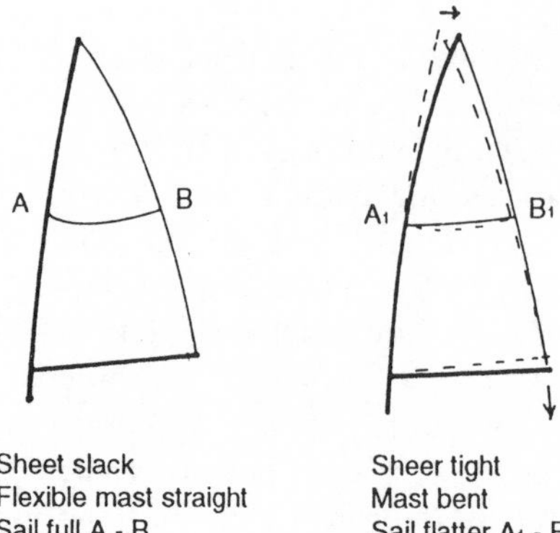

Fig 18.2 Bend of flexible unstayed mast controls fullness

Since a sail's fullness is set principally by the 'round' cut into its luff and foot, one obvious place to start was with reefs, pleats, pockets or zips up the luff of main and jib and along the boom. At its best, this approach worked in the technical sense, but it never began to be either simple, practical, or aerodynamically clean. Within a few years it had been abandoned except in a few specialized uses with headsails.

The now universally accepted method of bending the mast was viewed with suspicion at first. When 'bendy' masts first appeared greybeards muttered, 'any mast which bends will break', but they didn't. The search was on for the best method of control. In this brief note, I will touch only the eight mechanical arrangements which have survived because they are simple and efficient. Five of these are ways to bend the mast. The other three are ways to alter the tension of the forestay, and so control the fullness of the headsail.

Mainsails

1. The first way to bend the mast is the simple one – pull hard enough on the mainsheet to bend an unstayed mast enough to flatten the sail. Those who sail Lasers, Finns, OK's, etc. will be well familiar with this method. Its principle limitation is obvious – with this method you cannot have a flat sail without a tight leech! (Fig. 18.2)

2. A second way is to use a powerful vang. The exact effect of tightening the vang will vary according to whether the mast is free-standing or stayed, whether it is deck-stepped (pin jointed) or encastered in a mast socket or similar like a Laser or Finn mast, and the position of the boom. Use of vang enables the mainsail to be flattened independently of mainsheet tension, and it is the most effective of all controls for dynamic tuning.

3. A third method is to force the lower mast forward, usually by chocks or similar at the mast gate of an encastered mast. The upper mast is held back by shrouds or backstay(s). By varying the degree of chocking and so the amount of bend, any desired flatness of the lower sail can be achieved.

4. A fourth method, often used in conjunction with (3) above in the case of 'fractionally' rigged boats (i.e. with the forestay attached to the mast below the masthead) is to adjust the tension of a backstay attached to the masthead. The combination of forward force at the forestay attach point, and aft force at the masthead bends the upper mast. The extent to which the lower mast bends will depend upon the mechanical taper of the spar, and the rigging and any chocking arrangements lower down.

The principal advantage of methods 3 and 4 above is that the mast bend and hence the mainsail flattening is achieved without any tension in the sail itself, so in light air a crew can set a sail which is both flat and twisted. The principal disadvantage is that these methods are both dynamically inert.

5. The fifth method is to rig the mast with rigid swept-back spreaders, around which the shrouds or diamond stays or both are lead. If the tension in the shrouds is increased, the mast will bend according to the tension. The principal advantages of this method are that in practice, it is dynamically efficient, and that in addition it enables a big dinghy rig to be set up as a 'two-rate spring' with the elastic mode tuned to cut in exactly at the design wind.

Headsails

The fullness of headsails can be adjusted by varying the extent to which the forestay sags. A slack forestay implies much sag and a full headsail. Tightening the forestay reduces the sag and flattens the sail. It will be obvious that tightening the mainsheet will to some extent tighten the forestay. This may be regarded as desirable in the light air to moderate breeze range. But in stronger winds, as the mainsheet is eased, the forestay needs to remain tight. There are three customary methods of adjusting its tension:

6. In small dinghies, if the vang anchor point is suitably chosen, tensioning the vang can increase the forestay tension(but not independently of the mainsail leech tension).

7. The preferred method in larger boats is to tighten the forestay by increasing the backstay tension. The disadvantage of both these methods is that the control is not independent. Both controls necessarily flatten the mainsail at the same time as they tension the forestay to flatten the headsail. This may be exactly what you want. But if, sometimes, it isn't, these methods are not for you.

8. The third method is to adjust the shroud tension. As the shrouds are tightened, the forestay will necessarily be tightened and the headsail flattened. The advantage of this method is that it is independent of controls which affect other sails.

These eight methods have survived, and most modern sailboats use two or more of these in combination.

This section summarises the basics. Two examples of how these have been applied in individual cases appear in the 'wingmast development' story in the previous chapter, and the 'Eighteen Footer rig development' story which concludes this chapter.

18.5 Objects and dynamics

During the experimental years, sailors learned much more than how to adjust. Initially we started with simple observations and questions, such as:

Why was it that sailboats with low forestays and smaller jibs usually beat ones with higher forestays and larger jibs?

Why was it that boats with very flexible masts usually won on hot days?

Why was it that in stronger winds, boats with their spreaders pointed somewhat aft usually beat boats with their spreaders angled sideways?

As we unravelled the answers to these questions we found that there are three (at least) dynamic levels at which a rig can respond. We learned also that, to be fast, a rig's dynamic behaviour needs to be 'right' at all three of these levels. If the wind were always steady and the water always smooth, the dynamic behaviour of the rig would be of no importance. There would be one best rig shape for each wind strength and each point of sailing. This shape would be suggested by calculation and confirmed by experiment. All that would then remain would be for racing crews to repeat these known shapes accurately, in the manner in which a race-car driver repeats gear-shifts at exact speeds.

In real life things are different. From hour to hour the wind strength can change from light air to strong breeze and back to light air. From minute to minute, except in the case of steady light air, the wind speed changes continuously. Its gusts and lulls constantly sweep a range of speed, and a smaller (in the vector sense) change of direction. From second to second the wind's behaviour also changes. In cool-surface conditions the speed usually increases and decreases smoothly from lull to gust and vice versa. But in hot-surface conditions the gust onslaught can be harsh and abrupt.

These three situations – slow wind speed change, normal gusts and lulls, and the very short-term differences in gust onslaught – are three which have so far been identified. In each of these a rig which responds elastically and in the 'right' sense will be faster than one which is rigid. Conversely, an elastic rig, but one which gives the 'wrong' dynamic response, will be slower.

1. Slow Changes

When the wind speed changes slowly, the way the sails change shape with increasing force is important. Fig. 18.3(a) and (b) show the elastic response of two different rig types as wind speed increases. The low forestay of rig (a) allows the masthead of the flexible mast to flex backwards as the tension in the leech increases in stronger wind: this both flattens the upper mainsail and also allows the leech to fall to leeward. If the forestay attachment point is low enough, the increasing backwards force at the masthead tightens the forestay sufficiently to reduce its sag, and so flattens the headsail as well. All three of these responses are

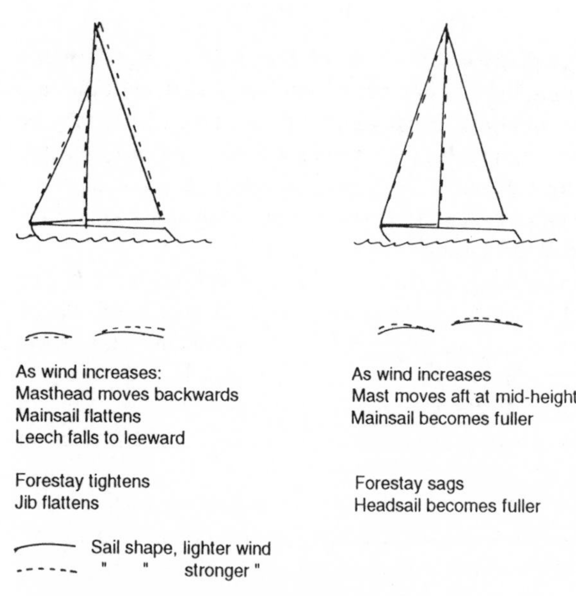

Fig 18.3 Dynamic responses of different rig types

correct in the 'fast' sense. As the wind speed increases, the crew of this boat will need to make infrequent and relatively small adjustments to maintain their sails at their optimum shapes. (The masthead will need to be held firmly sideways, otherwise it will bend to leeward, and the sail will twist too much.)

The masthead forestay of rig (b) produces the reverse effect. As the wind speed increases the forestay sag will increase and the headsail will become fuller. The mast at mid-height will tend to be drawn aft by the increasing sailcloth tension, and this will cause the mainsail to become fuller also. The masthead cannot move aft, so the leech will remain firm. The firm leech is a neutral response. The tendency for both the headsail and the mainsail to become fuller as the wind speed increases are both 'slow' responses. The crew of this boat will need to make frequent and substantial adjustments as the wind speed changes in order to maintain or restore the optimum shapes to their sails. It can be done but they will be busy if they wish to do it well.

A slow wind speed change is sometimes so subtle that even skilled crews fail to sense it until a substantial change has already occurred. It is for this reason that a rig which responds dynamically in the 'fast' sense will in practice sail faster than one which doesn't – a crew who sail with a 'fast' rig can be more relaxed about their rig and spend more of their time scanning the environment outside the boat. They will usually sense change sooner and adjust more accurately.

The simple responses noted above are correct in the general sense – a flexible rig which responds in the 'fast' sense is likely to be faster than any other in a wind of changing strength. What, then, is the optimum flexibility? This leads us to the concept of the design wind.

The design wind concept

If we consider the case of a sailboat which sails to windward, first in light air and then in progressively stronger breezes, the sideways force developed by the sails will (other things remaining constant) increase as the square of the speed of the Apparent Wind. At some wind speed the sail force will just balance the crew of a dinghy who are hiked or trapezed to extreme, or the sailboarder whose body is just skimming the water, or a catamaran with its windward hull just lifting, or a yacht which has reached its optimum angle of heel. This will be the design wind for each of those craft when close-hauled. Fig. 18.4 gives the dynamics. The design wind divides the performance of every sailboat into one lighter-wind part in which the crew will be 'looking for power', and a stronger-wind part in which the crew must 'shed power' because the 'power' potentially available exceeds what the boat can accept.

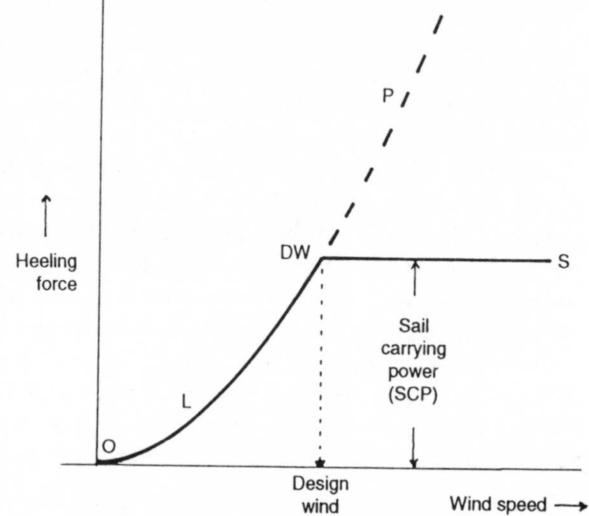

O - L - DW - P = Maximum heeling force which can be developed by sails.
SCP (Sail carrying power) = $\frac{\text{righting moment}}{\text{arm}}$ (Sect. 16.3 etc).
DW = Design wind.
O - L - DW = Wind speed range in which crew *look for power.*
DW - S = Stronger wind speed range in which crew must *shed power.*

Fig 18.4 Elements of the *design wind* concept

If we now imagine that the boat bears away

until it sails first a close reach and then a broad reach, exactly the same arguments will continue to apply – there must be a wind speed above which the crew must shed power, but it will not be the same windspeed.

In the case of a keelboat, it will be almost up to its hull speed at the design wind when close-hauled, and as it bears away it cannot sail faster and so the Apparent Wind will move toward the beam and must become lighter. The design wind when reaching will therefore be a stronger True Wind than when sailing close-hauled. It is probable that a stiffer rig would be faster

In the case of a high performance boat, typical boat speeds would be about 1.2 x wind speed when close-hauled, and approaching 1.8 x wind speed when beam reaching. In this case the Apparent Wind may not move toward the beam at all. It will certainly increase. All that will happen with the sails is that they will be sheeted a little further out from the centreline in the stronger Apparent Wind. In this case the design wind may be a lesser True Wind speed than the close-hauled wind speed, and a 'softer' rig may be faster. Fig 18.5 extends Fig 18.4 to close and broad reach in the case of a typical dinghy.

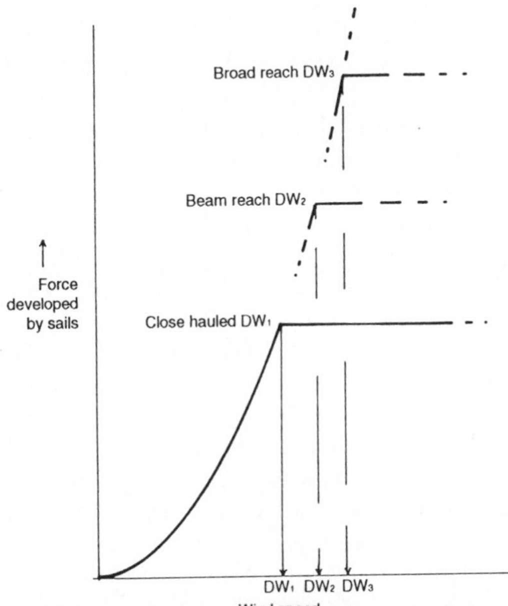
Broad reach DW3
Beam reach DW2
Close hauled DW1
Force developed by sails
DW1 DW2 DW3
Wind speed
This diagram is conceptual only.
There will be very great differences between the directions and speeds of the Apparent Winds on broad reaches as between a skiff and a keelboat.
Despite these differences, the principles will remain true.

Fig 18.5 Design wind concept extended to close and broad reach

When broad reaching or running, sailboats divide into two groups: those which sail slowly with the Apparent Wind aft, and those few which sail faster than the wind and so sail with the Apparent Wind always from ahead of the beam. The 'design wind and rig response' concept ceases to be relevant with the slower boats, but remains a vital factor in handling the fast ones.

The ideal rig response

Fig. 18.6 shows the ideal dynamic rig response. There are three components:

1) In winds lighter than the design wind, the rig should not yield.

2) In winds stronger than the design wind, the rig should yield elastically and at a precise rate.

3) The rig itself should be adjustable to accommodate changes in wind and sea-state condition, because the design wind will be different on different points of sailing, and in different wind and wave roughnesses.

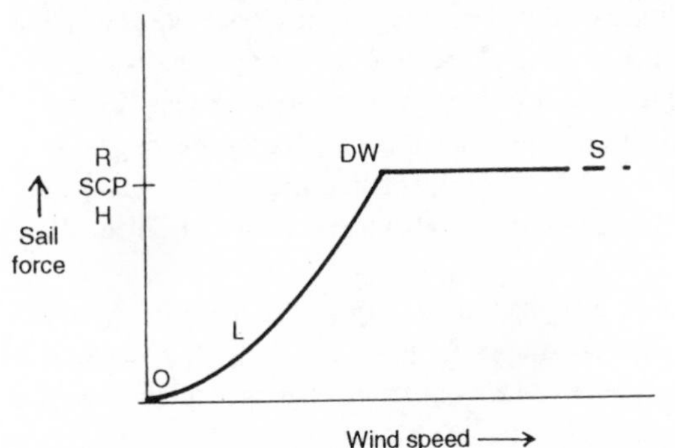
R
SCP
H
Sail force
DW
S
L
O
Wind speed

1) In the sailforce/windspeed range O - L - DW, the rig should not yield.
2) " " " " " DW - S the rig should yield.
3) In the range DW - S, the rig should yield in a manner so that:-
i) The cross-boat force does not exceed SCP.
ii) The sails' shapes are efficient at each wind speed

R In rough water a stiffer rig will be faster.
H In hot harsh winds a softer rig will be faster.

Fig 18.6 The ideal dynamic response of a rig

2. Gusts and Lulls

If we consider a typical situation that a boat with a design wind, close-hauled, of 10 knots is sailing in a True Wind of 10 knots in which gusts of 12 knots and lulls of 8 knots alternate every 30 seconds, then the force developed by the sails will sweep from the 'looking for power range'and into the'must shed power' range and vice versa between two and three hundred times during a typical two hour race.

The ideal rig response – the response which will sail fastest with least technical demand on the crew – is that the rig should not yield in winds up to the design wind, but that it should yield and in a precise manner at all higher wind speeds, i.e.

1. Up to the design wind speed for the boat the rig should yield not at all or only a trivial amount.

2.Thereafter it should yield relatively freely. The degree to which it yields should give the optimum sail shape for approximately constant cross-boat sail force. However -

3. The capability should remain to reset the system for the stronger design winds appropriate for rough water, or the lighter break-out point appropriate to the harsh gusts of thermally excited winds.

Technically, such a rig is a pre-loaded spring system with an adjustable pre-load. This response can be achieved quite simply if we assume that the flexible components of the rig – the mast, the sailcloth (but not if it is Kevlar), and the battens – blend together into a system of springs. Ideal rig performance can then be achieved by pre-loading the primary spring – the mast – by bending it backwards by appropriate tensions on shrouds, spreaders, diamond stays or backstays. Such a rig can then be tuned so that it gives the desired performance.

3. The rough-air, gust-onslaught response

So long as the rate of change of wind speed from lull to gust remains slow enough for a crew to respond to it as it occurs, it is possible for a boat to be sailed smoothly and fast through these changes and for a crew to adjust the sail shape on a gust by gust basis. Not many crews try, but these are usually the ones who win.

But as the gusts become harsher and strike harder, a point must be reached at which the rate of change of force exceeds the speed with which even the most skilled crew can respond. At this point the priorities change. A rig which yields automatically ceases to be a convenience. It becomes a necessity for speed. The fastest rig becomes the one which, by yielding easily and elastically to the gust's onslaught and for the moment thereafter, gives the crew added time in which to respond – sufficient time to ease sheets, etc. to keep the boat 'on its feet' and moving fast.

The concept of the design wind remains valid, in the sense that there remains a wind strength below which a rig should not yield. But the practicalities of strong harsh winds, with their forceful gusts, light lulls and fierce gust onslaughts are that the fastest rig will be one which yields sooner than is optimum in smoother-wind conditions. It is therefore desirable that a rig should be adjustable in the sense of being able to make it 'softer' in these conditions, as well as stiffer for the reasons noted above.

I first recognised the full importance of this factor when sailing with a university group on Tuttle Lake near Manhattan, Kansas. The 'Ka' in Kansas means 'south wind' and on summer afternoons it frequently blows at about 25 knots, and is fiercely heated by the adjacent hot land surface. The lake is too small to cool the wind significantly, so the wind over the water is extremely rough. Prof. Lucas had a Moth with a beautifully efficient wingmast, years ahead of its time. He also had an old bamboo mast, soft and springy and about as primitive as they come. In the smoother winds of the cool mornings and evenings that wingmast was magic, and the Moth beat everything else on the lake. In the hot afternoons, the Moth still won – but only when the stiff wingmast was discarded, and the old soft whippy bamboo stick was fitted.

In those days, twenty years ago, nobody ever talked about wind roughness, let alone degrees of roughness, so we did not really understand what was going on. Now that we can compare Fig. 7.1(a) with 7.1(b) the picture has become clearer. Softer rigs still go faster in rough winds than stiff ones. The difference is that now we know why.

To sail fast in harsh gusts, the short-period yield response of a rig has to be very fast indeed. A rig which blows 'open' and stays open for about one third to one half a second appears to be about right, because this is long enough for a crew to begin to free the sheets and so prevent the boat from heeling excessively and 'staggering'.

A rig with a very low forestay and a topmast free to move aft can easily be too soft and stay open for too long. As the forestay attachment point is progressively raised (or the movement of the masthead otherwise restricted) the yielding of the rig becomes less and the time it stays 'open' becomes shorter until, when the attach point is at about 85 to 88% of the mast height, the response becomes neutral. (The mechanical advantage of this set-up is that it permits use of the lightest mast, other things, such as staying, being equal. A Tornado rig is a good example of this arrangement.) As the forestay is raised toward the masthead the mast begins to bend the wrong way and the rig response makes the boat heel excessively, 'stagger', and sail more slowly unless the crew react very quickly indeed.

What we are talking about here, is that ideal short-term dynamic response itself has three components:

1. The break-out force at which the rig begins to yield.

2. The way it alters the sails' shapes as it yields.

3. The time it stays 'open' following onslaught.

The angle at which spreaders are swept back or forwards is also important. It is sometimes overlooked that spreader sweep has a short-term as well as a long-term effect. It is normal to vary spreader sweep to change the bend of the mast and therefore fine-tune the fullness and 'power' of the mainsail. This is the long-term effect, and within a certain range of sweep angle it works well and can still give a 'fast' response. A gust will cause the windward shrouds and/or diamond stays to become momentarily tighter. But if the spreader sweep is moved forward of some critical angle, there will be an added effect. The momentarily tighter shroud will force the mast backwards relative to the sail, thus making it momentarily fuller and also inhibiting the masthead from moving back and flattening the head. This will cause a 'slow' gust response even though the long-term response may be perfect. It is not easy to recognise when first encountered, and it can turn a previously well-mannered boat into a hard-mouthed brute in harsh winds. It is most likely to occur if spreader adjustment has been used to power-up too-flat a sail. It does not occur if added sweep is used to depower too-full a sail.

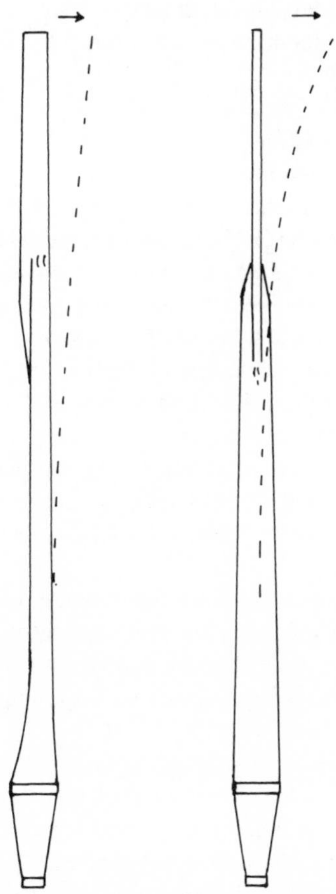

Upper mast is thinned sideways until it yields easily. Sail is cut so that upper leech batten *flips* to leeward when yield caused by design wind is reached.

Fig 18.7 Finn rig c1970

18.6 Modern rigs

Four examples will show how rigs have progressed over the past two decades.

1. The unstayed mast

Fig. 18.7 shows the mechanical arrangements of a simple Finn dinghy mast which was popular about 1965 to 1970. This wooden mast was shaped with a transverse elliptical cross section for about two-thirds of its height, and as a thin fore and aft blade above that height. The blade was progressively thinned sideways until it began to yield significantly at a wind speed just below the design wind when sailing to windward. The cut of the upper leech was adjusted so that the leeward bend of the topmast as the helmsman applied his maximum hiking force would just 'flip' the upper leech battens to leeward. It was an ingenious arrangement which endeavoured to secure the benefits of a two-rate spring from a single spring. It could be very fast in one chosen condition, e.g. to windward in flat water. However, because its response could not be changed, it could be disappointing in all other conditions. Particularly when broad reaching in waves, these rigs shed power far too soon.

2. The modern wingmast

The Tasar rig described in Section 17.11 represents the state of the art for a lightweight fourteen foot waterline dinghy designed in 1975. Since then we have learned to sail with more twist in light airs, and with much higher forestay tensions in stronger winds, and we have learned and are still learning much about the importance of elasticity. Because of the fluent adjustability of the basic rig, all three changes called for by the developing technique have been accommodated without requiring any mechanical change to the rig.

3. Recent Eighteen Footer

Fig. 18.8 shows the mechanical arrangements of a highly developed Eighteen footer rig of about the 1986 era. Each boat has a big rig for light air, a No. 2 for moderate breezes and a No. 3 rig for strong winds. These rigs, when handled skilfully, could be very fast in all conditions. Points of interest are:

a) The height of attachment of the forestay is chosen solely for the right yield response at the desired wind speed.

b) The lower mast is a tube of the hardest aluminium alloy and the highest temper available.

c) The topmast is a relatively stiff tapered carbon fibre tube.

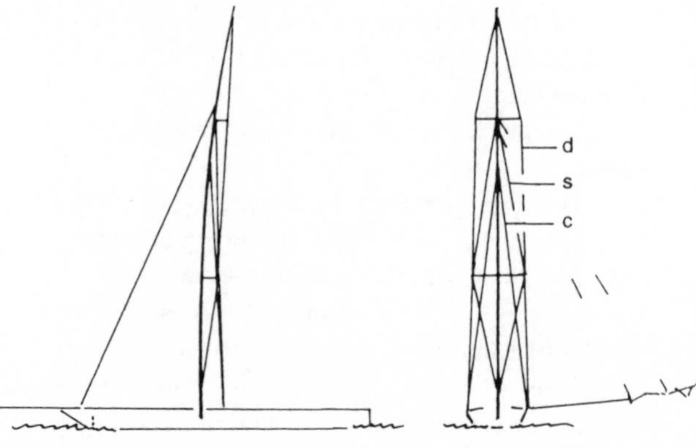

Lower mast - alloy tube
Upper mast - carbon fibre tube
d = Diamond stays around swept spreaders pre-bend mast
s = Shrouds
c = Check stays

Fig 18.8 Mechanical arrangements of *Eighteen* rig c1986

d) The diamond (cap) stays to the topmast are set around two sets of swept spreaders, and are tensioned sufficiently to bend the mast out of column by about 4.5 to 5 diameters.

e) The diamond stays allow the masthead to fall backwards under load, but hold it firmly sideways.

f) The fully battened mainsail has a large upper roach. This approximates the aerodynamically optimum elliptical shape.

g) It is deliberately cut over-full.

h) The stiffness of each full-length batten is adjusted so that the final camber of the sail in no wind is about 12% top to bottom.

This is the fastest shape in winds from calm up to the design wind. Because of the built-in mast-bend preload and batten-stiffness preload, this mast-sail-batten combination holds its shape almost unchanged in winds up to the design wind.

In stronger winds the mast and topmast begin to bend more, and the sail flattens and the upper leech falls off.

Fig. 17.29 shows how the pressure over a sail moves toward the leech at lower angles of attack. This shift of pressure toward the leech as the sail trim is eased in increasing wind is one of the primary triggers which starts the rig yielding at exactly the right time.

The shrouds are held by hydraulic rams, so that as the mast shortens as it bends further, the basic shroud tensions can be reset. This eliminates 'pumping' (a slow vibration or oscillation which if unchecked, amplifies and leads to destruction) and so keeps the whole rig securely in the boat. It also keeps the forestay taut.

Some practical points are:

Back to the importance of twist. A masthead which is bent back over the centreline appears to be hooked to windward when viewed from the angle at which the Apparent Wind approaches, and so makes it easier to control twist in exactly the same way as a masthead which is hooked out to windward such as the ice yacht or Tasar.

Experience confirms that the more the masts are pre-bent, the faster the boats go.

If a mast is pre-bent more than five diameters, it breaks. This seems to have something to do with more than materials. Carbon masts break just the same as alloy, but usually a little later.

For fine adjustment, check stays are attached to the mast at an appropriate distance below the forestay attachment point. The tension in these check stays can be adjusted whilst sailing (by a second smaller set of hydraulics). Tightening the check stays has the effect of stiffening the mast by preventing the lower mast from moving forward freely, and so prevents the topmast from falling back. By adjusting the tension in these check stays the point at which the rig begins to yield can be adjusted – stiffer in rough water when more power is needed and softer in the brutal heated Sydney westerlies with their savage onslaughts.

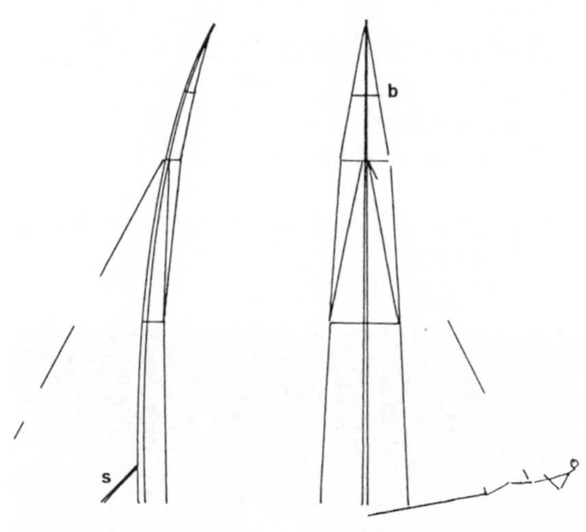

Lower mast - alloy tube
Upper mast - glass fibre tube
s = Strut to hold lower mast rigid
b = Baby spreaders to position diamonds as topmast flexes.

Fig 18.9 Simplified arrangements of champion *B18* rig - 1990

Fig 20.16 shows how this sort of rig works in strong winds.

Any crew who have developed, tuned and become fluent with the control of a rig such as this have an enormous advantage over their rivals. After they have tuned their rig correctly, they need thereafter make only minimal control and adjustment efforts as they race through the constantly changing wind with a rig which is both correct in shape, and also yields easily and efficiently to the wind's changes. Because their rig responds so well, they can achieve and maintain high boat speeds easily. They can then direct their attention to exploiting their speed, rather than struggling to maintain it.

4. Modern Eighteen Footer – further development and simplification

The complex rig described in '3' above is typical of rigs at the conclusion of the extraordinary development phase described in Sections 16.10, -11, -12 and -13. Every part of that rig is logically justifiable. These boats raced hard and regularly. They were reliable. They won. Fig 20.16 shows a boat moving at about 35 knots down a long 25 knot gust on Auckland Harbour on its way to winning a world championship. The extreme loads on the rig are clear to see, but these boats can accept this sort of punishment week after week and come back for more. If only some keelboats were half as reliable.

At the end of this period the unfortunate attempt to gain commercial control of skiff racing occurred, which lead to the rethink referred to in Section 16.10.

The need to reduce cost was welcomed by one designer as an opportunity to simplify. Fig 18.9 is the rig he produced, Fig 18.10 is a photograph of the boat under construction and Fig 18.11 shows it in action. This low-cost boat, now a one-design class, has also proved to be a design breakthrough which is substantially faster than all its predecessors.

As this book goes to press it is the current world champion for its second year.

The principle differences between *AAMI*, one of the new B18 class and the ENTRAD generation are:

1. The B18 is a much smaller boat, about two thirds the weight.

2. The lower mast is pre-bent almost to the extreme and then locked almost solid by its rigging.

3. The topmast is not stiff alloy or carbon but flexible fibreglass.

4. All the rig-spring dynamics are handled by the topmast.

5. Because the bend of the lower mast does not alter, the shrouds do not go slack, and there is no longer need for hydraulic shroud tension adjustment.

6. The main hydraulics, and their weight and cost, have been discarded.

7. The fine adjustment capability provided by the check stays in the ENTRAD generation rigs is, in *AAMI*, provided by a firmly roped mainsail luff and a powerful downhaul. Severe downhaul tension first stretches the bolt rope, then puts tension into the sailcloth between the battens. This pre-bends the topmast and so adjusts the wind speed at which the rig begins to yield.

8. The auxiliary hydraulics and their weight and cost have been discarded.

9. Very thorough development of the FRP topmast's flexibility characteristics have resulted in an overall short-term rig response which is superior to anything previously achieved with the stiffer alloy or graphite topmasts. The boat is beautifully easy to sail. The crew can look outside the boat to exploit their speed, rather than having to concentrate on controlling the boat.

10. Every effort has been made to exploit the cube/square law in reverse (Sect 16.5). The result is a much lighter boat with superior ratios of sail-carrying-power / total weight.

11. Further, the smaller hull has a much finer entry wedge angle at the bow. This gives it superior

windward-going performance into waves.

Fig 20.19 shows a B18 moving downwind off Nice in a 20 to 25 knot Mistral and big waves. It is a more compact, more controllable, faster boat.

When it is considered that the ENTRAD generation were state-of-the-art in 1986, and that the list above represents only the major developments during the following four years, and that the end result is that much less expensive boats now sail faster than ever, the sheer vitality and energy of this extraordinary class, and its ability to find ever-faster ways of sailing around the buoys in all wind and sea-state conditions, commands respect.

Note how the rig is being engineered so that the plane of the leech, top to bottom, is parallel with the centreline.

Fig 18.10 A *Fig 18.9* type rig approaching completion
As the book goes to press, this boat is the current world champion.

Note how all leeches are approximately parallel with the centreline.

Fig 18.11 1990 rig at work

Chapter Nineteen
Foils

19.1 The foils – the centreboard, keel and rudder

The task of the centreboard is to develop a cross-boat force. When sailing close-hauled or close reaching this is almost equal and opposite to the sails' force. Unlike the sails, which work at large angles in thin air, the centreboard or keel can work at a small angle in water nearly a thousand times more dense.

We saw in the 'Sails' section that gliders' wings are superbly efficient because they are long and slender, they are not twisted, they are big enough to work at very small angles, and their sections enable the air to flow smoothly around them.

Centreboards and rudder blades can approach the efficiency of glider wings. Only their length is limited, mainly for the practical reason that a centreboard of exaggerated depth hits the bottom too often. Twist is eliminated because they can be made of stiff material. It is fortunate that due to the great density of water, they do not have to be very big, and foils which remain practical and convenient in size are big enough to work at the small angles needed for efficiency. This factor makes it possible to use section shapes of unusually low-drag.

19.2 Laminar flow sections

Early aircraft lacked power, and flew slowly. Their wings needed to lift strongly at low speeds and large angles. High lift implies large suctions over the upper surface of the wings, and also that the flow should remain attached to the wing as it moves from the area of greatest suction to the higher pressure at the trailing edge. The 'scrubbing' action of a turbulent boundary layer can progress against an adverse pressure gradient about five times greater than is possible with laminar flow. For this reason the second generation of wing sections – the thicker tear-drop like sections which superseded the original thin curved sections – were all designed to run with turbulent boundary layers. These wings certainly lifted well, but they were hard to push through the air – their drag was high – because their surfaces were continuously scrubbed by high speed particles of air as is characteristic of all turbulent boundary layers.

The power of turbine engines made possible the much higher runway accelerations, cruising speeds and altitudes of modern aircraft, and called for wings with the absolute minimum of resistance. One of the aeronautical revolutions of some decades ago was the development of practical laminar flow wing sections. Laminar flow was achieved by developing slender wing sections which do not promote a turbulent boundary layer. Instead, they suppress it, to the point where they work almost entirely within a cocoon of slow-moving surface air which is characteristic of laminar flow. The advantage of this is that the wing 'feels' only the viscous drag of this slowly moving air, despite the fact that the full stream speed outside the boundary layer is many times faster. The end result is that the resistance of these wings can be as little as half that of the earlier turbulent flow sections.

The difference in the way these two sorts of sections work is shown by the solid lines in Figs 19.1(a) and 19.1(b). The drag curve of the turbulent flow section, Fig. 19.1(a), shows that the drag is at its minimum at zero angle of attack, and increases smoothly with increase of either positive or negative angle to the oncoming stream.

Fig. 19.1(b) is completely different. At angles greater than about plus or minus 3 degrees the drag, and the shape of the curve, is not much different from that in Fig. 19.1(a). But at the smaller angles the curve drops suddenly to about half this value, in a characteristic 'bucket' shape. This is due to the fact that a low-drag laminar boundary layer can develop over both the upper and the lower surfaces at these small angles. It is this development, as much as the turbine engine, which has made possible the astonishing efficiency of the modern transport aircraft.

19.3 Surface texture

Standard texts on the performance of wing sections all indicate that a rougher surface will give a poorer performance, in the sense that the rougher the surface the less will be the maximum lift and the greater the drag. One study of the effects of roughness went to the trouble of finishing a test foil with brilliantly polished chromium plate, on the grounds that it was not possible to do better than that. Sure enough, that foil developed both greater lift and lesser drag than the surface texture next in line, which was a polished painted finish.

Many wind tunnel performance diagrams now indicate both the performance measurements when the section is 'clean', together with those at two standard levels of roughness. These correspond roughly to extreme dirt, and minor blemish such as frost. Fig. 19.1 is from Abbott and Doenhoff; Ira Abbott was for many years Director of what is now NASA. I have shown both the 'clean' curves (solid line) and those at the second level of roughness (dotted line). Note that the low-drag laminar flow 'bucket' in Fig. 19.1(b) has completely disappeared, and that as a result the drag of the laminar flow section when roughened has approximately trebled over its narrow working range. In practice, this is exactly what happens if you let your centreboard or rudder become rough or dull – or when you pick up weed or a plastic bag. The loss of performance is much greater than would normally be expected. To sum up – no polish (or weed), no laminar flow, and no extra speed!

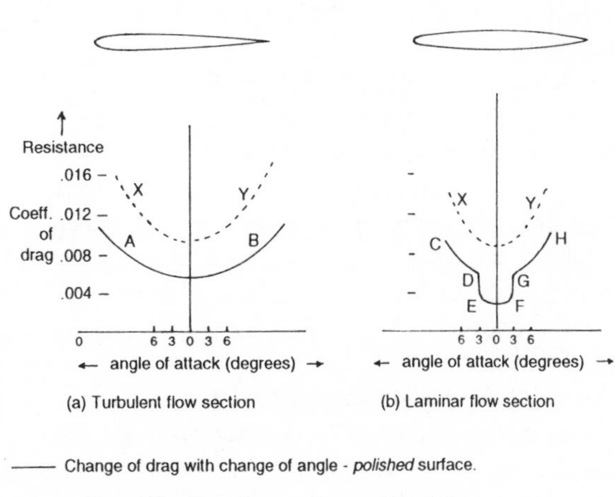

Fig 19.1 Shape of drag curves - turbulent and laminar sections

In sailing literature, this principle has been challenged on two counts. One challenge – which I suspect may have started with a wish to avoid hard work – notes that on a mirror-like surface the surface tension of water causes a thin water film to break up into 'beads', but on a slightly roughened surface it lies as an unbroken film. It is asserted that the drag of water flowing over such a slightly roughened surface should be less than the drag over a polished surface, and that a high polish is therefore undesirable.

The other challenge is more solidly based. It notes that most of the 'flow through straight pipes' studies show that the resistance to flow of fluid through pipes with rough inside surfaces is greater than the resistance through smoother pipes, but only up to some degree of smoothness. Once that smoothness has been reached at which the roughness lies entirely within the boundary layer, no further reduction of resistance occurs if the pipes are made smoother yet. What is deemed to be 'smooth enough' thus depends upon the thickness of the boundary layer, which starts very thin and becomes thicker with increasing distance downstream from the pipe entrance. As regards water at sailboat speeds this approach suggests that a fair paint surface which may include brushmarks and a little dust is smooth enough at the speeds and dimensions of most keelboats. As always with experiments which have been repeated many times, most measurements fall closely together and a few favour one extreme or the other.

We deemed that these two assertions merited a fair trial, particularly because – as noted below – we know that the results from straight pipes are not always valid for accelerating flow over curved surfaces.

We took two identical Laser rudder blades of modified NASA 0009 section, filled and faired and surfaced them flawlessly and progressed them towards a mirror surface. Near the end of the process, when both had been wet-sanded with 1200 grit 'wet' sandpaper and were ready for final buffing, we buffed one and polished it to a mirror finish, but left the other flawless but not buffed nor polished. The roughness caused by 1200 grit paper is such that the surface is smooth enough to reflect objects sighted 'along' it, but appears dull and will not reflect when viewed 'squarely'.

Fig. 19.2 shows the cross-flow 'lift' forces developed by these two foils. The 23% reduction in cross-flow lift force, i.e. the steering force, at 11 knots by the dull rudder-blade is exactly as expected from all NASA work and from all responsible standard texts. At the other extreme, it is the practical expression of the Fig. 17.11 kitchen experiment with a rough tumbler.

It certainly contradicts both of the 'unpolished is better' assertions. It doesn't take much dullness to make a substantial difference. Our measurements merely confirm again that the higher the polish, the better the control.

Note particularly that the NASA 0009 section is a turbulent-flow section. Laminar flow sections are even more demanding (Fig. 19.1) – they simply cannot work properly unless they are well maintained. They must be kept smooth and highly polished, otherwise the drag increase due to dullness with laminar flow sections is likely to be even more severe.

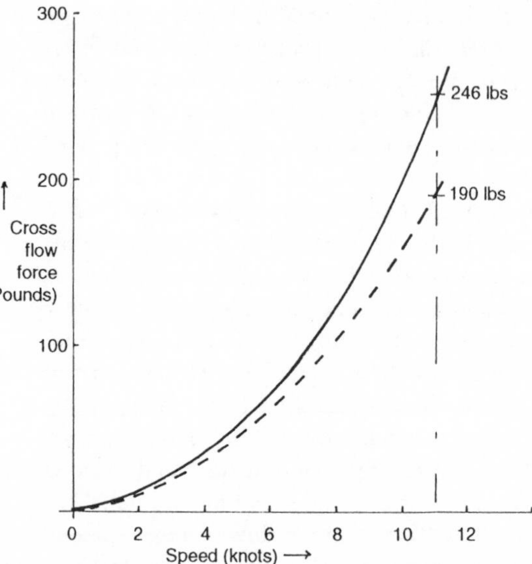
300
200
100
Cross flow force (Pounds)
246 lbs
190 lbs
0
2
4
6
8
10
12
Speed (knots)
Maximum steering force developed by Laser rudder blade. Blade varnished 10 coats, wet-sanded with 1200 grit paper, then buffed to mirror finish.
Maximum steering force developed by identical rudder blade, but not buffed.

Fig 19.2 Measured steering force of polished and dull blades.

19.4 Modern foil development

In the, 'Sails', section it was described how the modern rig was developed by drawing on aeronautical high-lift know-how of adjusting camber, eliminating twist, eliminating separation bubbles, and the use of trip turbulators.

In the development of the centreboard and rudder, we have drawn on aeronautical low-drag know-how, and have developed laminar flow centreboard and rudder blade sections of greatly reduced drag. But exactly as the end result in a modern wingmast rig looks a little different from a Jumbo's wing, so also the path to smallest centreboard and rudder blade drag encountered similar surprises.

It turns out that to achieve least drag seems to be a three-stage process.

The first stage has to do with what is called 'form drag'. This is what we are thinking about when we sense, intuitively, that if we pull two shapes through the water at the same speed, one a 'streamline' shape like a slender fish, and the other a square box of the same cross section area and volume, the streamline shape will disturb the water less as it slips through it, and so will be easier to pull. Why this should be so can be understood if we imagine them to be towed through a tube which is full of motionless water, as in Fig. 19.3. As the streamline shape is towed toward the left, the water is accelerated smoothly toward the right in order to pass through the restricted area between the shape and the tube wall. From the forward point of the shape to the point of its maximum cross section area energy is being expended to accelerate the water. As the speed increases the pressure drops. (Kitchen experiment Fig 17.5) From the point of maximum cross section area to the trailing point the process reverses – the water is slowed smoothly against the mass of water behind the shape, and as it slows and stops, its pressure rises, and this increased pressure forces the tapered after part of the shape forward. In this way the aft end of the streamline shape recovers almost all the energy which the forward half expended in accelerating the water 'backwards'. The greater the energy recovery the less the drag.

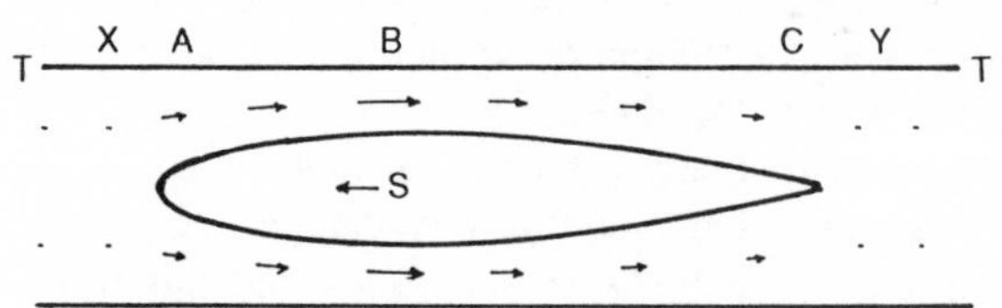
T
X
A
B
C
Y
T
S

T - T = Tube full of water.
S = Streamline shape moves through tube.
X, Y = Water at rest.
A to B = Displaced water accelerates to pass through annulus at B. As speed of water increases, its pressure falls.
B to C = Water slows and stops against water at rest at Y. As water speed falls, its pressure rises, and forces the tapered afterbody BC forward. This recovers most of the energy used to accelerate the water from A to B.

Fig 19.3 Energy demand and recovery around streamline shape

When we tow the boxy shape the situation is different. The square end of the box, as it advances, requires the water to accelerate with a great jolt, and to flow round square corners at speed. The water, very reasonably, refuses to do so. Instead it separates from the sharp corners and develops a very thick boundary layer with massive turbulence which slows the water and absorbs the energy and destroys the area of low pressure. So when the back end of the box passes there is no pressure increase to drive it forward – there is no pressure energy recovery. There is only more turbulence, and more drag.

This situation will remain true regardless of the diameter of the tube, so we can think of the shores of the harbour or the ocean as the tube walls. It will also remain true if we imagine the streamline 'fish' shape to grow downwards until it looks like a glider's wing or a winglike centreboard. The vital point is that whenever a body moves through water (or air), energy must be expended to move the mass of fluid aside as the body passes. The more smoothly this mass is accelerated and then slowed, the greater will be the recovery of energy, and this is what low drag is all about. Summed up, low form drag requires a good streamline shape. And even the best streamline shape will not work well if its surface is rough.

The second stage involves mighty wind tunnels and hundreds of man-years of research effort, at the end of which reports are published which will document to the fourth decimal place the lowest-drag wing section or fuselage shape to use in a given environment. If an aeroplane or a boat were just a single chromium-plated brilliantly polished wing, without ends, without engines, without control surface hinges, without a fuselage, etc, the wind tunnel results would be right. But in the real world an aeroplane is an assembly of parts, none of them quite perfect and they all interfere somewhat with the flow over some adjacent part. So there is more to designing a good aeroplane than just assembling parts all of which are shaped as recommended by prestigious but specialised reports. This is even more true of boats because sailboats work in a more complex environment.

This second level of development is a much more practical process, and it has its limitations. Three experiences gave me the insight to tackle the third stage in a sensible manner.

During a visit to England in the late 1940's to pick up some new flying boats, I spent some time flying high-performance gliders, and learned of an interesting method used by researchers in the British Gliding Association to examine the real flows over the wing of an experimental glider. They had found that if they left their machine on a cool grassy surface after sunset, dew formed on the varnished wing. If they then flew the glider at the speed of interest for about two minutes, the dew was scrubbed off by turbulent flow but not by laminar flow. Photographs taken against the light of the still-bright sky immediately after landing revealed both the general areas washed by laminar flow and by turbulent flow, and also the 'gaps' in the dew wherever some fly-speck surface blemish or interference effect had caused turbulence where the flow ought to have been laminar. As they eliminated each area of turbulent flow their machine flew better.

A little later I used this 'dew' technique to eliminate systematically as much of the turbulence as possible from my model gliders. After five years of development I managed to achieve laminar flow, and so hold the dew over the whole of the wing and tailplane and rudder surfaces except for the aftermost 10% on the upper surfaces, and over most of the fuselage. I could not help but observe that every time I reduced the area scrubbed by turbulent flow, my gliders flew a little higher above the seagulls. The final model's sinking speed – the most direct measure of drag – was about half that of my first cliff soaring glider.

Some years later a university group in the United States refined the British work with a clever adaptation – they dusted their glider with naphtha dust, and 'flew' it, at the speeds and angles they were interested in, by tying it to the top of a truck and driving up and down the taxiways of the local airport in windless conditions. While it was being driven for periods long enough for the areas of turbulent boundary layer to evaporate the naphtha dust, those interested could either stand alongside or be driven alongside close enough to watch and touch, so they were able to do a more thorough job than the Dunstable group. They reported results which were the same. They had been able to achieve very substantial increases in the areas swept by laminar flow, and as the area scrubbed by turbulent boundary layer was reduced so was the drag. They claimed to have almost halved the drag of their experimental glider.

What comes out of this is that no matter how well a machine is designed on the drawing board, in practice there are likely to be large areas of residual turbulence. However, if the original design is basically good, it will respond well to further development aimed at eliminating the residual turbulence.

It turns out that the same approach can be adapted to water flows. I had been corresponding about my work with dew on my model gliders, and also the trip turbulator development on wingmast rigs, with Prof. Oliver. When we met in Hobart (where he had an unusually extensive hydraulic laboratory) he set up a model wing in one of his water channels at an angle and flow speed at which it developed a turbulent boundary layer. He drew a line of ink across its surface with a squeeze-bottle with a long fine nozzle. I was astonished and impressed by the abrupt harsh streakiness which instantly formed, and at the speed with which it was swept downstream. The scrubbing action, the high speed of the particles which did the scrubbing, and the speed and completeness with which all of the ink was swept away were surprising. He then adjusted the angle of the model so that it operated with laminar flow in the same water-flow speed, and drew another line of ink across it. A smooth and gentle shading formed and drifted slowly downstream. The slowness of the process was as arresting as its smoothness. The differences between the natures of the two types of boundary layer flow were so unexpectedly obvious. Fig. 19.4(a) and (b) are sketches of the appearance of the two flows. I decided to use this approach for foil development.

Dew and naphtha dust were not of much use for centreboards – and nor was ink. So I settled on a slowly soluble tracer of glycerine mixed with gentian violet. When this slimy goo is smeared over the surface of a test foil, and the foil is then run through the water at the correct speeds and angles, turbulent flow looks exactly like Fig. 19.4(a), and all the tracer will have been scrubbed away in, typically, 3 to 6 seconds. Under laminar flow it soon looks like Fig. 19.4(b), and everything happens very slowly. There is still a shading of violet tracer around the trailing edge after 30 seconds. These are not easy subjects to photograph in a way that will show what you can so easily see under the water, so in this case I have resorted to sketches.

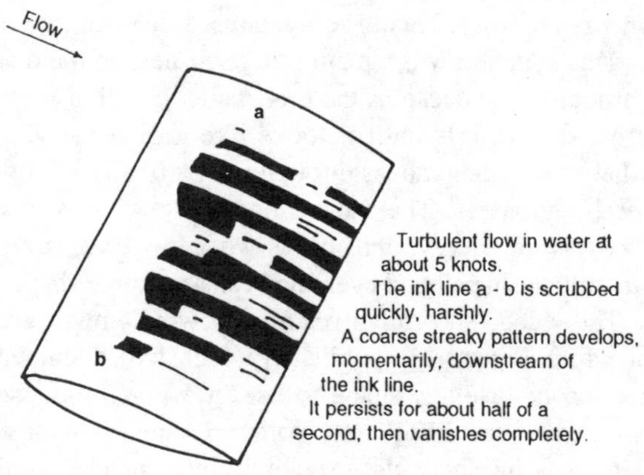

Flow
a
b
Turbulent flow in water at about 5 knots.
The ink line a - b is scrubbed quickly, harshly.
A coarse streaky pattern develops, momentarily, downstream of the ink line.
It persists for about half of a second, then vanishes completely.

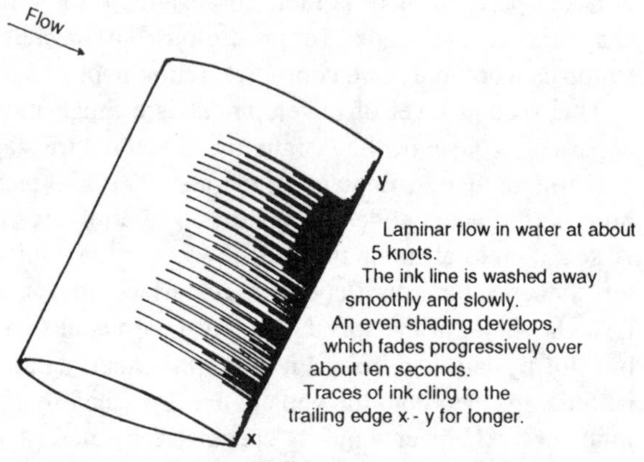

Flow
y
x
Laminar flow in water at about 5 knots.
The ink line is washed away smoothly and slowly.
An even shading develops, which fades progressively over about ten seconds.
Traces of ink cling to the trailing edge x - y for longer.

Fig 19.4 Boundary layer visualisation in water

We used this technique to look at the boundary layers of the classic NASA family of turbulent-flow sections (we started with 0009), and also one of the more recent laminar flow sections. The 0009 ran fully turbulent except for the forward ten percent or so where the flow accelerates. The laminar flow section ran laminar for about 50% of its chord when run at 3 degrees. This was about the performance of my early glider wings, so I was encouraged. We made a centreboard of each section and tried them, as described in Section 7.8, in boat against boat tests, in which two boats which were identical in all respects except for their centreboards were sailed close alongside each other. One boat used either the 0009 centreboard or the laminar foil, alternating at random. The other boat changed nothing. We measured the number of seconds needed to gain or lose one or two metres. Without exception, the laminar flow foil proved consistently faster.

From that start I repeated the approach I had used with my model gliders. We played with the leading edge radius, the blending parabola, the section thickness, the fore and aft position of the maximum thickness and the nature of the curves.

An explanatory note may be useful here. Central in standard boundary layer texts is a diagram which indicates how far along a pipe a fluid will flow with its boundary layer laminar. At some point (except at very slow speeds) that boundary layer will trigger into turbulence. The faster the flow the shorter the distance. These distances are surprisingly short. This diagram has been repeated in sailing reference books, and conclusions have been drawn that only the forward few inches of a hull are likely to run laminar. On this sort of reasoning efficient low-drag laminar flow wings on Jumbos are impossible, and like the bumble bee, they shouldn't be able to fly efficiently.

The facts are, of course, different. The diagram is correct – but only for steady flow through straight pipes. Over real wings and centreboards there are two differences. The first is that, from the leading edge and for some distance downstream the flow is not steady. It is accelerating, and in general an accelerating flow will run laminar. Usually, turbulence will set in where the acceleration stops. The second difference is that the flow is not straight. It is curved, and in general a fluid which follows a curve with the faster flow on the 'outside' will run laminar, because centrifugal force keeps the faster particles from sweeping inwards. It is surprising how far competent engineers can extend laminar flow by playing games with acceleration and curvature. Like right across Jumbo aeroplanes' wings. And right across centreboards, too.

Little by little we developed sections which would run laminar over about 90% of their suction surfaces at angles up to about 3.5 degrees, and the whole of their pressure surfaces (except for a tiny strip right at the leading edge where the flow is divergent, and so the faster flow is on the 'inside' for a few millimetres, and the flow becomes locally turbulent). This again echoed the model glider development experience. We kept testing the performance of the developing sections by 'boat against boat' tests on the water. Exactly as with the full-size and the model gliders, the more we increased the area swept by laminar flow, the better became the performance. With our boats this appeared as an ability to point higher at hull speed and so to increase the windward-going VMG.

There was one further occasional observation which confirmed the differences we were achieving in an unusual way, and I pass it on for its interest. At the time we were involved in this work, a few of my friends and I kept our dinghies at a local commercial boat shed which was accessible only by water. Trailed or roof-racked boats could be launched a few hundred yards away. Sometimes we returned our boats to the boat shed at night. Anyone who has rowed or paddled on a dark night will be familiar with the phosphorescence which is triggered by the turbulence caused by oars, paddles and bow wave. Very early we were delighted by the ghostly shadings of each other's centreboards and rudders as we paddled side by side in the stillness.

As the years passed the shadings changed to outlines! As our foils ran more and more laminar, we lost the 'front to back' phosphorescent illumination which was caused by the 'front to back' turbulent boundary layer, and watched instead the thin line which marked the turbulence of the divergent flow at the leading edge, and some flecks near the trailing edge. Between these, the laminar flow foils ran dark.

The end result of this work was that we developed sections for dinghy centreboards and rudders which would run with laminar flow up to a 'bucket width' of about +/- 3.5 degrees. Centreboards need do no more. Rudder blades need the same low drag but they also need, occasionally, to produce large forces for manoeuvring, so the final sections and plan forms should not be expected to be the same.

19.5 Control at higher speeds

Some years later we moved into a second stage of foil development. We were asked to do our best for the 470 class, which was then one of the 'new' Olympic classes. The rules dictate strange flat-sided sections. In this case there was no question of efficiency. All that we could do was to reduce the drag to the minimum within the rules. At the other end of the performance scale the Eighteen footers were beginning to move really fast and two problems were beginning to show up. The first was that a 'normal' leading edge radius was proving slower in practice than a much finer one at the higher speeds at which they raced in fresh breezes – but not at lower speeds. This was not consistent with wind tunnel data at the same Reynolds numbers, and we wanted to know why? The second was that they were beginning to suffer from ventilation problems – air is sucked downwards from the surface and splits attached flow away from the suction side. When this occurs effective steering control is lost until the flow reattaches.

For this second stage of the work we again decided that a completely practical 'hands on' approach was called for. We made a model holder with 'lift' and 'drag' spring balances, and bolted it to the stern of a relatively light seventeen foot planing motor-boat with a 70hp motor, which was capable of speeds up to 25 knots. We spent the weekends of one winter measuring the minimum drags, the maximum lifts, and the ventilation properties of ten different foils. One was a Tornado rudder blade of proven excellent performance. One was a Tornado rudder blade which had been badly scored. Two were NASA 0009 section Laser rudder blades. The other six were experimental, as sketched. From a practical programme such as this, one cannot approach the precision of measurement possible in the wind tunnel or the hydraulics laboratory, but it is possible to learn some very useful and practical things. What we learned is as follows. I do not know what happens at different foil sizes but suspect that it will be similar.

Concerning ventilation and control, we found that at speeds up to about 6 knots the situation is as shown in Fig. 19.5. As the rudder angle increases from 'A' to 'B', the steering force increases from nothing at 'A' to a maximum at 'E', where the flow looks like Fig. 19.6. If the rudder angle is then increased to 'C' the flow separates as in Fig. 19.7. Against the suction side of the rudder a mass of swirling water can be seen, and the steering force reduces from 'E' to 'F' because of the loss of suction.

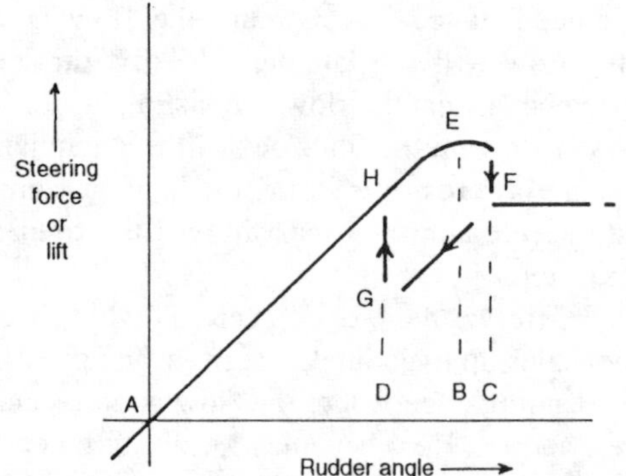

Fig 19.5 Rudder angles and steering forces at low speeds.

Before the flow can reattach and full control can be regained, the rudder angle must be reduced from 'C' to 'D'. This will cause the steering force to become even less during the time that the angle is reduced from 'C' to 'D'.

At angle 'D', the flow will abruptly reattach to the suction side, and the steering force will increase from 'G' to 'H'. Increase of angle will again achieve force 'E'. Note that once the flow separates and the force falls from 'E' to 'F', the only way to regain force 'E' is via the route 'F', 'G', 'H', to 'E'. This is called a 'hysteresis loop'.

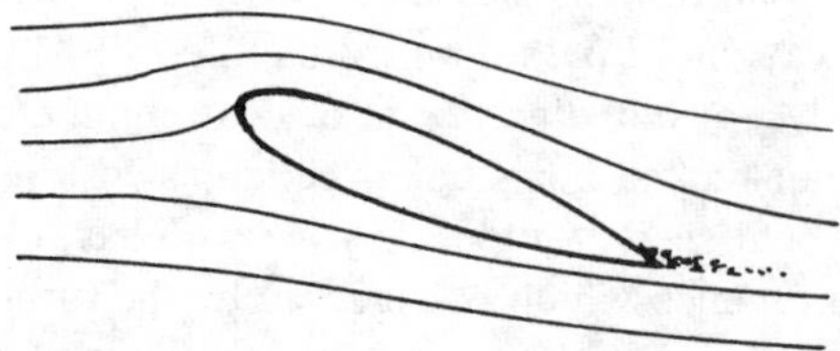
Fig 19.6 Appearance of attached flow (Point E, Fig 19.5)

Fortunately, with all symmetrical sections at low speeds, the reduction of force from 'E' to 'F' is quite small, and the reduction of angle from 'C' to 'D' is also quite small. In practice , a quick waggle of the tiller will usually re-attach the flow, and restore control.

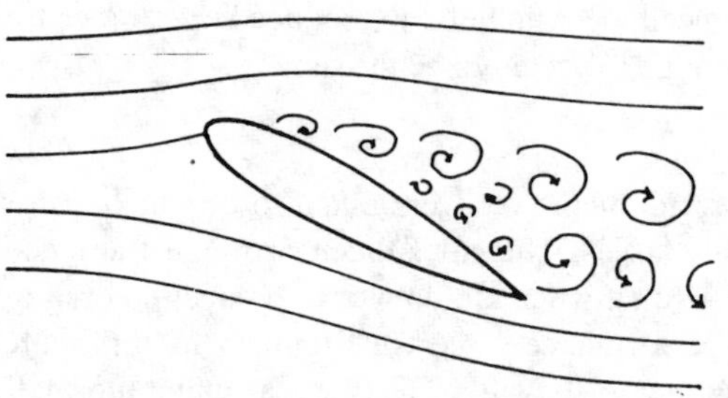
Fig 19.7 Appearance of separated flow (Point F, Fig 19.5)

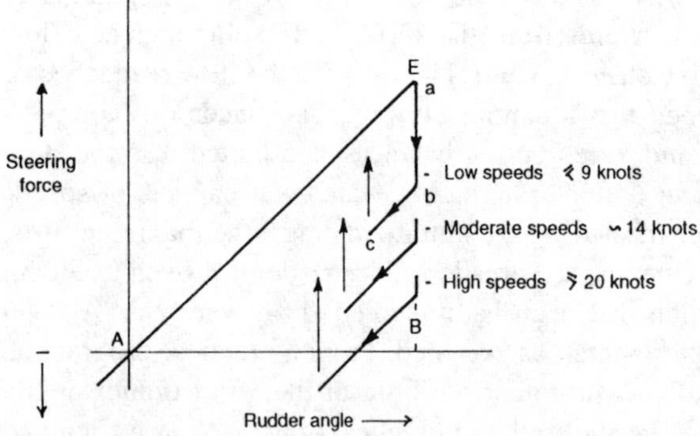

Fig 19.8 Rudder angles and steering forces at higher speeds

At speeds greater than about 9 knots, the whole mechanism changes, and is shown in Fig. 19.8 and those following. As rudder angle is increased from 'A' to 'B', Fig. 19.8, the steering force increases from 'A' to 'E', and the flow looks like Fig. 19.6. But once 'B' is exceeded, the water flow separates and at this speed a pocket of air is drawn down from the surface to occupy the space previously filled with water, as in Fig. 19.9. The loss of steering force is sudden and substantial, and the greater the speed the greater is the loss. Typical figures for rudders of normal shape would be 8 knots 20%, 14 knots 50%, and 20 knots 100%. At speeds of the order of 20 knots, both the separation, and the reattachment, occurred with a 'crack' noise like a loud cap pistol, and the stern of the motor boat jolted sideways. In these situations, wiggling the tiller is about as useful as whistling in the wind.

That last figure of 100% needs explaining, because it lies at the heart of the problem of control. Three factors are involved:

1. As speed is increased, the rudder angle at which ventilation occurs becomes progressively smaller until, at some limiting speed, any streamline section will ventilate on both sides

simultaneously, as shown in Fig. 19.10. For this reason fast motor-boats use a rudder section such as Fig. 19.11.

2. The shape and condition of the leading edge is absolutely critical in determining the onset of ventilation. Any imperfect shape, or perfect shape blemished by roughness, paint edges or weed will trigger ventilation many degrees earlier than would be expected with a perfect section in good condition.

3. The thicker the section, the greater will be the loss of control. Figs 19.12 and 19.13 show the reason. In Fig. 19.12, a flat plate at a small angle is shown in ventilated flow. The water which impinges on the lower surface clearly develops a force upwards in the diagram, even if it is a much reduced force. In Fig. 19.13, a thick section is shown which has reached a speed at which the upper surface has ventilated at a small angle. This section may easily develop a force downwards in the diagram, because the downward force of the suction from the water following the curved lower surface may equal or exceed the upward force due to the small upward angle. The thicker the section, the greater will be the curve and the more likely it will be that this will happen.

The overall picture, then, will usually look like Fig. 19.8. At 6 knots the stall and unstall characteristics are not severe, and may often pass unnoticed, particularly in unresponsive boats. At 9 knots the reduction in control as the steering force falls from 'a' through 'b' to 'c' is substantial and may often be the cause of broaching. At about 15 knots ventilation will result in almost total temporary loss of control, and is the cause of much broaching and not a little capsizing. Few classes of sailboat are capable of speeds of 20 knots, but these are all classes of great importance to the future of sailing. At these speeds, ventilation will occur quite easily unless steps are taken to prevent it. Further, when it occurs, an actual reversal of steering force can occur before attached flow is re-established. In the worst case, at really high speeds – say approaching 30 knots – it may be necessary to slow down to enable the flow to reattach.

There are two ways to delay separation, and one to prevent it.

The first way to delay it is to use a thin and highly polished section, with a fine leading edge radius, a blending parabola, and its maximum thickness well aft. Ten years ago we looked at control at speeds up to 20 knots. I believed that

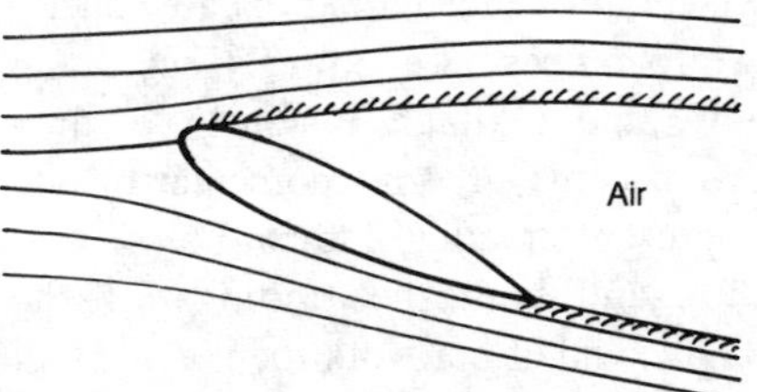

Fig 19.9 Appearance of ventilated flow

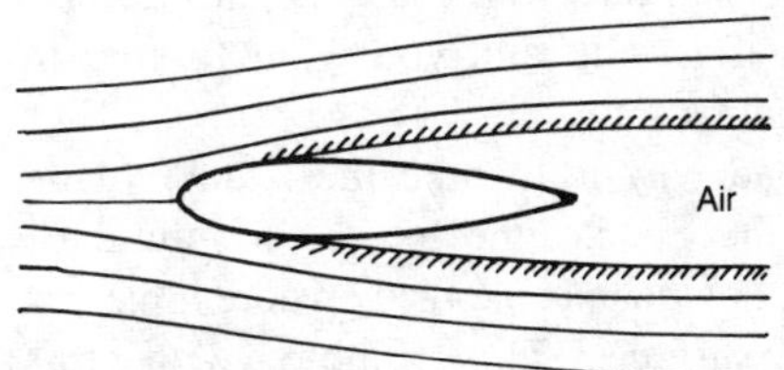

Fig 19.10 Flow with both sides ventilated

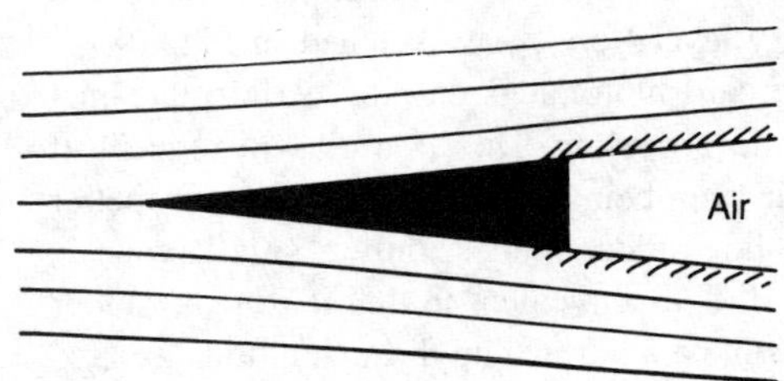

Fig 19.11 *Thin delta* rudder section

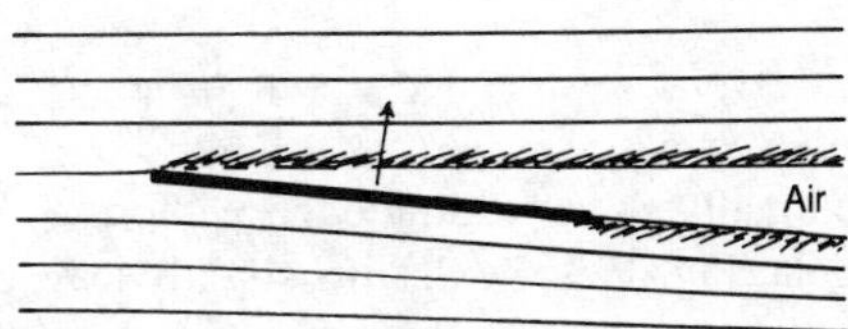

Fig 19.12 Flat plate - force when one side ventilated

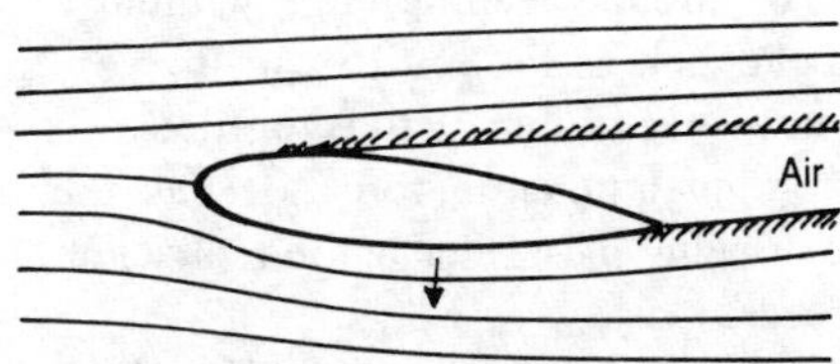

Thick streamline section ventilated one side at small angle.
Upward angles develops small upward force.
Flow attached to lower surface can develop larger downward force.
When this situation occurs, steering force can reverse.

Fig 19.13 Reversal of steering force.

would be adequate for awhile. How wrong I was! But I find it interesting that the foils used by speed sailboards which now exceed 40 knots are exactly the shapes we found best at 20 knots. They retain attached flow, and reattach instantly if they happen to have become airborne momentarily, and they are the present practical indicators of what works. And again, both the findings of the sailboarders now, and of our work then, agree that the thicker the section and the further forward the maximum thickness, the lower will be the speed at which simultaneous separation from both sides will occur. If your boat won't sail fast, this doesn't matter. But if it will, and you want to stay in control, forget fat foils.

The second way is to rake the rudder blade forward at the tip, i.e. the lower tip should be closer to the bow than is the blade where it pierces the water surface. The trouble with this arrangement is that it picks up the maximum number of plastic bags.

The way to prevent separation is to fit a boundary layer 'fence', as sketched in Fig. 19.14. All outboard motor legs employ a flat plate just above the propeller. This is a classic fence – it stops air from being sucked down to the propeller blades. For rudder blades, only a small fence is needed. It is inconvenient in that it stops a rudder blade from being drawn up through a housing, and it spoils the flow if the blade is pivoted and swung half up in shallow water. But it works, and it is the only one which keeps on working when all the other arrangements have stopped working.

Some of the lessons we learned about flows at reasonably high speeds are:

1. An abnormally sharp leading edge without a fairing parabola (Fig. 19.15) will 'lift' slightly less and drag a little more than an optimum section at low speeds. At high speeds it will ventilate at about 80% of the maximum force attainable, but has the advantage of reattaching easily.

2. A blunt or circular leading edge without a fairing parabola such as Fig. 19.16 can lift very strongly at low speeds, but it too ventilates at about 80% of the attainable force. It has the disadvantage of being most reluctant to reattach at all at high speeds.

3. A parabolic leading edge such as Fig. 19.17 appears to be the best compromise for both low and high speeds. A slightly blunter parabola will give greatest force at low speeds. A slightly finer parabola will give the greatest force before

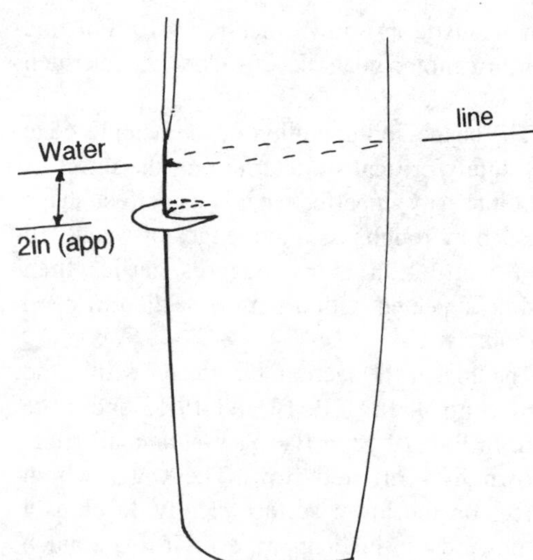

Fig 19.14 *Fence* arrangement

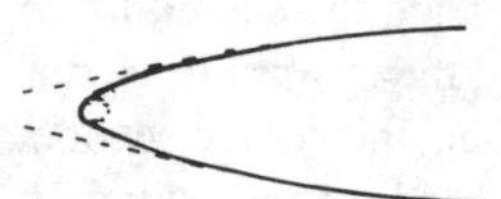

Fig 19.15 Sharp leading edge

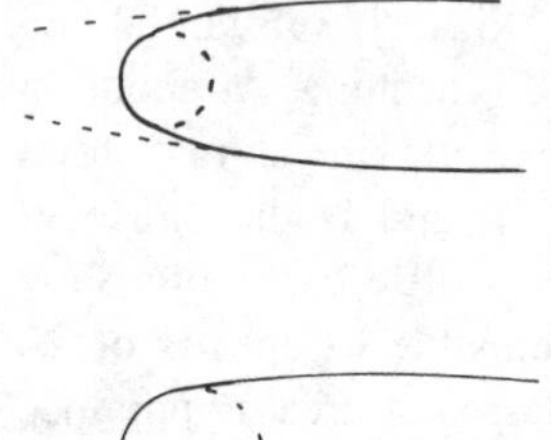

Fig 19.16 Blunt or circular leading edges

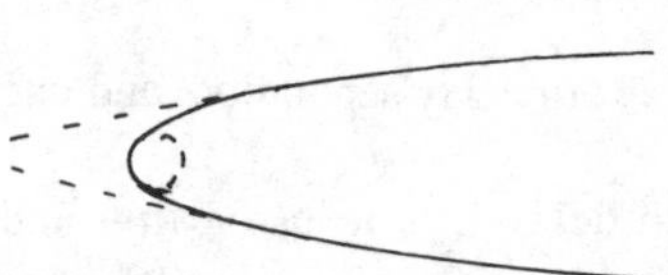

Fig 19.17 Parabolic leading edge

ventilation at higher speeds.

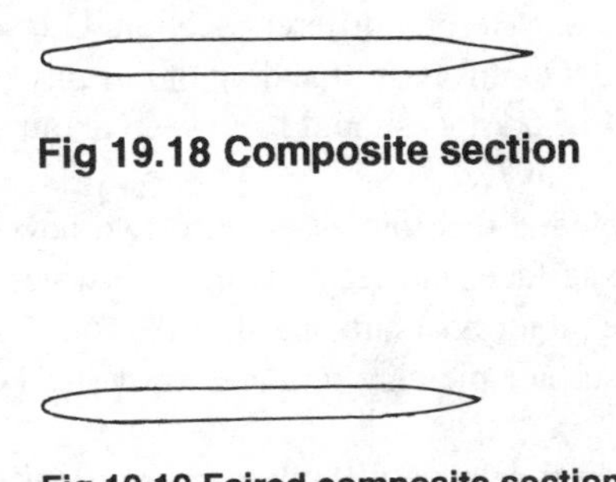

Fig 19.18 Composite section

Fig 19.19 Faired composite section

4. A 9% or 10% thick section with a small leading edge radius followed by a fairing parabola over the forward 15% of the chord gives the best blend of both low and high speed behaviour. The faster the design speed, the finer the leading edge radius should be. For example, Eighteen footers with three rigs used to use three centreboards. In light airs the big rig and big board are expected to handle the speed range between about 4 and 10 knots. A leading edge radius of about 1% of the chord seems to work best in this range. In moderate winds the boat will spend 90% of its racing time at speeds between about 12 and 20 knots. If the boat uses a centreboard with a 1% radius leading edge, it will not achieve speeds as high as similar boats with foils with leading edge radii of about 0.5% i.e. about twice as sharp. A board almost as big as the big one but of about half the leading edge radius is fastest in practice. For strong winds, only a tiny board is needed. It will spend its racing life at speeds of about 14 knots to windward, and sometimes up to double that in gusts downwind. The leading edge radius needs to be a little finer yet, at about 0.4%. This is also the shape to which the rudder blade is finished. At high speed, any blemish will trigger separation, and loss of control and probable capsize will follow unless the crew are very smart. A plastic bag spells instant disaster.

5. A thick section – 18% to 20% – such as Fig. 19.13 will have greater drag at low speeds, and will ventilate at 80-85% of the force attained by the thinner sections. At high speeds it can reverse its force before reattachment. It is slow to reattach.

6. A 'Composite' section such as Fig. 19.18 is pure disaster for any fast boat. It ventilates early and unventilates late. When shaped like Fig. 19.19 it is better, but is still not nearly as good as the optimum.

7. The effects of blemish or scoring tend to reverse at speed. At low speed the condition of the leading edge is vital for superior performance.

Further back, a blemish in the form of projections can destroy organised flow, but blemishes in the form of depressions seems to be much less important.

At high speeds this is not true. A Tornado rudder blade with a perfect leading edge but with heavy vertical scores down one side half way back gave respectable low-speed performance. But at high speed it repeatedly ventilated at 130 lbs, instead of the 215-220 lbs generated by a similar unscored blade at the same speed. It appeared that the scores were acting as feed channels for the air.

19.6 The drag of surface-piercing foils in wake

Substantial drag is caused both by the presence of the water surface itself, and also by the existence of the boundary layer which is formed by a hull ahead of the foil. This must always be the situation with a stern-hung rudder.

The object of the 'motor-boat' tests was to examine the mechanisms, and improve the equipment in whatever way was necessary to improve steering control at higher speeds. Our primary focus was to measure and compare the 'lift' (steering force) properties of different sections at both the low speeds achieved by all boats and also at the higher speeds which are now beginning to be achieved by modern high-performance craft.

The lift forces we measured were about what we expected up to the point at which ventilation occurred. Beyond that point the ground rules were altered, and even negative lifts became understandable and not too surprising.

But the drag forces we measured were much greater than expected.

In the next section, 'Hulls', a programme of tow tests is described. In one of these we compared the drag of a hull without a centreboard, with the drag of the same hull with a centreboard fitted.

The difference, at a speed of 5 knots, was about 1 pound, which is consistent with the wind tunnel prediction of a good laminar flow section working at zero lift. It is also consistent with the work of other researchers, such as Tom Tanner's measurements of the drag of a sailing canoe (full-size) in the National

Physical Laboratory's tank. He measured the drag both without any centreboard and with each of four centreboard's, each of a different section. Our results were consistent with his and we felt that we were on firm ground. On this basis, the drag of our tiny (6 inch chord and 12 inches immersed depth) test sections at speeds of 4 or 5 knots should have been about one sixth of a pound. They were not. They were more than one pound! Why?

We concluded that this was due to two new factors – first that they were measurements of foils which pierced the surface, and secondly that the water which flowed over them necessarily included the boundary layer of the motor boat hull ahead of the foil. This is a perfectly normal situation – every stern-hung rudder must be a surface-piercing foil, and must also be swept by the boundary layer of the hull which is ahead of it.

Our 17 foot, relatively flat-bottomed motor-boat had a reasonably smooth painted bottom. At a speed of 5 knots the boundary layer, fully turbulent, looked to be about 2.5 to 3.0 inches thick. At 20 knots it was easy to see the whitish intensely turbulent boundary layer every time a foil ventilated and we looked into the void in the water. At this speed the boundary layer was a little less than 1 inch thick.

We found ourselves wondering about the detail of the boundary layer over the test foil. The part below the motor boat's boundary layer appeared normal in all respects. But what happens when an intensely energetic 'fine-grain turbulence' boundary layer flow sweeps over a laminar flow section? In this case, a turbulent boundary layer had started near the bow of the motor boat when it was not planing, and from progressively further back as it planed faster, and had been growing thicker and more energetic with every foot of run from bow to stern. It therefore possessed within its three inch thickness (at 4 knots) much more turbulent energy than could possibly be developed by any foil across six inches of chord during which the boundary layer might grow to a thickness of about one tenth of an inch. Was it so strange that the drag was several times greater than expected? A minor but not unimportant fact is that the bottom of the motor boat was not as smooth as that of a racing dinghy, and its boundary layer was thicker than we were accustomed to observing behind our sailboats, so the bias we were considering would not be as great in the case of a well-maintained sailboat.

The second factor was that the foil pierced the surface. The way in which completely immersed bodies like fish, airships or gliders' wings move with minimum resistance because they recover almost all of the energy that they expend has been described above in Section 19.4. The critical point about stern-hung rudders is that they pierce the surface. Like ventilation, the presence of the surface alters the ground rules. The water in the tube had nowhere to go but to accelerate backwards, and so the energy added to it was conserved and could be recovered. But the water at and near the surface can escape upwards and outwards as spray, and the energy expended in accelerating this spray can never be recovered. In the extreme, a thick foil which ventilates on both sides simultaneously at and above some critical speed can recover no energy whatever, and its resistance will necessarily be horrendous. So it is not surprising that our relatively shallow test foils suffered more than deeper foils would suffer from the surface-piercing effect as well as from the launch's boundary layer effect.

We contemplated for awhile repeating the tests from a catamaran platform with the foil holder between the hulls so that the foils would pierce undisturbed water. After further thought we discarded that idea for two reasons:

(a) It would have eliminated the turbulent boundary layer but it would not have eliminated the surface-piercing factor; and

(b) The results of any such programme would not have been practical. Our object was to learn how to steer fast boats reliably, and all the fast boats we know have stern-hung rudders, except for sailboards which have similar problems such as becoming airborne from time to time.

It seemed to us that these two factors, together, completely explained the very high drags of our tiny test foils, because they were so shallow (only 12 inches immersed), and also that such a high proportion of their depth was both near the surface and also washed by the launch's thick turbulent boundary layer at low speeds.

We concluded:

1. There was nothing that we could do about it. Further, there was nothing that we ought to try to do about it, because it was the normal situation. All surface-piercing foils will suffer this very high drag but

only for the inch or two nearest the surface. The deeper they are the less will the abnormal behaviour of this thin layer bias the behaviour expected from fully immersed (i.e. wind tunnel, etc) measurements.

2. The thickness and energy of the hull's boundary layer will change constantly according to the speed of the boat, and the smoothness of its bottom. As between different designs of boats it will be governed partly by the length and partly by the curvature of the bottom. It is not the sort of thing that it is either practical or profitable to try to predict.

3. The adverse surface-piercing component will be smallest with thin sections at low speed and greatest with thick sections at high speeds. In the ultimate, a thick foil which ventilates on both sides simultaneously can recover no energy at all.

4. The effect of these two factors is considerable. For example, our test sections were 6 inches wide and were immersed to a depth of 12 inches. At a speed of 4 knots, any reasonable section with a drag coefficient at zero lift of about 0.01 or less would have been expected to have a measured drag of about 0.25 pounds or less. In fact they ran at this speed with drags of about 1 pound.

5. Whatever the reason, the appearance of this abnormally high drag when a foil is exposed to the turbulent boundary layer of another body suggests:

(a) Don't sail in the wakes of other boats.

(b) Don't run your rudder blade in the wake of the centreboard, i.e.think twice before you use a gybing centreboard.

19.7 Centreboard area, point of sailing, wind speed and experience

From Fig. 19.1, it is clear that the advantage of the reduced drag of a laminar flow section occurs only when the centreboard is operating at an angle of attack of less than about 3.5 degrees. The size of the centreboard should be chosen so that it will work comfortably 'within the bucket' when sailing to windward at hull speed, with the crew fully hiked, plus a small added margin to defend inexperienced crews who occasionally lose speed. (I regard the fact that we were not able to measure a realistic leeway angle to be an interesting quirk. It had never occurred to me that it is not in fact there.)

Experienced crews who do not lose speed may sail fractionally faster if they pull their centreboards up a few inches – lighter crews can raise the board with advantage a little further than heavy crews, because they apply less side load.

In lighter winds, the side load decreases rapidly while the boat speed decreases only slowly, and so, technically, less centreboard area is needed. Despite this, the boat will lose no speed (due to less tip loss) and will point higher (due to less leeway) if the full centreboard area is used.

In Section 17.7, reference was made to super-critical and sub-critical flow over sails in very light airs. The same phenomenon can affect centreboards at very low speeds – say at some fraction of one knot. Very strange things can then happen, such as a turbulent flow section working better backwards (sharp edge first), and other wierdos. These are of no practical significance for normal sailing.

In stronger winds and rougher water, many crews elect to sail a little faster than hull speed. As the speed increases, the centreboard may be drawn up progressively higher, and still operate, 'within the bucket'. The advantage of raising the centreboard is that it reduces the vertical distance between the centre of pressure of the centreboard and the centre of pressure of the sails (Fig. 16.2 etc), and so increases the total sail force which a crew can accept and the drive force they can achieve. In the trade-off, as the centreboard is raised, between increasing drag from greater tip loss and increasing leeway from smaller area, and increasing drive force – drive force wins every time, particularly in rough water. The limit is reached when the centreboard is pulled so high that the angle of attack increases to the point where it moves, 'out of the bucket', and the boat suffers the resistance 'C-D' or 'G-H' instead of 'E-F'. Any trace of weed on the centreboard (or rudder) will have the same effect.

As the point of sailing moves away from close-hauled through close reach, reach, and broad reach, the simultaneous increase in boat speed and reduction in side force means that only a fraction of the centreboard area required for close-hauled sailing will be needed for control of leeway. However, if the centreboard is lifted too high when the hull is broad-reaching or running fast, the hull's 'steer for balance' characteristics will progressively reverse. For this reason the practical limit for raising the centreboard is to ensure that enough depth (say 18 inches) remains in the water below the hull for adequate 'steer for balance' stability.

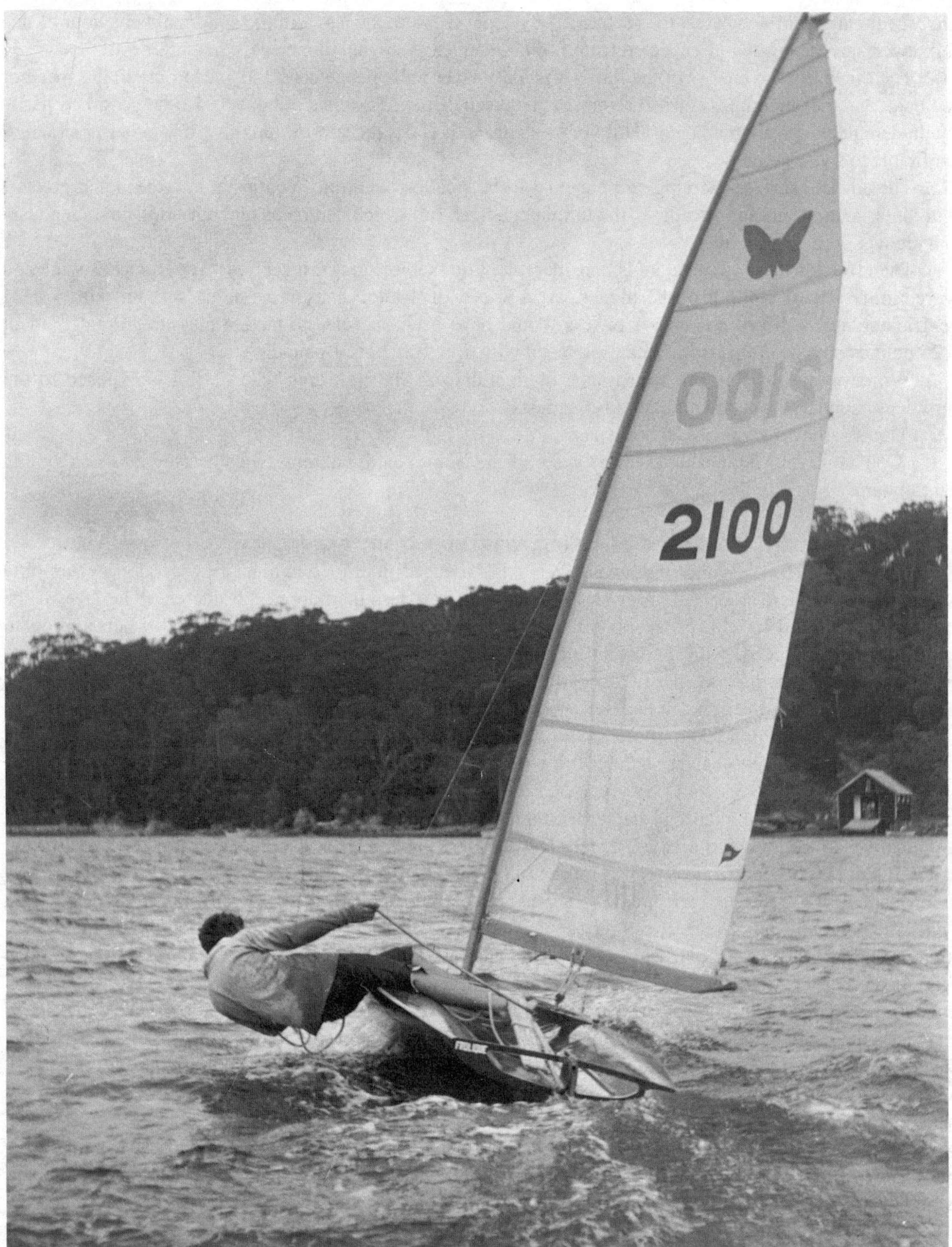

One of two identical moths used to compare the performance of cambered and uncambered centreboards.

Fig 19.20 *Mouldie* moth c1965

19.8 Cambered centreboards

Birds and aircraft both use deeply cambered wings at low speeds. As speed is increased, the wings become flatter, but even the fastest machines – such as the *Concorde* – still find it efficient to use wings which are slightly cambered in the lifting sense. Centreboards do the same job as wings. Would our boats sail faster if we used slightly cambered centreboards? We felt that the possibility justified the effort of finding out.

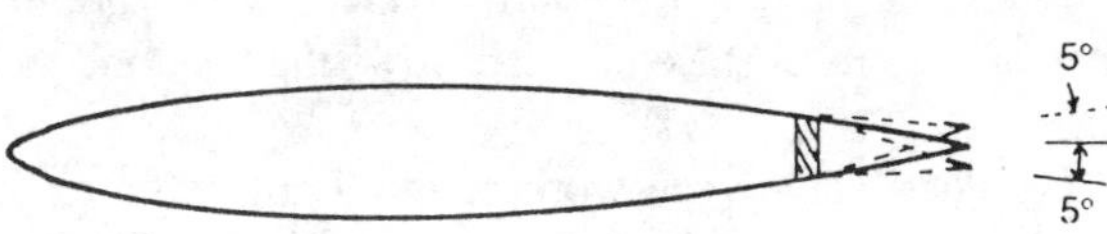

Fig 19.21 Centreboard with adjustable trim tab

At that time, about 1965, my elder son and daughter both sailed identical Moths. One is shown in Fig. 19.20. We made a third centreboard, identical to the other two, but cut off the aft 15% and reattached it with a piece of dense foam rubber in place of the saw cut, as in Fig. 19.21. We fitted a spring-loaded catch which enabled the helmsman to set the flap, while sailing, at either zero or at plus or minus 5 degrees. The rubber at the hinge line was shaved exactly to the level of the surface at the zero setting. While the surface across the rubber hinge was not as smooth as the surface of the highly polished 'solid' foils, the test foil was equally polished and the discontinuity was very small.

We fitted this test foil to either boat and sailed boat against boat until we were sure of our facts. In retrospect, it was this work which gave us the experience to develop the more exact 'boat against boat' technique which is described in Section 7.8 and which has given us such precise results in later years. In this case we towed no markers and punched no stopwatches, but we did alternate tests with the foil cambered with tests with the foil set straight. There was very little if any difference in the critical area so it took us a long time before we were certain of our facts, which were:

1. Flap at zero degrees. No detectable difference, but in the sense that the test foil was never better and occasionally it fell back a shade but not enough nor often enough to come to any conclusion.
2. Flap at plus 5 degrees. No detectable difference.
3. Flap at minus 5 degrees. Boat consistently fell away to leeward.

This principle has subsequently been developed with the use of trim tabs behind the smaller keels of some yachts. Shallow keels work at greater angles, similar to slow-flying birds, and in this situation trim tabs work well. Deep centreboards work at very small angles, and are different.

It was only years later that I realised that we had conducted the wrong experiment. The aerodynamic advantage of cambered wings over flat wings is that smaller cambered wings can do the same job as bigger flat wings, and the slightly increased drag of the cambered surface is more than offset by the reduced skin friction of the smaller area. (There are obviously other advantages such as the lesser weight and cost of smaller wings.) I now believe that we should have compared the performance of a series of progressively smaller cambered centreboards against that of a bigger uncambered one. When looked at in this way, the skin friction drag of a good laminar flow centreboard is already so low that some small percentage reduction of an already small component of the total drag would be unlikely to make a detectable improvement in performance. With larger boats with smaller keels which sail at larger leeway angles the situation is different. Trim tabs on yacht keels can certainly be beneficial

19.9 The rudder blade

When a boat is trimmed and handled properly, the rudder should carry a positive but much smaller side load than the centreboard. Our experience suggests that for maximum speed a boat should be balanced so that the rudder, which is typically about 30% of the area of the centreboard, will carry about 10% of the total side load. We experimented to establish the effect of rake on speed, and found that highest speeds were attained when the leading edge of the rudder blade was vertical, but that positive or negative rakes of up to 10 degrees made little difference. When the rake was greater than that, the boat sailed measurably more slowly. The rudder should always be designed so that it operates 'within the bucket', except for brief periods during manoeuvres.

19.10 Summary

The centreboard and rudder blade develop the same sort of forces as the sails. They are just as important as the sails in achieving high performance. They work in water which is about one thousand times more dense than air, so any surface blemish slows the boat one thousand times more than a similar blemish in the rig or sails.

Fortunately they can work at small angles more like gliders' wings than sails, so there is nothing one need do with them other than maintain them in flawless condition, and adjust the area of the centreboard in the water while sailing, and ensure that they stay free from weed.

They do their work quietly and efficiently. Generally they do not call attention to themselves in the same way as flapping sails or a crack on the head with the boom, and they therefore tend to be overlooked. If you seek high performance it is not wise to overlook them. They are just as important as your sails in providing the force which drives your boat, and they reward care and understanding.

For fastest sailing:

Keep them highly polished.
Keep them vertical.
Keep them free from blemish.
Keep them free from weed.

Skiff in light air with big rig on Brisbane River

Chapter Twenty
Hulls

20.1 Experimental background

The notes which follow flow from the unusual circumstances mentioned previously, in that an unusual group gathered together to develop a new dinghy class for their own use. This group of men and women included pilots, scientists, engineers and aerodynamicists. Between them, they enjoyed access to all the principal research and test facilities then available in Australia.

At that time there existed good sailing dinghies for children, and good sailing dinghies for athletic young males – the Australian Skiff classes and the Olympic classes. But no sailing dinghy which was truly suitable for a man and woman crew existed. This was why we had decided to develop a new class for our own use. In the beginning, we evaluated our concepts with two jointly-owned prototypes. We liked what we saw. We established class rules which encouraged experimentation and development within broad limits of length, beam, hull weight and sail area in a manner similar to the principles which had guided the International Fourteen Class but with three important differences.

The first was that all measurements were absolute and all assumptions based on historical precedent were removed – for example in this class 'sail area' meant 'actual measured area of sail-cloth, and the historical implications of 'fore-triangle', 'overlap is free', and 'roach is free' vanished. Whether any designer chose to put his allowable sail area all into a single jib or all into a single mainsail (and both were tried) or to divide it in any other way he chose between two or more sails was his business.

The second was that the structure weight, which had by that time become accepted in Australia as adequate for a robust hull with a long racing life, had already fallen to about ten pounds per foot of length, i.e. to between one half and one third of the traditional northern hemisphere hull weights. Sydney's average summer afternoon sea breeze is a brisk twelve knots. Light weight and the promise of wind suggested some lively times ahead!

The third was that the women for whom we were developing this new class stated very firmly that their preference was for no spinnakers and no trapezes, so these were excluded by rule from the outset.

Three decisions, all spontaneous, gave direction to the project.

First, we were interested only in the real speed increases achievable from planing dinghies. This concentrated our focus on 'light dinghies only' and saved us from all the customary 'heavy yacht' distractions which are irrelevant when one is considering speed.

Secondly, we co-operated from the beginning by publishing and freely sharing all new technical information, even though several of us were at the same time competing in developing our own individual design marques.

Thirdly, whenever a common problem was recognised, a core group of us co-operated spontaneously in mounting and completing semi-formal programmes of measurements to establish the facts as accurately as we could. These experiments provided an invaluable base in our search for higher performance.

This whole movement was started by a small group of enthusiasts for our own pleasure and recreational enjoyment. It never occurred to any of us that others might be interested. The initial boats were pleasant to handle, delightfully responsive, and surprisingly fast. The women for whom they had been designed were happy, sailed as competitively as any of the men, shared the trophies, and assumed and shared the responsibilities of office. Their organisational and experienced social skills made the class a most pleasant body to belong to. There are those who now say that we were one of the very early women's movements. If so, none of us noticed. Others observed that we were happy, and joined us. Soon there were a thousand, and a new class had been born. The originators maintained a philosophical influence but let others organise the class – which they did very well. We kept right on doing what we had started – finding out more about how light sailboats work, and developing them to make them sail faster.

The sail and rig experiments, and the foil developments, have been described elsewhere. Hull development was primarily comparative, by exposing progressively developed hull shapes to competitive fleet racing in the full variety of wind and sea-state conditions. However, to provide a base of absolute performance measurements, we conducted an extended programme in the late 1960's and the early 1970's in which we towed and measured the drags of four hulls of different styles, each ballasted to either 450, 525, or 600 pounds total weight, at speeds from one to eighteen knots.

One hull was a minimum-wetted-area style, smoothly rounded and with fine ends. Hulls of this shape are competitive in light airs, but their planing performance tends to be poor. They are often known as 'river' dinghies.

The second was almost like a small motor boat, with shallow 'Vee' and a reasonable bow, but otherwise an extreme, very flat, planing style. In moderate and strong winds this design planed so freely that it could be unbeatable, but its performance in non-planing wind speeds was disappointing, and its performance in conditions of 'waves and light air' was a disaster area.

The third was an early compromise, adapted from the 'Javelin' hull by the New Zealand designer, John Spencer. This hull combined some of the advantages of the first and second styles without the severe disadvantages of either. It was popular with us, we understood it well, and for several years this became our reference hull. It proved a useful 'test-bed' to use while we experimented and developed better ideas.

The fourth hull was designed in 1969 by Mark Bethwaite, and was the beginning of the truly modern stream. Its rationale flowed partly from the observed performance of the Finn, and partly from a little theorising. Its performance proved so unusual that this background is worth explaining.

One of Sydney's sailing features is an annual 'Two of a Kind' weekend regatta in which the national champion and the state champion of each class are invited to sail three long scratch races around a triangular course. Australian 'yardsticks' are drawn partly from this regatta, and partly from similar confrontations in Melbourne. In the years before the Eighteens developed their higher ratios, the winner was usually an FD or 505 or Lightweight Sharpie (the 'College' boat) or an Eighteen or a Tornado (the catamarans did not shine on the triangular courses). For several years I had compared the speed of each class with the speed which would logically be expected in view of each boat's length, total weight, sail area, and the wind and sea-state conditions in each of the three races. I had noted that the Finn, a heavy boat with little sail, consistently sailed faster than expected, particularly in the 'light air and waves' conditions in which so many boats fail to perform well. When we looked for a possible reason, the most obvious difference between the Finn design and all other boats was the shape of its hull. In the 1960's there were few classes which did not have the relatively symmetrical shapes developed over the years by the International Fourteens and other development classes, as in Fig. 20.1. In such designs the forward part of the bow wedge was often surprisingly blunt. The Finn was somewhat ahead of its time in having long almost-straight waterlines forward which gave a wedge angle which was both constant and much finer than was normal at that time, as in Fig. 20.2. It seemed to us that the wave impact drag which is one of the consequences of sailing through rough water was probably proportional to the square of the 'bluntness' of the bow wedge angle, that the Finn's finer entry-wedge angle could be a real factor for its relatively superior performance, and that this feature was worth trying.

The theorising had to do with energy recovery in waves. In Section 19.4, the motion of a 'streamline' section is described – how energy has to be expended to accelerate the air or water aside in order to make room for the wing or centreboard or whatever, and the manner in which almost all of this energy is subsequently recovered. In Section 20.4, the application of this principle to hulls in the displacement mode is described – while the energy expended in making the surface waves which roll away from the boat is lost forever, we can recover much of what is left, and the more we recover, the faster we will sail. It occurred to us that the crest of the stern wave is 'focussed' into a surprisingly small area and position. In flat water it has to lie at the distance behind the bow determined by the boat's speed, and it will necessarily lie centrally between the quarter waves. At hull speed it will be exactly under the stern of the boat. In this situation the hull will recover as much energy as is possible.

But when we thought about the position of the crest of the stern wave in rougher water, we realised that the orbital motions and momentums of waves, and particularly chaotic waves, must continuously displace the position of the crest of the stern wave both fore and aft and sideways. In this case, while a boat shaped as Fig. 20.1 might recover everything possible when sailing in flat water when the crest would be at 'A', it would recover little or nothing whenever the crest was moved by waves to 'C', 'D' or 'E'. Could this be one of the reasons for the poor performance of so many designs in light air and waves? My response was to try shaping the hull to keep the water accelerating further toward the stern, to make the crest harder to displace. Mark tried a different tack. He reasoned that an after bottom shaped like Fig. 20.3 would continue to recover a substantial fraction of the recoverable energy whenever the crest of the stern wave was positioned not only at 'A', but also at 'B', 'C' or 'D' as well. The advantage looked as if it could be substantial, and this approach was also worth trying. So he designed a boat with a long fine entry forward, and a long flat run between wider and almost parallel chines aft. When I watched it take shape I reflected that there is little new in this world. I recalled the 'cod's head and mackerel tail' that English Bristol Channel pilot cutters developed through the nineteenth century, which had the same asymmetric 'deepest forward and widest aft' general shape.(FIG 20.3)

There was another point. Toward the end of Section 17.11, I mentioned that a point was reached where frustration with a theoretical approach to mast shape caused me to discard it and try instead a mix of theory and practice – that I discarded the ovoid mast and went intuitively to a 'long squareback' wingmast. Mark's new hull appeared at exactly the right time, and this was the boat to which this flatter, softer, more intuitively logical rig was first fitted. Three changes in the one design? This could be dangerous. He christened this machine '*Medium Dribbly*', partly to indicate maturity somewhat beyond extreme youth, but partly, I sense, as an insurance. (The hull shape is shown in Fig.20.6 and the boat is shown sailing in Fig 20.12.)

This boat needed no insurance!

The performance of this hull on tow test was impressive. It was the equivalent of the 'river' hull in drift conditions, much superior as hull speed was approached, and in a different class when planing. At the other end of the range, it matched the 'flat planer' at high speeds, and was much superior to it at all lower speeds. These performance differences suggested that we were beginning to understand the dynamics of these new lightweight hulls.

In open competition, this design (shown in Fig 20.12) immediately won both the Australian and then the NSW championships – the latter with five wins and a second in a 100 boat fleet. Its performance through waves was indeed different. I recall several races which started in flat water. In light or moderate winds and flat water there was little speed difference between the River designs and the Javelins and the Dribbly's. But as soon as we reached the slop of the harbour, the new ones just kept on sailing fast while all the other hull shapes dropped back. The speed difference was of the order of 5 per cent, and sometimes up to 10% when all the factors – the greater power of the rig, the finer entry, and the greater pressure recovery – could all work to advantage.

The class as a whole sensed a breakthrough. All subsequent design work by other designers in the class focussed on further development of the new ideas introduced in this boat. Figures 20.6(a) and 20.6(b) show

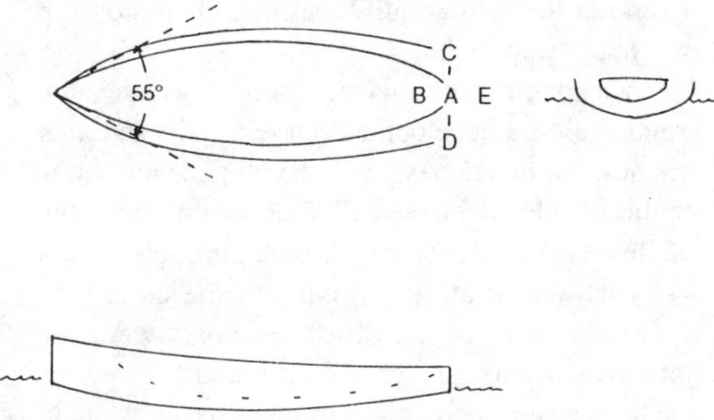

Fig 20.1 Conventional dinghy hull - c1960

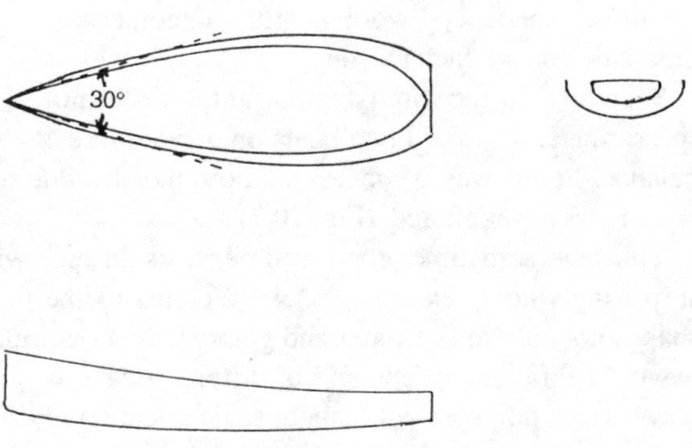

Fig 20.2 Characteristics of Finn dinghy hull

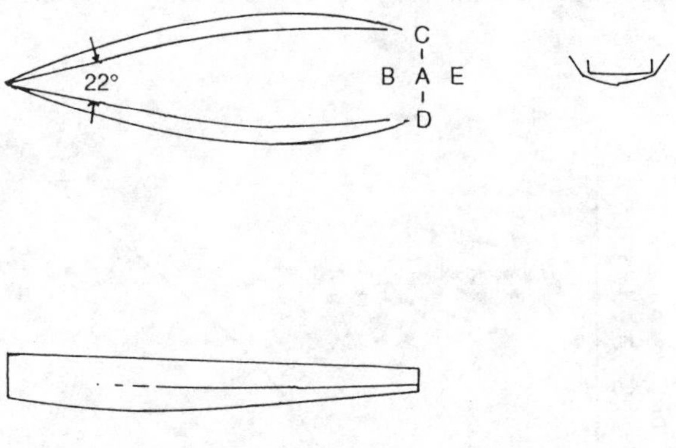

Fig 20.3 Medium Dribbly 1969

several of the similar hull types at a championship two years later.

(An economic note is of interest. Those who argue against a development class usually cite that whenever a better design is developed, the value of the obsoleted boats will fall. In this case the excitement generated by the breakthrough design was such that it attracted many to the class, and the resale value of the obsoleted boats went up, not down, due to the increased demand.)

The measurement programme was unusual in five respects:

First, we towed only real hulls which were ballasted to real sailing weights. We never trusted models because such unpredictable things happen in the scale change from model to full size. Even the most experienced workers still sometimes get this scale-change factor wrong.

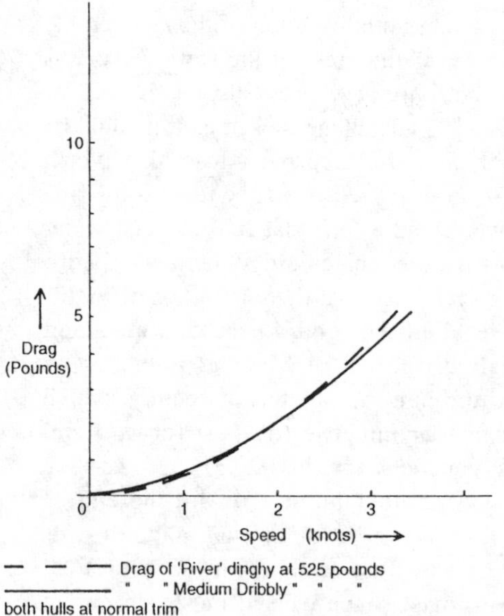

Fig 20.4 Drag comparison - 'River' dinghy and 'Medium Dribbly'.

Secondly, in the vitally important 1 to 5 knot speed range, we towed two boats on a beam like a balance. In this way we measured both the absolute drag and also the drag compared with a reference hull which was never altered. (Fig. 20.7)

Third, we sometimes continued our tests through wind and waves. As a result, we were able to develop a surprisingly complete set of measurements of the drag performance of real hulls of different but typical shapes not only in flat water and glassy calm conditions, but also when being towed 'into wave' and 'down wave' at different speeds and in different wave heights. These were real hulls at real weights and in real waves, with no guess-work about scale effect! (Figs 20.8 and 20.9)

Even so, a caution is justified about both the figures themselves and also the interpretation of the 'down-wave at speed' drags shown in Fig 20.8, because the way we tested the drags was different from the way we sail our boats. We tested by towing each boat behind an outboard-powered light aluminium dinghy. When the test speed was just a little faster than the wave speed, the boat almost surfed down each face very quickly and the drag was small for one or two seconds, but it then took an age to haul it up the back of the next wave and the drag was very high for the whole of the time the boat was being pulled uphill. The end result was that the faster hulls went downhill quickest but were just as hard and took just as long to pull uphill, so in terms of average drag (over time) the fastest hulls showed up worst. Anyone who repeats these tests would get the same result. But since in the tests we pulled the boats uphill for most of the time, but in the real world we sail them downhill for as much of the time as we can, this is just one more example of a scientific trap.

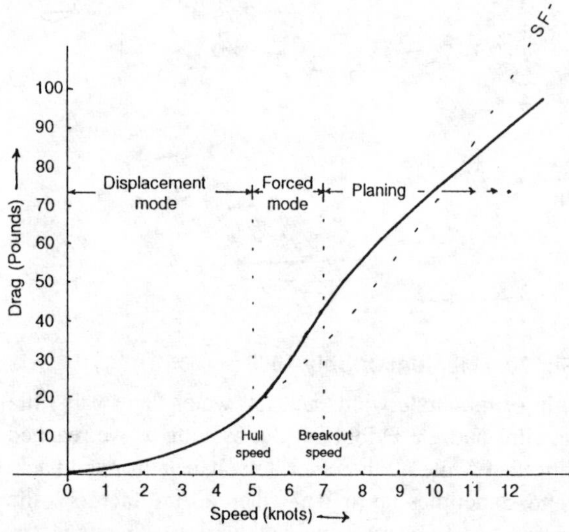

Fig 20.5 Drag curve, Dribbly 1, flat water

Fourth, we towed the hulls, not only at their proper trim, but also out of trim, i.e. bow down, stern down, and heeled. From these tests we learned that at one extreme the shape of the 'river' boat is not much disadvantaged by sailing out of trim. But at the other extreme, the flat planing shape suffered very large drag increase with even a small bow-down or stern-down trim or heel. Because the action of small waves in light air is to cause a hull to sail continuously out of trim as each wave crest washes onto and away from the

C 'River' hull
A Dribbly Mk I
D Dribbly Mk III

Fig 20.6 (a) Six different hull types

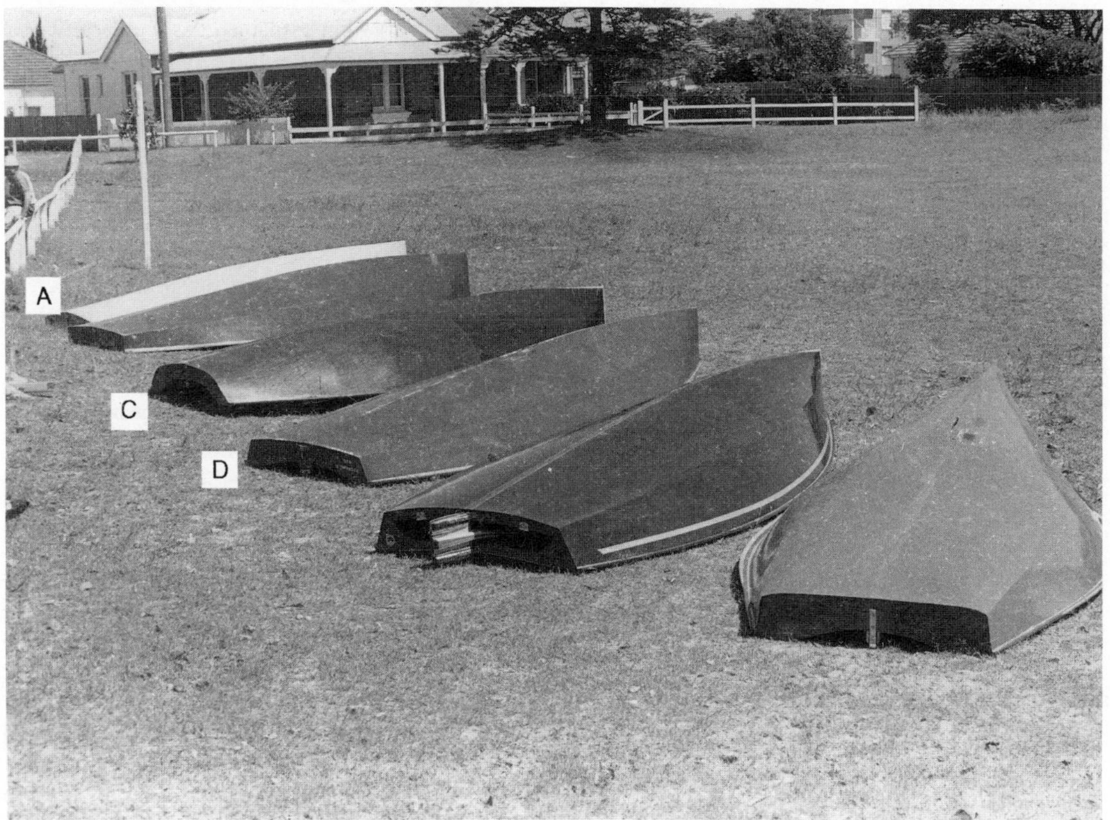

Fig 20.6 (b) Six different hull types

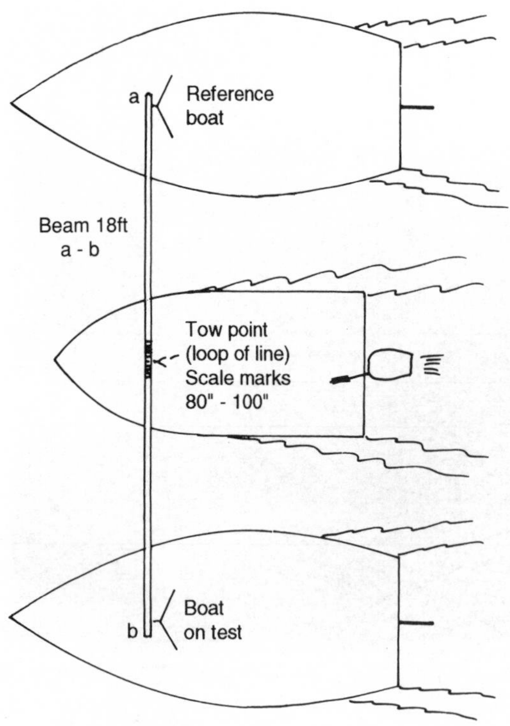

Fig 20.7 'Balance' method of tow-testing

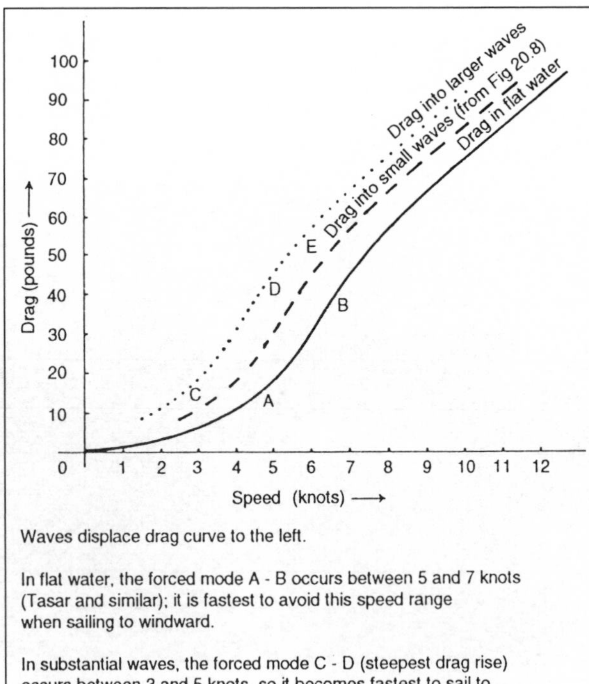

Waves displace drag curve to the left.

In flat water, the forced mode A - B occurs between 5 and 7 knots (Tasar and similar); it is fastest to avoid this speed range when sailing to windward.

In substantial waves, the forced mode C - D (steepest drag rise) occurs between 3 and 5 knots, so it becomes fastest to sail to windward at more than 5 knots to avoid the steep drag rise C - D. The fastest speed will depend on the waves and the boat.

In substantial waves, sail to windward free and fast, to enjoy the freedom in the range D - E. (Sect 20.12 refers.)

Fig 20.9 Effect of waves on forced mode - upwind

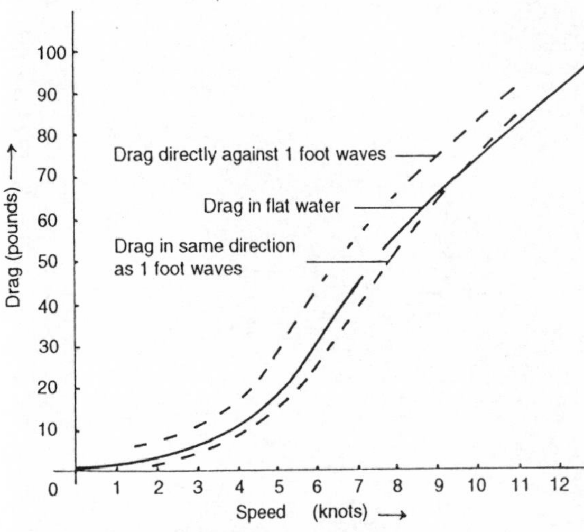

Differences in mean drag measured when towed by small motor boat directly against and down regular waves about 1 foot high.

Fig 20.8 Drag through small waves

hull, this observation explained the historically poor performance of too-flat hulls in light air and waves.

Finally, the accuracy of the flat-water, calm-air, comparative drag measurements was surprisingly sensitive. As an example, during the programme, every seventh measurement was a repeat of some previous measurement to check consistency. One repeat happened to call for a hull identical to the reference hull. On this 2 knot repeat test, these two hulls, which had previously recorded identical resistances, proved to be consistently different by a drag of about 1 oz or 2%. Both were ballasted to 450lbs. We repeated this measurement programme. Again, the test hull dragged 2% higher than previously. When we thought carefully about what could have happened, we realised that both dinghies had visited Canberra for a regatta the previous weekend. Both had trailed the 200 miles back to Sydney over dry sealed pavement. Both appeared clean. But the reference boat turned out to have been washed and the test boat had not. When we checked, road film was invisible to the eye, but just detectable to the hand. We washed both boats and repeated the test a third time. In this condition, the drags once again became identical. From this, we learned that even invisible grit can cause detectable slowing. We also learned to respect the sensitivity

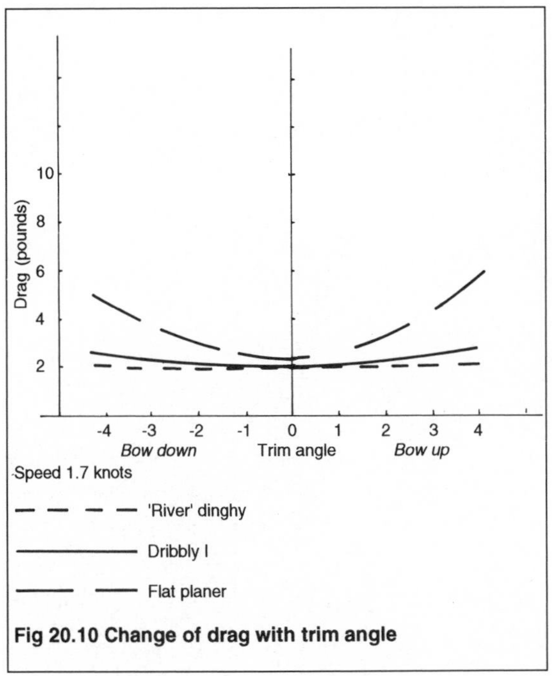

Fig 20.10 Change of drag with trim angle

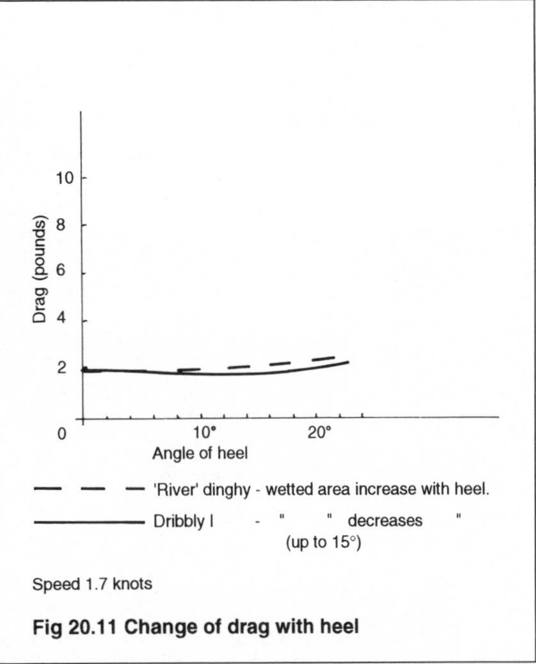

Fig 20.11 Change of drag with heel

and repeatability of our own work.

As a matter of record, my own contribution in the years that followed was to refine the Dribbly hull in three respects. Mk 2 incorporated a fractional adjustment of keel curvature to accommodate the average weight of two mature adults rather than the two younger adults for whom the boat had originally been personally designed. Mk 3 incorporated a slight broadening of the aft chine beam and slight flattening and reshaping of the aft bottom for further pressure recovery and also to promote earlier planing. This boat – shown as 'D' in Fig 20.6 – became the first non-trapeze windward planer, and achieved a reputation for consistent high performance across the entire range of wind and sea-state conditions. Mk 4 was an extension of this modification. By increasing the bottom roundness fractionally we achieved a smoother transition from 'hull speed' through 'forced sailing' to 'breakout' and 'full plane'. An unexpected advantage was that this slightly rounder hull proved able to carry heavier crews with less performance loss than would normally be expected. In open competition this hull established itself as dominant in the class, and it is the underwater shape of this Mark IV Dribbly hull which I incorporated into the design of the Tasar in 1975.

During this period my younger daughter sailed in the Cherub class, so I tried the ideas outlined above in this internationally popular and even lighter weight trapeze and spinnaker adolescents' class. The design principles continued to apply. She won several Australian championships, was runner up in the light-air world championships at Torquay in 1974, and won the open world championships in a strong-wind big-wave series in Adelaide in 1976.

Two years later I designed and developed the Laser II. The dynamics of this boat fall about midway between the two-adult Tasar and the more lightly crewed two-adolescent Cherub. I was fortunate in being able to draw upon a background so rich in both innovative development and competitive confirmation when asked to design what was clearly going to be a very important boat

At about this time David Porter – a personal friend – brought his three-hander Eighteen on line. My younger son Julian had grown up with, been central in and enjoyed all our experimental work. He sensed the ferment of further development ahead, joined the Eighteen footer class, and learned how it worked and shared its ongoing triumphs and disasters from the inside. It was not long before he was designing his own boats. The hulls of three most innovative two-hander Eighteens had their origins in the Tasar/Laser II dynamics. Fig. 20.18 shows the second of these three boats. As the Eighteens have increased their speeds year by year it has become my challenge to back up Julian's design work and to keep up with the technology. The present situation is that Julian's compact B18's are the fastest boats on the water and

Fig 20.12 Dribbly Mk I.

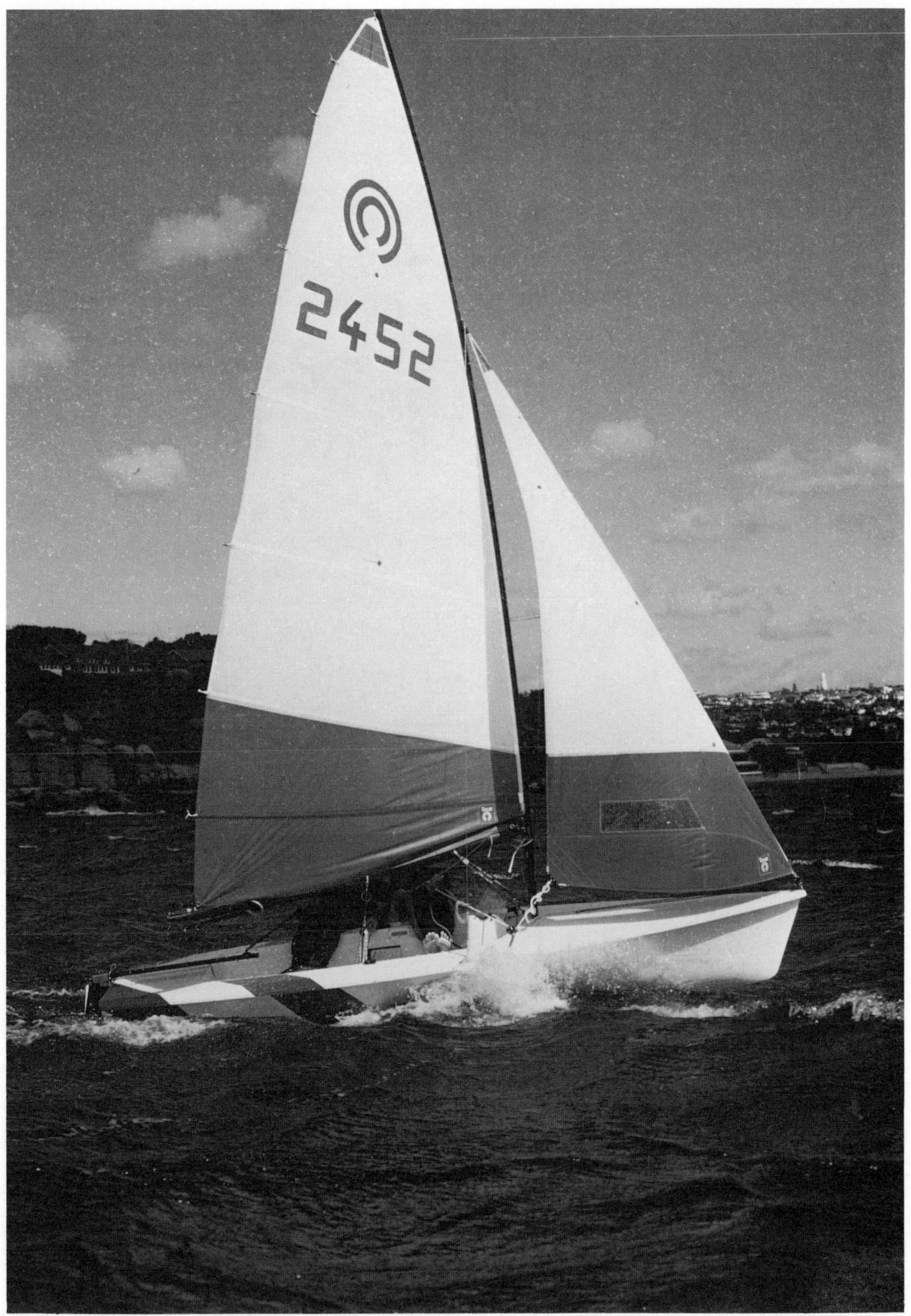

Fig 20.13 Rig set-up for windward planing

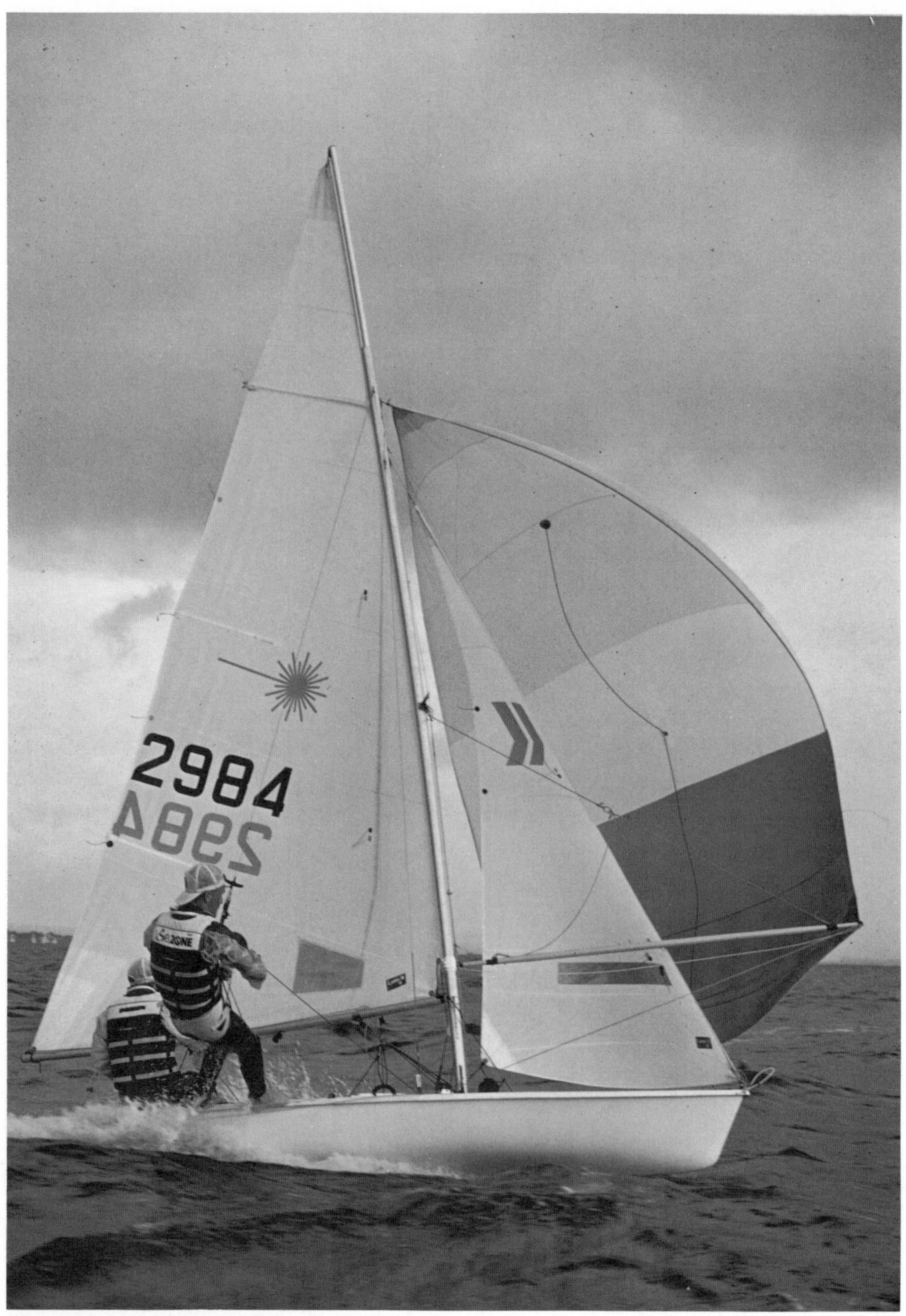

Fig 20.14 Laser II hull planes cleanly

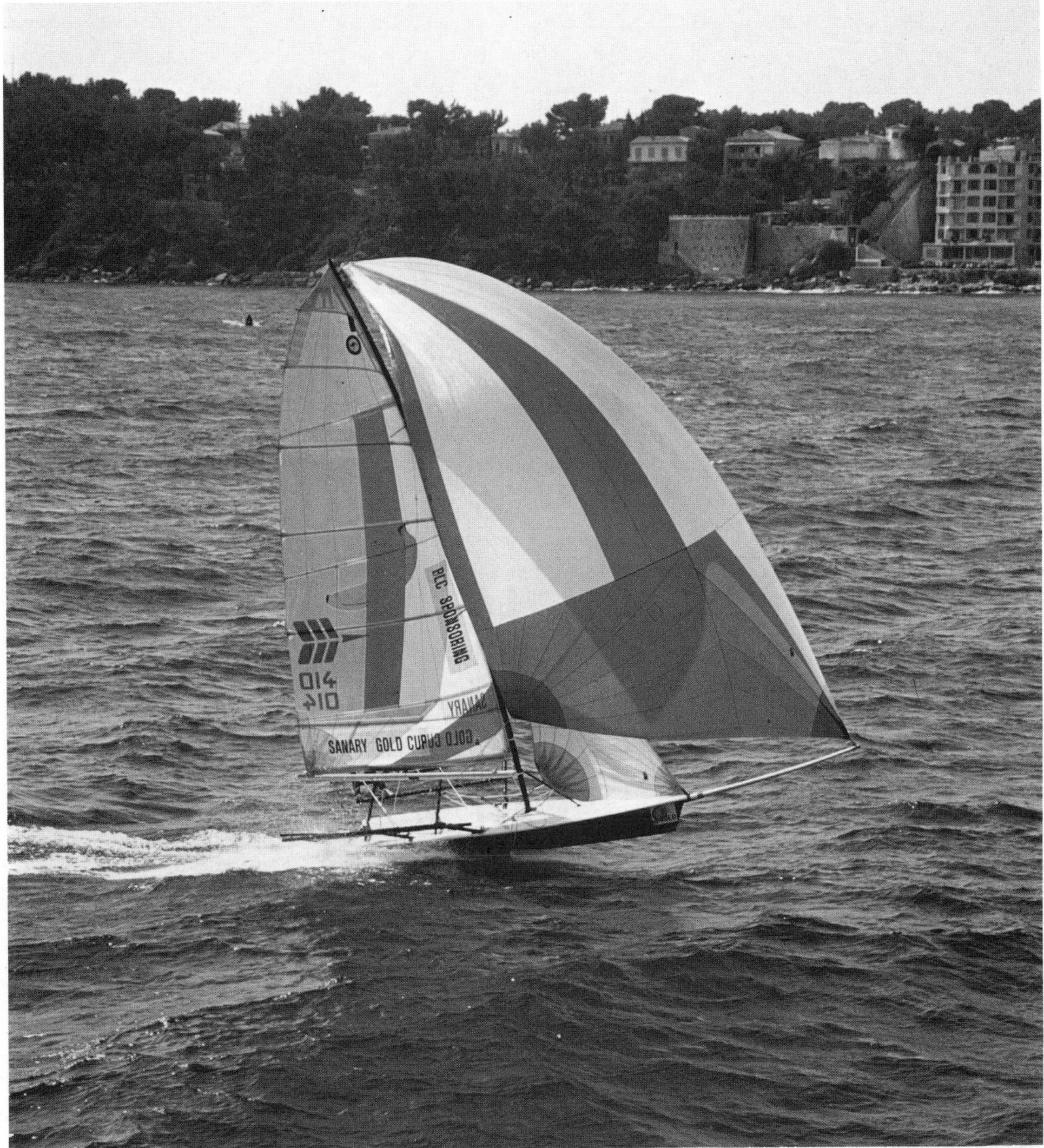

Fig 20.15 Prototype B18 at Sanary, South of France

Julian is the current world champion for the second year.

Reference to Julian's invention of the asymmetric spinnaker was made in Section 16.13. Fig 20.18 shows one of Julian's early two-hander Eighteens with this rig..

Fig **20.15** is a helicopter picture of a B18 moving fast downwind in strong wind and big waves at a regatta near Nice in the south of France. Video pictures show that the boats are moving downwind at about three times the wave speed.

Fig **20.19** shows one of my HSP's. The speed of about 22 knots is shown by the spray still rising at the stern of the 20 foot hull. The wind speed is given by the small angle of heel of the yachts in the background – about 12 knots.

Photo taken from distance in heavy rain. Skiff moving at 30 - 35 knots, sometimes faster, under smallest rig which is also reefed (ie no 4 rig).
Note skipper scanning ahead and to windward for approaching gusts. Sheethand and forward hands are watching their sails and the bow. Rob Brown (skipper), Matt Coleman and Julian Bethwaite.

Fig 20.16 1986 skiff at speed: Auckland,NZ

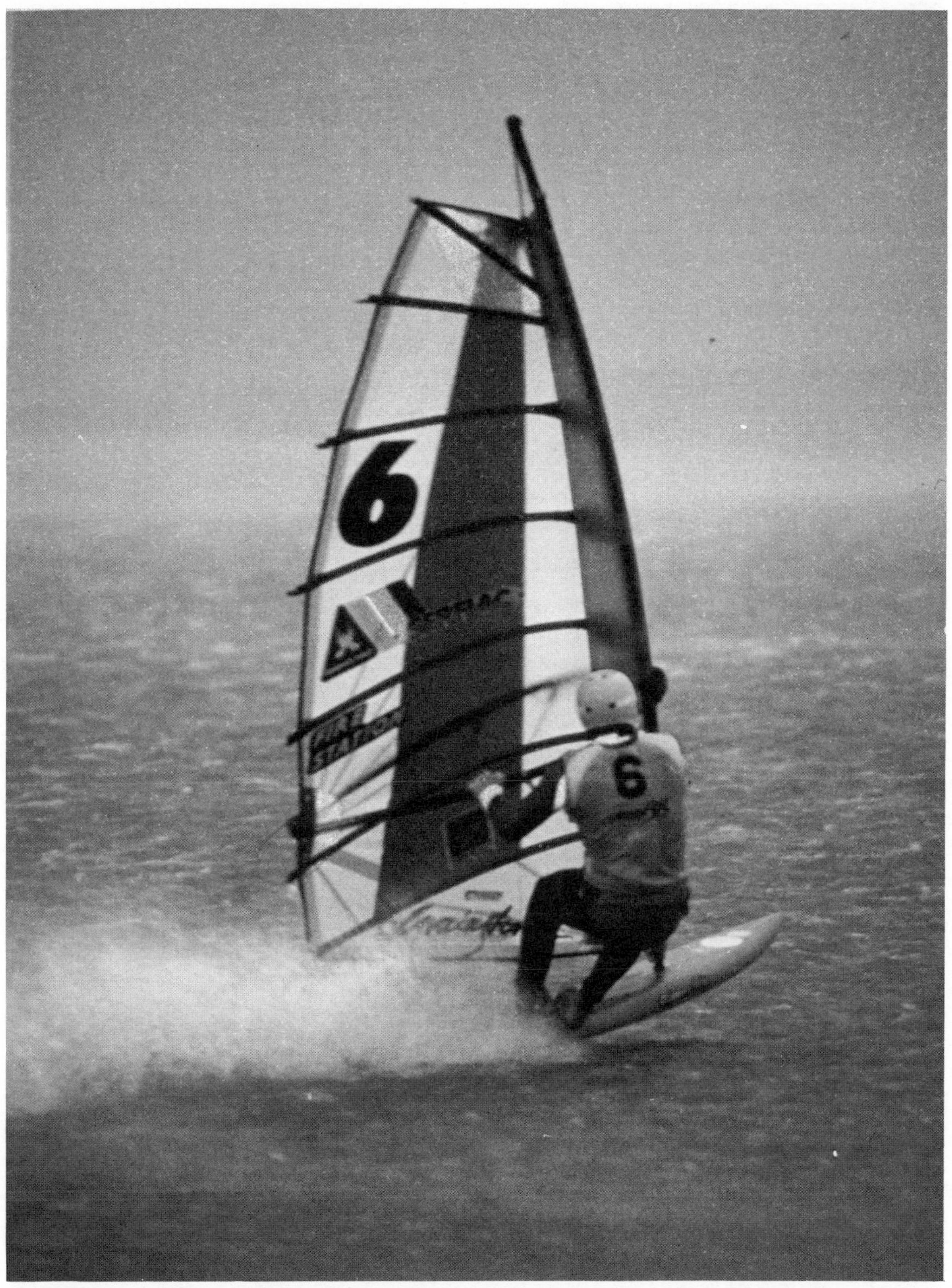

Mal Wright, holder for a while of the world speed record at 42 knots, photographed during one of his record-breaking runs, at Wilson's Promontory, Victoria.

Fig 20.17 Sailboard at speed
Photograph by courtesy of Michael Ellem - *Infocus Downunder*

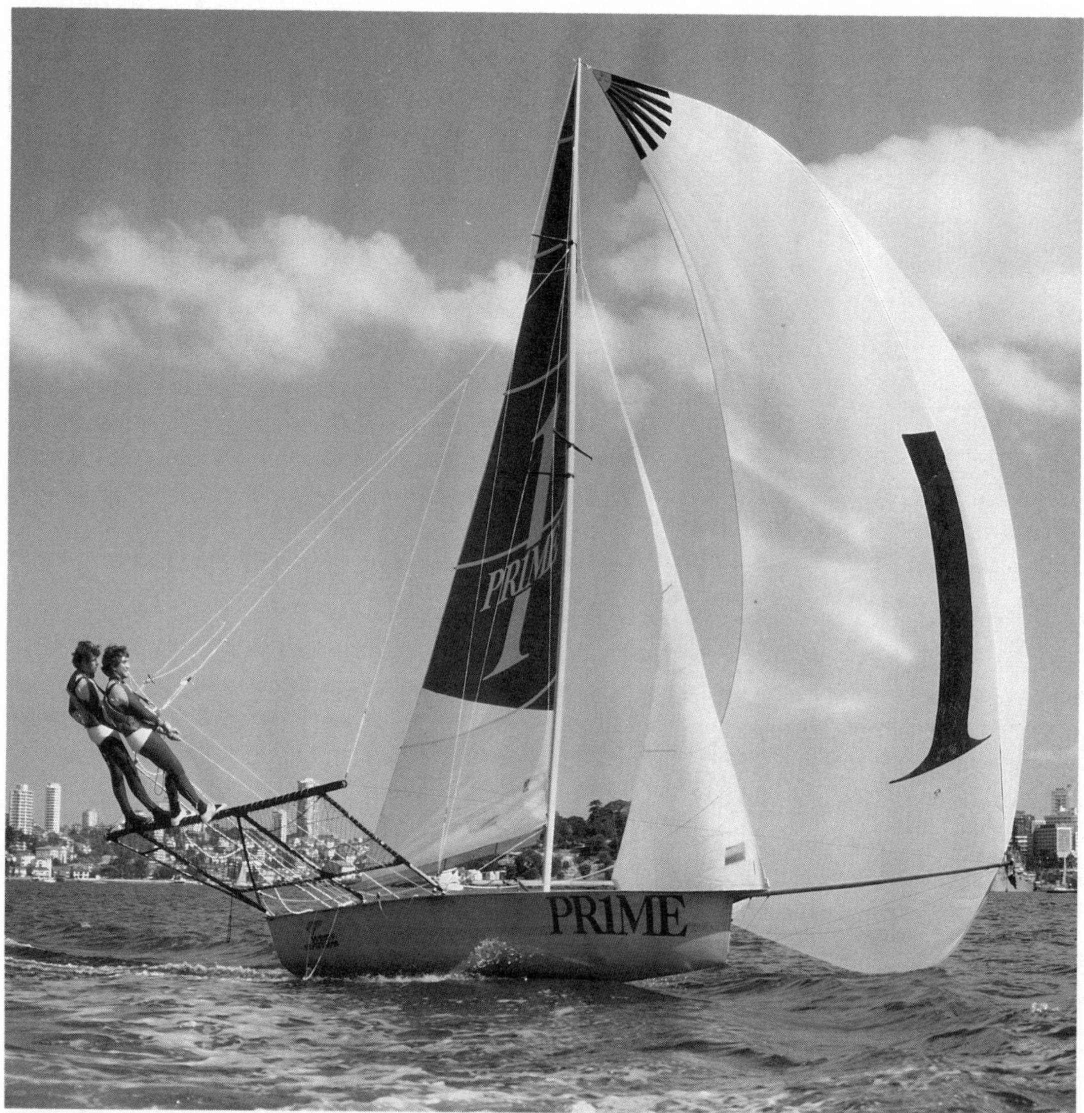

Julian Bethwaite and (Dr) Michael Wilson sailing *Prime II,* one of Julian's three two-hander Eighteens.

Fig 20.18 Early asymmetric spinnaker

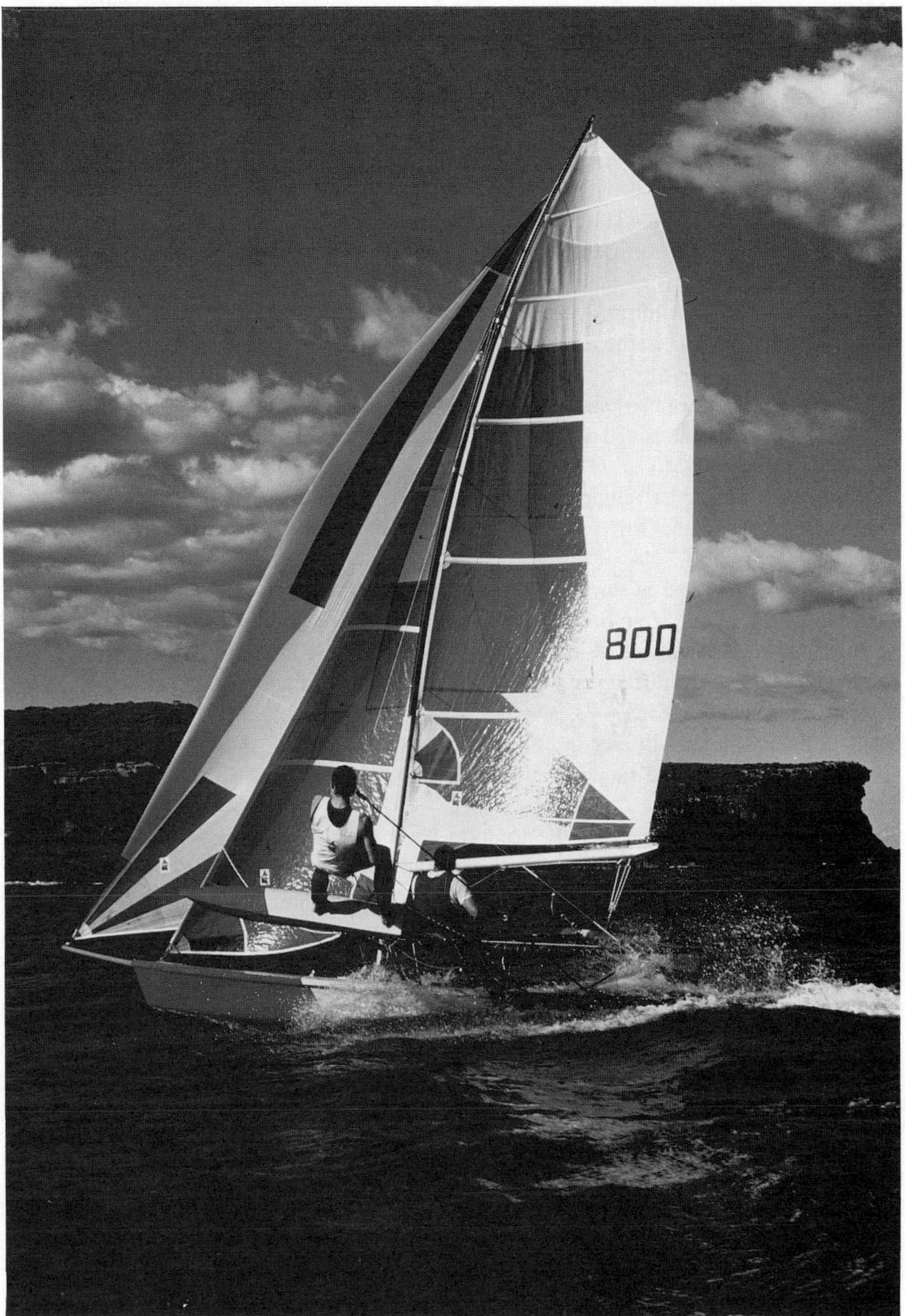

Cruising at nearly twice wind speed. This picture was taken within a few minutes of the photo on page 319. Wind speed is about 12 knots (as indicated by the yachts in the background on page 319). Boatspeed (about 22 knots) is indicated above by the spray still rising at the stern of a 20 foot hull.

Fig 20.19 HSP Duo Mk XVIII

The motion of a dinghy hull

20.2 Summary

Water impedes the movement and reduces the speed of a hull and its keel or centreboard and rudder, in six ways. These are:

1) Skin friction

A boat covered with weed and barnacles will sail more slowly than one which is clean and polished. The added drag is due to the difference in skin friction between a smooth and a rough surface.

2) Form drag

An outboard motor will push a slender yacht faster than a square-ended barge of the same length and weight. The added drag is due to the difference in form, or shape.

3) Induced drag or leeway

A hull which is towed straight will be easier to tow than one which is dragged sideways, even when the yaw angle is small. The added drag is the induced drag of the keel or centreboard.

4) Rudder deflection drag

A hull with its rudder aligned at the angle for minimum drag will be easier to tow than one with its rudder angled across the flow. The added drag is the induced drag of the rudder.

5) Wave making drag

If a short heavy boat is towed at progressively higher speeds, a speed zone will be reached at which, simultaneously, it will begin to make very big waves and its resistance will increase greatly. If a longer hull of the same weight is towed at that same speed, it will tow more easily and will make smaller waves. The difference is due to the difference in wave making drag between hulls of different lengths.

6) Drag due to waves

An outboard motor will push a hull faster through flat water than through any wave system (other than slowly down-wave). The increase in drag is due to the surface slopes, motions and momentums of the waves.

'Wave-making drag', refers to the complex wave system which is made by the moving hull itself. This is called the wake. In flat water wave making drag will be present, but drag due to external waves will be absent. 'Drag due to waves', refers to the situation of a hull which sails in waves, and will be a factor only in waves. In flat water it will be absent.

All six factors are to some degree under the influence of the crew. However, it is primarily wave making drag and drag due to waves which are of the greatest practical importance. Fortunately, these are the two factors over which the crew have greatest control.

Crews who understand how each of these factors work can adopt the handling techniques which will most reduce the drag as they sail through changing wind and sea-state conditions. In this way they can significantly increase their average speed.

20.3 Skin friction

Skin friction is the downstream force exerted on any surface when a fluid washes over it. This is one of the principle forces which governs the speed of ships through the sea, of aircraft through the air, and of oil, gas or water through pipelines which are sometimes hundreds of kilometres long. Fluid drag is of great economic importance, so it has been studied extensively.

The skin friction of a yacht or dinghy hull will depend on the wetted area and the roughness of the surface. It will be greater if the wetted area is large, and it will be greater again if the surface is rougher than an acceptable minimum.

The wetted area of a yacht hull is fixed by design. The wetted area of some dinghy hulls can be reduced by the use of the 'fourth mode' technique referred to later.

With respect to the minimum acceptable roughness, the information available to us falls into two categories – the steady speed, straight-line situation typical of a long pipeline, and the accelerating or decelerating speed, curved surface situation typical of the flow over an aeroplane's wing, a yacht's hull, or a dinghy's centreboard.

The laws which connect fluid mass, speed and viscosity, and surface roughness – with the final nature of flow in straight lines, have been measured and are published in standard texts on fluid dynamics. This information will suggest that at practical yacht or dinghy speeds, only the bow area of the hull can hope to run with a laminar boundary layer. Under this area the surface should certainly be highly polished. But beyond this zone the flow will become turbulent and under turbulent flow a highly polished surface will not be any faster than some rougher surface, provided always that the roughness is less than some small fraction of the boundary layer thickness.

My experience with model aeroplane wings, centreboards and the hulls of small boats, leads me to believe that as flows curve and accelerate and decelerate around small hulls they can remain laminar for much further than the straight-line measurements suggest. I question whether any surface is 'smooth enough' for a racing dinghy or skiff.

Two examples have been quoted. In Section 20.1 the detectable difference in hull drag as between a polished hull and one with invisible traffic film suggests that the boundary layer over both hulls was laminar all the way along the fourteen foot hulls, and not turbulent. The much improved steering force from a polished, as compared with an almost-polished rudder (Fig. 19.2), suggests that the 'rough surface' factor demonstrated by the rough tumbler kitchen experiment (Fig. 17.11), was still significant even with microscopic roughness and at relatively high speeds. Another factor is that the degrading effect of slight roughness on efficiency, is one of the constant observations when wing sections are tested in wind tunnels.

A classical experiment, and a simple kitchen experiment are worth thinking about:

1. If the annular space between two concentric tubes of different diameters is filled with liquid, and the inner one is rotated while the outer one is held still, the liquid between them will very quickly become turbulent because in addition to the normal shear forces the faster-moving particles adjacent to the inner tube are impelled outwards by centrifugal force. This situation repeats wherever fluid (air or water) flows with the slower flow on the 'outside' of the curve, as in the diverging flow for 2 or 3mm at the extreme leading edge of a centreboard.

However, if the inner tube is held still, and the outer one rotated, the liquid between them will remain laminar and turbulence-free for very much longer than would be expected from the straight-line measurements.This is because inward movement of the faster-moving particles, adjacent to the outer tube, is resisted by centrifugal force. This situation repeats wherever air or water flow over a convex surface such as an aircraft's wing, a centreboard, a curved hull or the leeward side of a jib.

2. All that the kitchen experiment needs is a cup of coffee. Create a swirl with a spoon. Note that every swirl has two parts. There is an inner core in which the rotational speed of the fluid increases with increasing distance from the centre, and within which the liquid flows smoothly. Surrounding this is an outer region in which the spin speed decreases with increasing distance from the centre. In this region the turbulence is clear to see.

We think that the boundary layer flow around convex bodies like hulls, can be and often is laminar over a much greater area than is predicted by the straight-line measurements. The skin friction resistance of a laminar boundary layer is substantially less than that of a turbulent one, provided that the underlying surface is highly polished. (Fig. 19.1)

Crews who want to go faster in smaller boats should ensure that the whole of their wetted surface is highly polished, and should keep it highly polished. For larger yachts, the forward parts of the hulls certainly should be polished.

20.4 Form drag

The primary aim in the design of racing sailboats is the reduction of form drag. When all other factors are reasonably equal – as with the yachts which race for the *America*'s Cup – it is usually the boat with the lowest form drag which will win.

To discover the shape which will move most easily through the water is relatively simple when the design requirement is for a single operating condition, but it rapidly becomes an uncertain science when multiple operating modes are needed. A single-scull rowing hull needs to carry the weight of one man at about 10 mph through smooth water, and rowing shells world-wide all look much the same. So do the hulls of most light, planing outboard runabouts. These are two of the simplest situations.

But the rowing skiff performs poorly in waves and at high speeds. The runabout hull is most inefficient when moving slowly. As soon as we need a hull which can sail efficiently at every speed between a light air drift and the highest speeds attainable in strong winds, and to do so both in flat water and in a variety of waves – then we cannot use either of these shapes, and the design problem suddenly becomes interesting.

Some of the broad effects on performance of changes to the shape (form) of the hull have been referred to in the tow tests described in Sect 20.1.

Historically, the fastest design has usually been developed by invention, measurement and competition of the kind described in Section 20.1. In that case we started with the best designs which had been developed during the past 70 or 80 years for dinghies of about the same size but which were heavier and which sailed in mostly lighter winds. Our contribution has been to extend efficient sailing to a substantially faster speed and to do this without sacrificing efficiency at the low speed end of the range. As we developed the new designs, we also found that they performed best when their attitude in the water was controlled in special ways. These are introduced in the 'mode sailing' sections of this chapter and are developed in the 'handling' notes in Part Four.

20.5 Induced drag and leeway

If a yacht with a keel or a dinghy with a centreboard is towed straight ahead, skin friction and form drag will develop. Drive force equal to that drag will then be needed to keep it going. This would represent the sailing situation of no leeway, as when running straight downwind in flat water. If the boat is then towed somewhat sideways, to represent the sideways sail force and consequent leeway which occurs when sailing to windward, the drag will increase, and extra drive force will be needed. The greater the leeway angle, then the greater will be the increase in drag. This extra drag is 'induced drag'. It is the price we pay for the sideways force from the keel/centreboard, that is necessary to balance the sideways force created by the sails.

Skin friction and form drag both change as speed (Squared), i.e. at double the speed, there will be four times the drag and at half the speed, there will be one quarter the drag.

Induced drag changes the other way. It will be greatest when sailing at low speeds and with large leeway angles, as when pinching to round a mark. It becomes rapidly less as speed is increased.

What is happening is that the keel or centreboard must be run at an angle to the oncoming water in order to develop the pressure on one side and suction on the other, which gives the cross-boat force to balance that of the sails. This angle is one part of the leeway angle. The pressure difference then drives the water in a spiral around the bottom of the keel or the tip of the centreboard. The shallower the keel, the greater will be the pressure loss due to this leakage around the tip. This leakage allows the hull to move sideways some more, and this adds to the leeway. The spiralling water continues to spin after the boat has moved on – this is the tip vortex. The energy needed to start the vortex lives on as the momentum contained in the spinning mass of that tip vortex. This energy can never be recovered, and is felt by the boat as drag. The slower the boat sails, the more time there is for the pressure difference to accelerate the water in its spiral, so more energy will be lost. As speed increases the process reverses and induced drag rapidly decreases.

When a boat has either a deep, well-shaped centreboard or ample keel area (such as a Soling or Etchells), it makes relatively little leeway, even at low speed. Then, no handling problems arise.

Boats which have either unusually small keels(as do some IOR designs) or shallow, 'bustles', (as some catamarans) , are different. Below a certain speed these boats develop so much leeway and induced drag that they cannot accelerate while pointing high. To get these boats going, needs a different approach – a close reach for one or two lengths to acquire sufficient speed for the keel to begin to work efficiently, and then to bring her up to the pointing angle for best VMG. This difference is of no consequence in one-design racing, but in mixed fleets, woe betide any small-keel boat which engages a big-keel boat in a tacking duel or who is unwise enough to be to windward of a deep-keel boat at the start.

20.6 Rudder deflection drag

It is self evident that if two identical boats sail side by side, and one has its rudder aligned with the keel or centreboard, and the other has its rudder angled at some substantial angle to the centreline, the boat with the angled rudder will fall behind. The angled rudder 'puts the brake on'. The technical reason is that the angled rudder develops excess induced drag.

There will be a fastest angle at which to carry the rudder. This is not always central.

The hull with its centreboard or keel and rudder, should be considered as a single system, exactly as are the fuselage, wing and tailplane of a glider. The principles are identical. The sailboat with the lowest drag and which makes the least leeway (lowest induced drag) will sail fastest to windward, and the glider with the lowest drag and the least tip loss (again lowest induced drag) will have the lowest sinking speed. Exactly the same factors are responsible for superior performance in both cases. In many ways the glider is simpler to visualise. Model gliders are certainly easier to experiment with.

If a model glider is ballasted so that its point of balance is under the centre of pressure of the wing, and its performance measured at the optimum forward speed, it will have a particular sinking speed. In this trim the tailplane carries no load. If the ballast is then moved back, so that the tailplane begins to carry some of the load, and the tailplane angle is increased a little to carry this load, the sinking speed will become less. What is happening is that the load is now shared between the wing and the tailplane. Up to a certain point the reduction in the wing's induced drag will be more than the increase in the tailplane's induced drag, so the total induced drag will become smaller, and the sinking speed will be reduced.

The important conclusion here, is that the more the tailplane is asked to carry its fair share of the load (within reason), the more efficient the glider becomes. (The *Voyager* light aeroplane which flew around the world without refuelling, carried its smaller wing ahead of the main wing so that it could carry its share of the load.) This is the key principle in deciding what is the fastest angle for the rudder.

If, in your imagination, you turn the glider onto its edge and put half of it into the water, you have the centreboard or keel, hull, and rudder of a sailboat sailing to windward. Sailforce substitutes for gravity, and exactly the same principles apply. All our experience suggests that, when sailing to windward, the fastest trim is that which calls for the tiller to lie at an angle of about 0.75 to 1.0 degree to windward of the centreline. (For dinghies with gybing centreboards, this becomes about 0.75 to 1.0 degree more positive than the centreboard. For yachts with trim tabs the same principle will apply.) This slightly positive angle compensates almost exactly for the sideways movement of the water – downwash from the wing in aeronautical terms – behind the centreboard.

If a rubber band or similar marker is put around the tiller extension so that it lies exactly over the gunwale when the tiller is fore-and-aft, its position can be felt when sailing. With a tiller of typical length (about three feet) the marker should lie about half an inch, and no more, to windward of the gunwale when the boat is being driven hard and upright.

On all other points of sailing, the rudder should be central. The boat speed will be higher and the side force required from the centreboard will be less, and for practical purposes, induced drag will become negligible.

Wave making drag

20.7 The three modes

Slender-hulled craft such as catamarans sail always in one mode – displacement sailing. Wider-hull craft of substantial weight (i.e. all typical keelboats) sail in either of two modes – the displacement mode and (occasionally), the forced mode. Craft which are light in weight and suitably shaped, such as light motor-boats and light sailing dinghies and all sailboards, sail in one of three modes – displacement, forced and planing. Some light craft of a particular shape can make use of a fourth mode in light airs

In displacement sailing, the resistance to forward motion (drag), increases approximately as the square of the speed. So, for example, during a prolonged gust which offers twice the drive force, offwind speed can be increased, with alert and skilful handling, by a maximum of about 40%.

In the forced mode, the drag increases at least as the cube of the speed for light boats, and at up to the fourth power for heavy boats. In the example above, the maximum offwind speed increase achievable in a gust which doubles the drive force would be about 25% for light boats and 20% for heavier ones.

When planing, the drag increases approximately as the speed increases. Again using the same example as above, an alert crew, in a gust which doubles the drive force, can *double* their speed for as long as they sail within that gust.

Crews who are aware of these three modes, and of the enormous differences in performances achievable within each of them, can often bias their sailing to spend more of their time in the displacement and planing modes, and waste less of their time in the forced mode, and in this way finish ahead of those who do not.

20.8 Displacement sailing

A hull at rest supports its weight by displacing its own weight of water. When it moves, every time it sails one boat-length, it must first move a mass of water its own weight sufficiently far aside to allow its hull to pass and must then return that water to approximately its original position. This is called displacement sailing.

When it moves very slowly, the water flow around it is so gentle that there is negligible wave-making activity. At speeds of about two knots and more, all dinghy and small yacht hulls will make a wave system which consists of the bow wave on each side, the close and parallel but separate quarter wave on each side, and the stern waves which lie between them. (Fig. 20.21) Slender hulls like rowing skiffs make trivial disturbance – the tubbier the shape, the bigger the waves become.

The bow wave is caused by the wedge action of the bow. This forces water sideways and forwards, and so increases its pressure and heaps it up in the familiar wave under the bow on each side. From this starting point, the heaped-up water flows 'downhill' away from the boat on each side to form the bow wave system which streams continuously outwards and backwards (relative to the moving hull), with small transverse waves inside them.

Beneath the surface and further back, as the main bulk of the hull moves forward, the water in its path is forced to move towards the only place where there is room for it – backwards towards the stern where the hull, by moving forward, creates a continuous void. As the water is accelerated backwards, its pressure is reduced and the nearby water level (at the sides of the boat) drops. As it approaches the void at the stern, it is slowed. This increases its pressure and so it rises again. From this heaped-up water near the stern, the two quarter-waves stream outwards and backwards, close to and parallel with the bow waves, but always remaining one or two wave-lengths inside and behind them.

This process can be watched in the simplest of kitchen experiments. Fill the usual basin with water, and sprinkle tracer flecks on the surface. Move your half immersed fist through it. Note how the water heaps up at the 'bow'. Note how much the surface water is accelerated backwards and how it is sucked downwards in the middle. Note how it comes to rest and heaps up again at the 'stern'. The flow around hulls is similar.

In the section on 'water', the reason why there is an exact relationship between the length and speed of gravity waves is described. The waves which move at 1 knot are 1.32 feet between crests. Two knot waves are 2.3 feet long. For 3 knots the wave-length is 5 feet; for 4 knots, 9 feet; for 5 knots, 14 feet; and for 6 knots it is 21 feet.

As a result, when a 14 ft waterline length hull such as any 14ft dinghy moves at 1 knot, about ten crests of the wave train started by the bow wave will be alongside the hull. (They may be only a millimetre high, and are completely negligible.) At two knots, there are 6 crests between bow and stern. At 3 knots about 3 crests are developed and the wave system around the hull will look like Fig 20.21. At 4 knots the second crest of the bow wave lies 9 ft behind the bow, and in fact helps to, 'fill in', the trough which will cause the stern wave.

At 5 knots, a combination which is unique for a 14 ft hull occurs. The second crest of the bow wave, 14 feet behind the bow, combines with the stern wave and so makes a single larger wave with its crest exactly under the transom. (Fig. 20.22(a)). To understand the importance of this, consider what happens at 6 knots. The second, and now very substantial crest of the bow wave lies 21 feet behind the bow. This crest combines with the stern wave system to form a single crest about 17-18 feet behind the bow. But the hull is only 14 feet long, and so the crest of the first stern wave has now fallen behind the stern of the boat. As a result, the stern has begun to sink into the trough. This is the critical difference. The hull, quite suddenly, has become supported by water at one level at the bow, and at a lower level at the stern. It has become a heavy body which is being continuously pushed up a, 'hill', of water, and this hill is of its own making. (Fig. 20.22(b))

The faster the boat sails, the further the first crest of the combined bow and stern wave system will fall behind the stern, the more deeply will the stern sink into the trough, and the steeper will be the slope the

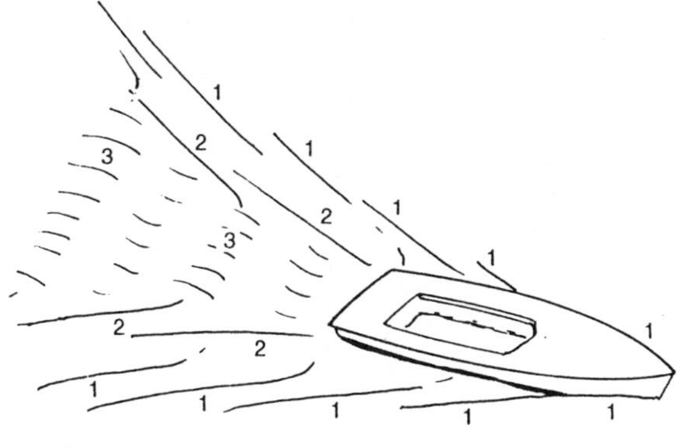

Fig 20.21 Wave system around 14 ft hull at 3.5 knots

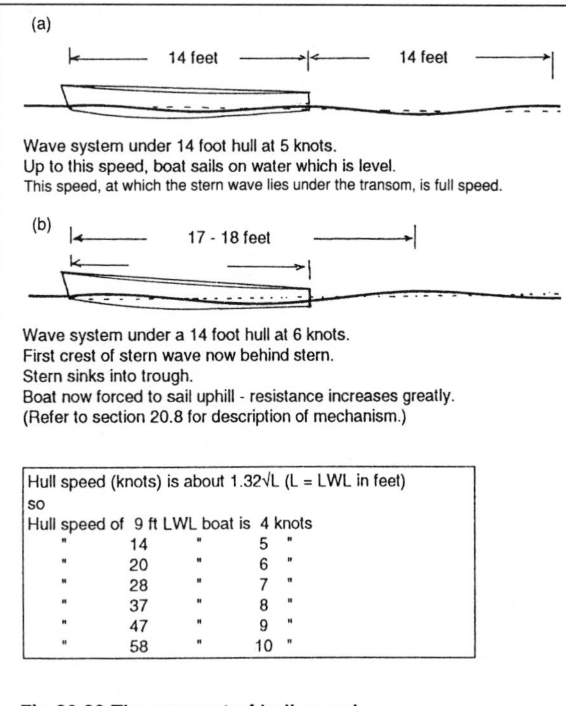

(a)
14 feet
14 feet
Wave system under 14 foot hull at 5 knots.
Up to this speed, boat sails on water which is level.
This speed, at which the stern wave lies under the transom, is full speed.
(b)
17 - 18 feet
Wave system under a 14 foot hull at 6 knots.
First crest of stern wave now behind stern.
Stern sinks into trough.
Boat now forced to sail uphill - resistance increases greatly.
(Refer to section 20.8 for description of mechanism.)
Hull speed (knots) is about 1.32√L (L = LWL in feet)
so
Hull speed of 9 ft LWL boat is 4 knots
" 14 " 5 "
" 20 " 6 "
" 28 " 7 "
" 37 " 8 "
" 47 " 9 "
" 58 " 10 "

Fig 20.22 The concept of hull speed

hull must climb. The heavier and tubbier the boat, the higher will be the bow wave and the deeper will be the trough.

The importance of that 5 knot speed is now clear. It is the highest speed at which a 14 foot waterline boat can sail 'level'. At this, and at all lower speeds, the stern will be supported by water at the same level as the bow. At hull speed, the particular situation occurs where the after half of the boat is surfing down the advancing face of its own stern wave, and in this way it recovers much of the energy needed to push the forward half of the boat up the back of its own bow wave. This highest speed for 'level' sailing is called 'hull speed'. It is always the speed of the wave train which has the length between crests equal to the waterline length of the hull. Sailing at any speed from zero to hull speed is *displacement sailing*. Fig. 20.5 shows how the resistance of our best hull, when ballasted to 525 pounds and towed upright in flat water, increased approximately as the speed (squared) through the displacement sailing mode(which for all 14ft waterline boats must be from 0 to 4.95 knots).

20.9 The forced mode

This is where heavy boats stop and high performance boats keep going.

As soon as hull speed is exceeded, the boat enters the 'forced sailing' mode, in which it is forced to sail up the progressively steeper slope of the back of its own bow wave. Fig. 20.23 shows the way the drag increases for a heavy yacht. The weight and bulk of the boat creates a big bow wave and a big hollow for the hull to sink into and the consequent increase in resistance as speed is increased is massive – it can be as high as the fourth power of speed.

This increase in resistance can be so great as to be an effective barrier to all faster sailing. One example of this was demonstrated during the first two days of a Sydney to Hobart yacht race some years ago, in which *Kialoa* and *Windward Passage*, two 'maxi' yachts of about 64 ft waterline length and so with hull speeds of 1.32 x sq. root of 64 = 10.56 knots, raced south for two

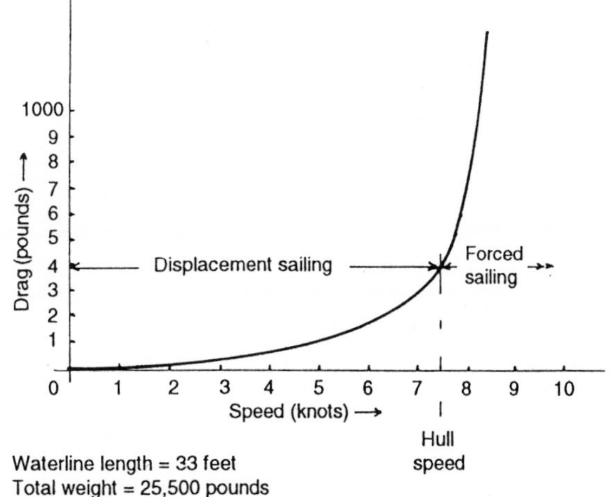

Fig 20.23 Drag curve of heavy keelboat

days in ideal racing conditions of very strong north-easterly winds on the port quarter. Their navigation logs both showed 240 miles each day, or an average speed of 10 knots for both days. Despite ideal racing conditions, neither heavy yacht could even achieve average hull speed, let alone exceed it. All other yachts in the fleet recorded similar performances of hull speed, or slightly less, during those two days.

Fig. 20.5 shows the very different shape of the drag curve for a light planing dinghy. Between 5 knots and 7.5 knots, the total drag (solid line) shows the increasing drag component due to the hull being forced uphill. Because the hull is light and relatively slender, the water is not disturbed as much as in the case of the heavy keelboat of Fig. 20.23 and so the 'hill' is relatively small and the slope not steep. Because of the light total weight, the increased drive force necessary is well within the capability of powerful sails to provide. Nevertheless, between 5 knots and 8 knots the drag triples from 18 lbs to 54 lbs – in this range it increases at about speed (cubed) instead of the almost uniform speed (squared) from 0 to 5 knots. The reduced 'freedom' in this narrow speed range is easy to feel when sailing.

At about 7.5 – 8 knots, the 'feel' changes. As soon as it is clear of the forced mode, the boat no longer baulks but accelerates cleanly with each gust. This change of 'feel' shows up on the drag curve of Fig. 20.5 as the reversing of the slope: instead of rising more steeply, the slope of the line reverses and begins to curve downwards again.

What happens at this point depends upon the design of the boat. Boats which are heavy and round behave like Fig. 20.23 and never reach it. Boats which are very thin, like catamarans, suffer little form drag and little of the drag increase due to forced sailing, but on the other hand they cannot plane, and so their wetted area does not diminish. As a result their performance remains dominated by the speed-squared increase of skin friction plus a little form drag – this is shown by the dashed line labelled 'SF' (for Skin Friction) in Fig. 20.5. This explains the catamaran's good performance up to a boat speed of about 10 or 12 knots and also its increasing reluctance to go much faster except in very special conditions.

Hulls which are light and have bottoms designed for planing can progress from 'displacement sailing', through 'forced sailing' and into 'full planing'.

20.10 Breakout and planing

Provided that the bottom of the hull is properly shaped for planing, it turns out that planing can be much more efficient than would appear possible at first sight.

As speed increases, the pressure which causes the bow wave becomes sufficient to force the bow itself to rise. Provided that there is sufficient horizontal or near-horizontal surface area far enough forward, the hull then begins to move over the water rather than through it. The water which is now trapped under the hull continues to be forced forward, partly pushed by the inclined bottom of the boat and partly pulled by the action of skin friction. Both these actions increase the pressure of the water affected and cause it to rise. But this bow wave is now under the boat. The pressure which forces the water upwards is not trivial and as a result the boat is lifted bodily on top of this rising water. So the remarkable fact emerges that the planing hull is lifted not by one force, but by two.

The first force – the action of the inclined bottom against static water – is easy enough to understand. It behaves like the undersurface of an aeroplane's wing. There will be a minimum speed at which it will support the total weight of the boat. At all higher speeds the boat can either lift further out of the water or plane at a flatter angle.

The second force is more subtle. Except for the pressure which escapes as waves and spray at the sides, the total effect of the boat on the water – forcing the water forward and also dragging it forward – has the effect of creating a wave crest under the boat. The faster the boat sails, the greater the movement of the water forwards and greater the upward pressure of this wave crest and the higher it will lift the boat. This action permits the boat to plane efficiently at a much flatter angle than would be the case if the hull were not lifted in this way. It also lifts the boat far higher out of the water than would otherwise be expected.

It is this action which is the key to the efficiency of planing. The faster the boat planes, the higher it is lifted and the smaller the wetted area becomes. It remains true that the resistance of skin friction continues to increase as the square of the speed – twice as fast means four times the resistance for each square foot of wetted area. This is what holds slender non-planing boats like catamarans back. But the lifting of the boat out of the water by the planing action alters the ground rules. When you plane, if you double your speed you will halve your wetted area. So the reduction of wetted area compensates for the increase in skin friction to the point where the increase in total resistance is about the same as the increase in speed, i.e. for double the speed you suffer only double the drag. So if the wind gives you double the drive force, when you are planing the boat can sail almost twice as fast. The 'almost' is because factors such as spray drag and foil drag are also present and they still follow the speed (squared) law.

During the past fifteen years, two groups of sailboats have been successful in increasing their average speeds. Each has concentrated on a particular object. The first group, the sailboards, have concentrated on broad reaching, 'dash', speeds in very strong winds and their success on this point of sailing has been spectacular. The other group, the bigger Australian skiffs, have concentrated on increasing their average 'round-the-buoys' speeds in all wind strengths and they too have been spectacularly successful. Both groups use planing hulls. It is interesting to note that the designs of the hulls of both groups have followed the same development paths to the extent that these have been appropriate.

Twenty five years ago, the skiff hulls were smoothly rounded boats with long sharp bows. They were crewed by four men and were not light. They carried vast sail area but because of their weight, they seldom planed. In those days they could sometimes be beaten by an FD, 505 or Tornado. The first change was a slow shift towards a flatter-bottomed planing hull. Because of their weight and the fact that their rigs, albeit of great area, twisted too much to be truly efficient, the newer boats tended to be faster, but not by much.

The second change was worked through in the years 1970 to '75 with the introduction of the much more compact three-hander. These boats were lighter with compact, taut, relatively untwisted rigs. Due to their lighter weight, they possessed a sail-carrying power to total weight ratio much greater than that of any earlier boat. Their smaller, tighter rigs were better controlled and twisted less and were much more efficient. They began to plane cleanly in all winds of 8 knots or more. In strong winds they were capable of dash speeds of 25 to 30 knots. These much higher average speeds quickly showed up the defects in traditional hull-design thinking and a series of technically important changes began.

The first change was the elimination of the small stern. A small transom was usually associated with good light-air performance but the inward curves to the narrow transom lead to uncontrollable 'dutch rolling' at speed. Those who have sailed Finns, GP14's, Lasers and most small yachts will recognise the problem. At some speed the rudder is overpowered by the turning tendency of the curved hull when it either heels or is washed by a wave on one side and not the other. It then goes its own oscillating way and the faster it goes the more violent the oscillations become. Skill is no answer. The complete fix was to adopt straighter aft topside lines more like those of a small motor-boat.

The wider transom logically called for gentle upward curving of the buttock lines to ensure that the bottom of the transom just skimmed the water at low speed. Boats designed like this certainly possessed better light-air performance and did not roll. However, as the wind speed increased, these boats would move freely to a speed of only 10 or 15 knots. They would adopt a progressively steeper bow-high attitude and tend to be sucked down at the stern. At some speed they would 'stick' and thereafter go no faster.

The fix for this was to flatten the aft bottom completely in the fore-and-aft sense. (It remained slightly 'Vee'd' athwartships.) This resulted in superb planing performance together with absolutely true steering control and no Dutch rolling. Average speeds in planing breezes were greatly increased. Dash speeds in the occasional ideal conditions became spectacular. Because they tended to drag their transoms at low speeds, the light-air performance of these boats was disappointing but they were clearly a giant step in the right direction.

The response to the light-air problem was the development of the two-mode hull. These boats are designed so that their shapes and immersed volumes are efficient for displacement sailing in light airs when the boat is heeled and trimmed bow-down. In stronger breezes the crew pull them upright and allow the bow to lift and in this changed attitude they are superbly efficient planing machines. This technique was simplified by the introduction first of gunwale extensions, then of stub wings, then of wider wings, and then these wings were swept back so that the crew could themselves lift the bow to the desired attitude by trapezing from a position which was not only outboard but was also behind the transom.

The two-mode hull marked the end-point of the quest for control and efficiency.

They go well in light airs. In breezes they are spectacular. They steer perfectly at even the highest speeds and in the roughest water. They have proved surprisingly seaworthy. The shapes of their after bottoms – some use strakes and some use fractionally concave surfaces – are almost identical with the shapes of the after bottoms of the very fast 'sinker' sailboards. On the basis of these hulls, designers have experimented and developed the optimum wing-spans, sail areas, rig controls and ever-lighter hull structures for highest round-the-buoys speeds.

The most recent chapter comes straight from sailboard technology. There is an optimum planing angle for very high speeds. If the planing surface is too big, the craft adopts too flat an angle, there is too much wetted area and skin friction, and the excess drag makes really high speeds impossible.

The sailboard's answer to this is the 'sinker' or 'speed' board – a planing surface designed solely to be efficient at the highest speeds and so small that it is unable even to support its rider at rest. The big skiff answer is similar to the sailboards, except that they don't sink when the wind becomes lighter. They now use a substantially smaller hull with a narrower bottom which by design does not begin to plane until it is moving much more quickly than has been customary in the past. Because of their relatively light weight, slender shape and enormous power, these boats find that they can gain more at the high-speed end of their planing mode than they suffer in the extended forced mode. This is a trade-off which applies to 'high performance sailboats' only.

In the introduction, it was suggested that one of the reasons why these big skiffs, and the sailboards too, have enjoyed so great an increase in performance may have had something to do with the freedom from rule restrictions which they enjoy. One has only to compare the sailboard and skiff developments described above and in the 'rig section' with the prohibitions which would be faced if a 470 or even an International 14 owner tried to do the same thing, to appreciate the truth of this suggestion.

20.11 The fourth mode

The concept of this has been touched upon in the description of the Eighteen's two-mode hull design, and the reasons why it was adopted.

Many higher-performance designs are now characterised by an underwater shape which tends to be triangular, i.e. they have fine deeper bows and wider flatter bottoms aft. These boats can achieve higher speeds in very light airs if they are handled in a special way.

At the near-calm end of the displacement mode, when the boat's speed is about one knot or less, and more in small waves, four advantages will follow if the crew adopt a bow-down and heeled attitude:

1. The wetted area of the hull will be reduced, and so skin friction drag (which is dominant at very low speeds) becomes less, and speed will increase.

2. When the hull is heeled about 15 degrees to leeward, sails can fall, by gravity, into smoothly twisted shapes even in a calm. Twisted sails are efficient in light air and this single fact enables many dinghies to keep moving, and moving well, when the wind is near-calm. The problem with all boats which cannot heel in light air, such as keelboats and catamarans, is that at and below some critical wind speed their headsails fall centrally by gravity. At that point a rig necessarily loses almost all drive force and the boat stops.

3. Given an underwater shape which is broader and more stable aft, and finely tapered towards the bow, the stability of such a hull will change according to where the crew position their weight. If a crew sit well aft, the hull behaves like a piece of plywood floating on the surface, and will rock to and fro as it follows the advancing and receding slopes of each wave. This rocking shakes the rig around, and in light air this movement of the sails in the air will prevent any organised airflow from establishing, and so the sail 'power' will remain feeble and the boat will sail slowly. But if the crew move their weight forward over the progressively narrower forward underbody, the hull stability will decrease to the point where it will become neutral. If, at the same time, the crew separate their weights in the sideways sense, this will stabilise the boat in roll (technically, by separating their weights they increase the angular inertia).

In small waves these three actions – heeling the boat, pitching it bow-down, and separating the weights of the crew's bodies – can steady the boat in roll and substantially reduce pitch. The more the crew can so stabilize the hull and steady the rig in the air, the more efficient and powerful can the airflow over the sails become, and the faster the boat will sail.

4. The fourth advantage is that the added resistance caused by waves is much reduced. Hulls which are flat can plane well, but their light air performance, always poor even in flat water because of large wetted area, becomes slower when they are sailed in waves because of the 'out of trim' effect of each wave as it washes onto and away from the flat bottom. But if a dinghy such as a Laser II, Tasar, B14, Eighteen Footer etc is heeled and trimmed bow down, it becomes, in effect, a boat with a narrow stern as well as a narrow bow, i.e. like a River Dinghy or a single catamaran hull. In this trim it becomes much less sensitive to small waves, and sails faster.

Note that the successful use of this 'fourth mode' technique will be entirely dependent upon the design of the hull you sail. Fig. 20.11 shows that at very low speeds, as between a smoothly rounded 'River' design with flared topsides, and the more triangular-bottomed 'Dribbly' design, the resistance becomes greater when a River boat is heeled, but it becomes less when the triangular boat is heeled. Fig 20.24 shows how the wetted shape changes.

The drag of the River hull increases because its wetted surface increases as the wide flared topside is immersed. This will be true regardless of whether it is also trimmed bow-down or stern-down.

The drag of the triangular-bottomed hull decreases at first because the wetted surface becomes less as the wider aft bottom is lifted out of the water. Judicious bow-down trim will reduce the wetted surface even more. Once the gunwale and deck go under water the drag increases again, so there is an optimum heel angle at which boats of this shape will sail fastest in light airs.

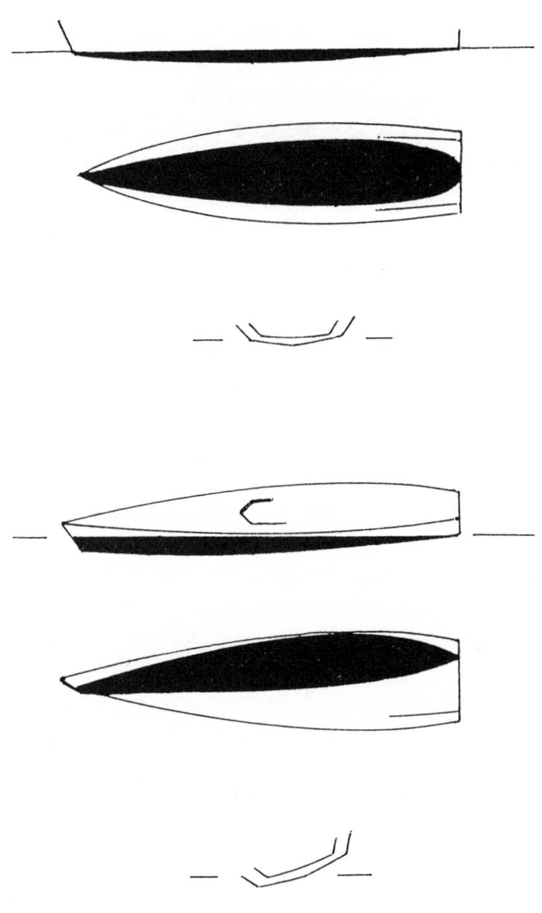

Change of immersed shape and wetted area when triangular-type hull is heeled.

Fig 20.24 Fourth mode technique

Drag in waves

20.12 Drag in regular waves – upwind and downwind

The information contained in Figs 20.4 and the following diagrams was obtained from tow tests, and primarily from an initial series of tests which extended over about two years. Sailors' Bay, a steep-sided arm of Sydney's Middle Harbour, is about half a mile long and 300 yards wide. It offered a number of advantages. Northbridge Sailing Club is built over the water on its south side, and has a rectangular rigging deck about 200 feet long. Markers placed at each end of the deck give parallel transits out from the shore. We towed parallel to the shore, timed the interval as we crossed these transits, and so could calculate the speed of each pass. My home was just above the club, so between the club's facilities and workboats, the specialist equipment which I could store nearby, plus a powerful ski-boat owned by a cooperative neighbour which we used for the higher speed tows, we were completely equipped. We maintained ourselves 'set to go' at very short notice, for the whole of the period until the programme was complete. We towed most often in the calms of early morning or evenings, but occasionally in winter we enjoyed whole days of calm. The programme was designed by Pat Smith. I seemed to be the one who provided the motivation and the hardware. Many interested friends and club members made up the teams and participated from time to time during the course of this long programme.

Our object was to measure the performance of each hull sufficiently accurately to know and understand the performance differences between the hulls. We always knew that it would be a long process to measure the drags of each of the four boats at three separate weights and at sufficient points over a wide speed range. It never occurred to us to expect to tow in other than flat water, and work in waves was never included in the programme. Just towing in waves would be meaningless unless the waves were all the same, and who could reasonably expect waves 'to specification' to appear at the right time?

On one winter's day which was expected to be calm, this whole scenario changed. We had started early. Soon an easterly wind developed. We considered cancelling, but instead took a snap decision to carry on. From that point onwards, everything went right for the whole day. We completed 86 individual runs. The wind built steadily to about 10 knots, held steady for several hours, then died slowly. It remained steady in direction along the bay. We chose to spend one third of the daylight hours available with each of three hulls, we towed upwind and down and we obtained as much information as we could in that time. As a result, we have a superb record of the differences between towing in flat water, and towing in waves up to about one foot high. Because the differences between waves and flat water are much greater than the differences between hulls, and because of the unsteadiness of all readings taken in waves, the most helpful presentation is to give the average of all the readings, and this is what is shown in Fig. 20.8. The figures have been corrected for the effect of the wind.

The lessons from that day were:

1. Drag through waves is unsteady. In flat water we were accustomed to towing either two boats, balanced on a beam, at speeds of up to five knots, or a single boat at all higher speeds, but in both cases, once we had stabilised the boats on course and on speed (and with two boats on a beam this could take several minutes), the drag figure was then steady. In waves it was different. The tension in the tow-line changed continuously. We could not hope to balance two boats on a beam. So we towed single hulls. We tried long skeins of shock cord – these helped but did not eliminate the unsteadiness. Instead of recording one figure, we recorded three – the maximum, the minimum, and an estimate of the mean over about 30 seconds.

2. Drag when towing down-wave was much more unsteady than drag when towing into-wave. Particularly at speeds close to the wave speed, the drag could vary from almost nothing as the boat almost surfed down the advancing face, to something approaching double the mean as it was dragged up and over the receding face.

3 (a) When a hull is towed into the waves, the drag is increased (compared with flat water).

(b) At low speeds, the increase due to waves about one foot high can be to double or even treble the flat water drag, i.e. a drag increase of 100 to 200 per cent is normal. Waves very greatly reduce light air, low speed performance.

(c) At higher speeds the drag increase due to one foot waves becomes smaller in percentage terms. Drag increases of 15 then 10 per cent are to be expected as planing speeds are approached. Waves have a much smaller effect in stronger winds than in lighter winds.

(d) Typical figures for our 14 foot dinghy hulls, when ballasted to 525 pounds total weight and towed into waves one foot high, were:

Speed (knots)	Flat water drag (pounds)	Drag in one foot waves (pounds)	Increase %
2	2.9	6.6	128
4	11	16	46
6	29	33	15
8	56	65	15
10	75	83	11

4. (a) When a hull is towed down-wave at low and moderate speeds, waves reduce the drag of the hull compared with flat water. At high speeds the drag is increased. (Fig. 20.8)

(b) The reduction of drag at low speeds down-wave is about half as great as the increase of drag into-wave.

(c) Mean drag figures at about wave speed are of little practical use because of the enormous variations. A boat which is surfing down the advancing face of a wave may have zero or negative drag. An adjacent boat which is trying to sail up and over the receding face of the same wave may have a drag more than double its flat-water drag. The practical response to this situation lies in developing good wave-surfing technique, rather than looking for small differences in the designed hull drag in flat water.

(d) At speeds of about double the wave speed, the drag down-wave of the boat in waves became the same as the boat in flat water. At all higher speeds, up to the highest speed measured, the drag became slightly greater.

The reason for this reversal is that at low speeds a boat which is sailing down-wave is accelerated by each advancing wave face, and slowed by each wave 'back', and the effect of this is that it often spends more time 'surfing' downhill than climbing uphill. There will be a very great difference between the wave by wave behaviour of a boat which is being towed and one which is being driven by its own sails.

A further factor is that the orbital motion within the waves moves the water in every crest downwind, and the convex wave crests engulf more of a hull's surface than the concave troughs. The effect is to reduce the relative speed between the hull and the water in the crests, and this reduces the skin friction. At increasing speeds the boat's increasing momentum stabilises its speed and the acceleration/deceleration factor is lost. At higher speeds yet, the boat simply overtakes the waves at considerable speed, and the 'roughness of the water' effect becomes greater than the 'crests moving downwind' effect.

A point of particular interest which is shown by Fig. 20.8 is that the effect of towing into the waves is to shift the whole drag curve to the left, so that the steep 'forced sailing' drag rise is encountered, passed through, and left behind at lower speeds when sailing into the waves. When sailing down-wave the reverse situation applies. These differences are important in understanding the fastest boat-handling techniques to use in waves. We will look at the into-wave and down-wave situations separately.

In Part Two, 'Waves', Fig. 13.2 shows the orbital speed of the water in waves up to 3 feet high. The table below extends this to 5 feet – perfectly reasonable waves to expect when racing in open water in winds of about 20 knots.

Wave Height (ft)	Typical Wave Speed (knots)	Orbital Speed of Water in Wave Crests (knots)
1	4.3	1.4
2	6.7	1.7
3	8.5	2.0
4	10.2	2.2
5	12.2	2.25

The importance of Fig. 20.8 is that it makes it clear that a completely different approach to mode sailing must be adopted when sailing in waves. In boats which are just capable of windward planing like the Fireball, 470, Tasar, etc, in flat water it will be fastest to sail to windward at speeds of either up to 5 knots, or at about 8 knots when conditions are right for windward planing. It will never be fastest to sail in the forced mode between 5 and 7.5 knots. In rough water the whole picture changes. The drag is greater at all speeds, so the boat must be pointed lower to achieve and maintain useful speed. More importantly, the steep drag rise which in flat water is associated with the 5 to 7.5 kt forced mode, will be encountered in rough water in the speed range 3.5 to about 6 knots when sailing to windward. Even more importantly, a speed of only 5.5 to 6 knots is needed for the boat to enter the range of freedom normally associated with the planing mode. Fig. 20.9 develops Fig. 20.8 to show what happens when you sail into bigger waves. Note the way increasing wave size affects the speeds at which the forced mode is reached and left behind. In the tests displayed in Fig. 20.8 we towed the hulls directly into the waves. I have assumed that the drag of a boat which sails at close-hauled angles into waves is broadly similar.

Fig. 20.9 confirms the conventional wisdom 'When sailing upwind in rough water, sail free'. I do not suggest that, in all the commotion of racing to windward through 3 to 5 ft waves, that one can be either too precise about speed, or that one can plane at any speed less than about 7.5 knots. What I do suggest with the conviction of both theory and experience, is that in planing dinghies the close-sheeted high pointing techniques which win in flat water produce only moderate success in big waves. But if one frees off a little the boat suddenly 'feels free', and on such days, this technique will be the fastest way to the windward mark. Unfortunately, it doesn't always work. Sometimes, the pattern of the waves is subtly different, the boat does not feel in any way free, and on such days sailing too low merely reduces VMG. Ultimately, selecting the fastest technique upwind through waves remains a matter of judgment, experience and feel.

When sailing downwind in waves, conventional dinghies and catamarans enjoy a particular advantage. The basic situation is that dinghies and catamarans of moderate performance usually sail downwind at speeds of about half the wind speed. Waves which are well developed (have enjoyed a sufficient 'fetch'), usually roll downwind at about two thirds of the wind speed. When sailing downwind in these boats, each wave will pass the boat relatively slowly, and the way the drag curve changes on a wave-by-wave basis will become glaringly apparent. While the boat is surfing down the wave's advancing face or being carried forward by the downwind-moving water in the wave's crest the drag will be least and the speed greatest. When it is climbing up the wave's back, or trapped in the windward-moving water in the wave's trough, its drag will be greatest and its speed least.

In these conditions a handling technique which enables a crew to spend the maximum time in the faster parts of each wave will override absolutely any small differences in hull drag. The displacing of the drag curve to the right in Fig. 20.8, makes it easier to 'catch' the waves. The logic is that the curve in Fig. 20.8 is the mean. It is more accurate to think of it as a combination of an increased drag on the backs and in the troughs of waves, and a very great decrease of drag on their faces and in their crests. The key to good wave-catching technique lies in accelerating the boat from its 'half wind speed' average speed to a momentary speed of about two-thirds of the wind speed at exactly the instant when the approaching crest reaches the transom. This technique will match the boat's speed with the wave's speed, and the boat can then surf down the face of that wave and maintain the higher speed of the wave for a prolonged period. When this technique is repeated many times during a downwind leg, the average speed can become closer to the waves' speeds than the flat-water boat's speed. An Olympic skipper put it another way: 'If you're not sweating at the end of a downwind leg, you're not trying hard enough'.

The details of wave-catching technique are given in the 'handling' sections in Part Four. They will be useful only in those boats of moderate performance which can turn and respond quickly enough – which will be most dinghies and some catamarans. High performance boats which overtake the waves will obviously call for different thinking.

20.13 Drag in regular waves - crosswind

The slopes of waves, the orbital motion of the water, and (as part of this) the special importance of the speed of water within the wave crest all operate within a few degrees of the upwind-downwind direction. As a result, the primary effects of the downwind speed of water in the wave crests, and the ability to surf 'downhill' downwind for prolonged periods fall almost to zero when sailing crosswind. The extra drag of having to push the topsides through wave crests, and the extra drag due to the displacement of the crest of the stern wave (mainly sideways when sailing cross-wave) and consequent loss of pressure recovery, remain. A small loss of speed, as compared with flat water, occurs in all three modes. Secondary effects, such as the wave-by-wave change of Apparent Wind – lighter and further ahead in the crests, and stronger and more on the beam in the troughs, call for particular sail handling and balance activity to exploit or compensate, but this is not due to the effect of waves on the hull per se.

When, in light air and flat water, a substantial wake from a passing motor boat approaches, the waves will slow the boat with maximum effect if they are encountered head on. The effect on performance becomes almost negligible if the boat is briefly turned so that the centreline is nearly parallel with the wave crests as they pass.

20.14 Drag in chaotic waves

Because chaotic waves, by definition, have no regular direction, they will increase the drag, and reduce the speed at which both hull speed and breakout occur, equally on all points of sailing.

In general, sailing in all directions in chaotic waves can be thought about in much the same way as sailing to windward in regular waves.

But in finer detail, only some of the waves of a chaotic system will come from ahead. This opens the possibility that many of the others can be sailed 'downhill' if a particular technique is practised and mastered. This is discussed in the 'handling' section in Part Four.

20.15 Drag in swell

The primary characteristic of swell is the long wave length, and very slow frequency of repetition. Fortunately, the wave heights are low, and the slopes correspondingly small. The practical effect is that the boat sails up and down long but gentle slopes of water. While it is sailing uphill its resistance must increase slightly, and vice versa. In moderate and strong winds, the effect of swell is negligible. The wind-formed waves on the swell will probably be more important.

The situation in light airs is completely different.

A boat can spend several seconds on each up-slope and down-slope. If it is sailing only slowly when it starts each climb, it may stop half-way up unless extra power is applied. Finding extra power is always a problem in light air, even in flat water.

In the case of swell the problem becomes much worse. It is worst when the light air blows from the same direction as the swell. In this case the orbital action of the waves will profoundly affect the Apparent Wind in the light air – and in exactly the wrong way. The advancing face and crest of each wave will carry the boat downwind and so will reduce the Apparent Wind towards zero at exactly the time when the crew need extra power to climb the rest of the slope to the crest. When the light air is from any other direction the situation will be less difficult.

Notes about useful techniques appear in the 'handling' chapters in Part Four.

20.16 Concepts of mode sailing

To recapitulate:

In the displacement mode, drag changes approximately as speed (squared).

For double the speed, four times the drive force will be needed.

If the drive force doubles in a gust, then speed can be increased by about 40 per cent.

In the forced mode, drag changes approximately as speed (cubed) for light boats, and closer to speed (to the fourth power) for heavy boats.

For double the speed, nine times the drive force will be needed for a light boat, and sixteen times for a heavier one. This does not sound much when you say it quickly, but just think about it for a moment.

If the drive force doubles in a gust, the speed of a light boat can be increased about 26 per cent, and a heavy one by about 19 per cent.

In the planing mode, drag changes almost directly as speed changes. For double the speed, double the drive force will be needed.

If the drive force doubles, speed can be increased by about 100 per cent.

The fourth mode is a different handling technique at the low-speed end of the displacement mode, of which it is a part.

For practical purposes, the change in the way the drag changes as between the three modes is so dominated by the speed (cubed or more) drag rise in the forced mode that, by comparison, the displacement mode and the planing mode appear almost similar.

For the sake of example, let us assume a very typical day in which the wind speed in the gusts is 40% faster than in the lulls, and that the boat has sufficient righting moment to make full use of the added wind speed. If we ignore second order effects such as the change in the angle of the Apparent Wind (which may change either way), we can reasonably assume that in the gusts the crew will be able to achieve double the drive force they enjoy in the lulls.

Mode sailing is the blending of performance with gust-lull probability to achieve a shorter-time path to the next mark. This will generally be accomplished by minimising the time spent in the forced mode. Obvious examples are:

1. To windward in moderate to strong winds – windward plane the gusts, displacement sail the lulls. Avoid the forced mode completely.

2. Close reach in light to moderate wind. Sail high at hull speed in the lulls. Bear away and plane in the gusts. Avoid the forced mode completely.

3. Broad reach in light to moderate winds. Sail below the rhumb line at hull speed in the gusts. Sail above the rhumb line to maintain hull speed in the lulls. Avoid the forced mode completely.

In each of the examples above, a boat which sails the composite courses suggested will arrive at the next mark sooner than a similar boat which displacement sails to windward or sails the rhumb line offwind. Other examples are given in the 'Handling' sections in Part Four.

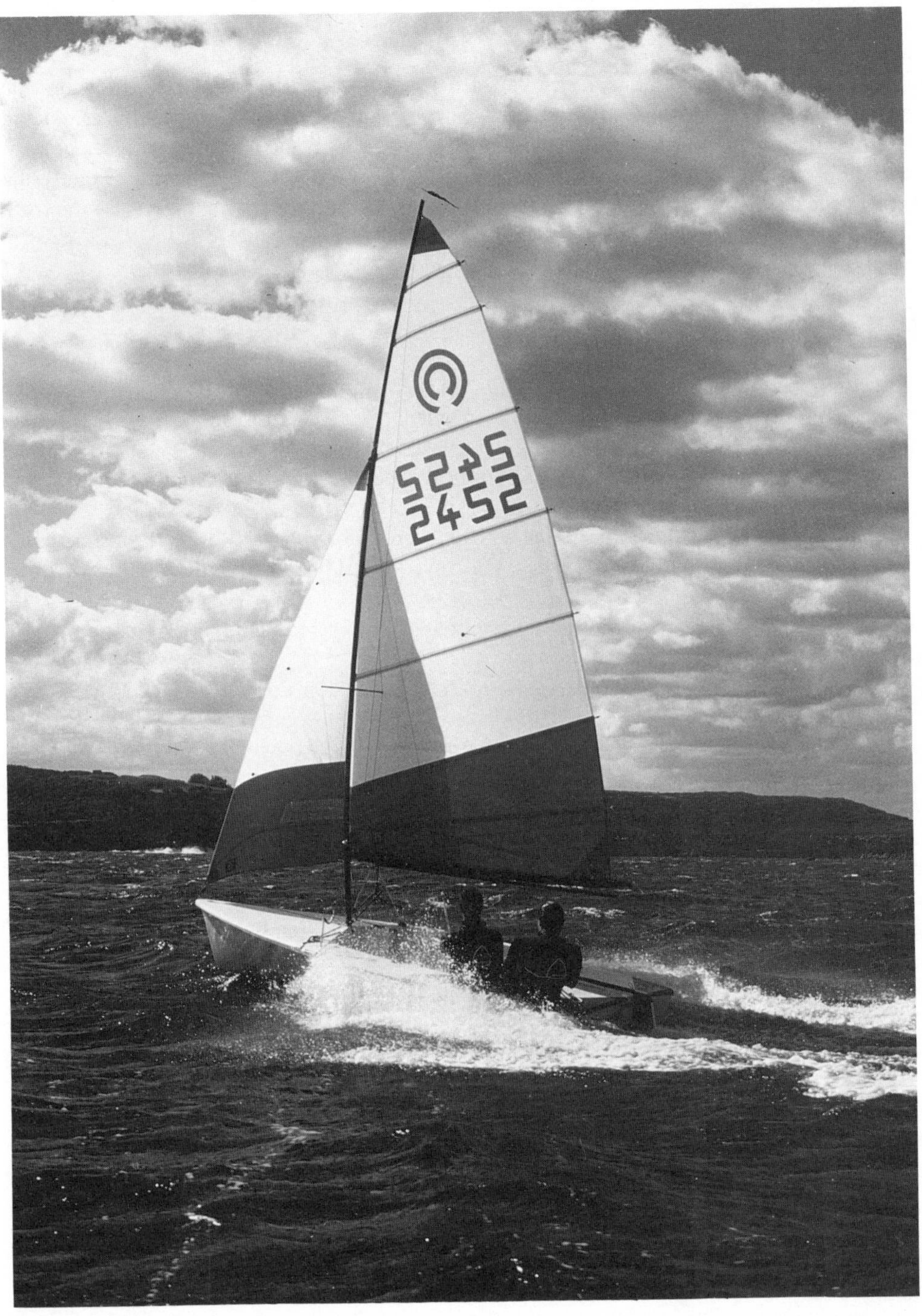

Light, fast and fun!

Part Four
Handling

Chapter Twenty One
Scope

21.1 Relevant conditions

This section is best expressed by an analogy. I spent 30 years commanding big aircraft. I enjoy flying high-performance gliders. The technical skills and questing mental approach one brings to a gliding competition on a holiday morning, are utterly different from the conservative professionalism and cautious mental approach with which one prepares for a foul night departure for a far-distant destination.

The handling suggestions which follow are directed primarily to the vitality and challenge of daytime round-the-buoys racing in relatively small sailboats.

21.2 High performance and other sailboats

The object of this book is to introduce the technical concepts which have made high-performance sailing possible. During the past two decades, these craft have evolved as a clearly recognisable group.

All of them have in common:

1. Light weight.
2. Aerodynamically efficient rigs and sails.
3. Fluent adjustability of their rigs.

In performance capability they range from the recreational skiff Moths, NS 14's and Tasars (which are light in weight and so achieve a sail-carrying-power / total-weight ratio of about the same as an FD or 505 and sail about as fast as conventional racing boats of about the same size such as Fireballs and 470's despite their lack of trapezes and spinnakers), through a variety of intermediate boats, to the high-powered Eighteens which command drive forces more than double those of any conventional boat.

The 'handling' suggestions which follow will describe the techniques used by successful crews of both low-power and high-power high performance boats and will also describe those used by winning crews in a number of conventional classes. Usually the techniques are broadly similar. But where they are different, the differences, and the reasons for them, are illuminating.

21.3 Physical principles and administrative restrictions

The notes which follow are concerned with sailing for speed. Particularly in the case of lighter boats, periodic application of muscle power and movement of body weight is essential for control and so is an integral part of sailing. In addition to the movements needed for control, further brief application of muscle power and movement of body mass in any of a number of ways can accelerate and/or turn the boat momentarily and this faster speed and manoeuvrability can be vital at critical times to establish planing, to 'catch' waves for surfing, and to flick the boat into the faster mode when two-mode sailing is possible. The crude practices of rocking, pumping and 'ooching' have been known for decades but in more recent years top level sailboarders and helmsmen from the Laser class in particular have developed the practise of generating extra speed from muscle power into an art form which is now known as 'kinetics'. It is as different from the earlier crudities as is a computer from an abacus. Its most skilful application is observed when sailboarders lift their craft off the water and perform spectacular gyrations when airborne, or when a gifted helmsman sails a light boat like a Laser through chaotic waves and manages, by positioning his boat with incredible rapidity on a succession of ephemeral downward slopes, to gain speed in conditions which stop lesser mortals. My white-haired opinion is conservative. I regard the activities of the aerial sailboarder as fun but outside the scope of yacht racing. But I can only applaud the skill of any helm who can turn chaotic waves to his advantage. I believe his cultured art should be applauded and encouraged by the rules. Certainly this sort of skill should never be penalised.

From time to time the Racing Rules have been changed or amended in an effort to limit the gross application of muscle power in undesirable ways. Unfortunately, since sailboard sailing and small-boat sailing is by its nature energetic, the form of these restrictive rules always seems to miss the point – they fail to distinguish between legitimate skill and illegitimate cheating. I have therefore decided to ignore present rules and include kinetics within and as an integral part of handling. Some of the reasons for this approach are:

1. The basic rules which govern all boats including sailboats are the ' International Regulations for Preventing Collisions at Sea'. These govern all sailboats which are not racing and all sailboats which continue to race between sunset and sunrise (unless other special arrangements are in force). These rules have not been changed in principle in decades. They do not concern themselves with either advertising or kinetics. The boat may be signwritten in any manner. The crew may apply whatever effort they choose to hull, paddles or sails.

2. The IYRU 'Yacht Racing Rules' apply between sunrise and sunset as between those boats which have mutually agreed to set aside the Collision Regulations. It is in the nature of the mechanism which generates the IYRU rules, that they change continuously because they are revised every four years. These revisions represent the collective wisdom, experience, personal preferences plus the current political pressures brought to bear upon the present office holders world-wide, and all of these factors change with time.

An example was cited in Section 16.10 of the IYRU's approach to advertising and promotion. This shifted from benign tolerance beyond the rules up to the late 1960's, to the most Corinthian restrictions in the early 1970's. These restrictions went too far and proved unenforceable. So the official position retreated progressively to the point where we are now back to benign tolerance again, but this time within the rules. The basic lesson here is that the Racing Rules follow fashion. The rules of today will not be the rules we will sail under tomorrow.

3. In recent years the IYRU approach to kinetics has also become increasingly restrictive. There are many who believe that these prohibitions may also have gone too far – that while they may be relevant and enforceable in the case of heavier craft (except at night), they may be both indefensible with respect to the seamanlike handling of light craft such as sailboards and very fast sailboats, and they may also be unenforceable. A sailboard cannot be raced in rough water and an unsteady strong wind without a lot of muscular effort and movement of the body and sail. It is reasonable to ask how it is proposed to achieve consistent rulings across the world as to which particular movements are deemed not permissible? In light air and waves, the subtlest applications of kinetics are intended to reduce the movement of the sail and rig. and to achieve this object may need considerable body movement. Again it is reasonable to ask what criteria will be applied in deeming this reduced movement not permissible, and in what way uniform application world wide will be achieved?

These reservations are present and practical. In considering the future there are more important considerations:

4. Political Logic. At a deeper level, the logic of building fierce prohibition against kinetics into the rules may be flawed. The implication that all sailors should be satisfied to ape the wooden immobility of those who steer heavy boats is offensive to a large group of sailors, and to offend so large a part of your constituency is politically unwise. There are millions who jog, not because they lack other means of transport but because they prefer the pleasure of exercise, of breathing and of running free in the open air. There are millions who sail sailboards and light high performance craft, not because they lack the wherewithal to purchase heavy yachts but because they prefer speed and intimate exposure to and physical participation with and control through the wind and the waves. The handling of sailboards and fast sailboats through the full range of wind and sea-state conditions is a cultured physical art form which is valued by those who have worked to perfect it. The endeavour by rulemakers to prohibit by rule those actions which are natural and proper in the control and handling of light fast craft does not encourage respect for the rules – nor for the rulemakers.

The notes which follow will focus on what makes a boat sail fastest. It will be for the reader to decide to what extent if any the techniques suggested should not be applied in view of such rules as may remain in force.

Chapter Twenty Two
Handling to Windward

22.1 Conventional and high performance handling

Conventional handling is based on the culture of the days of sail. In big sailing ships, time was needed to set sail, and more time to trim sail. Canvas was spread so that the craft was fully powered in the gusts. There was neither time nor manpower to ease sails to each gust nor to retrim between gusts. Most sailing literature assumes that small boats should be handled in the same way as big ships were. Sailboats handled in this manner will sail comfortably, but will necessarily coast under-powered through the lulls, i.e. for at least half of the time. Their average speed will be less than the maximum possible.

High-performance handling reverses conventional handling in several major respects:

1. Additional sail is spread and trimmed so that the craft is fully powered not in the gusts but in the lulls. The surplus 'power' is then shed during each gust and fluctuation puff. A well handled sailboard is an example. If the rider were not fully powered in the lulls, he would fall backwards into the water. To maintain his balance, he must first generate and maintain adequate power in the lulls, and then shed the surplus 'power' in the stronger fluctuations and gusts. With this technique he maintains full 'power' continuously and enjoys a performance which is surprising in view of the small size of his craft. Because he maintains full 'power' for all of the time, he necessarily averages a higher speed than he would if he coasted more slowly through the lulls. Other craft which adopt this 'fully powered for all of the time' technique will similarly enjoy a faster average speed.

2. In conventional handling, sail shape is adjusted infrequently, for the simple reason that the rewards for adjustment are small. In Section 17.9 some early efforts in the search for better rigs are described – the end result was that much work in learning how to adjust the shape of a mainsail set behind a conventional mast gave positive but small rewards because the separation bubbles tended to dominate the flow and the rig remained relatively insensitive regardless of the sail shape. At that time we seem to have suffered a form of tunnel vision in that we focussed almost entirely on the mainsails. It was just as well that we did because ultimately we developed the superbly sensitive and efficient flexible wingmast rigs and also the understanding of how they should be handled in order to sail fastest. Soon thereafter we came to realise that knife-edge separation was just as undesirable and that headsails would similarly reward intelligent handling. As soon as we learned to untwist and flatten the other sails exactly as we untwisted and flattened our mainsails, we added more speed.

All boats can therefore share in this speed increase. The techniques suggested in the following sections are directly applicable not only to high performance boats but to all boats with headsails and all boats which use reaching spinnakers.

3. The justification for frequent sail shape adjustment when sailing to windward is shown in Fig. 22.1.1 which repeats Figs 17.32 and 17.33 but adds the characteristics of a sail which is deeper yet, to approximate the performance of a headsail with an eased sheet.

Let us look at the performance of one of the simplest of all high-performance boats – a Skiff Moth with a wingmast rig. Let us imagine that two such boats sail side by side to windward in a 10 knot wind which has 12 knot gusts and 8 knot lulls. Fig. 16.2 suggests that a trim angle of the sail to the Apparent Wind of about 17.5 degrees is a reasonable maximum to expect when a boat is moving well and pointing high in a wind of about 10 knots. Let us say that a helmsman needs a coefficient of lift of 1.15 for 'full power' in the 8 knot lulls. He can get this at 17.5 degrees with a sail of 11% camber, point 'B', and drag 'B1', Fig. 22.1.1. In the gusts he will need a coefficient of lift of only 0.6, point 'A' and drag 'A1'. But look at the smaller drag – 'A2' – of the 7% camber wingmasted mainsail in the gust. If one of the two otherwise identical boats continues to use the 11% camber sail in the gusts, and the other adjusts to 7% camber in the gusts, the flatter-sailed boat will develop about 4 pounds less drag. This will be 10% or more of the total windward-going drag of both the hull and the rig and so the boat with the flattened sail will be able to point several degrees higher through each gust while sailing at the same speed through the water and so (other things being equal) will gain many lengths on each windward leg.

How to do it? In dinghies the headsail sheet will be adjusted by hand. In yachts there is usually adequate machinery in the form of winches and tweakers to enable the headsail to be sheeted closer and fuller in the lulls. For mainsails, a primitive technique I developed when wingmasts were new was to tune the tension of a wire hawse until the shackle which was the sheet block traveller would 'stay put' by friction so long as firm sheet tension was held. In each wind strength we established the optimum traveller position for both gust and lull. At the start of each windward leg we set each traveller control line in its cleat to the 'gust' (i.e. outboard) position. When each lull arrived we pulled the traveller inboard – to windward if necessary – by pulling the line between the cleat and the traveller but we left the line untouched in the cleat. Through the lull we sailed with the mainsail sheeted closer and fuller and the traveller remained in position by friction. As each gust hit, a momentary sharp easing of the sheet was all that was needed for the traveller to flick out to its outboard 'gust' position and I then pulled the sheet harder to flatten the mainsail. The added sheet tension also tightened the forestay and so flattened the jib. Fig. 20.12 shows this system in a gust. Those were early days, it was a rough system, but it worked and we flew and we won. Over the years, traveller systems which are curved plus rig dynamics which yield in the right way in gusts have been further developed and these now do the whole job automatically and so much more easily.

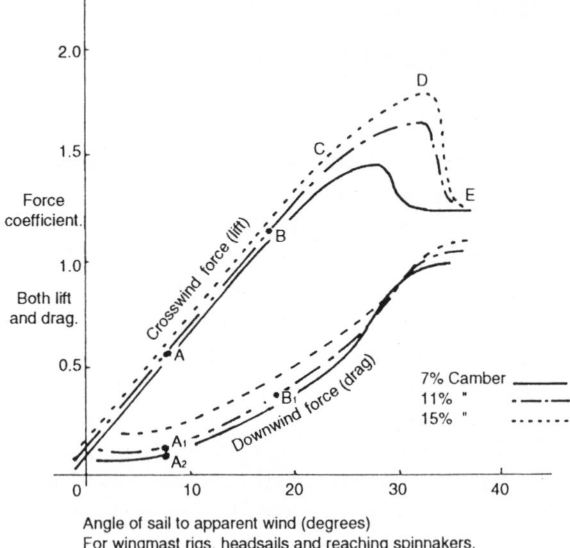

FIG 22.1.1 Change of sail forces with change of camber.

4. Offwind, it pays even more to adjust trim continuously, but for different reasons. From Fig 17.9 it is clear that there is little difference in the maximum force attainable from a flat sail or a full sail if it is set behind a conventional mast. Again, the separation bubbles are the culprits. Fig. 17.31 is typical: it shows that there will be little change of force whether the sail is trimmed at 20 degrees (Point C), or at 25 degrees (Point D), or at 35 degrees (Point E) when it is reaching or broad reaching.

Fig. 22.1.1 is conspicuously different. With both wingmasted sails and headsails, fuller sails give much greater forces at peak, so if sail shape is adjusted fuller offwind (up to the design wind), and the whole sail is trimmed to point D, the boat will sail faster because of the greater drive force. The peak of the lift curve is sharp and there is obviously great difference in drive force as between sails trimmed at 'C', at 'D' or at 'E'. For greatest speed, trim at point 'D' is clearly the optimum. But when sailing offwind, not only every change of wind direction, but every change of wind speed and every change of boat speed as well will all appear to the helmsman as a change in the direction of the Apparent Wind, so in the real world point 'D' is always a fairly rapidly moving target. The winning crews are those who adjust to optimum fullness and who keep their sails trimmed at or near Point 'D' for more of the time than their rivals in the rapidly shifting Apparent Wind. And in order that the whole sail should be trimmed at point 'D' in any breeze, it had better not be twisted.

There are many other elements in high performance sailing, but these four – spreading and trimming sail for full power in the lulls and shedding the excess power in the gusts; frequent adjustment of sail shape to windward; conscious adjustment of sail fullness for maximum potential power offwind; and near-continuous adjustment of trim to achieve that power – are basic.

22.2 Sailing for speed, comfort and survival

There are three ways of sailing: Sailing for speed, sailing for comfort and sailing for survival.

Sailing for speed involves applying the maximum possible drive force continuously, regardless of all other considerations – such as risk of capsize or risk of gear failure.

Sailing for survival involves maximising stability and control, by minimising the wind and wave forces. This is not consistent with speed.

Sailing for comfort is anything in between and cannot be defined.

These notes describe sailing for speed, except where the contrary is stated.

22.3 The three handling regimes

These divide naturally into light airs (0-5 knots), moderate breezes (6-10 knots approx.) and strong breezes (11 knots and stronger). (Fig. 18.4.)

The light air regime is obvious, by definition. In light airs, a crew will seek the greatest 'power' possible from their sails. The trim and contribution to total force of the upper sails will be dominant, as is shown in Fig. 5.1.

The moderate breeze regime covers the wind speed range from the onset of turbulence up to the design wind. In the practical sense, moderate breezes are those between light airs and the design wind, in which the crew are still 'looking for power'.

The strong breeze regime is that in which the wind speed is stronger than the design wind. By definition, in these breezes a crew always have available to them more 'power' than they can use.

To windward in flat water

22.4 In light airs

Starting from rest

1. Note the wind direction at the top of the sails. A balanced feather at the masthead is the most sensitive wind indicator. Indicators at a lower level, such as wool threads tied to the shrouds, or a wind indicator on the foredeck, are not reliable in very light air (Fig. 3.1(d)), and in any case it is the direction of the stronger Apparent Wind at *upper* level that is important.

Because of the great difference in wind speed at the levels of the upper and lower sails, the upper and lower Apparent Winds will be the same when the boat is at rest, but will become most different in their directions when the boat speed is about half the wind speed (Fig. 3.1), and will thereafter become less different as the boat accelerates to some higher speed. Maximum sail twist will be called for when the boat is moving relatively slowly.

2. Turn the boat until its centreline lies at about 45 to 50 degrees to the upper wind direction.

3. Set the mainsail to a fullness of about 8% (Section 17.7).

4. Set the traveller centrally or to windward and hold the mainsheet lightly by hand.

5. Heel the boat to leeward and ease both jib and main sheets so that the upper leeches of both sails fall to leeward to twist the sails. In the case of any boat with fully battened sails and substantial roach, the inbuilt fabric tension natural in any fully battened mainsail will cause the upper roach to 'hook' to windward when the boat is upright, and so boats with fully battened sails will need to be heeled further to achieve the same twist.

6. For approximate initial trim ease the sheets until both the upper jib and the upper mainsail are trimmed at an angle of about 20 degrees to the feather. For optimum continuing trim adjust the boat's heading and/or the sheet tensions so that the leeward forward tufts (tell-tales) stream but occasionally agitate. (These tufts are in the area of highest flow speed (Fig. 17.2), so in near-calm conditions these will be the tufts which 'come alive' first.) This will trim the sail between points 'C' and 'D', and nearer point 'D', in (Fig. 22.1.1.).

7. If sailing a boat which responds to *fourth mode* handling – (Section 20.11.) move forward until the bottom or chine at the transom just skims the surface. This will be a substantially bow-down hull attitude.

8. *Keep still.*

The boat will begin to move.

Sail trim

The optimum sail shapes for light air are shown in Figs 22.4.2 and those which follow. The symbols used are shown in Fig. 22.4.1. The meaning of each symbol is:

'Chord' – A line from the luff or mast, across the sail to the leech in the direction of the wind flow (i.e. somewhat upwards if the boat is heeled), is called the 'chord'.

'H' is the heading, the direction of the centreline(s) of the keel or centreboard(s). It is also the direction of travel through the water, except that a correction to leeward should be made for boats which make measurable leeway. For boats which use gybing centreboards, the direction of the hull becomes irrelevant, but the sheeting angles of the sails will be rotated with respect to 'H' by an amount equal to the gybing angle of the centreboard.

'T' is the trim angle of the sails. It is the angle between 'H' and the chord.

'C' is the camber of the sail – it is the greatest distance of the fabric from the chord, and is expressed as a percentage of the chord.

'L' is the angle between 'H' and the plane of the sailcloth at the leech.

Fig. 22.4.2 shows the approximate trim angles, cambers, and sail twists with which high performance boats sail fastest in light airs. The optimum trim angles at all times in light air and on all points of sailing (except when running 'square') will be with the forward leeward tufts streaming and occasionally agitating (flat water only). Sail twist should be adjusted so that both the lower and the upper tufts of both jib and mainsail all stream and occasionally all agitate together.

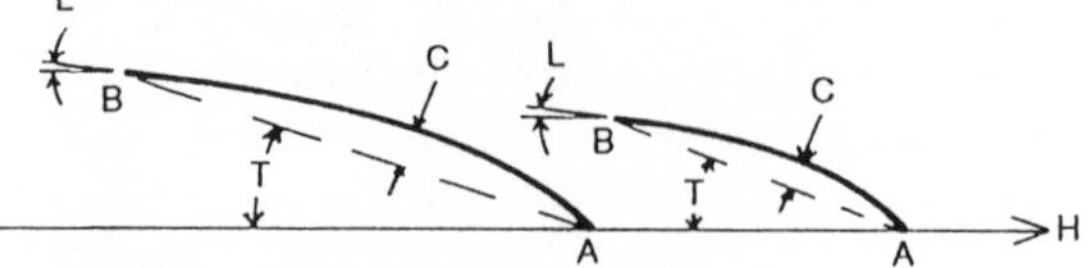

In Fig 22.4.2. and similar following figures:
At A - B (Chords of mainsail and jib at stated heights)
H = Heading, also direction of travel (leeway and current ignored).
T = Sail trim angle: Angle between H and chord, degrees.
C = Camber of sail, as percent of chord.
L = Angle between H and sail at leech, degrees.

Fig 22.4.1 Key for Figs 22.4.2 and similar.

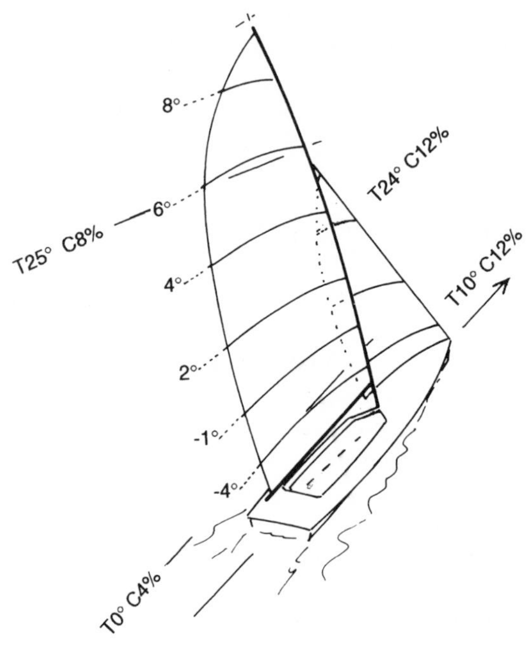

Fig 22.4.2 Sail trim for 0 - 5 knots, flat water.

Force dynamics in light airs

At the 'drift' end of the light air regime, the practical effect of the wind-speed difference between the upper and the lower sails is at its maximum. When the boat is at rest, or is sailing only slowly, very little force can be developed by the lower half of the sails. For example, if the upper sails of a typical 14 foot dinghy enjoy 4 knots of Apparent Wind and the lower sails only 1.5 knots then the upper half of the rig can develop about 4 pounds of total force while the lower half can contribute less than one half a pound of total force, and thus only an ounce or two of forward thrust, despite its much greater area (Fig. 5.1).

But if this boat is accelerated by close reaching to a boat speed of 2 knots and is then pointed only as high as is consistent with maintaining 2 knots through the water, the Apparent Wind speed across the upper sails will increase to about 5.5 knots and across the lower sails to about 3 knots. The total force developed will more than double compared with that available from the sails of an unaccelerated boat (because the force developed will increase as the square of the speed of the Apparent Wind), and this doubled force will give a boat speed increase of about 50%. This is why, when very light air returns after a near-calm period, it will always pay to accelerate by sailing free at first, and to 'wind up' to a higher pointing angle only after speed has been acquired. A boat which is pointed high from the outset can stabilise at some lower speed and will accelerate no further.

Boats which cannot be heeled significantly, such as keelboats and catamarans, should ignore the feeble lower wind and concentrate solely on trimming their upper and mid-level sails as efficiently as is possible to the stronger airs at those levels.

As the boat gathers speed, the Apparent Winds affecting both the upper and lower sails will each change direction. Both will move towards the bow. The lower wind, particularly, will begin to blow from nearly ahead and so the boom will need to be drawn in almost to the centreline. From near-zero speed up to about half the wind speed the directions will diverge to a maximum (Fig. 3.1) and increasing twist will be needed. As the speed exceeds half the wind speed they will tend to converge again. Most boats sail at about one third to one half of the wind speed, and so suffer the maximum possible difference in direction.

As the boat 'winds up' in its own Apparent Wind, the forces developed by the upper mainsail and jib will nearly double. More sheet tension will be needed just to hold the sails where they are and extra again when the speed calls for reduction of twist.

The fastest technique when a puff returns will be to sail the boat on a close reaching heading for one or two lengths. As soon as, but not before, it has accelerated to a reasonable speed, it should be pointed progressively closer to the wind and the boom drawn in a lot and the upper sail(s) trimmed in a little until speed loss is sensed, or sensed to be imminent. The fastest technique to windward will always be first to sail free to acquire speed and only then to 'wind up' and point as high as is possible consistent with maintaining reasonable speed.

So long as the light air holds its speed, and the boat maintains its speed, the trim and pointing angle described above and indicated in Fig. 22.4.2 will remain the fastest trim.

Whenever the wind speed falls lighter, and/or the boat loses speed, e.g. by passing through the waves of a substantial wake, then in the lighter Apparent Wind the elasticity of the rig can pull the upper leeches too far to windward unless the sheets are deliberately eased. This is particularly true if the boat has a fully battened sail with a big roach because the fabric tension pulls the upper leech of these sails to windward more than is the case with conventional sails. Fully battened sails need much more conscious easing in lighter patches than do conventional sails. Always look and ease the sheet so that the upper leeward tuft remains 'alive'. If,the sheets are not eased, the boat may fail to accelerate, or accelerate only slowly, when moving air returns.

Always be careful never to oversheet in very light air.

Always ease sheets deliberately when the air falls lighter.

In these very light airs, sheets should be eased, the boat should be turned a little away from the wind, and the basic starting technique of 'first accelerate with free sheets and then wind up,' described above, should be repeated whenever the wind returns after falling to near zero.

The notes above have described what to do whenever the Apparent Wind speed increases or decreases. In real life this will certainly happen. In addition, the direction of the wind will change as well, The 'feature size' of light air unsteadiness is about 100m, so a boat which sails at 3 to 4 knots (5 to 7 feet per second) will usually experience two changes of speed and two changes of direction every 60 seconds – about a change every fifteen seconds on average. The nature of these changes is shown in Figs 4.6, 4.7, and 4.8.

It is absolutely vital that the boat should be steered, in response to the changes in wind direction, so that the angle of the Apparent Wind over the upper sails remains approximately as it would have been had the wind not changed in direction. In either the unsteady pattern, or the oscillating pattern (See Part One), this will result in the boat following a 'snaking' course through the water. Observation of and understanding which wind pattern you are sailing in will greatly assist in anticipating these changes. Failure to follow the wind's changes of direction will result in the boat stopping each time the wind changes direction in the sense which causes it to blow more from ahead. As between two boats, one of which maintains good speed by 'snaking' and periodically steers lower than expected for a few seconds, and another which often points higher but which stops much more frequently, the boat which keeps moving will always win.

So the crew, and particularly the helmsman, have two primary tasks. The first is to acquire speed and then 'wind up' and thereafter maintain the best speed and pointing angle possible through the changes of wind speed. The second is to steer, in response to the changes in wind direction, whatever course is necessary from moment to moment to maintain the sail trim angles to the Apparent Wind which will give that best speed.

At the stronger end of the light air range, when the wind speed is 4 to 5 knots, all of the foregoing remains true, but the emphasis changes. Instead of needing to re-accelerate from near-zero speed periodically, which is quite normal in the very light unsteady or pulsing airs, it is more usual to alternate between, say, a 6 knot puff and a 3 knot lull. If we regard 4 knots over the upper sails and 1 1/2 knots over the lowers as a 3 knot lull, and that a 5-6 knot puff may well see 6-7 knots of Apparent Wind over the upper sails and 3 knots over the lower half, then in the puff a light efficient dinghy or catamaran can easily accelerate to about 4 knots through the water. This will give an Apparent Wind of about 9.5 knots across the upper half of the rig and 5.5 knots across the lower half. The forces at realistic trim angles will then become 24 pounds and 8 pounds – a total of 32 pounds, and this is more than enough to drive the boat at 4 knots of boat speed at a reasonably high pointing angle in flat water. To trim the mainsail firmly for high pointing against the 24 pound force on the upper mainsail will require a respectable sheet tension. This may feel like a breeze.

In this situation, it is vital to look at the water surface. Unless it shows the characteristic ripple and energy of the breeze's turbulent boundary layer it will still be light air, and you will still be sailing in a linear velocity gradient, i.e. the wind at the masthead will be much stronger than the wind at the surface. In these conditions, the boat will sail fastest and point highest if the mainsail is left slightly twisted.

Not until you are certain of the breeze's full wind strength low down should you consider sheeting firmly.

The 'circular airflow' effect

Every so often you will need to tack. When a boat turns, the action of turning causes a change in the directions of the Apparent Winds at the bow and the stern. and this effect is greatest in light airs. Imagine a boat of exaggerated length, with one sail at the extreme bow, a centreboard in the middle, and another sail at the extreme stern. If such a boat, in light air, were to hold a steady course on port tack, then the Apparent Winds over the sails at both ends will be from the same direction, Fig. 22.4.3(a). But when the boat tacks by pivoting on its centreboard in a turn to the left with little forward speed, then as the bow swings to the left, the Apparent Wind at the bow will blow more from the port beam (as 'x'), while that at the stern will change sides and blow more from the starboard beam (as 'y'). This is the 'circular airflow' component. It is important to aerodynamicists because it changes the direction of airflow over the tail surfaces of long aircraft when they turn. When sailboats turn quickly in light air the effects are much more pronounced.

If you now imagine a boat, say on port tack, to sail with speed from a puff into a near-calm lull, then the headsails will stream almost directly aft. If the boat is at this time turned to starboard, then the Apparent Wind over the headsails will appear to come from starboard for as long as the turn is continued, while that over the mainsail will blow more from the port side. There are numerous traps in this situation: the old adage 'never tack when the wind goes light' defends you from most of them. The higher the performance and manoeuvrability of your boat, the more relevant will circular airflow components become.

On another level, many texts on handling encourage a tacking technique based on easing the headsail and firming the mainsheet in the initial stages of the tack. If your object is power and speed, this is exactly what you should not do. During any light-air tack, your mainsail will lose drive immediately you begin to turn, while the headsail will continue to provide forward drive far into the turn.

Practical handling techniques

The basic techniques suggested above assume that the boat you sail is fluently adjustable and that you can in fact do the things suggested. Sometimes this is not possible, and you have to 'make do'. Sometimes the dynamics of your boat call for different priorities.

I asked an Enterprise class world champion who is currently sailing 505's at top level, what he did to regain movement and speed after the wind dropped out during a race.

''This is exactly the situation which occurred in one heat of the Australian 505 championships in Adelaide. The wind died completely for awhile and then returned as the lightest air. We tightened the rig to extreme: this bent the topmast back and flattened the upper mainsail and allowed the leech to twist off. We flattened the lower mainsail – it is not possible to flatten a captive-foot sail much, but we did what we could. We moved the jib slides forward, for more power in the lower jib. We heeled as much as was

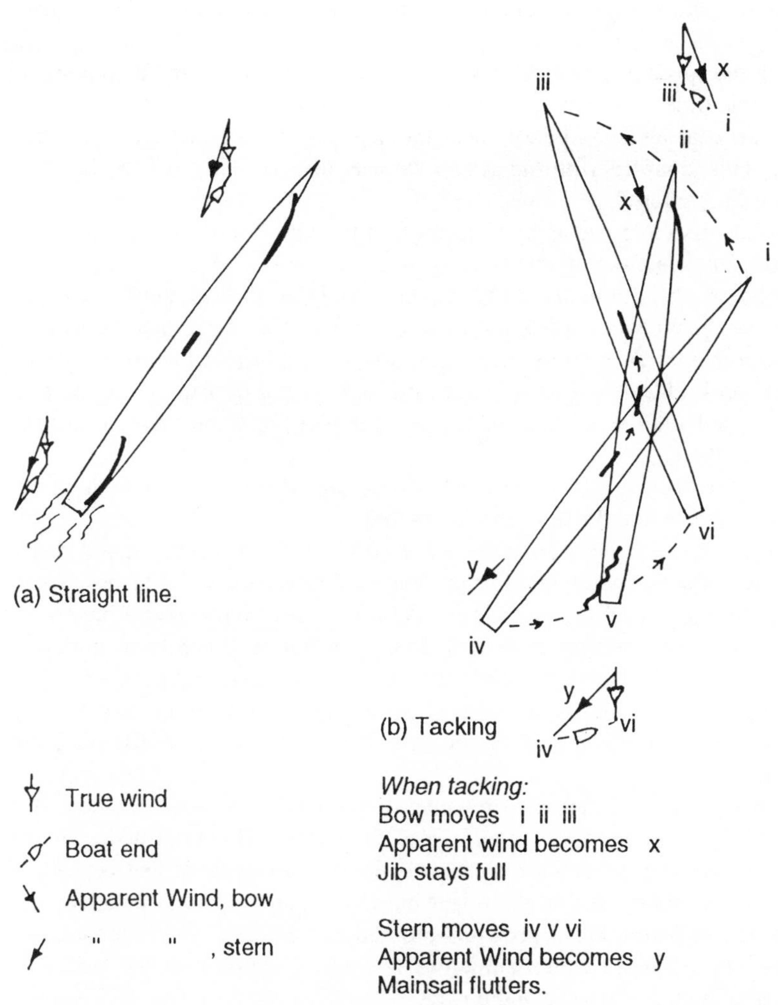

Fig 22.4.3 The circular airflow effect

necessary for adequate twist in the mainsail – surprisingly, the 505 does not need much heel. I held the mainsheet directly from the boom, to hold the boom on or fractionally to windward of the centreline with no downward force. The 505 is too symmetrical, too full forward to be responsive to fourth mode technique, so we did not move forward. We were the only crew to have a sensitive masthead wind indicator – a balanced feather – and we used it to the full. With this trim we were the only boat which could maintain reasonable speed while pointing reasonably high. We moved from fifth to first and continued to stretch our lead – but it did us no good in the end because in the adverse current the time limit ran out before we reached the next mark.'

And again 'In the Enterprise I applied exactly the same principles, but because there was no way of adjusting anything I had to resort to unusual practices. More heel was needed to twist the mainsail adequately. To position the boom on or near the centreline was only possible if I held it by hand, like a windsurfer. The Enterprise, like the 505, is a symmetrical boat and there is no point in trimming it nose down. But with sufficient twist (from exaggerated heel) and the boom held centrally by hand we could sail as fast as anyone else and point higher through the drifty bits.'

Mark Mendelblatt (Laser II world champion) – adds: 'In light air and flat water, I set the boat up for most power. The mast is right forward, and both main and jib downhauls are right off. The mainsail tack is not shackled to the boom. It is secured with a line as a floating tack. This enables us to free all tension from the luff in light air. The sails set with horizontal wrinkles and the fullness is well back. The outhaul is tight.'

'Right off the start line I pick up the speed necessary to match the boat to windward, and then point as high as possible at that speed. At this time I sail solely by feel – with practise you can sense when the boat is likely to lose speed and can bear away and ease sheet momentarily before that happens, then immediately start pinching again. This, coupled with the set-up we use, usually clears off the boats to weather and creates a gap to leeward for safety.'

'Once we judge that we are sufficiently clear, we apply Cunningham to remove most of the horizontal wrinkles and from that point on we sail as fast as possible.'

The Eighteen footer world champion comments; 'The basic principles always apply, but the differences in application are interesting. We will assume a skiff with a crew of three and that the wind is between 2 and 5 knots. In this variable light air with its near-calm lulls, even an Eighteen will be 'dead' in the lulls, but in the feeble puffs an Eighteen sailing to windward with its big rig can accelerate to a speed of about 1.5 times the wind speed and the differences in Apparent Wind between puff and lull are so great that they call for unusual handling.

The forward hand lies along the foredeck to get the bow down and the transom just skimming, for fourth mode sailing. This leaves two people, not three, to handle the boat.

The skipper adopts a position far enough out along the wing to keep the boat flat in the mean wind. He does not move and in this way maintains a constant frame of reference so as to be able to read the water surface upwind in the variable conditions. He plays the mainsheet himself to optimise feel and co-ordination. The third hand tends the jib sheets and moves fluently to maintain balance.

The rig is set up with little vang tension – the upper leech is encouraged to fall to leeward but the tension is set to optimise twist for maximum acceleration in the first seconds of each puff. Cunningham is relatively slack to set camber 'full'.

As each puff arrives heading is not altered and the third crewman does not move for the first second or so – not until the skipper has eased the sheet and has begun to draw it in again. This brief delay allows the upper leech to blow well open. The skipper eases mainsheet quickly – about three to five feet in about one second. The boat accelerates rapidly during the following few seconds. As it accelerates the skipper draws the mainsheet in as the Apparent Wind goes forward and also luffs to 'wind the boat up' to a pointing angle as high as possible consistent with maintaining the new speed through the puff. The third hand moves to windward as necessary for balance and power.

When the boat enters the next lull, the third hand moves rapidly to leeward, right out onto the leeward wing if necessary, to maintain balance. The sails stream down the centreline. There is no point in bearing away – the sails will continue to stream whatever the heading until the boat slows. Any substantial turn to leeward will in fact cause the Apparent Wind at the bow to appear to blow from even further to leeward – (refer to the note about circular airflow above). In any sharp lull, it is fastest to hold the heading, pointing high, until the speed washes off. The skipper then bears away gently and eases the sheet to establish efficient sailing through the much reduced Apparent Wind of the lull. The third hand returns from the leeward wing as sail force is re-established.'

This problem of how to handle the Apparent Wind when it blows from ahead when entering a light-air lull is common to all boats. It is merely a bigger problem with high performance craft, because the difference between the puff and the lull Apparent Winds is so much greater.

Summary

In light airs, both jib and mainsail should be trimmed continuously by hand so that maximum 'power' is maintained continuously over the entire height of both sails (point D, 7% camber, Fig. 22.1.1).

In light air and flat water, highest speed to windward will be achieved by consciously sailing the boat more loosely sheeted and pointed lower in the lulls and by allowing the boat to accelerate to a higher speed before pointing it higher and sheeting slightly more tightly in the puffs.

All my coaching experience suggests that most crews can 'read' approaching puffs on the water, recognise their effect on the boat, and respond correctly to them. Conversely, very few are at first mentally attuned to recognising the reduction of wind which signals a lull, and responding to it before the boat loses substantial speed. When you sail a high performance boat, the cost of losing speed – vis a vis a competitor who doesn't – is so great that high average speed and the winners' circle usually reward those who respond first to each *lull*.

22.5 In moderate breezes – the vital changes

As the wind speed increases through the critical 5-6kt speed range, turbulence will become fully established in the surface flow. As a result, three important changes take place:

First, full wind speed affects the lower sails as well as the upper sails (Fig. 3.2). Because of this, the total force on an efficient rig 'jumps' by about 300% instead of the 50% or so which would be expected from the speed increase from 5 knots to 6 knots alone. When you know what to expect, you can feel this extra force cut in as if a switch had been thrown.

Secondly, since all wind speeds at all heights above about one metre have now become approximately the same, the directions of the Apparent Winds at all heights will also become approximately the same. As a result, there is no longer any need for the extreme twist which was so necessary in light air to compensate for the differences in the directions of the Apparent Winds at different heights.

Third, the normal turbulent breeze pattern of fluctuations, gusts and lulls establishes.

Steering indicators

Because the wind speeds and directions at all levels are now the same, the absolute dominance of the masthead wind and hence the need to watch primarily the masthead wind indicator and the upper sails and tufts – and be blinded by the sun and suffer a stiff neck as well – no longer applies. The lower jib tufts now become the primary source of steering and trimming information.

Tufts near the luff of the jib are a much more precise indicator of the wind angle than might at first be thought. This is because of the way the mainsail spills air around its luff when it is trimmed in and the fact that the jib is in the area of this deflected flow. You can check the way this works in the case of your own boat with two simple experiments:

1. Trim the jib normally but let the mainsail stream with slack sheets. Sail to windward, and luff until the windward jib tuft(s) just agitate. Bear away until the leeward tufts just agitate. Note the difference in heading (compass or landmarks). Now sheet the mainsail normally, and repeat. The difference in heading will be about half – the bigger the mainsail the smaller will be the difference. The reason is that the mainsail, as you bear away, develops pressure over its windward surface and suction over its leeward surface and this pressure difference drives the air ahead of the mainsail to leeward – and this is where the jib is. You can see this working in another way in Fig. 20.12. The masthead feather shows that in this photograph the masthead is directly upwind of the camera. But you can see the windward surface of the upper jib – the part nearest the mast, and it is not flapping. It is setting perfectly in the local wind just ahead of the mast which is deflected to leeward as it approaches the mainsail.

2. Sail to windward with all sails trimmed normally. Suddenly let the main sheet go free, but hold your heading. The windward jib tuft(s) will agitate. Repeat, but this time suddenly pull the mainsail far to windward with the traveller (or vang the sail firmly and pull the boom to windward with your hands like a sailboard). The grossly overtrimmed sail will deflect more air to leeward ahead of itself, and the leeward jib tuft(s) will indicate this by agitating, despite the fact that there has been no change in heading nor jib trim.

These experiments show that the angle at which the local wind approaches the luff of the jib changes by up to twice as much as the change of angle of the whole boat to the wind, so the jib luff becomes the most sensitive area of the whole boat to use as a trimming guide to hold or restore a particular angle between the boat's heading and the wind direction at any instant.

This is what the jib tufts indicate so sensitively. They indicate equally sensitively when the trim angle of the mainsail changes for any other reason – such as a change in the wind direction, or an error in steering.

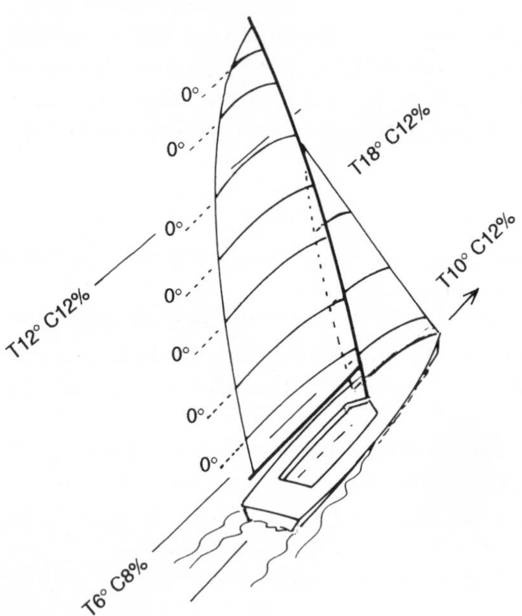

Fig 22.6.1 Sail trim for 6 - 8 knots, flat water

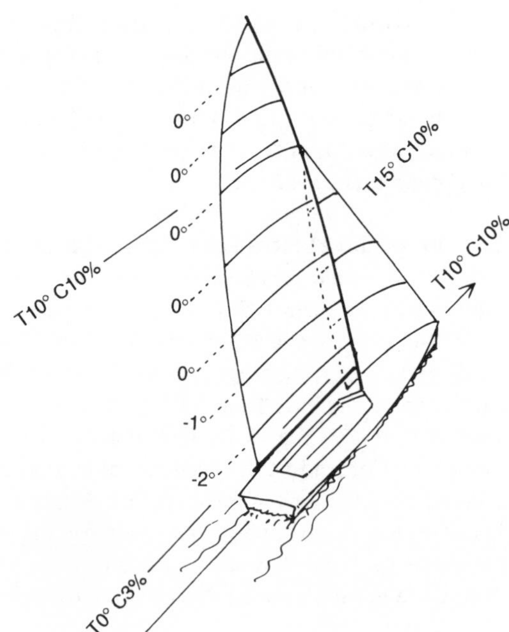

Fig 22.6.2 Sail trim for 8 - 11 knots, flat water

22.6 Sail trim techniques

Precise and continuous adjustment of the trim of the upper mainsail leech in response to the longer-term wind speed changes (one minute or more), is essential for peak performance in the 6 to 10 knot regime. Although the substantial twist needed in light air (to compensate for the change of direction of the Apparent Wind with height) is no longer needed, a small amount of twist will remain essential for other reasons. These are:

1. The presence of the jib in fractional rigs deflects the air in which the lower mainsail operates. No such deflection occurs above the jib. As a rule of thumb, the upper mainsail should be sheeted at about the same fullness and trim angle as the lower jib – because both sails enjoy the same flow of undisturbed air. The lower mainsail is an exception. It should be trimmed further to windward and flatter – but never to windward of the centreline – by the amount by which the jib deflects the oncoming air. Note two points:

(a) The more tightly the jib is sheeted, the greater will be the mainsail twist needed to compensate, and so the further to windward the boom should be and the slacker the main sheet, and vice versa;

(b) Adjustment of the jib sheet from time to time logically calls for simultaneous, smaller, adjustment of the mainsheet.

2. The change of fullness of the mainsail – normal fullness in the upper sail (10% for wingmast rigs, and about 13% for conventional rigs) and flattened as necessary behind the jib (to avoid backwind in the mainsail) itself calls for some twist to ensure that the leech of the upper mainsail does not 'hook' because of its greater fullness.

All these factors are shown in Figs 22.6.1 and 22.6.2.

3. A third practical factor is important when sailing in very harsh rough air. In these conditions a dinghy or catamaran with a more loosely-sheeted 'springy' rig which can twist open automatically and momentarily in the harsh gusts will far out perform a more tightly-sheeted boat with rigid sails. This subject is covered later.

As between any three adjacent boats which sail to windward at the same speed through the water, the one which is sheeted most accurately for the existing conditions will point highest.

Any boat with more mainsail twist must point lower to achieve the same speed because at the same pointing angle it will lack power from its upper mainsail.

Any boat sheeted too tightly, i.e. with less twist, will lack the proper forward drive from its upper mainsail and will, therefore, also have to point lower to achieve the same speed.

Fig. 22.6.1 shows the basic trim which sails fastest in a 6 to 8 knot breeze and flat water. The three primary differences between the light air trim of Fig. 22.4.2 and the breeze trim of Fig 22.6.1 are:

1. Both jib and mainsail are sheeted much more closely.
2. Both jib and mainsail are sheeted with very little twist.
3. Sail fullness and sheet tension are both adjusted so that the leeches of both sails are everywhere about parallel to the centreline – and this requires that the lower mainsail be substantially flattened to avoid 'hooking'.

Note that the trim angle and fullness of the upper mainsail is about the same as the trim angle and fullness of the lower jib. The lower mainsail is sheeted more closely and flattened sufficiently to avoid backwind in the mainsail from the air deflected by the jib.

The shift from the light air shape (Fig. 22.4.2) to the breeze shape (Fig. 22.6.1) – and vice versa – should occur whenever the wind changes from light air to breeze and vice versa. It should occur suddenly. An intermediate shape can never be the most efficient.

Fig. 22.6.2 shows the fastest trim as the wind speed increases to 8-9-10 knots. As the rig's 'power' increases, the boat can be pointed higher without losing speed. The changes in shape called for are small – the boom is trimmed in until it lies along the centreline and the lower mainsail is flattened further to avoid 'hooking' at the leech. (As the boom is trimmed in to lie along the centreline, a small area of the lower leech just above the clew will inevitably 'hook' slightly unless the sail is flattened to extreme. This seems to do no harm. In practice some fullness plus fractional hooking is faster than absolute flatness and no hooking.)

These small changes of shape mask the quite big changes in handling called for by the extra force in the sails. In the 6-7 knots of Fig. 22.6.1, the total force on a typical rig would be about 60-70 pounds. In the 10 knots of Fig. 22.6.2 this force will have doubled to about 140 pounds. Because the masthead is springy, the upper mainsail leech will blow to leeward under this increased force unless the mainsheet (and jib sheet also) are tightened. Given equal handling in all other respects, a boat will point highest (at the optimum boat speed) when it is sheeted so that all its leeches lie approximately parallel with its centreline. As the wind speed increases, the sheets *must be tightened to maintain this trim.* More importantly, when the breeze dies a little, they *must be eased,* otherwise the masthead will spring forward and pull the upper leech too far to windward. This is a trap, because the sail, thus oversheeted, still 'feels' powerful in the sense that a crew will have to 'swing' harder to keep the boat upright than they do when the sail is sheeted with the leeches parallel with the centreline. But because the force from the oversheeted upper mainsail is directed too much across the boat, and too little forward, the total drive force is less, and the boat will sail more slowly. This factor will be important in all boats, but will be doubly so in boats with fully battened mainsails because of the sensitivity of their upper leeches to mainsheet tension.

In light airs, which are so often unsteady, it was inevitable that speed would frequently be lost, so the fastest technique becomes 'first regain speed, and only then wind up to the optimum pointing angle'.

Breezes, because of the evenness of texture which results from their thorough mixing, are about 30 times more consistent in speed and direction, and so windless 'holes', in which substantial speed is likely to be lost, are about 30 times less likely. Instead, there will be the fluctuations and gusts of the normal breezes, or the fluctuations and slow speed changes of the wandering breeze to deal with. A glance at the traces of all the heated breezes from Fig. 7.1 to 7.22 (Part One) show that, except in the relatively rarely occurring 'steady' conditions, the wind speed will change both frequently and substantially. Throughout these changes, those crews will sail fastest to windward who accelerate to a reasonably high boat speed to gain the advantage of the strongest Apparent Wind which is practicably attainable and then make every endeavour to keep their sails accurately shaped in the changing wind speed and so maintain the highest possible pointing angle in every wind strength at the chosen boat speed.

Inevitably, they will point lower with fuller sails and slacker sheets in the lighter patches, and point higher with flatter sails and tighter sheets when the wind is stronger. Those crews who sense each small but significant wind speed change and adjust mainsheet and jib sheet tensions to maintain optimum sail trim as well as adjusting total rig shape for the longer lasting changes, will be able to point higher, in each wind strength, than any of their rivals.

A tactical point must be made here. In big fleet racing, in the period immediately after the start, the entire fleet customarily points higher than the pointing angle which yields VMG(max). In this situation a helmsman, in order to maintain his position, has no option but to match the pointing angle of the boat to leeward. For as long as a competitor sails close to leeward of him and he cannot tack or does not wish to tack he has no option but to sail higher and slower than he would prefer – and he had better practise this until he is as good at it as anyone else, or he will not survive any start in good position. Only when he has reached a clear air situation, will it be possible for him to adopt the faster boat speed which will give maximum VMG.

It is in this 'higher and slower' mode particularly, that oversheeting can lead to loss of speed and simultaneous loss of pointing ability. A boat which is sailing more slowly than usual begins to make significant leeway. The cure for this is to sheet slightly wider and with slightly flatter sails – when pinching,there is little drive force, so drag should be reduced to the absolute minimum. The ability to match and stay with and beat an opponent who either pinches or foots is an advanced racing skill that demands intense practise, but pays great dividends.

22.7 Effects of fluctuations and gusts on technique

In my youth – in the early days of non-adjustable Bermudan rigs – we put up one rig and used it in all conditions. We adjusted nothing, because nothing was adjustable.

It will by now be self evident that different sail shapes will be faster at different wind speeds. Sections 22.4, 22.5 and 22.6 suggest which particular shape would win if the wind were to blow steadily at a particular speed. A crew can easily and quickly tune a modern adjustable rig to any of these shapes, and can retune it to a different shape whenever the wind speed changes, provided that the wind speed changes relatively slowly. We have progressed, and can sail faster.

But out on the water the wind speed is not steady, nor does the speed always change slowly. Gusts repeat about every 30 seconds on average. Sometimes the interval can be 60 seconds, sometimes five. Skilled crews should and normally will 'power up' during the more prolonged lulls. But many gusts repeat much more quickly and the fluctuations normal to every breeze repeat more quickly again. These faster gust and fluctuation changes repeat so quickly that it is not possible to use the deliberate techniques of rig adjustment described above.

How then should we handle these faster changes?

For these quickly repeating changes, we must develop the second of two parallel skills. The first is the sail-tuning skill of deciding what will be the fastest sail shape in the existing mean wind speed, and setting up the rig to get that shape. The second will be a manipulative skill – a technique which will enable us to sail as fast as possible through the quicker wind speed changes caused by the quicker gusts and fluctuations without the need to move any control other than the three fundamental 'fast response' controls of steering, sail trimming and balance by body movement.

22.8 Handling in moderate breezes

The moderate breeze is that speed range of the turbulent breeze in which a crew can hold a boat upright by body balance alone. Because it is so simple to hold the sheet tightly, or cleat it, and 'swing' with body weight and energy to each gust, it is not surprising to find that this is the most common approach.

While this technique is simple and safe, it wins no races because it is slow. There are several reasons for this.

The first is the action of the upper mainsail leech. If the mainsheet is either cleated, or held in a fixed position, there is nothing to prevent the springy upper leech from hooking in the lulls (slow) and blowing too open in the puffs (poor pointing).

Another reason has been touched on in the light air section – whenever a crew move their weight rapidly, the boat's momentum is disturbed, and it loses speed.

A third reason is that whenever a boat rolls, its resistance increases. For example, during our tow tests, we were returning to the pontoon one afternoon after a series of runs. I was busy with a pencil near the balance when I saw it suddenly jump from 19 to 27 pounds. When I looked up to see what had gone wrong,

I saw that the crew in the towed boat had started to roll it from side to side for kicks. This was unexpected. We repeated the 'steady' and 'rolling' drags to make sure. That hull, a Dribbly 1, ballasted to 525 pounds total weight, with centreboard and rudder fully down, dragged 19 pounds at 5 knots when it was steady, and 27 pounds when it was rolled back and forth. Enough said.

It is the nature of gusts to hit hard. Their speed changes occur abruptly. It follows that if bodies are moved sufficiently fast to stop the boat from heeling, speed will be lost because such vigorous movement will disturb momentum. If bodies are moved more slowly and smoothly, the boat will roll to the gust in the meantime, and speed will be lost because of the increased drag. If the boat is turned either way, it will again lose performance. If it is turned to windward, there will be a time delay of about two seconds before it comes upright, and in the meantime boat speed will be lost. If it is turned downwind, VMG will suffer.

A moment's thought reveals that the basic reasons why these penalties are incurred are:

1. The change in wind speed is usually abrupt.
2. No boat can sail fast if it is handled harshly or unsteadily through these abrupt changes.
3. For a different wind speed, a different sail setting will be faster, and no amount of wishful thinking will alter this fact.

What is needed then, is a technique which will:

1. Accept a sudden gust, or the sudden cessation of a gust, without losing efficiency.
2. Compensate for the sudden change of force smoothly, without roll, and without sudden body movement.
3. Allow sufficient time for bodies to be moved smoothly to new positions proper for the new wind speed.
4. Approximate closely the, 'ideal' sail shapes which would be set up for the different lull and gust wind speeds if there were ample time to do so.

All of these can be achieved by the following techniques. The first technique works with high-performance boats at the low-end of the 'power' range. The second works with the high-power boats.

Technique for high performance boats of low power, i.e. those which do not routinely plane to windward.

Set up the rig for optimum windward-going boat speed and best possible pointing angle in the wind speed of the *lulls*.

The simplest way to set up the rig shape fastest for each wind strength in your boat is to 'do it by numbers'. The outhaul, downhaul etc control lines and the sheets should be marked so that the optimum shapes for light air, moderate breeze etc can all be repeated accurately. A simple system which works well is to put a knot in the line and paint tiny dots on the spars – the 'One dot' mark is for 5 knots, 'Two dots' is for 10 knots, and 'Three dots' for 20 knots and you interpolate in between. Both jib and mainsail should have both upper and lower tufts near their luffs (tufts on mainsails behind conventional masts will need to be back far enough to be clear of the separation bubble), and the mainsail should have leech ribbons.

To arrive at the fastest rig set-up for either the light air or the moderate breeze regime:-

1. Acquire the desired speed by pointing low.
2. While holding the desired speed systematically improve pointing angle by optimising sail trim. Adjust the fullness and the twist of the lower main, then the upper main, then the lower jib etc, then go round again and again until the whole rig is at peak.
3. Highest pointing at the desired speed will occur when all sails are set as full as possible providing that:

(a) All tufts are streaming,

(b) All leeches are parallel with the centreline, and none are hooked (except for a small area just above the clew.)

(c) The boat can be held upright.

A second check is that if the boat is luffed a little *all* the windward tufts should flutter simultaneously

Note that this technique needs flat water and relatively steady wind. Any wave motion or unsteadiness of wind will destabilise the tufts. But in the right conditions this method, worked through systematically, will result in the optimum rig shapes for every class. The final shapes will be similar to those shown in Figs 22.6.1 and 22.6.2 – smaller rigs will be more open and bigger rigs will lie closer to the centreline.

In winds stronger than the design wind the method will remain valid, but as the sails are eased to shed power the leeches will no longer remain parallel with the centreline.

Let us now assume that we are sailing a low-power boat which has alternative sheet or traveller control for the mainsail, that the mean wind speed is about 8 to 9 knots, that the lulls are about 7 knots and the puffs are about 10 to 11 knots. Set up the boat for the lulls (Fig. 22.6.1) and sail it thus in the 7 knot lulls. When the puff or gust comes, the object will be to achieve a set-up as close as possible to Fig. 22.6.2 during the puff, but without making any rig adjustments.

The principle factors will be:

1. In the stronger puffs the rig will develop about 30-40% more 'power', than in the lulls. Therefore –

2. In the puffs the sails can be sheeted more closely, and the boat can be pointed higher without loss of speed.

3. Because fluctuation puffs do not mark the water, the fluctuation puffs and lulls must be sensed by the boat beginning to roll to leeward as the puff is encountered, and to windward at the onset of the lull.

Sail the boat with the mainsheet cleated and the traveller hand-held and with the arm slightly bent. Whenever the boat begins to heel in stronger air, *immediately* free the traveller several inches (by straightening the arm – this avoids any delay in changing the grip) and simultaneously begin to luff *slowly* towards an aiming point 8-10 degrees further to windward.

Note that the initial action is that both hands move simultaneously to leeward. The traveller hand moves a long way and quickly – far enough to check the roll before the masthead has moved more than a few inches – while the tiller hand moves delicately and smoothly.

Starting at the same time, but with absolute smoothness, the crews' bodies should begin to move outwards to balance the force of the new wind. As the bodies move, the traveller should be drawn to windward again in such a manner that balance is preserved between the outwardly-moving bodies and the increasing sail force. The windward movement of the traveller should stop at the point at which the boom lies along the centreline. This whole process normally occupies up to about two seconds. During this period the boat is in a state of dynamic balance. (A convenient way to position the boom automatically is to hold the traveller line at a position so that the boom is central when the arm is fully bent. I put a knot in the traveller line and pick it up at that knot. In this way I always know where the boom is without needing to look at it.) During the puff, the sails should be sheeted as closely as is possible and the boat should be pointed as high as is possible *provided that it does not lose speed.* A useful way in which to judge speed is to listen to the characteristic hiss and slosh – this changes to a lower pitch and becomes quieter if speed is lost. Sheet the sails closer to the centreline and point higher only as much as is consistent with maintaining speed.

The set-up which results, during the puff, turns out to be not much different from Fig. 22.6.2. The boom has come closer to, or along, the centreline. The extra force increases the mainsail's twist, so the all-important upper leech remains in its correct position. The lower mainsail is a little too full. The upper jib is a little under-sheeted. (Alert crews adjust the jib sheet a little to each gust and lull.) The performance penalty from each of these errors is small.

Fluctuation puffs last, typically, about 7 seconds. Towards the end of this time, the crew should start moving their bodies inwards, and the traveller should be eased a little to leeward, in anticipation of the fluctuation lull. As this occurs, and is signalled by the boat beginning to roll to windward, immediately draw the traveller well to windward (deliberately over-trimming for a second or so, if necessary) and simultaneously bear away to the original lower pointing angle which was fastest in the 7 knots of the lull. Never bear away further than the angle at which the leeward jib tuft just begins to agitate.

During this period, the crew should smoothly resume the positions which balance the lull wind speed. The traveller should simultaneously and equally smoothly move to leeward to restore the Fig. 22.6.1 set-up.

To summarise:

As the masthead begins to move to leeward, both of the helmsman's hands move to leeward. In the seconds which follow, the crew move their bodies smoothly to windward and retrim the sail by drawing the traveller to windward.

When the wind speed decreases and the masthead begins to move to windward, both hands move to windward. Again, deliberate crew movement, and sail retrim, follow.

The traveller hand should make big, fluid movements. The tiller movements should remain small and delicate.

The key feature of this technique is that it provides a time-delay mechanism which keeps the boat upright and under full power, and at the same time enables the crew to move their bodies so smoothly that momentum is preserved.

In breeze, in all wind strengths less than the design wind, mainsail control should be by traveller, with the sheet cleated.

Sheet control from a fixed traveller position cannot put the upper and lower mainsail trims and leech angles in the right positions at two different wind speeds, In boat-against-boat tests, both with the primitively sheeted NS14 (Fig 20.12) and in the FD class (on which we developed the more sophisticated traveller control which is now on the Tasar), and in the Tasar class, and in the Soling class, this technique has proved several percent faster to windward than the hand-held sheet plus 'body movement only' technique.

The wind changes direction as well as speed. In addition to the gust/lull (change of speed) technique described above, a helmsman will need to follow the constant, usually small, changes of direction. The smooth luffing and bearing away steering responses called for by the gust/lull technique will, in practice, be superimposed on top of the continuous steering responses which are needed to follow the wind direction. When first practising this technique, this dual requirement is easily accommodated if the helmsman concentrates first on becoming fluent in following the changes in wind direction. Adopt survival sailing (i.e. keep the boat upright by use of sheet) for this period of practise. Once fluency has been achieved to the point where steering to follow the wind direction changes as indicated by the jib tufts has become automatic, the helmsman can then concentrate on practising the co-ordinated traveller-and-tiller gust/lull technique. If he adopts this sequence he will be unaware (except when he deliberately thinks about it) that he will already be 'following' the wind direction without conscious thought.

Note that this is a 'breeze' technique only. It is not appropriate for light air, because in those conditions, direct sheet control of twist is essential to allow the upper leeches to twist open in the drifty patches

Technique for high performance boats of high power.

The detail for handling boats of high power changes because the object changes.

When sailing to windward in flat water in any monohull boat which does not windward plane, the object is to achieve hull speed as soon as the wind speed is adequate to do so. The fact that the pointing angle will be low, will be more than compensated by the higher boat speed which is made possible by the stronger Apparent Wind. As the wind speed increases above this 'adequate' level, the object changes. Greatest VMG will now be achieved if the boat speed is held steady, and the boat is pointed progressively higher in the stronger winds. (The reason for this is to avoid the high hull drags of the forced mode.) Fig. 22.8.1(a) shows this concept visually. All the helming and sail handling detail suggested above has been directed to this object.

This concept applies to a high performance boat only in light air. As soon as the turbulence of the breeze establishes, its ratios are such that it moves through the forced mode and establishes itself in the planing mode. As the wind speed then progressively increases, maximum VMG will be achieved at progressively higher boat speeds until some other factor presents a limit. Fig. 22.8.1(b) shows this very different concept.

Summed up – with a low-power boat, your fastest response to a gust is to point higher without acceleration. With a high power boat, your fastest response to a gust is to accelerate to some higher preferred speed, and not to point higher. The notes below explain how champions in different classes apply these principles.

Laser Two (Mark Mendelblatt)

'For sailing to weather in a 6 to 11 knot breeze the set-up remains the same as for light air – mast forward and Cunninghams set for some horizontal wrinkles in the sails, for maximum power.

Set the outhaul for 2 inches maximum camber in the foot of the mainsail.

The traveller is important. Set its position so that when the sheet is tight, the upper batten leech ribbon is stalled completely (limp), but when the sheet is eased three inches it streams intermittently. Watch this ribbon constantly, and power up and depower in this way. Use a tight sheet and point higher in each puff. In the lulls ease sheet until the ribbon streams intermittently and point a little lower to keep going.

The most important thing in this breeze is to go for speed and get your crew on the trapeze (and sit in yourself if necessary) so that you can enjoy the strongest possible Apparent Wind'.

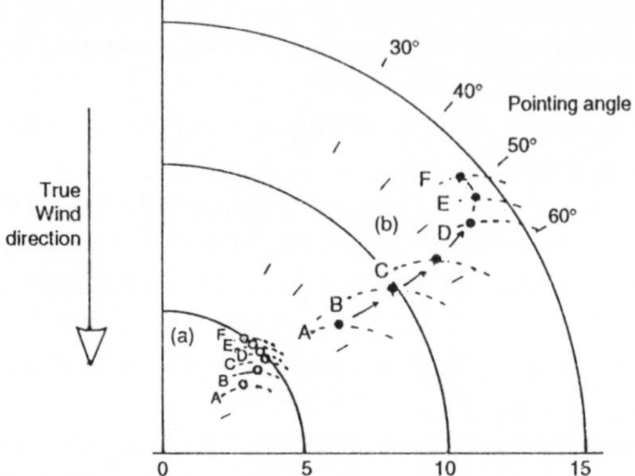

Optimum speeds and pointing angles
for maximum VMG in increasing winds and flat water.

(a) Non windward planning - Limit hull speed

(b) High performance skiffs - Limit dynamic conflict

A For True Wind of 6 knots
B " " " 7 "
C " " " 8 "
D " " " 10 "
E " " " 12 "
F " " " 14 "

Fig 22.8.1 Optimum performance points in increasing winds.

Soling, J24 etc.

'When sailing to windward in flat water and moderate air, we observe the approaching wind and estimate where it will blow most strongly. We sail to and remain in the strongest air to maximise the use of the available wind. We anticipate changes in the wind's strength and we move crew weight in anticipation of the greater or lesser heeling force.'

'We approximate the effect of the roll tack of a dinghy by allowing the boat to heel more than the optimum just prior to the tack. The extra heel turns the boat into the tack without need of excessive tiller movement or force. We sweep the mast to windward as the boat approaches head to wind, and do not let the jib sheet go until the jib ceases to be full of wind, to maximise the circular airflow effect.'

'We set the fastest mainsail shape for the lull wind speed, by use of backstay tension to shape the upper sail, vang (in stronger winds) for the middle and lower part, and outhaul for the foot. As the windspeed increases in each gust, in flat water we luff to point very high and ease traveller so as not to exceed the desired angle of heel, and at the same time we use vang as the primary control to flatten and depower the mainsail on a gust by gust basis. As the water becomes rougher we shift to sheet control because it is no longer possible to point high and maintain speed, and also because in rougher conditions a faster control is needed than is possible with traveller. Easing the sheet frees the upper leech with least delay and gives virtually instantaneous control of heel. Judging when to shift from traveller to sheet control is vitally important, as is the combination of backstay and vang to use for shaping the sail in the stronger winds and different seastate conditions. When the water is flatter and/or the waves are regular we use more backstay. As the water becomes rougher and/or the waves more chaotic we use more vang, which gives a more elastic rig.'

'With these heavier boats a delicate and precise approach to steering is fastest. I use absolute minimum rudder movement. We encourage the boat to steer itself by accurate control of heel. I almost never use force to push the tiller to leeward because I find that this luffs the boat more quickly than is optimum for speed.'

Eighteen Footer

'Let us assume that we are sailing an Eighteen footer to windward with its big rig in a 7 to 10 knot wind. This is in fact a particularly challenging wind speed range to race in for two separate reasons neither of which is at first obvious.

The first is that the very high speed of closing between the boat and the gusts and fluctuations causes them to repeat so quickly that the boat becomes excessively demanding physically. In a True Wind of 7 to 9 knots the boat can easily achieve 10 to 12 knots through the water. This doubles the speed of closing and causes gusts to repeat on average every ten to fifteen seconds and fluctuations several times faster. At the same time the boat will be sailing 'two and a half strings' with the skipper and sheet hand on trapeze, while the forward hand will move as necessary for balance. No matter how fit the forward hand, movement onto and off trapeze every few seconds is too much to contemplate throughout a race.

Further, the fastest sail trim will be with the mainsail 'vang sheeted' which calls for large excursions of the boom with every wind change, and this too is too much for even the fittest sheet hand to accomplish over a prolonged period. The practical response is to ease the vang and allow the mainsail to twist, so that a relatively small movement of the mainsheet will cause a big change of trim of the upper leech – this enables the sheet hand to control balance with a smaller excursion of mainsheet movement and this is physically acceptable over prolonged periods. When the occasional unexpected very light lull occurs, the upper leech is deliberately oversheeted and pumped for long enough to enable the forward hand to move to the leeward wing to restore balance. In stronger winds all three crew are on trapeze and the control movements become smaller so these techniques are no longer necessary.

The second difficulty is that the very high ratio of boat speed to wind speed together with the boat's free acceleration makes it difficult in some lights to judge your pointing angle with respect to the True Wind. If you bear away a little the boat obligingly goes faster. Because of the increase of speed, the angle of the Apparent Wind does not change. If you bear away a little further yet you may think that you are sailing to windward fast but in fact you will be beam reaching at about double wind speed and going to windward not at all. The sails will still be sheeted, and look, exactly as they do when sailing to windward, but beam reaching back and forth when you are meant to be sailing to windward wins no races.'

'So it turns out that sailing to windward in these lighter breezes becomes an 'intellect and judgment' exercise rather than a 'feel' response. The mental picture is that of Fig 22.8.1(b) – as the wind speed increases the boat should be driven from A to B to C to D, and only then should it be 'wound up' in the gusts by pointing higher.

As soon as the wind reaches about ten knots the characteristic upwind/downwind streaks on the surface (wind lanes) appear, and the 'vagueness' of direction which characterises the lighter breezes vanishes.

The high-power boats are all handled with sheet control and not traveller control. Traveller control is faster when you are displacement sailing at hull speed and steering within a very narrow 'groove' (range of pointing angle). A combination of sheet control plus vang is faster when you are windward planing (i.e. close reaching) and steering within a wider range of pointing angles.

Vang and Cunningham tensions are critical. With these active-batten rigs and sails the effect of Cunningham is to bend the mast and so flatten and depower the sail. It has no effect on the position of the maximum depth of the camber – the battens are far too stiff to be influenced. The vang is set sufficiently firmly and adjusted continuously, to limit twist so that the upper leech can open only as far as is desired in the conditions of the moment when the sheet is eased.

As each gust arrives, the heading is held steady and the sheet eased slightly for two or three seconds – a few inches only, just enough to open the upper leech. The boat which will have been sailing at 11 to 12 knots will accelerate to about 14 knots, which is the preferred windward-going speed when there is enough wind. Only when the forward hand has moved onto trapeze and the boat has accelerated to its new preferred speed is it luffed – 'wound up' – to point as high as possible while holding that higher speed. In strong winds and flat water the boats are capable of much higher windward-going boat speeds, but at higher speeds the 'steer for balance' effect – (chapter 24) – begins to roll the boat the wrong way when it is 'luffed in a puff'. In practice the boats sail to windward fastest by achieving about 14 knots as soon as there is enough wind, and thereafter they simply point higher as the wind becomes stronger.)

The lull, like the gust, is anticipated as much as possible. The problem is the same in principle as that in light air – that as the boat, with speed, enters the lull the Apparent Wind goes so far forward that the forward hand has to go in a long way to preserve balance. The boat cannot bear away too quickly or it will roll to windward under 'steer for balance' forces. So the forward hand anticipates the lull by dropping from trapeze to the outer wing beam *before* the boat enters the lull, and then goes in as far as is necessary for balance to enable the boat to bear away slowly as it slows. As the Apparent Wind of the lull re-establishes he moves some of the way to windward again as needed for balance.'

22.9 In stronger breezes – the new factors

The strong-wind technique is appropriate for all wind speeds stronger than the design wind. In the strong wind regime the potentially available sail power is by definition greater than the crew can hold upright. The key elements of this regime are:

1. Sail 'power' ceases to be relevant. There will always be more power available than a crew can use.

2. Body movement ceases to be relevant. The crew should maintain their bodies fully 'hiked' or trapezed continuously.

3. Since balance can no longer be achieved by body movement, it must be achieved otherwise. Fortunately, the same technique of co-ordinated steering and sail trimming, which is used to provide dynamic balance during the slowed body-movement periods in moderate breezes, turns out to be the fastest and simplest technique for maintaining balance for all of the time in strong breezes.

Stated in principles:

In light airs, a dinghy or sailboard is in a state of static balance all the time.

In moderate breezes, it is in static balance most of the time, but in dynamic balance whilst bodies are moving.

In strong breezes it must necessarily be controlled by dynamic balance for all of the time.

4. In strongbreezes, the aerodynamic drag of the rig becomes the dominant consideration in determining windward-going performance. Other things being equal, as between two identical boats which sail together at the optimum speed through the water, the boat with the lesser aerodynamic drag will be able to point higher and so will achieve the higher VMG.

22.10 The trims for 'most power' and 'least drag'

Fortunately, the properties of a typical fractional rig enables a crew to adjust it for either 'most power' or 'least drag'. This is because a jib without overlap can be operated in either of two modes, and also because the sailplan arrangement 'small jib and large mainsail' happens to be particularly efficient when it is set either way.

Without delving too deeply into the aerodynamics, greatest 'power' is achieved when the leech of the jib is set in the lowest pressure/highest speed area of the flow pattern around the mainsail and both jib and mainsail are trimmed for maximum coefficient of lift. The presence of the jib will itself affect the total flow pattern, but there must always remain a lowest-pressure area just to leeward of the mast, and this is where the jib leech should be positioned. When it is handled in this way, the jib becomes one of those strange aerofoils – like turbine blades – which have lower airspeeds and higher pressures at their leading edges and higher airspeeds and lower pressures at their trailing edges. The result is that the wind flows around their leeward sides much faster than is usual.

This is because in the normal situation the air slows as it approaches the leech because the air pressure at the leech is greater than the pressure further upstream across the lee side (Figs 17.2, 17.3, 17.7, 17.8, 17.15 etc). But when the jib leech is itself positioned in the area of lowest pressure caused by the mainsail, the air will keep accelerating towards that contrived lower pressure at the leech. The resultant higher average flow speed develops a very much higher aerodynamic force (because of the 'speed squared' dynamic law). Every crew who have had a jib sheet accidentally uncleat when they were sailing hard for 'power' in a moderate wind will have experienced how great a proportion of the total force was lost, despite the jib's relatively small size. The aerodynamic drag of this mode of operation is quite high, but in the moderate wind regime, in which the object is to achieve greatest drive force, the aerodynamic drag considerations are secondary, because the aerodynamic drag is so small a proportion of the total drag of the whole boat. In practice it is always faster to trim for maximum power and accept the drag. This is the normal trim to use between the light air regime and the design wind – hence the name – the 'normal' regime.

As soon as the wind speed exceeds the design wind, the whole picture changes, and suddenly.

The low-drag mode has, as its base, the fact that in very strong winds, in which a sail must necessarily be set at a very small angle to the oncoming wind, the lowest drag shape is one with no jib and no twist at all. Good examples are gliders' wings, centreboards, and the rigid wing-sails of some 'C' Class catamarans. As the wind speed reduces to the merely strong, and the angle of the sail to the wind increases from the glider's or centreboard's one or two degrees towards the sailor's 5 to 10 degrees in strong winds, it begins to be more efficient to use a small (not full-span, i.e. not masthead) supplementary aerofoil, which is trimmed so lightly that it provides only about one tenth of the total force. This fact is the basis of the surprisingly good strong-wind, windward-going performance of boats with well-designed fractional rigs.

As soon as the lull wind speed exceeds the design wind, it will pay to:

1. Ease the jib sheet substantially to shift the jib from its 'power' setting of providing nearly half the total power, into its 'low drag' setting, where it should provide only about one tenth of the total force.

2. Allow the boom to move to leeward substantially, by traveller, because the eased jib will deflect the wind which approaches the lower mainsail much less than it did when it was sheeted more firmly.

3. Tighten the mainsheet substantially, to reduce the twist in the mainsail, and so hold the upper mainsail leech at a useful and efficient angle to the wind, despite the eased boom, and also to flatten the upper mainsail by bending the masthead back.

4. Flatten both jib and mainsail. Flatten the jib by tightening the forestay. The mainsail should be flattened by outhaul and vang but only as much as is needed to ensure that the *windward* tufts remain streaming in the lulls. The leeward tufts cease to be relevant – in strong breezes they cannot do other than stream continuously.

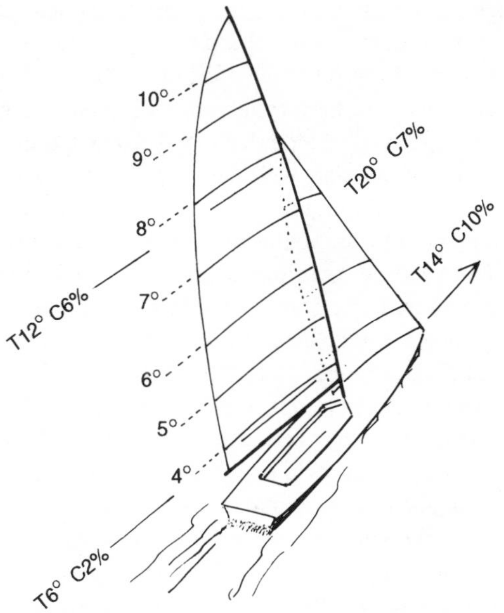

Fig 22.10.1 Sail trim for 12 - 16 knots, flat water

Fig. 22.10.1 shows the rig shape which results. The boom is no longer along the centreline, and the leeches of the sails are no longer parallel to the centreline. The mainsail has been much flattened and at the same time its twist has been reduced. The trim angle of the middle and upper jib has been allowed to open as the sheet has been eased.

22.11 Sail trim in 12 – 16 knots

As the wind speed increases through the design wind, the shift from the moderate wind to the strong wind rig shape, i.e. from the Fig. 22.6.2 'maximum power' shape to the Fig. 22.10.1 'minimum drag', shape should be made quickly. The practicalities of the change when the wind is increasing will be:

1. So long as you find it necessary to 'sit up' a little in the lulls, stay with the moderate wind, Fig. 22.6.2 shape. It is always faster to drive at maximum power in the lulls, and feather as needed in the gusts. Never deprive yourself of power in the lulls.

2. When, in marginal conditions, you find yourself in unexpectedly strong short-term winds, such as prolonged gusts of unexpected strength,

(a) Let the jib sheet go a little. For the reasons given earlier, this will reduce the 'power' of the whole rig by a surprising amount, and it will also enable you to point a little higher without loss of speed.

(b) Further depower by flattening the upper mainsail as necessary with vang.

These two adjustments can be applied and released quickly, and should be routinely used on a gust by gust basis when racing.

3. As soon as it is judged, from the increasing lull wind speeds, that the increasing wind strength justifies shifting to the low drag rig shape:

Ease the jib sheet and tighten the mainsheet.

Let the boom fall to leeward as necessary.

Flatten the lower mainsail (outhaul).

Flatten the upper mainsail (vang).

Apply firm downhaul (Cunningham) to further flatten the upper leech area.

Raise the centreboard 6 – 8 inches.

Increase shroud tension to tighten the forestay and flatten the jib if you have shroud adjustment – otherwise run with tighter shrouds when you expect stronger winds.

To use this set-up well, it is necessary to know what you want, and it will probably be necessary to fiddle a little until you get it. I recall a time in the late 1960's when photographs of FD's sailing to windward all over the world showed the mainsail fabric fluttering near the mast. Then one or two crews worked on their rig adjustments until they could get a taut mainsail when sailing to windward – and these boats 'took off' with such a speed advantage that they set a new trend which lasts to this day.

The practicalities start with the angle of the boom. It should be eased far enough to leeward so that the boat can be sailed upright and at the desired speed when the crew are fully 'hiked'. The jib sheet should then be eased and the mainsail flattened, each just sufficiently so that in the lulls the mainsail fabric remains taut and neither flutters nor shows backwind from the jib, while in the stronger gusts it may both flutter a little and also show some 'blowback' from the jib. The jib luff may flutter in the lulls, and will certainly flutter in the gusts. As the wind becomes stronger the mainsail should be progressively flattened further, and the jib sheeting angle set a little wider. Trimmed thus, with a flat, almost untwisted mainsail, sheeted well out, and a very lightly sheeted jib, the boat can be pointed very high without loss of speed. Boats with efficient rigs can tack through 70 to 75 degrees in steady 12-14 knot winds and flat water. Fig. 20.13(b) shows a Tasar rig perfectly set up in the low drag configuration. The boat is planing to windward in a wind of about 20 to 25 knots.

In decreasing wind, the immediate actions when it is realized that more power is needed are:

1. Tighten the jib sheet, and ease the vang.
2. Draw in the traveller to 'boom along centreline'.
3. Ease the mainsheet, to restore fullness and power to the upper mainsail, and to restore accurate 'leech parallel to centreline' trim to the upper mainsail leech.

Later, as opportunity offers:

4. Ease the outhaul and the Cunningham.
5. Lower the centreboard.
6. Ease shroud tension to make the jib a little fuller.

The sail trims described above are the fastest when the water is flat and the wind is steady. As the wind roughness and/or the water roughness increases, the considerations discussed in and following Section 22.15 will become increasingly important.

22.12 Sail trim in 17 – 25 knots

As the wind speed increases towards 20 knots, the rapidly rising force of the wind's resistance across the rig, the hull, and the crew will begin to slow, substantially, the boat's progress to windward even in flat water. To maintain speed against this increasing air resistance, it will be necessary to point a little lower. The jib sheet travellers should be set 2 or 3 degrees further outboard to sheet the jib more widely, and the mainsail should be set flatter and trimmed more widely – in each case just enough to maintain the desired speed through the water.

If the wind were truly steady and the water always flat, it would all be very simple. Alas, the wind and the water are never simple.

As the wind speed increases, the gusts in even the steadiest wind become harsher. This leads to large and rapidly changing heeling forces, which are regarded as tremendous fun by experienced crews, but which call for careful handling by novice crews. And the conditions in which the water remains flat in winds of 20 knots are rare. It follows that, between the extremes of, 'flat water speed' and 'survival' techniques there are a whole range of sail trims and handling techniques. Fortunately, it turns out that while the 'survival' technique is always the same, the trim for maximum speed changes in a simple way as the wind becomes stronger, the air becomes rougher, and the waves become bigger, and we consider crews who are progressively less experienced.

It therefore seems more helpful, in discussing the sail trims for strong wind sailing, to consider what to do as the wind becomes rougher, and the waves become bigger. For this reason, the changing sail trims will be described in the 'handling' section which follows.

22.13 Handling in stronger breezes

When the wind speed approaches 20 knots even the smoothest gusts will begin to hit hard, and while waters near a weather shore can remain flat, it will be unusual to sail far before they become rough. In these stronger winds the most practical approach will be to set the boat up initially with the rig in its most elastic mode. This will make the boat easiest and most pleasant to handle. There will be a small speed penalty. The crew should then progressively increase the rig's rigidity, until the boat's increasingly 'hard mouthed' behaviour becomes as much as they care to handle in the conditions of the moment. This will be the rig set-up which will sail fastest for them, with their level of experience, and in those wind and sea-state conditions.

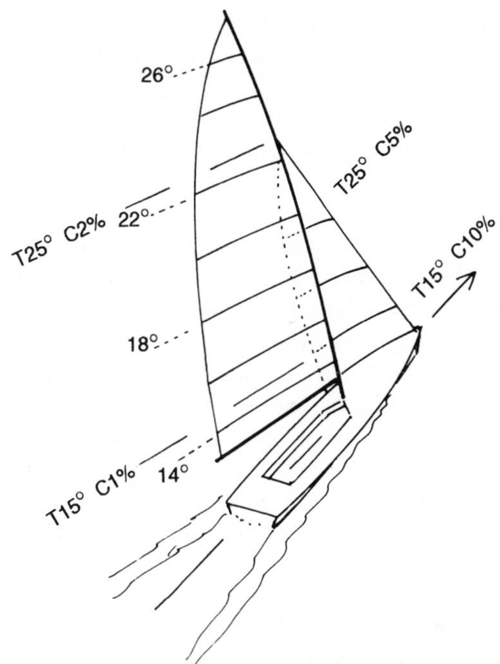

Fig 22.13.1 Sail trim 17 - 25 knots, flat water.

Start by tightening the vang towards '3-dots' to flatten the upper mainsail, cleat the mainsheet 'slack', i.e. with the black mark (you should have datum marks on your sheets) in or through the boom block, and control the mainsail by traveller. The jib sheet should be eased until there is just no backwind in the mainsail in the gusts, and the jib sheet should be cleated in that position in the lulls. When a fully adjustable boat with a springy rig is set up like this, with its mainsail flattened by vang and trimmed with a slack sheet, the leech tension will be at a minimum, and the whole sail will set in a soft and springy manner. It will twist somewhat under the aerodynamic load. More importantly, the springy leech will yield to leeward as each gust strikes, and in this way the rig will absorb automatically the initial shock of each gust onslaught. The leech doesn't stay open – the crew still have to play the traveller in response to the gusts, lulls and fluctuations – but the elastic springy sail smooths out the shocks, gives time to ease the trim, and makes the boat relatively docile and pleasant to handle.

This 'tight vang, slack sheet' set-up is the best setting for crews to use while they become practised in the strong-wind technique described later in this section, and until they are confident of their boat handling and control in vigorous conditions. It is much faster than the 'survival' technique can ever be.

However, in conditions in which the wind is relatively steady, and the water relatively flat, a boat will point higher at the same speed if it is set up more rigidly with a tighter sheet and slacker vang. As the sheet is progressively tightened, the vang can be progressively slackened and in this way the shape of the sail will remain unaltered.

So it turns out that, for any desired sail shape and fullness – and small variations remain very important, even when the whole sail is relatively flat – it is possible to set the sail at either the 'tight vang, slack sheet, elastic' extreme, or the 'tight sheet, slack vang, rigid' extreme, or at any intermediate setting. When the sail is set 'tight sheet, slack vang' the leech will be at its tightest, and the sail will set with the least twist. The relatively untwisted sail, coupled with the very lightly sheeted jib, will result in the smallest loss of pointing angle from the spilling of wind over the top of the rig (lowest induced drag) and for this reason the boat can point higher at the same speed through the water. But the tight leech also results in the sail being relatively 'hard' and inelastic. It does not yield to leeward as each gust strikes. Instead, the rig transmits the shock immediately and the boat heels unless the crew's control is very quick and skilful.

The relatively steady-strong-wind, flat-water situation, summarised, is:

For crews who are skilled and practised, the fastest windward-going performance will be achieved with a very tight mainsheet and the boom trimmed well to leeward of the centreline. This will give a 'hard' sail and little twist, but the crew must respond very fast and accurately to keep the boat upright and moving smoothly through the increasingly harsh wind-speed changes. This is exactly the same as a sailboard with a stiff mast and 'hard' sail – this combination is only for the expert when the wind blows strongly.

Crews who have not yet developed this skill will sail fastest with a more elastic sail. Whenever they encounter these conditions, they should start from the more elastic 'tight-vang, slack-sheet' setting, and progressively tighten the sheet and slacken the vang, and point progressively higher, until the boat begins to 'stagger' – to roll and heel excessively at gust onslaught and cessation, and in consequence to lose speed. For their level of skill, and those conditions, that is their limit. They should revert a little towards a more elastic setting to restore smoothness, and that will be their fastest setting.

Fig. 22.13.1 shows the key factors of the fastest rig shape.

Basic handling technique for high performance boats of low power.

Let us assume a breeze well into the strong-breeze regime, say 16 knots mean, with lulls at 13 knots, gusts to 18-19 knots, and fluctuations of about 2 knots and that the water is relatively flat.

Set up the rig to be at minimum drag, i.e. to have the 'cleanest' airflow, in the lulls, in this way:

Progressively flatten the lower mainsail until the lower windward tuft just streams in the lulls.

Progressively tighten the vang until, with a slack sheet, the upper windward tuft just streams in the lulls. With 'soft' sails, downhaul tension is customarily the primary control of the upper leech – little tension gives a firm upper leech and vice versa, so in strong winds a very firm downhaul tension will be needed. Fully battened sails behave differently, in that application of firm downhaul will bend the mast and flatten the entire sail, but with a much less specific effect on the upper leech. These effects will in any case change according to the stiffness of the mast and the age and elasticity of the sailcloth, so no hard and fast advice is possible.

Flatten the jib by tightening the shrouds (or setting the boat up with them very tight). Set the jib sheeting angle to about 11 to 12 degrees (out about 2 degrees from the normal 9 degree extreme inboard setting). Set the jib sheet into the lowest hole in the clewboard. Start with the jib sheet very slack. Sheet the jib progressively more tightly until backwind just appears in the mainsail, then ease it until the backwind just disappears.

On strong-wind days, the jib luff should be tightened before leaving shore, particularly with older sails.

Sail to windward. Start by sailing free and fast. Adopt the body-hiking stance which you propose to hold for the balance of the windward leg. (The further out you hike, the higher you will be able to point at the same speed.) Progressively point higher, and trim in the sails in the manner outlined above, until speed reduces to about hull speed. This is your 'basic' trim, speed, and pointing angle. Now systematically improve your pointing angle, by progressively tightening the sheet, and slackening the vang (to control the upper mainsail fullness so that the upper windward tuft continues to just stream in the lulls) until either:

(a) The vang becomes slack, or

(b) The boat begins to 'stagger' in the gust onslaughts, despite the best technique you can apply.

If (a), sail with that rig set-up. This is the fastest shape for that crew in those conditions. If (b), revert a little towards a more elastic sail for smoother sailing. This will be the fastest set-up for that crew in those conditions.

Both crew should be fully 'hiked'. Depending on confidence, strength, fitness, and motivation, this may vary from the timid to the 'far out, bodies horizontal' stance of the champion crew. The important thing is that each crew should decide how aggressively they wish to swing throughout the remainder of the windward leg, adopt that stance, and *hold it steadily*. It is of the greatest importance, once confident handling to maintain balance has been mastered, that neither crew sit up to even the slightest degree as each lull and fluctuation lull is encountered, because this action reduces speed so much. When an unexpected momentary lull occasionally rolls the boat to windward a little, both crew members should simply raise their forward shoulders a little, to 'slide' their backs across the water for the moment it takes to trim in the traveller and bear away a little and so restore 'power' and uprightnness.

The helmsman's hand actions should be exactly as described earlier for the moderate wind technique – as each gust or fluctuation puff is encountered, and the boat begins to heel, immediately free the traveller several inches (enough to stop the roll) and simultaneously begin to luff slowly towards an aiming point 5 to 10 degrees higher. As the turn to windward begins to reduce the sail's force, draw the traveller in sufficiently to maintain balance in the new wind. Balance the traveller position and the pointing angle so that the speed through the water remains constant.

In moderate winds, the combination of more sail power and the crew swinging harder in the gusts usually resulted in the boat being able to point so much higher that the traveller position, in the gusts, finished up well to windward of the 'eased for speed' lull position.

In strong winds, this can never happen. The crew remain fully hiked. The sail's heeling force cannot be other than constant – the maximum that the crew can accept. In the gust, the traveller will always settle to leeward of its lull position, so as to ease the gust's added sail force.

Tiller and traveller movements should be proportioned so that the boat speed remains constant. Again, use your ears to sense any change of speed – if you use too much tiller and too little traveller, the boat will luff too high and slow down in the puffs. The gain by pointing higher will not begin to compensate for the loss of speed. If you use too much traveller and not enough tiller, your speed must theoretically increase, but in practice this increase is only fractional and it does not begin to make up for the weather gauge forfeited by not pointing higher at constant speed. (When windward planing is possible the situation is different.)

Always point as high as you can provided that you maintain your desired speed. For more speed, point a shade lower and ease traveller slightly, and vice versa. It will be necessary to adjust pointing to maintain speed almost continuously, as the boat speed will be periodically slowed by 'sets' of bigger waves, motor-boat wakes, etc. Once these are behind you, point higher again until the next hindrance is encountered.

Continuously balance the sails' force, which you control with your traveller hand, against the crew's weight. The strong-wind regime becomes the dynamic balance of the cyclist, the skier, the sailboard rider. It transcends the static equilibrium of the trolley, toboggan, or catamaran.

The absolute rule is that the sails should be trimmed so that the mainsail, set as flat as is necessary, is taut and inflated, i.e. with no backwind, while the jib is sheeted as lightly as is necessary to ensure no backwind in the mainsail. The windward jib tufts will certainly agitate. Several inches of the jib luff may also flutter, particularly in gusts in strong winds. This is normal.

As a rule of thumb, the jib sheet position is about right if just a shimmer of backwind appears in the mainsail during the strongest gusts. If the jib leech flogs audibly, it has been eased too far. Sheet it until it becomes quiet, and hike harder, or furl it.

Notes re flexible wingmasts

Particularly with lighter crews, there may be some combinations of windspeed, sheet tension, and vang tension, which cause a wingmast to 'flip' out of rotation and into the anti-rotated position during the stronger gusts. If this occurs, lock the mast into the 'full-rotation' setting (rotation stop beyond cage), or shift to a tighter-vang set-up. But when severe vang tension is applied, it can become difficult to rotate the mast after a tack has been completed. When this situation occurs, wait until the next lull, ease the vang momentarily, re-set the rotation, and re-apply vang. The easy, simple, and best technique for handling rotation is to reverse the mast rotation at the *beginning* of the tack. The hand which releases the jib sheet should hold the sheet a few inches from the cams immediately prior to release, and that hand should continue upwards and reverse the rotation as a part of the same movement. At this point midway through the tacking process, it is both mechanically easier to move the rotation lever to its new position, and it is physically easier to pull it towards you as you go under the vang, rather than try to push it away from you, later, and against the much greater force which develops as soon as the sail fills on the new tack.

Again, the differences in approach between champions in different classes are revealing;

Laser Two (Mark Mendelblatt)

'When the breeze increases to 12 to 18 knots, I alter the set-up. Drop the mast well back. This opens the slot and promotes windward planing. Flatten the mainsail by pulling the outhaul on hard, and the Cunningham on hard. From the time that the crew is all the way out, apply firm vang for vang- sheeting. When the sheet is eased, the boom should swing out and not move up. Set the traveller well down.'

'Trim the jib pretty hard with the slides right in – always right in.'

'In waves, use the same set-up, except that both crew members move aft as far as is necessary to lift the bow above the wave crests.'

'The further the crew can get his weight out on trapeze, the higher the boat will point. So the crew should 'stand tall', on his toes in the gusts if necessary, and should also carry his arms above his head particularly when extra drive is needed. Similarly the skipper should body-hike far out continuously to add to the righting force of the crew on trapeze.'

When the wind increases to 20 to 25 knots

'Set the mast rake all the way back. The outhaul should be very tight – this is critical. Vang should be tight – but remember to ease it before reaching the windward mark, or else a boom dragging momentarily in the water can capsize you. Set Cunningham down hard and set traveller all the way out.'

'The forward hand should move his/her weight back until the forward foot is about 12 inches behind the shrouds.'

'For maximum speed in these conditions, it is critical that the boat be sailed upright, or be heeled slightly to windward.'

Eighteen Footer

'We will assume that we are sailing an Eighteen footer with either the second rig up in 15 to 20 knots of wind, or the third rig in 18 to 30 knots. For reasons noted later, there is no change of technique, apart from a small variation in pointing angle, between relatively flat water conditions and sailing in waves. The crew will be *three strings* – all on and remaining on trapeze. At the upper end of the wind speed range for each rig, the technique is biased towards keeping the stick in the boat. Any fool can smash a Ferrari into a brick wall if he drives it stupidly. Any fool can tear the rig out of a high performance boat in strong winds if he similarly mishandles it. Substantial vang and substantial Cunningham are used to 'blade the whole mainsail off' (virtually dead flat).

The forward hand calls the wind continuously upwind. In moderate winds the sails are eased and the heading is held steady for acceleration to a higher preferred speed at the beginning of each gust. The boat is then luffed to a higher pointing angle. But as the wind becomes stronger a point is reached beyond which it is not possible to ease the mainsheet fast enough to compensate for the gust onslaught, so the jib sheet is eased with each gust as well. Continuous handling of the sheets in this manner throughout a race calls for strength and fitness. As the wind becomes one or two knots stronger it is no longer reasonable to rely on the trimming of both sails to keep the boat upright, and very positive steering becomes the primary technique for balance. In practice it is found that a boat speed of about 14 knots is the maximum reasonable speed at which this works properly. If the boat is pushed faster – which is very easy, particularly in steadier winds and flat water – then the dynamics conflict. A gust hits, the boat begins to heel, it is luffed to reduce the angle of the sails to the wind and so reduce the heel, but at progressively higher speeds the boat will roll progressively more strongly to leeward because of the centrifugal force of the turn on the rig mass, rather that to windward as is desired. The solution, at the present state of development, is to limit the boat speed to about 14 knots. Ths calls for careful restraint – never the blood and guts approach.'

22.14 In rough air

Figs 7.1(a) and 7.1(b) (Part One) show how heating makes the wind rougher over open water. In addition to this thermal roughness, the wind in the area downstream of any physical barrier such as hills, headlands, and particularly high-rise buildings will be reduced in speed but increased in its roughness for a distance up to about thirty times the height of the barrier.

When the wind is rough, and the gust factor reaches or exceeds 100%, for example in a wind with harsh 15 knot gusts and 6 knot lulls, the distinctions between moderate breezes, the design wind, and strong breezes becomes blurred.

This does not matter, because the basic technique does not change. The crew which will sail fastest and with most confident control will be the crew which keeps their boat moving at its best in the lulls, will shed the excess power as necessary in the gusts, and will handle their boat so that it does not heel to the point where it slows – 'staggers' – during the onslaught and abrupt cessation of each gust.

The strong-wind situation is the easiest to describe. If we look at Fig. 7.1(a) (Part One), a skilled crew would expect to handle this 'steady' wind with a 'tight sheet, slack vang, point high' technique. But as the gust factor progressively increases towards and beyond the roughness shown in Fig. 7.1(b) (Part One), at some point even the most practised crew will be unable to respond fast enough to stop their boat from staggering. As soon as this situation is sensed, a simple shift towards a springier, more elastic leech, which will allow the sail to twist open but only during the gust onslaughts, will eliminate the staggering as if by magic. (Some helmsmen describe this as 'setting up for a wider groove'.) Tighten the vang, ease the sheet, and draw the traveller to windward, but only enough to provide sufficient elasticity to eliminate staggering *in those conditions*. The benefit will be a higher average speed. The penalty will be a small loss of pointing angle. In boats which cannot be set up elastically, a deliberate trim with more twist will give 'a wider groove' and better speed, but because the leech will not then close automatically between the puffs, the loss in pointing angle will be much greater."

Summed up, the response to rough wind is elasticity. The rig design and controls should enable you to select exactly as much as you require to compensate for the wind's changing roughness, and so maintain steady speed.

Simple elasticity ceases to be adequate for control at both the very strong wind and the lighter-wind extremes. When control is in doubt, speed ceases to be a priority, even when racing. Neither a capsized dinghy nor catamaran, nor a broaching yacht which is charging at high speed but in the wrong direction, win any races. As soon as control is in doubt, it is faster to revert to survival sailing and maintain control.

Examples will be as numerous as localities, but the sort of situation in which this technique is useful is very well exemplified in Sydney's occasional strong summer westerlies. These winds arrive at the Harbour after blowing over fifty miles of dry-land which is strongly heated by the afternoon sun and cloudless skies, and are further roughened by the steep 100m high scarp-like shorelines of some parts of the harbour.

In these conditions, in strong winds, occasional gusts occur which turn the water glittering black. Because of vertical and swirl motions, wind direction within the gust is changeable and uncertain. My own technique, and my advice, is that when unsteadiness such as this appears just upwind, cleat the traveller, uncleat and substantially ease the mainsheet (and the jib sheet also) sit up a little, and bear away a little towards a close reach. This preparation puts the boat in the best state to survive the onslaught of the approaching gust, regardless of whether its direction lifts, heads or stays steady. Extremes of sheet easing may be necessary at gust onslaught. Once the gust onslaught has passed, and the boat is within the relatively steadier conditions within the gust, it is a matter of choice whether to return to the 'sailing for speed', technique with its accompanying better performance while still within the gust, or to await its passing. Typically, only about every fifth or tenth gust would merit such extreme care.

Tacking is another matter. If you need to tack when any really strong gust is imminent – or you are in it – uncleat the sheet and revert to survival sailing both through the tack and during the few seconds of acceleration immediately afterwards, until the boat is up to speed on its new tack. During the tack – while the boat is moving slowly – it is vulnerable to freak gust. The defense is sheet control and the ability to shed power instantly. As soon as the boat has regained speed, the tiller and steering become the quickest-acting way of shedding power, and the boat sails more safely.

In lighter winds, the problem is different. When conditions are such that gusts strong enough to capsize an unwary crew – say 12-15 knots – can occur occasionally in a wind which is usually between 5 and 10 knots, they are possible only because of massive vertical motions within the air. In this situation the direction within the gust may be 30 degrees or more backed or veered from the mean wind direction. The first problem here is that the change in wind direction may exceed the excursion of the traveller. Accordingly, prudence dictates reverting to mainsheet control as in survival sailing, so that the upper mainsail in particular can accommodate very quickly to whatever the new wind direction may turn out to be. (I know that you can usually read the wind direction from the appearance of the water surface, but sometimes, in particular lights, you just can't. Further, there will always be that gust in a hundred which reaches the surface exactly where you are, and in this case you have no warning at all. This situation is most probable when the air is strongly heated.)

The second problem is that a boat can stagger just as badly when the wind suddenly stops as when it starts. The classic case is the two-on-trapeze youth's skiff in which two youngsters, frustrated by a fickle light breeze with random gusts, seize the opportunity of a gust to start trapezing – only to have the gust cut off sharply five or ten seconds later. This is the worst possible technique, because the boat then 'flops' to windward, one or more bodies become at least half immersed and cause such drag that they stop the boat completely. By the time they have clambered aboard and regained their positions and balance, have the sails set and drawing, and have again accelerated up to their desired speed through the lull, at least fifteen or twenty seconds will have passed. During this period any crew who entered the lull on speed and maintained, say, 4 knots, will have sailed nearly fifty yards. Years ago Colin Thorne was a champion at a club which sailed in an upriver part of Sydney Harbour, which was surrounded by built up city and suburbs. These areas became very hot in the afternoon sun, and in these conditions the area was notable for short, harsh, thermally excited gusts. Colin coined the phrase, 'throw the gust away'. He developed a technique which did almost exactly that. He prepared for the lull early during the gust and so ensured that he entered the following lull with full speed and smooth efficiency. He won far more than his share of the races.

22.15 Survival

Whenever the combination of water roughness and wind roughness increases to the point where a crew do not feel confident of control with 'sail for speed' technique, they should shift toward survival sailing. The basic set-up for survival sailing to windward, and also for reaching, is:

Lower Mainsail	–	Flat
Mainsail Control	–	By Mainsheet, hand held, i.e. never cleated.
Traveller	–	Cleated centrally.
Vang	–	Slack.
Centreboard	–	Half up.
Crew	–	Sit well aft, for maximum stability.
Jib	–	Furled, or if not furled, sheeted lightly by hand, *never cleated.*
Rotation (Wingmast Rigs)	–	Ignore it.

Trimmed like this, the upper mainsail will stream in the wind. Only the lower mainsail will hold wind (plus a little of the jib, if set). Total sail force will be so reduced that the moderate-wind control technique described in Section 22.7 and 22.8 above can be used, i.e. the crew can play the sheets and also move their bodies to each gust and fluctuation. Full body 'hiking' will seldom or never be required. Sailing like this minimises the forces when sailing to windward, or reaching, and offers the crew the maximum reserve of stability at all times. By easing both jib and mainsheets as far as necessary, a crew can sail as slowly and as carefully as they wish.

Survival sailing as described above is useful whenever especial care and safety are needed for a brief and limited period which is unexpected, as in prolonged gusts which are stronger than anticipated or in unpredictable squalls such as the fall-out from high-based raining clouds. It is also useful for brief but critical periods. For example even the most experienced crews who are racing in extreme conditions often find it prudent to adopt survival technique for the few seconds of each tack and the subsequent acceleration, because in extreme conditions a boat without speed and little steering control is more vulnerable and needs much more careful handling than a boat which is up to speed.

In the case of progressively deteriorating conditions, survival sailing can restore confident control, but only for awhile. For crews who are 'caught out' in such conditions there must come a time when shortening sail will be essential for safety. It should always be remembered that the action of shortening sail in an unballasted dinghy will itself pre-occupy the crew and reduce their ability to balance the boat. Prudence therefore demands that sail be shortened early, well before it is essential for control, otherwise the boat may capsize during the process.

When it is necessary to sail downwind in conditions so severe that control under full sail is in doubt, it is essential to shorten sail before turning downwind, because sails cannot be eased in strong gusts when sailing downwind, and sail cannot be shortened in an unballasted dinghy which is running.

In a two-sail boat it will be safer if the mainsail is lowered and only the much smaller jib left set. The control factors of the 'balance position' in sail trim, the 'steer for balance' helming technique, and the way boats which are round near the stern 'Dutch roll' at and above some critical speed – and boats with straighter lines do not – are all discussed in the reaching and running chapters. It is more difficult to retain secure control when sailing downwind in survival conditions than when sailing upwind, and downwind sailing should be treated with the greatest respect.

A practical point is that most two-sail dinghies will sail very well under jib alone. They will sail upwind and crosswind as well as downwind, and they will tack and gybe without fuss. Whenever it is necessary to shorten sail, it is usually simpler and safer to drop the mainsail and go straight to the jib alone, than to think of lowering or furling the jib and sailing on the mainsail alone for awhile and then to have to make the second shift of lowering the mainsail and re-setting the jib later, and in worse conditions.

Because survival sailing necessarily results in lower speed and poor pointing, it wins no races of itself. But it is useful in enabling a crew to progress steadily and survive in squalls which capsize other dinghy and catamaran competitors, or in which yachts broach and go the wrong way and break their rigs. The simple capacity to survive sometimes wins races.

Survival technique in high performance boats is based more on dynamics. As the wind strength increases to the point where control by steering becomes uncertain (end of Section 22.13), the crew shift to survival mode. The vang is released, the centreboard raised until only a little is exposed to the water, the crew all move aft for maximum stability, the jib sheet is never cleated. A lower speed on a more close reaching heading is adopted. Only the lower sails now 'hold wind'. The upper sails stream. The mainsails, fully battened with stiff battens, do not flog. Most of the jibs have battens built into their seams for the same reason. Handled like this and with the windward wing and crew either skimming or lightly dragging in the water, these craft can survive surprisingly strong squalls. At this low speed, co-ordinated sail trimming is essential because the sails steer the boat in the sense that if either sail were to be trimmed firmly when the other is released, the resultant turning force would overpower the rudder and steering control would be lost.

22.16 To windward in waves

Regular waves

When wind blows over open water, waves form. These are the commonest of all waves. Their primary characteristic is their regularity. They are aligned crosswind and roll downwind. Their speed is always exactly related to the spacing between their crests – the wave length. Within any one system the speeds and lengths of all waves are all about the same, and this uniformity gives the system its characteristic regularity. (The thin warm surface layer is a special case of two such systems which combine in an irregular manner.) Waves start small at windward shore-lines, or when the wind starts. They grow in size with distance from their starting point (fetch), with increasing wind speed, and with time since the present wind began to blow. While shore-lines, shallow water, a warm surface layer and current can all affect the size and spacing of regular waves, they can never change either their direction nor their basic regularity and predictability.

Chaotic waves

The water surface of a busy harbour will become rough as the wakes of all the moving vessels combine in a random manner. The resultant wave system has no pattern and cannot be predicted. These are chaotic waves. They are caused mechanically, by traffic, and can exist whether the wind is blowing or not.

Standing waves

These are caused by current such as river flow and tidal stream. While almost always small in themselves, their principle effect is to combine with any regular waves, and skew the direction of the resulting waves so that their crests lie more across the current than across the wind.

Swell

Swell is the attenuated regular wave system of some earlier and distant storm.

In practice, in the busy waterways in which so much of our recreational sailing takes place, the wave system at any time and place will often be a blend of regular and chaotic waves, plus possibly swell. This mix of wave systems poses what is probably the most subtle challenge to a crew's skill in handling a sailboat, because in such a system the handling which will sail fastest, second by second, is so hard to define. A simple example will indicate the problem.

Typically, a windward leg might start at a downwind mark in a bay in which regular waves will be dominant. The helmsman who handles this situation best will be the one most skilled in the practised rhythmic technique which is fastest through regular waves. Mid-harbour, the water will remain rough, but the mix will be different. The regular waves, if they are still recognisable, will be smaller. Here, in the busy channels of the harbour, chaotic waves will be dominant. These cannot be predicted, and the helmsmen who sail fastest in this situation will be those who have best developed the spontaneous skill of steering 'down' whatever slope each wave offers for more of the time than their rivals, and in adopting the 'wider groove' sail trims which are faster in these conditions. Nearer the windward shore the waves will usually become small, but the wind pattern will usually become more unsteady because the land surface now close upwind may be aerodynamically rough and will probably be heated. In this situation the crew who trim their sails and handle their boat best in the smoother water but rougher wind will sail fastest.

Not only will there be these three 'clear cut' sets of conditions. In between each pair there will be an area in which elements of both will be blended.

So it turns out that this simple and typical fifteen minute windward leg not only rewards, one after the other, three separate skills – first regular-wave rhythmic technique, then chaotic-wave spontaneous technique, and finally flat-water rough-air sail handling. (Anywhere near open water, swell might also be a factor.) It also rewards those who can best handle the intermediate blends of waves with blends of techniques. And all of these skills will be needed to sail fastest in these very ordinary conditions.

22.17 The effects of waves on performance

Waves affect the performance of a sailboat which sails to windward in five different ways. All of them make the boat sail more slowly.

1. The water surface slopes as the crests advance and recede, and inertia-lag effects cause the boat both to bury its bow too deeply into the advancing faces of the waves, and to spend longer sailing on the uphill rather than the downhill slopes.

2. The downwind moving water in the wave crests hits the angled windward topside of the hull with much more force than any other mass of water in any other place. These wave-crest impacts develop a backwards force.

3. The water in the wave crests moves downwind and the water in the troughs moves upwind at significant speed due to orbital circulation. When sailing to windward a boat which is handled normally will tend to be 'captured' for an unexpectedly long period in the downwind-moving water adjacent to each crest.

4. The curved surface of waves makes it impossible for a boat to sail on its designed lines. When it is poised on a crest a hull will appear, to the water, to be a fat-bellied tub as both the bow and the stern tend to emerge into fresh air. When it is in a trough, both ends will be buried deeply, and an otherwise slender hull will look, to the water, like a barge with squarish ends. Tubs and barges are unfortunate shapes, and sail woefully slowly.

5. Waves shake the rig around in the air, and this can reduce sail force substantially, as was explained earlier.

22.18 In waves and light airs

All waves will increase hull drag when sailing to windward. This means that, in waves, it will be harder to accelerate the boat, harder to keep it moving, and it will sail more slowly.

The action of the waves oscillates the rig. The masthead moves most. This means that the Apparent Wind which drives the upper sails changes speed and direction with each oscillation; and the greater the oscillation, the greater the changes in the Apparent Wind. As the bow rises to each wave the masthead moves backwards and the Apparent Wind at the top of the rig falls to some much lower speed. As the bow falls, the masthead sweeps forward and the Apparent Wind becomes stronger for that part of each cycle. In light airs sails take several seconds to build up to their maximum force, but only a second or so to lose it. For this reason, when a sail is being shaken about by waves and so is washed by a rapidly fluctuating Apparent Wind, the average force obtainable is unfortunately much closer to the force expected at the lowest recurring wind speed than the force expected from the average wind speed.

Further, in light airs it is only the upper sails which develop useful force. But in waves it is the upper sails which oscillate most. So the reduction in force caused by waves in light air is sometimes dramatic.

For this reason, the first priority in light air and rough water will be to reduce the oscillation of the rig.

An extreme example illustrates this.

A championship race in Adelaide's St Vincent's Gulf started in a 10 knot breeze. Near the windward mark, the air fell light and backed 45 degrees. The left-over waves were about 6 to 8 inches high, regular, and at exactly the right frequency to cause all the boats in the fleet to pitch bow-up, bow-down at their natural frequency. The speed of the light air was about the speed at which the upper sails moved aft with each oscillation – about 1 to 1.5 knots. As a result, the fleet, necessarily all on port tack, virtually stopped with all boats bobbing up and down in the same place and the sails developing almost no force at all. After a minute or so, I worked out what was happening, and asked my forward hand (Julian) to move as far forward as he could – he lay along the foredeck with his head forward of the bow. I moved right aft to preserve trim, as in Fig. 22.18.1. (The boat was the one shown in Fig. 20.12) With our weights thus separated, the boat's angular inertia was greatly increased and its 'natural frequency' slowed sufficiently for its resonance with the waves to be broken. The pitching was immediately damped to almost nothing. The hull, which had previously oscillated on the waves in silence, began to make sloshing noises as the waves washed onto and off the now-steadied bow and stern. *But* the sails, now steady, began to draw properly, and the boat began to move. The 50 yard lead gained before others woke up and copied the technique was a sufficient margin to win what turned out to be a long and difficult race.

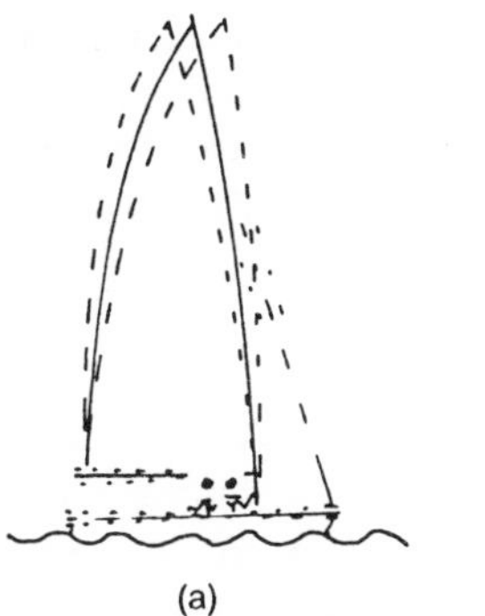

(a)

(b)

(a) Crew weights together allow hull to pitch.
(b) Crew weights separated de-tune hull from waves.

Fig 22.18.1 Suppression of pitching.

Note carefully the conflict between hull need and rig need. With the 'crew weight concentrated' technique, the hulls bobbed smoothly and noiselessly on the waves, accommodating perfectly to their slopes. This is the technique usually recommended for least hull resistance, and to this extent it works. The only trouble is that so often, as in this case, it deprives the rig of so much of its power. Summed up, even zero hull resistance wins no races if it occurs at zero speed because of zero drive force. There are faster ways.

Holding the rig steadier in the air is almost always the higher priority in light air. Fortunately, almost all high performance designs have very fine bows, and can be sailed in the fourth mode. This is what fourth mode sailing is all about. The principles and the technique are given in Section 20.11.(Part Three)

In flat water the fourth mode technique is useful only at very low speeds – say up to about 2 knots. In waves its ability to reduce, significantly, the out-of-trim drag suffered by a flattish hull means that it can be used with advantage up to speeds closer to 4 knots.

When sailing towards waves (usually but not always this means 'to windward'), resistance will always be greater than in flat water. To provide the necessary added drive force, the sails should be set slightly fuller and sheeted wider and the boat pointed correspondingly lower. In these conditions the sail trim requirement will always be for maximum available force – forward leeward tufts just agitating – if they are reading usefully.

When the waves are sufficiently small for the rig to be held reasonably steady in the air by the techniques described above, the tufts will continue to be accurate indicators of airflow and trim, and can be used with confidence. But as soon as wave size becomes such that the hull and rig can no longer be held steady, then in light airs the oscillating movement of the rig will cause such great changes in both the Apparent Wind and also the airflow pattern around the sails from moment to moment that the tufts will begin to flick around unsteadily. In these conditions they are not only ineffective as trim aids – they accurately indicate that there is no longer any attached lee-side flow at all.

When these conditions occur the trim for maximum force must be found and maintained primarily by 'feel'. The best technique is to make the upper mainsail progressively fuller and at the same time allow it to twist more. The boom should be kept close to or on the centreline – in practice, if it is allowed to fall to leeward 'for better speed' all that seems to happen is that pointing is lost but without any better speed. The trim for the jib follows identical principles – sheet the foot closely but very slack so that the upper leech twists off to leeward similarly to the twist of the mainsail. Fig. 22.18.2 shows this typical 'light air and waves' rig trim. Summed up, the lighter the wind and the lumpier the water, the fuller and the more twisted the sails should be.

Handling

Mark Mendelblatt – Laser II – clearly has normal waves in mind when he suggests;

'If the wind is light and the water is choppy, I use the same set-up as for light air and flat water, except that we ease the outhaul a little and set the jib slides out a little. This makes the boat more forgiving. We drive off as necessary for adequate speed'

Because light air and rough water can adopt an infinite number of combinations, it is not possible to advise the best trim for each. The best practical approach is to set the sails full for power, point low and close reach for two or three lengths until speed which is judged adequate for those conditions is achieved. Then systematically point higher – very slowly – and sheet in to reduce twist and simultaneously flatten the sails to avoid 'hooking' until speed loss is sensed. Immediately this happens, revert to the last setting which yielded adequate speed. In normal waves this will lead to the handling described above. But in extreme conditions the results can be surprising.

Many years ago Peter Hollis was a speaker at a 'Sailing Performance' seminar. He had just won the world Contender championship for the second time. One of his comments, 'The fourth race was held in three foot breaking waves and a wind of five knots' jolted me out of complacency. How could there be such waves when there was no wind?'

I thought about it and began to realise how it was possible. Some years later it was my turn to experience this particular wind and sea-state condition, and the fact that I had previously thought about it helped me keep a clear mind when it mattered.

During a Canadian Tasar championships at Sarnia, at the southern end of Lake Huron, sailing was abandoned late one afternoon in thunderstorms and rising wind as a front approached. The front swept over in the early evening, and a 40 knot northerly blew straight down the 200 mile length of the lake all night. It abated suddenly in the morning. At the start of the first race the wind had diminished to a near-calm light northerly drift, but the water still offered mixed three to four foot regular waves which sometimes broke.

You get just as many points for winning in unusual conditions as when conditions are ideal, so we set about finding out how to go to windward – and downwind – in these conditions. We first adopted a 'conventional' attitude and trim – with the boat at about 45 to 50 degrees to the wind direction and the sails set as in Fig. 22.18.2. The boat scarcely moved. The sails sawed around in the air and developed virtually no 'power' at all. I turned onto a beam reach, and set the sails to maximum fullness. The boat began to move. So far so good. The wind seemed puffy. Little by little it dawned on me that the puffs were correlated with the waves. I had read somewhere that in big waves more wind was to be expected when a boat was on the crests, because it was then more 'exposed', so I tried pumping at each crest. It didn't work. We nearly fell in backwards, so I stopped, and looked harder. Suddenly, the penny dropped. There were puffs, but they blew when we

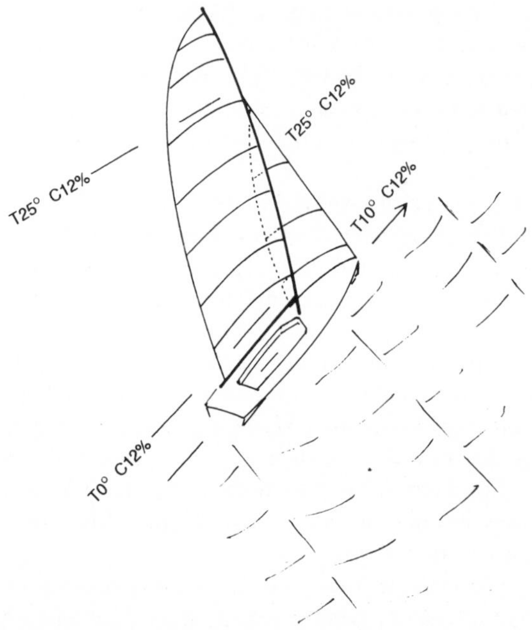

Fig 22.18.2 Sail trim 0 - 5 knots, in waves.

were in each *trough*, and not when we were on the crests at all. I tried pumping in the troughs. The boat shot forward!

That was the key. In conditions of big waves and very light winds, the sailboat by itself and without the aid of what we now call kinetics was helpless on all points of sailing. As each wave washed by, we were carried downwind when we were in each crest and this made the Apparent Wind about zero, so there was no help there.

But we were carried to windward when we were in each trough by what I now recognise as the upwind part of the upwind/downwind surge of the orbital motion of the water within all regular wave systems. This windward movement of the water forced us against the feeble wind at about two knots for a period of about one second during each wave cycle of about three seconds. By applying two or three very quick and increasingly powerful impulse-pumps during this period, we suddenly acquired useful 'power' during one part of each rhythmic wave cycle, and this regularly repeated thrust gave us movement and the ability to do whatever we wanted to. In that case, the interval between waves was about three seconds, so it was all very civilized and easy to apply both upwind and down once we had worked it out.

22.19 In waves and breeze - *sail trim in 6 to 14 knots*

When a boat sails from flat water into waves in a breeze, the effect of the waves on its performance will be as described in Section 22.17, but the application as between light air and breeze is different.

As described in the previous section, in light airs and waves the attached lee-side flows which are normal when sailing in flat water or small waves cannot establish or are separated by the motion of larger waves. The unstable motions of the tufts indicate this.

In breezes and waves the flows re-attach and the tufts become useful tools again – except in one situation which is as follows.

When the wind speed is only just into the turbulent regime (6 to 7 knots) and the waves happen to be irregular and big enough the same situation can arise. It will be indicated accurately by the tufts – they cease to indicate any steady lee-side flow at reasonable trim angles, despite your best efforts to trim the sails sensibly. When this occurs, do not assume that leeside flow is there but the tufts don't show it. Read what is there – that there is no organised lee side flow. In these conditions set the sails even fuller, twist them more, bear away a little for whatever speed you can develop in these conditions – and be alert for the next change of either more wind or less waves.

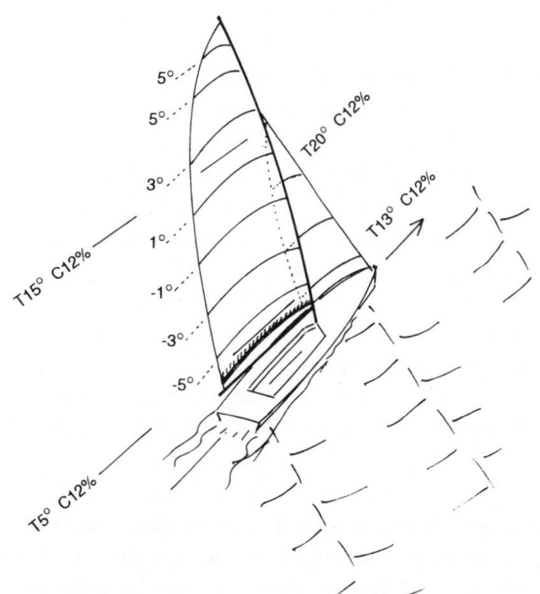

Fig 22.19.1 Sail trim 6 - 14 knots, in waves.

Apart from the exception above, the wind flow over the sails remains normal. But its power is not normal. The reason for this is described in Section 23.2 ('The part-power pause') Briefly, the Apparent Wind speed slows and sail force is lost each time the masthead moves backward. Only a little of this loss is recovered during the half-cycle during which the masthead moves forward and the Apparent Wind becomes stronger. The loss in total rig power is substantial. So more power is needed from a rig which has become less able to deliver it.

Changes in sail handling are needed as well as changes in boat handling. To provide the extra drive force to maintain reasonable boat speed through waves, all three areas of the sail plan, lower mainsail, upper mainsail, and jib, should be set fuller and then fine-trimmed so that in the lulls the leeches all lie parallel with the centreline. Because the power loss is substantial, the degree to which the sails should be set fuller in order to maintain the desired speed is sometimes surprising. Even more surprising is the increase in the speed of the design wind. You will find yourself still 'looking for power' in the lulls in winds already several knots stronger than the design wind in flat water. Because there can be big waves when the wind is light, and small waves near weather shores in stronger winds, no hard and fast rules can apply. The practical answer to the question 'What is the fastest rig shape?' is found by applying the fundamental technique; 'Sail free to acquire the speed you want. Then point as high as possible consistent with maintaining this speed, and fine-trim the sails as full as possible provided that:

(a) The tufts are all streaming in the lulls (except in patches of lighter breeze and lumpier waves).

(b) The leeches are not hooked.

(c) The boat can be kept upright.

Fig. 22.19.1 shows the sort of shape which will sail fastest.

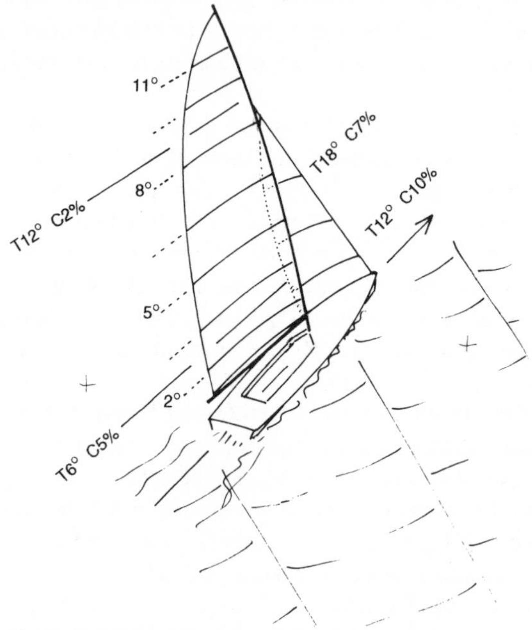

Fig 22.20 1 Sail trim for 20 - 25 knots, in waves

22.20 In waves and breeze - *sail trim in 15 to 25 knots*

In strong winds, by definition, there will never be any lack of power. But first, a warning about assuming that you are sailing in the strong wind regime. The waves may be big. The water may look angry. The surface marks of the wind over the water may be far beyond normal indications of the design wind. No matter. If you cannot hike to extreme in the full wave cycle in the lulls, you are not yet in the strong wind regime in that particular rough water, and you will sail fastest in these conditions by retaining your moderate-wind 'power' setting and handling technique. In conditions such as those just described, the design wind may well be four or five knots stronger than the design wind in flat water – it's hard to judge. But a too-early shift to 'strong wind' technique will merely lose both speed and pointing angle.

Once the wind strength in the lulls has exceeded the design wind for those wave conditions, then exactly the same 'jump' to the low-drag, strong-wind sail shape should be made *except that*, in waves, the lower mainsail and jib should be set a little fuller – as full as is necessary to provide the extra drive force to keep the boat moving through the rougher water.

The logic behind this set-up has three bases. The first is the practical one. If you have a choice, the last place you want to draw extra force from is the top of the rig. Extra aerodynamic force there will merely heel you quickly, and you would have to ease the traveller significantly to stay upright for only a small gain in drive force. Extra aerodynamic force from the fuller jib and lower mainsail is another matter entirely. It will heel you little, and almost all of it will be available for extra drive. The second reason is geometric. If you use more fullness in the lower sail than the upper, it will be necessary to use a little more twist to avoid hooking the upper leech, and this allows you to even further reduce heeling force by allowing the flattened upper mainsail – and jib – to twist away a little, and so heel you even less. The third is dynamic. The fore and aft motion of the lower sails due to the wave action will be less than that of the upper sails, so the rig will work more 'steadily' when the lower sails are relied on for most of the force. Fig. 22.20.1 shows the shape of rig which is fastest in these fresh breezes and waves.

As the wind speed continues to increase, the effect of the wave-induced mast movements on the Apparent Wind at the masthead becomes progressively less significant. In a few knots stronger than the new, rough-water design wind, the boat will sail fastest if the sails are trimmed progressively flatter and sheeted progressively wider exactly as in flat water. In winds of 20 to 25 knots the fastest sail shapes in flat water and in waves become indistinguishable, but the sheeting angle in waves will be slightly wider.

Waves can vary from nothing to huge, so no hard and fast rules about fullness can be given. The lower windward mainsail tuft will be the best indicator; the mainsail should be as full as possible, provided that this tuft just continues to stream in the lulls. The fundamental technique for setting up remains true. Sail free for the speed desired, then point progressively higher and flatten and reduce twist progressively until speed loss is sensed, then revert to the last setting and pointing angle which gave the desired speed.

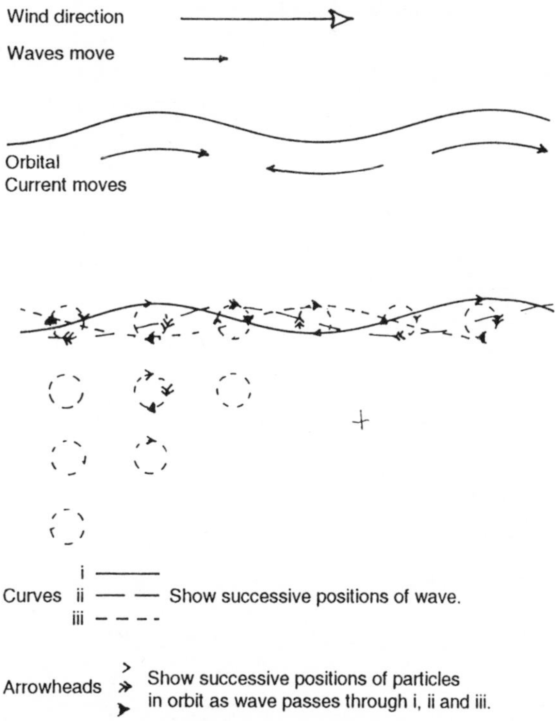
Wind direction
Waves move
Orbital
Current moves
Curves i ——— ii — — iii - - - - Show successive positions of wave.
Arrowheads Show successive positions of particles in orbit as wave passes through i, ii and iii.
The wave form moves horizontally.
The particles orbit, and do not move horizontally.

Fig 22.21.1 The nature of regular waves.

22.21 Handling in regular waves

Regular wind-waves on the water's surface form a 'gravity-wave' system in which the wave-shape moves horizontally downwind while individual water-particles move in a circular orbit but do not move horizontally. The practical effect of this is that all wave crests become zones of strong local down-wind current, while all wave troughs become zones of strong local windward-going current. Fig. 22.21.1 shows how the wave shape and orbiting particles interact as the wave-system rolls forward. Fig 22.21.2 (repeats Fig 13.2) shows the dimensions of the waves after two hours of the wind noted; these would be reasonably typical of waves in racing areas which are well off-shore in a harbour or large-lake situation.

In winds of 10 knots and less, the waves are so small and so short that they are encountered faster than one each second. Even if the helmsman could respond fast enough, the mass and angular inertia of the boat itself prevents it from turning though any significant arc and back again twice per second. For this reason the helmsman has no option but to ignore all small waves.

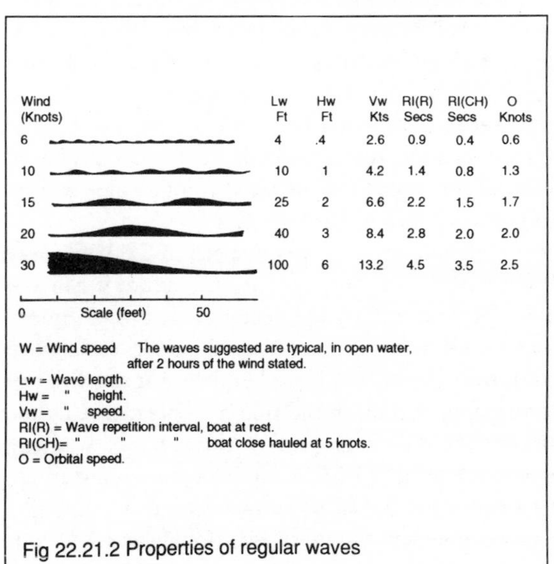

Wind (Knots)	Lw Ft	Hw Ft	Vw Kts	RI(R) Secs	RI(CH) Secs	O Knots
6	4	.4	2.6	0.9	0.4	0.6
10	10	1	4.2	1.4	0.8	1.3
15	25	2	6.6	2.2	1.5	1.7
20	40	3	8.4	2.8	2.0	2.0
30	100	6	13.2	4.5	3.5	2.5

0 Scale (feet) 50

W = Wind speed The waves suggested are typical, in open water, after 2 hours of the wind stated.
Lw = Wave length.
Hw = " height.
Vw = " speed.
RI(R) = Wave repetition interval, boat at rest.
RI(CH)= " " " boat close hauled at 5 knots.
O = Orbital speed.

Fig 22.21.2 Properties of regular waves

By way of contrast, in winds of 25 knots, the 100 foot length of a typical wave means that a crest will be encountered every three and a half seconds by a boat sailing to windward at about 5 knots boat speed and 3.5 knots VMG. Further, the difference in the speed at which a typical dinghy will approach the windward mark between the periods when it is sailing through the crests of the waves, and the periods when it is sailing in the troughs, is a substantial 5.2 knots – it varies from 0.9 knots through the crests (3.5 knots – 2.6 knots) – to 6.1 knots through the troughs (3.5 knots + 2.6 knots) – if the heading is held steady.

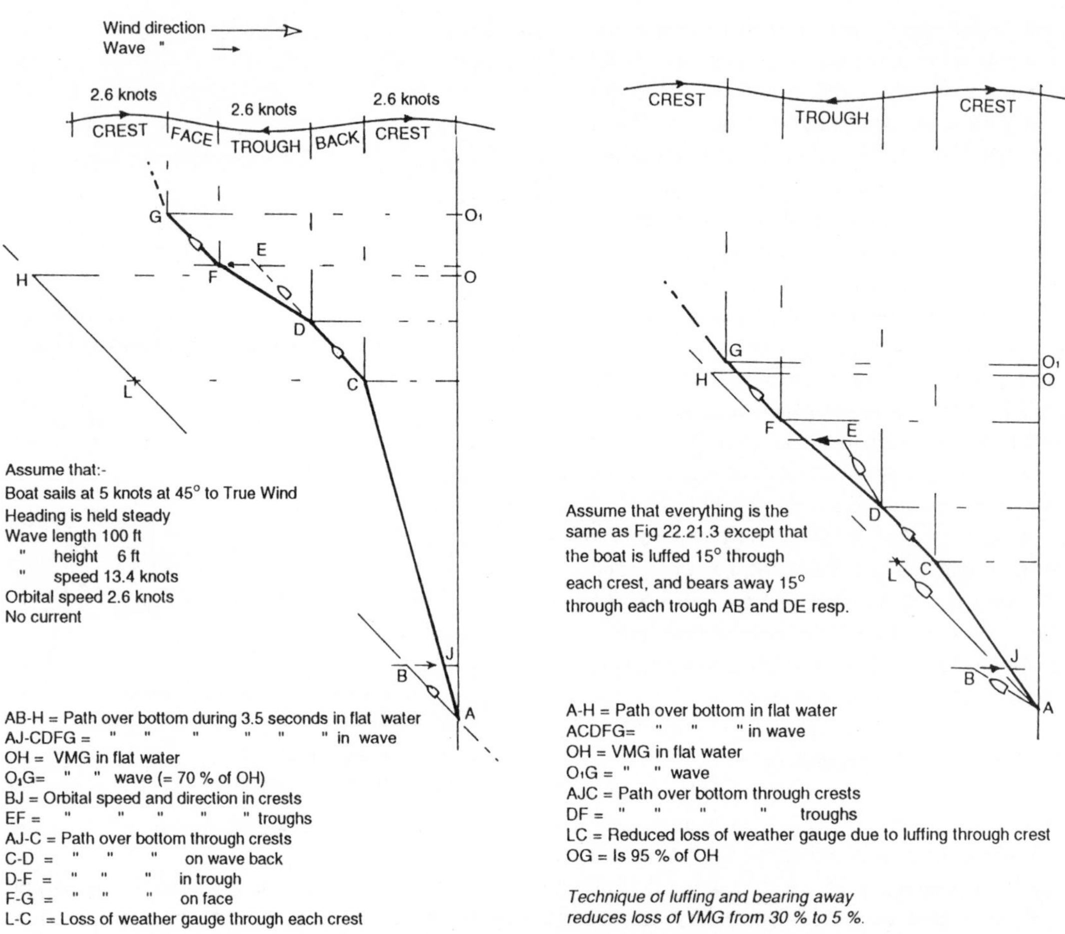

Fig 22.21.3 Track and VMG through wave - heading steady

Fig 22.21.4 Track and VMG through waves when *snaking*.

Unfortunately, the plusses and the minusses do not average out. The reason for this is that the boat tends to be 'captured' by and so spend far longer than it should in the downwind-going water in the crests in which its windward-going speed is so much slowed. It is revealing to look closely at this mechanism – a useful approach is to look at what would happen if the wave were 'frozen' in one place, but with its orbital flows still intact. Figs 22.21.3 and 22.21.4 do exactly this and show the differences between the windward-going performance in flat water and in waves, and Fig 22.21.4 suggests a useful technique.

If we assume that the average VMG to windward in a breeze and flat water is 3.5 knots – 5 knots through the water but on a heading of 45 degrees to the True Wind – then the average speed of a 14 foot dinghy of reasonable performance which sails on a constant heading of 45 degrees to the wind in flat water will be represented by the line 'AH' in Fig. 22.21.3, and its VMG to windward by the line 'OH'.

But if we assume 100-foot long waves which are 6 feet high and have an orbital speed of 2.6 knots (say 2.5 knots component), then a boat which starts at 'A' will have to sail from 'A' to 'C' before it can sail clear of the strong downwind-moving current in the crests (represented by the vector 'B-J' in the figure). During this prolonged period the VMG will be only about 1 knot. From 'C' to 'D' on the back of the wave – and also from 'F' to 'G' on its face, the orbital current lowers or lifts the boat, but does not retard it nor advance it. From 'D' to 'F' it enjoys the strong windward-going current in the trough, represented by the vector 'E-F'. This increases the boat's VMG, but also moves the boat very quickly towards the advancing face of the next wave and so reduces the time which the boat spends in this favourable current. Summed up, the boat will spend about half of its time at a VMG of 1 knot in the crests, about one sixth of its time at a VMG of 6 knots in the troughs; and the remaining third of its time between crests and troughs at a VMG of 3.5 knots.

Fig. 22.21.3 is drawn to scale, and shows dramatically how the boat is 'captured' by the downwind-moving orbital current of the wave crests 'BJ'. The difference between the path over the bottom in flat water 'A-L', and the path whilst within the influence of the crest 'AJ-C', absolutely dominates the diagram. The equal-and-opposite speed gain 'D-F' through the troughs does not begin to compensate for the loss caused by 'B-J', because this favourable factor acts for so short a time segment of each cycle, whilst the influence of 'B-J' is so prolonged.

In real life these 100 foot long waves roll downwind at nearly 14 knots and the whole sequence 'ACDFG' is compressed into and repeats every 3.5 seconds. This speeding-up does not alter the way in which the downwind movement of water in each wave crest still 'captures' the boat and holds it in this most unfavourable current for an inordinately long part of each cycle. The fact that the boat slows a little as it climbs each wave face and approaches each crest merely increases the time it takes to pass through each crest and so exacerbates the problem.

The time difference suggests the remedy, which is to 'snake' through the waves by luffing through the crests and bearing away through the troughs. Fig. 22.21.4 repeats Fig 22.21.3 exactly except that the boat is assumed to luff 15 degrees to heading 'A-B' as it sails through the crest segment 'AC', and to bear away 15 degrees to the heading 'D-E' as it sails through the trough segment 'DF'. This reduces the distance it sails in the adverse current (A-C) from 58% to 39% of each wave cycle. It increases the distance it sails in favourable current (D-F) from 18% to 29% of each cycle. As a result 'OiG' becomes 95% of 'OH', and the overall performance loss has been reduced from 30% to 5%, an increase in speed of a full 25% of the flat water speed.

The period during which the boat should be luffed is only about one and one quarter seconds when sailing in 100 foot waves. It is slightly less than one second in 50 foot waves. For practical purposes, momentum will maintain speed for a period as short as this, so the assumption of uniform speed on which the figures are based is reasonable.

The basic technique is to bear away and ease sheets across the trough, and use the extra time in favourable current – which causes a more favourable Apparent Wind – to accelerate to a speed slightly greater than would be used in flat water, and then to turn smoothly but firmly into the advancing crest and firm sheets as you turn so as to cross it and pass through its downwind-going current as quickly as possible. This technique calls for practised skill in timing the luff through each wave so that the crossing of the crest is accomplished as quickly as is possible, consistent with smoothness of rudder control, smoothness in the manner the bow encounters the crest, and sustained power from the sails. 'Power' is better sustained when luffed if the mainsail is deliberately over-trimmed *momentarily* with the traveller. In the trade-off between moderate luffing to the limit of losing heeling force from the sails if the mainsail is not over-trimmed, and extreme luffing together with momentary over-trimming to maintain steady heeling force, the extreme luff is the faster technique because it enables the crest to be crossed more directly and thus more quickly.

The trough should be handled by a correspondingly more extreme bearing away. The object will be to increase the proportion of time which is spent in the windward-going current in the trough. Depending upon the characteristics of the boat, it is normal to start bearing away at about the instant that the bow starts to fall. Both the wider angle of the boat to the wind as the boat bears away plus the windward movement of the water in the trough will develop a stronger Apparent Wind more from the beam, and the sails should be eased slightly both for balance and for maximum acceleration. A vigorous pump will further boost the acceleration in lighter winds. A final point is that if the boat is allowed to accommodate first to the slope of the back of the wave, then to the hollow of the trough, and then to the slope of the face of the wave, the resultant roll will move the masthead to leeward, and so deprive the boat of power. A technique which either rolls the boat somewhat against the wave, or at least maintains it at a constant heel, will be faster, particularly in winds lighter than the design wind. All told, skilful handling of the trough is a fairly cultured art form. It is also very energetic. But this is the way to ensure that every crest is approached with adequate speed.

A practical point is that a helmsman who endeavours to 'pick by eye' each advancing face when sailing through the slightly uneven waves of real life can tend to become a little mesmerised and inefficient after more than ten or fifteen minutes of sustained concentration, particularly when the light is difficult. Fortunately, there is a very simple solution. It is very much easier to see and feel the bow rising to each advancing face and falling to each back than to pick the approaching slopes. If you 'let the boat tell you' and start to luff as the bow starts to rise, and bear away as it starts to fall, the task becomes much easier. You can then focus your concentration not just on the bow meeting the present wave but also on the approaching two or three waves next to be encountered. In this way you can pick the occasional non-regular one before it arrives, and so be ready to handle it with least loss of rhythm.

The lower part of Fig. 20.9 draws attention to the way the drag rise of the forced mode begins at a lower speed when sailing to windward in waves; this factor will affect all boats except the bigger catamarans which are relatively insensitive to waves. It also notes that in waves boats emerge from the 'steep drag-rise' zone, and begin to feel 'free' at a lower speed. In practice, this factor creates an abnormal situation which occurs only when relatively fine-lined boats which are capable of useful but conventional speed – examples would be FD, 505, Laser ii, Tasar etc – sail to windward in waves which are quite big but so short that the 'snaking' technique cannot be used. In these conditions a point is reached at which, if the 'jump' in sail setting to the strong-wind shapes is made much sooner than would seem reasonable, the boat will accept it and begin to sail faster and point higher in a manner which is surprising at first. I can suggest no way other than experience to find out whether it will work with the boat you sail, and the range of conditions in which it will work.

In light airs the 'snaking' technique cannot be used by any boat because at low speed no boat can turn quickly enough.

It cannot be used by catamarans because their long slender hulls cannot turn quickly at any speed.

High performance boats cannot use it either, because their higher speed through the water increases their speed of closing with the wave system so much that there is no longer sufficient time in which to turn. For example, if we consider a day with 20 knot winds and 50 foot waves which roll at 9.5 knots, then the interval between successive crests experienced by a race officer in a moored boat, by the crew of a moderate performance boat which sails to windward at 3.5 knots VMG, and the crew of a high performance boat which sails at a VMG of 10 knots would be 3.1, 2.5 and 1.5 seconds respectively. 1.5 seconds full cycle is not long enough in which to do much turning.

Practical techniques

Laser Two (Mark Mendelblatt)

'In winds of 15 to 25 knots and waves, I change to and use the same rig set-up as I use in flat water except, that in 15 to 20 knot winds both crew members move aft as necessary to lift the bow above the wave crests. and in winds of 20 to 25 knots and waves both crew move back as far as is possible.'

Soling, Etchells etc.

'With keelboats, their increased mass and length makes it more difficult to turn through an adequate angle, but the advantages to be gained from even a slight turn are still very great.'

'As the years pass and the competition becomes more skilful we find that even in flat water it is fastest for the helmsman to concentrate on the factors directly related to steering. As soon as the water becomes rougher – even when it is just a jobble – you take your eyes off the focus at the front of the boat at your peril. By this I mean the field of vision which includes the jib and its tufts, the bow meeting the current wave, the two or three oncoming waves, and the marks of the wind on the water in that area. It is up to the crew to scan the wind and the sea-state over the broader area, and above all to watch the fleet.'

'In these heavier boats you cannot plane off in a private gust, you cannot crack a long surf down a fortunate wave, so differences in speed between the leading boats are minuscule and they are never far apart. Success in racing in these fleets reduces to developing the skills, techniques, team-work, equipment, concentration and stamina to sail at the same speed or marginally faster than your opponents from the start of the race right through to the finish, and to miss no opportunity to exploit even the slightest advantage. In this area the experience, skill, and team-work of the whole crew are critical. While you are concentrating on your job of maintaining competitive speed you have to rely on them to observe and recognise all the other things that matter – and only the things that matter. They must convey this information clearly and succinctly to you and to each other so that as the critical boats move into your field of vision each boat is where you expect it to be, and your whole crew is ready to exploit any tactical advantage, or defend against any attack, in a co-ordinated manner.'

22.22 Handling in chaotic waves

A single wave system takes the form of a series of continuous regular parallel cross-wind crests, separated by troughs, all of which advance at a constant speed. Because all waves within the system advance in a known direction at a constant speed, the future position of any wave can be anticipated, and a practised, rhythmic technique can be developed and employed.

When two wave systems intersect, there are three possible outcomes:

When they meet at some speed and angle which are not equal and opposite, the continuous crests are transformed into lines of individual hillocks, and the valleys become lines of 'holes'. Hillocks and holes all advance in some intermediate direction at a constant speed, so again their future position can be anticipated, but with some difficulty.

A second possibility is that the second wave system is equal and opposite to the first. This situation routinely occurs just to windward of any crosswind vertical water barrier such as a cliff or a man-made sea-wall, which will reflect any wave system unchanged, in the same way as a mirror reflects light. When this situation occurs, the result becomes a series of standing waves which do not move. Instead, the water pulses up and down, with the peaks twice as high, the holes twice as deep and the *slopes four times as steep* as those of regular waves of the wind-driven system. The local current alternates: initially it flows towards the forming peak, and later it flows away (in all directions) from the collapsing peak. No rhythmic sailing technique to compensate for the massive increase in drag is possible.

The third possibility is that both wave systems can move in the same direction, and that one is a little faster than the other. This is a very normal situation and is described in more detail later.

When three or more wave systems interact, the situation abruptly changes into one in which no anticipation at all is possible. Individual hills and holes appear suddenly, exist for a second or two, and vanish. They may or may not move. If they move, each individual hill or hole may move in any direction. Their sizes become uneven, with high hills and low mounds and deep holes and shallow hollows. But, characteristic of all chaotic systems is the much increased steepness of slope which is an integral part of the 'equal and opposite' standing wave system. This sort of seaway is characteristic of any busy harbour – and the wakes of your own fleet can also be the cause of much of the roughness.

The effect on total performance of the regular-wave situation is mixed. The relatively well-shaped waves slow the boat a little. The downwind-going currents within the wave crests are much more damaging to windward-going performance. However, it turns out that these effects can be largely compensated for by a practised, rhythmic technique.

The effect on total performance of the chaotic-wave situation is quite different. The waves are rougher. Their effects on the boat's dynamics and speed are more damaging. There is a technique to compensate, but its application is the reverse of the regular wave technique.

The principle is subtle. If we regard the water surface at any instant as a series of flat plateaux on the tops of the hills, of flat floors at the bottoms of the holes, and of slopes joining the two, then five important facts follow:

1. This moment's hole will be the next moment's hill, and vice versa.

2. Because 'holes' last only momentarily, any boat presently entering a 'hole' will be lifted bodily in the next second or so.

3. Any boat steered toward the nearest 'hole' will necessarily sail downhill and so increase its speed.

4. As the water surface rises, it can rise as:

(a) A part of a hill behind;

(b) a part of a hill ahead; or

(c) a part of a hill to one side, or to the other.

5. The boat therefore has one chance in four of being lifted in a bow-up attitude and slowing; one chance of being lifted in a bow-down attitude and accelerating; and two chances of being lifted in a level attitude on a slope but with a potentially useful downslope and hole to one side or the other.

The key to the chaotic-wave technique lies in those last two chances of the four, each with a potentially useful downslope and hole to one side or the other. If a helmsman can develop the skill of observing sufficiently quickly on which side the next hole is forming, and sufficient quickness of response to turn the boat significantly 'downhill' toward the hole during the useful life of that slope, he can treble the time that he spends sailing downhill. The gain in performance is magic!

If the hills and holes surged and collapsed in slow motion, a helmsman could so easily watch the developing peaks and holes just ahead and to either side of his bow, and turn either right or left to sail downhill towards and into the nearest developing hole. He would feel the boat begin to accelerate as it sails downhill, and a moment later would feel it rise as the hole fills and the surface surged upwards underneath him. He could repeat this manoeuvre (to either right or left, it can never be predicted) and at the same time bias his choices so as to remain on headings reasonably close to his chosen track. It would become obvious how this technique, skilfully applied, can greatly increase the proportion of time that the boat spends sailing downhill and faster, as compared with the boat of any rival who steers straight ahead, and 'takes what comes'.

In practice, the hills and holes form and change so quickly that no advantage can be expected until a threshold level of skill and speed of response is attained. However, once sufficient skill in all the factors is acquired – observation, fast recognition of developing holes, and very quick response with firm, positive steering – crews skilled in these conditions can weave through chaotic waves in a manner and at a speed which leaves normal crews helpless with envy.

Note the difference between the two techniques. In regular waves, the boat is turned toward the hill. In chaotic waves, the boat is turned away from the hill. In regular waves, the technique is rhythmic; you can do it, with practise, with your eyes closed. In chaotic waves, the technique is spontaneous – you have to see and recognise each individual developing hole, and then turn towards it, either right or left, never rhythmic and never predictable, always a conscious choice. It is essential that the boat be moving reasonably quickly so that it can be turned quickly – so this can never be a light air technique. It is essential for this sort of handling that the rig should be set up very flexibly, and for a 'wide groove'.

There is more to it yet!

Let us look again at that typical windward leg. At the downwind mark, there are regular wind waves. These call for regular-wave technique, with the boat always turned 'toward the hill'. As the mechanically generated chaotic waves of mid-harbour are approached, the changing wave mix calls for the most subtle, wave by wave handling. Occasional big, chaotic waves will appear, with increasing frequency, and will form and move in some other direction in the midst of the still dominant regular wind-waves. This area will call for a mixed technique, and I question whether it is possible to describe it in any helpful way. Mid-harbour, in chaotic waves, it will be pure 'turn toward the holes'. As the flatter waters nearer the upwind shore are approached, there will be a point at which, abruptly, it will pay to ignore the progressively more trivial waves, and concentrate instead on steady, accurate handling of a more rigid rig for peak power and efficiency in the probably increasingly unsteady wind conditions.

So, not only does the well-rounded helmsman need to know both the regular-wave and the chaotic-wave techniques. He also needs sufficient practise to be confident of his judgement as to when to apply each, and above all, how to handle them when they are mixed.

Like so many other situations, competence in waves is all in the mind. My unstinted admiration goes to those flat-water champions who, when faced with a rough water championship can smile in anticipation, say 'Isn't it good to have some waves to play in!' – and win.

22.23 Handling in swell

Swell is the attenuated wave system of some recent but distant storm. It is a regular wave system in which the wave speed is usually substantially faster than the wind speed.

The principle factors which distinguish swell are:

1. The wave length is very long (typically 500-2000 ft).
2. Wave height is usually small (typically 5-10 ft).
3. The slopes of face and back are not steep (typically less than 1 degree).
4. The wave speed is always fast (typically 30-60 knots).
5. The interval between successive crests is long (typically 10-20 secs).
6. The swell direction is constant over a period of many hours.

The swell direction is in no way related to the local wind direction, and may be completely different. As between swells which may be either vigorous or much attenuated, over which blow winds which may be either strong or light, and which may blow in a direction either with, or against, or across the swell, the number of possible situations which the racing helmsman may meet is endless. But some things remain common:

1. The shallow slope means that the extra resistance whilst sailing uphill, and the extra thrust whilst sailing downhill, will be small – typically of the order of about 1% of the total weight (boat plus crew) or say 10 pounds for a heavy dinghy and 5 pounds for a light one.

2. The long interval between crests means that the time spent climbing each face or descending each back will be up to 5 to 10 seconds.

3. The orbital motion of the water can become very important indeed when sailing in light airs.

To put these factors into perspective, here are noted some situations and examples as they effect a dinghy of 500 pounds total (boat plus crew) weight as it sails upwind, downwind, and crosswind in swell, in winds which are either moderate or light.

To windward in swell and moderate air

Wind direction same as swell direction.

Throughout the discussion of regular wind waves, the principle has been developed that maximum windward-going VMG will result if the boat is steered so that it spends the minimum of time in the downwind moving water in the crests, and the maximum of time in the windward moving water in the troughs – hence the basic technique of luffing through the crests and bearing away in the troughs. In all regular wind-wave situations, the period which a boat spends on the uphill or downhill sloping water is so short that the boat's momentum is dominant and speed changes little. In the case of moderate wind and relatively small swell, the time on the uphill slope will become longer, but the boat speed at the start of each climb will still be fast, and the sail power substantial, and so the worst that will happen is that the boat will noticeably lose speed as it approaches and reaches each crest. In these conditions, the basic, 'luff through the crests' will still be the fastest technique. (If there is reserve centreboard area available, this is the time to use it).

However, as the wind becomes lighter, the starting speed must become slower, and the sail power more feeble. As the swell becomes longer, the time spent climbing the hill will increase. At some point the inevitable must happen in that any boat which is luffed up the advancing face will simply run out of speed before it gets to the top. When the swell and the local wind are both from the same direction, the fact that the Apparent Wind both heads and becomes lighter in the downwind-going water in and near the crest is not helpful. Exactly when you run out of speed because you are sailing uphill, you also run out of wind and so have no power to accelerate again regardless of which way you steer. The physical situation is bad enough. But the worst news is more subtle. It is only when you stop to think about it that the realization dawns that because you now sail so slowly through each crest, and much faster through each trough, that you are in fact spending more time in the downwind going water in the crests than in the windward going water in the troughs.

Anything is better than this.

The principle remains true. Spend the least time near the crests. Least time will be spent by adopting the best compromise between boat speed and pointing angle which can be achieved under the circumstances.

Generally this will involve what appears at first sight to be a reversal of technique:

In the lighter winds as the boat begins to climb don't luff, but bear away to a close reach to provide sufficient drive force to maintain speed up the hill. Only when the stern comes up as the crest is reached, should you luff firmly and use the retained speed to minimise the time in the rest of the crest.

Because the Apparent Wind will free and become stronger in each trough, it will be not only possible but also essential to re-accelerate through each trough.

To windward in swell and light air

Let us assume the worst case – that light air blows in the same direction as the swell.

As light air fades toward calm, a point must be reached at which the downwind (orbital) speed of water in the crests will match or equal the speed of the wind. In this situation, the Apparent Wind will become calm or even reverse as each crest is approached and traversed. Clearly, the boat speed which can be acquired on the way downhill, and in the restored very light air through the trough, cannot be much. This very small starting speed will soon be lost as the boat climbs the next long face and at the same time loses all power due to being deprived of Apparent Wind. The end result will be that a boat which is handled normally will either stop completely, or even begin to sail backwards. Fortunately, these conditions are not encountered often, but when they are, those boats which can maintain some sort of movement will draw away from all the rest. The key in this situation is to turn beam-on to the waves whilst on each advancing face. In this way the boat will be lifted bodily but will suffer no resistance increase, and so will maintain some speed and manoeuvre capability as the crest approaches. At the crest, the boat should be turned on to a close reaching course while it sails down the receding back of the wave and through the trough, where there will be increased Apparent Wind. It can then be turned cross-wave again across the next rising face. It's tedious and it's slow, but it's the fastest technique and it works.

To windward when the swell rolls across the wind

The Apparent Wind will change wave by wave due to the cross-wind orbital flows within each crest and trough. The lighter the wind, the more important will this factor become. To keep the sails full and driving it will be necessary to both steer and retrim sails on a wave by wave basis, Depending on the relative directions of the wind and the swell it will sometimes be possible to gain advantage by steering so as to maximise the time spent in stronger wind, or in favourably moving orbital current, or sailing downhill. Each situation will be different. A practical example – one which increases performance – will illustrate the strange things that can happen when the wind direction and the swell direction are not the same..

Strong sustained winds around deep depressions in the Southern Ocean – the roaring forties – sometimes generate huge waves which later arrive at the New South Wales coast as a southerly swell with an interval between crests of eight to ten seconds. The orientation of the harbour entrance focusses this swell, still from the south. The most common summer wind is the north-easterly sea breeze. So boats which race near the Heads frequently encounter a large ESE swell while sailing in a NE wind.

When close-hauled on port tack in these conditions the boat is carried to the left by each crest, so the Apparent Wind backs and strengthens for three or four seconds in eight to ten knot winds and a great deal longer in lighter airs. In the troughs the boat is carried to the right and the Apparent Wind veers. The fastest technique is to steer a snaking course which not only maintains a constant angle to the Apparent Wind, but also maximises the time spent in the windward-going flow in the crests, and minimises the time in the downwind-going flow in the troughs. (This is the exact reverse of the dynamics to windward in regular waves.)

As each crest approaches the Apparent Wind backs and strengthens as the boat is carried bodily to the left. The boat can be luffed and sailed, slightly bow down as it traverses across the advancing face, and pointed high to extreme – the higher you can point it the longer you will stay in the crest where the orbital flow carries you to windward. After the crest has passed but a little before the Apparent Wind goes lighter, you need to bear away very firmly and ease sheets slightly. The turn downwind needed to keep the sails full and the hiking crew fully loaded is far more than would be expected, but there are two advantages in doing so. The first is that it keeps the crew fully 'hiked' and so maintains a constant drive force and constant speed, But far more importantly the turn moves the boat quickly across the trough in which the water is moving to leeward, and so reduces the time that the boat spends in the adversely moving water. The end result is that this technique greatly increases the proportion of time that the boat spends in the favourably moving water in and near the wave crests and similarly reduces the time in adverse flow. I can vouch from race experience that this technique will outpoint and outfoot any other.

22.24 Handling in waves and rough air

The practical effect of rough water is that the rig oscillates fore and aft in the air as the hull pitches bow-up, bow-down through the waves. This has the effect of momentarily increasing the Apparent Wind speed at the top of the rig by about two knots in the peak gusts as the rig pitches forward, and vice versa as it pitches backwards in the lulls.

That this must increase the gust factor of the Apparent Wind, and therefore the roughness of the wind, is obvious. What is not so obvious is that the distracting commotion of the waves is so dominant that the wind no longer 'feels' rough.

Put simply, all experience indicates that for greatest speed in flat water, the stronger the wind the tighter the sheet should be until the point is reached at which the boat is felt to begin to stagger. Only when this point is reached should the sheet begin to be eased and the vang tightened to increase elasticity. Obviously, this point will be reached much sooner when the wind is rough than when it is normal.

When the water is rough, the situation is different. It turns out to be perfectly easy to sail in strong winds and rough water with a tight sheet and rigid sails and without any sensation of staggering at all, and this is equally true whether the wind is rough or normal. However, we are now certain, from well established and repeated experience, that in these conditions it is faster to use a more elastic rig.

We were particularly fortunate that, in the months preceding the Sydney Tasar world championships in 1985, a number of top-level crews from many classes raced regularly in the same waters. We compared notes freely. It was a boisterous spring and early summer with a good mixture of relatively steady but usually strong north-easterly sea breezes; harsh, rough, thermally-excited and always-strong westerlies; and cool but strong cross-harbour southerlies. When wind was against tide, the water was rough, and wind-waves were everywhere substantial. Traffic created chaotic waves mid-channel. When southerly winds blew across the harbour, we sailed the 'typical' windward legs referred to earlier, with wind-waves at the leeward end, chaotic waves mid harbour, and flat water at the windward end.

This concentrated experience and note-sharing confirmed that, when the water was smooth, and the wind was normal, tight sheets won all the way. However, as soon as the water became rough, the fastest technique proved to be to introduce the twist-open-in-the gust of elasticity long before it was felt to be necessary and this was true whether the wind was normal or rough. Use of taut shrouds is essential to retain a reasonably taut forestay when the mainsheet is eased, and, as always in strong winds, the jib should be sheeted very lightly to ensure no backwind in the mainsail. This has the double advantage – it achieves lowest aerodynamic drag and highest speed to windward as described earlier, and as well it enables the forestay to remain reasonably straight (despite the slacker mainsheet), and the jib to remain well shaped, which makes all this possible.

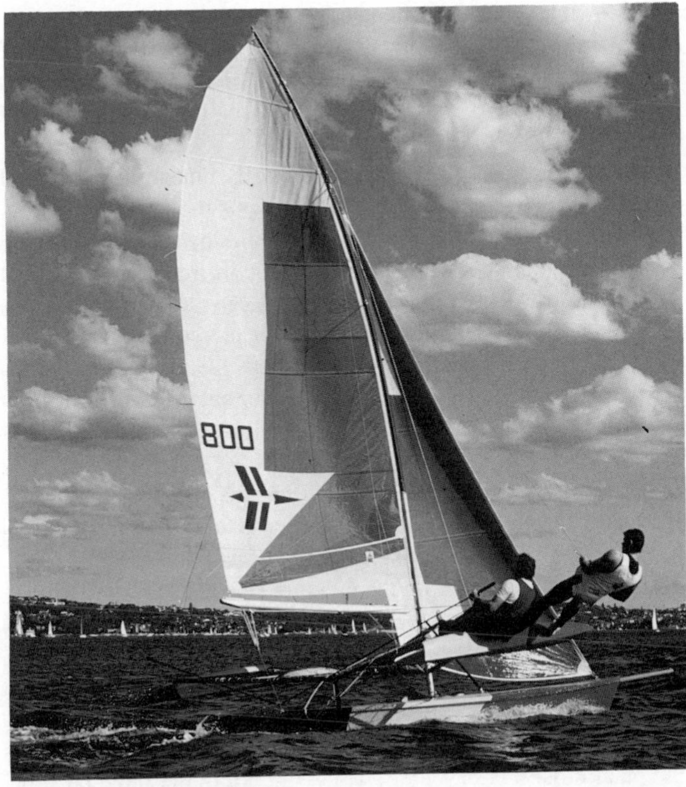

HSP Duo Mk XVIII

Narrow hull scarcely marks the water. Note the length of the bow wave feather.
(Refer also to Fig 20.19, page 261.)

Chapter Twenty Three
Kinetics

23.1 Introduction

When sailing offwind in stronger winds, and on all points of sailing in lighter winds, crews can increase their speed by using the same principles as a bird or insect uses when it applies muscle power to its wings. The lighter the boat, the greater is the opportunity to boost performance beyond that available from the basics of sail shape, sail trim, hull trim, gusts and lulls and also fluctuations.

Kinetics – the co-ordinated movement of sails, steering and body weight – is a subject which has been developed to a high expertise by top-level sailboard and Laser sailors. It can sometimes be a primary determinant of speed when sailing light craft in lighter conditions. All other sailboats can respond to some extent. When skilfully applied at particular times, kinetics can be a critical factor even when racing surprisingly heavy boats.

At the present state of knowledge we can recognise seven separate kinetic mechanisms. Five are understood. Of these, one is negative, and four are positive. The sixth and seventh we know about, but as yet we have no idea how they work. There may be others.

This chapter will focus on the mechanisms – on how kinetics work. Their detailed application will be suggested in later chapters.

23.2 Negative kinetics – the part power pause

If a sail streams in the wind as when tacking, Fig. 23.2.1(a), and is then suddenly trimmed to its working angle, a force is developed instantly but it is only about half the final force. Fig. 23.2.1(b) shows the streamlines at the instant of trimming. Fig. 23.2.1(c) shows the flow pattern a few seconds later after the sail has moved through the wind about six of its own lengths. For example, if a sail has an average chord of six feet, and is sailing to windward in a True Wind of 7 knots – say an Apparent Wind of 10 knots or 17 feet per second – flow (b) will develop as the sail is trimmed, but flow (c) will not be fully developed until at least 40 feet of wind has flowed past the sail. This will take about three seconds. In light airs it will take six to ten seconds.

The difference between the flow and pressure patterns of (b) and (c) above is that in (b) no speed differences have had time to develop – the flow speed is everywhere still about the same as in Fig. 23.2.1(a). In (c) an area of high pressure has developed to windward of the sail. This slows the approaching air which further increases its pressure. This pressure field deflects the air not only in front of the sail, but also in front of itself. Over the suction surface the reverse action has taken place – a suction area has developed and the approaching air accelerates as it approaches this area of lower pressure and so further lowers the pressure due to the increased speed. So the fully developed flow pattern has a pressure field, a suction field, the air deflected through bigger angles, and faster flow over its suction surface. This approximately doubles the initial force. This 'part power' period after trimming can be thought of as a 'part power pause'.

These changes can be watched and felt in the simplest kitchen experiment. (For this one, the bathroom is probably better unless you have a very big basin.) If you take something shaped like a sail such as a big server or small saucer, and move it steadily through the water from a standing start and at a sensible angle, you can see how the flow changes and the water builds up higher on the pressure side and falls away lower on the suction side as the foil moves a few lengths from its starting point. Once you get the feel for it, you can feel the force increase against your fingers.

If the sail were to suddenly vanish, momentum would preserve the flow pattern for awhile, but without the sail to fix its position, the whole pattern would be swept downwind. An analogy is to hold a stick in a flowing stream. So long as the stick is there it makes a pattern of swirls in the water which start at the stick. When you take the stick out of the water the pattern itself persists for awhile, but not in the same position. It is instantly swept downstream. So it is with the sail. If anything happens to reduce the sail's efficiency – if it is allowed to stream for a moment (you dropped the sheet), or if the wind flow slows for a moment (as when the masthead sweeps backwards when the bow rises in waves) – the fully developed flow pattern will immediately begin to wash downstream with respect to the sail. It needs only half a second for it to wash right across the sail and off the leech in a ten knot Apparent Wind. This is why force is lost so quickly when the rig saws backwards and forwards in the air when the hull pitches in waves.

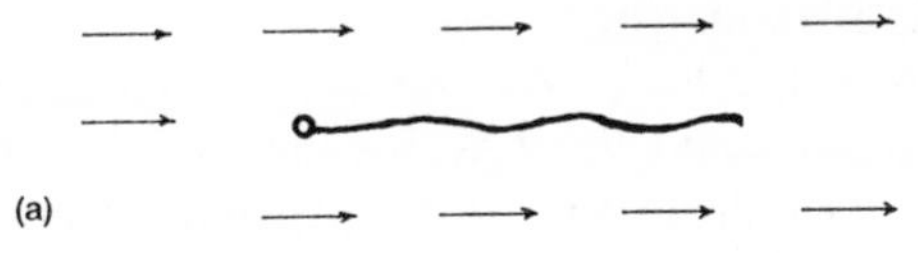

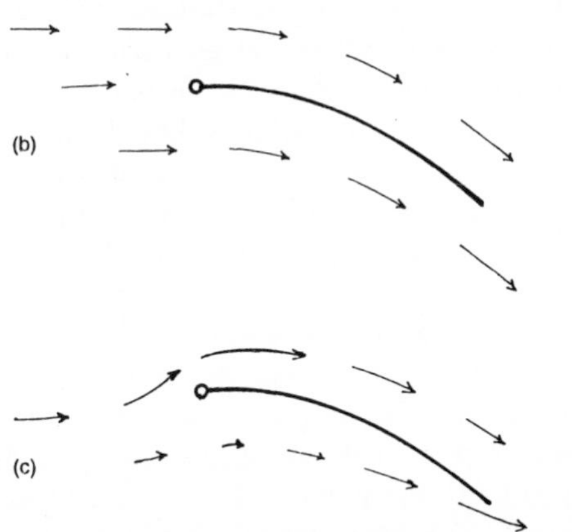

(a) Trim and flow while tacking. Speed direction and pressure everywhere the same.
(b) Flow at instant of trimming after tack. Direction has changed. Speed and pressure have not yet had time to change. Force developed is small.
(c) Flow a few seconds later. Speed, direction and pressure have all changed. Force developed is about double force at (b).

Fig 23.2.1 Change of airflow immediately after trimming

Fig. 23.2.2 shows these two concepts as impulse – how force changes with time. Let us assume that a dinghy with 125 square feet of sail area tacks and sails to windward in a 7 knot True Wind – say 10 knots or 17 feet per second of Apparent Wind speed, and flat water. A total sail force of 20 pounds would be typical at the instant that the sail was trimmed. Fig. 23.2.2(a) shows this, and how the total force develops and becomes 40 pounds after three or four seconds.

Let us now assume that the boat sails past a point and into waves 14 feet long and one foot high which it meets once each second. If the pitching causes the masthead to move backwards and forwards one foot, then the maximum speed of the masthead relative to the wind will be about 4 feet per second (it will move forward one foot in one quarter of a second, be steady for one quarter of a second, etc.) so the minimum Apparent Wind speed will fall from 17 feet per second to 13 feet per second for one quarter of a second each second. Force changes as the square of the speed. 13 times 13 is only about half 17 times 17. So whether the force falls because the Apparent Wind speed falls or because the pattern has been swept backwards makes no difference – the force drops to about half, the sail is in a 'part power pause' state and the flow pattern has to start building again. In the next three quarters of a second the sail will pass through about 12 feet or two 'chord wind-runs' of wind, and will recover some of the force lost. Then the masthead will sweep backwards again as the cycle repeats. This is shown in Fig. 23.2.2(b). The mean force developed in these waves will be about 27 pounds, or only about 67% of the force developed in flat water. The power loss due to small waves in a moderate breeze is as great as that!

This is kinetics in reverse – the negative mechanism. I have included it to emphasise the point that whatever the conditions and however you sail, every effort should be made to keep the rig as steady as possible in the wind, so that it can develop *and retain* force, flow and pattern in their right position across the sail. Otherwise the slow build from about half-power has to start again every time they are lost.

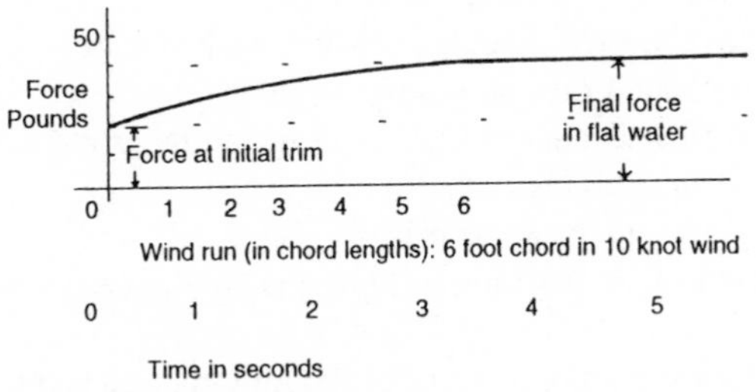

(a) Change of force with time after initial trim.

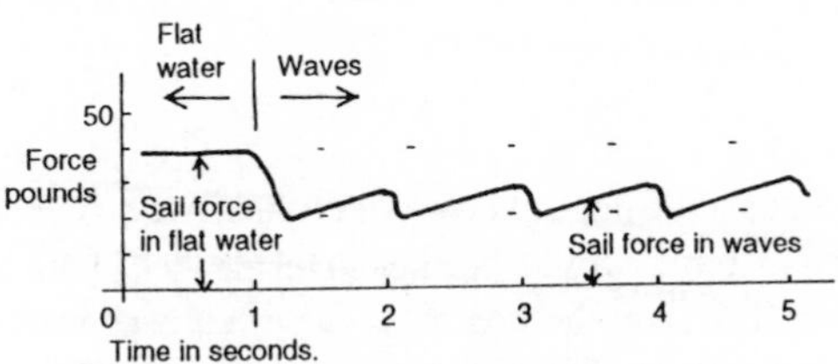

(b) Change of sail force due to pitching in waves.

Fig 23.2.2. Change of sail force after trimming and in waves

23.3 Positive kinetics

Let us now look at the positive kinetic mechanisms. We can do no better than to consult the experts – the bee, the humming bird, the eagle, the albatross – and some fish.

Creatures like the mosquito, the bee and the humming bird are prepared to work to fly. They use their own muscles. They can fly for as long as their energy lasts. Beating their wings to support their weight requires intense and sustained effort. Not surprisingly they have developed very efficient techniques to give them the greatest lift for the least work.

At the other end of the scale, sea-birds such as the albatross and the gannet can fly effortlessly by using dynamic soaring when there is enough wind; they use the difference in speed between the slowed wind within a few inches of the surface and the much stronger wind a few metres higher up. So long as the mean wind speed is stronger than six knots these birds can fly indefinitely. As soon as it falls lighter than six knots the nature of the boundary layer changes (Figs 3.1 and 3.2)(Part One) and the speed difference becomes smaller and blurred and is no longer adequate for dynamic soaring. In winds of six knots or more these birds can fly indefinitely. In light airs of five knots or less they must either beat their wings to fly, or stop flying.

Sailboats have some of the characteristics of both groups. They exploit the difference in speed between the wind and the water. When they are running straight downwind they are like the hovering insect. When they are sailing crosswind they are more like the sea-birds. And like the albatross, in stronger winds they have available to them more power than they can use. But as the wind becomes lighter, they have two choices. Either they can sail more slowly as the wind fails, or their crews can start 'beating their wings'. If they beat them skilfully, they can sail significantly faster.

In the natural aerodynamics sense, the notes in Chapter 17 (How Sails Work)(Part Three) apply to the steady state conditions of an aircraft in cruising flight, or an albatross soaring effortlessly in a breeze. To the sailor this approach is absolutely basic, because accurate sail shape and sail trim is the primary determinant of boat speed. What follows here is the icing on the cake – how best to achieve extra speed at critical moments, particularly in the lighter winds.

Birds and insects which beat their wings apply their muscle power to the wind in four different ways. These are:

Impulse
Impulse + energy-recovery
Impulse + pumping
Surging.

No insect nor bird bothers to use pumping in isolation; it is always combined with impulse.

Impulse, and the more sophisticated impulse + energy-recovery, can be applied by the helmsman or crew of any boat when it is running square or nearly so, i.e. with separated flow across the sails.

When boats are broad reaching or reaching, i.e. when the flow is attached to the sails, pumping can be used by the crews of boats which cannot be rolled (yachts and catamarans).

Impulse + pumping can be used by crews of lightweight boats which can be rolled.

Surging can be used when sailing close-hauled, close reaching or reaching in light airs by the crews of lightweight boats which can be rolled.

(Note – The word 'pumping' is so well established in sailing literature to describe the moving of a sail to windward by a crew in situations where kinetics are employed, that I will continue to use it in this sense. It also has the special technical meaning 'the momentary retention of attached flow at abnormally large trim angles'. It will be obvious from the text which meaning applies, and that there are many different ways of pumping.)

23.4 Impulse

The inefficient extreme of impulse is the butterfly, a light insect with huge wings which beat with feeble uncoordinated strokes to achieve erratic flight. The efficient extreme would be the hovering bee, which moves its wings so rapidly on the downstroke that, despite their tiny size, the tips move at some respectable fraction of the speed of sound and so develop a considerable pressure pulse with each downstroke. This is the buzz that we hear. The bee can support both its own weight plus its payload on its diminutive wings solely because it beats them downwards so fast. The upstrokes are relatively languid.

The sailing analogy of the hovering bee is the sailboat or sailboard which is running 'square' when sailing downwind. The Apparent Wind is at about right angles to the sail, so the force on the sail is pure 'flat plate drag' and is proportional to the square of the speed of the Apparent Wind. If a sail is set square across the wind and held steady, the force will be steady. But if the sail is moved back and forth against the wind the movement will change the speed of the Apparent Wind from moment to moment and the force will not be steady. Because of the 'speed squared' factor the increases in force will be greater than the decreases. Some examples will show how this works.

Let us imagine that a boat is running square at four knots directly down an eight knot breeze. The Apparent Wind will be four knots and the force per square foot of sail area will be about one ounce. Now imagine that the crew start pumping their sails by drawing them sharply back against the wind at a speed of four knots – 6.9 feet per second – for half a second and then allow them to blow forward for the next half second. The force in the doubled Apparent Wind speed of the back-stroke would then be four times as great, or four ounces per square foot for half the time and nothing for the other half. This would give an average of two ounces per square foot, or double the steady-state drive force. If the 'pump' speed were to be faster yet – say 20 feet per second, or 2 feet in one tenth of a second, followed by a pause of three tenths of a second, then the force during the backstroke would be 16 ounces per square foot, and nothing for the other three quarters of the time, and the average force would become 4 ounces per square foot. This is how bees and mosquitoes fly. The fact that they make a lot of noise – compared with butterflies which don't – indicates how sharp and forceful are their downstrokes. At about this point the analogy ceases to be useful. Insects turn their wings through about 90 degrees so that they cut through the air 'edge first' on their relatively languid upstroke.

Sails cannot do this. Another point is that if a sail is pumped too vigorously in very light winds it so stirs up the air in its vicinity as to turn what was a tailwind into a virtual headwind until the fuss dies down. In the meantime the boat stops. This puts a practical limit to enthusiasm. This is another 'part power pause', but is due to a different mechanism.

This principle can be experienced directly if you draw a saucer through water in the manner of a mainsail which is running 'square'. First move it steadily, and feel the force. Then move it in a series of pulses. As you get the feel, use all your strength to make the pulses as short and as sharp as possible. It will become obvious that the sharper the impulse, the greater will be the resistance of the saucer, and that its feel of 'solidity' in the water when it is pulsed in this way is many times the force of the slow steady-state stroke.

While the principle above holds true, regardless of whether the wing or sail is moved a few inches or several feet, the practical consequence of moving a sail too far is the break-up of airflow mentioned above. Impulse pumping, when running square, has to be tuned to the wind and the waves of the moment, and adjustment of the mainsail to its optimum elasticity is critical. The powerful single sweep of the mainsail, timed to promote surfing on one particular wave in stronger winds, is well known. But in lighter winds all that this technique does is to create such a swirl in the air that the mainsail lies 'dead' in an area of no wind until the swirl lives its local life and then blows away, and the boat slows instead of sailing faster. In light winds very short, sharp subtle movements, which from the outside appear no more than a shimmering of a springy leech, are much more effective, and they are even more effective when they are synchronised with the pitching of the boat in tiny waves.

23.5 Energy recovery

The humming bird, when hovering, is a perfect example of the combination of impulse plus recovery of energy. Another kitchen experiment will introduce the important factors. If you repeat the pulsing experiment suggested above, and watch the action of the water, you will note that with each pulse, from 'a' to 'b' in Fig. 23.5.1(a), two swirls form close to the edges as sketched at 'i' and 'i'. These both move away 'downwards' as indicated at positions 'ii' and 'iii'. But if the foil is angled a little and then pulsed, as from 'a' to 'b' in Fig. 23.5.1(b), the swirl nearer the edge which trails becomes much larger and initially it moves away in an 'upward' direction as indicated by 'i', 'ii' and 'iii' before it curves and begins to move downwards as at 'iv' and 'v'. In this situation much of the energy initially put into the down stroke appears as the momentum of the spin in this large swirl.

The hovering humming bird moves its wings in a special pattern which enables it to recover almost all of this momentum. This is sketched in Fig. 23.5.2. The first strong downstroke of the slightly angled wing is represented by positions 1, 2 and 3. The wings then turn to feather edge-on, like a sculler's oar, for the upstroke at 4 as they move toward position 5. 5, 6 and 7 represent the second sharp downstroke. Note that the wing tip has displaced itself far enough from the initial downstroke to take full advantage of the upward speed of the up-going half of the swirl – at 'x', 'x', 'x' in Fig 23.5.1 – caused by the previous downstroke. The down-going wing meets this up-going air and so enjoys the 'solidity' of almost double the stroke speed. The wing is also angled slightly the other way so that the swirl from the second stroke appears at the right time and spinning the other way at position 9 or 1. The wing feathers again, but the other way, for the second upstroke from 7 through 8 to 9 or 1 and the cycle repeats.

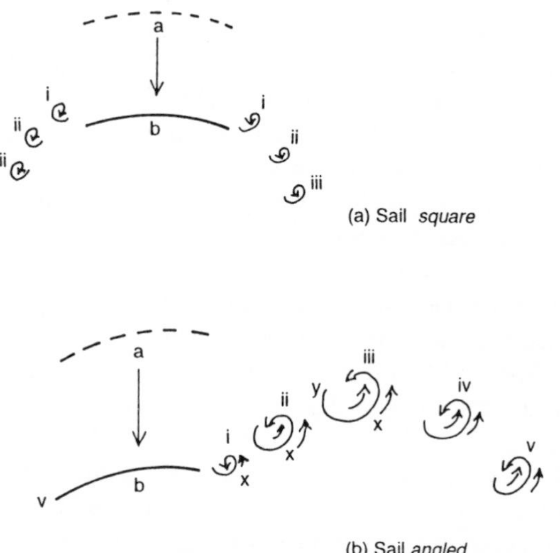

(a) Sail *square*

(b) Sail *angled*

Fig 23.5.1 Flows near *Square* and *Angled* pulsed sails.

(9)
1 5
2 6
3 4 8 7

(a) Angle of wing at each stage of cycle.

9
1 8 5
2 6
3 4 7

(b) Locus of wing tip movement during each cycle.

Fig 23.5.2 Movement of Humming Bird's wing.

The sailing analogy of the hovering humming bird is again the yacht or sailboard running square. While even the most skilled sailboard sailor is unlikely to match the humming bird's mastery of technique, the principles remain valid. Whenever a sail is pumped, the air over the area of the sail will be accelerated 'backwards', while that around the edges of the sail will be accelerated forwards. Particularly in moderate windspeeds and when on a point of sailing which is close to a square run, i.e. when either running slightly by the lee as in Lasers, Finns, etc, or slightly toward a broad reach, a situation can sometimes be created where the downwind-going part of a swirl from the previous pump will be positioned close to the leech. A pump applied against this momentarily stronger wind will give a very much more powerful impulse than one which is applied at any other time. Every helmsman will be familiar with the experience, when applying a succession of pumps, that they sometimes become more 'solid' and effective. This is what is happening.

At the other extreme, sometimes the force progressively diminishes to the point where the sail just 'comes back' because there no longer seems to be any wind speed to work against. This will occur either because the pumping has been too vigorous as noted above, or because the leech is in the windward-going part of the swirl ('y' in Fig. 23.5.1) instead of the downwind-going part.

The optimum stroke and frequency will depend upon the size of the mainsail, the wind speed and the exact point of sailing. The important fact is that whenever you run near-square, there must always be some unique combination of stroke length and frequency which will add more speed than any other. All that is needed to find it, is a very open mind and a little experimenting.

Start with a very tight leech and a sensible stroke length – very short in lighter airs, progressively longer in stronger winds. Use very sharp back movements but slow frequency. Speed up the frequency until you feel the back-load increase and then keep speeding up until you feel it diminish – which it will. Having found the optimum frequency, systematically change the stroke length and the elasticity of the leech and optimise both. Always keep the back-stroke sharp. If you repeat this sequence in flat water and different wind strengths, you will soon develop a feel for what works best in your boat in each condition. Keep a very open mind about what may be the fastest technique, because so often it bears no resemblance to the vigorous 'rowing with the sails' which is so often assumed. Particularly in lighter airs, an almost invisible shimmering of the leech seems to be the fastest technique.

Two examples from personal experience indicate the more delicate end of the range. At a European championships at an English Channel port, the downwind legs in one light air race were in 3 to 6 inch waves and against a 1.5 knot tide, so were unusually long. In the light air, any gross pumping or coarse body movement would have slowed the boat. But a little experimenting paid off. I adjusted the vang until the springiness of the mast-mainsail system was such that a sharp tug applied to the mid-point of the vang sent a 2 to 3 inch ripple up the leech. I found that if I tugged twice at about a one second interval each time the bow dipped to the following waves, the boat speed increased perceptibly. At the end of each run I was sweating but we had gained about 100 metres on adjacent boats. (At that time three pumps per wave were legal.)

Another unusual example was at an Australian championships in Melbourne. In this case, on the last leg of one race a failing northerly died and was replaced by the faint beginnings of a southerly sea breeze, so the final 'beat' became a light-air run, but against tiny waves left over from the earlier northerly. All the boats in the fleet pitched bow-up, bow-down in these waves and the performance loss was severe. I experimented and found that an adaptation of the humming bird's beat worked best. I used the same 'leech ripple' technique noted above but in these conditions timed each pulse so that the backward-going ripple arrived at the upper leech at the same instant that the upper sail was already being driven backwards by the bow-up pitch of the boat. Performance increase in this case was dramatic.

Techniques such as these cause no movements of the boat and rig which are perceptibly different from those of adjacent boats. All boats pitch in waves – all you can do is suppress the movement as much as possible. All leeches ripple a little due to the pitching motion. All that is different is that these leeches ripple in a different way.

My observations at a recent Australian Olympic selection trials make an interesting commentary on the notes above. The waters of St Vincent's Gulf, near Adelaide, South Australia, are in constant movement, so in all the lighter-wind races the wind and sea conditions on the downwind legs were such that kinetics were dominant. In these conditions the techniques of the 470 and the Finn sailors fell into four groups.

Some used no kinetics and relied upon smoothness. They didn't win.

Some used one particular stroke and frequency to catch selected waves. They did well.

Some used one particular stroke and frequency almost all the time. They did less well.

I overheard one coach's comments: 'Just because pumping occasionally makes you go faster, pumping ten times as much doesn't make you go ten times faster. Back off a bit. Sail smoothly until you select the wave you want to catch.'

One or two crews used kinetics almost all of the time, but they used different techniques which ranged from the vigorous to the delicate. They matched their kinetics to the constantly changing wind and sea state conditions. They won.

23.6 Overtrimming (pumping)

If the trim angle of a full sail is increased slowly, the force will increase to a maximum as at 'e' in Fig. 17.33 (Part Three). As the trim angle is further increased the flow will separate and the force will fall to a lower level as at 'f'. Fig. 23.6.1(a) repeats part of Fig. 17.33.

If a sail is trimmed to the angle which gives maximum force, 'e' in Fig. 23.6.1(a), and the wind remains steady, the force will remain constant as at 'e' in Figs 23.6.1(b), (c), etc. This is representative of the reaching and broad reaching situation, in which you will be looking for the absolute maximum of power when the flow is attached.

If the trim angle is increased very quickly, momentum will keep the flow over the suction surface moving toward the leech for a brief period – perhaps half a second to one second – and until the flow comes to rest it will not separate. During this period the sail will develop greater force than its normal maximum, as at 'g' in Fig. 23.6.1(a). As soon as the suction-side flow comes to rest, the flow will separate and the force will fall to 'f'. Fig. 23.6.1(b) shows this mechanism, again as an impulse. The extra power (shown shaded) is there, but it is only momentary.

If the trim angle is increased very quickly, held for an instant, and then reduced at a rate so that the flow never quite stops and so never separates, the extra power can be enjoyed for an instant, and relinquished without sacrificing the sail's pre-pump 'maximum power' trim. Fig. 23.6.1(c) shows one cycle of this mechanism, again as an impulse. Again, the extra power is indicated by shading. It can be repeated indefinitely. A second cycle is indicated, dotted.

The drive force on the boat will normally be proportional to the area under the curve. Fig 23.6.1(c) suggests that, compared with the maximum steady force that can be achieved with accurate trimming, skilful 'pumping' (overtrimming followed by almost immediate release) can increase the drive force from most sails by a useful amount. There will be big difference in the penalty for poor technique (shown in (b)). It will be negligible for mainsails behind conventional masts because there will be little difference between forces 'e' and 'f'. It will be severe for headsails and spinnakers and wingmast rigs where the difference between 'e' and 'f' is substantial.

If you move a sail-like foil through a big basin of water, not 'square' nor slightly angled off-square as in Fig. 23.5.1(b) but angled for maximum lift with attached flow, you can get a feel through your fingers for the maximum force. If you then try suddenly increasing the angle a little, you will be able to feel the surge in force and feel also its almost immediate collapse as you see the flow separate. If you suddenly increase the angle and as quickly reduce it again, you will be able to feel the Fig. 23.6.1(c) pulse, and also see how this technique enables the flow to remain attached.

In craft such as keelboats and catamarans in which the weight of the crew can do little to roll the boat, pumping as described is about the limit to which a crew can make the boat go faster on any reaching leg. In lighter and more sensitive craft, more is possible.

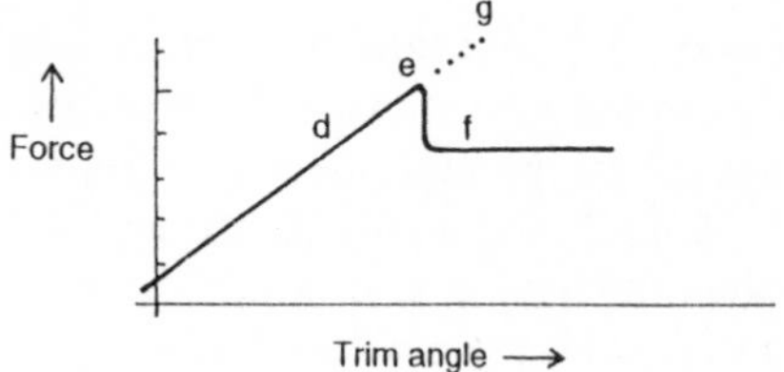

(a) Change of force with trim angle (from Fig 17.33).

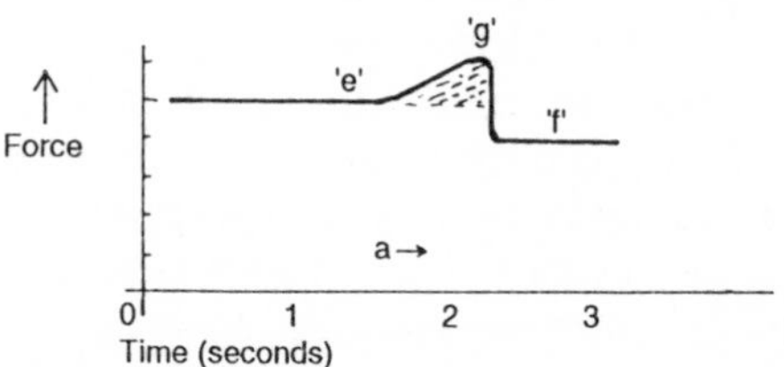

Change of force with time when trim angle is increased suddenly and held steady.
'e' = Sail trimmed as e above.
a = Trim angle suddenly increased.
'g' = Momentary higher force, prior to separation of flow.
'f' = Final force after separation

(b)

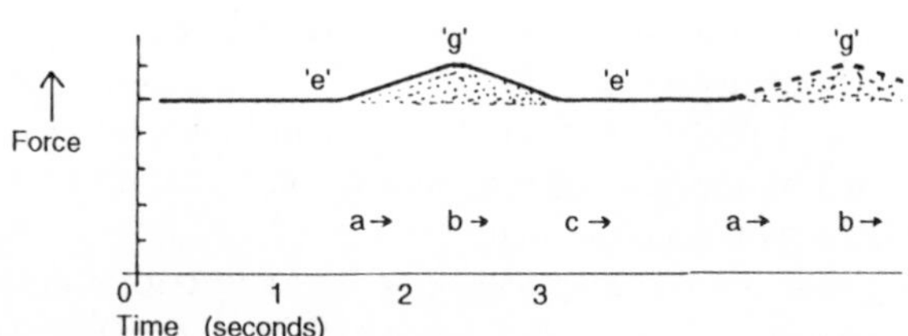

Change of force with time when trim angle is increased suddenly, and then released.
'e' = Sail trimmed as at e in (a) above.
a = Trim angle suddenly increased.
'g' = Momentarily higher force.
b = Trim angle reduced to about d in (a) above.
c = Trim angle restored to e

(c)

Fig 23.6.1 Overtrimming *pumping* mechanism

23.7 Combined impulse and pumping

I am not certain who coined the term 'kinetics' but it encapsulates perfectly the difference between the relatively gross pumping, rocking and 'ooching' which have figured in sailing literature for decades and which various rules have endeavoured to govern from time to time, and the skilled subtlety of modern practice. An example: the paragraphs above have described 'pumping'. Pumping by itself, at best, can give a slight urge to a boat. The added sail force will also roll the boat to leeward slightly, But if a pump of the sails is combined with a movement of the body which flicks the topmast of a light boat to windward by only a few inches – much less than the pump would have moved it to leeward – the result can be a massive kick which can propel the boat from behind a wave onto its face.

Many years ago I introduced the Tasar to a very good Laser sailor. We were tacking downwind in a 15 knot sea breeze and sparkling waves off Brisbane. Martin asked me how the Tasar responded to kinetics. I responded that I didn't know, and what were kinetics? He said 'let's find out'. What followed I have never seen duplicated. He picked a set of approaching waves, turned somewhat crosswind in the preceding trough, pumped hard twice, then applied a third pump together with a co-ordinated turn to put the boat neatly onto the advancing wave face. We surfed cleanly for the life of that wave. He caught the next similarly, and the next. So far so good. This was the expert pumping and surfing which I expected from a top-level sailor.

But what happened next surprised me. Inevitably the time came when he missed one. Instead of conceding and going for the next wave behind us, he applied about four quick, powerful 'urges'. Each was a combination of a sharp impulsive roll to windward plus a snap pump which stopped and reversed the roll. The sheet was released almost immediately – it was not held 'in' for more than an instant. Each roll was achieved by contracting the stomach muscles sharply and would not have moved the topmast to windward by more than about six inches. With each urge, the Tasar jumped forward about two feet, and by the third or fourth urge – they were all delivered within the space of about two seconds – we were established and surfing down the face of a wave which a moment before had been ahead and unattainable. Martin is not a big man. What he applied was skill, not brawn.

You can get a 'feel' for this technique with another kitchen experiment. For this one set yourself up with the biggest area of water possible – I used the corner of an outdoor pool. Take a slightly curved server; ideally it should be about the size of your hand. Get a feel for the maximum steady-state force achievable by moving the server through the water at steady speed – say one foot per second – at the maximum angle which will retain attached flow. Note particularly that the water some inches ahead of the server is not moved by its approach, regardless of the speed at which you move it.

Now for the fun. The object is to increase the force developed by the server to the point where the water ahead of it moves. It is worth taking this experiment seriously, because what works with the server will work with your sails when you race. I find it best to repeat rapidly a series of short, sharp strokes, in each of which the whole server starts by moving toward me about half an inch, at which point the 'leading edge' stops but the trailing edge continues to move toward me for another half inch. It is vital that the stroke starts with the 'impulse' action and finishes with the 'pumping' action. Immediately relax and let the server wash away from you and return to its optimum angle, to restore the normal flow pattern. The optimum frequency seems to be about three per second. The added force when I found the optimum stroke and frequency was easily felt. Most importantly, the water well ahead of the server began to move to 'leeward'. This was absolute proof that substantial extra force was being developed. Keep experimenting until you find and can repeat the effective technique, and can recognise when it is and when it isn't working – and why.

Apply this knowledge in sailing your boat on the water. Practise until you know exactly what rate of movement and what degree of movement applies the greatest propulsive force to your boat in particular conditions and on particular points of sailing. Charlie McKee is a 470 bronze medallist. He suggests that the sail should be drawn in about twice as fast as it is let out, and that the repetitions should be as fast as possible. Martin McLean makes the point that the impulsive roll to windward must precede the pump, and that it is ideal if the masthead moves no more than about four inches. Those who race boats hard in Adelaide's big waves make the psychological point 'You should never give up, mentally, the determination to catch the wave ahead'. The relaxed attitude which I most admire is that of one world champion – 'Isn't it nice to have some waves to play in'.

As a coach, I observe that the concept of 'pumping' which is commonly held, is wrong. It may be helpful to describe what I usually see when I ask somebody to show me how he/she pumps. The helmsman leans inwards to initiate a roll to leeward and frees the sheet a little, then leans outwards to roll the boat to windward *but brings the sheet with him as he leans out.* This action is repeated. The boat does not sail faster, because the sail is pumped before the roll. The flow separates, and stays separated until the sheet is eased momentarily prior to the next roll to windward. The force developed by the roll is too much across the boat, and does not drive it forward. The repetition frequency is far too slow. The contrast between this and the explosive thrusts that Martin McLean achieved, reveals just how important it is to develop the proper technique.

In recent years a number of wildlife programmes with truly superb close-up photography of birds in flight have appeared on TV and in the cinemas. I can offer the student of kinetics no better advice than to watch the way in which these masters of flight apply kinetics. During the final phase of slowing as they approach to alight at the nest, eagles employ a powerful but delicate blend of impulse plus pumping. This is very powerful but the strokes are so short and quick that they produce a rhythmic rippling of the feather tips at the wings' trailing edges. The ruffling of tuft-like feathers on the wings' upper surfaces show that this technique does indeed maintain attached flow at impossibly slow speeds and very large angles.

Sailboarders are able to use this action almost exactly during the acceleration phase of a beach-start race. The contestants run, carrying their sailboards, from dry land into the water, where they leap on board and pump to accelerate. Except in the strongest winds they vibrate their wishbones with great strength at a high frequency and through a small angle. The tensed leeches vibrate to and fro a few inches in sympathy, with wavelike motions of the sailcloth starting at the clew and flowing both up the leech to the masthead, and down the leech to the tack. This 'leech shimmer', like the fast rhythmic ripple of the eagle's trailing edge feathers, is a very efficient mechanism and the sailboarders accelerate quickly. As soon as they reach the 'Design Apparent Wind' speed, the overt kinetics cease. There is no point in working to add more energy after the speed has been reached where nature already provides more than enough.

Another situation where this sort of leech-ripple pumping is routinely used is in Eighteen footer sailing just after tacking in moderate winds. These very light boats lose way during the tack, but the crews move out onto the wing without hesitation. As soon as the mainsail fills the sheet hand starts pumping the mainsheet with sharp, very quickly repeated movements. The resultant leech ripple both supports the crew's weight on the wing, and also accelerates the boat very quickly. As with the sailboarders, as soon as the boat is up to design Apparent Wind speed, the pumping stops. But if the boat enters a lull which is lighter than anticipated, the response is to bear away slowly and start pumping again. This holds the wing up and maintains speed and gives the forward hand enough time to move smoothly as he goes inboard far enough to restore balance.

The availability of this kind of added thrust makes it possible for light boats which move freely on the surface of the water to surf surprisingly small waves in lighter winds. The basic situation is that except for the faster high-performance craft, boats usually sail downwind at about half the wind speed, while the waves typically roll at about two thirds of the wind speed. Surfing the bigger waves in stronger winds has been part of sailing for decades. But with skilful kinetics it is often possible to match the speed of and surf a surprising proportion of small waves too.

23.8 Surging

Surging is the only kinetic technique which can be used when sailing to windward.

When an eagle, a pelican, or any of the great ocean-ranging sea-birds takes off it uses the same impulse and/or pumping techniques with relatively fast wing-beats to become airborne and accelerate as are routinely employed by the bee or the humming bird. But as soon as its speed is sufficient for its wings to carry its weight without 'pumping', its wing-beats slow and it adopts an altogether different mechanism. It no longer needs extra lift. The bird's dynamic purpose changes from the 'lift regardless of the effort needed' required for take-off, to the 'forward thrust with minimum effort and minimum drag' needed for steady sustained flight. I call this mechanism 'surging'.

The mechanism which is revealed by the wildlife pictures of great birds in flight is the obvious model. When photographed from directly behind, the wing action is seen to be:

An upbeat during which the wings are untwisted and are at about the angle which one would expect them to be if the bird were gliding. Indeed, on the occasions when beating stops, the wings simply maintain this shape while the bird glides or soars.

A downbeat which starts with the whole wing twisting down a little. From directly behind the underside of the wing cannot be seen during the upstroke, but during the downstroke the trailing edge rises and you can see a little of the underside. On those occasions when there is sufficient time and repetition to observe closely, it can be seen that during the downstroke the wing is twisted least at the root and a little more at the tip.

At the end of each downbeat the wingtip of an eagle makes a separate triple action; it simultaneously twists its leading edge downwards further, and makes a strong 'impulse' movement which is both downwards and also backwards. This tip action is distinct from the rest of the wing and the rest of the stroke. The end-of-stroke tip action of the longer-winged albatross is similar but not nearly so pronounced. At the conclusion of this 'tip-flick' the whole wing smoothly untwists and commences its relatively languid upstroke.

This surging motion is a very efficient propulsive mechanism which is used for cruising flight. It has nothing to do with the explosive outburst of beating energy which is needed for take-off or for acceleration for the hunt or to evade the hunter.

A sailboat can duplicate the surging motion almost exactly, particularly if it has a relatively tall rig with plenty of mainsail area high up (elliptical is better than triangular) and the ability to roll gently without too much drag penalty. The technique is to allow the boat to roll, very slowly, to leeward. In light air the roll should be so slow and smooth that the sail continues to drive in its normal manner. If the point of sailing is close- hauled, it will be necessary to point a little lower than the steady-state optimum to compensate for the leeward-going motion of the upper sail during this slow roll to leeward. At whatever point is judged to be the leeward extreme of the roll, the sheet should be eased a few inches to allow the leech to twist a little more open, and the boat rolled gently to windward. A rate of roll about double that of the leeward-going roll is about right. It must be so gentle and smooth that the fragile attached flow across the sail is not disturbed. As the boat reaches the vertical, a firm but not abrupt pull on the mainsheet will give an added impulse of thrust, and will stop the windward-going roll. The cycle can be repeated immediately because the flow has remained attached throughout. There is nothing critical about this technique; it can be used with long strokes or with short strokes, intermittently or continuously. In suitable craft – Ten square metre sliding-seat canoes would be close to the ideal, but most dinghies surge well – it can provide a tremendous performance boost on the light air, close-hauled, close reaching and reaching points of sailing.

It is a particularly useful technique to use when, during a light air race, a wave set from a passing motor-boat slows your boat. In this situation the rolling of the boat on the waves is natural. There is no ethical reason why you should not adjust the last two or three rolls to your own advantage, and use them as part of a surging sequence to reaccelerate your boat to regain speed.

23.9 Other possible techniques

All the techniques described above have involved a horizontal movement of the sail which has been achieved by either pumping – swinging the leech but not the mast to windward; or rolling – moving the upper sails but not the lower sails to windward; or impulse – moving the whole sail bodily to windward by pulling the whole wishbone to windward in the case of a sailboard sailor, or by simultaneous pumping of both the spinnaker sheet and brace (guy) in the case of a spinnaker trimmer. It is not generally appreciated that there are other planes in which to work, and other ways in which kinetic effort can be applied to achieve forward thrust.

One is demonstrated in nature by the up and down movement of the horizontal tail of a whale, and in human watersports by the similar action of the flexible flippers worn by underwater swimmers. While there is no present way in which the full dynamic cycle can be used by sailboat or sailboard sailors, a part of the cycle is used very effectively by surfboard riders. I refer to the way skilled board riders and some sailboard sailors can accelerate or re-accelerate themselves with the powerful short quickly-repeated downward thrusts which they also call 'pumping'. With this technique they can catch and use waves which are otherwise marginal or unusable, and they can greatly prolong the distance of their surf on a wave which is decaying. There is no technical reason why the crew of a light dinghy should not use similar dynamics for similar advantage.

If you imagine the motion of a whale which swims on its side, you then have the action of every fish with a vertical tail. This can be used by the sailor in two ways: either by sculling with a swept-back rudder, or by pumping with a sail at the stern of a turning boat. The dynamics of sculling are that if strong force us used to drive a swept-back rudder from extreme angle to central, and application of force is then stopped, the rudder action will both drive the boat forward and also start it turning or pivoting. The pivoting causes circular waterflow (and airflow) and in this flow the released rudder will stream to the opposite extreme. Strong force applied the other way, (but, again, only from extreme angle to centre) will drive the boat forward and also start it turning the other way. This cycle, repeated, can propel a boat forward very efficiently. As a handling technique when sailboat racing, this crude sculling is universally frowned upon, but let us look at the further dynamic possibilities.

A crew can use their own body weight to roll a boat for impulse pumping or surging, and they can similarly use it to turn a light boat or sailboard. If, when sailing in flat water, a crew were to turn a boat sharply with body effort, the streaming rudder would immediately deflect in the circular waterflow, and if force were then to be applied to the tiller to arrest the turn by centring the rudder, forward thrust would result. In short, it is not necessary to initiate any turn by hydrodynamic force from the rudder. Momentum will do equally well. Once the boat is turning, the action of centring the rudder will convert much of the angular momentum of the turn into forward thrust.

If we consider this principle as it could apply in waves, the situation becomes really interesting. Think of a fourteen foot boat which is broad reaching at 5 or 6 knots on port tack in an 8 knot breeze. The waves are 8 inches high, 14 feet long and roll downwind at 5 knots, and their orbital speed is approaching one knot.

When the stern is on a crest and the bow in a trough, the orbital flows turn the boat to port by pushing the bow upwind and the stern downwind. This is exactly what you do not want, so you use the rudder to keep the boat heading down the wave face. There is a problem here. The wave crest's orbital flow under the stern already causes the rudder to stream 'no load' at about ten degrees with the tiller to port before you apply further rudder angle to start the boat turning. Let us say that you need another ten degrees of angle to turn to starboard, partly to counter the turn to the left due to the orbital wave action and the rest to start the turn to the right that you want. The rudder angle of 20 degrees across the boat – much more than is usual because it started angled – means that no less than one third of the total rudder force will act in a backward direction.

When the bow is high on a crest and the stern in a trough, wave action turns the boat to the right – again exactly what you do not want, and again an unusually large rudder angle with correspondingly high drag will be needed to turn the bow away from the back of the wave.

If we guess at sensible figures, it might need a ten to fifteen pound force applied for about one quarter of the wave cycle to turn the boat each way, so in this case we estimate at least a three pound drag for half the time, say 1.5 pounds average drag. In the conditions stated the drag of a Laser Two or a Tasar would be about 20 pounds, so in these very typical conditions the rudder drag developed from just steering the boat will be between 5 and 10 per cent of the total drag.

If two boats are racing side by side, and one is steered with the rudder and the other is steered with kinetics, the boat steered with kinetics will escape this rudder drag and sail about 3.5 per cent faster.

If a third boat joins them, and the crew of this boat steer with kinetics but turn the boat more than is needed, so that the rudder streams momentarily the other way, and they immediately arrest these turns by centring he rudder as described above but in this case against the orbital cross-flow , they will sail much faster yet. And if as they turn downwind they give their mainsail a healthy pump, this is just another boost from a good impulse-pump – it is just as effective to drive the leech to windward prior to the pump by turning downwind as by rolling the mast to windward.

We have come a long way from crude sculling.

If we observe nature closely, fish and birds use a number of other kinetic techniques which we do not yet understand. Cyril Bryant noted that pigeons emit a characteristic 'whir' during the downbeat as they fly. He recorded this and measured the frequency by oscilloscope and photographs and noted that the frequency was about 670 cycles per second and further noted that the wavelength of this frequency is a shade bigger than the bird's span. He reasoned from a number of other observations that the bird was generating its own micro pressure field as it flew, in the sense that it would always be flying into the rarefied part of the sound wave which it was itself generating. He identified the source of the whir as the free ends of the covet feathers on its back between its wings. these resonated at this frequency. He checked those feathers on both bigger and smaller birds some of which were water birds, and found that in each case the frequency was such as gave the wave-length which was about the bird's span or a shade more. Because of the differences in the nature and amount of oil and therefore the resonant behaviour of feathers from land and sea birds, this is unlikely to be a coincidence.

If this is important for birds now it may in future be important for us. Some day it may enable us to sail faster

Dr Bernard Smith, who wrote *'The 40 knot Sailboat'* showed me an oddity in the wake of a guppy fish. If you move a round stick through the water, swirls sweep away from it from alternate sides. But after a guppy has swum by, it leaves swirls which are exactly aligned. It is unlikely that this particular arrangement should be the result of chance. There will be some dynamic reason for it which helps the fish to swim faster with less work. As yet we do not know what it is.

These are two examples of what Alan Payne means when he says 'but we haven't found all the links just yet'. When we do, we will be able to blend the benefits into our designs and/or techniques, and we will then be able to sail faster.

23.10 Summary

The different kinetic mechanisms apply naturally to the different points of sailing and to different types of sailboats.

Impulse, or the better *impulse + energy recovery* can be used with advantage by all boats which are running square or nearly so, and in all winds up to survival wind strength. All that a sailboarder or helmsman can do is to pull the whole sailboard rig back impulsively, or pull the boom or spinnaker back impulsively. Rolling the boat makes no difference when the wind is behind you. But tensing the rig until the leech vibrates at the rate which is right for the wind at the moment, and adjusting the angle of your sail and your point of sailing and the repetition frequency of your stroke until you achieve the nearly doubled force from energy recovery, can make a very big difference. It isn't easy, but it works, and for those who take their sailing seriously it is well worth the effort of practising until you know exactly how best to do it.

Pumping or the better *impulse + pumping* can be used with advantage by all boats which are sailing crosswind, and in all strengths of wind up to the design wind for that point of sailing. The lighter the wind the smaller and faster the movements should be. They finish as something almost invisible and astonishingly effective. I refer again to the videos of humming birds, eagles and albatross. The enormous power that an eagle can put into rapid shimmering of its wings as it approaches its nest at low speed – with the effect that the eagle can carry its whole weight with attached flow at almost no speed and with its wings pointing nearly straight upwards – commands my absolute respect. We cannot match this technique. All that we can do is to copy it as well as we can. And it is astonishing how much extra power we can achieve with even our poor copying.

Surging is in the province of the mobile sailboard, and of the lightweight sailboat which can be rolled by its crew. It calls for a gentle, delicate mental and physical approach. It is a precise, controlled, very efficient technique which racing crews can employ in light airs with great advantage on all points of sailing. Wherever racing sailboats roll in waves, the nature of the rolling can be adjusted by an alert crew to that needed for optimum surging. Crews who make use of this will draw ahead of crews who do not.

This does not pretend to be a complete coverage of kinetics. I have outlined something of the theory and as much as I know at present of the practice. Friends who have sailed the light-air lakes of Europe and North America more than I, advise me of local crews with legendary local reputations who achieve superior speed in drift conditions with near-invisible techniques. Of these I know nothing. But I know that when crews at Olympic medal level meet around the world, and the wind goes to light air (which it very often does) nobody seems to be able to do much better than anybody else, so it may be that I have not missed too much.

An occasion which excellently demonstrated the usefulness of kinetics was motivated by my wish to rejoin my family and friends in time for a lakeside celebration lunch. Lake Macquarie is a coastal lagoon north of Sydney, about twenty miles north-south and three miles east-west. I was holidaying with my family and friends on one shore. I had taken one of my HSP prototypes to see how it impressed as a holiday toy. (It impressed very well indeed, proving easy and pleasant to sail, challenging to get the best out of it particularly downwind, and much faster than anything else on the lake in winds of any strength). But I was not prepared for what happened in light airs.

Other friends were staying on the other side of the lake, and had asked if they could sail it.

One cloudy morning, I sailed over to them early, and they enjoyed the forenoon with it in a dying westerly breeze. As lunchtime approached, I took my leave and set out to return in a near calm. That boat had a sail area of about 170 square feet and a wetted area of about 17 square feet, a higher ratio of sail area to wetted area than any other design that I know of. It responded superbly to surging. In the glassy conditions I ghosted along close to a warming shoreline (the clouds had cleared) and by using surging in the onshore drift was able to achieve a respectable two knots or more for the half mile to the point. By that time there was a faint movement of the air form the north-east, just enough to enable me to continue surging. Each roll to leeward would have taken say ten seconds. I then waited for the speed to wash off until the Apparent Wind moved from near the bow far enough toward the beam for the sail to assume its proper shape. I hesitate to use the word 'fill' because there just wasn't enough wind near the surface to fill anything. However, there must have been enough movement aloft, because the boat kept going. The roll upright would have occupied another four seconds or so.

The 'power' I was putting into the boat amounted to no more than a to and fro sway of my upper body through about five to ten inches. The crews of three catamarans and two yachts which I passed close by clearly thought it was still a flat calm – their jibs hung central and lifeless, their boats were motionless in the water, and when they realised that I was neither paddling nor motoring they were astonished. (This has repeated many times since.) Within a little while, the first fingers of a sea breeze appeared. I used my mobility to surge to the edge of the nearest finger. In its two to four knots I sailed at about five knots. I picked and sailed towards the narrowest parts of the calms between the fingers of the moving air, and alternated between surging through the calms toward the nearest moving air, and sailing in the fingers of moving air toward the narrowest part of the next calm. After a mile or so of this I reached the southern point of my 'home' bay, and sailed the shoreline drift again to join my friends for lunch on time.

The facts that I could use kinetics effectively in conditions as light as these; that a modern very high performance boat plus kinetics could maintain useful movement in conditions in which conventional boats lay motionless; that I could sail three miles across a lake in about an hour in what others regarded as flat calm conditions; and that I had more fun in doing so than anyone else in a boat was having at that time – these facts have to be important pointers to some of the future directions in sailing.

High performance in action. B14 at Sanary, South of France.
Shortened sail in strong wind and long waves. Wake streaming back across three wave crests indicates how quickly this broad reaching boat is overtaking waves.

Chapter Twenty Four
Sailing Crosswind

Crosswind sailing

24.1 Crosswind sailing

Figure 24.1 shows the speed polars on all points of sailing of a keelboat, a dinghy and a skiff, in True Winds of 6, 10 and 15 knots. Polars for light airs are not shown because I do not have reliable measurements other than for one class.

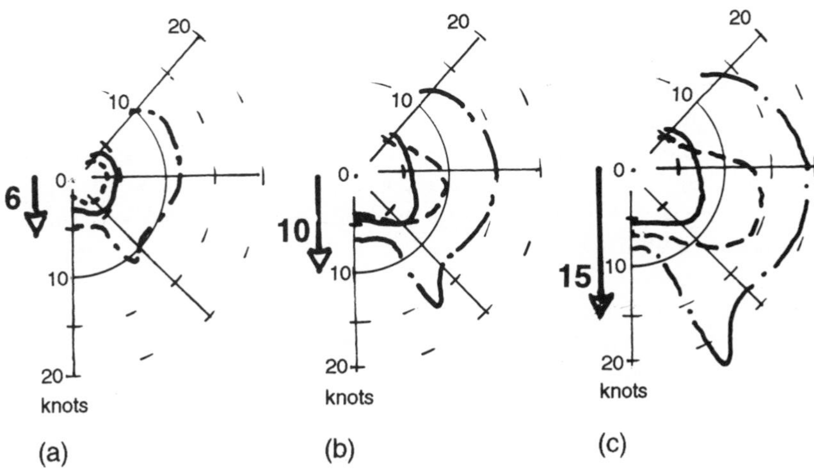

Speeds of Soling, Tasar, and Eighteen Footer on all points of sailing.

(a) In true wind of 6 knots
(b) " " " " 10 "
(c) " " " " 15 "

——— Soling
- - - - - Tasar
—.—. Eighteen foot skiff

Fig 24.1 Speeds of keelboat, dinghy and skiff

In the breezes of Fig 24.1, several facts become clear:

1. The Soling's hull is not a planing shape, and so it cannot much exceed its hull speed of six knots on any point of sailing. Even when the wind is strong and on the quarter, it can sail only about two knots faster.

2. The Eighteen footer can and does plane in all winds of six knots and stronger. The speed diagram of the Eighteen footer shows a consistent speed advantage over the Soling from about two to one in the lighter breezes, to about three to one as the wind becomes stronger (except when it runs square).

3. As a result, the relative performances of the Soling and the Eighteen footer do not change much.

4. By way of contrast, the performance of the high performance but low power Tasar changes dramatically with respect to both. Its ratios are too low to enable it to plane in the lighter breezes, so it displacement sails like a Soling but it is smaller and so has a slower hull speed. But as the breeze freshens it

planes freely and its reaching performance approaches that of the Eighteen footer. It is held back upwind by its lack of sail carrying power and downwind by its lack of extra sail area.

5. The Eighteen footer's diagram shows two factors which are typical of all high performance craft:

(a) The sharpness of the 'spinnaker lobe' may be surprising. The practicality is that the slower the boat, the wider is this lobe. With increasing speed it becomes progressively sharper as the Apparent Wind draws further ahead. Ultimately – as in the ice yacht which has no use for a spinnaker – it vanishes.

(b) There is enormous speed difference (approaching three to one), between the speeds achieved when tacking downwind and when running 'square'. This ability to achieve significant speed increase by tacking downwind is one of the two characteristics of all high performance craft. The other is the ability to achieve speeds substantially faster than hull speed when close-hauled.

When sailing to windward, the basic technique is to accelerate to the speed desired, and then point higher. The windward-going speeds and speed differences so evident in Fig 24.1 are all achieved with this same basic technique. The examples quoted in the previous chapter of the ways in which different classes are handled revealed interesting differences of detail, but no new principles.

The situation when sailing crosswind is different. The great majority of sailing literature focuses on the handling of keelboats, and documents very thoroughly how to sail at the low speeds from drift up to hull speed. But all of the lighter craft can sail at several times the speed of any yacht. In the extreme case a sailboard in winds of 40 knots and more can sail five times as fast as Soling crews who win gold medals. This tremendous speed range introduces completely new elements in handling – ones which call for a different approach. At present it is only in a few sailboard magazines that you can you find sensible discussion about how to sail at these higher speeds. In the general yachting literature there is little enlightenment offered to those who would like to sail faster and who want to know how to control a high performance sailboat at high speed.

The world is obsessed with speed. The number of sailboats which can sail relatively fast is increasing. It is time to discuss the fundamentals of high speed sailing.

In these notes, the polars of five classes are shown or referred to.

I have measured the performance of both the Tasar and the Eighteen footers, and can vouch for the accuracy of these plots.

The Tornado plot has been estimated by Chris Cairns, a Tornado world champion and Olympic bronze medallist. Chris did a lot of sailing against the Eighteens in the years when I was measuring their performance, and his estimate is a bias of my Eighteen footer plots to accommodate the differences he observed between the performance of his Tornado and the top Eighteens.

The Soling plot has been estimated by an ex dinghy champion in many classes including two Olympic selections in FD's, who has since won the world championship of both the J24 and the Soling classes. A technical point is that this is likely to be an unusually accurate estimate, simply because the hull speed of any keelboat is so predictable, and that of the app. 20 foot waterline length Soling is about six knots.

Australian sailboard speed enthusiasts have relatively recently found a venue which gives them what they dream about – frequent 50 knot 'steady' winds plus a stretch of flat water exposed to the prevailing winds at the proper angle for speed dashes. The references to sailboards come from this group, one of whom (Mal Wright) won and held for awhile the world speed record with a run of 42 knots.

24.2 Reaching dynamics

The differences between the off-wind dynamics of conventional sailboats and high performance craft are the consequences of:

1. The greater shift in the direction of the Apparent Wind with higher speed.
2. The increase in strength of the Apparent Wind with higher speed.
3. The fact that momentum effects become dominant at higher speed.

Fig 24.2 shows the Apparent Winds developed by the Soling and the Eighteen footer on points of sailing progressively further offwind in a True Wind of 15 knots. Points of particular note are:

1. The Soling crew will sail the offwind legs with the Apparent Wind on the beam or over the quarter. The Eighteen crew will sail the whole race with the Apparent Wind coming from ahead.

2. The Soling crew will experience a shift of the Apparent Wind direction from the True Wind direction of a maximum of 32 degrees. For the Eighteen footer the comparable figure is 110 degrees. You need a

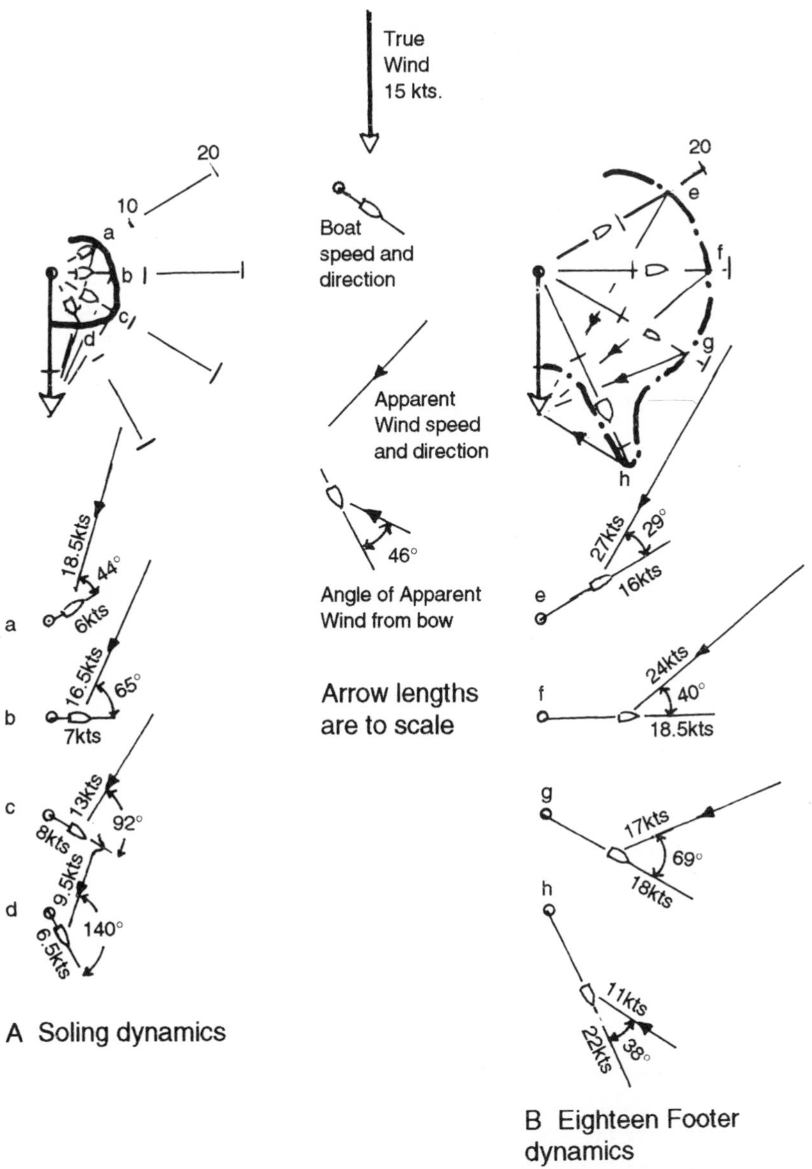

Fig 24.2 Offwind dynamics of keelboat and skiff

very highly developed sense of orientation to be able to sense the lifts and headers when you are racing downwind with the Apparent Wind coming from nearly ahead.

3. In a True Wind of 15 knots, the Soling crew will sail the close reach and reaching legs in Apparent Winds little stronger than the True Wind. If the boat was pressed when sailing to windward, it will be comfortable across the wind. On the broad reaching and tacking downwind legs the 15 knot True Wind falls to an Apparent Wind of the strength of a gentle breeze. The skiff crew sail the crosswind legs in much stronger Apparent Winds which approach 30 knots. Even on the broad reaching legs they must still sail in a strong Apparent Wind which blows from ahead, so they still need to use strong-wind 'going-to-windward' handling technique even although they are sailing downwind. On the same point of sailing on which the Soling crew have gentler Apparent Winds from the quarter and are 'looking for power'. The Eighteen therefore needs a harder, flatter, lower-drag rig to slice against strong Apparent Winds at boat speeds up to three times as fast as the keelboat.

Except for the 'tacking downwind' mode with spinnaker set, the Eighteen sails in a much stronger Apparent Wind which blows from much closer to the bow than the Soling. Both the Eighteen's rig and sail carrying power are optimised for close- hauled and close reaching sailing, because it never sails in any other way.

4. When tacking downwind, the Apparent Wind is still only 40 degrees or so from the bow. The powerful but relatively flat reaching spinnaker trebles the sail area. In practice the crew control the heeling force by steering through the gusts and lulls so as to maintain an almost constant 'cross-boat' component of the Apparent Wind. This results in the very sharp lobes in the polar diagram of the high-power, high-performance boats on this point of sailing.

There is enough in the paragraphs above and associated figures to indicate just how different high performance sailing is from conventional sailing. It is not surprising that different handling techniques are needed to control these high performance craft. We will be able to focus on the principles better if we look at a more moderate boat which has some of the properties of both the others. The third boat in Fig 24.1 – the Tasar, has no trapeze nor spinnaker and is as moderate as the Soling in light airs and light breezes. But its light weight and unusually efficient rig give it very high crosswind speeds in the stronger breezes. At these speeds it responds to high performance handling techniques. As an example to use in this and the following chapters, it has two particular advantages: it sails at about the same speed around-the-buoys as the majority of trapeze and spinnaker racing dinghies and some catamarans of about its size, so the techniques which work with the Tasar will be helpful to a very large number of sailors; and its performance has been measured and so can be discussed with confidence.

Let us look first at the vital principles, then at basic crosswind handling, and then at examples from different classes.

The principles are:

The design wind zones
The balance position
Steering for balance
The four balance techniques:

1. Feathering –	Up and Ease (in gusts)
2. Close reaching –	Aim and Ease
3. Reaching –	Down and Ease
4. Tacking down wind and running –	Down and Hold

The fastest sail trims
Kinetics considerations.

24.3 The design wind zones

Fig 24.3 shows the performance of a Tasar in winds from 2 to 20 knots. Flat water and the steadiest of real winds are assumed. In the lower wind speeds – say up to about 8 knots – it sails in the displacement mode and its performance is a little slower than that of the longer Soling. In this wind-speed range the shift of the Apparent Wind is similar to that of the Soling in Fig 24.2. As the boat bears away to beam reach and broad reach the Apparent Wind continues to blow from much the same direction as the True Wind, and so the Apparent Wind quickly shifts aft of the beam and becomes lighter.

In stronger breezes the boat planes freely and can achieve relatively high speeds. These higher speeds cause the behaviour of the Apparent Wind to become very different. The table below Fig 24.3 gives the details for a True Wind of 14 knots. The fourth, fifth, sixth and seventh lines are of particular interest – the speed of the boat, the speed of the Apparent Wind, the deflection of the Apparent Wind direction from the True Wind direction, and the angle of the Apparent Wind direction from the bow. From a close reaching course at 60 degrees to the True Wind (point 'B' in the diagram and column 'B' in the table), to a broad reaching course at 105 degrees to the True Wind (point and table 'E'), every few degrees of bearing away enables the boat to accelerate to a higher speed. This added boat speed so deflects the Apparent Wind direction and influences its speed that there is only trivial change in the speed and angle of the Apparent Wind 'across the deck' through the whole sector from B to E. As is shown in the vector diagrams (line 8), between heading B at 60 degrees to the True Wind, and heading E at 105 degrees to the True Wind – a change of heading of 45 degrees, there is a change in the angle of the Apparent Wind to the centreline of the boat of only 12 degrees and a change of only +/- 1 knot in the Apparent Wind speed.

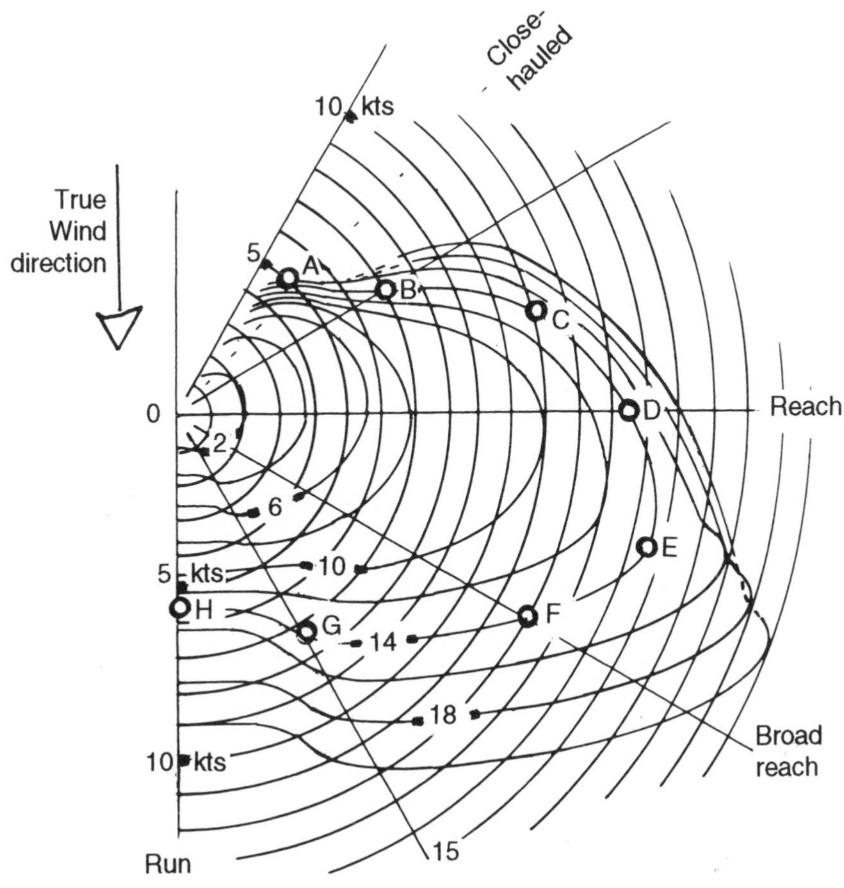

Performance of light dinghy in winds from 2 to 20 knots.

Boat speed in True Wind of 10 knots is curve labelled —▪ 10 ▪—
and in 6 " " " " —▪ 6 ▪— etc

Note how unusual reaching speed holds Apparent Wind forward almost to broad reach, for example in true wind of 14 knots:

At points	A	B	C	D	E	F	G	H	
True Wind speed	14	14	14	14	14	14	14	14	kts
Heading relative to True Wind	45	60	75	90	105	120	150	180	degs
Boat speed	5	7	11	13.5	14.5	11.5	8	6.5	kts
Apparent Wind speed	18.5	19	19.6	20	18	13.5	9	7.5	kts
Deflection of Apparent Wind) from dir'n of True Wind)	11	18	31	42	51	48	27	0	degs
Angle of Appn't wind from bow	29	42	44	48	54	72	123	180	degs
Vector diagram									

Fig 24.3 Performance polars of Tasar

There are two surprising results from all this.

The first is that the boat needs to be handled as if it were close reaching through the whole range of sailing angles from close reach to broad reach.

The second is that the concept of the design wind continues to apply almost as if the boat were sailing to windward all the way from close-hauled to broad reach.

In Section 18.5(Part Three) the design wind was introduced. The 'going-to-windward' design wind was defined as that wind speed at which – with optimum sail trim and without easing anything – a crew can just hold a dinghy upright or a yacht reaches its optimum angle of heel or a catamaran lifts one hull.

Exactly the same concept can be applied on all other points of sailing. Fig 24.4(a) repeats Fig 24.3 but shows the figure divided into three zones. Zone A designates those wind speeds and points of sailing in which the boat will be overpowered for all of the time, and within which a crew will need to shed power in exactly the same way as when going to windward in stronger winds. Zone C shows those areas within the performance diagram within which a crew will always be 'looking for power'. Zone B is shaded; this is the zone within which a crew will sometimes be overpowered and sometimes not, because of the natural unsteadiness of the wind. The design wind is shown as the solid line at the edge of the shading which defines zone B.

As this light boat bears away from close-hauled it initially begins to plane so freely on a close reach that the design wind falls a knot or so and then rises again between close reach and beam reach – this behaviour is unusual. Thereafter as the boat continues to bear away and sail progressively further offwind it can be held upright in progressively stronger winds.

The absolutely vital point is that any boat which sails in a wind stronger than the design wind (i.e. in zone A) will sail fastest when it is sailed with flat sails for minimum drag. This remains true on all points of sailing. The fact that the boat may be broad reaching or tacking downwind does not invalidate this truth.

If we consider this concept as it applies to boats across the whole performance range from the low-performance heavy boats to high-performance skiffs and ice yachts, the positions of the design wind zones change systematically. Refer to the insets in Fig 24.4. In Fig 24.4(b) (keelboat) the division between zones A and C is more nearly horizontal. The Tasar plot given in 24.4(a) is intermediate. The skiff plot of Fig 24.4(c) wraps almost completely around the diagram – the break is where the reaching spinnaker is hoisted. For an ice yacht it must be near-circular.

Sailboats sail fastest when the combination of wind speed and sail area is such that they can be sailed on the point of being overpowered on whatever point of sailing is called for at the moment. *A truth which emerges from Fig 24.4 is that the higher the performance of the boat, the less will be its need of extra sails, because the boat's own speed generates an Apparent Wind strong enough to keep the boat fully powered.*

In Fig 24.4(a) the heavy boat ceases to be overpowered as soon as it begins to turn crosswind. The ocean racer's response to this is to carry a sail locker full of progressively bigger and fuller headsails. Further offwind the broad reaching and running arc through which it can carry a spinnaker with advantage is very wide, but within this arc the differences in boat speed and downwind VMG between tacking downwind and running are small.

In Fig 24.4(c) the way the design wind of the high-performance skiff wraps around the diagram correctly represents the way the skiff 'makes its own wind'. The crew stay on trapeze far out on their wings as the boat sails fast enough not only when reaching, but also when broad reaching and also when tacking downwind with spinnaker up, to generate an Apparent Wind strong enough to keep them there. With these boats the 'spinnaker lobe' is very narrow and the differences in boat speed and downwind VMG between tacking downwind (where the boat generates much of its own Apparent Wind), and running (where it doesn't) are enormous. As a point of interest, the quickest way to slow down in any emergency is simply to bear away towards a square run. From the crew's point of view, the boat seems to stop.

What we see from Fig24.4(a), (b) and (c) is that the very high 'round-the-buoys' speeds of the high performance boats flow not only from their higher ratios, but also from the fact that their own dynamics enable them to sail fully powered for so much more of the time. When it is possible for them to do so crews will change their sail area to match the wind strength of the day. Technically they reconfigure their boats so that they sail in a dynamic state which is as close to the design wind for that rig as is possible. Sailboards and skiffs change to smaller rigs as the wind speed increases. Many keelboat classes shift to smaller headsails. In classes which carry spinnakers these extra sails are hoisted when the Apparent Wind becomes

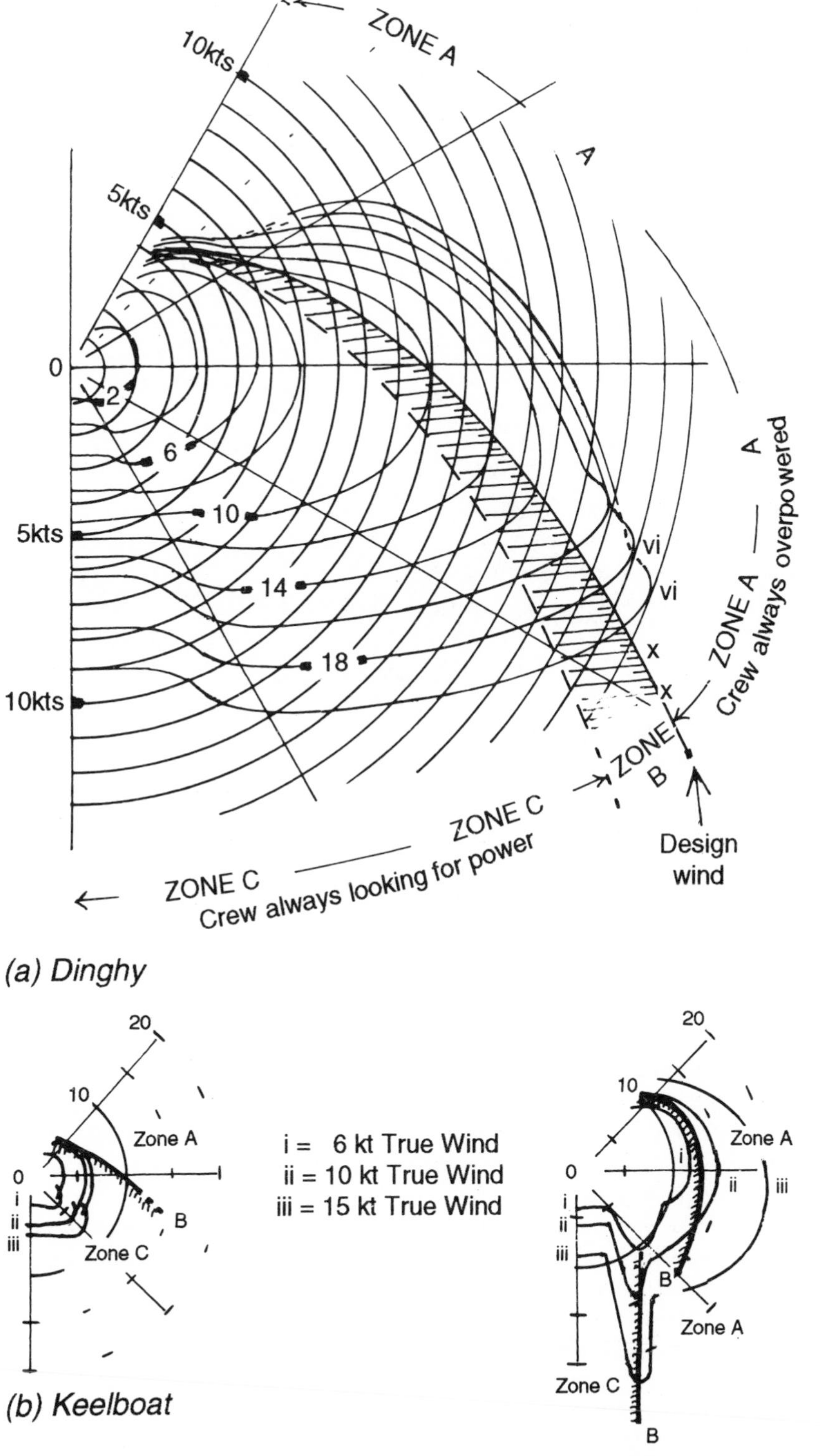

In Zone A, use flat sails for minimum drag
In Zone C, use fuller sails for maximum drive force (except when running square)

Fig 24.4 The design wind zones

lighter when sailing downwind. Technically, each change of sail area will change the boat's design wind zones, but they will not change them much, nor will they alter the fundamental characteristics. As an example, the break in Fig 24.4(c) shows the change due to nearly trebling the sail area as a close-reaching spinnaker is set. Clearly, any difference due to reefing a mainsail or changing a jib will be small. For simplicity, in Fig 24.4 and its insets the design wind zones for only one rig is shown on each diagram. This is all that is needed to show the essential differences between the three groups.

Let us summarise the fundamental principles: Any boat which sails in zone 'A' will sail fastest if it is set up and handled for minimum drag. A crew in zone 'C' will always be 'looking for power' and will shape and trim their sails accordingly. If the real wind were steady, there would be no zone 'B'. The unsteadier the wind on the day, the wider zone B will become.

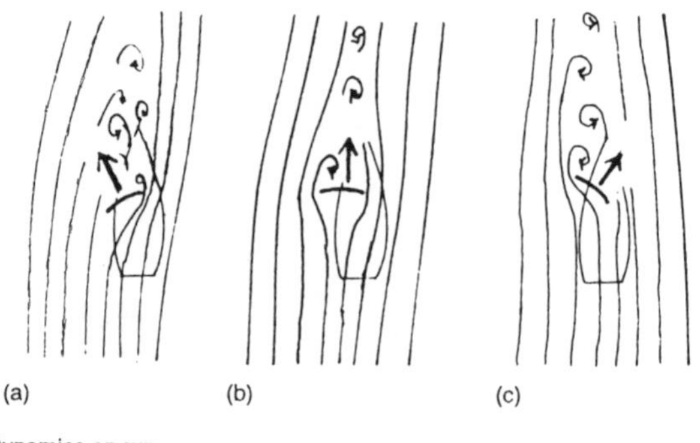

Dynamics on run

(d) (e) (f)

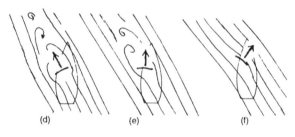

Dynamics on broad reach similar

in (a) & (d) upper mainsail oversheeted, boat rolls to left in gusts.
" (c) & (f) " " eased too far, " " " right " "
" (b) & (e) " " square across boat, boat does not roll.

Fig 24.5 The balance position

24.4 The balance position

It is a truism when sailing, that when a boat is overpowered by either a gust or a rising wind, that the heeling force can be reduced by easing the sheets.

There are two exceptions to this.

The first is that if a sheet is eased so far in a strong wind that the sail begins to flutter like a flag, the drag of fluttering fabric can be up to ten times the drag of steady fabric. If the fabric has a weight attached to its free end (like heavy jib sheets) this can cause the sail to 'flog' and the drag of flogging fabric can be much greater again. Any increase of drag will increase the heeling force, and not reduce it, when the wind is abeam.

The second exception is that when the Apparent Wind is aft of the beam, the sails can roll the boat either way. The principle is shown in Fig 24.5. If, when broad reaching or running in a strong wind, the upper mainsail is not trimmed out far enough (Fig 24.5(a)) the pressure force from the upper sail will be directed forwards and to leeward. The leeward-directed force will roll the boat to leeward (towards the boom) in the gusts, and it will roll to windward in the lulls.

If the mainsheet is eased so far that the upper leech can blow forward of the mast as in Fig 24.5(c) the rolling force will be reversed. The boat will roll to windward, and will be rolled to windward very strongly in gusts because the force of the gust will drive the upper leech even further forward.

These principles will remain true when broad-reaching as well as when running (Fig 24.5 (d), (e) and (f)).

Between the extremes of (a) and (d), and (c) and (f), there must necessarily be a 'balance position' which will occur when the upper mainsail is trimmed square across the boat, and the drive force is directed straight forward as in Fig 24.5(b) and (e). When the sail is trimmed to this 'balance position', the effect of gusts is simply to drive the boat straight forward and faster, and not to roll it at all.

Boats with unusually flexible rigs such as Finns, OK's and Lasers merit special mention. With these rigs the difference in force between lull and gust can so flex the rig that an upper leech in the balance position in the lull will flex forward into the 'heel to windward' trim in each gust. The technique to handle this is to draw the sheet in in the gusts sufficiently to hold the upper leech dynamically steady in the balance position.

Fig 24.6 displays the points of sailing as two arcs. Within the 'upwind' arc heel in gusts can be reduced by easing sails. Within the 'downwind' arc heel cannot be reduced by easing sheets but it can be controlled by adopting and holding the 'balance position'. This principle will apply to all boats. The slower the boat, the nearer to a beam reach will be the sailing angle at which the changeover occurs (Fig 24.6(a)). The arcs shown as (b) are about right for an intermediate boat like a Tasar. Fast skiffs and ice yachts race downwind with the Apparent Wind forward of the beam so they never approach the balance position and for these boats when racing it is of no practical importance.

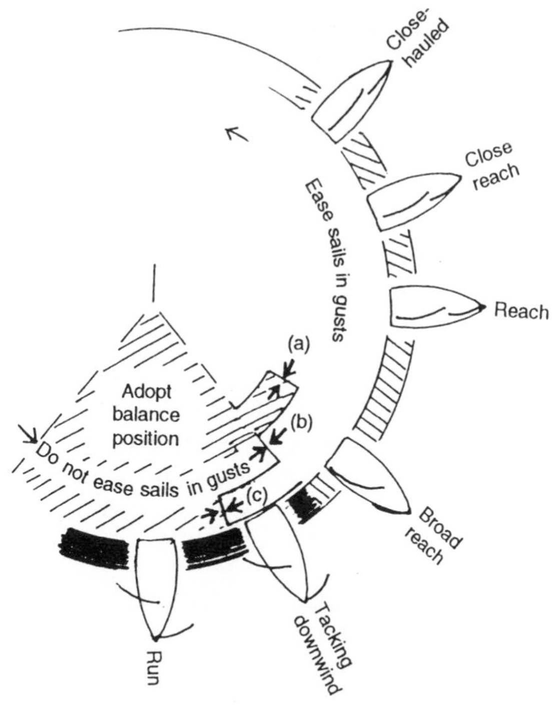

(a) Slower boats adopt balance position nearer beam reach.
(c) Faster boats (VMG downwind = wind speed or faster) never approach the balance position because the Apparent Wind is always from forward, so for them the balance position vanishes.

Fig 24.6 Sail trim technique for balance on all points of sailing.

24.5 Steering for balance

This is the most important of all the balance controls when sailing at higher speeds.

If any boat of normal monohull shape such as an outboard dinghy or light motor-boat is driven at planing speed across the water, and then turned, it will roll 'inwards' – i.e. if it is turned to the left, it will roll to the left.

When it is turned to the left at speed, its initial response will be for it to continue to slide in its original direction (Fig 24.7(b)). Water will heap up under the advancing right hand side of the 'Vee' bottom – which is the 'outside' side of the turn. The upward and inward pressure of this heaped up water will both roll the hull to the left, and also provide the inwards force which will guide it into and around the turn. (Fig 24.7(c)).

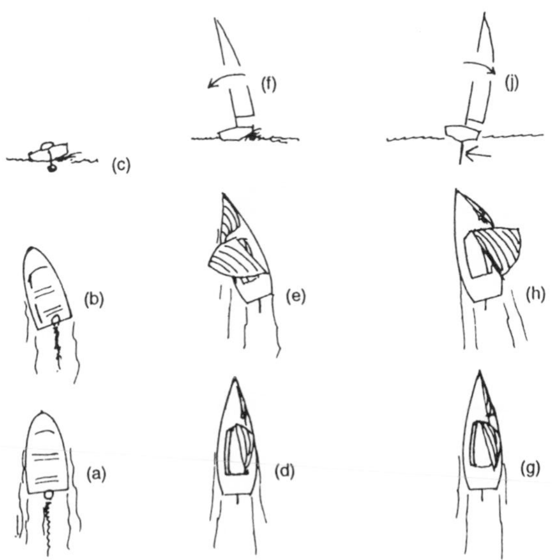

(a) (b) (c) (d) (e) (f) Hull with no centreboard rolls toward turn.

(g) (h) (j) Hull with centreboard down rolls away from turn so *steering hull under rig* willl roll boat upright.

Fig 24.7 Steering technique for balance

A sailboat which is driven at the same speed by its sails will react similarly if its centreboard is raised or is down only a little. Fig 24.7 (d), (e) and (f) repeat (a) (b) and (c) but with a sailboat with negligible centreboard down as the example.

As soon as the centreboard is put down further, the dynamics change completely and the direction of roll reverses.

The presence of a centreboard in the water limits the leeway of a light boat almost absolutely. The sideways slide is eliminated, as shown in Fig 24.7(h). Instead of the sideways slide and the heaped up water on the right, the initial action of a turn to the left will be that the centreboard will immediately develop a strong sideways force to the left. This will accelerate the boat to the left with a force which acts below the centre of gravity of the hull and rig, and so will roll the boat to the right. Vice versa, a turn to the right will roll the boat to the left. The end result is that when a boat which is reaching or broad-reaching fast is heeled by a gust, it can be brought upright most certainly *not* by luffing but by *bearing away* and turning downwind. This technique is summed up perfectly by the old adage 'at high speed, always steer the hull under the rig'.

The amount of centreboard which it is necessary to expose to achieve this reversal of dynamics will vary according to the shape and weight of your boat. If you experiment some brisk day by running straight downwind and systematically raise your centreboard two or three inches at a time while you steer a snaking course, it will become very obvious as you approach the neutral point – that depth of centreboard exposed below the hull at which your boat will roll neither way. In light winds you can raise the board as far as you like, but in stronger breezes you had better leave it down some way further than whatever is the neutral point for your class, or your control will become unreliable in the gusts.

The faster the boat moves, the more powerful will this 'steer for balance' rolling force become. At high speeds, it becomes absolutely dominant. In principle it is identical with the balance control used when riding a bicycle. It is a vitally important technique for control when sailing in gusty winds and through rough water and big waves.

A very practical point is that the reversal of 'steer for balance' roll which occurs when the centreboard is raised completely is responsible for many capsizes when they are least expected – when coming ashore. If, after the centreboard has been raised as shoal water is approached, the boat accelerates in any gust or begins to surf down a wave, it will roll suddenly and powerfully the way you don't expect when you turn it. The cure for this is to realise that steer-for-balance and also anti-steer-for-balance both operate only at speed. If you drag a leg over the side to keep your final approach speed slow, no significant force to roll you either way can develop.

When we consider how steer-for-balance can be combined with other balance techniques and also look at these combinations across different performance levels of boat, a fascinating picture emerges.

While most keelboats can turn quickly, their speeds are too low for 'steer for balance' to be of much use. They will normally bear away in gusts as if steering for balance for the reasons shown in Fig 24.4 – the further offwind they steer, the more wind they can stand; and in addition they will then spend more time in the gusts.

Catamarans march to a different drummer. Their long hulls resist turning quickly and so they cannot develop any strong righting force – for them the technique is of only limited use. They will normally steer downwind in gusts for the same reasons as the keelboats. But their fine bows bury if pressed too hard so when the point is reached where safety becomes paramount to stay afloat they reverse their turns and luff and ease sails in the gusts instead.

Dinghies fall into two groups. Fig 24.8 shows how 'steer for balance' applies to all craft up to intermediate performance – say up to 505 and FD level. The figure shows three arcs.

In the reaching, broad reaching and running arc there are no surprises. This is where 'steer for balance' is supreme for all of the reasons so far given. Note that boats of low and moderate performance will generally be 'looking for power' in this arc. Their sails will usually be trimmed to about point E in either Fig 17.32 or 17.33. As the boat turns downwind the sails should be eased to maintain this point E trim, but note that any error either way will result in reduced sail force and reduced heeling force.

The situation can be different in the 'close-hauled and windward planing' arc. For those boats

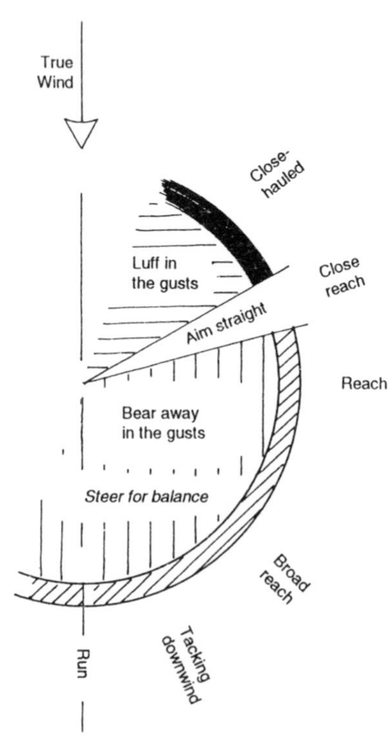

Fig 24.8 Steering technique for balance on all points of sailing

which cannot sail fast, no problem will ever arise, because steer for balance and anti-steer-for-balance operate only at higher speeds. But for boats which can achieve windward planing speeds or faster, a basic conflict occurs between the heeling force of the sails and the righting force of 'steer for balance' whenever a boat is turned in stronger winds.

Let us assume that a dinghy such as an FD is windward planing at about 9 knots in a 15 knot wind. Its sails would be working at about point A in Fig 17.31. Let it enter a gust of 20 knots. The heeling force from the sails will approximately double, so the boat will begin to heel.

If the boat is luffed smoothly about 5 degrees, the angle of the sails to the (slightly wider) Apparent Wind will decrease by about 4 degrees to about point 'x' in Fig 17.31. This luff, plus some slight easing of the sheet, will reduce the sail force and restore balance provided that the luff has been slow and smooth. Note that this turn is the wrong way for 'steer for balance' If it is too quick, even at 9 knots the 'anti steer for balance' force will roll the boat even further to leeward to the point where the out-of-trim boat slows significantly before the wind force is reduced and it rolls upright again – and this is what so often happens.

If we imagine the boat to be turned sharply downwind instead in an effort to use 'steer for balance' to bring it upright, the action of bearing away will increase the angle of the sails to the 20 knot gust to between points B and E in Fig 17.31 unless the sheets are eased. In this case 'eased' would mean a major re-trim of about 15 degrees of boom and jib foot angle. For the most practical of reasons any substantial easing of the jib sheet will result in an over-full jib, and this, in the gusts, is exactly what you need least. Handling several metres of mainsheet on a gust by gust basis is equally impractical.

So a conflict is emerging when sailing close-hauled. At this moderate level of performance the fastest technique in gusts is to ease sheet to reduce the sail heeling force immediately, and simultaneously to luff, but slowly enough to suppress the 'steer for balance' roll force which acts the wrong way, and while luffing recover the sheet so as to establish the trim desired through each gust.

Fig 24.3 shows how rapidly boats of about this performance level increase their speed as they bear away from close-hauled towards close reach. 'Steer for balance' is a momentum effect and its force increases as the square of the boat speed. As speed increases a point is soon reached at which the steer for balance effect is about equal and opposite to the change in sail force brought about by the turn. Once this point is reached there is no purpose served in turning either way when the boat heels in a gust. At and near this point of sailing the fastest technique is simply to aim the boat straight, and play the sheets to keep the boat upright.

This is the third arc – the close reach arc which lies between the close-hauled arc in which it is fastest to luff in a gust, and the reaching to running arc in which it is fastest to steer for balance by bearing away in a gust. The positions of the arcs shown in Fig 24.8 are about right for planing dinghies of moderate performance.

The situation with the high performance skiffs is, at present, a stalemate. If the wind were steady and the water flat, they could sail at upwind speeds considerably greater than the 14 knots which I consistently measured. In fact, there was one world championship which was held in particularly smooth waters and steady sea breeze winds off Brisbane, Queensland. The crews found that they could control their boats easily in these steadier prevailing conditions, and began to add about a metre a night to their wingspans, and to carry their big and intermediate rigs into progressively stronger winds. Four things then happened:

1. The boats sailed faster. I wasn't there and nobody else measured the absolute speeds, so I do not know how much faster, but the boats with wider wings were much faster upwind than those boats which chose not to modify and which had previously been competitive.

2. A rash of breakages of masts, centreboards, and spinnaker poles occurred. These boats are designed close to the limits in that there is not much margin beyond the strength normally needed, and they responded predictably to the greater static and acceleration (turning) loads imposed by the increased sail carrying forces and greater speeds on their structures.

3. When they returned to their various home ports, all of which have more congested and rougher waters and more variable winds, the wider-winged boats lost their speed advantage. The practicality was that in more variable conditions they proved slower, – and not faster, – than their unmodified rivals. The lesson here was that the more unsteady the wind and congested the waters, the smaller was the fastest wingspan.

4. Even the independent Eighteen footer movement decided after this that enough was enough, and brought in a rule to limit future wing width.

Which brings us back to balance control. Fourteen knots of boat speed seems to be about the present limit at which it is practical to control an Eighteen foot skiff when it is sailing close-hauled in winds of normal unsteadiness. It cannot bear away and steer for balance because of the increase of wind force on its sails noted above. What applies to the moderate performance boat applies with even greater force to the more powerful skiff. As the winds become stronger it is essential for a skiff to luff and bear away aggressively in order to control its sail force. There is only so much that a strong, fit and skilful sheet hand can contribute to control. The practical observation is, that at speeds greater than 14 knots of boat speed, in the real world any luff in a gust which is quick enough to be aerodynamically useful rolls the boat to leeward with unacceptable force and/or drags a wing momentarily.

So for high performance boats the diagram of Fig 24.8 is not far wrong. Both the upwind and the 'aim straight' arcs are much smaller and closer to close-hauled. The 'steer for balance' arc is correspondingly bigger.

In view of this current limitation on skiff performance, it is reasonable to ask whether any other boat can do better. In recent years there have been a series of approaches, such as the 42 foot 'Professional Sailors Class', the 'Formula 40' boats, and the 30 foot 'Ultimate' class. Section 16.5 suggested that these bigger boats would find the cube/square law difficult to bypass, and the evidence to date confirms this. The 42 foot keelboats sail no faster than any other good 42 foot keelboats, and in the stronger winds they stick at a hull speed of about 8.5 knots as expected, just like a Soling. The Formula 40 multihulls all have disappointing ratios of sail area to wetted area, so in light fickle airs a good child's dinghy which is well handled can sail around them. The 30 footers are as yet too new to evaluate. Nobody suggests that eighteen feet is some magical number. It is just that, as we approach the end of this century, these are the high performance boats which have been most rigourously developed, and at present they possess a performance which is head and shoulders faster around-the-buoys in all conditions of wind and water than anything else in sight anywhere in the world.

We know that specialist sailboards can exceed 40 knots when reaching in very strong winds. We know that the sailboard fraternity are working confidently towards 50 knots, and that there is no technical reason to doubt that they will achieve 50 knots, but at the cost of near-zero performance on all other points of sailing and in all lighter winds. We know that as we measure the speeds of present craft, the 14 foot skiffs are faster than the 12's, the 16's are faster than the 14's, and the Eighteens are much faster than the 16's. There are political reasons why the development of the 16's has been held back. In my opinion the 16's have the technical potential to become very quick boats indeed, but it would need an administrative revolution and twenty years' development to achieve it. As we either tabulate the performance of existing progressively bigger boats, or imagine the potential performance of bigger boats which are not yet built, all the observations and the calculations lead to slower average speeds. The cube/square law looks very secure.

In addition to these measured and calculated slower speeds, there is the sort of logic discussed above which sees even the Eighteens now up against an unexpected speed barrier in the unsteady winds of the open water. If the featherweight Eighteen has already developed these dynamic conflicts within its performance envelope, just imagine the trim and control problems which will beset any bigger boat with bigger spars and sails which take added seconds to trim in the same, rapidly fluctuating, unsteady wind. The hand-held, minimum-weight, minimum-response-time wishbone of the sailboard is looking more and more like a winner.

In case there are readers who wonder 'what about an all-out big catamaran?', that question has been answered. Dennis Connor and his *'Stars and Stripes' America*'s Cup winning catamaran was invited to the south of France to sail against their then latest maxi. He beat the maxi as easily as he beat the giant New Zealand keelboat. But an Eighteen joined the race too, and beat them both with sheer speed both upwind and downwind in a long upwind/downwind race in a steady moderate breeze. It was all shown in detail on French and European television. For my part, I would have expected that particular 45 foot catamaran, in those conditions which were ideal , to beat the Eighteen upwind but not downwind. But on the water, boat against boat, it couldn't. The Eighteen proved itself faster both ways.

24.6 Control at high speeds

Control for balance

Fig 24.9 combines the information from Figs 24.6 and 24.8 and shows how the sail trim and steering factors combine to form four arcs. Higher performance boats sail in only three of these arcs because, in their case, the Apparent Wind never moves aft of the beam so they never approach the balance position.

Control of boats at high boat speeds in unsteady winds is achieved by using a particular co-ordination of steering and sail trimming. The higher the boat speed, the more important does the steering component become. This co-ordination changes systematically with point of sailing in the following manner:

When the boat rolls to leeward in each gust, to restore balance:

In arc 1 – Luff smoothly and ease sails *'Up and Ease'*
In arc 2 – Aim straight ahead and ease *'Aim and Ease'*
In arc 3 – Bear away and ease sails *'Down and Ease'*
In arc 4 – Bear away and DO NOT ease *'Down and Hold'*

Use the reverse co-ordination when the boat rolls to windward as it enters each lull. When any boat enters a lull, with speed, in arcs 3 and 4 (and even in arc 2), a firm luff will hold the boat upright for long enough for the crew to move inboard provided they are quick.

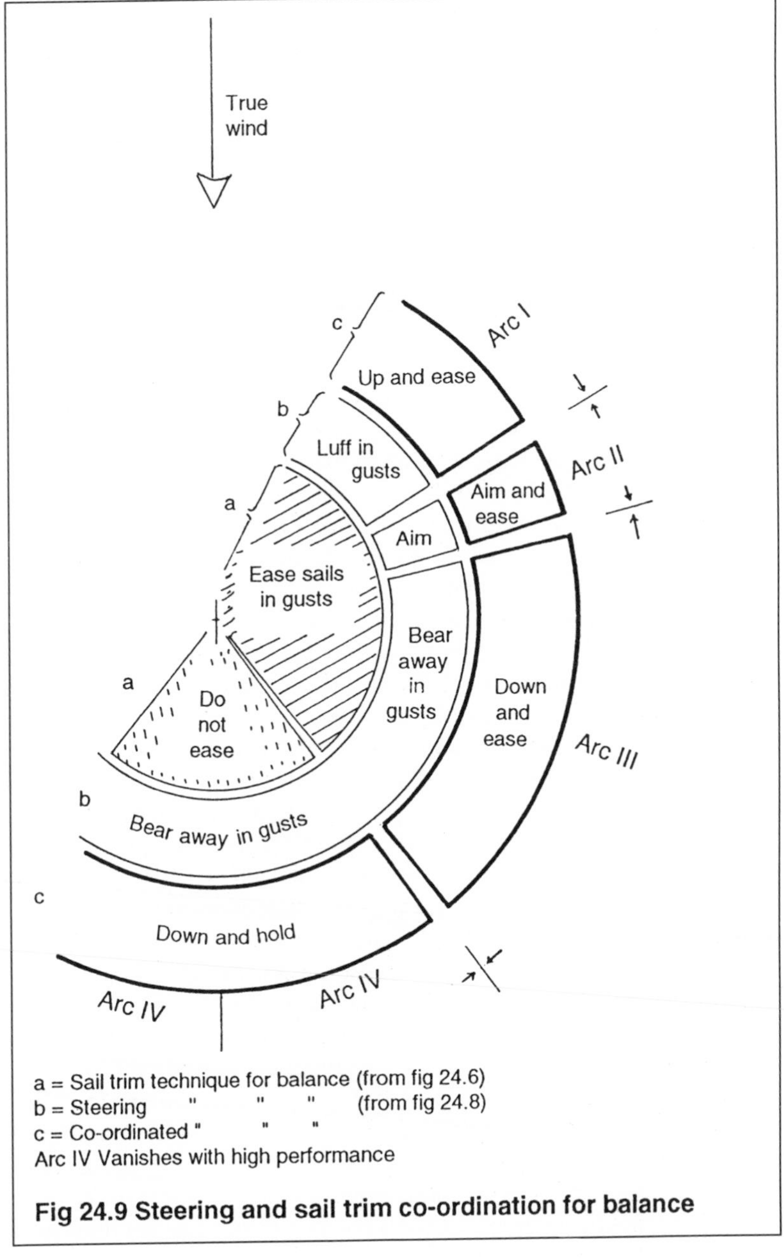

a = Sail trim technique for balance (from fig 24.6)
b = Steering " " " (from fig 24.8)
c = Co-ordinated " " "
Arc IV Vanishes with high performance

Fig 24.9 Steering and sail trim co-ordination for balance

The fastest sail shapes

Fig 24.10 adds the 'design wind' information which relates to sail shape from Fig 24.4 to the balance technique information of Fig 24.9. It shows the sail shapes used by high performance boats to achieve their speeds, as well as the steering and sail trim techniques used to control them at those speeds. The zones from 24.4 and the arcs from 24.9 intersect to give a number of sectors. Within each sector maximum speed with secure control will be achieved by handling in the way suggested under the figure. The broad principles become surprisingly simple:

In zone A Use flat, minimum-drag sail shapes in all arcs.

In zone C Trim sails for maximum drive force. This means maximum fullness except when close-hauled or nearly so in arcs 1 and 2 where moderation is called for, (refer to chapter 22 for the detail); and also when running square or nearly so in the extreme downwind part of arc 4, where trim for maximum projected area will be fastest.

In zone B Use Intermediate fullness -

EXCEPT When the gust harshness is such that there is doubt about the ability to hold the boat upright in the gusts, then use flatter and more elastic sails. The loss from being under-powered with too-flat sails in the lulls will be in metres.The loss from being over-powered and broaching in any strong gust because of too-full sails can be hundreds of metres.

This summarises the principles of balance control and sail trim when sailing crosswind in sailboats capable of high performance. The sections which follow will look at the detail of the techniques.

Handling crosswind in light and moderate air

24.7 In light air and flat water

Light air sailing is all zone 'C' sailing. The dynamics of speed and the technique differences associated with the design wind are remote from light air considerations.

In light air, the handling techniques crosswind are virtually identical with the light air close-hauled techniques described earlier. The boat should be heeled so that the sails adopt a twisted shape. Both jib and mainsail should be set and trimmed for maximum drive force – in light air this is achieved with a camber of no more than about 10% about midway back in the sail. It should be trimmed for Cl max, i.e. with the forward leeward tufts streaming but occasionally agitating. As when close-hauled, the upper sails are dominant because that is where most of the wind is, and every effort should be directed towards maintaining the trim which yields Cl max over the upper mainsail and upper jib. The point of this remark is that in a reach/broad-reach situation in flat water, the fact that the boat speed can be much greater than the wind speed at low level means that the Apparent Wind at deck level can blow from a direction surprisingly close to the bow even when broad reaching. (Refer to Figs 3.1 and 3.2. in Part One) The feather, in the stronger wind at the masthead, may indicate an Apparent Wind about 50 degrees from the bow, and in this the upper mainsail will be ideally trimmed at about 30 degrees from the centreline (i.e. at a trim angle of 20 degrees to the Apparent Wind). This situation calls for 20 to 25 degrees of twist in the mainsail. In light air this may not be possible to achieve because of the weight of the boom and the fabric in all sails, the fabric tensions natural in fully battened sails, inadequate adjustment capability, etc.

In practice, in these conditions the lower jib and lower mainsail sometimes get wafted aback momentarily when the boat, with a speed of 2 or 3 knots, runs into a particularly dead patch of lower air. To attempt to correct this by sheeting more closely is folly, because it over-sheets the all-important upper sails. All coaching and racing experience suggests that the angle of heel should be increased as the boat is sailed further offwind so that gravity can increase the mainsail twist. A heel angle of about 10 to 15 degrees appears about right for most classes for close-hauled and close reach sailing. The heel angle should be progressively increased until the gunwale is skimming the water for broad-reach sailing. Bow-down, fourth mode sailing technique should be adopted when sailing boats with fine bows. This will require the helmsman to position him/herself close to the mast. When sailing from this position it is sometimes not possible to control the mainsail efficiently by the sheet,and it is often more comfortable and convenient to

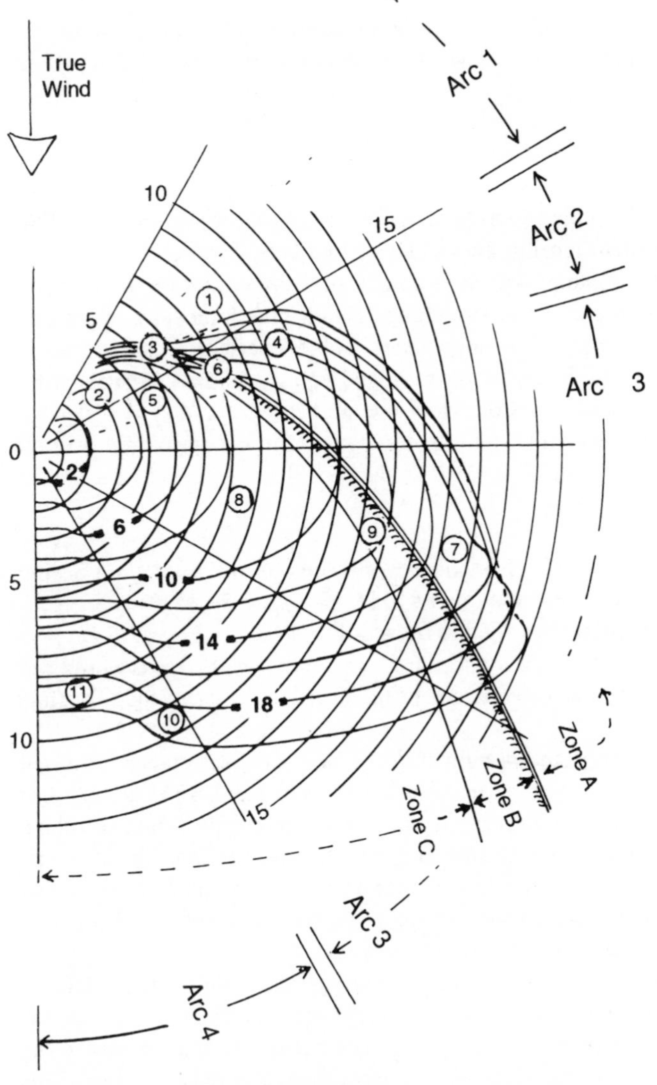

Combination of Fig 24.4. with Fig 24.9 gives the key handling elements for every point of sailing and every wind strength within the performance envelope.

Point	Arc and zone	Balance control in gusts	Sail dynamics	Reference
1	Arc 1 Zone A	Up and ease	Flat for min. drag	} CH22
2	" 1 " C	" " "	Fuller for max. drive force	
3	" 1 " B	" " "	Flatter in harsher winds	
4	Arc 2 Zone A	Aim and ease	Flat for min. drag	
5	" 2 " C	" " "	Fuller for max. drive force	
6	" 2 " B	" " "	Flatter in harsher winds	
7	Arc 3 Zone A	Down and ease	Flat for min. drag	
8	" 3 " C	" " "	Fullest for max. drive force	
9	" 3 " B	" " "	Flatter in harsher winds	
10	" 4 zoneC	Down and hold	Unstalled i.e.Tacking downwind Fullest for max. drive force	
11	" 5 zoneC	" " "	Stalled,ie Running square - or nearly so Flattest sails for max. projected area	

Fig 24.10 Key handling and sail trim dynamics - offwind

control it by holding the boom end of the vang assembly, or the boom itself, directly in the sailboard style. The jib clew can similarly be held by hand, and the twist of the jib can then be assisted by lifting the clew.

Handling

470 class

I asked a Cherub world champion and 470 Olympic representative about light-air reaching in the 470. 'The mainsail should be set with no Cunningham tension and with the foot soft. Trim continuously to keep the upper leech ribbon alive as much as possible. Adjust twist and fullness so that the middle and lower mainsail tufts on both sides of the sail are alive and streaming. These three indicators prove that the twist is correct. When in doubt oversheet rather than undersheet. The forward hand should be to leeward and forward. This handling technique will give you all the speed you can expect, Position your eyes as high as possible with the best possible field of vision. How you perform in the race will depend primarily on your own observation, and how successfully you position yourself in stronger air as a result of what you see.'

OK class

I asked Glenn Collings, an OK world champion who has since won a number of Australian Soling championships how he moved his boat so fast crosswind and downwind?

'I won the OK world's in Denmark. It was necessary to use the right sail to do it.

In light air the OK rig has the same problem as the Finn and the Laser, in that if the rig is optimised for moderate breezes it will have too tight a leech to be efficient in light airs. As a result the OK class has developed two different types of sail.

One, the 'European', has no luff curve. All the shape is built into the sail with seam taper. This sail will set, perfectly shaped for light air, twisted and with a free leech, in a near calm, so it is very fast upwind and crosswind in the light airs and wandering breezes which are so frequently found in inland sailing. As the wind speed increases to moderate it is difficult to get good shape without twist, so its pointing performance to windward and its power on the reaches tend to be disappointing. In winds stronger than the design wind its twisted shape becomes efficient again, so this rig is optimised for light airs and strong breezes, and it is not really competitive in moderate breezes.

The other sail, the 'Australian' style, has moderate luff curve and moderate seam taper. It sets up perfectly in a moderate breeze, and can be flattened progressively as the breeze becomes stronger, so it is very fast in all breezes (i.e. winds of 6 knots and more). The Laser sail is a perfect example of this style. In light airs it cannot be both flattened and twisted, so in light airs its performance is disappointing. This rig is optimised for breezes, and it is not really competitive upwind and crosswind in light airs.

In the regatta area in Denmark the prevailing winds were light, so I chose a European sail for the world's there. Had I been able to sail in the following year's championships at Medemblik on the Ijsselmeer where the prevailing wind is much stronger, I would have chosen an Australian style of sail for best speed in the expected stronger winds'.

Laser Two class

(Mark Mendelblatt). 'On light air reaches I sail with the Cunningham off, the lower mainsail flatter on tighter reaches and fuller on broader reaches, and the vang tension set so that the mainsail is still soft enough for the leech to move and be 'alive' but the boom must never go up in a puff. This is critical. The centreboard is raised about one quarter of its length; I never raise it further than this in any circumstances. Locate the puffs which are approaching, and position yourself to intercept them and use them. Sail high in the lulls between them, and low within the puffs to stay with them for longer, but never steer too aggressively. Excessive steering disturbs the flow over the spinnaker and is slow.'

24.8 In light air and waves

As wave action begins to move the rig unsteadily in the air, it will become more difficult to maintain attached leeward-side flow. As described in the 'close-hauled' section, the technique of heeling in a bow-down attitude to achieve sail twist also minimises rig movement due to waves when sailing a fourth-mode boat. Every effort should be made to hold the rig steady and so to retain attached lee-side flow for as long as is possible. The 470 champion again – 'In light air and waves try to keep the rig still by steering either more along or more down the bigger waves, depending upon their alignment, and trim the sails each time you turn'.

As the waves increase in size, at some point the rig will begin to move so much in the air, that attached suction-side flow will be lost. This will be indicated by the tufts. When this occurs, the sails should be set fuller – to about 16% camber, – and sheeted more closely to that point at which the windward tufts usually stream, and occasionally flutter. Trim for maximum drive force in unsteady light air conditions and separated flow occurs with much fuller sails and at a closer sheeting angle than for attached flow.

Since there is no longer any penalty for moving the rig in the air, every effort should now be directed toward using kinetics to add some muscular energy to the feeble drive force. In very light air, wave action crosswind often shakes the sails to the point where they are not steadily full of wind. In this situation, use of body movement to suppress roll for one or two waves – until the sail is full – and then allowing the boat to roll unchecked to sweep the sails to windward will usually kick it along. On broader reaches where wave action is sweeping the masthead more forwards and backwards, very careful adjustment of leech tension with the vang will enable the mainsail to respond with maximum force to broadly the same technique.

24.9 In moderate breeze and flat water

For the purposes of this section we will consider as 'moderate' those breezes lighter than the design wind, in which the boat's performance remains in zone 'C', Fig 24.10.

As soon as the breeze establishes, with its stronger wind to lower levels, the handling technique for fastest sailing changes abruptly. The boat should be held upright. Sails should be shaped and trimmed to achieve maximum drive force with attached flow. The basic rule always applies:- set the sails as full as possible provided that, in the lulls;

1) The tufts stream
2) The leeches are not hooked, and
3) The boat can be held upright,
(i.e. Don't make the sails too full, don't oversheet, and don't overpower).

The detail of setting up a rig for sailing crosswind is:

1. The jib sheet should be adjusted until the lower leeward jib tuft is streaming but occasionally agitating.

2. The jib fairlead slide should be adjusted in or out so that (1) above is achieved with the lower jib leech parallel with the centreline. (The slide will be well inboard for a close reach and much further outboard for a broad reach.)

3(a) If the wind speed and point of sailing is such that the forward hand can sit inboard and to leeward, the jib sheet should be held near the clew by hand, and should be held downwards to reduce twist so that the upper leeward jib tuft also streams but occasionally agitates in a manner similar to the lower tuft.

(b) If the wind speed and point of sailing is such that the forward hand needs to be on the windward side, the boat will sail faster if the jib is sheeted until both windward and leeward *upper* jib tufts stream. This may result in moderate or severe oversheeting of the lower jib. If so, move the jib slide out sufficiently for attached flow to be restored across the lower leeward surface of the jib while the upper tufts also stream.

4. Set the mainsail as full as possible (16% except on a close reach, where a flatter sail will be needed to avoid a hooked leech) and sheet so that -

(a) The *upper* leeward mainsail tuft streams and occasionally agitates, and/or the upper leech ribbon(s) 'just pop in and out' This trim is essential.

(b) The lower leeward tuft streams and occasionally agitates. (This trim is desirable if possible.)

(c) Control twist with sheet, traveller and/or vang until the leech, top to bottom, lies parallel with the centreline of the boat, if this can be achieved at the same time as the leeward tufts usually stream and occasionally agitate. If (c) is not possible (broad reach) ease sheets to achieve (a) and (b) above.

Fig 24.11 shows the essential details of this set-up, and Fig 24.12 shows a practical example being engineered and tuned in the workshop.

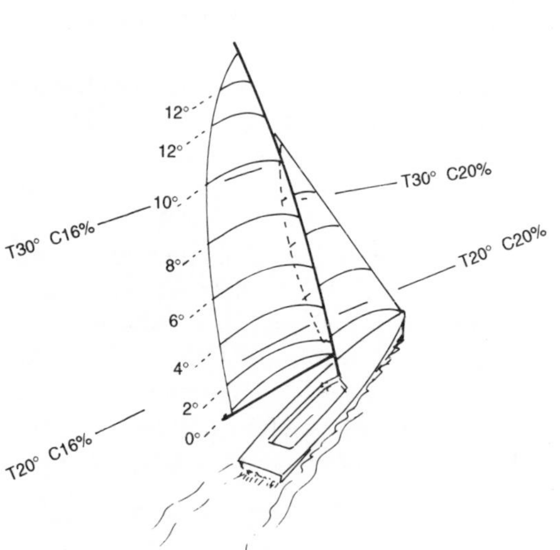

Fig 24.11 Fastest sail trim for reaching in zone C

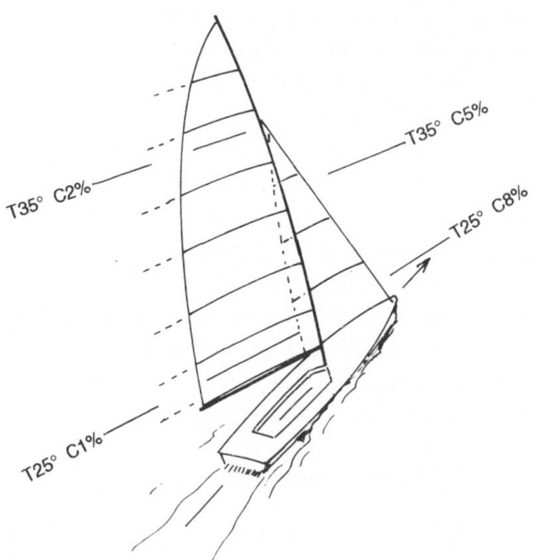

Fig 24.13 Fastest sail trim for reaching in zone A

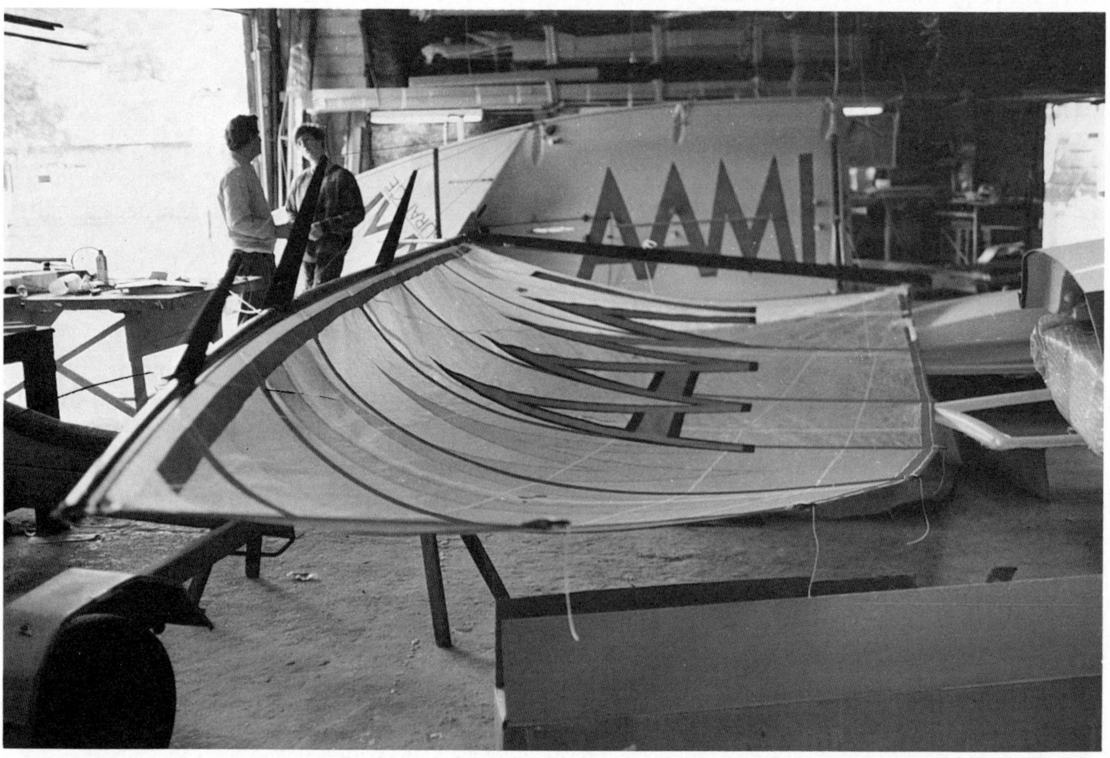

An Eighteen approaching completion. This active-batten sail will adopt this shape from light airs up to the design wind. Note how all parts of the leech are parallel to the centreline. (As this book goes to press this boat is the world champion.)

Fig 24.12 Example of Fig 24.11 sail shape

The sails should be trimmed continuously in response to the Apparent Wind's continuous changes of direction, so as to maintain Cl max accurately.

A practical point. If the mainsail is not back-lighted, and the glare is such that it is difficult to see the leeward tufts' behaviour, trim for 'the leech ribbons just popping in and out'. (Charlie McKee). The logic behind this trim technique is given in section 17.5 in Part Three.

470 class

'As the breeze establishes, reduce twist. The vang comes on, the boom goes out, leave the Cunningham slack for the most powerful upper leech possible. Pump to the limit of the rules to start driving the boat in the gusts, and to surf even the smallest waves.'

Exploiting the forced and planing modes

In boats of moderate performance, i.e. boats which sometimes plane, an interesting situation often occurs in moderate breezes when the course to the next mark is a close reach (i.e. in arc 2). Fig 24.14 repeats some of Fig 24.10. Let us imagine the case of a boat which is steering for a mark at 75 degrees to the True Wind, and that the wind speed alternates between 6 knots in the lulls and 10 knots in the gusts. If the helmsman steers straight for the mark, he will sail at 5.4 knots in the lull (point A, Fig 24.14), and 7.6 knots in the gust (point B) – an average speed of 6.5 knots. But if he steers 15 degrees higher in the lulls and sails at 4.5 knots (point C), and 15 degrees lower in the gusts, he will in this way systematically enter the planing mode in each gust and sail at a speed of 10.3 knots (point D) for as long as each gust lasts. This will give him an average speed of 7.4 knots, or almost 14% faster. Further, the fact that he will be steering more downwind in each gust will preferentially increase the time he will spend in the stronger winds of the gusts, and so even further increase his average speed. Since the distance penalty incurred in deviating +/- 15 degrees from the rhumb line is only about 4%, it is clear that this technique, when skilfully used, can deliver large gains. The detail will change from class to class according to the characteristics of each hull, but the principle will remain true.

24.10 In moderate air and waves

In lighter air, the difference between sailing in flat water and sailing in waves is a quantum jump.

This is not true in a breeze. With the onset of the stronger wind, the breeze's turbulence, the stronger wind at lower levels, the stronger tendency of the turbulent air of the breeze to remain attached to the leeward sides of the sails, and above all the stabilizing influence on the motion of the boat of the greater wind force on the sails, will all mean that the unsteadying influence of the waves will be greatly damped. Only a minor variation in technique will be called for, rather than a total change.

In waves, use fuller sails, and oversheet slightly.

The rig movement due to waves will cause the tufts to agitate more than they otherwise would. If this movement becomes substantial, the fastest trim will be that at which the leeward tufts *occasionally* stream. In harsh chaotic waves and a 6-8 knot breeze, the flow can break down completely on a broad reach, but this is rare. Perhaps the simplest practical advice is: 'In flat water, the Cl max trim, as indicated by the tufts, will be fastest. As the water becomes progressively rougher, progressively oversheet, rely more on 'feel', and use kinetics to the limit'.

Laser Two class

(Mark Mendelblatt) 'I use no Cunningham and the centreboard is up one quarter, i.e.the same set-up as in light air, except that the vang needs to be tighter to achieve the same balance between a leech which is 'alive' and 'springy' for pumping, and the boom not going up. In this breeze on all spinnaker reaches when there are even the smallest waves I sit to leeward and the crew moves out on trapeze. We find that from the trapeze the crew can not only see the spinnaker better, but also see the small waves better and can feel the boat's response to each wave better. We therefore make it his responsibility to steer the boat to place it on each advancing wave face. He steers it with his feet. He does not pump the spinnaker; we find that pumping the spinnaker on reaches is slow. I co-ordinate with him by steering and trimming the mainsail as he turns the boat, and by pumping the mainsail with one good hard pump per wave. I steer the boat with my aft hand and trim the mainsail by holding the boom directly with my forward hand. The mainsheet lies ready over my thumb so for pumping I grasp the mainsheet and pump with the fastest hardest full-arm sweep I can make.

At the worlds at Hayling Island in England, the courses were set with very long reaches which were correspondingly tight. About half the races were in light breezes, but there were always small waves which came through the entrance to the bay from the rougher water of the English Channel. We used the technique described above to use the small waves and gained consistently on the crews who sat on their windward decks and did not appear to be able to take the same advantage of the small waves'.

Handling crosswind in stronger breezes

24.11 Sail trim crosswind in stronger breezes

In chapter 22 it was stressed that when sailing close-hauled, the loss of pointing performance from being underpowered in a lull was far greater than the loss of speed performance from being slightly overpowered in a gust; hence the invariable advice for sailing upwind, 'Trim so that you are comfortable but fully powered in the lulls, and *feather* as necessary through the gusts'.

When sailing crosswind in light air and in the moderate breezes, balance is not a problem even in the gusts. The same principle applies – make the sails as full and as powerful as possible (consistent with attached flow and no hooked leeches), so as to achieve the maximum possible drive force in the lulls.

As the breeze becomes stronger, this situation abruptly reverses in zone A (Figs 24.4 and 24.10). Zone A is the zone in which the wind speed is stronger than the design wind.

In the case of displacement boats they will be up to hull speed. Fuller sails will make them go no faster in the lulls, and the increased drag of eased fuller sails will only make them sail more slowly in the gusts, (except for a few very tender keelboats – such as Stars – which can still be in zone A with the Apparent Wind aft of the beam.

In the case of boats which can plane freely, the boat's high speed in the gust will hold the Apparent Wind far forward of the beam, and it will become stronger. In this situation, the limit to speed is set not by the hull, which can plane freely to any speed, but by the aerodynamic drag of the rig. The drag of an over-full sail in a strong wind is substantial, and will increase as the square of the speed of the Apparent Wind. Worse, when an over-full sail is eased until it makes only a small angle with the Apparent Wind, (as will inevitably happen when the sail is eased to keep the boat upright), the drive force suffers badly because much of the forward-directed suction is lost. (The forward part of the sail flutters, and only the leech remains fully inflated. The pressure difference then becomes primarily across the boat, and not forward.) The effect of these two factors – high aerodynamic drag and poor drive force at the smaller trim angles – is that a boat which is set up with sails full, so as to be comfortable but fully powered in the lulls, can accelerate only a little in the gusts. The increasing drag and collapsing drive force result in only a modest increase of speed. A practical point is that a boat which is handled in this way is much more likely to broach when only the sails' leeches are full than one with flatter sails with the drive force further forward.

By way of contrast, a boat which is trimmed with much flatter sails, so that it is comfortable and efficient in the gusts (and not the lulls) may sail a little slower in the lulls, (depending on kinetics), but will sail very much faster in the gusts. Compared with the full-sail boat, it may in practice lose ten metres in the lull but can often gain one hundred metres in the gust.

The consequence of this is that, as soon as the wind and boat speed reach the point where a flat sail is justified in the gusts, it usually pays to flatten quickly and to extreme. Delicate shades of adjustment to minimise the average drag are the hallmark of the winner when sailing to windward. Not so when sailing crosswind in zone A. Once flat sails are justified, they should be very flat! Figs 24.11 and 24.13 show the two shapes. Fig 24.12 shows a good example of the Fig 24.11 shape.

In zone C, the dynamics are such that balance will never be a problem, and so (except in very light air) the sails should be set at a camber of about 16% to achieve Cl max, be vanged firmly to limit twist, and be trimmed continuously to maintain Cl max in the continuously shifting Apparent Wind.

Between the flat sail, maximum-hiking zone A, and the full-sail, crew inboard zone C, lies the transition zone B. In steady winds this zone will be narrow. In rough unsteady winds it will be wide. In zone B, a technique of using moderately full sails plus sailing further offwind in the gusts than is advantageous in either zone A or C, will usually be fastest. But on days with harsh gusts, flat sails will win every time.

24.12 Arc 1 – flat water and windward planing

In arc 1 (Fig 24.10), the handling techniques will be exactly the same as for close-hauled. In gusts the boat should be pointed higher and the sails eased. Boats of low and moderate performance will sail faster if their mainsails are controlled by traveller.

The vital trim difference between close-hauled and close reach sailing in arc 1 is that much less centreboard area will be needed because of the higher speed. The centreboard should be raised. How far? There are usually two practical limits. The first is that in boats fitted with dagger boards it is convenient to raise the centreboard no further than will permit the boat to be tacked or gybed without the top of the centreboard fouling the vang assembly. The second is that enough centreboard area should be left in the water so that 'steer for balance' will still be strongly effective. This position should be found by experiment, and marked in some way so that it can be repeated with confidence.

In winds of about 12 knots or more, if the centreboard is raised half-up and the boat steered lower and the traveller eased, boats with reasonable performance will accelerate immediately and start planing freely. Once the boat is planing, it can be pointed a little higher if desired without loss of speed provided the crew hike to the limit of their ability and the sail trim is accurate, or its rig can be optimised for slightly higher speed at a lower pointing angle along the rhumb line.

The further out the crew can carry their weight, the higher the boat will point without loss of speed, or the faster it will go when pointing lower. So the trapezing forward hand should 'stand tall', on his toes on the rail if necessary, and carry his arms above his head. The helm should 'hike' his body out as far as is possible consistent with the strength to stay there for the duration of the leg.

In steady winds, the mainsail twist should be very small, so the mainsheet should, if anything, be tightened, and the mainsail trimmed outboard as necessary with traveller. As the wind speed increases, the mainsail should be flattened to extreme with outhaul and vang. As the wind becomes stronger it inevitably becomes rougher and the boat will at some point begin to 'stagger' in the gust onslaughts and will cease to feel 'free'. At this point, the feeling of freedom, together with regained speed, will be restored immediately if elasticity is introduced by progressively tightening the vang and easing the mainsheet. Only two or three inches of mainsheet movement are usually needed. A fractional additional fullness in the lower mainsail can also be useful for greater steadiness and speed in harsh winds. Shroud tension, if adjustable, should be increased to tighten the forestay and flatten the jib. Jib traveller slides should be set as far outboard as possible consistent with not losing jib 'power' in the lulls. Typical 'fastest' jib sheet fairlead settings are about a 9 degree angle between the centreline of the boat and the chordline of the lower jib in zone C (arc 1), 12 degrees approximately in zone A in winds of 12 knots, increasing to up to 22 degrees in winds of 25 knots.

Windward planing

The performance polars of all sailboats will necessarily fall into one of three groups, which are well exemplified by the Soling, the Tasar, and the Eighteen footer plots of Fig 24.4

The Soling inset shows that, in strong winds, the fastest windward-going VMG will be achieved by sailing at one precise speed. In flat water this will be very close to hull speed. In waves, depending upon the size and type of the waves, it may be a little faster. The graph at this point has a sharp peak. Any endeavour to sail faster results in a lower VMG. In practical terms this means that when keelboats and the heavier dinghies race to windward in strong winds, it is not possible to 'over-run' a competitor to leeward and slightly ahead who is sailing as well as you are. If you bear away a little, you will merely fall to leeward and finish behind him and not ahead of him, because your speed will not increase more than minimally. The whole tactical area of gaining advantage through speed variation when sailing to windward is not open to sailors of these boats, and the surrendering of this advantage is one of the principal mental adjustments which have to be made by sailors of fast dinghies and catamarans when they choose to sail and race in these heavier boats.

The Eighteen footer inset is different in three respects:

The speeds are much higher

The speeds are always in the planing mode.

The VMG graph is much flatter.

With boats with high 'sail-carrying-power / total weight' ratios, you cannot sail them to windward without planing. There is no question of needing to point low to initiate the plane. At normal pointing angles, as soon as you sheet your sails in, they just go. You cannot stop them. Further, you have a wide range of pointing angles available from which to choose. Depending upon the traffic and the tactical situation you can point higher and sail more slowly, or sail lower and faster, and provided that you handle the boat properly your VMG will not change much. The VMG plot is relatively flat, and there is little penalty either way. This is also true of the faster big catamarans. This is the practical reason why these faster boats can mix relatively easily with all the slower boats in a crowded harbour. By tacit agreement, crews adopt a different interpretation of the rules. In open water the fast boats give way to almost everything else by bearing away and flashing behind them, and never mind who is on port tack and who is on starboard. They do this because they can do so without significant loss. Near their rounding marks the tacit rules change: everything else keeps clear, and they apply the rules strictly as between themselves. It's a fair and reasonable arrangement.

The third group, the intermediate boats, are technically interesting. These boats have two peaks in their windward-going VMG curves; examples are the FD, 5O5, 470, Laser 2, Tasar etc. The Tasar polar is typical. The first VMG peak is in the displacement mode, and is as precise as that of the Soling and for the same reason. Through the speed range of the forced mode the VMG falls. As soon as free planing establishes in winds which are strong enough a second peak occurs which is flatter. This means that in stronger winds the crews of these boats have a choice – point or plane. A number of factors go into this decision:

1. It is essential to sail at one or the other of the two efficient speeds. In flat water the speed range in the forced mode between them gives a slower VMG than either of the peaks.

2. In the real world, there are three extraneous factors all of which slow the windward planer more than the boat which is displacement sailing. These are:

(a) Because the boat points lower it will normally tack more often, and each tack will take a little longer because in addition to the tack it will be necessary to re-acquire planing speed before 'winding up' to the higher pointing angle on the plane.

The planer loses more in tacking.

(b) Because the boat will make longer wider crosswind sweeps and its crew will generally be more reluctant to tack, it will frequently sail through lulls between the gusts which are necessarily oriented upwind/downwind in any stronger wind. If the lulls are pronounced, a higher-pointing rival will probably tack to avoid them.

The planer spends more time in the lulls.

(c) The lower the pointing angle, the more severe is the penalty for sailing in any header. In thermally excited strong winds in which individual gusts can be skewed at random, any mistake of lift and header, or any reluctance to tack once a header is identified, can lead to massive loss.

The planer is penalised more severely by any header.

Because of the practical penalties noted above, a boat of intermediate performance will usually achieve a lower VMG when planing to windward than is indicated by it's polar diagram. Conversely, spectacular gains become possible on those occasions when lulls and headers can be avoided.

Because the high-performance boat sails faster and points higher, it tacks no more often, suffers less from sailing any header, and has the power to keep moving fast through the lulls. It suffers little disadvantage.

24.13 Arc 1 – rough water

When close reaching in steady stronger winds, rough water will call for surprisingly little difference in technique. While the difference in hull drag between flat water and waves can be very large at low speeds, it becomes relatively small when planing, and this explains why there is so little difference in the 'feel' of the boat.

In rough winds with harsh gust onslaughts a boat which is set up 'hard' will begin to 'stagger' and so sail more slowly. Control and speed will be restored if the mainsail is allowed to yield more elastically. This will be necessary at some stage in flat water, and sooner in waves. The mainsail should therefore be set with progressively tighter vang and slacker sheet, to increase its elasticity until the boat can be controlled to remain upright in the gust onslaughts. In strong winds – 20 knots plus – the boat will sail faster if the jib as well as the mainsheet is eased *slightly* as each gust strikes. It must never be eased too much, or speed loss will become substantial.

24.14 Arc 2

In arc 2 (Fig 24.10) the technique for fastest speed is to control balance solely by easing sails in gusts. The boat should be aimed directly at the chosen aiming point, and neither luffed nor steered downwind other than for tactical reasons or to chase gusts. Boats of lower and moderate performance will sail fastest if the mainsail is controlled by traveller. Because of the greater power options and speed range of high performance boats they sail faster with the greater flexibility of sheet control rather than the greater precision of traveller control.

Because the Apparent Wind angle scarcely changes between arcs 1 and 2, the sail shapes and trims for fastest speed change little. In winds of 10-12 knots the sails can be shaped a little fuller. But in winds of 14 knots and more, they should be as flat, and for the same reason, as in arc 1. They will need to be trimmed several degrees further outboard, primarily because of the need to ease them in the stronger Apparent Winds at the higher speeds. Exactly the same remarks apply with respect to rough water and rough winds as applied in arc 1.

Arc 3

Arc 3 covers the widest range of speed and sailing angles of all the arcs. Fortunately, it divides logically into zones A, B and C, and so becomes easier to visualize and handle.

24.15 Arc 3 – zone A and flat water

In zone A the handling remains broadly similar to that in arcs 1 and 2, but with three vitally important differences.

1. Steer-for-balance becomes dominant, and so the boat can be driven much harder and still be held upright.

2. Because of (1) above, there is advantage in allowing the mainsail to set slightly fuller for a second or two at each gust onslaught, to secure extra drive force for faster acceleration.

3. The performance lobes (vi-vi in Fig 24.4) invite special handling.

The advantage to be gained from setting the mainsail slightly fuller in gusts (2, above) is the key to the primary handling difference. In arcs 1 and 2, stronger-wind control of the mainsail should be by traveller, except for the highest performance boats. In arc 3, it should be by sheet. The effect of this change is that as the sheet is eased in each gust onslaught, the upper mainsail twists to leeward and becomes slightly fuller (as the masthead flexes forward), and this occurs at the same time as the boat is turning more downwind. This is exactly the right combination for maximum acceleration.

The detail of arc 3, zone A handling is as follows.

As soon as the windspeed increases to the point where, when using the moderate-breeze set-up described in 24.9 above, the windward mainsail tufts flutter in the gusts, the set-up should be quickly changed towards:

Sheet:	Adopt sheet control of mainsail.
Traveller:	Cleat about half-way between centre and leeward extreme.
Outhaul:	Flatten lower mainsail to extreme.
Vang:	Apply severe vang, to flatten upper mainsail to extreme.
Rotation:	(Wingmast Rigs) Set at about 45 degrees (Use 70 degrees only if the 45 degree position will not remain locked in. This may be necessary with lighter crews and/or harsher gusts).
Shrouds:	Tight
Jib Slides:	As far outboard as possible provided windward jib tufts do not agitate in the lulls.

Centreboard: Up to extreme consistent with maintaining steer-for-balance capability.
Crew: For highest speeds, both crew members should move aft as far as possible, and hike directly outboard and not half backwards.

This set-up enables very high speeds to be achieved and maintained in strong winds and gusts.

When the wind is rough with strong gusts and pronounced lulls, the forward hand needs to be fluently mobile in moving forward as necessary to preserve trim in the lulls. As the next gust is watched approaching, the forward hand should anticipate as necessary so that both crew members are in position to hike to extreme as the gust strikes.

As the gust hits, the helmsman should ease mainsheet and turn downwind as firmly as is necessary to keep the boat absolutely upright. The forward hand should ease the jib sheet to maintain Cl max trim. This handling will give very fast acceleration, and the Apparent Wind will move forward quickly. Acceleration will be even faster if the mainsail is, 'pumped' vigorously. As the speed stabilizes, the boat can be turned gently back towards the rhumb line, and the sheets tightened, for optimum speed and heading through the body of the gust. Fastest heading will usually be a little downwind of the rhumb line – normally, a crew will adjust their heading so as to remain within the area of that gust's stronger wind for as long as possible.

As the gust fades, the reverse sequence should be used. As the boat begins to heel to windward, the sails should be trimmed in and the boat luffed, as firmly as necessary, to keep it upright by steer-for-balance dynamics while the crew move their bodies inboard. The boat will sail faster through the lull if it is steered a little above the rhumb line.

If the gust terminates abruptly, a fast-moving boat should be luffed sharply to preserve balance. If, in this situation, a helmsman inadvertently reverts to the normal 'slow-boat' technique, and bears away, he will roll any fast-moving boat further and forcefully to windward (because a turn away from the direction of roll is anti-steer-for-balance). This trap is a common cause of capsizes when helms move into high performance boats. If, when you are moving fast, the boat rolls to windward, the automatic response must be to *luff*. In this way lies survival and the highest speeds.

The performance lobes (vi – vi, Fig 24.4) occur at those combinations of wind strength and points of sailing at which it becomes unnecessary to ease sheet to keep upright – these are the points where the application of steer-for-balance is itself sufficient. The practical effect is that the speed increases a little, but the ability to maintain this very high speed for longer periods is enhanced greatly, because the helmsman can simply adjust his sail trim and point of sailing for gust or lull, and never has to ease.

When these conditions occur in the presence of waves big enough to surf in the traversing sense, very much higher speeds yet can be achieved. In this situation the Apparent Wind can move so far forward that crews who find themselves enjoying these conditions for the first time often find that they cannot sheet their sails closely enough to maintain optimum trim. Experience suggests that when the waves are big enough to surf, the mainsheet traveller should be sheeted more centrally, and the jib slides should be set closer inboard, so that efficient sail trim can be maintained no matter how far forward the Apparent Wind may move.

470 class

The way these principles are applied in a 470 becomes:

'In breezes between 12 and 16 knots, apply Cunningham sufficient only to take the wrinkles out. Trim for absolute maximum power by playing the vang on a gust-by-gust basis; apply vang with each gust, the stronger the wind the more severe the vang. Ease for greater fullness and power in the lulls. This will allow some twist, so co-ordinate mainsheet trim with vang adjustment – bring the mainsheet in as the vang is eased – to keep the power on.

As the wind increases through about 17 knots, apply severe Cunningham to open the upper leech. The vang is not now so necessary, because the boat is now sailing de-powered all the time. 'Flatten the foot to make the mark' i.e. adjust the foot as full as possible consistent with the point of sailing required'.

24.16 Arc 3 – zone A and rough water

The effect of regular waves will be at a minimum when sailing cross-wind because the heading will be more or less aligned along their crests and troughs. Further, in stronger-wind zone A sailing, the sail forces are at their most dominant. Fast boats are not noticeably slowed by waves when reaching, and no change in handling technique will be needed as far as achieving the greatest speed is concerned, beyond minimising the time spent sailing 'uphill'.

If short, steep chaotic waves are encountered, the crew should move even further back to lift the bow higher, so that the hull drives over, and not through, the steep wave faces or backs.

When sailing further downwind, towards the strong-wind extremes of zone A, surfing opportunities will occur, and these should be exploited to the greatest possible extent. When reaching in zone A, the downwind speed of normal wind-waves will usually be too great to allow continuous surfing. But if we imagine that a boat were to surf one unbroken wave, and head as far crosswind as possible whilst remaining on that wave face, then the extra speed due to surfing will deflect the Apparent Wind further forward, and displace the very high speed 'lobes' (vi – vi Fig 24.4) further downwind and with even higher speeds to positions X – X, Fig 24.4. This can be very exhilarating sailing indeed.

Out on the water, waves tend to occur in 'sets' – a few large and well-formed waves are followed by a period of smaller and confused waves, and then follow the next 'set' of larger waves. This means that, in practice, the extreme speeds of lobes 'X' can be enjoyed only periodically. The tactical consequences of this are far-reaching. In any group of close-spaced boats on a reaching leg, there will be a tendency to sail above the rhumb line as each crew ensure that they are not over-run by the boats to windward and astern. In this situation, a crew who can pick the moment when a suitable bigger wave of a set coincides with a gust, can elect suddenly to bear away, accelerate and surf to leeward with lobe 'X' performance. In this way they can separate themselves both downwind and forward from adjacent boats and also return towards the rhumb line. No other boat will be able to match that high speed downwind 'dash' performance until a similar combination of simultaneous big wave and gust repeats, and this will probably not occur until the next set of big waves.

In rough air

The very fact of moving fast crosswind through gusts, lulls and channels which are oriented up-and-down-wind, will mean that the moving boat will experience changes in wind speed which are more abrupt and which will occur more frequently than those experienced by an observer at rest or on a slower boat. The consequence of this is that the crew will have to respond more frequently, more quickly, and more forcefully in keeping the boat upright. No other change of technique will be called for.

24.17 Arc 3 – zone B

If the wind were always steady and the water always flat, zone B would not exist. The boundary between the 'stability limited' zone A, and the 'power-dominant' zone C, would be clear-cut. In the real world, the natural unsteadiness of wind and water means that the boundary is blurred and indistinct. This reality is acknowledged by zone B.

There are no 'zone B ' handling techniques. A boat will sail fastest in conditions which alternate between those of zone A and zone C if it is handled as for either zone A or zone C as appropriate at that instant. Further, zone B is one of those 'opportunity areas' which often occur in sailing in which a combination of tactical and handling considerations can from time to time be skilfully blended to achieve, briefly, higher speeds than can otherwise be expected. One very common example of this occurs when broad-reaching in conditions of well-defined gusts. In this situation, a crew who sail the rhumb line will sail faster through the gusts and more slowly through the lulls. As a result they will probably spend more of their time in the lulls. Another crew may sail more downwind in the gusts, and so increase the proportion of the time that they spend sailing faster in the gusts' stronger winds. They may sail more crosswind in the lulls, and in addition adjust their heading so as to intercept the next suitable gust more quickly and also to enter that gust at the most favourable point – through its advancing, 'shoulder' – and in this way they will reduce the proportion of their time that they spend sailing more slowly in the lulls' lighter winds. For this crew, the increase in average speed which they achieve by increasing the proportion of the time that they spend in the gusts' stronger winds will probably be much greater than the extra distance they will cover by sailing alternately above and below the rhumb line. In handling their boat, they will probably alternate between zone C strong-wind technique, and zone A moderate-wind technique. Looked at in the broader aspect, this is classic zone B sailing, with the alternating techniques called for solely by the wind's unsteadiness.

24.18 Introduction to arc 3 – zone C

In stronger winds – say 12 knots or more – this is the broad reaching zone. In an ideal world of steady wind and flat water, sailing fast in this zone would be simple. In the real world, local wind speed differences due to pronounced gusts and lulls, and channelling; the effects of waves; the skill of the crew at further exploiting wave opportunities by combining surfing with kinetics; the effects of wind direction change; and (when racing) tactical considerations, all become important and sometimes conflicting considerations in deciding what will be the fastest way to the next mark. Not surprisingly, it is on these downwind legs that most races are won. It would probably be a truer statement to say that, usually, they are lost by everybody except the winner.

For clarity, we will look at each of the factors separately.

The common factors

In zone C two factors remain common by definition. Since the boat is no longer stability-limited, it will never be necessary to ease the sails (except as is advantageous in pumping). Further, since the Apparent Wind direction will be either on or aft of the beam (except for high-performance boats), the higher drag of full sails will not slow the boat. The sails should therefore be set at their fullest and trimmed for maximum Cl for maximum total force and maximum drive force.

24.19 Arc 3 – zone C in steady wind and flat water

In these conditions the fastest sail trim and boat handling technique will be the simplest possible combination. The rig set-up described in Section 24.9 will provide greatest drive force. The steer-for-balance technique will provide dynamic lateral stability. The crew should separate their body-weights laterally, i.e. they should sit one on each gunwale and not crouch both in the middle of the boat. The 'body weights laterally separated' position keeps the rig steadier in the air – (maximum angular inertia), gives each crew member room to move, and above all raises the eye levels so that both can see better. The crew should position their bodies, fore and aft, so that, up to planing speeds, the transom just skims the water, for minimum hull drag. At boat speeds of eight knots or more – free planing – the helmsman should move progressively further aft, to lift the bow. When the wind speed approaches 'survival' force, both crew members should move right aft for maximum possible lateral stability. (Nothing is slower than an inverted boat). This is the arc in which the biggest changes in the direction of the Apparent Wind occur continuously, as shown in Fig 24.3. Even in flat water and the steadiest winds, the degree to which the Apparent Wind changes direction is surprising. Those crews will sail fastest who are most attentive in continuously trimming their sails to maintain Cl max.

Relatively steady winds and flat water do sometimes occur. If, in these conditions, you find yourself in the lead, enjoy the privilege of clear wind and straight lines, – sail accurately and increase your lead.

24.20 Arc 3 – zone C in gusts and channelling

Conventional wisdom usually advises that, when gusts or channels are readily identifiable, a crew will risk nothing and will usually reach the next mark sooner if they bear away in the gusts and so sail faster in the stronger wind for more of the time. This is true in zone A, which is stability limited. It is certainly true in arc 4, the downwind situation. But it is not nearly so true when broad reaching in zone C.

A careful play with Fig 24.10 will confirm that, while luffing in the lulls and bearing away in the gusts is fastest in zones A and B, and also in arc 4, it can be slower than straight lines when broad reaching in zone C. The reason is that in this zone it is so much harder to maintain, let alone improve, your speed as you return to the rhumb line. Racing experience also suggests that, in the absence of other factors, straighter lines are often faster when broad reaching.

This simply raises the stakes a little higher. If the gusts and channels are well defined and you can get them consistently right, you can still gain. And the tactical effect of the fleet bunching near the leeward mark usually favours the windward, i.e. upwind, boats. But if you don't handle the gusts and channels flawlessly, or the fleet just doesn't 'gel' this time, then on broad reaches you can lose. So when broad reaching in flat water and clear air, be much more careful before you abandon straight lines.

24.21 Arc 3 – zone C in waves

In this case we are considering regular waves which can be surfed. Chaotic waves, standing waves, and swell cannot be surfed, for obvious reasons.

These notes apply not only to broad reaching. They apply with equal force to downwind sailing as well.

The basic facts are that in the generally sheltered waters in which unballasted sailboats usually sail, regular waves will normally grow until they stabilize at a wave-speed which is about two-thirds to three-quarters of the wind speed. A glance at Fig 24.10 indicates that a modern high-performance dinghy of low power (Laser II, Tasar etc) and many other racing boats of similar size can achieve, in flat water, a downwind speed of about one half the wind speed when they are broad reaching or running.

The importance of waves is that they can be surfed. Successful surfing can significantly increase boat speed periodically, from about one half of the wind speed to about two thirds or three quarters of the wind speed, both when broad-reaching and running.

To surf any wave successfully requires that the boat be accelerated to a speed little different from the speed of an approaching wave, and then turned down-wave at the exact instant that will position the boat on its advancing face and preferably nearer its crest. The boat will then enjoy not only the drive force of the wind on its sails, but, in addition, the drive force from both sailing downhill, and also the assistance of the down-wind movement of the water near the crest due to the orbital motion of water in the wave. If this total drive force is sufficient to maintain the boat's speed at the wave's speed, prolonged surfing will be possible. If, with skilful sail trimming, it can maintain a greater speed, then broad reaching at substantially greater speeds than are attainable in flat water become possible, by the technique of traversing.

The technique of surfing depends upon the combination of several factors:

1. The hull must be capable of achieving high speeds without much increase in drag. Light planing dinghies and sailboards are ideally suited to surfing.
2. The wave system should be of the normal type, in which sets of three or four well formed big waves recur periodically.
3. It should be easy to observe the approach of gusts (No oil slicks).
4. The crew should be skilled in surfing.
5. The crew should be skilled in kinetics.

The basic technique is given in Fig 24.14. If we assume that the wind is 15 knots, it would be reasonable, in open water and the larger bays, to assume that regular waves would have developed after a few hours which move downwind at about 10 knots, and with a length, crest to crest, of about 60 feet. This wave speed is indicated as W – W. In 15 knots and flat water a Tasar or similar dinghy when broad-reaching on a heading 0 – O would sail at about 10 knots, point 'O'. If, in the trough just prior to the first of a set of big waves, the boat is sailed more crosswind say on the heading 0 – P it will accelerate to 12 knots, point 'P'. If with this speed it is turned downwind and downwave at exactly that instant which places it on the advancing face, say at 'Q', it will 'catch' that wave, and can then be luffed to 'traverse' across the wave-face 0 – R. It will be driven partly by the wave-slope and partly by the downwind-moving water near the wave crest and partly by the increased Apparent Wind. Its speed at 'R' is 13.5 knots! So long as the wind keeps blowing, and that wave maintains its form, the boat can continue to surf at 13.5 knots in the direction 0 – R. Its notional competitors are still sailing at 10 knots on the same heading 0 – O. This is where and how many dinghy races are won.

Note that it is possible to achieve the performance of position 'R' only by proceeding from 'O' through 'P' then 'Q' to finally arrive at 'R'. It is not possible to sail straight from 'O' to 'R'.

Laser Two class

(Mark Mendelblatt) 'Catch every wave possible. Steer with the tiller to spear the boat down the advancing faces. So long as you are reaching with unstalled sails, pump the mainsail as you turn down the wave but do not pump the spinnaker. In a Laser II take nothing for granted; its light weight makes it easier to 'lose' and flip in wave or gust than heavier boats.'

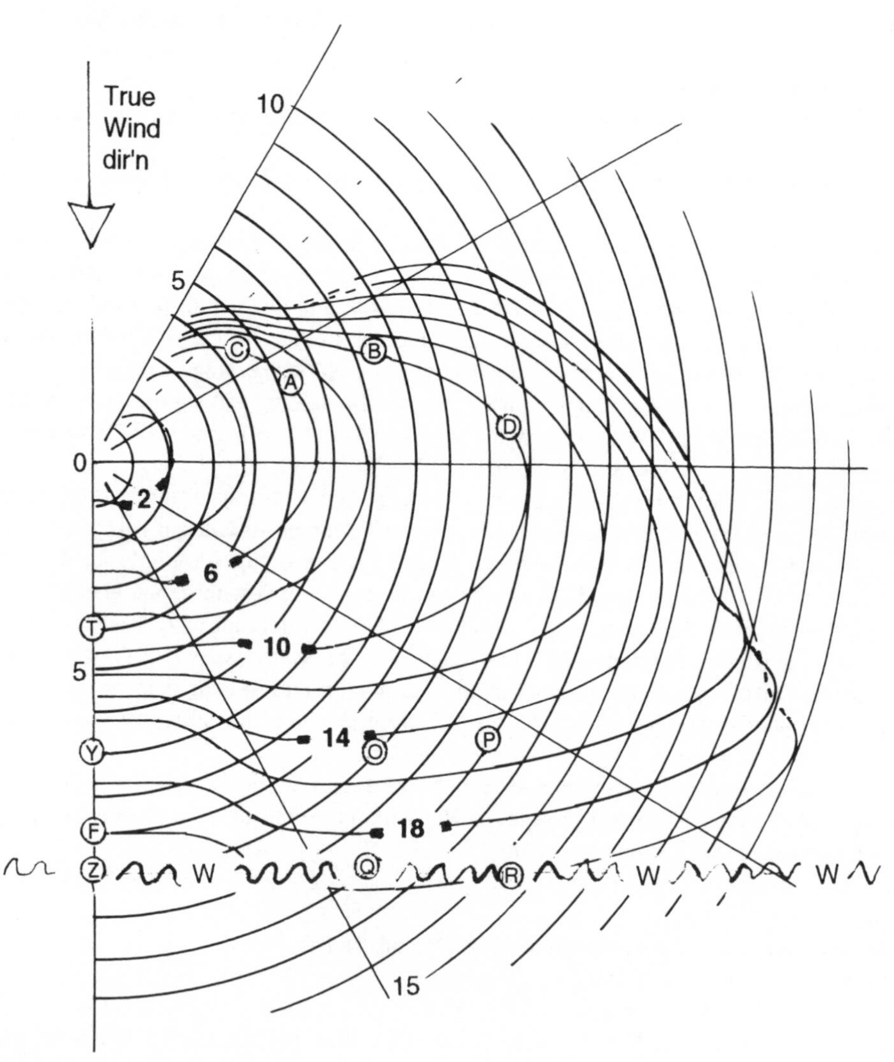

ABCD Technique for avoiding the forced mode.
OPQR " " catching waves when broad reaching.
YOZ " " " " " running.
W Wave speed, 10 knots in downwind direction in 15 knot wind.

Fig 24.14 Techniques for catching waves - and for avoiding the forced mode

470 class

'Use waves to the limit. Use the sets of bigger waves to get 'depth' – use them to sail faster on a more downwind angle to a position below the rhumb line so that you can sail faster at a higher angle through the smaller waves between the sets.'

OK class

Glenn Collings, world OK champion, described his exact technique well: 'I found that it was possible to achieve superior broad reaching and downwind performance in the OK by using a precise co-ordination of body movement, steering and sail trimming. This was a technique which came from a determination to sail faster downwind by employing all three factors simultaneously. I spent a lot of time practising and there was a lot of trial and error before I could feel and hear the boat beginning to respond properly. In essence I alternated as rapidly as conditions permitted between steering downwind, down every available wave, and luffing to a broad reaching course to maintain speed whenever the wave-drive was lost. As I accelerated down each wave I deliberately moved my body into the boat. It was essential to be almost central in the cockpit before each turn was started. When the boat reached maximum speed – well before it began to lose speed – I luffed very quickly across the wind sufficiently to maintain the drive, but so smoothly that the speed was not checked. I simultaneously used both body movement to control the roll and trimmed the sail to maintain optimum sail angle to the wind through the turn, and co-ordinated all three movements into a kinetic urge which gave me a speed boost which sometimes drove me over the wave ahead. I was very fit and needed to be, because the body movements needed to stabilise and optimise the boat's attitude through the wave crests and down the slopes, and to give the urge through the turn, was so intense. This does not mean that I handled the boat coarsely – the exact reverse is true. I think that I had learned to co-ordinate steering, sail trimming and balance in down-wave situations better than others had at that time. Other helms pumped better than I did, and put more effort into it, but they lacked the co-ordination to use all three factors simultaneously and more subtly. I was able to gain three or four waves on them on each downwind leg, and that was sufficient to win.'

'The same technique works with the Tasar, but it is more difficult because of the presence and weight of the second person. It also works with the Soling, but to a lesser extent again.'

Other helms pick up the story with bigger boats. Surfing can be used momentarily to achieve a critical performance increase at a critical moment even in craft which cannot normally surf.

Probably the most famous example of this occurred when Jock Sturrock surfed *Gretel 1* past Bus Mosbacher during Australia's first challenge for the *America's* Cup. With that single, swift, skilful, passing manoeuvre, Australia, and the world, knew that the Americans could ultimately be beaten. After that, it was just a matter of time. It came as no surprise that, ultimately, the American's were beaten downwind.

Another more recent example occurred in the final race of a J24 world championships. The points situation was that whichever of two crews beat the other would win the series. These two possible winners lay second and third as they turned downwind on the first broad reaching leg. Ahead was a helmsman who could not win on points, but who was known as a compulsive luffer, and so could not safely be passed to windward. The crew who were second sailed slightly low, as if to attempt to pass later and well to leeward. They waited until a combination of gust and wave-set approached, anticipated their moment brilliantly, and luffed sharply to accelerate towards the lee quarter of the leader. As they closed to within half a length, their timing paid off. Both the approaching gust and the first big wave of the approaching set arrived at that instant. The leader assumed that they intended to cross his stern to blanket him from windward, and luffed sharply to defend. As he luffed the attackers curved away down the wave-face with their higher initial speed boosted by the wave slope, plus the wave crest, plus the gust, plus all the skilful effort they could put into kinetics (at that time three pumps per wave were legal).

Never mind that the boat was a rather insensitive 24 foot keelboat. They co-ordinated all the factors plus the pumping perfectly. They caught that wave, surfed straight through the lee of the leader, and thereafter increased their lead with straight lines and clear air. The luffer, now second, was well stimulated to block any repetition, and so defended the new leader's position very efficiently. The leaders went on to win that race and the world championship. Such is the power of a wave, a gust, imagination, anticipation, and the ability to exploit two natural advantages simultaneously.

Chapter Twenty Five
Sailing Downwind

25.1 Sailing downwind – the principles and the performance factors

Sailing originated thousands of years ago with the hoisting of rudimentary sails on oar-powered vessels on those occasions when, 'the wind was fair'. Sailing downwind is thus the oldest form of sailing, and so could reasonably be expected to be the point of sailing best understood. Until relatively recently this was probably true. The great sailing ships which 'hunted the trade winds' so that they could broad reach around the world certainly developed these skills into a fine art. The traditional yacht racing approach to the downwind leg has been to set all sail possible and head straight for the leeward mark. This leads to the traditional procession of yachts, all sailing at about the same speed, and all following one another.

High-performance sailing changes all this. To the traditional 'square running' sail power, lightweight high-performance boats add the low drag of planing hulls, which can surf as a routine, kinetic thrust for rapid acceleration to match wave speed prior to surfing, the added broad reaching sail power which can often make it faster to tack downwind and a new understanding of the wind's patterns and the waves' patterns, to guide a crew in choosing which of several possible options is more likely to be faster at any particular time. Gone are the boring processions. In their individual search for wind and speed, crews fan widely over the course. After the tactical straight-jacket of the 'barrier effect' of the fleet on the broad reaching legs, the downwind legs can now offer freedom, opportunity, excitement, individual challenge and race success.

How recently this new understanding has appeared, may be judged by the fact that in the 1960's the Tornado catamaran – still one of the world's fastest boats – was designed with a whisker pole to goose-wing the jib on the side opposite to the mainsail when the catamaran was running 'square'. And again – at that time, no sailing book on handling or tactics ever discussed tacking downwind other than as a temporary escape from being blanketed by a close follower.

During the past thirty years there has been a revolution in the way successful crews have thought about downwind capability, technique and performance. The new key fact is, that the new breed of boats can, in some circumstances, reach the downwind mark more quickly by tacking downwind than by running square. Our new problem, once it is acknowledged that to run square may not be the fastest technique in all winds and on all occasions, is that several additional factors come into play. These are all inter-related.

As a result, the fastest way to the leeward mark has ceased to be 'just sail the rhumb line'. Further, it has become a choice not just between the rhumb line and one other single alternative. Instead, it has become a choice between a number of possible options, all of which need to be considered.

Downwind sailing is now a point of sailing that is not at all well understood.

Life is simplest for the crews of boats at both extremes of performance. For the heavier and slower boats there is little problem. With these craft it almost *never* pays to steer other than directly for the downwind mark, so there is seldom any uncertainty. For the helm or crew of an ice yacht or a high-performance boat such as an Eighteen footer, it almost *always* pays to tack downwind with the sails unstalled, so again there is seldom any uncertainty.

However, for the crews of all the sailboats in between, from 12 Metres, IACC's, Etchells and Solings to Laser II's, 470's, FD's and 505's, the fastest technique in the wind and sea-state conditions of the moment may involve running square, broad reaching or any of the intermediate headings which lie between these two. A further point is, that because of the natural unsteadiness of wind and water, the fastest point of sailing can never be one single compass course, any more than the fastest way to windward in a shifty breeze can ever be a constant heading.

As a general principle it will be faster to sail wider angles in the lighter airs and to steer more directly downwind in the stronger breezes.

The principles are:

1. In an imaginary, simple, steady wind and flat water situation, tacking downwind will be faster if – and only if:

(a) The rig can develop extra drive force.
(b) The hull can develop extra speed from the extra drive force.
(c) The extra speed will more than compensate for the extra distance sailed.

2. In the real world of winds which are unsteady, waves and kinetics, there are five further factors:
   (d) Added speed from kinetics.
   (e) Added speed from surfing the waves.
   (f) Added downwind VMG from tacking down the headers.
   (g) Loss of speed through lulls.
   (h) Loss of speed in gybes.
3. Regardless of the conditions, it will *never* pay to tack downwind unless the total extra speed from all sources, both positive and negative, will more than compensate for the extra distance sailed.
   The performance factors, all of which are inter-related, are:
   (j) Rig characteristics and delta characteristics.
   (k) Hull characteristics.
   (l) Kinetics.
   (m) Surfing.
   (n) Sailing the gusts.
   (o) Sailing the shifts.

The consideration of these factors may lead to the conclusion that in the prevailing wind and sea-state conditions, the fastest way to the leeward mark is either straight down the rhumb line; a little divergence from it to promote surfing, to take advantage of gusts or for kinetic reasons; or alternatively to diverge from it widely for aerodynamic plus windshift reasons.

Now that we have abandoned the downwind processions, it is probably true that more races are won downwind than on any other point of sailing. So the decision of how and where to sail to reach the leeward mark most quickly had better not be taken too lightly. Note also that the fastest way will change as conditions change, and conditions can sometimes change surprisingly fast. I have slipped-in Section 25.2 which follows, as an example of the fluency of challenge and response which we now enjoy.

As in previous chapters, we will focus on each of the performance factors in turn, so that we can know what we can and cannot expect from our particular boat in any combination of wind and waves. But because when sailing downwind these six factors all become inter-related – e.g. there is no point in trying to surf if the hull won't go fast enough – the handling suggestions necessarily have to consider all six factors together. Any attempt otherwise becomes unrealistic.

I have asked many successful helms to contribute to these handling chapters. It is significant that almost all of them are less confident about the fastest techniques to use when sailing the downwind legs than on all other points of sailing. Their general message is 'observe, remain flexible, use whatever works best at the moment, be prepared to change as conditions change'. Most refer to the downwind legs as those on which it is hardest to be confident that they are matching the performance of an opponent. It is not really surprising that so many of the gains and losses in yacht racing now occur on the downwind legs.

It is reasonable to make two points.

The first is that the polar diagrams of Fig 24.3 etc are as accurate as measurement in flat water and the temporarily 'steady' winds within a gust or a lull can make them. But the true effects of gusts, waves and kinetics when sailing downwind can be so dominant that the real racing performance of an aggressively-handled boat may become significantly faster.

The second point biases the picture the other way. Exactly as extraneous effects reduce the upwind VMG of a windward planer more than that of a displacement sailer (Section 24.12), so do the effects of waves, gusts and kinetics conspire against the downwind tacker and shift the fastest point of sailing downwind more toward a square run. These are just two of the reasons why certainty of decision when sailing downwind can never be as definite as on other points of sailing.

25.2 The fleeting dynamics of wind and wave

If we look at the tacking downwind techniques which win in the flat water or negligible wave conditions assumed in Sections 25.4, 25.5 and 25.6, they are very different from the more nearly straight downwind techniques which win in the significant wave conditions which are discussed in Sections 25.7, -.8, -.9, and

-.10. It becomes obvious that any simplistic question such as 'In your class of boat, is it faster to tack downwind or run square?' makes no sense. Depending upon the prevailing wind speed, wave height and wave speed, the fastest way downwind may lie anywhere between a square run and (in the extreme) a course luffed even further from direct downwind, than that of 'flat water' tacking downwind. A very practical example will show the way in which even small changes in wind and sea-state condition will call for a progression of techniques, and how the successful downwind sailor needs to keep an open mind and be adaptable.

Gradient winds of 8 to 12 knots which are heated often tend towards a pattern of 'stronger – weaker – stronger – weaker' with a repetition frequency of twenty to forty minutes. I have raced in this pattern in regattas as far apart as Elbow, on Lake Diefenbaker in Saskatchewan, and Lake Macquarie on the New South Wales coast in an offshore breeze. When such a wind blows over relatively open water, the wind takes time to generate growing waves, and the waves persist for awhile after the wind dies, and this alternation of wind strength plus the time lag in the growth and decay of the waves develops a wind-wave cycle which becomes:

1 Light air over flat water.
2 Increasing wind over nearly flat water.
3 Breeze over increasing waves.
4 Breeze over waves.
5 Fading wind over waves.
6 Dying wind over decreasing waves.
7 Light air over feeble waves.
8 (& 1) Light air over flat water.

Given a thirty to forty minute 'stronger – weaker – stronger' repetition cycle, each of the segments will last for only four to five minutes. In a wind which averages five knots a typical downwind leg may occupy thirty minutes. In a boat such as the Tasar and many racing classes of similar performance, the fastest way downwind in each five-minute (approximately) segment of this cycle becomes:

1 Tack downwind with normal angles.
2 Tack downwind with reduced angles.
3 Use blocking wave technique.
4 Use blocking or surfing technique as appropriate.
5 Use surfing technique.
6 Use surfing technique.
7 Tack downwind but use abnormally wide angles for adequate Apparent Wind.
8 (& 1) Tack downwind with normal angles.

It was noted in the introduction to this chapter that when sailing downwind, more than on any other point of sailing, everything affects everything-else – the wind, the waves, the boat characteristics and the trends. The full force of this inter-relationship is very well shown by the sequential responses called for by this very typical wind and wave pattern.

25.3 Rig characteristics and the properties of the delta planform

Let us imagine that a boat sails straight downwind in a moderate wind. Its speed will stabilise at some speed between about one third of the wind speed for slow boats, and half the wind speed for faster boats, as shown in Fig 24.1. If it is then luffed (turned away from the directly downwind direction) little by little toward a broad reach, several changes will take place. The Apparent Wind will gradually become stronger. The boat speed will increase a little. Then, at some point, the direction of the Apparent Wind will have moved far enough forward towards the beam for attached flow to establish over the leeward surfaces of the sails. At this point the relative performances between different types of sailboats will change profoundly.

In the case of boats with hulls of a weight and shape which makes them too hard to push much faster and rigs which are not particularly efficient, nothing much will happen, as is evident from the keelboat plots of Fig 24.1. It is clear that for these classes in these conditions it will not pay to tack downwind except in light airs.

In the case of boats with efficient rigs, and hulls which are easy to push to higher speeds, the boat speed can double or treble, as is shown in the skiff plots of Fig 24.1. These are dramatically different from the keelboat plots. For classes with this sort of performance, it makes no sense at all to sail downwind other than by tacking downwind.

Most classes fall somewhere in between these two extremes. At some point their sails will cease stalling, suction force will be added to pressure force and their boat speed through the water will increase. But very often the extra speed which is gained by luffing to this point is little different from the extra distance which has to be covered. In these cases the choice of whether you will reach the leeward mark sooner by running 'square' or by doing something else will usually be far from self-evident.

The reasons for the tremendous differences between the keelboat and the skiff plots in Fig 24.1 at the point where their sails stop stalling, lie partly in the characteristics of their rigs and partly with their hulls.

The principle characteristics with respect to downwind sailing of some of the more usual rigs and sailplan shapes are:

1. Headsails on stays, reaching spinnakers set from bowsprits and mainsails set behind wingmasts need be turned only until they make an angle of about 35 degrees with the Apparent Wind. Further, there is great drive force advantage to be gained in achieving attached flow ('unstalling'); for example in Fig 17.33 the force at point 'E' is more than 50% greater than the force at point 'F', and this extra force is due entirely to the addition of the suction of the attached flow. So skiffs with reaching spinnakers, advanced dinghies with wingmast rigs, catamarans with wingmast rigs such as the Tornado, and advanced A-class catamarans and the 'C' class catamarans with 'solid' glider-wing type rigs will all sail faster downwind in most conditions by tacking downwind with their sails not stalled.

2. Sails set behind conventional masts have to be turned further until they make the smaller angle of about 25 degrees to the Apparent Wind before they will operate with attached flow. To achieve this lesser angle to the Apparent Wind the boat needs to be turned ten degrees more from the direct downwind heading, and so will have to sail a greater distance. Further, there is little benefit from doing this; in Fig 17.31 the force at point 'D' is little more than the force at point 'E', so very little extra speed can be expected. (The separation bubble is the villain.) So Lasers, Finns, OK's, Stars, Enterprises, Albacores etc will usually win by sailing straight for the downwind mark. Not at any angle to the Apparent Wind can their sails develop the extra force needed to achieve the higher speed which alone would justify sailing the longer distance, so they cannot improve their downwind VMG by tacking downwind. Their sail characteristics are not the whole story, but they are most of it, as we shall see.

3. Sails which have long leading edges angled to the Apparent Wind like the leading edges of delta-winged aircraft can develop 'roll-over' vortices which scrub stagnant air off their suction surfaces. This mechanism can maintain attached flow over the suction surface up to abnormally high angles, and at these high angles the forces developed also become much greater than 'normal' maximum forces. The surprisingly low speed and extreme nose-high attitude of the *Concorde* and the space shuttles as they approach to land, and the very high force lobe developed by the gaff sail (Fig 25.1), are examples of the roll-over vortex at work. This was also the key factor which enabled the square-rigged sailing ships to achieve their surprising broad reaching speeds. At these very high trim angles of sail to Apparent Wind the drag is fearsome – but note that at low angles of attack (trim angle) such as the *Concorde* in cruising flight, the drag is as low and the wing as efficient as a wing of any other shape.

This is another mechanism which can be observed in a simple kitchen experiment. As before, fill a basin with water and add a generous amount of ground pepper as a tracer. Move the square corner of something thin and flat, point-first, at not too great an angle a little below the surface. Vortices will form behind each leading edge, and the way their rolling action reaches inward to 'scrub' stagnant water off the suction surface can be seen at work. If the square-cornered plate is sharp-edged and flat the mechanism will work only up to a small angle. But if the advancing edges are bent down like the leading edges of an aeroplane's wing – or the rolled edges of a spinnaker – the maximum angle at which this mechanism will retain attached flow will become much greater than any other arrangement.

The head of a spinnaker which is trimmed to float more horizontally than vertically at its head can and should develop these roll-over vortices. The critical point here is that the boat does not have to be luffed at all from the direct downwind heading to achieve attached suction-side flow over a useful fraction of its spinnaker's area, and the pressure difference across this part of the sail will be much greater than where the flow is separated. This technique is necessarily limited to boats which sail downwind more slowly than the wind. Note that when you let the spinnaker 'sky' to achieve this stronger force you inevitably lose

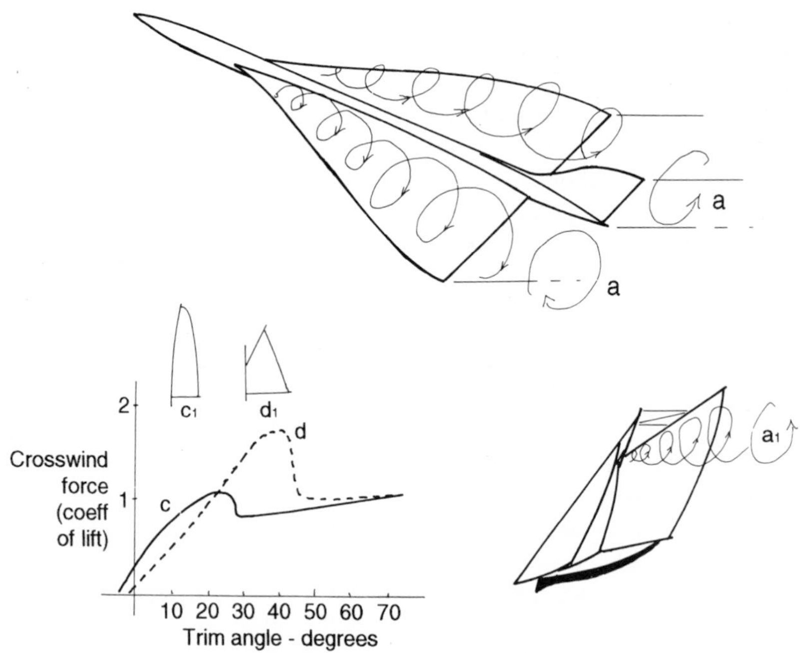

a - a = Spiral 'roll-over' vortices develop behind swept-back leading edges.
c = Force developed by marconi sail c_1.
d = " " " gaff " d_1.
Lobe d is due to roll-over vortex a_1
(from Manfred Curry's 1925 book)

Fig 25.1 The roll-over vortex

projected area, so there is a price to be paid. It may be faster in some conditions to strap it down for maximum projected area. Only with experience with your own boat will you will develop a feel for when it is fastest to sky it for attached flow and when it is fastest to strap it down for projected area, and the borderline cases will never be obvious.

There is another approach. If the boat is luffed just a little, and the spinnaker sheet is eased to achieve a 'lower luff just breaking' trim, the windward roll-over vortex at the head will extend almost all the way down the sloping luff of the spinnaker and its scrubbing action will encourage attached flow over a much larger fraction of the spinnaker's area despite the very large trim angles. If the spinnaker area is large with respect to the rest of the sail plan, this technique can achieve a substantially increased 'attached flow' sail force without luffing much from the 'direct downwind' heading nor sailing much extra distance.

The same principle can apply to the clew of a goose-winged jib (Fig 25.2). In this case the unstalled jib will also act as an aerodynamic slot to help unstall the mainsail. If the mainsail happens to be set behind an efficient wingmast, the downwind performance of such a rig can be surprisingly fast. The same principle will apply to a leading edge which is swept back the other way. The reaching spinnaker of a modern skiff is set from a long bowsprit. In this case the Apparent Wind when sailing downwind will blow from ahead rather than from astern, and the initiating delta point will be at the tack with the wind from ahead rather than at the head with the wind from behind, as shown in Fig 25.3. The same principle of developing a roll-over vortex up the rest of the luff will then apply when large forces are needed (such as to hold the crew up on the wings in a lull). In the gusts the boat accelerates, the Apparent Wind goes far forward, the trim angle of the sail to the wind becomes much smaller, the roll-over vortex vanishes, and the drag of the sail becomes small like the *Concorde's* wing at speed.

When it is used intelligently, the delta can be a very versatile shape indeed.

From the point of view of downwind sailing, we can now recognise that rigs will divide into four categories:

(a) Rigs which sail fastest when running straight downwind. Typical of these are the rigs of most keelboats which have relatively small mainsails and relatively large masthead spinnakers. The spinnaker will normally develop a roll-over vortex at the top of and for some distance down both luffs when the head is allowed to float near-horizontally. The downwind VMG of these boats will become smaller if they turn either way because any turn will suppress the roll-over vortex on the leeward spinnaker luff.

(b) Rigs which sail faster when sailed a few degrees to windward of the straight downwind heading. These can develop roll-over vortices down a substantial fraction of the windward edges of their spinnakers, as described above. Typical of these are all the classes which use goose-winged jibs such as the Star and the Tasar, and all classes which set spinnakers on relatively short spinnaker poles, such as the Olympic 470, FD and Soling classes, 12 Metres and IACC boats. An impressive example of the skilful use of this technique in marginal conditions was the winning of the last race of the 1983 *America*'s Cup series by *Australia II*. As all the world could see from the TV coverage, *Australia II* had developed, and was using in an efficient manner, a flatter spinnaker which was smaller in area but was shaped to develop attached flow by using the roll-over vortex with its increased Cl(max) and increased drive force and speed in those sorts of light winds and slop. *Liberty's* spinnaker was unstable because it was too full to develop attached flow, and it developed no extra attached-flow drive force. *Liberty* could not match *Australia II's* extra downwind speed, fell behind and lost that race and the series. This sort of tacking downwind is discussed more fully in later sections.

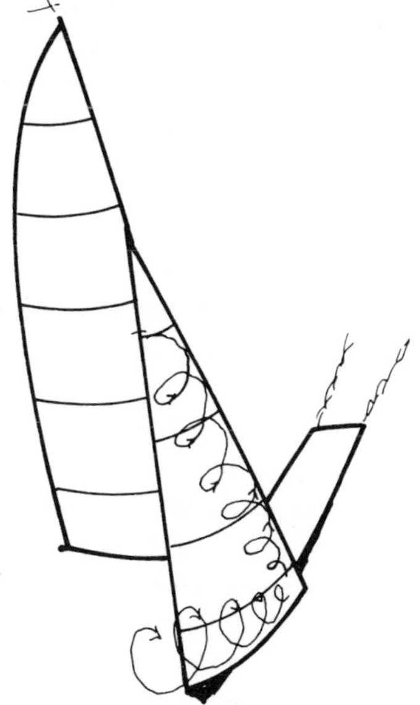

A poled-out jib can offer delta characteristics, and develop one or two spiral vortices.

Fig 25.2 Spiral vortices on jibs

Spiral vortices form behind the swept-back luff and near the foot of an asymmetric spinnaker when power is needed in the lulls.

Fig 25.3 Roll-over vortices form over asymmetric spinnakers

(c) As a variant of this, some rigs can sail faster when sailed 'by the lee'. Typical of these are the single-sail (no jib and no spinnaker) rigs with unstayed masts such as Lasers, Finns, OK's, Sabres etc., and also all sailboards. Particularly in light airs, these craft can be heeled away from the boom. This has the effect of raising the sail and exposing more of the sail's area to the stronger wind at greater height, with a consequent increase in drive force and speed, particularly in light air. The practical difficulty – that in light air the boom will fall to leeward under its own weight – is solved by allowing it to swing forward sufficiently for gravity to make it want to fall towards the bow instead of the stern. The sheet prevents this, and so this configuration is stable in even the lightest air. To fill the sail properly, the boat is then steered a few degrees by the lee. This has a second advantage in that the flow then becomes leech to luff. When set and trimmed in this way the sail will behave like any other sail with a 'clean' leading edge (such as a headsail on a stay), i.e. it can unstall sooner. Whether or not it will pay to sail that high (by the lee) will depend on the characteristics of the hull and the conditions of the moment.

(d) Rigs which can develop so much extra drive force when trimmed for broad reaching so that the extra speed, will always more than justify sailing the extra distance . However, it can work only if the hull can sail freely to the speed needed. Ice yachts and high performance planing craft such as the big skiffs enjoy this performance in all winds. The better catamarans can enjoy it in winds which drive them at up to moderate hull speeds, except that catamarans usually have problems in light air because of poor sail-area / wetted-area ratios. Keelboat classes which have tidy hulls and relatively big sails and big spinnakers can enjoy it in winds which are so light that they are sailing at speeds well below their hull speeds and are therefore still able to accelerate reasonably freely to some higher speed, as in the 12 Metre example above.

25.4 Hull characteristics

The purpose of this note is to focus on those hull characteristics which will enable their crews to benefit, on some occasions, from tacking downwind.

Regardless of hull type, no boats with relatively small rigs will ever be able to reach the leeward mark sooner by tacking downwind. The reason for this is that with a small rig they can sail only relatively slowly, and even when sailing crosswind, a slow speed does not deflect the Apparent Wind to any great degree. So they need to turn through a large angle (60 degrees minus the deflection of the Apparent Wind) from the direct downwind heading before they can achieve the 30 degrees (approx.) of sail trim to the Apparent Wind at which their sails will 'unstall' and can develop the extra force of Cl max trim. In this situation, the extra distance to be covered must always be large. In practice it is always far too large ever to be justified by the extra speed.

Conversely, the larger the rig and the greater the natural speed of the hull, the faster the boat will broad reach, the more will the Apparent Wind be deflected towards the beam or forward of it, and the smaller will be the angle through which the boat must luff before the sails 'unstall'.

The important ratio is the speed of the boat compared with the speed of the wind. The more closely the boat speed approaches the wind speed, the less the angle through which it must luff to achieve attached flow and develop Cl max sail force, and so the smaller will be the extra distance it must sail. Those boats which can exceed wind speed – ice yachts, land yachts, Eighteen footers etc – simply choose to steer that angle which they find from experience gives them the fastest downwind VMG.

Because the drag of each different type of hull increases in a different way, there are several typical performance patterns.

(a) Keelboats which have relatively big type 'd' rigs (Sec. 25.3 above) will usually be able to benefit from tacking downwind in light airs. The prohibitive drag rise which occurs as hull speed is exceeded precludes all possibility of advantage from tacking downwind in moderate or strong breezes.

(b) Catamarans which have relatively big type 'd' rigs will usually be able to benefit in light airs and moderate breezes because the speed increase to be gained from luffing sufficiently to unstall the sails will be greater than the extra distance sailed. However as boat speed increases in stronger winds the 'speed squared' increase in hull drag will progressively reduce the advantage until the point is reached at which the extra speed no more than matches the extra distance. At this point the advantage from tacking downwind ceases, and in all stronger winds it will be faster to run square.

For catamarans with fine bows this may not be a realistic option because of their tendency to nose-dive. So for survival reasons many catamarans continue to tack downwind in all winds.

(c) Light dinghies which plane freely and which have relatively big type 'd' rigs may be able to sail faster by tacking downwind in all winds and modes. Depending upon the hull characteristics and whether the rig is big enough, and also upon the present wave and gust situation, tacking downwind may or may not be justified in the forced and planing modes. Fast dinghies therefore fall into two broad groups;

(i) Those in which tacking downwind is always faster in light airs (i.e.in the displacement mode) but may become marginal or slower in breezes (i.e. in the forced and planing modes). The Tasar polars in Fig 24.1(a), (b) and (c) are typical of this group. This is an excellent example of the situation where the measured 'steady wind and flat water' performances show that tacking downwind is always faster by a small margin, but the real world of gusts, waves, kinetics and windshifts usually biases the performance to the point where it is usually faster to do something else.
(ii) Those in which tacking downwind is always faster. The skiff polars in Fig 24.1 are typical of this group.

This is really an exercise in two important ratios. The ratio 'Sail Area / Wetted Area' tends to govern light air performance. The ratio 'Sail Area / Total Weight' tends to govern planing performance. Boats with heavy hulls (most conventional dinghies) and particularly smaller boats which are sailed by heavier crews (the classic 'grown-ups in children's boats' situation) are too heavy for that hull design to 'unstick' in the forced mode, and so cannot plane freely and cannot develop their own stronger broad-reaching Apparent Winds. Boats which are light and well shaped and not overloaded can plane freely and can often benefit even though their rig size may be modest. These are the low-power, high performance boats. Boats which are light and have very powerful rigs, i.e. the high-power high-performance boats, simply never run square because they go downwind more than twice as fast by tacking downwind regardless of any other factors.

25.5 Handling in light airs and flat water

In all light air sailing the importance of the upper sails is dominant. When sailing downwind this is doubly true. The hull and lower sails of an easily-driven boat which runs square can easily exceed the speed of the low-level wind, in the manner indicated by the ribbons in Fig 3.1(d) (Part One).

In Fig 5.1(Part One) the boat was assumed to be at rest. Fig 25.4 repeats Fig 5.1 except that the boat is now assumed to be moving straight downwind at the correct speeds for both the light air and the breeze situations. Note that in (a), the light air running case, only the top of the sail provides any significant drive force. Most of the sail – about 75% of the area in the case of a fast boat – has either become useless or it actually impedes the boat. The faster a boat can move downwind, the more pronounced will be this reversal of sail force from drive at the upper levels to impedance at the lower levels. This is the primary reason why all high performance boats have no option but to tack downwind not only in light air but also in the lighter breezes.

When this very light air situation occurs suddenly and unexpectedly it can offer opportunity for quick thinking. As an example, in one of the Soling races at a pre-Olympic regatta at Tallinn, several boats converged to windward of the downwind mark and then ran square to preserve their tactical rights in what had been a light breeze. At that point the wind became light air. The sails of the closely grouped boats further slowed the air over and near what had suddenly become an open barrier, which at that point was about 30 metres from the mark. The wind became a virtual calm. Spinnakers fell limp. One crew toward the back of the group analysed this new situation correctly, and luffed smoothly about 60 degrees. There was just enough wind to fill their spinnaker on the broad reach. Their boat accelerated, very slowly at first and then faster as they drew clear of the stagnant air. They sailed, accelerating, for about 40 metres, gybed smoothly and kept their boat moving well until they reached the dead air to leeward of the group. By that time their momentum was sufficient to carry them through the calm air and they rounded the mark ahead of the whole group.

When running square, the wind flow onto sails (other than the tops of spinnakers) will necessarily be at about 90 degrees, i.e. totally separated. Since all practical sail shapes seem to produce about the same 'flat plate' drag (which when running square becomes the drive force) the fastest technique is to flatten the mainsail to achieve maximum projected area.

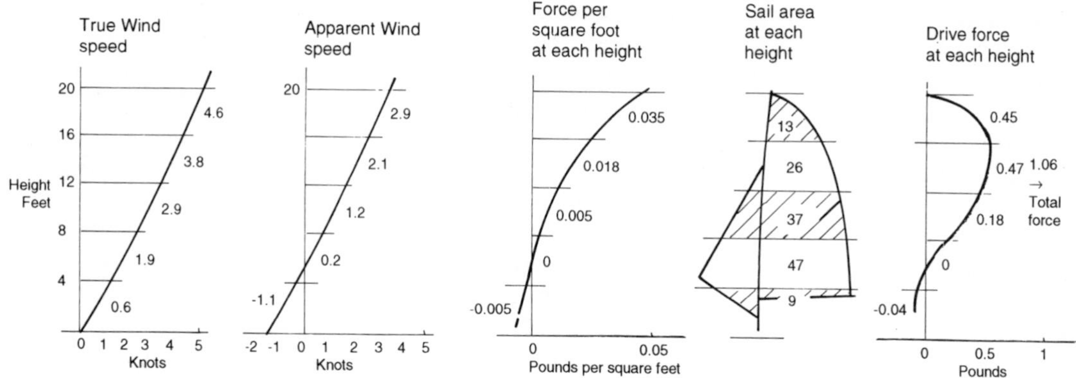

(a) Dynamics of 'running square' in light air of 5 knots.
Only upper sails provide significant drive force. Total force 1.06 pounds.
Boat speed 1.7 knots. Lower sails retard boat.

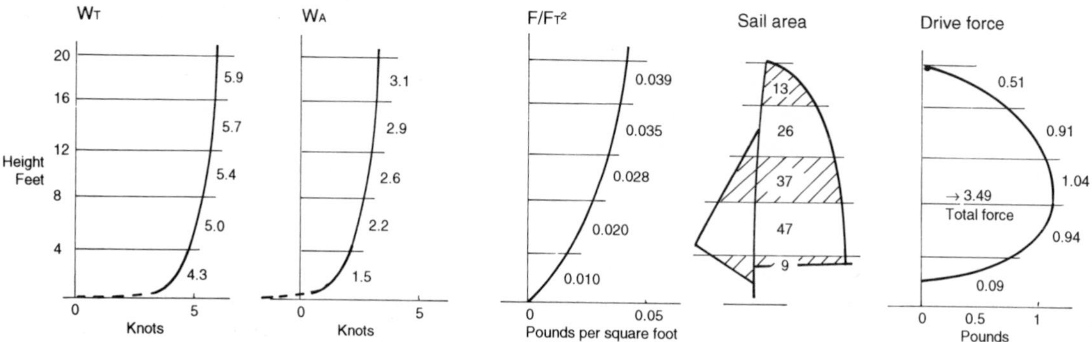

(b) Dynamics of *running square* in breeze of 6 knots.
All sails provide useful drive force. Total force 3.49 pounds.
Boat speed 2.75 knots.

Fig 25.4 Dynamics of *running square* in light air and in breeze

Spinnakers require particularly enlightened handling when running square in light airs.

In very light airs there will be insufficient wind to fill the sail and it will hang limp. In this situation the boat will sail faster without it. Note that the bigger the spinnaker, the more will this be true, and also the stronger the air which will be needed before it can be set and filled with advantage.

Once it is set, it should be flown as high as possible partly because there is more wind up there, and partly to develop the roll-over vortices with their attached lee-side flow and greater pressure difference and drive force. The problem is that the attached flow will be curved downwards and as it descends it will not only encounter dead air, but as the boat gathers speed it will in fact be opposed by the reversed pressure gradient as it approaches the foot. This will bring the moving air to rest, and at that point it will separate exactly as does the water in Fig 17.11. A little below that point the spinnakers of fast boats will begin to blow back. Spinnakers may be 'mystery sails' but they are not magic. Remember that the better you exploit the faster air aloft, the more trouble you must expect from the impeding air at lower levels. Look at your speed relative to your competitors, keep an open mind, keep the head of the sail working well, and don't expect miracles.

On the water light air is seldom steady, and any boat must periodically sail from stronger into lighter air. When this happens on a square run much of the spinnaker will collapse. If the boat is luffed onto a more broad-reaching heading to create an Apparent Wind more from the beam it may be possible to keep it full. This is one of the situations in which a boat which would not normally win by tacking downwind can indeed tack downwind briefly with great advantage. But watch out for the occasional trap. If you run out of good air with speed into not just lighter air but into a calm patch, there will be no advantage in turning because in a calm the Apparent Wind will always come from ahead no matter which way you turn. If only the world were a simpler place, and somebody would paint all the 'holes' blue!

In between the 'always run square' group and the 'always tack downwind with the Apparent Wind from ahead' very high performance group, there will lie the vast majority of boats which will sometimes sail faster in some light air conditions by tacking downwind if they do it well. To get an idea of the principles and the technique let us look at the actions of the crew of a low-power, high-performance dinghy. Let us assume that they have just rounded the windward mark in steady light air conditions, and have elected to gybe away from the fleet, for clear air.

The rounding and the gybe should be made smoothly so as to retain all the speed possible – which, in light air, will not be much. The turn should be arrested when the heading is about 40 to 45 degrees from the directly downwind heading. The mainsail should be set at about 12% camber. Downhaul and vang should be slack. If shroud tension is adjustable it should be eased to allow the mast to rake forward. Either the spinnaker should be set or the jib should be goose-winged on its whisker pole, and the sheet eased until the jib adopts about a 16% camber (a little more than the mainsail). If the hull is of a design which benefits from fourth mode handling at very low speeds it should be heeled and trimmed with the bow well down The leeward jib sheet should be tightened – gravity will twist a mainsail or spinnaker the right way but will twist a goose-winged jib the wrong way.

Throughout the turn and the jib or spinnaker-set sequence, the crew should make every possible effort to sail the boat absolutely steadily, at optimum trim, smoothly, and above all without harsh body movement. In very light air, and particularly when sailing downwind, once speed has been lost it is very difficult and time consuming to re-acquire it. This is a supreme example of prevention being better than cure. *Don't lose your speed in the first place.* A sharp turn around the mark to a downwind heading, followed by a lighting-fast spinnaker-set by two vigorous athletes, will leave the boat dead in the water with waves rolling away from it in all directions, and it will take considerable time to re-acquire its speed. In light air a smooth open turn with the sails trimmed progressively for close reach, reach and broad reach – and with the turn arrested at broad reach – can increase speed. Thereafter it is much faster in terms of downwind VMG to set up the jib on its whisker pole, or to set the spinnaker, no faster than is consistent with the deliberate smoothness of body movement which alone will enable the boat to maintain its speed. Hull trim should be preserved carefully as the crew shift positions. Under no circumstances should the transom be dragged low by a too-far-aft crew position. Both crew members should move smoothly forward, one onto each side deck. This lateral separation of their weights ensures that the boat and rig will be held as steady as possible in the rolling sense. The helm sitting on the deck will have his eyes at maximum reasonable height above the water, and so will enjoy the best field of vision and the least foreshortening in his search for pattern in the wind ruffles. There is no law against standing up to get a wider view – but do it smoothly

Beginners often sit or crouch in the cockpit, centrally, one behind the other. This positioning has absolutely nothing to recommend it. Weight is too far aft. Eyes are too low, so pattern is harder to pick because of the foreshortening. Further, it is difficult to look at the all-important water surface behind the boat for approaching puffs. Control movement is cramped. The boat is not held steady laterally by the separation of weights.

As a heading of about 50 to 60 degrees from the direct downwind heading is approached, the leeward tufts on the leech of the jib – which is now the upwind edge – will begin to agitate. This agitation indicates that the jib has unstalled and developed attached flow, and is operating at close to Cl maximum. In the case of spinnaker-rigged boats, the windward luff of the spinnaker will begin to 'roll'.

As soon as agitation of the jib leech tufts or the roll of the spinnaker luff is observed, the turn should be arrested, and the boat held on a steady heading for a few seconds. During this period, four things will happen which do *not* happen when running, 'square':

1) The leeward jib tufts will agitate, or the spinnaker luff will 'come alive'.
2) The upper mainsail leech ribbons will begin to stream – ('just popping in and out' – Charlie McKee).
3) The boat will be felt and heard to accelerate.
4) The Apparent Wind will become noticeably stronger.

As the boat accelerates, the direction of the Apparent Wind will move toward the bow. As the direction of the Apparent Wind changes, it will be necessary to bear away, as the boat gains speed, in order to maintain the trim angle at which the jib leech tufts just agitate or the spinnaker sets with the luff just off the 'roll' (Cl Max). In practice the angle through which it will be necessary to bear away can be as much as 15 to 25 degrees – two to two and a half hand-widths at arm's length – and when the boat is up to speed, it will be found to be sailing at only about 25 to 30 degrees from the direct downwind direction. The Apparent Wind direction (as shown by the feather) will be about 20 to 30 degrees aft of the beam. When the sails unstall, and begin to operate at Cl max, the extra thrust and acceleration appear suddenly, as if a motor had been switched on. If the helmsman does not bear away as the boat accelerates and the Apparent Wind moves forward, the jib or spinnaker will be blown aback, and the boat will slow as the jib or spinnaker force reverses.

Once the boat has been brought up to speed and established on its correct heading, the art of tacking downwind is to refine the sail trim to achieve attached flow over as much of the sail area as possible and so enjoy the maximum increased speed, and then to steer as far downwind as is possible while maintaining this added speed. This is the ideal in that it achieves the best compromise between added speed and extra distance sailed. Any heading more toward a broad reach will give slightly more speed but with the penalty of too much added distance. Any turn too far downwind will cause the attached flows to separate and the boat will be felt to go suddenly 'dead' as it loses the added performance. The whole technique calls for steering which is as delicate and as continually accurate as when sailing to windward.

Unless you sail with sufficient extra speed to justify the extra distance, there is no point whatever in sailing other than straight towards the downwind mark. The consequence of this is that in conditions of relatively steady air and flat water any heading intermediate between a square run and the heading at which the extra speed cuts-in should be avoided as it is likely to be slower than either the square run or tacking downwind.

So long as the light air remains relatively steady:

1) Steer to maintain Cl max trim as accurately as possible – and

2) Monitor the True Wind direction carefully and gybe whenever it is advantageous to do so.

Note the difference between the advantaged tack or gybe as between sailing to windward and tacking downwind. In both cases, the advantaged tack or gybe is the one which will take you most directly toward the mark. To windward, this will be the 'lifted' tack (i.e. a veer if you are on starboard tack). When tacking downwind, this will be the 'headed' gybe (i.e. a back if you are on starboard gybe).

Let us now look at what happens when light air is unsteady.

The crew's initial actions will be exactly as described above, but not for long.

In the 'wind' section we saw that unsteady light air and the pulsing pattern and the oscillating pattern all have a characteristic repetition dimension of about 100m. At a boat speed of, say, three knots or 5 feet per second or 100m per minute, this suggests that two major changes of speed and two major changes of direction will occur every 60 seconds. Put another way, it is reasonable to expect that either the speed or the direction will change substantially every 15 seconds or so.

(a) Let us assume that the first change is an increase of wind speed. This will cause the Apparent Wind to move aft, the lee-side flow will separate (i.e. the sails will 'stall') and the leeward jib tufts will fall limp or the spinnaker luff will become steady. In this case, the rig may not be felt to lose power, because the added wind speed will compensate for the reduced sail force. The helmsman should immediately respond to the 'limp tufts' indication and luff gently until the leeward tufts begin to agitate again or the spinnaker luff comes alive. The acceleration process, the moving of the Apparent Wind toward the bow, and the bearing away again to keep the sails trimmed at Cl max trim in the changing Apparent Wind direction, will then need to be repeated. During this stronger puff, the upper mainsail leech may blow forward slightly. If this occurs the upper mainsail (where most of the wind is) will operate at a trim angle less than Cl max. To correct this the vang should be tightened a fraction to reduce twist and so firm the trim of the upper mainsail leech until the leech ribbons again just pop in and out and indicate that it too is again operating at Cl max trim.

(b) Let us assume that the next change is that the wind direction moves a few degrees in the sense of heading the boat. This will cause the leeward jib leech tufts to stream, and may even cause the windward jib leech tufts to agitate, or it will cause the spinnaker luff to roll as if the sheet had been eased. *Immediately* bear away until the leeward tufts occasionally agitate, for Cl max trim. Always steer as close to the downwind mark as is possible consistent with maintaining Cl max trim and speed.

(c) Let us assume that the next change is that the wind goes light. In this case the lower jib or the spinnaker may blow aback, and the crew will feel the Apparent Wind coming from almost directly forward, as the boat, with speed, moves into a calmer patch. In this case the fastest action is to *do nothing and wait.* Until the boat slows to a speed which is less than the wind speed, the Apparent Wind at face level will continue to come from almost ahead, and this will remain true regardless of whether the boat is turned or not. After three or four seconds, the boat will have lost the extra speed it had acquired in the previous puff. As soon as the feather at the masthead indicates that the Apparent Wind direction is again aft of the beam, the boat should be turned until its centreline is at about 45 degrees to the feather, and then steered according to the leeward jib tufts or the roll of the spinnaker luff to re-acquire attached flow and stabilize in the new lighter wind, exactly as described in (a) above.

(d) Let us assume that the next change is a change of wind direction in the sense of freeing the boat (i.e. it is necessary to luff to maintain sail trim). If the helmsman does not alter his heading, the sails will stall, lose suction, and drop to 'pressure only' force with consequent loss of speed. The helmsman should immediately luff gently to unstall the sails and so restore Cl max Drive Force and speed. Alternately, he may elect to gybe and repeat the exercise on the other tack, if this heading is now more favourable.

The purpose in describing the crews' responses in this way is to emphasise the point which was made earlier – that *every* change – whether it be wind speed or wind direction or boat speed – will appear to the crew as a change in the direction of the Apparent Wind, and that the proper response to this for fastest sailing when tacking downwind, will always be to make the turn which is necessary to restore the Cl max sail trim in that changed direction of the Apparent Wind.

The angle through which the downwind tacking boat must be turned when the wind changes speed is surprisingly large. Usually the angle is about three times as large as when sailing to windward (Fig. 25.5).

The curves of Fig 24.1 all assume 'steady state', i.e. the hull speeds indicated along the 'tacking downwind', (and all other) lines assume that the boat has been steered for several seconds in a steady wind at the heading and sail trim which gives Cl max force from the sails.

In the changing winds so often found afloat, it is inevitable that speed will be lost from time to time. Whenever the wind speed falls to a near calm, speed loss cannot be avoided. Sometimes a smaller wind speed change combined with a direction change 'feels' like a calm patch, and speed will be lost until the situation is recognised and Cl max trim can be restored and the boat re-accelerated. Always, very positive but absolutely smooth steering is needed, first to re-acquire speed by broad reaching for one or two lengths, and then, with the regained speed, to turn more downwind onto that heading which gives maximum downwind Vmg. Fig 25.6 shows how a boat should be handled when the wind speed increases *without change of direction* from 3 knots to 5 knots.

The situation shown in 'a' assumes that a 3 knot lull has been blowing steadily for several seconds.

In 'b' the wind has just increased to 5 knots. The increase of total sail force, from about 2 pounds to about 4 pounds can accelerate the 500 pound mass of the boat plus crew only slowly, and so the helmsman initially luffs his boat 18 degrees to maintain Cl Max trim in response to the initial 18 degree shift toward the beam in the direction of the new Apparent Wind caused by the increase in wind speed. During the next three or four seconds as the boat accelerates from 2 knots to 3 knots the direction of the Apparent Wind moves toward the bow by 13 degrees, and so he bears away 13 degrees to maintain Cl max sail trim in response to this subsequent shift towards the bow in the direction of the Apparent Wind caused by the increase in boat speed. His final heading is indicated in diagram 'c' with his hull now moving at 3 knots and at a downwind Vmg of 2.4 knots.

There are two very interesting consequences which flow from the 'snaking' track which is so characteristic of tacking downwind in either unsteady light air or the wandering breeze.

The first is that it is not at all easy to decide which is the advantaged gybe, nor when it is most advantageous to gybe. There is much truth in Bertrand's comment that Connor fell behind on the critical last downwind leg of the 1983 *America's* Cup races because *Liberty* gybed eleven times and *Australia II* only five. Each boat suffered a distance penalty equivalent to about 5 seconds' sailing with each gybe. Because this is primarily a question of tactics we will pursue it no further here.

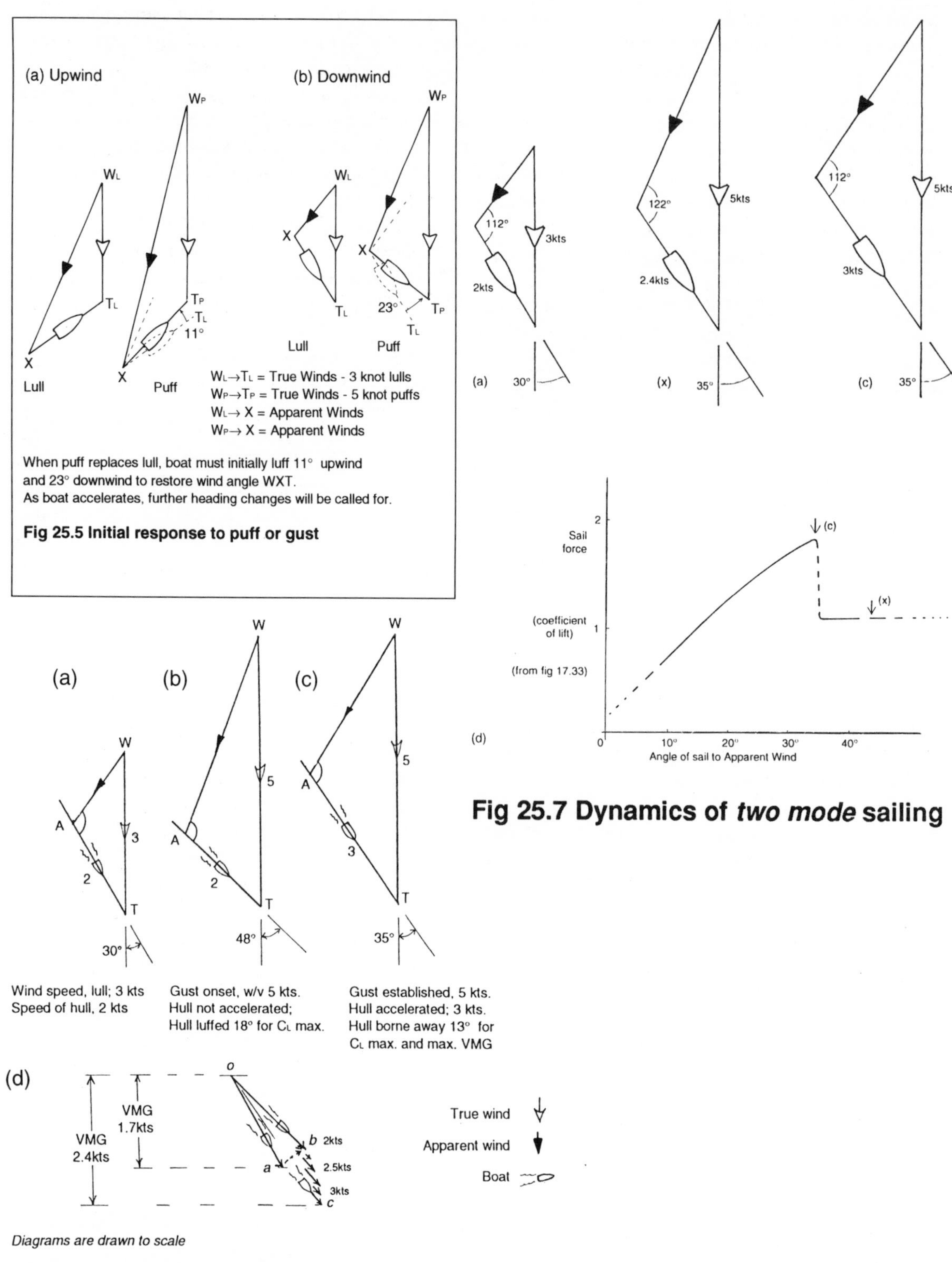

Fig 25.5 Initial response to puff or gust

Fig 25.7 Dynamics of *two mode* sailing

Diagrams are drawn to scale

Angle WAT= 112° - which gives trim angle for C_L max - is constant.
Diagrams A B & C are summarised in D which shows handling sequence for fastest speed downwind at gust onset.
To achieve performance *c*, boat must first be luffed 18° to *b*
(to re-acquire C_L max and increased drive force.). Only as it accelerates can it be turned downwind to *c*. *c* cannot be acquired except through *b*

Fig 25.6 Fastest handling sequence at onset of puff

The second consequence is the whole subject of two mode sailing.

At very low speeds, most of the hull drag will be due to skin friction. Hulls which offer less wetted area when heeled and sailed bow-down – i.e. hulls which respond to fourth mode handling – will sail faster heeled. As far as the hull is concerned, it matters not which way it is heeled. In light air, heeling to windward will result in a greater area of the mainsail being lifted higher and therefore being exposed to the stronger wind at increased height. Rudder drag will be reduced fractionally because the tendency of the sails to turn the boat away from the boom will be compensated for by the tendency of the hull to turn away from the immersed topside. This is the rationale behind the handing of boats such as the Laser.

In the case of yachts and catamarans, which cannot heel, or boats with narrow rounded hulls such as skiff moths which achieve no dynamic advantage from heeling, they either must be or should be sailed upright.

In the case of light dinghies with sloop (jib and mainsail) rigs, they should be heeled to leeward to induce twist in the sails by gravity when tacking downwind, and heeled to windward when running square. The hull trim which results in minimum drag is the same as has been described earlier for light air sailing to windward.

Provided that the centreboard and rudder blade are in flawless condition and highly polished, and so operate with full laminar flow, their combined drag at this sort of speed is less than about half an ounce, and practical experience suggests that there is no advantage in moving the rudder blade from its vertical fully-down position, nor raising the centreboard above about half-way.

The importance of stillness cannot be over-emphasised. As between two boats which are racing downwind in light air side by side, if the crew of either boat makes the slightest coarse movement, that boat will fall behind. For this reason it is very important that both crew members should take care to adopt, as a routine, a body position which is sufficiently comfortable for them to maintain it without movement for long periods. Nobody can predict how long any particular calm period will last. This point is equally important when sailing upwind and crosswind.

25.6 Two mode sailing

In Fig 25.6, inset (d) shows the dynamic progressions between the instantaneous situations shown 'frozen' in (a), (b) and (c). Performance (c) cannot be acquired except by passing through (b). This leads straight to the concept of two mode sailing which is shown in Fig 25.7. This concept applies to and can trap all sailboats except those which can never win by tacking downwind in any circumstances.

In Fig 25.7 'a' repeats 'a' in Fig 25.6. Fig 25.7 'c' also repeats the 'c' of Fig 25.6 – i.e. it shows the speed which has been acquired by passing first through the Fig 25.6 'b' situation of fastest sailing angle and the sail trim for best acceleration.

Fig 25.7 'x' is different. It shows the situation of a helmsman such as in 25.7 'a' who, when faced with the challenge of helmsman 'c' overtaking him at 3 knots, luffs 5 degrees to parallel the heading of 'c' who may by now be sailing through his lee. Boat 'x' after four or five seconds to accelerate, will stabilize at 2.4 knots. Boat 'c' alongside has stabilized at 3.0 knots.

This is 'two mode' sailing.

The reason for the different speeds is given by the difference in the angles of the Apparent Wind to the centrelines of the two boats. In the case of boat 'c' the wind angle is 112 degrees, and the sail trim angle is 33 degrees, i.e. point 'c' (Cl max) in Fig 25.7(d). In the case of boat 'x' the wind angle is 122 degrees and the sail trim angle is 43 degrees, i.e. point 'x' in Fig 25.7(d). The drive force at trim 'x' is only two thirds of the drive force at point 'c'.

Note again that both situations are completely stable. The True Wind is the same and the headings are the same. But the drive force is different and the boat speeds are different. They are not the same because the way the two helmsmen approached situations 'c' and 'x' were different.

The examples given are taken from Tasar figures. The performance of the Tasar has been so thoroughly measured and documented that it lends itself naturally as the model for these examples.

At first sight, spinnaker rigged dinghies such as the Laser II might be thought of as not needing these 'luff first for speed' techniques, because their spinnakers can obviously be trimmed for Cl max independently of turning the boat. However, all experience on the water indicates that trimming the spinnaker is almost useless unless it is driven by a stronger Apparent Wind – and only the turn across wind will provide this added wind speed. So it turns out in practice, that the principles and techniques described above are as applicable to Laser 2's, 470's, Cherubs and Eighteen Footers, as they are to the non-spinnaker but wing-masted Tasar. Three anecdotes are relevant:

1) The Yachting Association of New South Wales periodically conducts 'Centreboard Clinics' at which 90 or so leading helmsmen and crews from all classes enjoy two days of intensive coaching. My role one typical year was to coach 470 and Cherub crews one morning; Tasar crews the second morning; and two Australian children's trapeze and spinnaker classes, Flying Ants and Flying 11s, in the afternoons. The senior crews included several world champions. During the winter mornings the winds were light airs which increased to light breezes in the afternoons. The spinnaker-rigged 470's and Cherubs were the most interesting. In the predictable unsteady light air situation, I was able to forecast the wind patterns and discuss the principles above with the crews before they went on the water. I encouraged them to compare for themselves and with boat alongside boat the Fig 25.6 a-b-c approach with the Fig 25.7 a-x approach. In every case the results were absolutely supportive of the a-b-c approach. In the typical light-air conditions we experienced, the ability to compare was perfect. The two-mode situation occurred repeatedly. It usually took the form of one boat with virtually no speed and a near-collapsed spinnaker and *no acceleration* while the adjacent boat on the same heading enjoyed useful speed and enough Apparent Wind to keep its spinnaker inflated.

2) During that afternoon I left the 'sailing classroom' for awhile and observed the Sydney Eighteen Footer fleet racing. I measured two additional performance points to add to and compare with those I had measured previously, and I noted very carefully the detail of and the duration of several gybes in an 8 knot breeze. The situation prior to each gybe was that the boat sailed smoothly in a True Wind of about 8 knots at about 12 knots on a heading about 45 degrees from the direct downwind direction. The Apparent Wind blew from about 45 degrees from the bow. The turn to gybe was made smoothly – the hull turned through about 110 degrees in about 5 seconds. As the boat passed through the 'downwind' direction it was still moving substantially faster than the True Wind and all sails streamed *aft*. The helmsman (the then world champion) did not arrest his turn until the boat was heading within about 20 degrees of a beam reach. The spinnaker had at this point blown through to the new lee side and filled. At this instant the Apparent Wind was about 60 degrees from the bow at about 5 to 6 knots. Superb co-ordination between the helm and the forward hand maintained the trim of the spinnaker with its luff just on the point of rolling (Cl Max) while the boat accelerated fast and was at the same time turned downwind about 30 degrees to its new stable VMG Max (downwind) heading, with an *increased* Apparent Wind of 8 knots again blowing from 45 degrees from the bow.

During the turn downwind the sheet hand pumped the mainsheet with very quick forceful pumps which appeared almost as leech shimmers. The object of the pumping was to hold the crew up on the wing until the Apparent Wind and the sail forces had stabilised. This acceleration and turn downwind occupied about two lengths or three further seconds. Note the technique of making an ice-yacht like turn towards a beam reach for increased initial Apparent Wind speed and fastest acceleration. The detail of this whole manoeuvre underscores the challenge and the exultation of skiff racing which is so well summed up as *'In Eighteen footer racing all three people have to do exactly the right thing all the time'*.

3) Experimental craft are now sailing in Sydney which offer about the performance level of an Eighteen Footer with the portability, economy and convenience of a sailboard or Laser. They are slender planing craft with wide wings, but on the wingtips are tiny flying-boat type tip floats for static and/or emergency stability so that ordinary mortals can sail them. (Fig 16.11 and 20.20) The two-hander prototypes have spinnakers and the single-handed prototypes do not. Performance currently achieved with the simple jib and mainsail rig of the single-hander exhibits the extremes of two-mode sailing. If at the start of a downwind leg in 10 knots of wind this craft is not luffed as described above it will stabilize with separated flow at a downwind VMG of 5.5 to 6 knots, i.e. at about the same speed as any good conventional racing dinghy or catamaran. But if it is first luffed far enough to unstall and accelerate, it can then bear away and stabilise at a downwind boat speed of about 12 to 15 knots and a VMG of about 10 to 12 knots.

My point in describing this is that several helms who can sail superbly in Solings, Dragons, Tasars, 470's etc and who have sailed this craft, have all at first repeatedly settled for the 6 knot downwind performance, solely because it did not occur to them that double the speed was available. Only after they had been further briefed and the techniques demonstrated to them were they able to bring themselves to turn sufficiently far crosswind to take the Apparent Wind far enough forward to unstall the sails, then accelerate, and only then to turn downwind and only far enough to keep the speed.. Skiff helms, on the other hand, are already well indoctrinated. Those who have sailed this new craft have all exploited its full downwind performance capability expertly.

Nothing could be more different than downwind speeds of 6 knots and 12 knots. But I have watched helm after helm settle for 6 because it never occurred to them that 12 was available. This 'mindset' – the conviction that there is only one best way to handle a boat and that we already know it – appears to affect the crews of all classes, from dinghies to 12-Metres. So often, what holds us back from achieving what we want to achieve is our own rigidity of thinking.

The purpose of this book is to open a few windows.

Use of the compass

Some authors have recommended that the skill of tacking downwind can be mastered by using the compass. The technique suggested is to establish the wind speed and direction from instruments, and then to steer a series of headings, each a little further luffed from the direct downwind heading, and to calculate from instrument indications the VMG on each heading, and to compare this with the direct downwind VMG. A moment's thought will reveal that this approach can neither reveal nor achieve the fastest downwind VMG. In any steady wind it is most likely to adopt the slower stable point of two mode sailing. In any wind which is unsteady in direction it can only result in achieving, alternately, trim angles which are either less than or greater than Cl max. Both of these are necessarily slower than the optimum. It would be nice if tacking downwind could be handled on so simple a numbers basis, but in the real world the subtleties of wind and water are never so simple.

You can sail downwind with separated flow, and slowly. Or you can sail downwind with attached flow, and often much faster. The faster technique requires skill, concentration and understanding. It is an acquired art. It is a challenge. It is tremendous fun. And it wins races.

25.7 Handling in light air and waves

In a light air and flat water situation, it is relatively easy to acquire and maintain the C1 max trim. If at this trim your sails can develop a higher force than when running square, there will probably be times when running straight for the downwind mark will not be the fastest way to get there.

If on the way you sail past a point and into waves, the situation will change profoundly because the waves introduce so many new factors:

1. Waves will tend to rock the boat and oscillate the rig. In this situation the masthead and upper sail will move most.

2. This to and fro movement of the upper sails through the slowly moving light air will make the Apparent Wind over the upper sails unsteady. The movement caused by the waves therefore makes it no longer possible to maintain any sail trim at or near the angle which develops the extra sail force. Further, in light air it is primarily the upper sails which do most of the driving. Therefore in waves and light air it becomes no longer possible to develop much of the extra force which alone justifies tacking downwind, and so the whole rationale vanishes. What works in flat water does not work in waves.

The practical situation is that in waves up to some critical height (about six inches for a fourteen foot boat) the rig can be held steady enough by use of the fourth mode techniques described earlier to be able to maintain C1 max trim. Up to this point, tacking downwind will still be advantageous, other things being equal. But with further increase in wave size a point must be reached when the rig can no longer be held steady enough. Once C1 max can no longer be maintained, forget about tacking downwind in waves and light air – unless it is possible to bring some other factor into play.

Kinetics is such a factor. The technical possibility of applying kinetics will vary enormously as between a big yacht, which has heavy gear which cannot be 'fanned' fast enough and so it is not possible to apply kinetics at all, and a sailboard which can be driven at a respectable speed in almost no wind by applying a vigorous impulse-plus-pump every second or so synchronised with small waves. (As in chapter 23, we will discuss here what is technically possible. The proper response to future rules will be for the reader to decide at that time.)

While it is possible for any type of wave to occur in light air, it is customary for light air to be associated with small waves.

Sailboard sailors have no need to steer other than straight for the mark, and apply the most powerful impulse-pumps possible. There is one exception – this is one of the situations in which energy-recovery (as applied by the humming bird) is possible with the right combination of stroke-force, frequency and heading. When a skilled and enthusiastic youngster gets this right in light air his speed is impressive to watch. His heading, a little 'running by the lee', will be close to a square run but it will be governed by the need to position his leech correctly adjacent to the last swirl he developed from his sail, and will have nothing to do with the direction of the mark.

Catamarans cannot flick their mast-heads to windward on any point of sailing. Those with long booms can pump just as well when they head directly downwind as when broad reaching. Those with shorter booms may do better on balance in the stronger Apparent Winds on broad reaching headings. Special techniques sometimes become essential, e.g. in classes without vangs or indeed classes without booms. These are specific to particular classes, and involve no new principles.

The much greater mass of even small keelboats (e.g. Ynglings and Flying Fifteens) makes them relatively insensitive to small waves. The principles which apply to them are similar to those of catamarans, but the waves have to be bigger before they have to abandon tacking downwind.

Dinghies which run square can pump, but cannot flick their mast-heads to windward. Dinghies which broad reach can flick their mast-heads to windward and impulse-pump. A practical point is that the Apparent Wind will be strongest at the instant when the boat's centreboard is in the windward-going water of the wave trough, and an impulse-pump applied at that instant will deliver the most forceful drive forward. The fastest way downwind for a dinghy which employs impulse-pumping is therefore likely to be some broad reaching heading which may look like tacking downwind but which in fact is chosen by feel as that which gives the optimum downwind VMG in those conditions of wind, waves and kinetics.

In waves, a dinghy which can adopt fourth mode sailing should be sailed well heeled up to a speed of about three knots, instead of the one knot appropriate in flat water. The full reason for this is given in chapter 20, Hulls. (Summarised – a fourth-mode type hull which is heeled will suffer a smaller resistance increase due to the out-of-trim effect of the waves than one which is sailed upright.)

In light air and swell, a completely different set of circumstances can arise, in that whenever the wind speed becomes so low that the orbital speed of the water exceeds the wind speed, strange things will happen to the Apparent Wind on a wave-by-wave basis. The slow repetition frequency of a big swell enables a crew to respond in unusual ways. The best way to handle each situation will depend upon the orientation of the swell to the wind.

A personal example will illustrate the principles:-

I had been coaching in a Tasar off Enoshima (the sailing venue for the Japanese Olympics) in a 10 knot southerly sea breeze and a very long southerly swell which was all that was left of a typhoon near the Phillipines some days earlier. As evening approached we headed for the harbour in company with many boats which had finished their races. The sea breeze died as the late afternoon cooled. As it became lighter the wind-waves stilled, and all that was left was the southerly light air, becoming lighter, and the swell. Some of the larger spinnaker-rigged boats had been overtaking us.

As the wind speed fell below about 2 knots, the Apparent Wind began to blow from ahead as the boats were surged forward by the orbital motion of the water in each swell crest. Lower spinnakers were blown aback for a few seconds on each wave. This slowed the boats carrying them.

I worked out what was happening, and tried a technique of turning about 60 degrees crosswind in each trough. As the boat was swept to the south against the faint true wind by the south-going orbital flow in each trough, the Apparent Wind freshened for four or five seconds each wave cycle. I applied impulse-pumps in quick succession which accelerated the boat cross-wind to a respectable speed. As each crest approached from astern I turned straight downwind and surged. During this part of the cycle the Apparent Wind blew from ahead and the sails streamed aft as I was carried north, driven by the momentum of my own residual speed and the gentle swell-slope plus the north-going orbital current in the crest. This proved to be a very efficient way to progress in these conditions. We cleared out ahead of all other boats including those with spinnakers as if driven by a motor.

The above is a classic example of getting the priorities right in unusual circumstances. In waves and light air, wave technique plus kinetics will always be more important than sail trim.

A whimsical point is that a dinghy which does not employ kinetics at all may roll considerably when sailing downwind in unsteady winds in even small waves. In such circumstances crews of unstable craft (such as narrow Skiff Moths) may have to use substantial body movement to balance their boats. They have no option about this: their boats roll naturally and either they move their bodies to maintain balance or they do not survive. Nothing in this inadvertent but often substantial rolling or body movement seems to incur the official displeasure of the rule-makers, despite the fact that some of the rolling must necessarily be propulsive. By way of contrast, a dinghy or small keelboat which employs forceful kinetics skilfully will be deliberately stabilised and will roll less – not more – than those which do not. The body movements of their crews may even be imperceptible.

During recent years the changing rules concerning propulsion which have endeavoured to limit the use of kinetics have consistently waffled around the edges of the perceived problem and have failed to target the important dynamic principles. I respect the rules and applaud the intentions of the rule makers, but in this area I wish the rule-makers of the future better success than they have enjoyed in the past.

25.8 Downwind in breeze

The onset of the breeze means that air at full wind speed begins to drive the lower sails. Boat speed suddenly doubles. Sails can be sheeted more firmly. There is no longer need for excessive twist.

The fastest way to sail downwind in a breeze will depend primarily on the wind speed. There are three wind speed ranges which tend to govern in a practical way the techniques you can use for greatest speed. They are:

1) *From 6 knots to about 9 knots*

This is probably the most common of all breezes. Within this range:

(a) The hulls of most dinghies and yachts will be sailing within their displacement mode, so if tacking downwind was advantageous in light air, it will probably remain advantageous in these lighter breezes.

(b) This is the wind speed range of the wandering breeze, with its very large changes of speed and direction. It will be obvious that a downwind tacker who sails the big headers accurately will benefit from the added speed at little cost because the distance penalty will be much reduced. In these conditions the downwind VMG advantage of the downwind tacker can become massive.

In this wind speed range, the handling principles remain much the same as those described for light air. The principle differences are:

1. The increased sail force keeps the rig much steadier.
2. The boat sails faster and more steadily.
3. The boat can be turned smoothly and more quickly.
4. In the steadier conditions the crew can acquire and maintain Cl Max trim with ease.
5. The major changes of wind direction occur every few minutes instead of every few seconds. It is much easier to recognise and adopt the advantaged gybe.
6. The more skilful you become and the faster you sail, the slower will the Apparent Wind become and the more it will feel like light air. Don't be fooled. Look at the water. So long as the surface shows an energetic ruffle and not a smooth glassiness, that ruffle indicates that the turbulent boundary layer of the breeze is present. Trim your sails accordingly.

The combination of increased boat speed from broad reaching at Cl max trim, plus increased downwind VMG from intelligent tacking downwind in headers which are now better understood, easier to recognise and more predictable, has developed as a decisive race-winning technique in recent years.

In all winds (including light air) between calm and about 9 knots, most boats with reasonable to good performance can expect to gain in some conditions from tacking downwind, particularly on the warmer days with heated air and generally larger shifts in wind direction.

There is an overriding proviso. If, despite the light winds, there happen to be significant waves, then wave forces will dominate over subtle wind forces, and wave technique plus kinetics will become the decisive race-winning factor.

2. *From about 10 knots to about 15 knots*
   This is the wind speed range in which, when sailing downwind:
   (a) Most dinghies and all yachts will enter their forced mode. Increase in sail force from broad reaching will develop little extra boat speed, so for all except truly high performance boats the technique of tacking downwind will become at best marginal and at worst positively disastrous.
   (b) The wandering breeze will have disappeared. In its place will be any one of a number of patterns in which oscillations of wind direction of no more than +/- 6 degrees are normal. The very great downwind VMG advantages which can be enjoyed by sailing the headers in the wider direction swings of unsteady light air and the wandering breeze will have vanished.
   (c) Significant waves will develop in all except unusually enclosed waters. In any situation in which there are significant waves and only moderate winds, the blocking or surfing properties of the waves will override subtleties of heading and sail trim. As the waves grow in size, wave technique plus kinetics will become the dominant race-winning factors.

3. *From about 15 knots to about 25 knots.*
   This is the wind speed range in which:
   (a) The drive force available from the sails when sailing downwind increases greatly.
   (b) Planing craft will leave the forced mode and begin to plane cleanly.
   (c) Wave size and wave effect will increase, but to nothing like the extent that the wind force increases.

The end result is that for boats at and towards the high performance end of the scale – the boats with unlimited speed which can plane cleanly over the waves once they have enough power – wind forces and sail trim will again become dominant. For boats with performance limited by weight and shape and which cannot escape the forced mode, wave technique will remain the race winning factor.

Two recent examples from Sydney harbour indicate these extremes:

An Eighteen footer 'Grand Prix' circuit of six six-race regattas in each of six cities was televised with superb helicopter and chase boat footage, and was broadcast one hour each week on national TV. The Sydney races happened to coincide with a major keelboat event, and some of the keelboats appeared in some of the video sequences. Four of the six Sydney races were sailed in 20 to 25 knot north-easters. Within the confines of the harbour these winds kick up waves about three to four feet high, fifty to sixty feet long and they roll downwind at about ten knots.

Downwind, the keelboats, running square, could be seen to be sailing slightly more slowly than these growing waves. Occasionally one managed to catch and surf a bigger wave for 40 or 50 metres. Downwind race success was determined by these surfing boosts. For these competitors, wave technique was the primary race-winning factor downwind.

The Eighteens tacked downwind. Frame by frame measurement of the downwind progress of various Eighteens in comparison with fixed marks and wave crests showed that these sailboats, tacking downwind, overtook the waves at nearly three times the wave speed. Occasional frames showed hulls clear of the water. For these boats, speed and race success downwind were governed by gust and lull and heading and sail trim, and the waves were just a nuisance.

These are the extremes. For the great majority of boats of moderate performance, greatest speed downwind in the stronger winds will rely on some mix of both heading and sail trim and wave technique and kinetic technique, and can call for some very quick thinking indeed, as we shall see.

25.9 Handling in blocking waves

Often, when you sail downwind in waves, the waves roll faster than your flat-water speed. You can surf the biggest of these 'surfing' waves for extra speed. But sometimes the waves are smaller and roll slower than your flat water speed. These slower waves block you and hold you back. To pass them you have to look for the lowest crests, because these are the only ones which will let you through.

Imagine a day with a fifteen knot offshore wind. Near the shore the waves will be minuscule. Ten to fifteen miles offshore the waves will have grown to be about fifty to sixty feet long and two feet high, and will roll downwind at about ten knots. In waves such as these all those boats which sail downwind at about half wind speed (say from six to eight knots) will all be busy catching and surfing as many of the big ten-knot waves as possible on the downwind legs. But what happens nearer the shore?

As the waves grow from tiny and slow until they mature with a speed about two-thirds of the wind's speed (the size and speed noted above) they must at some point grow through the size at which they are about 32 feet long and 1.5 feet high and roll downwind at 7.5 knots. When a boat with a downwind VMG of 7.5 knots sails in waves which roll downwind at 7.5 knots, that boat will settle into and be captured by the troughs. Closer to the shore where the growing waves are a little shorter and slower – say 6.5 knots – the troughs of these slower waves will similarly capture and hold *at their slower speed* a boat which would in flat water sail at 7.5 knots in that wind. There are three factors which hold it captive:

The first is that in the lulls the boat will be driven by the crest behind.

The second is that in the gusts the boat will be blocked by the crest ahead.

The third is that the orbital speed of the wave's circulation is from ahead when a boat which is running is sailing in the troughs. So for as long as any boat remains trapped in a trough, it may well sail at its normal speed of 7.5 knots through the water, and its crew may think and its instruments (if it has any) may show its speed to be 7.5 knots and 'normal'. But its speed over the bottom will be slower by the 1 to 2 knot adverse component of the wave's orbital circulation.

This trap will be perfect whenever the waves themselves roll at this slightly slower speed, because the boat's reduced speed over the bottom will then exactly match the slower wave speed, yet all sensual impression or instrumental indication will suggest that the boat is up to speed and sailing at its normal (7.5 knot) speed toward the mark. This is a subtle trap indeed. It will occur wherever sailboats race offshore in brisk offshore winds. Near busy waterways it is sometimes masked by the chaotic wave component. But where the position of the course happens to coincide with these growing, steeper sloped, not yet fully developed waves, the fact that these waves will slow the boat is real. What to do about it?

If one side of the course has flatter water and the other side has bigger waves, then a general escape from blocking waves may be possible. Elect this option with caution. If the wind stays at 15 knots, the boat in flatter water will sail faster. But if the wind should lull for awhile to 10 knots, the waves which were blocking waves in the 15 knot breeze will become surfable waves at the slower boat speeds of the lighter winds, and the boat which stays in the waves can then surf some of them and so sail faster.

In conditions where waves are uniform across the course, speed can be increased by using local differences of both wind and wave. The wind situation is obvious: if areas of stronger and lighter wind can be detected, boats which sail to and within the stronger wind areas will sail faster.

The wave situation focuses on smaller detail, such as:

Any set of three or four big waves now will become an area of confused smaller waves soon and then big waves a little later as the underlying slightly different wave systems move into and out of phase.

The lateral extent of big wave is often limited. This will depend on whether the underlying systems are exactly aligned or not, and so it will change continually.

Crests are often serrated, with alternating higher and lower segments.

The escape technique is to move along the wave to where the crest is locally lower or the waves are smaller and confused. This is similar to the chaotic wave technique but reversed – instead of steering the boat into the deepest developing holes you steer it towards where the water is becoming flatter. Where the crests are lowest the orbital speed of the water will be slowest, the adverse current in the smaller troughs is slowest and the speed of the boat over the bottom becomes faster. The reward for your search is threefold. You sidestep the bigger blocking crests. You escape the stronger adverse current in the bigger troughs and so the boat sails faster over the bottom and through the smaller crests. You can gain waves, one at a time, on your opponents.

Pick the point where the crest is smallest, luff for extra speed as you approach, turn smoothly downwind and use the added momentum plus kinetics plus the sails' drive force to sail through the lower crest.

Summary:-

Situations sometimes occur wherein growing waves roll with a speed which is slower than the natural speed of the boat. In such situations:

1. These waves will block and slow a boat on the downwind legs.

2. Normal wave-catching techniques are futile.
3. The quickest escape from a blocking crest is by moving 'sideways' toward the lowest part of the crest.
4. The speed advantage from spontaneous and momentary broad reaching or running by the lee to escape blocking crests will far outweigh all other factors.

25.10 Handling in surfing waves

The principal difference between running in flat water and running in waves is that (apart from the blocking wave situation) the extra speed which can be achieved by surfing the waves will dominate all other factors except differences in wind strength.

If we accept the polar diagram of Fig 24.14 as reasonably typical of a very large group of dinghies and catamarans, then a boat which runs directly downwind in a wind of 15 knots in flat water will sail at about 7 knots – at about half the wind speed – i.e. at point Y. If it continues to run directly downwind in waves which roll at about 10 knots (and these would be typical), its speed will alternate between surging at about 9 knots as the boat accelerates down the advancing face of each wave (point 'F' face), and about 4 knots or less as the boat slows, sterndown, as it sinks down the back of each wave and into the trough (point 'T' trough). The deceleration while it is sailing 'uphill' is severe. Further, once the boat sinks into the trough, the orbital motion of the water in the trough is an adverse current for the boat so whatever the boat's speed through the water may be, for the period it remains 'caught' in the trough its speed over the bottom will be reduced by the orbital component. Because a boat which runs straight downwind will spend longer trapped in the troughs at this slower speed than it will near the crests at a higher speed, the average speed downwind will be slower in waves than in flat water.

But you can sail downwind in waves much faster.

Downwind in regular waves

The principles of wave-catching and surfing outlined in chapter 24 are as relevant to sailing downwind as they are to broad reaching. But boats sail more slowly when they are running than when they broad reaching, so they start from a slower speed. And crews of boats which are running can only pump, while crews in boats which are broad reaching can employ the much more efficient impulse-pump. So in practice it is more difficult to accelerate to the minimum wave-catching speed from the slower, running point of sailing, and most crews cannot catch and surf as many waves on the running legs as on the broad reaching legs. This difficulty places a very high premium on a crew's skill in catching and surfing waves because, as between two otherwise equally matched crews, the one which can catch and surf waves better will catch and surf more waves and open up a lead on the downwind legs, and so win the race. Glenn Collings' description of his technique in Sect 24.21 summarises years of experience by a highly motivated OK world champion. It is more exact in its detail than most others I have listened to. He has since been twice runner-up world champion in Tasars, and several times Australian champion in Solings, so his comments are worth reading twice.

The dynamics are shown in Fig 24.14. What Glenn is saying is that when the waves were too small to be useful, he ran directly downwind at about 7.0 knots average, alternating between points T and F. Point F, even with kinetics, is not fast enough to catch the wave, and the crest slides by. But whenever a larger wave – one which he judged to be large enough to surf – approached, he luffed at least 45 degrees and simultaneously both trimmed his sails and used forceful kinetics as he turned. Note that from the running heading he needed to turn through a much greater angle (from 0-Y to 0-P) much more quickly than when he started from a broad reaching heading (from 0-O to 0-P) and that his successful technique was based on practising and achieving the co-ordination which enabled him to do the three things simultaneously and efficiently. On the broad reaching heading 0-P he accelerated very quickly to the 10 knots necessary (point P or better). This is a big increase in speed from point Y, and his description makes it clear that this is not an easy task to accomplish in the second or so available and that he put a lot of muscular effort into it as well as skill. As soon as he had acquired the necessary speed, he again turned 45 degrees, swiftly and smoothly and at exactly the right moment to position himself on the advancing wave face on a square run at 10 knots, at point Z. Note that this is another case where it is not possible to move from point B or Y directly to point Z. Point Z can only be reached via point P.

Once you have 'caught' a wave, the object is to stay with it for as long as possible. The longer you surf and sail faster than your opponents, the further you will draw ahead, so stretch your time on each wave to the limit. Do not allow yourself to surf straight down the face into the trough again, because you will slow so quickly in the trough that the crest will overtake you and roll by just as if you had never tried to catch it. The art of surfing is to hold a position on the advancing face near the crest. Successful surfboard riders do this brilliantly, and TV sequences of surfboard carnivals are worth watching. It is only near the crest that the wave's orbital speed will add to your own speed. This is the boost which will give you a speed a little faster than the wave speed, and it is this performance margin which makes it relatively easy to maintain your position and prolong the surf.

It was interesting to see how these same principles were applied in a lighter, faster boat. It was my privilege to sail sometimes with Ian Bruce, of Laser fame. Ian was among the world's best helms in International Fourteens; in which he won the Prince of Wales' Cup twice. When he first sailed the Tasar prototype, his overwhelming impression was a freedom on the surface of the water unlike any other boat. Kinetics (as they are practised today) were then in their infancy, but the way he adapted his technique to the faster hull foreshadowed everything written above. He sailed the Nova downwind in waves with a silky-smooth, brilliantly accurate technique, singing quietly to himself as he concentrated; and occasionally muttering, 'You know when you get it right, because you don't need much rudder.

Acquiring the speed

He acquired the necessary speed by employing a technique which enabled him to retain most of the 'surge' speed which he had acquired from the previous wave ('F') (Fig 24.14). He turned very firmly away from the direct down-wind direction a little *before* the instant at which speed would normally begin to be lost. The turn was made primarily by rolling the boat smoothly to leeward, so that it turned, naturally and fast, without the use of rudder. Because the turn was made easily the boat was already broad reaching as the crest passed underneath the hull, and the angle was chosen so that the loss of wave-drive force as the boat slid, bow-up, down the receding face of the wave was almost exactly compensated by the extra drive force. By broad reaching thus, Ian reached the trough just ahead of the chosen wave with speed close to 'O' instead of 'T'. Next, he waited a moment for the increased Apparent Wind, (due to the windward-going orbital movement of the water in the trough,) and as soon as he sensed it, he pumped his mainsail twice, smoothly, but hard. This increased his speed from 'near O' to 'O'. Sometimes, if he sensed that his speed was still not quite enough for certainty of surfing, he held his heading and repeated this sequence for a second wave. By starting from a higher speed, he finished at a higher speed yet. Ultimately, by repeating this technique, he acquired the speed he wanted, point 'O'.or better.

Catching the wave

He caught the wave by turning the boat primarily by rolling it to windward, so that it turned cleanly and almost without the use of rudder. While it was turning, he pumped the mainsail once more, and simultaneously moved his weight forward. The turn was started sooner than I expected, and yet Ian got it exactly right, time after time, with the bow over the deepest part of the trough and the after part of the hull planing on the steepest part of the face, Point 'Z'. (Note how the combined windward roll and pump anticipated the modern understanding of kinetics). Ian then maintained the surf by angling along the face of the wave like a surfboard rider.

All my coaching experience suggests that beginners turn too late. They wait until they feel the wave face lift the boat before they begin their turn. By the time the turn is completed, the advancing crest has passed them and they have missed it. Anticipation and practise are the keys.

Maintaining the surf

Even before he caught his wave, Ian had scanned to the right and left, and decided which way to go. What he did *not* do was surf straight downwind. The drag of water on the boat is equally truly the drag of the boat on the water, and this disturbance will very quickly diminish the local size and steepness of even a big wave. Run a little to one side or the other of 'directly down-wave' so that the boat's weight is always borne by a 'new' part of the wave; this will affect the orbital circulation least and the wave will last longer. The logical choice will be to steer toward the side where the crest is higher. This may well change and there is no reason why you should not make one or more turns during the life of any one surf. There is no reason why a boat should not run by the lee when surfing. Some helms do this deliberately to compensate for the luff initially needed to gain the speed to catch the wave. In this way they 'use waves to gain depth' and stay close to the rhumb line without gybing.

Note that in those conditions when the direction of wind-waves is biassed by the standing waves caused by current, a boat which is steered straight downwind will automatically sail slightly cross-wave, and so can expect to enjoy long surfs. This situation often occurs when sailing in tidal estuaries.

Terminating the surf

How you terminate the surf is important. If you have caught the first big wave of a set, and as the present wave decays there is another suitable wave directly behind, the last thing you want to do is to slide backwards into the trough and have the speed fall to point T. This was the part of Ian's technique which surprised me most.

Glenn's description is exact (Sect 24.21) ' – well before it began to lose speed, I luffed very quickly across the wind sufficiently to maintain the drive. . .' i.e. as the wave died he went straight from point Z to point O and never to point B. In this way he both maintained a higher average speed, and at the same time put himself into the ideal position to catch the wave immediately following. This is how he caught and surfed more waves than his rivals.

The comment of another world champion reinforces this message; '- if you're not sweating at the end of a downwind leg you're not working hard enough.'

The drive force which makes waves grow is the speed difference between the wind and the wave crests. When the waves are small and the wave-speed slow, this difference is large and the waves grow rapidly. They grow quite quickly until they reach a size at which they roll downwind at about two thirds of the wind speed.

When conditions are suitable waves will continue to grow, but much more slowly, until they reach a practical limit which seems to be the size at which the wave speed is about nine tenths of the wind speed. For this second stage of growth to occur, a strong wind must blow steadily and from a reasonably steady direction for many hours over an uninterrupted fetch of water for many miles upwind. The water must be deep enough for big waves to form, and free from any warm surface layer. Such conditions are to be found routinely in open oceans. In more enclosed waters the presence of sluicing tidal currents which mix the water sufficiently to inhibit the development of a warm surface layer seem to be an essential factor. The tideless Great Lakes, the Baltic, and the waters off the Queensland coast within the Great Barrier reef are all examples of waters which develop warm surface layers because the tidal mixing is absent or feeble, and even their biggest waves remain relatively small. But in waters in which strong tidal currents mix the water sufficiently to inhibit the development of any warm surface layer, a fetch of only 40 or 50 km, such as in Melbourne's Port Phillip will enable waves to continue to grow to a size where you can lose sight of a nearby boat when both are in troughs.

These bigger waves roll faster and it is necessary to match these higher speeds to 'catch' them. Fortunately the advancing faces are bigger so there is a little more time available in which to accelerate. The higher the speed needed, the more skilful and forceful will be the kinetics needed. In big-wave conditions, a boat which planes freely will often exceed the wind speed when it enters areas where the wind is lighter as in a local fluctuation lull. The sails will stream aft. When this happens, ignore the sails and prolong the surf as much as possible by handling the hull exactly as you would handle a surfboard. Concentrate on poising your bodies for the fastest planing attitude, steer towards where the wave is steepest, and continue to maintain a position just ahead of the crest. If you had been considering gybing, this is the time when it can be done with the least effort; only a finger's force is needed to start the boom moving toward its new side as the Apparent Wind from aft returns.

25.11 Handling in mixed waves

The situation in which a stronger wind blows over a very thin warm surface layer and develops mixed waves merits special mention. This is the third wave situation described in Sect 14.2 (part Two). It is a mixture of larger faster waves and smaller slower waves. It is regular in the sense that all the waves go the same way, straight downwind. But the smaller waves sometimes get bunched together and sometimes become more openly spread by the orbital flows of the bigger waves, so it has no regular rythym. When sailing downwind, the small waves move more slowly than the boat and so are blocking waves, while the free fast waves move faster than the boat and can be surfed. The same skill and forceful kinetics will be needed to initiate the surf, but there will then be the added problem that it will continue to be necessary to sail through the smaller blocking waves while the boat is surfing the larger waves. This will call for a more complex technique than that which is fastest in free waves which are regular and simple in form. The best description of race-winning technique which I have been privileged to read was contributed by Charlie McKee, Olympic bronze medallist and winner of the Tasar world championship at Adelaide, to the class' newsletter:

'The classic theory of steering up and down in every crest and trough simply does not work in waves like Adelaide's. The waves are too irregular for rhythmic steering to be effective. Instead, I would look further ahead than the next wave, and try to discern areas of relatively flatter water. When running, our main advantage was our ability to sail lower than others. While this was not always possible, i.e. when other boats were controlling us, or when the runs weren't really runs, it was very effective when the situation permitted it. Mostly, sailing low is a matter of steering aggressively on the waves. Once we caught a wave I would sail as low as was physically possible and still stay on it. Frequently this would mean sailing well by-the-lee, and Becky would have to hold the boom forward to stop us from gybing. The basic principle of surfing was expressed best by Elvström: *always keep the boat pointing downhill.* There is always a tendency when faced with a wall of water ahead of you to head up. Faced with the irregular patterns of Adelaide's waves, there were many instances when you could continue carving down, and another gap would develop. Once you have lost too much speed, and there are no more gaps down low, then you need to head up and build speed. The key is to head up dramatically to build speed as quickly as possible, then immediately look for your opportunity to carve down again.'

'There are some things you can do to make it easier to sail lower. For instance, sailing with your board a little further down gives more control in the waves. The trick to sailing low in big waves is for the skipper to steer aggressively and for the crew to pay close attention to fore and aft trim. Take care, because sailing very low in short steep waves does leave one more susceptible to nosediving and swamping.'

'One of the great things about our sport is that the playing field is always changing, always different. Sailing well in big waves is still one of the greatest challenges'.

25.12 Handling in chaotic waves

Chaotic waves have no dominant direction, so the upwind handling techniques described in Sect 22.22 will continue to apply equally when sailing crosswind and downwind. In practice the main difference will be the way a crew apply kinetics. When sailing to windward the sails are already trimmed well in, and the only way kinetics can be applied is to force the masthead itself to windward. When sailing crosswind both windward movement of the masthead and pumping of the sails is possible and use of this impulse-pump is fastest. When sailing directly downwind moving the masthead by rolling the boat ceases to be effective – because the crosswind movement of the masthead does not increase the Apparent Wind speed – while pumping has maximum effect. For this reason it may be faster in practice to luff sufficiently to enable the full power and added speed of impulse-pumping to be used, rather than run square and be limited to pumping only.

When the wind is strong enough for you to sail at high speed through chaotic waves the bow should be trimmed higher than when sailing in flat water or regular waves, and the forward hand should adopt a stance which enables him/her to move aft very quickly on occasion. Chaotic waves characteristically have steeper faces and backs than regular waves, and any boat which drives its bow at high speed into a steep wave face or back will suffer very high drag for the period of deep immersion. It may also fill. The fastest trim will be to trim the bow as high as necessary for it to drive over, and not into, the wave slopes. Note that it is *only* at high speeds through chaotic waves that this 'bow higher than normal' trim is faster. Normally, a too-high bow merely signals a slow boat.

The chaotic wave situation calls for special mention in another respect. As mentioned in Section 20.12, (Part Three) the drag rise associated with the forced mode will occur earlier when the boat is sailed into waves. In the case of regular waves, this will occur when sailing to windward. Conversely, when sailing downwind in regular waves, the drag rise will be delayed until some higher speed is attained. But in chaotic waves the early drag rise will occur on every point of sailing – and so will the earlier release into the freedom usually associated with the planing mode. The effect of this will be to reduce the performance advantage to be expected when tacking downwind, because the hull at quite modest speeds will already be behaving as if it were in the forced mode.

Conversely, these are exactly the conditions when the 'steer into holes' technique described in Section 22.22 can be applied most effectively, and particularly so if it is used in conjunction with forceful kinetic technique. The fastest way downwind in chaotic waves and any breeze is to abandon tacking downwind early,and use kinetics plus chaotic wave technique as soon as the boat speed is sufficient for the boat to be turned fast enough. To do this really well takes a lot of practise. First you must learn to anticipate where the holes will form quickly enough. Then you must develop a response fast enough to turn your boat into them in time for it all to work properly. A second too late and that hole will be becoming a hill. Once it all begins to work properly that is only the beginning. Further practise will develop even faster anticipation and response, and better co-ordination of kinetics with the wave technique. More practise yet will enable you to do all this exactly right, and with all the muscle force you can muster.

All too hard? Just watch somebody who has done the work. The final results are magic.

25.13 Handling in swell

If the direction of the swell is from astern and the wind speed is marginal for planing, the gentle slopes of the swell can cause the boat to alternate between planing and the forced mode. The wave speed of the swell may be thirty or forty knots, so there will be no question of 'catching' the wave in the surfing sense. The best that can be done is to initiate each plane as quickly as possible and to extend it for as long as possible. Because the Apparent Wind will be stronger in the trough and will become less as the crest approaches, there is every reason to turn onto a broad reach while in the trough, pump on one or two smaller waves to build speed as the slope of the face approaches, and use a maximum pump to establish the plane. Once on the plane, turn straight downwind and poise your weight accurately for maximum speed and distance. As the boat slows on the back of the swell, move forward instantly (but smoothly) for fastest displacement trim. Repeat this sequence on a wave-by-wave basis

25.14 Sailing the shifts

The foregoing sections have suggested that in the real world of gusts and waves, the fastest way downwind for all boats will always have some crosswind component. Even those boats which sail fastest downwind by running square will sail faster yet if they deliberately seek and sail in sequential gusts, and in this way increase the proportion of time that they spend in stronger wind. As each gust decays, the only new gusts which can be of any use are the nearest approaching from upwind on the right and the nearest similar gust on the left, and to reach either it will be necessary to sail somewhat crosswind.

If the new gusts are equidistant and the present wind direction is the same as the mean direction, there will be no advantage either way. In Fig 25.8(a) A and B are two boats within the same gust. At A1 and B1 they leave the decaying gust simultaneously and sail, A to the left to intercept the new gust GL1, and B to the right towards the new gust GR1. Other things being equal they will still be an equal distance from the downwind mark when they reach each new gust at A2 and B2. So in this case it will be faster to sail to whichever new gust is stronger or closer. But if the present wind direction is veered only 10 degrees, the relative positions of A and B as they reach their new gusts will be changed. 'B' will now be closer to the downwind mark by one third of the distance from the decayed gust to either of the new gusts, as is shown in Fig 25.8(b). It is clear that to sail toward any gust to the right when the local wind is veered or to the left when the local wind is backed is unlikely to be the fastest way to the downwind mark.

Crews of boats which run square normally assume that windshifts are of little consequence to them when sailing downwind. But Fig 25.8 shows that a relatively small back or veer can lead to a very significant race advantage, even for those boats which normally run square. For boats which normally tack downwind and sweep more widely across the course these gains and losses will be correspondingly greater. Putting your head in the sand is no help – these losses will occur regardless of whether a crew realises that the wind is backed or veered or not.

What comes out of this is that for all boats there will always be an advantaged gybe. This leads us to the second problem. Which gybe is advantaged? Before you can adopt the advantaged gybe downwind, you need to know what the present wind direction is with respect to the mean.

When boats sail to windward close-hauled, they adopt a characteristic angle to the true wind which always repeats very closely in particular conditions. Crews become accustomed to these angles, bias the observed compass reading appropriately, and compare the result with the direction of the mean wind. Because the sailing angles repeat so accurately, there is seldom doubt about which is the advantaged tack.

This is not at all true when sailing downwind.

Whenever boats run square in the gusts, either from time to time or as a routine, the direct downwind heading can be noted, either from the compass or from some prominent downwind landmark, and mentally tracked. This is the easy way of remaining confident that you know what is the present wind direction, and which gybe is at present advantaged.

For downwind tackers who seldom or never run square, it is not easy to know the present wind direction within say 5 degrees. An uncertainty of 5 degrees can lead to a total error of 10 degrees, and such an error can lead to very big losses. Everything written in this chapter suggests that while the angle through which you should luff for fastest downwind VMG may be relatively constant in steady wind and flat water, in the reality of gusts and waves and kinetics and tactics it is anything but repeatable. I do not think that there is any simple answer other than awareness, experience, a growing sense of orientation and a determination to use many other factors as well as the compass. Observation of the sailing angles of the boats ahead is particularly valuable. In this way you become able to know and adopt the advantaged gybe more confidently in unsteady conditions, and less is heard of '..sailed fast but in the wrong direction, downwind.'

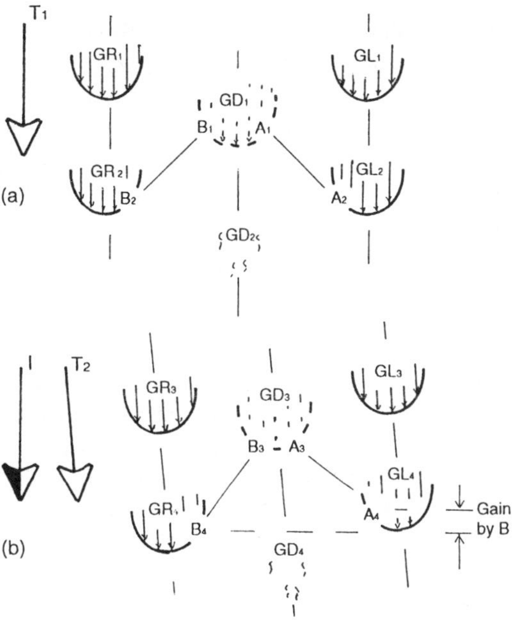

T_1 = True Wind 360° T
GD_1 = Decaying gust
A_1 B_1 = Two yachts side by side
GL_1 = New gust to left
GR_1 = New gust to right

In (a), A_1 and B_1 each sail from the decaying gust to the new gust each side. One minute or so later at A_2, B_2, GL_2, GR_2 (and GD_2) they are still even.

In (b), A_3 believes the True Wind still to be 360° (I)
- but " " " is actually 355° (T_2)

This 5° deg uncertainty can lead to a 10° tactical error, i.e.

A_3 sails to the nearer gust GL_3 arriving at A_4 and GL_4.
B_3 sails the header to GR_3, arriving at B_4 and GR_4.
At A_4 and B_4, B is ahead by about one sixth of the distance A_4 - B_4, due to the tactical error of 10° caused by the uncertainty of 5°.

Fig 25.8 Shifts and gusts

The race advantages which can flow from anticipating the windshift pattern and sailing the shortest-distance path to the windward mark have been discussed in chapter.12. The same advantages can be enjoyed when sailing downwind, particularly by downwind tackers.

On days when the *stability index* is low, no prediction will be possible. On these days it will be fastest to sense the wind direction as you go and gybe spontaneously as opportunity suggests, but bias your track so that you never sail too far from the rhumb line.

On days when the *stability index* is high, and you can predict the backs and veers with some confidence, you can plan your downwind legs with more certainty. The principles are identical with those which are fastest upwind; the shortest distance is to sail to the 'inside' of every curve. But because downwind you sail the headers and not the lifts to do this, and because the wind-waves tend to flow downwind at about one quarter of the wind speed, the practical application becomes different in time and space. In many ways this makes the game easier, because on the downwind leg you sail back through the wind-waves you have just sailed through on your way upwind. Let us follow an imaginary boat to see how this works.

Fig 25.9 shows diagrammatically 1,000 metres of a windward/leeward leg. On a day with a 12 knot sea breeze, the starter in the moored committee vessel notes that the direction backs for 4 minutes and veers for

4 minutes regularly. These would very likely be caused by wind-waves 400 metres long flowing downwind at 3 knots, or 500 metres long flowing at 2.5 knots, or some similar speed/wavelength combination. The sequential diagrams, 0, 1, 2 etc show the pattern as it would appear if photographed from above at one minute intervals, and how it changes as the backs and veers B1, V1, B2, etc. flow downwind.

The dotted line 0, 1 etc plots the track of a Soling which sails at 6 knots. From 0 to 1 it sails on port tack in the back B1. At 1 it tacks, and holds starboard tack in the veer V1 until a little after 2 when it tacks on to port again in back B2. It rounds the windward mark between 3 and 4.

In the 12 knot wind it will be up to hull speed, and will gain nothing from any attempt to tack downwind. But it will need to be luffed occasionally either to sail to a gust or to regain speed after a momentary lull or bad set of waves, or whenever a suitable wave offers for a semi-surf. It will therefore gain significantly if it is sailed on the advantaged gybe. So from the windward mark it adopts starboard gybe in back B2. (Note how the rule works – 'If port tack is favoured on approach to the mark, starboard gybe will be favoured after rounding' – and also that the rule works for both the windward and the leeward marks.) The Soling, sailing downwind at 6 knots will now be overtaking the wind-waves which are flowing in the same direction at three knots. Its speed of closing with the wind-waves will be three knots. It will therefore expect to sail for about three times as long between gybes as between tacks. By time '5' it has sailed through B2, and gybes on to port into V1 (which it sailed through between times '1' and '2'). It takes until time 9 to sail through V1 and into B1, which it was sailing in between times 'o' and '1'.

Note that while sailing downwind and overtaking the wind-waves, most crews will be able to look at the boats ahead to see the wind direction which they will soon enter. But they must look behind them to pick up the approaching gusts.

The exception is that crews of those high performance boats which sail downwind faster than the wind will look ahead and to windward for their next gust, and ahead and to leeward for their next direction.

25.15 Handling in gusts

The different types of gust which occur in different conditions have been described earlier. These are summarised below. They will affect the performance of sailboats which race downwind in a number of ways, some of which are inter-related.

In light airs

There are no gusts. In light air it is necessary to sail to and within the puffs.

In breezes

When racing downwind in breeze:

(a) All boats will sail faster in the stronger wind of the gust than the lull.

(b) Some boats will sail faster when tacking downwind than when running square.

(c) Many boats will sail faster when surfing waves.

There are essential conflicts between (a), (b) and (c) above. It is the compromises which have to be made between these three which make the downwind legs so interesting and unpredictable.

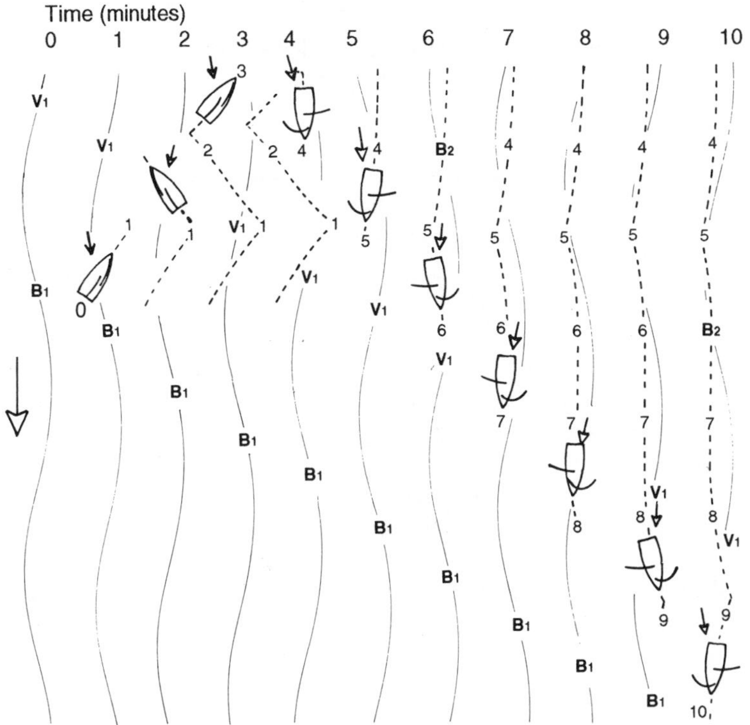

Wind speed = 12 knots
Boat speed (Soling) = 6 knots
Wind-wave speed = 3 knots
Wind-waves roll downwind 100m each minute, as indicated in 0,1,2,3 -- above.
Wind near boat at the stated time = ⟶
Boat meets backs and veers of the wind-waves every 80 seconds when sailing to windward - but overtakes the back or veer ahead only every 4 minutes downwind i.e.
Between times 0 and 1- boat sails in back 1, it overtakes back 1 again at time 9.
" " 1 " 2 " " " veer 1, it sails downwind in veer 1 between times 5 - 9.
" " 2 " 3 " " " back 2, it sails downwind in back 2 from time 3 to time 5.

This figure shows how a running boat overtakes friction driven wind-waves. The crew can observe by *looking ahead*, the wind direction that they will shortly be sailing in.This figure shows the dynamics when the wind-waves are regular. When the wind-waves are not regulaı, the principle will remain true - *look ahead* for your wind direction. (This principle will also remain true when the wind direction changes are driven by heat.)

Fig 25.9 Sailing the wind-waves downwind.

In cooled breezes

Gusts develop which are characteristically moderate and predictable.
All blow from the same direction as the lulls.
All blow about 50% faster than the lulls.
All display a typical near-circular lozenge shape on the surface which is aligned with its major axis upwind/downwind.

In heated breezes

Lighter heated breezes usually become wandering breezes.
Wandering breezes have no gusts.
Stronger heated breezes develop harsh gusts which are characteristically unpredictable.
Individual gusts blow from directions which can differ by up to plus or minus 30 degrees from the mean direction of the lulls.
These direction changes are random.
Gusts typically blow at double the lull speed or more.
The added momentum of these faster gusts takes longer to decay. In heated breezes gusts live longer
This longer life-span greatly extends the typical upwind/downwind dimension of each gust.
In cooled winds the pattern of each gust is near-circular.
In heated winds the pattern of each gust is more elongated in an upwind/downwind direction.
The more intense the heating, the more the surface pattern of each gust will approach a broad upwind/downwind stripe.
Regardless of the heating, the total area of the surface which is occupied by both the gusts and the intervening lulls remains at about 50% each.

In valley winds

Gusts tend to strike from the direction of the gradient wind aloft.
The 'base wind' (lulls) tends to be channelled along the direction of the valley.
This is one situation in which the wind direction tends to be correlated with the wind speed i.e. in which either 'Gusts will favour port tack',or 'Gusts will favour starboard tack' (depending upon the alignment of the valley axis with the gradient wind aloft.)
The effects of heating and cooling will be super-imposed on the basic direction pattern noted above.

If we divide all sailboats into three broad 'breeze performance' groups, we find that the interesting options lie primarily with the middle group.

Low performance sailboats

Keelboats, heavy dinghies and heavy catamarans cannot plane and so cannot tack downwind with advantage in breeze. Their fastest way downwind is simply to spend the maximum time possible in the areas of strongest wind, and to further boost their speed by surfing if possible. Everything else is of second order importance.

High-performance sailboats

These boats sail downwind faster than the waves and often faster than the wind. So in practice they simply sail through or over what are for them blocking waves, and the surfing skills they mastered years ago have been superseded and discarded. Further, at the speeds they sail the crosswind dimensions of typical gusts – 200 to 300 metres – are too small for crews to contemplate gybing back and forth within them in other than relatively light breezes. This means that they have no option but to sail through the intervening lulls. Fair enough. A little more sail area in the close-winded reaching spinnaker, and they equip themselves with a rig which is the right area for the gusts upwind, and also the right area for the lulls downwind. In the gusts downwind they simply run a little more square, and the Apparent Wind obligingly decreases in strength to match the extra area of the spinnaker, and they sail even faster provided their spinnakers are cut close-winded enough. It is all so simple when you can think laterally and adjust your Apparent Wind on a gust by gust basis to fit your rig rather than adjust your rig to a True Wind you cannot control, and never mind about traditional rules or mindsets.

Moderate-performance sailboats

It is these boats in the middle which are left with the options and the opportunities. These are the boats which can plane, which can sometimes sail faster by tacking downwind, which can be accelerated by kinetics, and which can surf. The crews who race these boats cannot escape the challenge, the responsibility and the exultation of considering the complex of facts of the moment, making the best decisions possible, and drawing ahead, matching their opponent, or falling behind in consequence.

We have looked at the principles involved in running square or tacking downwind. We have looked at the techniques of surfing. We have looked at the different kinetic techniques. Let us now look at the effects of gusts on the downwind performance of this group of sailboats, and keep in mind that where there are gusts there will sometimes be waves, i.e. let us try to look at the whole situation holistically.

In light airs

There are no gusts. Downwind performance will depend upon the extent to which the crew use and mix tacking downwind, wave surge if there are waves, kinetics and above all sailing to and remaining in the areas of stronger air for more of the time than their competitors.

In six to nine knot breezes

(a) In flat water and cooled air.

The gusts in these light breezes be the smallest of all the gusts. Boats which centre in the strongest core of each gust and run straight downwind with it for as long as it lasts will probably sail downwind faster than rivals who tack downwind and ignore the gusts. But as soon as one gust decays they should luff or gybe to tack downwind toward and into the nearest available next gust and centre themselves in it until it decays. These gusts are too small for even a slow boat to gybe back and forth within them, so a boat which tacks downwind will necessarily spend at least 50% of its time in the intervening lulls in a wind only two thirds as strong. Except for the very high performance boats, the increased speed from tacking downwind is unlikely to compensate for the decreased speed in the lulls between the gusts.

(b) In flat water and heated air.

These are the conditions in which the wandering breeze develops. In wandering breezes there are no gusts, but there are massive differences in wind speed and wind direction as between the peripheries and the centres of the cells. The fastest technique here will be to use the crosswind capability of tacking downwind to search for and centre in the wider bands of stronger air. This is the reverse of the advice in cooled air.

(c) In waves.

In both cooled and heated air, the priorities are:

1.Seek and centre in the strongest air.

2. Surf as many waves as possible.

Stronger air comes first. When surfing, bias the choice of right or left along the waves to move towards and/or stay within the stronger air.

In stronger breezes – say ten to fifteen knots

This is the wind speed range in which most moderate-performance boats get trapped in the forced mode when sailing downwind, and the speed advantage in tacking downwind becomes marginal at best and probably slower. So in all conditions – flat water and waves, cooled air and heated, it will probably be faster to sail to and centre in the stronger wind, and then run square in it. If there are waves, surf to the limit, and bias your direction as you surf to stay in the stronger wind.

In strong winds – say sixteen knots and stronger

In these winds the sizes of the individual gusts in cooled air will have become much bigger, and the fans (Sect. 5.5, Part One) will have become significant.

(d) In flat water and cooled air.

Sail to the nearest gust. At its edge, bear away and ride the fan for as long as possible. This will give the triple advantages of the extra boat speed from the stronger wind, the extra boat speed from tacking downwind, and the extra VMG from heading more closely toward the mark. As the fan fades, enter and sail in the gust proper. In gusts as big as this, it may be advantageous to tack downwind, gybing back and forth within the gust. This will depend upon the performance of your boat, how smartly you gybe, and the size of the gust.

(e) In waves and cooled air.

If you are riding the fan to its greatest advantage, what are surfable waves within and between the gusts will suddenly become blocking waves within the fan. In this situation the advantages of riding the fan are so great that it will probably be better to accept the occasional block for as long as it takes for the wave to decay, rather than risk losing the narrow fan. Within the gust, surf downwind to the limit. Run by the lee to stay within the gust if your boat has the performance to do so. If the gust is very long-lived and in your surfing you approach one edge and your gybing technique is adequate, simply gybe while you surf and begin to work back the other way.

(f) In flat water and heated air.

As above, sail to and centre in the strongest wind. The heated-air gusts are stronger and they are longer and they last longer. The lulls between them are lighter, so forget about tacking downwind. except while you hunt the next gust. The chance of finding a useful fan is smaller. Conversely, heated gusts tend to have very strong narrow lines of wind as cores. Sometimes there are more than one in the same gust. There is every advantage in sailing to, then centring in and sailing straight down these cores. Be prepared for the fact that their direction will often be skewed by up to thirty degrees either way from the mean downwind direction. Note that this does not invite tacking downwind because you cannot enjoy the advantage of the stronger wind within the narrow core of the gust unless you go where it goes, and this will be straight down the local wind at every point.

(g) In waves and heated air.

Again, sail to and centre in the strongest cores of the gusts. Add to your speed by surfing. The new fact with heated gusts is that in very strong cores the boat speed may sometimes exceed the wave speed, so be prepared to switch from surfing technique to blocking-wave technique whenever necessary.

In valley winds

Check the direction of the gradient wind aloft by noting the direction of the isobars on the current weather map, or (better) by observing the direction of movement of any lower clouds. When the wind direction aloft is backed from the axis of the valley, the gusts will probably be backed with respect to the lulls, and vice versa. All the considerations of flat water and waves, and of cooled and heated air which have been noted above will continue to apply. But there is another particular advantage which often occurs: When the direction of the downwind leg lies between the directions of the gusts and the lulls, crews can often enjoy the ideal situation of tacking downwind without gybing in the lulls, and running directly downwind in the gusts.

This logic is sometimes missed in the midst of other distractions.

25.16 Practical handling downwind

In the chapters about upwind and crosswind sailing, the more important dynamic principles in each of the primary combinations of wind, sea-state and point of sailing were described, and in the same sections examples contributed by champion sailors were given of the way these principles were applied in the handling of different classes of sailboats.

Downwind sailing has so many more variables that it would be unmanageable to try to repeat this format. Instead, I have asked each of five helms to discuss the downwind techniques which win in their classes, in different wind and sea-state conditions. One is a youth champion. The other four are world champions. Two are Olympic representatives.

One sails an Etchells 22, a non-planing keelboat. One sails an Eighteen footer. For the boats 'in the middle' I have chosen the 470 and the Laser Two.

25.16(a) Laser Two

Mark Mendelblatt comes from St Petersburg, Florida. While still a junior, he won the 1991 Laser Two world championships with a race to spare from a fleet of 170 starters at Hayling Island near Southampton in England. His earlier contributions and those which follow here reflect particularly the North American college environment in which crews sail twenty or thirty very short races per day, and there is very great emphasis on the detail handling of the boat.

'When sailing downwind in flat water and light air, we move our weight right forward. The crew is against the shroud to weather and I sit to leeward just behind the spinnaker sheet deck-eye. The centreboard is up one quarter, and the spinnaker pole is trimmed right aft for maximum projected area. I avoid any sharp turns as these disturb the flow over the spinnaker and in the extreme can collapse the spinnaker. I sail as low as possible in the puffs. My crew and I co-operate in that he advises me continuously how much tension there is on the spinnaker sheet, and in particular he warns me when the tension begins to go light. So I sail higher through the light patches that I can see, and regardless of anything else I also sail higher whenever my crew warns me that the spinnaker is beginning to go 'soft'.

When the waves are so small that we cannot catch them, nothing changes and we try to sail exactly as in flat water. But as the waves grow it becomes more difficult to keep the spinnaker flying in very light air, and it may be necessary to come up a little further. We do this to a minimum extent – we always sail as close to directly downwind as is possible consistent with reasonable drive from the spinnaker.'

'In breezes of 6 to 10 or 11 knots and flat water we use the same centreboard position, rig set-up and forward crew weight position as for light air. The wind is steadier and we can sail lower – almost by the lee. I use the jib as a guide. It should set to leeward with the sheet very slack; if it comes over to the weather side I am steering too low.'

'When there are waves big enough to catch, we find that one co-ordinated pump applied as the stern begins to lift will accelerate this light boat sufficiently to start surfing. I pump the mainsail with the fastest full-arm sweep on the mainsheet that I can apply. My crew simultaneously pulls both sheet and guy to pump the spinnaker. This action needs practise as it is critical that it be very fast, and also that the pulls be proportioned so that the spinnaker tack and clew both come back about the same distance. While it is obviously desirable that the pumps be synchronised, in practice it does not seem to matter very much when they are not. Once on the wave we sail, when it is possible, as low as is possible without gybing, When in the lighter winds and smaller waves it is not possible to surf directly downwind like this, we sail as high as is necessary to stay on the wave provided that this does not involve sailing too much away from the mark. Apart from the pumping action we do everything smoothly and nothing to extreme.'

'In breezes of 12 to 20 knots and flat water, we still keep the crew weight forward and sail straight downwind except for sailing to and into gusts which are close enough to be convenient. In waves we pump the mainsail and spinnaker simultaneously on every wave. We continue to sail almost straight downwind and even more so in gusts, and slightly by the lee when surfing. (Only in the lighter breezes do we ever tack downwind.) If the wave shape is such that the bow is likely to go under, the crew moves back on a wave by wave basis to keep the gunwale at the bow above the wave crest.'

'In strong winds we set the spinnaker pole higher and also move our weight back; both changes help keep the bow up in the bigger waves. The centreboard remains at no more than one quarter up'.

Jason Muir started his sailing in Hobart, Tasmania and in recent years he has sailed from Brisbane, Queensland. He comes from a family of top level sailors which reaches back for several generations. Jason was the fastest at the world youth championships in Amsterdam which was sailed in Laser Two's. His contributions reflect the Australian environment, in which it is customary to sail one ten or twelve mile race with long legs, and in which race success depends very largely on the observation, recognition and correct interpretation of distant clues.

Approach

'I find that you can make great gains downwind just by applying some basics:

1) Maintain your concentration.
2) Maintain your determination.
3) Develop the ability to make the right decisions.

This means that you must spend far more hours in the boat than most people, race against a fleet if possible but at least against a partner. You must record as many decisions as you can remember, analyse and re-analyse these to see which were right and why, – and then which were wrong and why. In this way you can develop the ability to make the right decisions for more of the time.'

Priorities

'For maximum advantage, the helm should scan both the distant water surface and the dynamics of other boats. These can reveal where the next line of breeze is likely to come from. I look for darker patches or shading on the water, the presence sometimes of ripple or tiny waves and the attitudes and/or speeds of other boats. These are all useful guides as to where the air is stronger.

As between boats sailing upwind and downwind, I find that boats sailing upwind are better indicators of the presence of stronger air. As between boats ahead and behind, I find that if you respond to what you can sense from the boat(s) ahead you can usually make useful gains. Boats directly behind do not seem to provide information anywhere near as useful.

Look for more than the nearest puff. Look for pattern. You can sometimes see that the positions of the darker patches reveal some arrangement of lines. If you sail to and along a line you will usually enjoy more wind than anywhere else. Be very careful of cloud shadows: they can be deceptive.'

Summed up:

'The crew which looks around the most will usually make the largest gains. In all wind strengths, sail towards and stay within the strongest air. Gybe on the headers. Sail in clear air; keep well away from the wind shadows of following boats.'

Sail trim

'Look at what your rig is doing'

Vang

'The Laser Two always needs some vang downwind, otherwise the head of the sail will twist forward and you will lose power. The fastest setting will depend on conditions. In light air use just sufficient vang to prevent the boom from moving around and spilling precious wind out of the sail. In winds of about 10 knots and choppy waves, if the vang is too slack the leech will twist forward whenever the boat hits a wave. This will spill pressure and lose speed. If the vang is too tight the leech will close and you will lose projected area. As wind speed increases vang tension should be increased to maintain the greatest projected area without unacceptable twist. If the vang is too slack, the boat will roll to windward in gusts.'

Outhaul

'The Laser Two mainsail is made from soft cloth which stretches. This stretch allows the leech to lie open in breeze unless the outhaul is pulled out tightly to stretch the fabric the other way, and enough vang is used to minimise twist.'

Jib

'On some occasions when running square or by the lee in light to medium airs the jib can be goose-winged for added area. Otherwise it plays little part in downwind sailing.'

Spinnaker

'The spinnaker area on the Laser Two is relatively big for the size of the boat. In 0 to 2 knots it will not set properly, and the boat will sail faster without it. The fastest trim is to set the spinnaker so that there can be free airflow between the spinnaker and the luff of the mainsail. The spinnaker halyard should be eased about 4 inches in winds from 2 to 10 knots, 2 inches from 11 to 20 knots, and not at all in strong winds. For the same reason the spinnaker pole should always be positioned somewhat forward of the beam. If it is too far aft the spinnaker will set too flat and too close to the mainsail, and this is slow. If it is too far forward projected area will be lost. The fastest position in each wind strength and sea-state condition can be sensed by feel. Whatever the spinnaker pole and halyard positions, the clews should always be at the same height.

The crew's eyes should never leave the spinnaker. You cannot make gains when the spinnaker is collapsing. You and your crew must be able to communicate with each other without uncertainty. As a crew you should make no errors due to misunderstanding.'

Handling

'The spinnaker should be hoisted quickly; it should be up and trimmed between one and four lengths of the mark depending on conditions. In light airs the spinnaker pole is usually set before rounding the mark, and the spinnaker is hoisted during the rounding. In breeze it is sometimes advantageous for the forward hand to steer from trapeze while the skipper sets the pole and hoists – this keeps the boat flat and moving fast and wastes no time. In heavy airs the priority is survival and the spinnaker should be set at the first reasonable opportunity.

As the breeze changes, spinnaker halyard, spinnaker pole, vang and centreboard should all be retrimmed periodically for fastest sailing.'

Gybing

'For fastest sailing through gybes, it is essential that the spinnaker should remain filled and not collapse. This calls for good technique and good co-ordination. Our technique is:

The forward hand stands up, uncleats the jib, grasps the vang to assist gybe the mainsail, and rolls the boat (toward the new leeward side) to help float the spinnaker to its new side. After the gybe he reaches for the pole, releases it from the mast and clips it to the new windward brace while the leeward sheet is still hooked to the other side. This balances the spinnaker so that the skipper can keep it full by steering away from either luff if it tends to collapse. The leeward sheet is then released and the spinnaker pole placed on the mast fitting. The forward hand, now on the windward side, fine-trims the brace and sheet, and the skipper, now on the leeward side, re-cleats the jib loosely. Throughout the gybe, skipper and forward hand should co-ordinate smoothly to preserve balance. We use this technique in all winds from 2 to 20 knots.

In stronger winds the technique is biassed more toward control of the boat, as it is more important to keep the boat flat and on its right course than to keep the spinnaker full.'

Wind and wave tactics

'We tack downwind when the breeze is shifty and/or gusty, but gusts always take precedence over shifts. We sail more across blocking waves, to get the boat speed to break through them whenever practical. We surf all waves possible. We chase gusts at every opportunity. Gusts give us our greatest gains. In medium winds we both chase gusts and gybe on the shifts. In stronger winds we sail more directly toward the mark, consistent with chasing and using gusts.'

25.16(b) 470 class

Rounding the windward mark

'The method of rounding the mark from sailing to windward to a reach or a run is critical. The quickest way to slow a boat is by turning too sharply. The ideal way to round the top mark is to turn smoothly, which will promote and sustain planing for as long as possible. If there is a gust, so much the better. Ignore all spinnaker setting action until the gust has been fully exploited. You will generally find that this technique will take you straight over the top of those boats that turned sharply immediately, lost speed in the turn, and then became preoccupied with setting spinnakers.'

Reaching

'In the absence of other boats, reaching from one point to the other can be accomplished fastest by 'scalloping', i.e. sail the boat closer to the wind in the light spots and bear away in the heavier patches. The stronger the breeze, the less pronounced the scalloping needs to be. In the presence of other boats, it is suicidal to allow first one boat, and then the next and the next and the next to go over the top of you. In any racing situation, the choice of whether to sail the fastest course or the tactical course will be governed by how close behind you the next boat is. If there is a bit of a break behind you, work on sailing the fastest course. If there is only a boat length or so between you and the next boat, with a bunch behind, think very carefully before you go too low.'

Running

'This is always a trade-off between going high for speed and going low for shortest distance. There are two situations – sailing faster than the waves or sailing slower than the waves.

Every time you turn downwind for a running leg, the fact that both the wind and wave conditions are constantly changeable means that there can be no one angle to the wind nor one wave riding technique which will give fastest VMG. Generally, the stronger the wind, the more directly downwind will be the fastest heading. In the lighter winds, and particularly when you are still displacing, some heading further from directly downwind will be faster. Whether the angle you are presently sailing is in fact the fastest must be constantly monitored relative to other boats. If a distant background is opening up behind another boat which is crosswind of you and on either gybe, that other boat must be sailing downwind faster, and you had better try some different combination of heading and sail trim, or find more wind.

When the light is uniform, we use the shading of the water surface to read the differences in wind speed across the area of vision. But in conditions of uneven light this method can be unreliable at increasing distances. We then look more at how hard the crews are leaning and how fast the boats are sailing to judge the wind strength in their area. Hunt the puffs and the gusts and the windier side of the course, but be sensible about it. If it turns out that one side of the course consistently has more wind, then go there. But don't waste time sailing toward any too-distant gust which will have decayed and vanished by the time you arrive.

The classic descriptions of wave catching techniques are generally understood to apply to waves of substantial size which are rolling faster than the boat. In this situation, by aggressive scalloping, the boat can be broad reached across the front of a wave for speed and then turned very square or even a little by the lee to stay on the face of the wave for as long as possible. Use running by the lee to regain the rhumb line and keep crosswind movement and the associated extra distance sailed to the minimum. The larger the waves, the easier they will be to catch and surf. Always leave a wave by heading 'up' for speed, otherwise the crest will roll under you and the boat will then slow very quickly, bow up, on the wave's back. Provided that you leave each wave with speed, a set of waves will often offer the opportunity to surf them one after the other.

When the waves roll downwind more slowly than the boat, exactly the same technique is used to acquire extra speed, but in this case the extra speed is used to sail through or over the lowest part of a crest ahead.

The fact that 470s and boats of similar size and manoeuvrability, can increase their downwind speed by making use of surprisingly small waves in lighter winds is not generally appreciated. Skilled crews can exploit waves as small as half a boat length. At these wave sizes there is no question of planing, the difference between surfing waves and blocking waves becomes blurred, and the technique for all waves becomes the same. The keys remain the extra speed which can be acquired by momentary broad reaching, and the use of this extra speed either to catch and position the boat on advancing faces from behind which are big enough, or to turn smoothly downwind and sail over a momentarily low part of the crest ahead. Sets of waves offer particular opportunity for surfing. The method is to turn downwind and carry as much of this extra speed as is possible as far downwind as is possible between waves. The level of success is how much you can increase your downwind VMG.

The technique is to turn much more quickly and through greater angles than might be expected would be advantageous in lighter conditions. As the wave size becomes smaller, the boat must be positioned on each wave more precisely. Further, because coarse use of the rudder will slow the boat, it is necessary to turn the boat partly by gentle use of the rudder, partly by heel and partly by body movement; between them these three factors can turn a boat very quickly and with minimum drag. Trim the sails as you turn and pump with each wave. It's a subtle technique, and it takes practise to develop, and more practise to use to advantage, but it works.'

25.16(c) Soling, Etchells, J24 etc.

Basics

'When sailing downwind, by far the most important factor is to look out of the boat more. Advice about how to steer or surf or trim the sails is of trivial importance compared with sailing to and staying in stronger wind and getting the windshifts right.

As you become more experienced, learn to sail better, sail more competitively and sail in fleets with a higher proportion of top-level crews, your mind needs to move progressively further ahead of the boat. At this level of competition it is not enough to be able to sail as fast as your competitors. If you sail as fast as your opponent and he makes a right decision and you make a wrong one, you lose. Fair enough. But what is not so obvious is that if he makes a right decision and you don't make any decision, you will lose just the same.

There is a simple learning progression to this:

Novice crews are preoccupied with the moment to moment control of their boats. They look out of their boats so little they sometimes collide with each other. Experienced crews look beyond their boats to watch out for other boats. Soon, they also learn to read the water surface immediately upwind, and so learn to observe and anticipate the gusts and lulls. They can then handle the wind speed changes better, and in this way they sail faster than the novices.

Advanced crews need to do two further things:

(i) They must extend their scan to look at the more distant water and note the present areas of stronger and lighter wind.

(ii) They must then start thinking ahead, in order to make the best use of this information. It is no use sailing to the present position of an area of distant stronger air. By the time you get there it will have moved downwind and be somewhere else, so you have to think ahead and estimate how fast it is moving so that you can sail to meet it and use it. And if the whole area begins to fade and a new area of stronger air begins to appear somewhere else you have to think fast about trends of growth and decay as well as movement of position.

Note the point made earlier – It makes no difference whether you make the decisions and get them wrong, or whether you simply don't make them. Either way you will be beaten by those crews who scan, and recognise distant differences which are often subtle, and who estimate where those differences which are advantageous will be when they reach them and so can sail to and use them – and are reasonably correct in their predictions for most of the time. These crews are already thinking well beyond their boats.

Top level crews have to go three steps further yet. When you sail in company in which, routinely, the boat handling is good, the gust/lull anticipation is good, and they all keep clear of the light patches and sail in good air, race success will go to those who most correctly anticipate the wind shifts. To do this you must:

1) Sense the shifts and their pattern,

2) Estimate the reliability of pattern repetition, and

3) Keep track of the pattern as you sail.

Windshifts cannot be seen. Their presence must be sensed and recognised by indirect means – either from the compass or the fleet or both. At a second level of difficulty their predictability needs to be estimated. Will the recent pattern probably repeat, or not?

When sailing to windward all boats sail at about the same angle to the wind. Wind shifts sensed from the angles of other boats in the fleet usually tie in well with what comes from your own compass, and so the windshift pattern can be mentally tracked without difficulty. But when sailing downwind the angle to the wind at which the fastest boats sail is not constant and does not necessarily repeat from boat to boat, so it is much harder to remain confident of where you are within a pattern.

A point needs to be made here. This note has to do with handling downwind. But remember that success on the next upwind leg can well depend on the accuracy with which you track the windshift pattern on the preceding downwind leg in exactly the same manner as you should track it before the start. This is no idle comment, as an example will show:

At the Tallinn pre Olympic regatta in 1979, as the Solings went into their last race any one of four boats could win. From the start of the first critical windward leg all four boats started well and were able to sail where they wished. They split. The second and third boats went to the right, and the fourth to the left. Which to cover? No question here of tactics, or of the fleet telling you which way to go. It was back to basics. Only the correct decision on windshift could win the regatta for us. We had tracked the windshifts for a long time before the race. Repetition was recognisable but not reliable. It was going to be a gamble. We believed that to go to the right was correct. We covered those two boats. But on this occasion we came second. Whether Willi Kuweide (who is a meteorologist) had sailed left because he had tracked the wind better we will never know, but he hooked into a big back out near the left hand wing, crossed the three of us, and went on to win. The fact that this particular situation happened directly after the start is immaterial. It could have been at the start of any windward leg, in which case the accuracy of tracking the shifts down the preceding run would have been just as vital.'

In light air

'He who has most wind runs fastest. This overrides all else. Ignore everything else and sail to stay in the strongest wind.

One crew member has the sole responsibility of continuously observing and reporting the positions of approaching and nearby puffs. In general, in light air – and probably in stronger winds also – crews tend to gybe too little. Because of its momentum, a keelboat loses very little distance from gybing in light air if the gybe is well executed.

When sailing downwind near adjacent boats, continually experiment with wind angle and sail trim and steering technique to achieve maximum downwind VMG in the conditions of the moment. No fixed wind angle nor sail settings should be held continuously. Variations in wind strength and wave patterns should always enable a boat which experiments to make marginal gains.

To sum up – downwind in light airs, always chase wind strength rather than wind direction.

As regards sail trim:- In light air a lower spinnaker pole position will give both a greater projected area and greater stability in waves and will sail fastest. As the wind becomes stronger a progressively higher pole position is fastest. The spinnaker can be made more stable yet in light air and waves by hoisting its head to the mast, but if it will set steadily with the halyard eased the head should be set about half a metre away from the mast for free flow of air between the spinnaker and the mainsail. In all downwind sailing, a rig which is allowed to rake forward will run faster than one raked more aft.

In waves and very light air, experiment to find out what works. If the spinnaker is hard to hold steady, keep the pole very low to flatten the spinnaker and reduce its mobility. Try running square to test for movement. Try aggressive higher angles to see if they will generate sufficient Apparent Wind to keep the rig fully pressured, and if so check by comparison with adjacent boats to see whether the downwind VMG is better. In these conditions intermediate angles are unlikely to be better than the extremes.

When the wind becomes stronger the compact gusts of the turbulent breeze replace the puffs of light air, but the priorities do not change. Very little distance is lost in a well-executed gybe, and a crew who hunt for the closest gust on either side will win more gusts during a running leg than a crew who hunt on one side only. Whenever a nearby gust offers – sail to it and gybe if necessary.

In stronger winds if the waves are surfable, broad reach to build speed, then run by the lee when on the wave. In very strong winds, and particularly when broad reaching between gusts, experiment with vang and sail trim to seek marginal speed advantage. In these conditions the risk of broaching is real, and good boat handling technique becomes essential for sustained speed. A broaching boat, at the very least, is conceding vital time to its rivals for as long as it flops around going the wrong way.

In our downwind sailing we measure our performance relative to the boats around us. We are very alert to the slightest difference in downwind VMG. We watch as the wind and wave conditions keep changing in their subtle way. We experiment continuously. We find that this approach leads to small losses but relatively big gains because surprisingly large differences in drive force and downwind VMG can often be wrung out of these changing conditions.

The continuous experimenting with sailing angle makes it hard to be certain of the advantaged gybe and to keep track of the windshift pattern. While this may not seem too important while we are sailing gusts with speed downwind, it is vital that the best estimate possible be made before the downwind mark is reached to enable us to act intelligently and adopt the advantaged tack immediately at the start of the next windward leg.

A caution is proper concerning the 'motherhood' adage 'always tack towards and gybe *away* from a new wind'. What is not stated in this advice is that it depends upon an implicit assumption that the wind speed across the course is constant and will remain so. So often it isn't and doesn't. It is our experience that wind gusts should be used in a different way from the use of wind shifts when racing downwind, and that the difference is one of distance. At the dimension of the distance between gusts, we usually find that the first boat into the next gust – i.e. the boat which gybed towards and not away from the new gust wind regardless of its direction – usually moves downwind faster. It is only at the much larger dimension of shifts that it pays to work across the course so as to be in the best position to take advantage of the back or veer next expected from the pattern.

We practise setting and gybing the spinnaker without the pole. When racing, on approach to the top mark we observe the approaching gusts and are able to keep our options open right up to the mark rounding itself because we are not committed by the present position of the pole to set the spinnaker on one side or the other. In this way we can set full sail instantly and on either gybe, and so can sail straight to and into the closest gust without delay. The spinnaker pole is set at leisure after we are established in the gust.'

25.16(d) Eighteen footer

'Let us imagine that as we approach the downwind mark on a lighter-wind day on which we are using the big rig, the wind goes light, then dies, then builds little by little from the other direction. The wind change has turned what we planned as a windward leg into another downwind leg, starting with a near calm.

Light air

In light air of less than about 2 knots the reaching spinnaker, tacked out on its long bowsprit, will not lift nor fill, or if it fills in the puffs it will collapse under its own weight in the lulls and fall all over the jib and choke the slot like a cobweb. In these conditions the boat will sail faster without it. As soon as there is movement in the air, the boat should be turned crosswind and heeled so that the sails twist toward the right angles. As it accelerates it should bear away and tack downwind with the sails unstalled like any two sail catamaran such as a Tornado.

As the wind increases the light-air range between about 2 and 5 knots is tricky. In recent years we have sailed a good deal at inland lake venues and have learned much about handling these big skiffs in light fickle air. The trick is to sail so that the spinnaker does not collapse, because whenever the spinnaker collapses it takes an age to get the boat going again. So the fastest way to the downwind mark, surprisingly, is to limit your speed so that the spinnaker can be kept inflated when the boat enters each lull.

If you consider the performance of two boats you can see how this works.

The first boat sails into a 4 knot puff, trims everything correctly for acceleration and speed, achieves about 8 knots very quickly, and shoots at 8 knots out of the puff and into the next 2 knot lull. The Apparent Wind will blow at 15 degrees or less from the bow. The spinnaker will collapse onto and all over the jib, the boat will stop, and it will stay stopped and lie dead in the water throughout the lull and until the next puff lifts the spinnaker off the jib.

The second boat sails into the 4 knot puff. As it begins to accelerate it is turned downwind as far as is possible without collapsing the spinnaker in the dead air behind the mainsail. Handled like this its speed will not exceed three or four knots and it will stay within the puff for longer. But the critical difference is that when it sails out of the puff and the spinnaker begins to stream and collapse in the Apparent Wind of the lull which is now from near ahead, a firm luff will sweep the end of the long bowsprit to windward and so feed air more from abeam into the spinnaker (circular airflow). With their slower starting speed plus this weapon this crew can keep their spinnaker inflated while the boat slows further and they then resume normal trim and heading for tacking downwind through the lull. So by a technique of both deliberately limiting their acceleration and also heading further downwind than the heading for maximum speed in the puffs, this second crew is able to keep its sails full and the boat moving, and moving reasonably well, for all of the time. This technique leaves the first 'stop-start' boat far behind.'

In waves

'In inland lakes and light air there are usually no waves. In more open waters with waves, if the light air is sufficient to keep the spinnaker inflated, it is faster to use it even though this may mean sailing almost a beam reach occasionally. Otherwise drop it and keep moving with two sail technique.'

Breeze

'When the wind speed increases through about six knots the breeze becomes steadier, and these boats then come into their own. But they have to be thought about, and handled, quite differently from anything I have ever sailed before, so it may help if I comment first on some of the less obvious differences between say a J24 and my Eighteen.

On boats with spinnaker poles such as the 'J' and which sail downwind with the Apparent Wind from behind, the spinnaker and mainsail can be trimmed to set efficiently at any sailing angle between a square run and a broad reach; and the performance polars in Fig 24.1 shows that the spinnaker can be used to give a small increase in speed at any sailing angle within this broad lobe.

The Eighteen sails downwind with the Apparent Wind from ahead. The fastest fullness for the spinnaker is dependent on the rig size and the crew weight, and the fastest spinnaker sheeting angle is governed by its fullness. Once these two have been optimised they are fixed, and the performance polar shows a lobe within which we can double or treble our speed, but it is so sharp that we have almost no flexibility at all. We have traded flexibility for speed. So in place of the 'broad lobe' thinking, normal to downwind sailing, we need to think more of the 'narrow groove' normal to upwind sailing. In practice this means that we direct all our effort toward sailing at or near what is for our boat the one, preferred, fastest angle to the Apparent Wind.'

Sail set and trim

'Our number one asymmetric spinnakers are about 950 square feet in area. Not only are they faster than the old designs – with their flat leeches they can point much higher into the Apparent Wind – they are also much quicker to handle. They have been responsible for a very big increase in average speed.

The old pole spinnakers, which were bigger, needed 30 to 35 seconds to set or drop, and about 15 to 20 seconds to handle the 24 foot long pole and associated braces through a gybe. The invention of the asymmetric spinnaker on its bowsprit has revolutionised not only the speed of the boat, but also the ease and quickness with which the spinnaker can be handled; it now needs only 12 seconds to set or drop and 6 to gybe. To put this into perspective, when the windspeed is above 12 to 15 knots, the boat speed with the spinnaker set is between 20 and 25 knots and the downwind VMG between 15 and 20 knots. At these speeds a two mile downwind leg takes 6 to 7 minutes plus sail handling and manoeuvring time. With the old pole system a set, three gybes and a drop totalled about two minutes. With the modern rig they total 40 to 45 seconds. In the minute and a quarter difference the boat with the new rig can sail about half a mile.

To Set: The sheet hand passes the mainsheet to the skipper while he hoists the spinnaker. The forward hand hauls the tack to the end of the bowsprit, then picks up and trims the appropriate spinnaker sheet.'

Routine technique

'The design proportions of the boats and rigs are such that the boats achieve their maximum downwind VMG with the mainsheet and forward hands fully trapezed and the skipper half way out on the wing. When overpowered – e.g. big rig up but the breeze has freshened – the skipper trapezes also.

The forward hand adopts a stable, feet-well-apart braced position from which he controls the spinnaker sheet. If the skipper is half way out on the wing, the forward hand will usually be close alongside the sheet hand at the aft extremity of the wing. If the skipper is out too, they will all be close together. To the greatest extent possible the skipper and the forward hand hold steady positions while they control the boat by co-ordinated steering and spinnaker trim. The sheet hand holds the mainsheet well in (pulled in hard then eased about two feet) because the mainsail becomes the backstay. He is as mobile across the wings as is necessary to maintain balance. In light airs this can mean tip to tip. The stronger the breeze, the less he needs to move.'

Gybing

A gybe in a light breeze has been described in Section 25.5. Note particularly that the 'old' spinnaker sheet is not released until the Apparent Wind begins to pressure the spinnaker from the new side. This technique prevents wineglasses from occurring.

Dropping

'Prior to dropping, the falls of the tackline and halyard are checked for clear run. To drop; the clew is hauled to windward of the mainsail. The tack is released and the foot gathered and stowage commenced. The halyard is then fired and stowage completed.'

Handling

'Trim for Speed – It was noted in the 'breeze' paragraph above that once the fastest spinnaker fullness and sheeting angle are established and set-up, the boat will sail very fast at that trim, and much more slowly at all other trims – hence the sharpness of the lobes in Fig 24.1.

The way the boat is trimmed in practice is that the crew move as far out onto the wings as is needed to achieve the highest speed in the wind of the moment. This is sensed by feel and experience. There comes a point where the boat begins to fly; the luff of the spinnaker is on the point of rolling with the spinnaker sheet well in but not hard. Once this crew position is found, it alters very little through the gusts and lulls and fluctuations.

Let us imagine for a moment a magical steady-wind, flat water situation.

If the crew stay too far in, the spinnaker sheet will need to be eased, and the boat will stabilise closer to a square run in a lesser Apparent Wind and at a slower boat speed and a slower VMG than the optimum. If safety and/or survival become the object, this is the configuration adopted.

As the crew move progressively out on the wing, the spinnaker can be trimmed in and the boat points a little higher into the Apparent Wind and sails a lot faster. The VMG increases until the optimum is reached.

If the crew move further out yet it will be necessary to trim the spinnaker in further yet, and while the total 'cross Apparent Wind' force will increase and this will hold the crew up on the wing, this will be at the expense of a higher trim angle to the Apparent Wind. At this higher angle a roll-over vortex will form and the total drag from both the roll-over vortex plus the increased induced drag from the higher trim angle increases so much that the boat slows severely, and smart action will be needed to keep it in the groove or it will slow to the point where the Apparent Wind from ahead will be lost and the boat will need to be re-accelerated.

In unsteady winds and waves, the boats that win have rigs of a size which go fastest downwind with the crews at 'two and a half', i.e. the forward and sheet hands are usually fully trapezed and the skipper is halfway out on the wing.'

Balance

'Sailing a fast skiff, with the spinnaker up, downwind through gusts and waves is the classic 'steer for balance' situation. In addition the lift of the swept-back spinnaker is used to control the height of the bow through any big waves. The skipper who is steering and the forward hand who is controlling the spinnaker keep their eyes on the waves ahead of the bow. The sheet hand keeps a continuous watch upwind (ahead and to windward) for gusts, and calls their approach.

As each gust hits the skipper bears away very positively, the forward hand eases spinnaker sheet as necessary, and the sheet hand moves out if not already fully trapezed. Acceleration is very fast. Within one to two seconds the added speed will have flicked the Apparent Wind forward again and the spinnaker trim and heading are optimised for stable poise through the body of the gust. Refinements are that the skipper will try to use the fan whenever possible, and that once within the gust he will use all of the little flexibility he has to sail as low as is possible consistent with speed so as to remain within the gust for as long as possible. In practice a boat which is heeled to windward sails lower, so it is normal to see the top skiffs sizzling downwind in the gusts with the windward wings just inches clear of the water.

As the boat enters each lull the skipper luffs and both forward hand and sheet hand retrim very positively to keep the wing out of the water. The boat is stabilised in the lull at a speed almost as fast as through the gusts, but at a lesser VMG because it is headed more crosswind. If the lull happens to be exceptionally light a bigger luff plus retrim plus pumping (of the mainsail – never the spinnaker because that is slow and ineffective) will hold the boat in balance with the wing out of the water for two or three seconds but at the expense of a roll-over vortex. If this is allowed to persist the drag of the vortex will slow the boat severely, so it is imperative for the sheet hand to move in quickly to restore balance with efficient sail trim. This is the emergency procedure – in normal gust-lull sequences the sheet hand does not need to move much.'

'A very practical point is that the dynamic response of the spinnaker appears to be of equal importance for sustained speed downwind as is the dynamic response of the rig for sustained speed upwind. As these notes are written (1991) the asymmetric spinnaker has not been around for very long, few sailmakers can yet make really fast asymmetric spinnakers for any boats, and most of these need a big strong forward hand who is fit enough to throw and recover metres of spinnaker sheet every gust throughout an 80 or 90 minute 20 mile race. But some designers and sailmakers have now thought about the realities of racing, and asymmetric spinnakers are beginning to be produced which are both fast and which control beautifully through gusts and lulls and fluctuations with relatively small giving and taking of the sheet. Those win.'

Rig selection

'The ideal is to select the rig size with which the boat will be just overpowered for almost all of the time. This is the sail area with which the boat will sail fastest.'

Downwind through waves

'If an Eighteen with the spinnaker set, is luffed a little and the spinnaker sheet eased, the bow of the boat will be lifted strongly by the upward force from the angled sail. When we race downwind through big waves we use this capability to hold the bow at whatever attitude is desired. In our 'South of France' circuits we sail about sixty races in thirty days and more than half of these are usually in 20 to 30 knot Mistrals. Where the angle of the coastline gives unlimited fetch the waves are typically 2 metres high and some are higher and are on the point of breaking or breaking. To windward the bowsprit and foredeck generally go through and just under each crest. These waves roll at about 16 knots. Downwind in these strong winds we sail at about 25 to 30 knots, and the helicopter videos show that we overtake a crest every few seconds. In these conditions we find it safest to sail wave by wave. The boat is driven fast up the back of the wave so that it 'launches' off the crest rather than topples nose-down over it. The boat is luffed fractionally and the spinnaker is eased to hold the bow high until the hull has settled into the trough ahead, then we bear away and sheet firmly to drive hard up the next back. This calls for nice co-ordination between skipper and forward hand, and bears out once more the adage 'In Eighteen footer racing *everybody* has to do the right thing *all* the time'. These are the most demanding waves we meet. In smaller and/or shorter waves we simply hold the bow a little higher and go for speed without other consideration.'

Wind tactics

'When the breeze is light and the areas of stronger and lighter air are sufficiently distinctive, the fastest way to the downwind mark is to hunt the stronger wind areas and to gybe as often as is necessary to stay in the breeze and away from the light patches. This technique wins in a small range of winds, such as the wandering breeze and the unstable areas just downwind of heated shores.

In stronger breezes the downwind VMG is fast and the distance penalty for any unjustified gybe (which will take 6 seconds at reduced speed – a penalty of about 50m to 60m and in practice probably 100m by the time the boat is re-established at speed and on heading) – is daunting. You have to be very confident before you throw away 200m (two extra gybes) in any race. This is where the champions emerge. They are the ones who seem to be able to look far ahead down a leg and to decide which side will probably be fastest, or what will be the fastest way through narrower waters, and they sail their races with minimum gybes. When there is no tactical reason to adopt either gybe first, we always go for a leeward set as this is easier and faster and so gets the boat up to speed more quickly.'

Boat against boat and fleet tactics.

'The other day a friend who sails at world masters level in Lasers and who has been sailing Tasars seriously for a year said, 'You can sit on the hip of a Laser all day and suffer no disadvantage, but if you try it with a Tasar you go out backwards very fast indeed'. He was really talking about how much a boat deflects the wind. His comment described accurately that a boat with a small righting moment cannot deflect the wind much, and that a much more powerful boat can deflect it by a surprising amount. An Eighteen footer is a very powerful boat indeed, and its wind shadow washes downwind for a long way. The end result is that, despite the speeds of these boats, Eighteen footer racing is fiercely and very effectively tactical at its top levels. This is the aspect which television producers exploit, and some would say over-exploit. The tactical plays are effective, and their execution is very public per the TV coverage, so this subject need be developed no further here.'

Have wings, can fly - only the stern is wet and the bow not even up.

Postscript

In the months while the editor has been turning my text and diagrams into a book, another season has passed. This one has offered interesting glimpses, some frivolous and some seminal, of the way principles hold true as they develop. On the frivolous side:

The Cube-Square law. The first challenge for the America's Cup under the IACC rules has confirmed that bigger heavy boats sail fractionally faster than smaller heavy boats, but at about ten times the cost.

Calculation versus human creativity. If computers could have analysed keel performance correctly, they would have got it right first try. They didn't. I am advised by those who have been involved that computers looked at any one of several keel designs and offered expensive vague suggestion disguised as hard figures. Wind tunnels measured the flows and forces around the same designs at about the right Reynolds numbers and their predictions proved closer. But in the water the real keels either couldn't turn, or couldn't accelerate fast after turning, or didn't want to sail straight through a swell, or could do all of these things but couldn't sail fast, or a variety of other practical delights. What this development effort has demonstrated once again is that prediction of performance in a complex fluid environment is not yet an exact science.

Corinthian isolation versus commercial involvement. Until recently, yachting went its own, quiet, elitist way, e.g. 'If you have to ask you can't afford it' and 'Watching a yacht race is like watching grass grow'. Not all boats are slow – some of the modern ones are spectacularly fast, but it may be years before their existence is acknowledged. History has few examples indeed of contemporary thought being welcomed by any bureaucracy.

The Olympic movement started in the same quiet way, but nationalistic fervour fanned by modern communications have taken over. 'The Olympics' has grown into a huge event, which is now economically viable, if and only if, it is structured as a television spectacular for which the rights can be sold. Commerce has become king. The real Olympic controllers are now the TV programme promoters. These men are driven by market forces and have scant regard for tradition, and watching grass grow has never been a profitable TV programme. The IOC has – not surprisingly – demanded that the IYRU, along with other sports presently perceived as dull, lift its game in this respect and turn the image of sailing into something closer to a television spectacular. Nothing could encapsulate this developing tension better than the jacket picture of this book – spectacular sailing close to large numbers of viewers by a truly modern class of boat – and one, moreover, which is sufficiently exciting to attract its own TV audience. A further subtle twist is that the owners of this particular boat happen also to have paid much fine gold to the Olympic financiers for the privilege of displaying the Olympic rings on their sails, and the Olympic controllers are only too happy to accept the money and be joint advertisers.

So much for frivolity. On the seminal side:

The second need – or 'power' alone is not enough. The Eighteen footer crowd are a turbulent lot. It pleased them this last year to divide into two camps. One group went for slightly bigger boats of increased 'power', and used wings which spanned eighteen feet to develop it. The others, mindful of the expectation of reasonable design stability by the growing numbers of non-Australian Eighteen footer sailors elsewhere in the world, stayed with the recently evolved smaller-boat wing span of sixteen feet. and busied themselves with further tidying their boats. Late in the season, the top boats of each group met head-on. To the surprise of most, the smaller span, lower-powered but cleaner sixteen foot wing-span boats proved faster.

Technically, this division and subsequent confrontation was fortunate because it has enabled us to learn so much more so soon.

In the 'Quest for Speed' chapter, I outlined both the theoretical reasoning and the associated technical development which we understood had made our modern 'faster than the wind' sailing possible. The vital factors were big sails, very great sail-carrying power, and light weight. That this list might not be complete is suggested by Fig 16.10, which points out that it is also necessary to be able to point very close to the wind with spinnakers set when sailing downwind in order to properly make use of the available power and speed. Little did I realise how prophetic that suggestion might be.

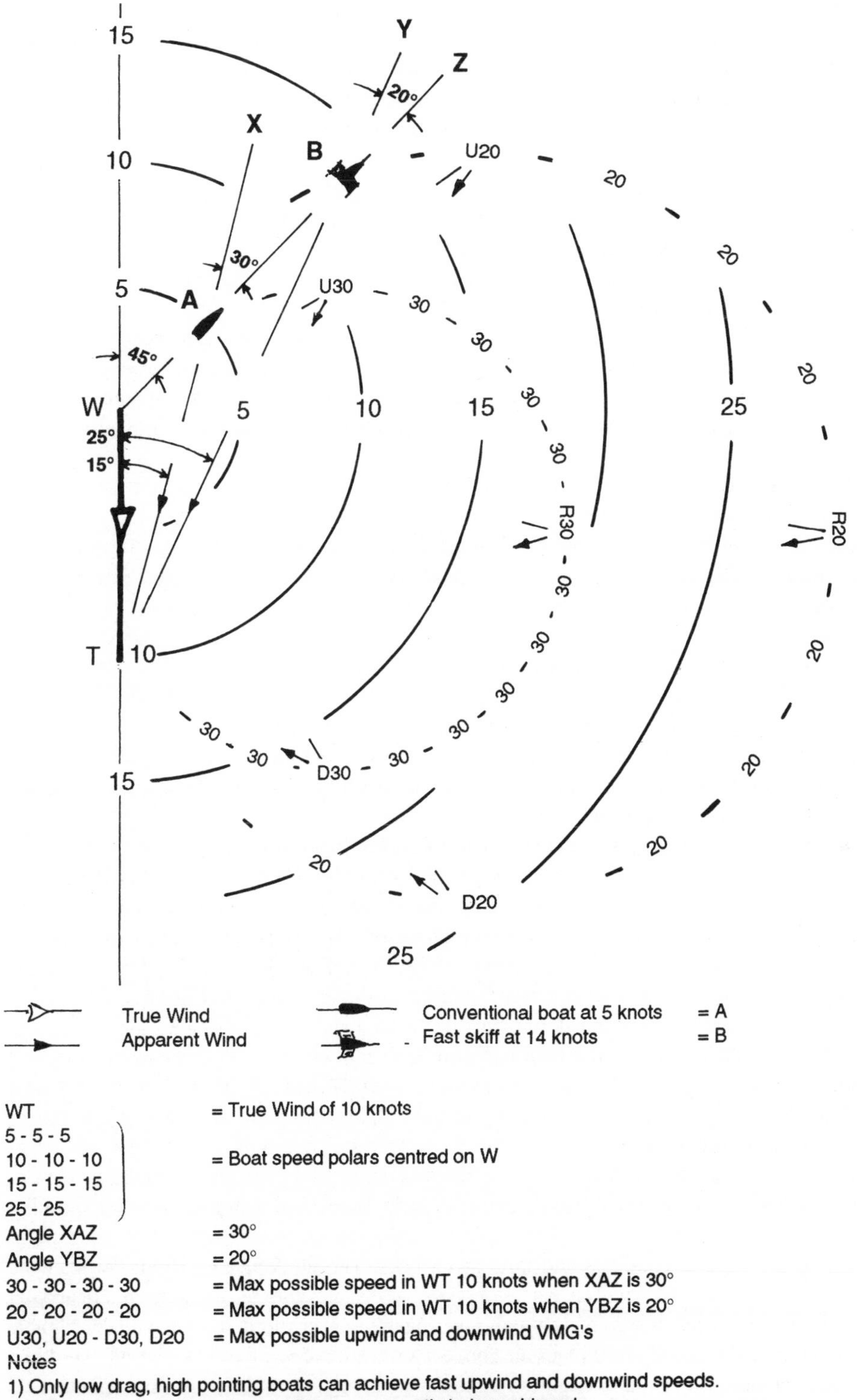

WT = True Wind of 10 knots
5 - 5 - 5
10 - 10 - 10
15 - 15 - 15
25 - 25 = Boat speed polars centred on W
Angle XAZ = 30°
Angle YBZ = 20°
30 - 30 - 30 - 30 = Max possible speed in WT 10 knots when XAZ is 30°
20 - 20 - 20 - 20 = Max possible speed in WT 10 knots when YBZ is 20°
U30, U20 - D30, D20 = Max possible upwind and downwind VMG's

Notes
1) Only low drag, high pointing boats can achieve fast upwind and downwind speeds.
2) The speeds A, B, U30 etc, and D30, are currently being achieved.
The speeds R30 and R20 are not yet being attained(in winds of 10 knots).

Fig PS1 *Pointing* as well as *power* is essential for fast upwind and downwind speeds

Refer also to Fig 16.10

When I drew Fig 16.10 a year ago it did not occur to me to continue the sweep and look at what happens upwind as well. Fig PS.1 now does this, and it opens a whole new Pandora's box.

The assumptions in Fig PS.1 are the very ordinary ones of a 10 knot breeze in which an Enterprise or a Soling can sail to windward at about 45 degrees to the True Wind at 5 or 6 knots (point A), and an Eighteen with its big rig which sails also at about 45 degrees to the True Wind but at 14 knots (point B). The point of interest – as in Fig 16.10 – is the angle of the Apparent Wind to the centreline of each boat. The 5 or 6 knot boat speed of the Enterprises and Solings deflects the Apparent Wind in the adverse direction by about 15 degrees, and so they – along with almost all conventional boats sail with their centrelines at an angle of about 30 degrees to the Apparent Wind. The skiff's higher speed deflects the Apparent Wind about 25 degrees, and so it sails with the apparent wind blowing at only about 20 degrees to its centreline. This is about 10 degrees higher than any conventional boat can manage! If any conventional boat could point even 5 degrees higher than its competitors it would win every race!

What Fig PS.1 makes clear is that the unthinking popular view – that these skiffs are fast because they are powerful, but that they are otherwise unremarkable – is very wrong. Instead, they are among the most efficient craft ever to sail on water! To put this into perspective, let us look at the critical sail trims and angles of attack of a Soling, an Eighteen, an ice yacht and a glider when sailing to windward (or the glider's equivalent).

The Soling sails with its sails trimmed at about 10 degrees from its centreline and at about 20 degrees to the Apparent Wind – total 30 degrees.

The Eighteen sails with its sails at about 10 degrees to its centreline, and at about 10 degrees to the Apparent Wind – total 20 degrees. It can do this because its sails are bigger, it sails faster so the Apparent Wind is stronger and its bent-back masthead enables it to set its sails almost twist-free in the lulls – refer to Sect 17.8.

The ice yacht sails with its sails at 3 to 4 degrees to its centreline and at about 3 to 4 degrees to the Apparent Wind – total about 7 degrees.

The glider manages to fly within about 1 degree of the horizontal.

The above examples show that the skiff is not an extreme machine. It fits naturally within a performance continuum of broadly similar wind machines each of which has less resistance and goes faster at a smaller angle to the wind than the one before.

What Fig PS.1, and Fig 16.10 together now make clear to us is that the ability to sail close to the wind both upwind and down is critical to good 'round-the-buoys' performance. We now know that the factors mentioned earlier – big sails, very great sail-carrying-power and light weight – while adequate for high crosswind speeds are by themselves not enough for high round-the-buoys speeds. We can now see that if a boat can sail no closer than, say, 30 degrees to the Apparent Wind, its performance on all points of sailing in a 10 knot breeze will be limited to speeds of not more than the curve 30..30..30 in Fig PS.1. Even if its 'power' were infinite, it could sail upwind and downwind no faster than the VMG's of points U30 and D30. But if the resistance is reduced so that the boat can point closer – say at 20 degrees to the apparent wind – the performance envelope 20..20..20 and the upwind and downwind VMG's of U20 and D20 become available – but only if there is enough power to achieve them. What we now see is that power alone is not enough. For highest round-the-buoys speeds a second factor – 'pointing' – is also essential, and it is self-evident that both these factors need to be matched most carefully if the fastest round-the-buoys speeds are to be achieved. This is the new realisation, and it unlocks the way to achieve very much higher on-the-water speeds yet.

An aeronautical analogy may help us understand how this works. The modern high-flying swept-wing transport aircraft can carry heavy loads for great distances at speeds not achievable by any other load-carrying aircraft. But unless such an aircraft has wings big enough and engines powerful enough, it will not be able even to climb high enough to make use of the thinner air above. Conventional sailboats, as a group, could be regarded as having wings not big enough and/or engines not powerful enough to enter this performance zone.

But big wings and powerful engines by themselves are still not enough. Imagine a Jumbo trying to fly fast around the world with its wheels still down and its flaps half way out! No amount of power would enable it to match the performance of cleaner rivals. Only when its design has been made 'slippery' enough to let it move freely can it begin to deliver its full potential, and the more slippery it can be made, the less power it will need (this is the 'matching' bit).

This is the post script message from the skiffs. We had already learned that, to achieve our 'faster than the wind' performance, we needed more sail, more sail carrying power and less weight than the world has so far regarded as customary. What we learned again last season is that we have to focus on drag as well, and that the fastest boats in the future will be those which best match adequate drive force with the lowest drag. Not just 'power', but the highest 'Pinching Drive Force to Planning Drag' ratio will be the essential characteristic of the boats which will be able to sail fastest in the future. This is why, this last season, the cleaner lower-powered boats were able to beat the bulkier higher-powered boats.

Little by little we keep on learning how to sail faster yet.

Postscript II The Free-Flowing Hull

The most important recent development is that we now recognise that, for some shapes which are slender, there is a weight at and below which the forced mode vanishes. Boats with this property sail with surprisingly high average speeds in light and moderate winds, because they do not baulk when they accelerate past hull speed in the puffs, and they do not slow all the way back to hull speed and so lose their apparent wind so badly in the lulls.

Julian and I came to recognise this truth more or less by chance. My experience in analysing race performance is that average 'round the buoys' speeds of almost all classes tend to increase as the wind speed increases to the point where the boats approach the hull speed for their length, and then they either baulk and sail no faster (Fig 20.23) or there is a hiatus until the wind becomes much stronger and planing can occur for a significant proportion of the race (Fig 20.5). All traditional dinghy classes seem to display this performance hiatus. An observation which interests me is that Tom Tanner's 1960 drag measurements in the NPL tow-tank of one of Uffa Fox's 10sq m canoes, a relatively light slender boat from the late 1930s, show the characteristic forced mode hump in its drag curve, and this is very similar to the drag curve we measured of the Tasar prototype shown in Fig 20.5. Also my HSP Mk 17 (pp 101, 187), a more recent light slender boat, similarly baulked quite badly, so I thought this property was probably universal, and was unprepared for what has followed.

The Sydney Eighteens race around or close to islands, so their course lengths have not changed for many decades. In measuring their 'round the buoys' speeds in lighter winds I suddenly realised that I was looking at average speeds through-the-water of 7 to 10 knots in winds of 5 to 7 knots. There was no way in which an 18ft waterline boat with a hull speed of 5.6 knots and a forced mode 'hump' in its drag curve which would be steepest at about 7 to 8 knots could sail at these speeds in light winds. So Julian and I took the two 1992/93 champion boats (both his design) and towed them at their fully-loaded sailing weight of 350kg in flat water and in waves, and into wind and down wind and over a useful range of speeds. Fig PSII shows what we measured that day, plus Tanner's and the Tasar's plots for comparison.

The Eighteens, in the cut and thrust of fierce competitive development, have achieved a design revolution. We have given it the technically correct name 'The Dynamically Humpless' hull, but this is too much of a mouthful, and 'Free-flowing' is equally expressive and sounds better.

Once I had digested the astonishing information in Fig PSII I took another look at my little single-hander HSP concept, and progressed the hull designs from Mk 17 through Mks 20 and 21 to my current Mk 22. (Mks 18 and 19 were two-handers.) In a breeze the performance of Mk 22 concedes little to an Eighteen, but the most important observation is that I sailed one day 10nm straight-line distance up the narrowing and tortuous Sydney Harbour/Parramatta River in 90 minutes in a fickle 4 to 8 knot following breeze, tacking downwind all the way. Through-the-water speed would have needed to average about 7 to 8 knots. This boat too now has superior free-flowing performance in the speed range where Mk 17, and the canoe, and the Tasar, all baulk. Its length and total sailing weight are little different from Mk 17, so we have learned something about the importance of shape. This was encouraging.

Julian has now designed a 4.9m two-hander. The shape of its bottom is shown in the photograph on the next page and we have progressively developed the shape and measured the performance of this boat most carefully. It too now sails with truly impressive light and light-moderate air performance, so we are beginning to understand this property.

The critical attribute of each of these boats is that they perform much better than expected in light to moderate winds, and are free-flowing and exciting to sail in conditions in which conventional boats baulk and are dull.

The importance of this recognition and development for the future of sailing is hard to overstate.

In the 1960s a new breed of dinghy was offered to the recreational public. The then-new fibreglass hulls were affordable in price and use of the newly developed trapeze offered better-than-expected performance. These boats appealed to the public as affordable and exciting, and the 1960s sailing boom was the result.

Since then the world has changed but sailing has not kept pace. As we approach 2000 new and more exciting toys are on offer in the leisure marketplace, but sailing in general still offers only boats with 1960s-type performance. The media and the public now generally ignore sailing, and sailing is losing market share to recreations perceived as more modern and exciting.

In this rather gloomy picture there is a brilliant ray of hope. The Sydney Eighteen-footers offer performance so exciting and spectacular that they – and they alone of all sailboats – routinely attract big TV audiences.

Until now, no other sailboat has been able to offer a level of performance which gives spectacle and excitement sufficient to attract any substantial routine audience.

Until now, the Eighteens have been rather special beasts, and pricey. In this book I have tried to explain something of high performance theory and the ratios they use and other factors that make them tick, but there is much in the brew that we do not know, not because only a handful of people can do it, but because they do not always recognise what it is that they are doing.

It has been my privilege, and Julian's, to separate out one more of these previously hidden factors, and to apply it to other sailboats and to prove that it is useful.

My little HSP, and Julian's sixteen and a half footer, demonstrate that the world can again look forward to a new generation of affordable, exciting sailboats which are creatures of their time and which sail with a performance better than expected. And look what happened last time!

Frank Bethwaite 1996

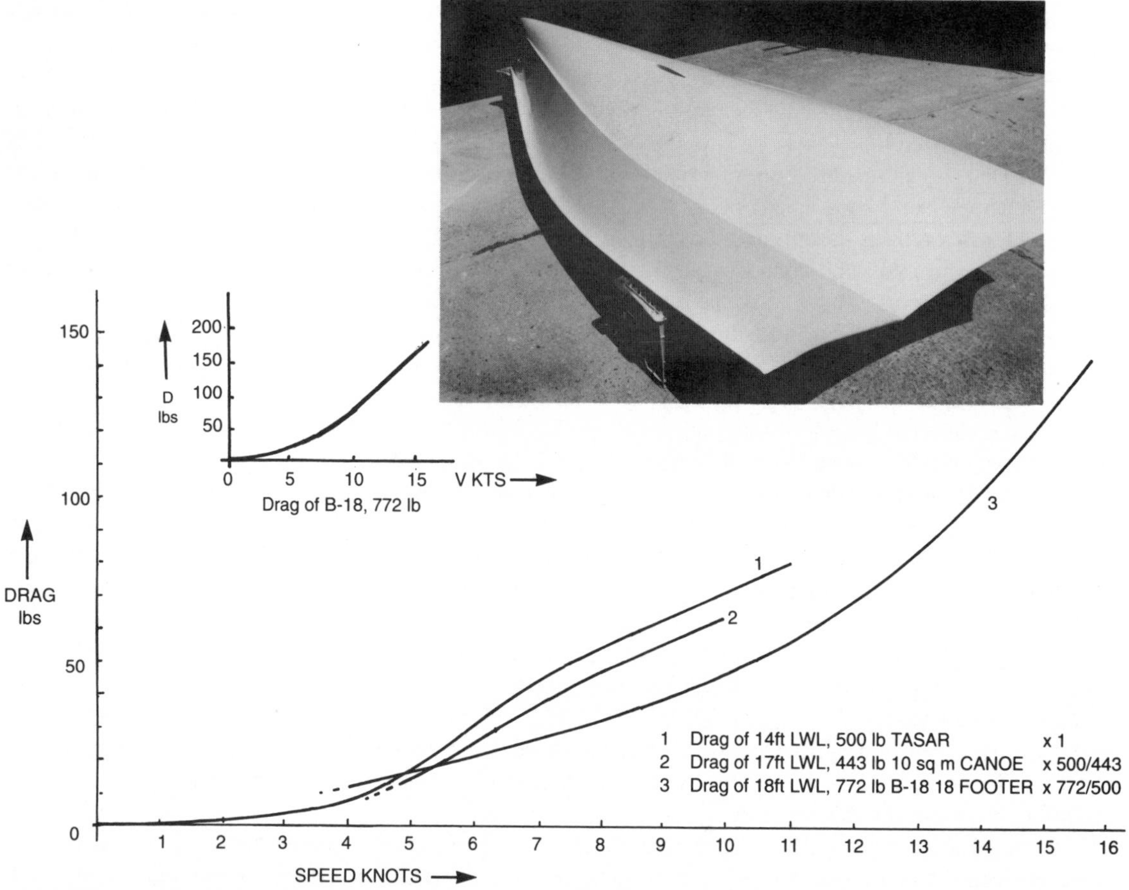

Fig PS2 Comparison of Conventional and Free-Flowing Drag Curves

Index

470, 175,237,273,348,351,356,360,376,395
505, 174,285

A
AAMI, 229
active batten rig, 209,295
adiabatic, 19,22
adjustable pre-load rig, 226
advancing face:wave, 148
advantaged gybe, 135,387
aerodynamic drag, 169,296
air roughness, 183
air temperature, 96
Albacore, 174,365
ana-front, 64
anabatic wind, 89,91
anemograph, 15
angle of attack, 190,228,243,
angular inertia, 270,307
anticyclone, 3 (See also'High')
Apparent Wind,10,167,181,214,283,334,368
arc 1-(Fig 24.9), 345
(Fig 24.10), 353
arc 2-(Fig 24.9), 345
(Fig24.10), 355
arc 3-(Fig24.10), 355
(Fig24.9), 345
arc 4-(Fig24.9), 345
aspect ratio, 201
asymmetric spinnaker, 182
atmospheric temperature, 18
attached flow, 191,366

B
B18, 229
back:wind, 128
backstay, 222
balance position, 340
bar, 159
barrier effect:leeward mark, 146
:reach, 146
:start, 144
batten, 226,228
batten-stiffness, 228
Bermudan, 220
blending parabola, 239
blocking wave, 381
boosted longitudinal roll, 26
boundary layer,10,16,99,191,232
bowsprit, 365
bow wave, 150,266
breeze, 10,32,309,379
bridging change:sea breeze, 80
bucket:laminar flow, 233
buoyancy, 19
by the lee:running, 368

C
camber, 222,234,282
:sail, 209
cambered centreboards, 245
capture:in waves, 312
carbon fibre, 228
catamaran, 183,268,368
cellular mechanism, 23
cellular pattern, 20
centreboard, 164,208,232,243,341
channel, 158
channelling:wind, 2,61
chaotic wave, 147,150,274,305,315,385
Cherub, 253,376
chilled: air, 63
: wind, 88
chock:mast, 222
circular airflow, 284
circulation:cloud, 67
:wind, 6
clew, 220
cloud, 64
cloud:base, 67,71
:core,22
:curled,37
:hunt, 138
:wind, 4
coefficient :of drag, 214
:of lift, 214
coefficients, 218
cold front, 137
comfort, 280
compass, 116,377
concertina effect:wind, 98
control for balance, 345
conventional handling, 279
convergent/divergent pattern:air, 59
cooled breeze, 390
core:cloud, 22
corner:course, 128
Coriolis effect, 7,58
cotton, 220
crest:wave, 148
crew weight, 172
crosswind force, 213

crosswind sailing, 333
cube/square law, 172
Cumulus, 8,64,66,137
Cunningham, 286,295
curlies, 37
current, 106,147,158
:gradient, 107
curtain:air, 24
curve:waterway, 160

D
deck-stepped:mast, 222
defensive sailing, 1,125,133
delta planform, 364
depth:boundary layer, 40
:water, 154
design wind, 4,122,167,224
:zone, 336
diamond stays, 227
displacement sailing, 169,265
downhaul, 229,291
downwind, 135,362,392
:force, 214
drag, 17,168,190,221,243,271
:due to waves, 262
drive force, 166
dry front, 64,137

E
eddy, 160
Eighteen footer, 180,228,286,294,302,333,376,399
elastic:mode, 222
:response- rig, 223,303
elasticity:sail shape, 210
energy recovery, 234,248
:kinetics, 323
Enterprise, 174,284,365
estuary, 158
Etchells, 314,396

F
fan, 39,122
fast response controls, 290
feature size:air, 283
fetch:wave, 149
fibreglass, 174
Finn, 227,340,365,368
Fireball, 175,273
flat:sail shape, 194,220
fleet sailing, 132
flexible mast, 208
flow speed:water, 158
fluctuation frequency:breeze, 33
Flying Dutchman, 174
foam sandwich, 175
foil, 232,240
forced mode, 265,267,380
forestay, 223
:sag, 224
form drag, 234,262,263
Formula 40, 344
fourth mode, 270,281
free shear layer, 194
frequency:kinetics, 324
friction:air, 43,86
frontal cloud, 64
full:sail shape, 194,220
full-wave technique, 93
fully-battened sail, 201,283
funnelling wind, 57,82

G
gaff, 220
girt, 220
glaciate, 8
goose-wing, 366
GP14, 174
gradient wind, 5,73,137
gravity wave, 148
Gulf of St Vincent, 156
gunter, 220
gust, 24,33,121,225,275,280,291,303,356,386,388
:mechanism, 36
:onslaught, 210,226
gybe, 363,371

H
hard rig, 210
harmonic oscillation:air, 54
header, 1,124
headsail, 196,223
heated breeze, 390
heeling moment, 165
hexagonal cloud, 22
High(antincyclone),8, 48
high-lift, 234
high-performance handling, 279
hook:sail, 289
hull, 247
hull speed, 141,148,267
hysteresis loop, 238

I
impulse:kinetics, 322,326
impulse + energy-recovery:kinetics, 322
impulse + pumping:kinetics, 322
induced drag, 262,264
intense layer:water, 156
International Fourteen, 247
International Regulations for Preventing Collisions at Sea, 278
interval:swell, 152
isobar, 111
isolated thermal, 20,22
IYRU, 174

J
J24, 294,361,396
jib tufts, 287

K
kata front, 64
katabatic wind, 89
keelboat, 365,368
Kimberley, 21
kinetics, 157,278,320,379
Kingston Tower, 15
knife-edge:mast, 210
knife-edge separation, 196

L
lake breeze, 57
laminar boundary layer, 232
laminar flow, 16,196,232
land breeze, 89
latent heat, 8
layline, 2,116,130
Laser, 340,365,368
Laser II,185,253,286,293,301,308,314,376,348, 351,359,392
leading edge:rudder, 239,240
least drag:sail trim, 296
leech, 220,291,303
:ribbon, 291,348,373
:ripple, 325,328
leeway, 164,262,264
lift, 1,125,190,213,221
light air, 10,20,306,317,346,369
:regime, 281
longitudinal roll, 25
looking for power:technique, 225
Low(Depression),8, 48
luff:downwind, 135
lull:breeze, 33,225,275,280,291,390

M
main sheet, 293
mainsail, 191,222
maintaining the surf, 384
marine ply, 175
Mark IV Dribbly, 253
mast, 191,226
:gate, 222
:bend, 228
mature wave, 149
maximum-safety technique, 93
mean wind direction, 116,124
Medium Dribbly, 249
Middle Harbour:Sydney, 159
minimum time: technique,93,102
:path, 126
mixed waves, 385
moderate breeze regime, 281
momentum:current, 158
Moorabbin, 80
most power:sail trim, 296
most power/least drag:sail trim, 296

N
natural fibres, 220
natural frequency, 307
negative kinetics, 320
node, 124
non-raining cloud, 139
North Polar High, 7

O
offshore counterflow:sea breeze, 74
OK, 340,348,360,365,368
open barriers, 143
opportunistic sailing, 119
orbital motion:wave, 148
orbital speed:water, 152
oscillating air, 25,28,126
outhaul, 209,291
over-critical:design 216
overtrimming:kinetics, 325

P
part power pause:kinetics, 320
part-wave technique, 93
persistent shift, 126,130
pinch, 290
plane, 169,268
pleat, 222
pocket, 222
pointing angle, 116

polar diagram, 333,363
Port Phillip Bay, 155
Port Stephens, 100
positive kinetics, 322
pre-loaded spring system:rig, 226
Professional Sailors Class, 344
progression:air pattern, 27
pulsing air, 25,28
pumping, 325,376

Q
quadrant effect, 75
quarter-wave, 150,266

R
race:preparation, 102
:strategy, 110
raining cloud, 69,140
ratio:power to weight, 177
:sail area to wetted area, 171,178,369
:sail area to total weight, 178,369
:sail carrying power to total weight,171, 178
reaching dynamics, 334
re-attachment, 191
receding face:wave, 148
reef, 222
regular wave, 147,305,311,382
remote wind, 137
repetition interval:wind, 116
resonance, 307
Reynolds numbers, 218
ribboning air, 26,29,61
rig response, 225
righting moment, 165,174
ripple:water, 32
River Dinghy, 248
RNSA Regatta, 176
roach, 228,283
roll-over vortex, 221,366
roll :cloud,47,64,65,137
:mechanism, 25
:pattern, 20,22
rough-air, 226,302,318,357
rough-textured surface, 194
rudder, 233,245
:angle, 238
:deflection drag, 262,264

S
Sabre, 368
sail, 188
sail carrying power, 166
sail carrying power to total weight' ratio, 175
sailboard, 171,183,334,368
sailcloth, 226
sail shape, 346
sail trim, 282,288,309,352
sail twist, 282 (See also'twist')
salt crystal, 71
sea breeze, 57,73
separation, 194
:air, 190
:bubble, 191,215,234
shed power:technique, 225
shift:wind, 386
shoal, 158
shoal depth, 154
shore effect:air, 26
shorten sail, 305
shroud, 222,300
:tension, 223
skiff, 175
Skiff Moth, 279,379
skin friction, 17,262
snaking:downwind, 373
Snipe, 220
soft rig, 210
Soling, 294,314,333,361,396
South Polar High, 7
speed, 280
speed to length ratio, 166
Spencer -John, 248
spinnaker, 182,329,340,365,370
spreader, 222
square run, 364
square-back:mast, 210
stability index,99,110,122,387
stable wind, 1
standing wave, 147,152,305
Star, 220,365
start,120, 126,144
steady wind, 114
steer for balance, 243,341
stern wave, 150,248
stern-hung rudder, 242
Strato Cumulus, 64
streamline shape, 235
stroke:kinetics, 324
strong breeze regime, 281
sub-critical flow, 198,210,243
subsidence:air, 22,74
subsidence inversion, 48
super-critical flow, 198,243
surf, 157,359,381
surface friction, 15

surface texture, 232
surface-piercing foils, 241
surfing, 147,272
surfing waves, 382
surging:kinetics, 322,328
survival, 280
survival sailing, 304
swell, 147,152,275,305,316,386
swept-back leading edge, 221
swept-back spreader, 222
swirl, 16
Sydney Harbour, 155
synoptic situation:weather, 95

T
tack, 132,284,303
:downwind, 135,183,334,362
Tallinn, 30
Tasar, 175,253,273,333,361,376
tear-drop:mast, 219
tell-tale, 194,206
thermal: excitation, 20
:pattern, 52
terminating the surf, 384
thickness:boundary layer, 191
throat, 220
tidal stream, 106,147,158
tip-leakage, 201
Tornado, 226
trace:wind, 3,121
transition:air flow, 198
transition zone B:(Fig24.10), 352
transom, 371
transverse roll, 25
:air, 49
trapeze, 174
traveller, 210,280,293
trim: angle, 282
:tab, 245
trip turbulator, 204,210,234
troposphere, 5
True Wind, 10,167
tuft, 194,206
turbulence:air, 32
:inversion, 43
turbulent flow, 17
turbulent mixing:air, 32
twist:sail shape, 200,215,228,234
two-hander Eighteen, 253
two-mode:hull, 270
:sailing, 375
two-rate spring, 222

U
U2A:wind trace, 14
Ultimate, 344
unstable:wind, 1
unstayed mast, 227
unsteady:light air, 119
:wind, 113,119

V
valley wind, 390
van Essen, 174
vang, 222,295
vang- sheeted:mainsail, 295
veer, 128
velocity: gradient, 18
: Made Good (VMG), 167,172,296,317
:times Length(VL), 218
ventilation, 237
viscosity:air, 15
vortex, 16

W
wake, 150
wandering breeze, 40,62,120
warm:front, 137
:surface layer:water, 105,147,154
water temperature, 96
wave:height, 154
:impact drag, 157
:making drag, 262,265
:speed, 148
:systems, 147
wave-by-wave technique, 157
wavelength, 148
wave-train, 149
weather map, 95
wedge angle:hull, 248
Westell, 174
wetted area, 268
wind:indicator, 281
:lane, 2,37,122
:pattern, 104,119
:recording, 15
:rose, 108
:shear, 160
:trace, 15
:tunnel, 233
wind up:light air, 283
windward planing, 353
windward-sailing technique, 133
wind-wave, 44,53,115,117,122,130
wind-wavelengths, 122

wingmast, 207,227,301,365
wire-drawing, 98
WMO:wind trace, 14
World Meteorological Organisation, 94

Y

Yacht Racing Rules, 278
Yarrawonga, 26
yield response:rig, 226
young wave, 149

Z

zip, 222
zones A,B &C:design wind, 338